50 Years of Central Banking in Kenya

50 Years of Central Banking in Kenya

Regional and Global Perspectives

Edited by

PATRICK NJOROGE

AND

VICTOR MURINDE

OXFORD
UNIVERSITY PRESS

OXFORD
UNIVERSITY PRESS

Great Clarendon Street, Oxford, OX2 6DP,
United Kingdom

Oxford University Press is a department of the University of Oxford.
It furthers the University's objective of excellence in research, scholarship, and education by publishing worldwide. Oxford is a registered trade mark of Oxford University Press in the UK and in certain other countries

First Edition published in 2021

Impression: 1

Published in the United States of America by Oxford University Press
198 Madison Avenue, New York, NY 10016, United States of America

British Library Cataloguing in Publication Data
Data available

Library of Congress Control Number: 2020945721

ISBN 978–0–19–885182–0

DOI: 10.1093/oso/9780198851820.001.0001

Printed and bound in the UK by
TJ Books Limited

Acknowledgements

The origin of this book goes back to the symposium to celebrate the 50-year anniversary of the Central Bank of Kenya on 13 September 2016 in Nairobi. In addition, the book features papers which were commissioned from the staff of Central Bank of Kenya, specifically to provide exceptional insight into the evolution of specific functions of the Central Bank and the financial sector over the last five or so decades in areas such as monetary policy, bank regulation, payment systems, financial innovation, and the interbank market. All the papers have since been updated in the light of comments received at the Conference and subsequent review of the draft versions.

The Central Bank of Kenya hopes that this book will provide exceptional insight into the evolution of the financial system in Kenya, in the context of regional and international developments in the last five or so decades. Most of the chapters contain original work which is not available elsewhere, which should be of special appeal to university researchers and students as well as policy-makers, practitioners, and civil society who are interested in the past, present, and future of the Kenyan financial sector. It is also hoped that the book will help generate momentum for the transformation of the financial system in Kenya in view of the ongoing digital revolution as well as global challenges such as the COVID-19 global pandemic.

Many people made this book possible. We are especially grateful to all the authors of the chapters featured in this book for sharing their papers at the Conference and contributing the additional chapters. Many colleagues helped by reviewing and providing helpful suggestions for improvement of the draft chapters; we would like to thank Laurence Harris, Andy Mullineux, Désiré Kanga, Ayse Demir, Meng Xie, Maryam Shloever, Anosi Ikimalo, and Ibo Murinde. We also acknowledge helpful comments and recommendations made by three anonymous reviewers from Oxford University Press during the initial stages of the book proposal. We are indebted to Adam Swallow, the commissioning editor, and his editorial team at the Oxford University Press, including John Smallman, Katie Bishop, and Samantha Downes; they supported our project from beginning to end with patience and professionalism. We also thank Bhavani Govindasamy for her meticulous work during the production process of the book.

No book project of this magnitude can be accomplished without research and logistical support; we would like to sincerely thank the staff in the Research Department of the Central Bank of Kenya, in particular Maureen Were, Anne Kamau, Raphael Otieno, Esman Nyamongo, and Julius Bett, who provided excellent support and input. Additional support from other departments of the Central Bank, in particular by Betty Gatere, is much appreciated.

Patrick Njoroge and Victor Murinde

Contents

PART II THE CENTRAL BANK OF KENYA

List of Figures

List of Tables

Notes on Contributors

Editors

Patrick Njoroge is the Governor of the Central Bank of Kenya. He holds a PhD in Economics from Yale University, and first and second degrees in Economics from the University of Nairobi. He worked in the Ministry of Planning in Kenya as a Planning Officer from 1985 to 1987. Upon completing his doctorate, he worked as an Economist at the Ministry of Finance from 1993 to 1994. From April 1995 to mid-June 2015 he was at the IMF in Washington, DC, where he served in various capacities: first as an Economist and later as a Senior Economist; IMF Mission Chief for Dominica; Deputy Division Chief, Finance Department; and Advisor to the Deputy Managing Director of the IMF. He has won several awards as a Central Bank Governor. He was named the 2018 Central Banker of the Year in Africa by an international UK-based publication, *The Banker* Magazine in recognition of his prudence and long-term vision for Kenya's economy and the banking sector. In October 2018, he received the Global Markets Central Banker Governor of the Year award for sub-Saharan Africa, and in May 2016 he was recognized as the Central Bank Governor of the year at the African Banker Award ceremony held in Lusaka, Zambia.

Victor Murinde is AXA Professor of Global Finance and founding Director of the Research Centre for Global Finance at SOAS University of London. He has contributed over 100 research papers to the financial economics literature, mainly in the areas of banking and finance, development finance, and financial markets. According to the UK Research Excellence Framework (REF2014), his research on 'Shaping Bank Regulatory Reforms in Africa' was recognized for exceptional impact. He is the Principal Investigator of a DFID-ESRC Research Grant on 'Inclusive Finance', 2016–21, leading a consortium of: SOAS University of London; University of Birmingham; Columbia University; University of Sussex; University of Nottingham; ODI London; University of Groningen; Laval University; University of Ghana, Legon; and the African Economic Research Consortium (AERC). He is co-investigator on ESRC–NSFC Grant on 'Research on China's Financial System towards Sustainable Growth', jointly with colleagues at SOAS University of London and Nankai University Tianjen, and Zhejiang University, Hangzou, in China. His other current roles include: Chair, Econometric Society Africa Region Standing Committee; Chair of Group C (Finance & Resource Mobilization) for the African Economic Research Consortium (AERC); Board Member of New Rules for Global Finance, a policy forum based in Washington, DC; and Visiting Professor of Financial Economics at the School of Economics, University of Nairobi. He was the founding Director of the African Development Institute, at the African Development Bank (2011–14).

Contributors

Babak Abbaszadeh is the President and CEO, Toronto Centre. Babak Abbaszadeh joined Toronto Centre as the President and Chief Executive Officer in June 2010. He is responsible for all aspects of the organization's strategic development, capacity development, and operational activities. On behalf of the Centre, Mr Abbaszadeh builds partnerships with the leadership of central banks, supervisory authorities, as well as international standard setting bodies and ministries of finance and foreign affairs globally. With almost 30 years of experience in management, public policy, and stakeholder relations in the private sector, government agencies, and NGOs, Babak has held leadership roles in highly regulated sectors such as financial services, energy, and natural resources. Prior to joining Toronto Centre, Babak held senior positions in internationally oriented Canadian financial institutions such as the Canada Pension Plan Investment Board and Sun Life Financial. Babak was also Chief of Staff to two senior cabinet ministers in the Government of Ontario.

Daniel Amanja is the head of External Sector Analysis Division in Research Department, Central Bank of Kenya. He joined the Bank in 2006 and has headed various Divisions within the Department. He is a member of the Bank's Foreign Reserves Investment Committee and has also been involved in the EAC regional integration initiatives. He teaches as part-time lecturer for postgraduate collaborative programmes at the Kenya School of Monetary Studies (KSMS). Before joining CBK he worked at Ministry of Finance in various capacities and was involved in many reforms, including introduction of medium-term budget framework, procurement reforms, and training of public officers on financial management, especially management of foreign aid in Sub-Saharan Africa.

Julius Bett works in the Macroeconomic Modelling Forecasting and Research Division, Research Department at the Central Bank of Kenya. His responsibilities include inflation analysis; near-term and medium-term inflation projections. He has a Master's degree in Banking and Finance from Moi University.

Federica Branca works with the Impact International Graduate Program at UniCredit in Milan, Lombardy, Italy. Previously, Federica worked as a Risk Analyst at the European Central Bank, Frankfurt Am Main, Germany, September 2017–June 2018; Financial Analyst at LIST SpA in Milan, Italy, during July 2017–August 2017; and a trainee in the Capital Markets-Monetary Policy Department at the European Central Bank, Frankfurt Am Main, Germany, during July 2016–June 2017. Federica holds a Master's degree in Economics from the University of Pavia, another Master's degree in Economics from Eberhard-Karls-Universität Tübingen and a Bachelor's degree in Economics from the University of Insubria.

Cappitus Chironga works in the Research Department of Central Bank of Kenya as a Manager. He joined the Bank in 2001. He worked in Financial Markets for eightyears before joining Research Department where he currently leads a team on financial stability and financial inclusion work. An alumnus of Warwick Business School, University of Warwick, UK (2005), where he studied Masters of Science in Economics and Finance and the University of Nairobi School of Economics for his first Masters of Arts degree in Economics (2003) and Bachelor of Arts in Economics. The author is an Accredited

Fellow of Macroeconomic and Financial Management Institute of Eastern and Southern Africa (MEFMI), Cheavening Scholar, Fellow of International Visitors Leadership Program of the US State Department and Germany Academic Exchange Services (KAAD) Scholar. He is also a UNCTAD Member of Consultants Team. He has wide experience on financial sector issues in Kenya and across East African region.

Bob Collymore sadly passed away when this book was in press. He was the CEO of Safaricom Limited, a leading communications company in Africa and pioneer of M-PESA, the world's most developed mobile payment system. Robert (Bob) Collymore's work experience spanned across diverse countries such as Japan, South Africa, and the United Kingdom where he held senior roles in marketing, purchasing, retail, and corporate affairs. Bob had more than 30 years of commercial experience working in the telecommunications sector and was passionate about how businesses can be catalysts in transforming communities. Under his leadership, Safaricom committed to utilize its infrastructure to achieve universal access to essential communications and leverage partnerships that aimed to tackle health and clean energy for a positive impact on economic growth. Mr Collymore was a member of the Board of Acumen and served as a Commissioner on the United Nations Commission on Life-Saving Commodities for women and children. In Kenya, he was on The Vision 2030 Delivery Board and was the founding trusteee of the National Road Safety Trust. He was also the Chairman of the TEAMS (The East African Marine System) Board. In recognition of outstanding services rendered to the nation of Kenya, Bob was awarded the Moran of the Order of the Burning Spear by the President of the Republic of Kenya.

David Ferrand is the Director of Financial Sector Deepening (FSD) Kenya, a multi-donor initiative to support the development of inclusive financial markets in Kenya. He has led the organization since its inception in 2005. FSD addresses opportunities and constraints to market development from the policy and regulatory level through industry infrastructure to innovation by financial service providers. Current funders are the UK's Department for International Development (DFID), the Bill & Melinda Gates Foundation, and the Swedish International Development Agency (SIDA). David has been engaged in work on financial inclusion and small and medium enterprise (SME) development since 1993. As financial sector specialist for DFID in the Eastern Africa region, he was involved in a wide range of activity from programme design and management to policy advice and analysis. He has also consulted on a range of financial inclusion projects around the world. In his earlier career he trained and worked as a banker in the UK and Kenya. Experiences included a formative period in Kenya as a lending manager dealing primarily with a portfolio of small and medium enterprises.

Mitsuhiro Furusawa has been Deputy Managing Director of the International Monetary Fund (IMF), since 2 March 2015. He joined the IMF after a distinguished career in the Japanese government, including several senior positions in the Ministry of Finance. Immediately before coming to the Fund, he served as Special Advisor to Japanese Prime Minister Shinzo Abe and Special Advisor to the Minister of Finance. Among his recent ministry postings, he served as Vice Minister of Finance for International Affairs (2013–14), Director-General of the Financial Bureau (2012–13), and Senior Deputy

Director-General of the International Bureau (2009–10). His overseas postings for the Japanese government have included IMF Executive Director (2010–12), Minister (Finance) at the Embassy of Japan in the United States (2007–09), and Counselor (Finance) at the Embassy of Japan in France (1997–99). He is a 1979 graduate of the University of Tokyo with an LLB degree; he also graduated in 1983 from the École Nationale d'Administration in Paris.

Mahesh Gheewala is now retired after a long and distinguished career in the financial sector in Kenya. He joined Government service as an Economist/Statistician in the Statistics Department of the Kenyan Treasury in January 1962. He retired as Deputy Secretary in Charge of the Monetary and Fiscal Division in 1975. Throughout his tenure, he handled many economic, monetary, fiscal, and other matters, and was instrumental in initiating and promoting major policies, programmes, and projects to their successful implementation. He was Treasury Officer responsible for establishment of the Central Bank of Kenya.

Anne Kamau is an economist at the Research Department of the Central Bank of Kenya with 10 years' experience in central banking—specifically in monetary policy, economic modelling, and forecasting. Her policy and banking career has been enriched by her experience in high level public policy engagements, at the Executive office of the President of the Republic of Kenya and internationally at the Brookings Institute based in Washington, DC. Currently she focuses on monetary and inflation research, essential inputs to the Monetary Policy Committee—a top decision-making organ at the bank. Prior to joining the Bank she worked for a commercial bank before joining a government think tank—Kenya Institute for Public Policy Research and Analysis, where she was part of a select team that was engaged in economic policy modelling, research, and providing public policy advice to key government officials. She has published several journal articles, discussions and working papers, policy briefs, and policy opinions. She also features in several topical podcasts. She holds a PhD in Economics from the University of Nairobi.

Désiré Kanga is a Senior Economist at the Central Bank of West African States (BCEAO), the issuing institute common to the eight member states of the West African Monetary Union (WAMU). Before that, he was a post-doctoral Research Fellow in the Research Centre for Global Finance (CGF) at SOAS University of London. Désiré joined the CGF at SOAS in 2018, under the AXA Chair in Global Finance. He holds a PhD in Economics from the University of Orléans (France), and an MSc in Statistics and Economics from ENSEA (Côte d'Ivoire). Before joining SOAS, he was involved in various research projects and teaching at ENSEA. His research focuses on the banking sector and monetary policy transmission mechanisms. His ongoing research seeks to uncover new evidence on how cross-border banking impacts the domestic credit market in the WAEMU region. His work has been published in highly rated journals including the *Journal of Banking and Finance*.

Esther Kariuki joined the Central Bank of Kenya in September 2011. She holds a Master's degree in Economics from the University of Malawi and a Bachelor's degree in Mathematics and Economics from the University of Nairobi, Kenya. She has also attended a wide range of professional courses organised by various institutions. Prior to joining the Central Bank, Ms. Kariuki worked for the National Treasury (2005–August 2011) where she rose through the ranks to the position of a Senior Economist. While at the National

Treasury, she was seconded to the World Bank Voice Secondment Programme (2009) in the East Asia and Pacific Region (Jakarta, Indonesia). Prior to joining the National Treasury, she worked for the Kenya Institute for Public Policy and Research Analysis (KIPPRA), 2002–04, where she served under various capacities. Her professional and research interests are in Macroeconomics, Monetary Policy, Fiscal and Debt Policy, and Regional Integration issues.

Louis A. Kasekende is former Deputy Governor, Bank of Uganda. From May 2006 to 2009, he served as Chief Economist of the African Development Bank (AfDB). As Chief Economist, he was the Bank's spokesperson on socio-economic and development issues of importance for Africa, and is credited for playing a leading role in the AfDB's efforts to help African economies withstand the impact of the global economic crisis. Between 2002 and 2004, he served as Alternate Executive Director and later as Executive Director at the World Bank for Africa Group 1, including 22 countries mostly from Anglophone Sub-Saharan Africa. Prior to joining the World Bank, he had worked for 17 years at the Bank of Uganda in several capacities, including as Director of Research Department, Executive Director responsible for Research and Policy and served as Deputy Governor between 1999 and 2002. He has previously served as a member of the United Nations Group of Eminent Persons for the Least Developed Countries and the World Bank Knowledge Advisory Commission. Currently, he is a Board Member of the African Export Import Bank (AFREXIMBANK), the International Economics Association (IEA), and the Africa Economic Research Consortium (AERC), and is a member of the National Steering Committee on Capital Markets Development in Uganda. He holds a PhD in Econometrics, from the University of Manchester. He has authored several articles in academic journals and books.

Evelyne Kilonzo has worked for the Central Bank of Kenya (CBK) for over 19 years and currently serves as a Manager and Portfolio Lead of the Financial Inclusion Section of Bank Supervision Department. She is also the lead of the 16-member interdepartmental Financial Innovation & Inclusion Team (FIIT) of CBK. She has led, coordinated, facilitated, and participated in critical milestone activities with various local, regional, and international partners towards fulfilling CBK's mandate of formulating innovative policy solutions to enhance financial inclusion in Kenya. She is versed in key policy, legal, and regulatory issues relating to financial inclusion, including microfinance, digital finance, agency banking, credit information sharing, financial education, consumer protection, and recently, Financial Technology (Fintech). Ms Kilonzo is an alumnus fellow of the Cornell Institute of African Development (IAD) and graduate of Cornell University, USA, having been awarded a Master's degree in International Development (focusing on Development Policy). She also has a Bachelor of Arts degree in International Relations from the United States International University—Africa (USIU-A), Kenya, and a diploma in Microfinance from Strathmore University, Kenya.

Charles Koori is the former Director, Research Department at the Central Bank of Kenya. He holds an MA degree (Economics) degree and BA degree (Economics) from the University of Nairobi. Mr Koori joined the Central Bank of Kenya in August 1984 and served in various capacities in the Research Department until his secondment as an

Economist, from the Central Bank of Kenya, to the Office of the IMF Senior Resident Representative (Nairobi) in August 2004. Mr Koori was appointed Director of Research in October 2008. The Research Department is responsible for economic analysis and research with the view to support the formulation and implementation of monetary policy for price stability, compiling, and disseminating economic data and related reports, providing advice on sound economic policies, and coordinating Central Bank of Kenya participation in the national economic policy dialogue and regional and international integration initiatives.

Isaya Maana is the head of the Monetary Policy Committee Secretariat in the Research Department at the Central Bank of Kenya. He is responsible for coordination and facilitation of the activities of the Monetary Policy Committee. He has wide experience in the Central Bank's operations spanning twenty years, has undertaken technical research and published on monetary and financial sector issues, public debt, and on Central Bank communications.

Anne W. Mariga is the Head of the National Payments System (NPS) Division of the Banking and NPS Department, a position she has held for the last year. Anne holds a Bachelor's degree in Finance from the University of Nairobi and an MBA in Strategic Management from the Moi University. She is also a qualified accountant, CPA (K) and a Certified Information Systems Auditor (CISA). Anne has been with the Central Bank of Kenya for 26 years, a period during which she worked in different departments of the Bank. She started her career in the Bank at the Finance department then moved on to the Internal Audit Department where she served for 15 years. She was later transferred back to Finance where she was in charge of the Bank's Payroll before she moved to her current position.

Ignacio Mas is an executive director and co-founder at the Digital Frontiers Institute, a new organization that is developing a professional development network and training course around digital money and payments. He is also a Senior Fellow at the Fletcher School's Council on Emerging Market Enterprises at Tufts University. Ignacio has been Deputy Director in the Financial Services for the Poor programme at the Bill & Melinda Gates Foundation, Senior Advisor at the Technology Program at CGAP, and Director of Global Business Strategy at Vodafone Group.

Ixart Miquel-Flores is a Banking Supervision Risk Analyst in the Quantitative Risk Analysis Department at the European Central Bank, Frankfurt Am Main Area, Germany. He works as part of a team which conducts and leads on-site inspection on market and IT risk, conducts regular analysis of findings to guide teams and JSTs in order to identify systemic weaknesses, develops and maintaining the on-site inspection methodology and organizing related training activities and workshops, and participates as necessary in international methodology and standards development working groups and committees. Ixart holds postgraduate qualifications in banking risk management from University College Dublin, a MSc. degree in Corporate Finance from the Frankfurt School of Finance & Management, and Bachelor of Business Administration degree in Business/Managerial Economics from the Universitat Rovira i Virgili.

Francesco Paolo Mongelli is Senior Adviser in the Directorate Monetary Policy, at the European Central Bank (ECB) and honorary Professor at the Johann Wolfgang Goethe

University of Frankfurt. He holds a BA in Economics from the Free University for Social Studies (LUISS) in Rome, and also a Master's degree and a PhD in Economics from the Johns Hopkins University in Baltimore. He has worked at the ECB since 1998. Prior to that, he spent several years as an economist at the IMF in Washington. His papers have been published in various outlets including *The Journal of Money Credit and Banking*, *The Journal of Common Market Studies*, *Economie Internationale*, *Bancaria*, and *The Journal of Economic Integration*.

Matu Mugo is an Assistant Director in Bank Supervision, Central Bank of Kenya. He leads teams responsible for the review and development of policies to promote safe, affordable, and inclusive financial services. He has held various positions in the Bank Supervision Department over the last 18 years. He has been involved in the development of legal and regulatory frameworks for sharia compliant banking, microfinance, digital financial services, credit information sharing, and agent banking. Before joining the Central Bank of Kenya, Mr Mugo worked as an auditor for KPMG, an international audit and consultancy firm. He holds First Class Bachelor of Commerce (Accounting) and MBA (Finance) degrees from the University of Nairobi and is a certified public accountant. Mr Mugo was a Fellow of the Financial Inclusion Leadership Program at the Fletcher School of Law and Diplomacy, Tufts University, USA in 2011.

Lydia Ndirangu is a researcher based at the Kenya School of Monetary Studies. She has a broad public policy research experience as a development economist. Before joining the CBK in 2010, she worked as a Policy Analyst at the Kenya Institute for Public Policy Research and Analysis (KIPPRA) for eight years, mainly focusing on the real sector and rural financial markets. Her initiation into economic policy work was at the Institute of Policy Analysis and Research (IPAR) and at the Coffee Research Foundation between 1991 and 2000. Her current research focus is on monetary policy, interbank markets, and financial inclusion. She holds a PhD degree in Development Economics from Wageningen University, the Netherlands; MSc in Agricultural Economics and BSc in Agriculture, both from the University of Nairobi.

Kethi Ngoka-Kisinguh is the Head of External Sector Development at the Central Bank of Kenya. She also worked as an economist in the office of the IMF Resident Representative to Kenya, on secondment from the Central Bank of Kenya and was part of a team that monitored macroeconomic developments and the implementation of Kenya's programme with the IMF. Kethi is also an accomplished researcher and has published in refereed journals and presented papers at both regional and international conferences. Kethi holds a BA (Hons) from the University of Nairobi and an MSc. in Economics from the University of Leeds. She has also undertaken short courses in Macroeconomics and Econometrics at the London School of Economics (LSE).

Esman Nyamongo is the Assistant Director and Head of the Real Sector Analysis Division, in the Research Department of the Central Bank of Kenya. Prior to joining the Bank in 2008, he was a Lecturer at the Department of Economics University of Pretoria, South Africa, for two years, where he lectured in econometrics, microeconomics, and public finance to both undergraduate and graduate students. Previously, he also worked as an economist in the Ministry of Finance and Planning and the Ministry of National

Development in Kenya. He has a solid publication record and has presented papers at both regional and international conferences. Esman holds a PhD from the University of Pretoria, South Africa, an MA (in Economics) from the University of Nairobi, an MA in Economic Policy Management from Makerere University and a BA from the University of Nairobi.

John Rwangombwa is the Governor, National Bank of Rwanda. He was appointed Central Bank Governor on 25 February 2013. His career started in Rwanda Revenue Authority where he grew through ranks to the Deputy Commissioner of Customs for Operations. He then joined the Ministry of Finance and Economic Planning in 2002 as the Director of the National Treasury Department. Having served as the Ministry's first Accountant General in 2005, Mr Rwangombwa was appointed Permanent Secretary and Secretary to the Treasury in the same year and in 2009 he became the Minister of Finance and Economic Planning. At that time, he oversaw the elaboration and implementation of Rwanda's first Economic Development and Poverty Reduction Strategy (EDPRS I), under which Rwanda's economy was able to achieve high growth at an average of 8 per cent and poverty was reduced by 12 per cent in five years from 2006 to 2011. In just three years at the helm of the Central Bank, Mr Rwangombwa has been able to maintain the stability of the Rwandan economy and its financial sector. He was further voted Governor of the Year 2015 for the Sub-Saharan Region by Emerging Markets. Mr Rwangombwa serves as member of various advisory bodies including the Presidential Advisory Council and World Economic Forum on Global Agenda Council.

Tavneet Suri is an Associate Professor of Applied Economics at the MIT Sloan School of Management. Suri is a development economist, with a regional focus on Sub-Saharan Africa. Her research centres on agriculture, household financial access, and informal risk sharing, and, more recently, governance and political participation. A large body of her work focuses on the constraints to technology adoption in agriculture. She has also conducted a lot of research on the impacts of mobile money (for example, M-PESA in Kenya) and applications of the mobile money platform for credit contracts (e.g. trade credit and credit for solar panels). Her most recent work has focused on governance issues in the Kibera slum in Nairobi and a large-scale field experiment she conducted in Kenya during the 2013 general election (the project where 'they sent a million text messages, literally!'). She spends a lot of time in the field, collecting her own data, primarily in Kenya, Sierra Leone, and Rwanda. She is the Scientific Director for Africa for J-PAL; a Faculty Research Fellow at the National Bureau of Economic Research; an affiliate of BREAD and CEPR; and co-director of the Agriculture Research Program at the International Growth Center. Suri holds a BA in economics from Trinity College, Cambridge University, as well as an MA in international and development economics, an MPhil in economics, and a PhD from Yale University.

Daniel Tallam is the Assistant Director and Head of the Financial Sector Analysis Division in the Research Department of the Central Bank of Kenya. He has over 15 years' experience at the Central Bank where he has held various senior positions in the Research Department, the Rural Finance Development and the Bank Supervision Department. He specializes in financial sector analysis and has deep understanding of the financial markets, financial legal, and regulatory environment. Daniel's career began with working as an Economist and

Statistician at the Long Range Planning Division in the Macro Planning Department of the Ministry of Finance and Planning, where he worked for one year, before moving to Egerton University as a Lecturer in Economics. He later joined the Ministry of Finance (The National Treasury) as a Deputy Director and Head of the Monetary Affairs Division in the Fiscal and Monetary Affairs Department for three years. Daniel has been instrumental in developing key financial sector policies, legal, and regulatory frameworks including chairing the Anti-Money Laundering Taskforce during 2001–04, policy and legal frameworks for microfinance banks and SACCO societies, and credit information sharing and agency banking frameworks. He holds an MA in Economics from the University of Nairobi.

Leonard Thotho joined the Central Bank of Kenya in June 2007 as a Graduate Trainee. He works in the Financial Markets Department, in the area of public debt management and financial market development and is a member of the CBK Financial Inclusion and Innovations Team (FIIT). He is a holder of Masters of Science in Finance from Kenyatta University, Master of Science (Demography), and Bachelor of Arts in Education (Statistics) both from the University of Nairobi. He is also a Certified Public Accountant Kenya (CPAK) and a member of ICPAK (Institute of Certified Public Accountants of Kenya) and Accredited Fellow of the Macroeconomic and Financial Management Institute of Eastern and Southern Africa (MEFMI), in the area of Sovereign Debt Management and Capital Market Development. Mr Thotho has over ten years work experience in public debt management, financial markets development and financial sector issues having worked at the Central Bank and with the National Treasury in Kenya, and facilitated in several international workshops in Africa as a resource person. He has participated in various regional initiatives such as the institutionalization of the Bank of South Sudan (BSS), an initiative of the Central Banks of South Sudan and Kenya; and the Financial Markets Subcommittee (FMS) of the Monetary Affairs Committee (MAC) of the East African Community (EAC) Central Banks.

Caroline Wanjiku is a graduate of Economics and Finance from Kenyatta University, currently pursuing a master's degree in Economics at the University of Nairobi. Her academic pursuit stretches to the fields of accounting and finance where she has attained Certified Public Accountants II certification. Having joined Central Bank of Kenya since 2014, she holds a wealth of knowledge and understanding in public debt management. Her keen interests are in public finance and debt sustainability and monetary analysis. Her passion for prudent public debt management cannot be overemphasized. Her current research is focusing on the interactions between public debt, public investment, and private investment.

Maureen Were works in the Research Department at the Central Bank of Kenya as a Manager, Macroeconomic Modelling and Forecasting Division. Dr Were is a seasoned economist with a conglomeration of experience in macroeconomic policy analysis, research, economic modelling, forecasting, and teaching. Before joining the Central Bank in 2008 she worked at the Kenya Institute for Public Policy Research and Analysis (KIPPRA) as a Policy Analyst in the Macroeconomics Division, taught Economics at the Egerton University and worked at the Institute for Policy Analysis and Research (IPAR). In 2013 she competitively won a one-year Mo Ibrahim Leadership Fellowship award that gave her a wealth of leadership and international work experience at the World Trade Organization in Geneva. She has written numerous research papers on various topics including macroeconomic policy issues, monetary policy, macro modelling, trade, growth, gender, and development, most of which are published in refereed journals. She has a PhD and Master's degree in Economics from the University of Dar-es-Salaam and University of Nairobi, respectively.

1
Introduction

Patrick Njoroge and Victor Murinde

1.1 Background

This book aims to document important milestones in the epic journey traversed by the Central Bank of Kenya (CBK) over the last 50 years, putting into perspective the evolution of central banking globally and within the East African region, and contemplating future prospects and challenges.

The book is timely, mainly because within the last 50 years, the global financial landscape has shifted. Central bankers have expanded their mandates beyond the singular focus on inflation and consider economic growth as their other important objective. Intermittent episodes of financial crises have continued to disrupt the functioning of financial institutions and markets, the most devastating one being the global financial crisis that broke out in 2008 and from which the global financial system has not fully recovered. Bank regulation has moved from Basel I, to Basel II, and some countries have fully migrated to Basel III while some are still at the crossroads. Economic theory has also gone through some serious rethinking, from Keynesian demand management to supply-side structuralism, rational expectations, and further to dynamic stochastic general equilibrium models that central banks are using for the new normal of monetary policy at zero-bound interest rates.

The book captures the wide-ranging discussions on central banking, from a symposium to celebrate the 50 year anniversary on 13 September 2016 in Nairobi. The participants at the symposium included current and former central bank governors from Kenya and the East Africa region, high-level officials from international organizations and multilateral financial institutions, policy-makers, executives of commercial banks in Kenya, private-sector practitioners, civil society agents, executives, and researchers from think tanks based in Kenya and the Africa region, leading academics in banking and finance, and university students.

Beyond the symposium, the book highlights the evolution of specific functions of the CBK over the last 50 years (such as monetary policy, bank regulation, and payments system), as well as developments in Kenya's financial system which strongly relate to the functionality of the CBK, such as financial innovation, the evolution of financial markets, and non-bank financial institutions in Kenya.

Patrick Njoroge and Victor Murinde, *Introduction* In: *50 Years of Central Banking in Kenya: Regional and Global Perspectives.* Edited by: Patrick Njoroge and Victor Murinde, Oxford University Press (2021).
DOI: 10.1093/oso/9780198851820.003.0001

1.2 The Chapters in Outline

The volume brings together leading scholars, policy-makers, and practitioners to provide a comprehensive and cutting-edge coverage of the epic journey travelled by the CBK from inception in 1966 to the present, in the process providing exceptional insight into Kenya's financial institutions, markets, and instruments. The book is structured into two parts. Part I provides a rich background of international issues, including theory as well as evidence, which relate to central banking in general. Part II builds on this background and provides specific insight into central banking in Kenya together with the other relevant components of Kenya's financial and fiscal architecture. For example, the thematic chapters in Part II cover topics such as commercial banking, development banking, the stock market, and insurance. It also includes examinations of banking regulation and supervision, and monetary policy.

Let us, for example, take three highlights from Part I, namely relating to reflections on central banking, financial inclusion, and mobile money. Chapter 3 by Njoroge and Murinde summarizes their reflections on central banking. It seeks to code the milestones on the epic journey of central banking from the initial conditions, through the transition to modern policy and practice today, both in a global context and in a Kenyan perspective. It is argued that although developments in economic theory, evidence, and policy have entrenched the robustness of central banking today (the good), some unresolved issues persist—five of these issues are highlighted. The note concludes with a futurology of central banking (the unknown) and some key highlights of our reflections.

In Chapter 8, David Ferrand and Ignacio Mas examine the role of central banks in financial inclusion, and pose the question: do central banks have a role in financial inclusion? The authors first look at the relationship between financial stability and financial inclusion before turning to the potential impact of financial inclusion on broader economic policy dimensions which some central banks regard as part of their remit. The discussion in this chapter provides an interesting case study of central bank engagement in financial inclusion, motivated in large part by the desire to support economic development objectives.

In Chapter 10, Tavneet Suri provides an overview of the operations and impacts of mobile money in the developing world. It is shown that over the past decade, mobile money has become a ubiquitous tool in some developing economies, allowing individuals to digitally transact money without formal bank accounts. It is interesting to note that the impacts, where documented, have been sizeable: For example, poverty decreased by two percentage points in Kenya. However, adoption still lags in many economies and, even where there is universal adoption, product innovation over the rails of these digital accounts has been slow. The review concludes by discussing what the future of mobile money in developing economies may look like and, thus, where the most exciting opportunities for research may be.

Part II of the volume offers plenty of highlights. For example, Chapter 13, by Maureen Were, Charles Koori, and Julius Bett, examines the evolution, challenges, and future prospects of central banking in Kenya. It is shown that the history of central banking in Kenya dates back to the pre-colonial period when the traditional central banking functions were performed by the East African Currency Board before the establishment of the CBK in 1966. Since then, central banking after independence was largely geared towards the development and expansion of the financial sector. Overall, the analysis in this chapter concludes that the central banks have achieved several milestones, including price and financial stability. It is argued that, going forward, the future of central banking in Kenya will have largely been shaped by the emerging financial and technological developments, regional integration initiatives, and the evolving global dynamics. The authors observe 'the Bank will have to think globally but act locally'.

Chapter 14, by Esman Nyamongo, Isaya Maana, and Anne Kamau, examines the dynamics of monetary policy in Kenya. The chapter chronicles the monetary policy phases and outcomes in Kenya since the establishment of the CBK in 1966. After detailed analysis of historical events and data spanning 50 years, it is found that monetary policy has evolved from an era of rudimentary monetary policy practice, a backward-looking monetary policy, to a regime best characterized as transitioning to inflation targeting. During this journey, the Bank has made major milestones. However, it is noted that the interest rate capping law which came into force in September 2016, as the Bank celebrated its 50th anniversary, is an area of concern for monetary policy, going forward.

Matu Mugo, Evelyne Kilonzo, and Anne W. Mariga, in Chapter 16, take these arguments a bit further and note that over the past half-a-century, Kenya's payments and banking systems have undergone incremental as well as revolutionary modifications that have transformed Kenya's financial landscape. From cash transactions to digital finance ecosystems, the most notable of these developments have taken place over the last two decades. These innovations include the reduction in clearing period for cheques, introduction of the Real Time Gross Settlement System for high-value payments, agency banking, and credit information sharing, among others. One of the most remarkable of these developments, M-PESA, rolled out in 2007, undoubtedly has earned its place in Kenya's Hall of Fame as well as placed Kenya among the technology innovative countries of the world. The developments in the payments system have culminated in a more accessible, effective, and efficient Kenyan payment system. For the first time ever, the chapter tells the M-PESA story from the lens of a regulator, the CBK, by key staff who have been actively monitoring and evaluating the innovation process. It details the fairly routine meeting that introduced the CBK to the product, review of the product, testing of the technology and its applications, the dilemmas faced, right up to the eventual launch in March 2007. More importantly, the chapter tells other understated stories of payments and related banking sector innovations that have seen the level of financial inclusion in Kenya triple from 26 per cent in 2006 to over 75 per cent in 2016. The chapter provides lessons that the CBK has learnt in this transformation journey. One of the most important lessons is the need for regulators to understand the business models underpinning innovations, risks thereon, and the risk mitigation measures in place.

In the deeper context of the monetary-fiscal arithmetic, namely the government budget constraint, discussion of the CBK would be incomplete without consideration of government securities. In Chapter 17, Leonard Thotho, Caroline Wanjiku, and Daniel Amanja examine the development of government securities market in Kenya. It is noted that a well-functioning domestic government securities market is not only a key determinant of a country's economic growth but also acts as a ready fall-back for the government to meet its budget financing needs at optimal cost and risk. This chapter evaluates developments in the domestic government securities market in Kenya during the period 1966–2016. The chapter traces the evolution of Kenya's government securities market starting with the legal and regulatory framework, evolution of the issuance policy, developments in both the primary and secondary market for government securities over time, and some of the milestones achieved during the period under review. Among the key milestones are: development of a reliable domestic financing programme for the government, development of benchmark bonds and a government securities yield curve, development of market infrastructure, and diversification of products in the market such as infrastructure bonds among others. For Kenya to further deepen her government securities market and capital markets in general, a couple of reforms have been proposed including launch of new products and further modernization of trading system and establishment of over the counter market for government securities.

It is indeed exciting to note that Part II of this volume ends with one key issue that policy makers and practitioners in the banking sector must watch: the structure of the interbank market in Kenya. Lydia Ndirangu, Kethi Ngoka-Kisinguh, and Esther Kariuki examine the prospects and challenges of this market in Chapter 18. It is noted that the overnight interbank market in Kenya has been in operation since 1995. This chapter discusses how the network structure of this market has evolved over time. The chapter invokes several measurements derived from network theory to uncover a number of interbank market microstructure characteristics in Kenya, including the nature of segmentation and associated asymmetric information in the interbank market. To the best of our knowledge, this chapter is the first to uncover the intrinsic structure of the interbank market in Kenya, using network theory. An important issue in the chapter is to understand what opportunities and challenges the structure of the interbank network presents for liquidity management, and therefore the implementation of monetary policy, the peer-to-peer mechanism of financial regulation and stability of the banking system.

1.3 More than a Golden Jubilee

The chapters that have been put together in this book provide a lot more than the coverage of the golden jubilee of the CBK. Many of the chapters provide original source material, from the archives of the Central Bank as well as the golden memories of long-serving government officials. For this matter, it is hoped that, in this volume, policy-makers in central banks and regulatory agencies will find invaluable insights about how some of the ideas in vogue today have evolved through time, and which of these ideas have worked very well, but also about some pitfalls in the context of Kenya. In addition, executives and practitioners in financial institutions and financial markets should be able to find interesting highlights about policy innovations and policy shifts that shape the economic and financial environment in which they ply their trade in financial services. Indeed, so will practitioners in agriculture, industry, and other sectors of the Kenyan economy, with implications for global lessons in many other countries. In the same manner, global and local investors should be able to gain rare insight into developments over the last 50 years in order to position their strategies for future investment in Kenya. Also, civil society agents should be able to find useful insights relevant to the third sector, such as the symmetry about policy success and unintended consequences. Importantly, researchers, think tanks, undergraduate and postgraduate students will find the book the key reference source on central banking in Kenya as well as developments in Kenya's financial sector.

The outbreak of the dreaded COVID-19 pandemic presented a global shock of unprecedented size and nature and sparked off somewhat globally synchronised economic restrictions, lockdowns and containment measures. These unprecedented events happened when this volume was already in print, rather too late to include any short analysis or even hazard a guess of the economic implications for the CBK, the Kenyan economy in a regional as well as a global perspective. The CBK, like many central banks around the world, reacted swiftly and forcefully to deploy the full range of crisis tools in order to ease financial stress and safeguard reasonable continuity of flow of funds within the economy, especially to the private non-financial sector. Detailed economic analysis, of the measures deployed by the CBK and the footprint of these measures on the Kenya economy and the East African region, will be the subject of a new volume in the near future.

PART I
CENTRAL BANKING
Global and Regional Perspectives

2
Monetary Policy and the Future of Central Banking
Implications for Africa

Mitsuhiro Furusawa

2.1 Introduction

I am honoured to join you today to commemorate the 50th anniversary of the Central Bank of Kenya.[1]

I have had the pleasure of working closely with Patrick—if I may call you Patrick, Governor—during his previous incarnation at the IMF, and it is truly a joy to share this moment with you.

Today marks an important milestone for Kenya, so I am very happy to have this opportunity to reflect upon your journey over the past half century—and to discuss with all of you the way forward.

In the time we have today, I would like to discuss the current state of central banking in Sub-Saharan Africa and to explore the challenges that this region's central bankers face as they address the increasingly complex forces at work in the global economy.

Of particular concern is a global economy marked by subpar growth with downside risks related to the ongoing adjustment in the global economy.

In addressing these challenges monetary policy has a central role to play. Along with government fiscal policies, well-designed and well-implemented monetary policies are essential for a country to achieve strong, sustainable, and inclusive growth.

2.2 Evolution of Central Banking

Let me begin by briefly taking stock of developments in central banking and monetary policy over the last 50 years, and then placing those developments in the African context.

[1] This chapter originates from the remarks made on the 50th Anniversary of the Central Bank of Kenya by Mitsuhiro Furusawa, IMF Deputy Managing Director.

Mitsuhiro Furusawa, *Monetary Policy and the Future of Central Banking: Implications for Africa* In: *50 Years of Central Banking in Kenya: Regional and Global Perspectives.* Edited by: Patrick Njoroge and Victor Murinde, Oxford University Press (2021).
 DOI: 10.1093/oso/9780198851820.003.0002

Traditionally, the primary objectives of monetary policy have been to maintain price and financial stability and to help achieve full employment.

At times there may appear to be a conflict between the goals of low inflation and economic growth. But we have learned from hard experience that high inflation distorts the private sector's savings and investment decisions—leading ultimately to slower growth.

That is why countries have increasingly placed greater emphasis on price stability, and many of them have made low and stable inflation the primary objective for monetary policy.

To achieve the price stability objective, we have seen monetary policy frameworks evolve over time. In the period after World War II, monetary policy operated in the context of fixed exchange rates under the Bretton Woods system.

Following the collapse of that system in 1972, central banks generally used monetary targets and soft exchange rate pegs to bring down the high inflation that the world experienced through the early 1980s.

However, as inflation fell, and financial innovation emerged, the link between money targets and inflation outcomes became increasingly tenuous. In addition, the increase in capital flows—and the market volatility that followed—created significant challenges for small, open economies operating soft exchange rate pegs to deal with external shocks while seeking to achieve price stability.

This is why central banks have gradually switched to forward-looking monetary policy frameworks to stabilize their economies. Starting with New Zealand in 1989, many central banks responded to these challenges by switching to formal inflation targeting as a framework for monetary policy.

This approach essentially combines an explicit inflation target with a commitment to use market-based instruments and a flexible exchange rate to achieve the inflation target over the medium term.

Not all central banks adopted formal inflation targeting frameworks. But in most cases the operational framework has been similar—that is to say, it was centred on adjusting short-term policy rates to maintain low and stable inflation over the medium term.

These forward-looking monetary policy frameworks have been supported by legislative mandates to give central banks operational independence. This has been coupled with procedures that ensure central bank transparency and public accountability.

2.3 African Central Banking in Perspective

These trends certainly have influenced the way central banking and monetary policy have evolved in Sub-Saharan Africa. In the immediate post-colonial era, the new central banks lacked independence from their governments: they were directed to finance large fiscal deficits. There were pervasive foreign exchange and interest rate controls.

Starting in the late 1980s and increasingly during the 1990s, the region largely adopted monetary policy frameworks based on either monetary targets or exchange rate pegs. These were supported by smaller fiscal deficits and reduced central bank financing of those deficits.

Now, however, the weaker relationship between money and inflation, and the changing financial landscape, are again calling on African central banks to adjust their strategies.

Ghana, South Africa, and Uganda have adopted formal inflation-targeting regimes. Other countries with flexible exchange rate regimes are de-emphasizing the role of monetary aggregates and incorporating elements of the monetary policy practices of industrial and emerging market countries.

These practices include greater reliance on interest rates for the transmission of the monetary policy stance, improved liquidity management, and greater focus on policy analysis, forecasting, and communications.

Kenya does not formally target inflation. But since 2011, Kenya has adopted a more forward-looking monetary policy framework centred around the CBK's policy rate, which is set by a monetary policy committee. As many of you know, this policy is aimed at maintaining inflation within the government's target range of 2.5 per cent on either side of the 5 per cent medium-term target. Using this framework, Kenya has successfully managed to keep inflation within the target range most of the time over the past several years.

Sub-Saharan Africa's shift towards more forward-looking monetary frameworks has been supported by reduced fiscal deficits, generally more flexible exchange rate regimes, and a more intensive use of market-based monetary instruments.

At the same time, financial systems in the region have experienced significant deepening over the past decade. This should translate into potentially stronger monetary transmission over time.

A key element of this deepening has been the region's emergence as a world leader in innovative financial services based on mobile phone technology. This has led to a breakthrough in financial inclusion, especially here in East Africa.

And as you know, Kenya has led the way: over 75 per cent of your population has now financial access, up from about 40 per cent just five years ago. This reflects the fast spread of M-PESA, M-Shwari, and M-Kesho, which has helped reduce transaction costs and facilitate personal transactions.

On top of this, Kenya also has one of the most diversified and deep financial sectors in Sub-Saharan Africa. Your well-established government bond market is providing key support for effective transmission of monetary policy. Other African countries are making similar progress.

2.4 Challenges Facing Africa

Nonetheless, many central banks in Sub-Saharan Africa are facing serious obstacles as they design and implement effective monetary policies—not least because of the combination of external and domestic challenges. Allow me to elaborate.

The external factors are well known to this audience. Many African countries have been feeling the pain of the collapse in commodity prices. Growth has fallen sharply, and inflation is rising as a result of exchange rate depreciation.

Countries that are less dependent on commodities exports—including Kenya—are doing better. But the room for manoeuvre that their central banks have enjoyed for the past several years is becoming more confined.

A key reason for this is the region's integration into global trade and financial networks. You are subject to forces well beyond your control.

For example, the uncertainty surrounding the timing of exit from unconventional monetary policies in advanced countries has increased the volatility of capital flows. The risk is that a sudden reversal of capital inflows could lead to a large and disorderly depreciation of the local currency, with adverse implications on both inflation and financial stability.

All of this greatly complicates the conduct of monetary policy. Still, the good news is that many of Sub-Saharan Africa's central banks have built adequate international reserve cushions. This includes Kenya, giving the CBK greater room for manoeuvre, and reducing the risk of a sudden reversal of capital flows in the first place.

This confluence of international developments is heightening the domestic challenges that central banks are facing. Many still have limited operational capacity. This partly reflects persistent weakness in government cash flow management, which makes it difficult for central banks to adequately manage liquidity conditions.

Together with restrictions on access to central bank standing facilities for lending to banks and allowing them to place deposits with the central bank, at times this results in large variances between policy rates and the market rates relevant for commercial bank liquidity managing. This risks rendering policy rates irrelevant for commercial bank pricing and lending decisions, thus reducing the effectiveness of monetary policy.

Another challenge facing many African countries is the persistence of very high spreads between the interest rates offered on deposits and those charged on loans. This has led to understandable frustration among borrowers about the cost of credit, and has produced political pressure for interest rate controls.

However, the politicization of monetary policy bears well-known risks—for the soundness of the financial system and for credit access, notably higher-risk borrowers. International experience suggests that, in many cases, interest rate controls may actually end up reducing access to the banking system for small borrowers—such as farmers, SMEs, and consumers—and may also revive informal lending at much higher cost for borrowers.

In addition, linking deposit and lending rates to the central bank's policy rate may compromise the independence of the central bank, and hamper its ability to enact monetary policy towards achieving its main objectives—that is to maintain price and financial stability and to support the economy.

Finally, the limitations of high-frequency economic indicators in many countries, especially on external trade and the real economy, constrain monetary authorities' ability to take corrective actions in a timely manner.

2.5 The Way Forward

So how can we best address these challenges? The answer will not be the same for different countries.

Where countries have chosen to belong to a currency union, or maintain a hard peg, the exchange rate will continue to anchor monetary policy. In countries where institutional capacity remains very weak, building that capacity should be the first priority.

But for many others, notably the frontier economies in Africa that are rapidly integrating into global financial markets, more forward-looking monetary policy frameworks will be needed in the coming years.

Let me now turn to seven principles to increase the effectiveness of monetary policy for countries seeking to move towards forward-looking monetary policy frameworks, which are based on the experience around the world on such frameworks. Here I would like to emphasize that I am making points that apply across the region. Kenya already has embraced many of these principles.

First, the central bank should have a clear legal mandate of policy goals and operational independence to pursue these goals.

Second, the primary, medium-term objective of monetary policy should be price stability. Monetary policy ultimately has a limited capability to directly influence real variables such as output growth over the long term.

Third, the central bank should make a medium-term numerical inflation objective the cornerstone for its monetary policy actions and communications. A transparent inflation objective provides a simple benchmark against which to measure performance.

Fourth, the central bank should carefully take into account the implications of monetary policy adjustments for financial stability. However, this should not come at the expense of undermining the central role of the medium-term inflation objective. Any significant erosion of central bank credibility can change inflationary expectations for the worse. This, in turn, could have an undesirable impact on real activity and financial stability.

Fifth, the central bank should have a clear and effective operational framework, by setting an operating target and clearly communicating the link between such an operating target and the medium-term inflation objective. This supports the functioning of money markets.

Sixth, the central bank should have a transparent, forward-looking monetary policy strategy that reflects timely and comprehensive assessments of the monetary transmission mechanism.

Seventh, central bank communications should be transparent and timely. This helps reduce uncertainty, improves monetary policy transmission, and facilitates accountability. The goal must be to build credibility.

2.6 Conclusion

Having listed these seven principles, I would like to stress that each country faces unique conditions and challenges that will dictate the pace at which they proceed. What is essential is to have internally consistent policy goals, the institutional arrangements that give the central bank the operational independence to pursue these goals, and transparency.

Many countries in Sub-Saharan Africa, including Kenya, are well advanced along this road. It is an important achievement. The IMF is fully committed to provide any assistance that the Kenyan authorities and those across Africa may need to continue upgrading the monetary policy frameworks to address the challenges of the future.

3

Reflections on Central Banking

Patrick Njoroge and Victor Murinde

3.1 Introduction

It is a great honour to participate in this historical celebration of the last 50 years of the Central Bank of Kenya (CBK).[1] Indeed, the CBK's golden jubilee is no trivial matter. The average corporate life expectancy of top institutions and corporate bodies in Africa is less than 50 years, and more than 80 per cent of small firms (e.g. *Jua Kali*) succumb to the Valley of Death in 0–3 years;[2] nevertheless, the CBK is right here at 50 and growing stronger!

We seek to reminisce about central banking. But, rather than trying to demonstrate our age advantage of being a tiny bit older than the CBK, we draw some boundary lines, perhaps superficially, in order to keep things manageable and also to keep off the 'neck of the woods' allocated to other speakers at this symposium.

We seek to code the policy milestones on the epic journey of central banking from the initial conditions, through the transition, to modern central banking today, both in a global context and in a Kenyan perspective. Then, we argue that throughout the twists and turns of the epic journey, although developments in economic theory, evidence, and policy have entrenched the robustness of central banking today, some unresolved issues persist—we highlight five of these issues. Futurology is often quite tempting when we reminisce, so we conclude with some important concerns today regarding the future of central banking.[3]

[1] This chapter was prepared for the Symposium to mark the Central Bank of Kenya 50th Anniversary celebrations. Murinde also acknowledges support of the research under grant ESRC Ref: ES/N013344/2 as well as funding by the AXA Chair at SOAS University of London. However, the views expressed in the paper are entirely our own and should not be construed to represent the official views of the Central Bank of Kenya or other institutions or organizations.

[2] See Cressy (2006) on why most firms die young. See also Green, Kimuyu, Manos, and Murinde (2008) on evidence from a large-scale survey of Kenyan micro and small scale enterprises (locally known as *Jua Kali*).

[3] Some of our predictions will be supported or rejected when CBK is celebrating its Centenary Anniversary. The tragedy of economic science is that our beautiful hypotheses may be easily assassinated by ugly facts!

Patrick Njoroge and Victor Murinde, *Reflections on Central Banking* In: *50 Years of Central Banking in Kenya: Regional and Global Perspectives*. Edited by: Patrick Njoroge and Victor Murinde, Oxford University Press (2021).
 DOI: 10.1093/oso/9780198851820.003.0003

3.2 The Epic Journey: Global and Local Milestones

3.2.1 Initial Conditions: The Swedish Riksbank (1668) and Bank of England (1694)

Economic historians trace the history of central banking to 1668 when the Swedish Riksbank was established as a joint stock bank, with a national charter to lend funds to government and act as a clearing house for commerce.[4] Later in 1694, the Bank of England (BoE) was established as a joint stock company, also to lend to government, by purchasing government debt. Other central banks followed, including the Banque de France, founded in 1800 to contain hyperinflation and foster renewed economic growth during the French Revolution.

What is interesting here is that these early central banks established three building blocks of the mandate of central banking today, namely the issuance of currency and protecting its value, lender to government and lender of last resort, and payments system (banks for bankers and providing a clearing system).

3.2.2 The Transition: The Walter Bagehot Milestone and the US Federal Reserve Milestone

The Walter Bagehot milestone: Major financial panics occurred during 1825–1857, when BoE turned away private claims for gold. To address these panics, Walter Bagehot proposed the 'responsibility doctrine', which required BoE to subsume its private interest to the public interest of the banking system as a whole, to lend freely on the basis of any sound collateral offered—but at a penalty rate (that is, above market rates) to prevent moral hazard. Hence, the Bagehot's dictum:

> to avert panic, central banks should lend early and freely (i.e. without limit), to solvent firms, against good collateral, and at high rates.[5]

It is worthwhile to note that the 'responsibility doctrine' worked well such that no major financial crises occurred in England for nearly 150 years after 1866, until August 2007 when the UK experienced the global financial crisis (GFC).

The US Federal Reserve milestone: The first central bank in the US, modelled after the BoE, was the Bank of the United States (1791–1811), followed by a second Bank of the United States (1816–1836). The latter was followed by the Free Banking Era, which had minimal regulation and allowed virtual free entry into

[4] See Bordo (2007) for an excellent summary of the history of central banks.

[5] See Bordo (2007). Note the mark-up pricing of funds, where the mark-up is risk-sensitive and stochastic over time.

and exit out of banking. The period was characterized by frequent bank failures, banking panics, and inefficient payments system, with thousands of dissimilar-looking state bank notes and counterfeits in circulation—hence, the central bank mandate of issuance of currency was at stake here.

The creation of the Federal Reserve in 1913, to provide a uniform currency and to serve as a lender of last resort, gave birth to a central banking system in the US. Hence, by 1913, the Federal Reserve System and other central banks emerged, to consolidate the various instruments used for currency, engender financial stability, and manage the gold standard (or price stability).

In addition, this transition period saw the birth of the world's oldest international financial institution—the Bank for International Settlements(BIS). The BIS was established in 1930 to 'foster international monetary and financial cooperation and serve as a bank for centralbanks'.[6] However, during the Great Depression, BIS was unable to play the role of lender of last resort and could not intervene to end exchange rate instability when Britain and the US printed more money and devalued their currencies. Subsequently BIS suspended all operations during WWII. What is to be noted here is the lack of coordination by central banks, when individual central banks pursue seemingly unrelated objective functions.

3.2.3 Modern Central Banking

Following the end of WWII, the International Monetary Fund (IMF) was created, mainly to monitor exchange rates and suppress possible currency warfare and to lend reserve currencies to nations in debt, hence addressing some of the difficulties that had crippled the BIS.

With the IMF in place, central banks started to refocus the policies. In the US, the Federal Reserve System refocused its stabilization policy from low inflation to high employment, perhaps underpinned by the theoretical persuasion of Keynesian macroeconomics and the Phillips curve trade-off between inflation and unemployment. There followed a difficult period of high inflation, recession, stagflation, until the early 1990s.

However, gradually central banks delivered the Great Moderation, with steady growth and low inflation in industrial economies and rapid growth and stable inflation in emerging economies, until the outbreak of the global financial crisis in 2008. The success is attributed to inflation targeting to ensure both economic growth and low inflation. Of course, the Fed has long had a dual (unemployment and price stability) mandate, as did Bank of Japan (to increase inflation).

[6] See BIS website at https://www.bis.org/about/index.htm

Another important evolution is the role of financial stability by modern central banks. It is now conventional wisdom that a healthy and well-functioning economy is built on trust and confidence in financial institutions, markets, and the financial system as a whole. For example, the financial stability roles of modern central banks, such as the BoE, European Central Bank, and the CBK, are reflected in the mandate of the Financial Stability Board (FSB), which:

> promotes global financial stability by *coordinating* development of regulatory, supervisory and other financial sector policies and conducts *outreach* to non-member countries.[7]

Two issues: first, in the financial stability deliberations, what role should be given to asset price inflation? Should central banks 'lean against the wind'? Second, coordination problems persist, in part due to implicit or explicit exchange rate targeting and, indeed, Quantitative Easing now largely works through relative devaluation effects, raising fears of 'beggar thy neighbour' policies that the IMF was set up to eliminate in the first place. Post-GFC, undershooting inflation target is a problem for the EU as well as Japan (the UK and the US, to a lesser extent). So, at Jackson Hole two weeks ago alternatives were considered, including raising the inflation target to say 4 per cent, as previously advocated by the IMF, or move to nominal gross domestic product (GDP) targeting, among other options, to avoid the zero-bound problem and the need for negative interest rate policy (NIRP).

3.2.4 From the 1919 Milestone to the 1966 Milestone in Kenya

The first stage of the evolution of central banking in Kenya was the establishment of the East African Currency Board (EACB) in 1919 for Kenya, Tanganyika, and Uganda, later joined by Zanzibar in 1936. The main role of the EACB was to issue the East African shilling, which replaced the rupee as currency in the region.[8]

The East African Shilling was issued at par with the shilling in the UK, strictly on the basis of sterling securities at the Bank of England. Hence, the EACB did not have any room for any kind of monetary policy or exchange rate policy or for regulating the activities of commercial banks. The EACB's hands were tied.[9]

The EACB was replaced by the independent central banks of Kenya, Tanzania, and Uganda in 1966. Consequently, the Central Bank of Kenya started issuing

[7] FSB website at https://www.bis.org/about/index.htm

[8] But, later during WWII, the East African shilling monetary area, expanded to include, albeit temporarily, Aden, British Somaliland, Eritrea, Ethiopia, and Somalia. See Symes (2004) for detailed coverage.

[9] Currency Boards have been described as a way of tying the hands of the monetary authority; see, for example, de Haan and Berger (2003), in Mullineux and Murinde (2003).

its own currency in 1966 under the mandate in the Central Bank of Kenya Act cap 491.

Unlike the EACB, each new central in Kenya, Tanzania, and Uganda, respectively, would:

- Serve as monetary authority, charged with the responsibility for policies that affect the supply of money and credit in the respective country.
- Have a mandate to use its tools of monetary policy (namely open market operations, discount window lending, changes in reserve requirements) in order to affect short-term interest rates and the monetary base (currency held by the public plus bank reserves).
- Have a mandate to use monetary policy to achieve important policy goals; for example, inflation, economic growth, and the exchange rate (or foreign reserves).

Notable among the consequences of the 1919 milestone is that central banking in East Africa followed the British central banking tradition and so did the entire banking system. The evolution of the mandate of the Central Bank of Kenya was influenced partly by its earlier connection with the Bank of England.

Overall, what has emerged from the epic journey of global and local (Kenyan) milestones is that the modern central bank now has three main goals:

- Safeguarding the value of money or maintaining price stability is the prime role. This is measured by a sustained low rate of inflation. Monetary policy is expected to achieve this goal. Notwithstanding quantitative easing (QE), NIRP, and the proposal to scrap cash so that only money is electronic bank money, so all savings can be 'taxed' using NIRP.
- Achieve high and sustainable economic growth. Here, monetary policy has an important role here, specifically smooth the business cycle and offset exogenous shocks.
- Financial regulation and maintaining financial stability. This goal includes maintaining regulatory and supervisory oversight of financial institutions, an efficient and smoothly running payments system, and the prevention of financial crises.[10]

In addition, the evolution above gives us the theory of central banking today. In a flow of funds framework, central banks address asymmetric information problems among financial sector agents (such as banks), real sector agents (households and companies), and between the domestic economy and the rest of the world.

[10] This is consistent with Griffith-Jones and Gottschalk (2016) on balancing financial stability and growth in Africa.

Information is used to level the playing field for all agents and to price risk by financial institutions and financial markets. Central banks also underpin the incentive structure for all agents, especially for financial intermediation models used by banks to balance profitability and risk, and the incentives for market discipline (e.g. via peer-monitoring).

3.3 Observations on Some Unresolved Issues

The epic journey for the evolution of central banks, described above, was characterized by many breakthrough developments. However, some challenges have persisted in economic theory, empirical evidence, policy, and practice. Let me consider five challenges.

3.3.1 Macroeconomic Policy Modelling

Central banks, the world over, have been at the forefront of macroeconomic policy modelling to underpin their policy decisions and forecasts. The most notable achievements include the flow of funds modelling approach pioneered at the Cowles Foundation for Research in Economics at Yale University,[11] the vector autoregressive work pioneered by Christopher Sims, among others, and the focus on monetary policy by Bernanke and others, and recently the dynamic stochastic general equilibrium (DSGE) approach that has proved popular with many central banks.[12]

Economic theory and econometric applications have thrown up at least five challenges:

- The objective function—what utility function are you maximizing?
- Model uncertainty—the functional form as well as parameter uncertainty.
- Lag structure for dynamics: shall we use Akaike Information Criterion (AIC) or Schwarz Information Criterion (SBC) or Hannan-Quin Information Criterion (HC) or co-integration? The results from AIC and SBC often conflict.
- Making forecasts: can we forecast structural breaks?
- Choice of policy instrument—the Tinbergen–Theil framework and the 'assignment problem'.

[11] See Brainard and Tobin (1968), for their seminal paper on pitfalls in financial model building; see also Stone (1984) and Klein (2000, 2003) on flow of funds—all three Nobel prizewinners (Klein in 1980, Tobin in 1981, and Stone in 1984). For a theoretical model, relevant to emerging market economies, see Green and Murinde (1998).

[12] These macroeconomic modelling approaches are covered in detail in Murinde (1992, 1993), Green and Murinde (1993, 1998), and Murinde (2011), among other studies. See also applications of flow of funds modelling to capital flight, in Murinde, Ochieng, and Meng (2015).

Nevertheless, what we have learnt from the macroeconomic modelling work by central banks over the last 50 years is that each approach has its major advantages as well as limitations. For example, the flow of funds approach to large scale macroeconomic models gives researchers the flexibility to calibrate the model to the structure of the respective economy with the central bank located at the core of the macro model, and to undertake policy experiments using stochastic simulations in order to generate what-if scenarios for the impact of a given policy package on each of three targets: inflation rate, economic growth rate, and exchange rate.[13] The central bank can easily pick the policy package of choice for the desired macroeconomic outcomes. However, the well-entrenched Lucas critique warns us that some parameters may change when policy changes. DSGE approach is very promising, but falls short of the forecasting power of Bayesian vector autoregressive (BVAR) models.

The CBK has featured actively in these developments, generating rigorous econometric models to support strategic financial policy at the macro and micro levels, thanks to the competent team in the Research Department, the Kenya School of Monetary Studies (KSMS), and the School of Economics at the University of Nairobi. Given this huge battery of research expertise, it appears worthwhile for the CBK to invest in a suite of the best three model vintages available to date, with each tailored to a special purpose, but offering the advantage of comparing outputs: the flow-of-funds model for macro and micro policy; the BVAR for forecasting and the DSGE for dealing with specific monetary policy questions.

3.3.2 Governance: Central Bank Independence and Other Governance Reforms

The governance of central banks is a major issue of interest today in industrial economies as well as developing countries. Indeed, a quick look at the structure, composition and roles of the Board of Directors and top management of many central banks points to some surviving commonalities (consistent with *the original sin hypothesis*), but the differences (mainly shaped by institutional environment such as legal and political factors) seem to suggest that no two central banks are the same, even within the East African region![14]

[13] See Murinde (1992, 1993) on modelling the potency of stabilization policy in Uganda, and Green and Murinde (1993) on Kenya, Tanzania, and Uganda. See also models based on flow of funds in Green and Murinde (1998, 2003, 2005). Bahra, Green, and Murinde (1999) present financial reform simulation experiments for Estonia and Poland. On flow of funds models of household portfolio behaviour, see Moore, Green, and Murinde (2005, 2006).

[14] The central bank governance structures are not homogenous of degree one among the five East African countries.

But, core to the governance of central banks is the issue of governance reforms designed to secure central bank independence (CBI).[15] The theoretical underpinnings are well represented in a government budget constraint.[16] A useful characterization defines CBI in terms of personnel independence, financial independence, and policy independence.[17] Personnel independence reflects limits to the government's influence on the central bank board's membership or tenure. Financial independence restricts the government's ability to use central bank's loans to fund its expenditures, to avoid monetary policy subordination to fiscal policy. Policy independence reflects the central bank's powers to select targets and instruments for monetary policy and to implement them. It is a sharp departure from the early experience in East Africa, where the hands of the EACB were tied.

But, what do we know about the dynamics of central bank reform in the world? Existing knowledge today suggests that CBI is linked to lower inflation, reduced variation in inflation and output, increased credibility of monetary policy, and lower uncertainty among economic agents.[18] However, it is not altogether true that African central banks have the highest marginal propensity to be manipulated by political ambitions. On the contrary, Kenya is featured as having the highest CBI in Africa during 1998–2010. Nevertheless, the measurement of CBI is still imperfect and it is not clear whether the three types of CBI identified above all have stabilizing potency.

3.3.3 Exchange Rate Regime and Natural Resources

Competitive devaluation of the exchange and beggar-thy-neighbour policies featured in our epic journey of central banking.[19] Post-WWII, the IMF has played a key coordination role with central banks in order to minimize the incidence of competitive devaluation, notwithstanding some intermittent currency wars.[20]

However, recent literature has flagged up an interesting aspect of exchange rate regime and CBI, which has important implications for African countries that are endowed with natural resources, including Kenya—given that central banks are at

[15] See, for example, Bernhard (2002) and Garriga (2016). See the time-inconsistency problem (Kydland and Prescott, 1977) can be overcome if the control of monetary policy is delegated to independent central banks; on 'rules versus discretion' debate (Barro and Gordon, 1983; Rogoff, 1985); and the fact that the IMF welcomed CBI (Bernhard, Broz, and Clark, 2002; International Monetary Fund, 1999; World Bank, 1992; and Garriga, 2016).

[16] See, for example, Murinde (1992, 1993).

[17] See Eijffinger and de Haan (1996) and de Haan and Berger (2003).

[18] See, in particular, Bodea and Hicks (2015a), and de Haan and Berger (2003).

[19] Specifically, using beggar-thy-neighbour policy, one country attempts to remedy its economic problems by means that tend to worsen the economic problems of other countries. The term is attributed to Adam Smith.

[20] See *IMF Annual Report on Exchange Rate Arrangements and Exchange Rate Restrictions* (IMF, 2014).

the core of managing natural resource rents as well as seigniorage.[21] It is argued that for countries which depend heavily on natural resources, the degree of exchange rate management tends to influence the relationship between seigniorage and governments' natural resource revenues. But, the exact influence seems to also reflect the various types of natural resources as well as the exchange rate regime. For example, it is found that under fixed or limited flexibility exchange rate regime, an increase in natural resource rents may trigger an increase in seigniorage. But, the same increase in natural resources has little effect on seigniorage under crawling currency bands and managed floating regime, while under freely flexible exchange rate regimes, an increase in natural resource rents allows less reliance on seigniorage. In terms of the various types of natural resources, it seems that the direct relationship between natural resource rents and seigniorage is driven mostly by oil and natural gas, with mixed evidence of a direct relationship for minerals and little evidence that coal and forestry influence seigniorage in the sample countries.

Researchers at the CBK, KSMS, and School of Economics of the University of Nairobi and other universities in Kenya may wish to pursue this line of research, with respect to Kenya and other countries that are *blessed* with natural resources.

3.3.4 Bank Regulation: Still at the Crossroads?

National central banks and BIS, the central banks' bank, have played a critical role in sustaining the dynamics of international banking regulation, codified in Basle Accords. Basel I was introduced in 1988 to create a bank asset classification system in order to deal with credit risk: banks were required to maintain a minimum amount of capital based on a percentage of risk-weighted assets (8 per cent). But, the Asian financial crisis highlighted deficiencies in monitoring credit risk and hence derailed Basel I.[22] An updated version was introduced in June 2004, coded Basel II, structured into three pillars: minimum capital requirements (for credit risk as in Basel I), supervisory review, and market discipline. But, before it could be fully implemented by many countries, Basel II reached the crossroads following the outbreak of the global financial crisis in 2008. From the crossroads many African countries are a bit apprehensive about Basel III, which is structured around bank capital adequacy, stress testing and market liquidity risk.

[21] See Elbahnasawy and Ellis (2015) on the inverse relationship of financial development and exchange rate management to seigniorage. See also Kamgnia and Murinde (2015) on the role of these natural resources for economic growth and employment creation for the youth in Africa.

[22] The CAR of 8 per cent was not very useful in identifying bank performance inefficiency; see Kirkpatrick, Murinde, and Tefula (2008) on the measurement and determinants of x-inefficiency in commercial banks in Africa. See also Lensink and Meesters (2014) on institutions and bank performance; and Zhao and Murinde (2011); Zhao, Matthews, and Murinde (2013); and Matthews, Murinde, and Zhao (2007).

The schedule for implementation has been extended to 31 March 2018 and again to 31 March 2019.[23]

But, why are bank regulators overstaying at the crossroads? Perhaps, it is the ownership of Basel III (or earlier versions in Basel I and II), involving wider membership and due consultations (voice), or simply that the small print of the accord are not well understood. Indeed, some researchers have called for Pillar 4 in designing post-crisis bank regulation.[24] Also, it may be the capacity building required to bridge the gap between bank regulation and bank supervision.

But, it may well be the case of the missing evidence:[25] some tenets of Basel III, such as capital buffers, are part of the unresolved issues in theory and empirical research today: specifically, the Basel accords have not reconciled three issues—bank capital, bank risk, and bank profitability. For example, recent research investigates the simultaneous relationship among bank capital, risk, and profitability, using bank level data from West African Economic and Monetary Union (WAEMU) countries during 2000–2014.[26] The 8 WAEMU countries are split into lower middle-income (LMIs) and low-income (LICs). It is found that:

- the sensitivity of bank profitability to changes in capital ratio is much higher in LICs (-0.39) than in LMIs (-0.07).
- on average, one unit percentage increase in capital ratio leads to 107 basis points decrease in bank risk (as per the *moral hazard hypothesis*); the impact is stronger in LICs than LMIs.
- banks are counter-cyclical in LICs, i.e. banks accumulate capital buffer during expansions and deplete the capital during recessions when risk is high, mimicking Basle III.
- Foreign bank ownership and cross-border banking reduce risk in the banking sector, but while the former is associated with an increase in capital ratios (0.005) in LICs the latter reduces the capital ratio in LMIs and increases profitability in LICs.

Jointly with the CBK, KSMS and the School of Economics at UoN, it will be interesting to investigate the case of Kenya, together with the regional member countries which host cross-border banks from Kenya.

[23] Murinde (2011) argues that financial regulation in Africa is at a crossroads: the road behind points to an expired Basel 1, the road ahead points to Basel 3 with so many unknowns, while the side roads have interesting aspects of Basel 2 and its weaknesses. See Murinde (2012) for wide coverage of bank regulatory reforms in Africa.

[24] See Llewellyn (2013) on the need for Pillar 4 in post-crisis bank regulation.

[25] The absence of evidence is not evidence of absence.

[26] See Kanga, Murinde, and Soumare (2016) on capital, risk, and profitability of WAEMU banks, with cross-border banking. For the debate on opening up to foreign bank entry, see Murinde and Ryan (2003).

3.3.5 Globalization (Cross-border) and Convergence of Banking Systems

The long historical dynamic of finance is to expand globally and transform local, regional, and international finance accordingly. Although that dynamic has experienced reverses periodically it has accelerated between the 1970s and now, and there are theoretical grounds for believing that the globalization of finance will continue and develop new forms in future decades. The future of central banks is inextricably linked to the dynamics of globalization and convergence of banking systems.[27] Existing evidence shows that banks have increasingly gone cross-border, but banking systems have not necessarily converged.[28] Hence, central banks will continue to play a key role in the design of financial regulation and supervision as banks increasing go cross-border.

With respect to Kenya in the Eastern Africa region, two questions arise: first, whether banking systems in the Eastern Africa region are converging into a single East African banking space; second, the dynamics of cross-border banking from Kenya. Convergence of banking systems is driven by institutional factors such as legal framework for banks but also by the behaviour of financial markets and non-bank financial intermediaries, mainly in terms of whether bank-based financing prevails over market-based financing. The experience for a series of studies on the EU countries[29] shows that corporate financing patterns in EU countries are converging towards increased dependence on equity and bond markets and a reduced share of borrowings from the banking sector. A single Eastern Africa banking space, in which Kenya is playing a leading role, is a long-term perspective. The CBK and other central banks in the region are already playing their coordination role to reduce asymmetric information and to promote the merits of 'relationship banking' in the region rather than over-reliance on sheer credit scoring.

Research conducted here in Kenya investigated the drivers of cross-border banking in East Africa.[30] Four main findings are relevant here:

- institutional quality is vital at the planning phase of banks' going-abroad decision;

[27] A broad view of the challenge of globalization for central banks includes financial globalization and supply-side developments, such as political instability and oil price shocks, which fall outside of the control of central banks.

[28] See, in particular, Mullineux and Murinde (2003), chapter 1; also Murinde, Agung and Mullineux (2004) on patterns of corporate financing and financial system convergence in Europe.

[29] See Murinde (1992), Murinde et al. (2004), and Mullineux and Murinde (2003). See also Brambila-Macias, Massa, and Murinde (2011) on cross-border bank lending versus FDI in Africa's growth story.

[30] See Kodongo, Natto, and Biekpe (2015) on explaining cross-border bank expansion in East Africa.

- relatively competitive markets and weak market power at home seem to 'push' banks abroad, but higher inflation in the host country is a deterrent;
- banks seek to exploit the benefits of their relative efficiency through regional expansion; and
- greater earnings, economic integration, and follow-the-client do not matter.

3.4 Futurology of Central Banking

3.4.1 The Future of Bank Regulation Cannot Ignore Peer Monitoring and Market Discipline

The architecture of Basel Accords I–III, since 1988 to the present, mimics the mechanical design of the n-speed of a manual transmission gearbox (where n is the number of forward gear ratios) in car manufacturing.[31] For the future, before Basel comes up with Basel IV, there is strong imperative to integrate the role of peer monitoring and market discipline as an integral component of official bank regulation. Indeed, as recent research shows, it takes more than simple regulation to achieve financial stability.[32]

As an example, in a recent empirical study, a team of Kenyan and other researchers investigated whether the interbank market in Kenya is effective as a peer monitoring and market discipline device and thus complements official bank regulation.[33] The research uses quarterly data on 43 banks which participated in interbank transactions during 2003Q1–2011Q4:

- A stable inverse relationship is uncovered between interbank activity and bank risk levels, even after controlling for differences in bank characteristics.
- The overall findings suggest that regulators can use the dynamic interbank borrowing activities among large and small banks as market signals to identify risky banks.
- However, if a bank continues to increase its net interbank position up a certain level, the impact on bank risk is reversed from risk-reducing to risk-increasing.

[31] Think of the gradual upgrade of gears of a manual transmission car: by 1900 with 1–2 gears; 1960s, cars had gears 1–3; in the 1980s, we got gears 1–4; in 2000, we got gears 1–5; now (2016), we have gears 1–7 on the Porsche 911. Gears 1–10 eventually or just automatic transmission?

[32] See recent path-breaking work by Griffith-Jones and Gottschalk (2016).

[33] See Green, Bai, Murinde, Ngoka, Maana, and Tiriongo (2016) for a survey on overnight interbank markets and the determination of the interbank rate. See also Murinde, Bai, Maana, Ngoka-Kisinguh, Tiriongo, and Green on peer monitoring role of the interbank market in Kenya and the implications for bank regulation.

Other non-formal regulatory mechanisms may be invoked, including the taxation of banks, as suggested by the new research on balancing the regulation and taxation of banks.[34] In addition, existing research seeks to draw regulatory lessons for emerging stock markets from an empirical study of the relationship between transactions costs and share price volatility in the London Stock Exchange.[35] The findings suggest that transactions taxes (e.g. stamp duty and brokerage charges) have a significant and dependable effect on share price volatility, such that the official regulatory regime needs to take account of the impact of regulation on such costs. For the future, this is important for financial regulators that rely on stamp duty or other transactions taxes as a regulatory tool—'throwing sand in the wheels' whenever the need arises.

3.4.2 The Mandate of a Central Bank

It is clear from the epic journey bank that since 1668 the mandate of central bank has been evolving, mainly influenced by economic and financial developments, globally and in Kenya. But, the economic and financial landscape has shifted and some conventional wisdom in economics has been challenged post-GFC, including the financial development and economic growth nexus; for example, recent research claims that too much finance can harm growth.[36]

The ever-changing world financial system generates international financial crises with widespread market failures of such a global magnitude that regulation machinery breaks down.[37] The co-existence of market failure (the market was unable to price risk) and regulatory failure translates into global financial risk; for example, the re-occurrence of financial crises:

- The Tequila crisis of December 1994 was a currency crisis ignited by capital flight.
- The financial crises across Asia in 1997–98 ignited fierce debate about domestic economic weaknesses and flaws in the international financial system.
- The Russian financial crisis (the Ruble Crisis or the Russian Flu), which hit Russia on 17 August 1998, resulted in the Russian government and the Russian Central Bank devaluing the currency and defaulting on its debt.

[34] See Chaudhry, Mullineux, and Agarwal (2015) on balancing the regulation and taxation of banking.

[35] See Green, Maggioni, and Murinde (2000) for 150 years of evidence on transactions costs and share price volatility in the London Stock Exchange.

[36] See Murinde (2012) for a survey of evidence on financial development and economic growth; and Law and Singh (2014) and Law, Azmani-Saini, and Mansor (2013) regarding evidence on how too much finance may harm growth.

[37] Banking crises generate contagion and pose a threat to financial integration; see Caballero (2015).

- The global financial crisis of 2008.
- The Eurozone crisis—the multi-year sovereign debt crisis since 2009, where the Eurozone member countries of Greece, Portugal, Ireland, Spain and Cyprus have been unable to refinance their debt or bail out over-indebted banks without intervention from other Eurozone member countries, the European Central Bank and the IMF.

The above financial crises have put to the test the traditional mandate of central banks and the conventional wisdom on moral hazard and adverse selection associated with deposit insurance and bank bail-outs, with new perspectives on too-big-to-fail (or too-big-to-exist).[38] Reforming the traditional structure of a central bank to cope with a financial crisis can be quite challenging, as can be learnt from the experience of the Bank of Thailand during the Asian financial crisis.[39]

Overall, for the future, there are five major global risks:[40]

1. *China's impact as a global investor:* the new context of China, setting 'new norms' in transforming the behaviour of financial markets, financial institutions, financial instruments, manufacturing, and commerce. How is Chinese outbound investment influencing industries abroad or shaping trade in Africa? The big world picture is shifting, including the setting of new rules for global finance. What does this mean for Kenya? What are the effects of financial disintermediation in China for Kenya banks?
2. *Technology-based financial innovation:* Electronic money (such as BITCOIN and block-chain technology). Also, how will the growth of non-traditional financial vehicles, including peer-to-peer lending, mobile payments systems, and mobile financial services (such as those developing from the M-PESA model) affect the theory and practice of finance and financial system stability? In this digital age, such Fintech innovations may herald a shift towards disintermediation that leads to the decline of traditional banks and financial institutions, but may lead to new forms of intermediation through new financial institutions or through emulation and incorporation by established financial firms.[41] It is to be noted that the move to a cashless society (e.g. mobile money) not only allows electronic money held in bank accounts to be taxes using NIRP, but may lead to loss of control of the

[38] See Griffith-Jones, Ocampo. and Stiglitz (2010) on lessons from the GFC and the need for 'a visible hand'.

[39] See Mullineux, Murinde, and Pinijkulviwat (2003) for further details.

[40] See Murinde (2016) on mega trends in global financial risks.

[41] In theory, the S-curve of financial innovation suggests that such innovations can derail financial stability; for example, securitization in the early 1990s and the recent subprime crisis. Central banks have to watch these innovations and how economic agents adjust their expectations.

money supply by central banks as it goes outside the banking system (perhaps to avoid the tax).

3. *New wave of political risk:* These risks are unconventional and mutative, posing threats to global business and finance. Some of the threats depart from convention, e.g. Brexit and uncertainty about the future of the EU, with implications for global economic security. The East Africa region and Kenya in particular are no exception. The global security context has serious implications for global investment; the question is whether financial markets are mispricing geopolitical risks.[42]
4. *Investment uncertainty and new rules for the regulation of global finance* arising from opaque rules for governing global finance, as in Basel III.[43] For example, when regulatory changes, technological and business model innovations are reshaping the global banking landscape, how can long-term investments be prioritized in Kenya?
5. *Islamic finance and shadow banking: different rules of the game?* This refers to the growth of Islamic banking and finance, as alternative forms of banking.[44] To what extent is expansion of 'Islamic' finance sustainable in East Africa and Kenya? Or will there be increased convergence with 'conventional' banking and finance as regulators and markets promote lower leverage ratios in the latter and create a conventional system which has features closer to equity based Islamic finance? The rapid growth of shadow banking globally means that there is an increasing need to monitor these non-bank financial intermediaries which provide financial services to traditional commercial banks but outside the oversight of official financial regulatory authorities.

In the face of the above five global risks, the central bank of the future is expected to be the 'brain' of the financial system, in a F-O-F framework, coordinating dissemination of information about resource availability at every level, evaluating the pricing of inherent risk, and so enabling the efficient allocation of resources for supporting economic growth.

Hence, future modern central bank should be modelled on a (1+*n*) design, where 1 is the universal goal to provide price stability (or low inflation over a long-run period) and *n* denotes a finite number of additional goals to be selected from among the following:

[42] Lensink, Hermes, and Murinde (2000) show that political risk is a key driver of capital flight. The new wave of political risk poses a threat to national and global financial systems.

[43] See Lensink and Murinde (2006) on the effect of uncertainty on investment.

[44] See, Al-Deehani, Karim, and Murinde (1999) on the capital structure of Islamic banks under the contractual obligation of profit sharing.

- *economic growth*: this is a separate goal, because low inflation does not guarantee economic growth; when the above mega exogenous shocks threaten to slow down economic growth, the central bank may temporarily ease monetary policy to restore the economy to its growth path. The most radical idea is that central banks should consider nominal GDP targeting rather than inflation targeting!
- *financial stability*: this is another separate goal, which addresses macro-prudential regulation, in order to mitigate systemic risk—the risk of the financial system as a whole. Also, in case of a financial crisis, as cited in the four examples above, it becomes necessary for the central bank to provide the required liquidity to ensure solvency and proper functioning of a stable market-based financial system—a modern variant of Walter Bagehot principle—even if it means a temporary departure from the low inflation goal.
- *Bank supervision and regulation*: this role includes the licensing, supervising, and regulation of commercial banks, as a mandate of the central bank.
- *Payment and settlement systems*: the central bank has an important role to ensure regulation and supervision of effective payment, clearing, and settlement systems.

Nevertheless, some questions remain; for example, what should the inflation target level be (above 2 per cent) and should this level be ditched in place of nominal GDP growth or other nominal targets (or perhaps real targets—which is implicitly what we have with interest rate policy under Quantitative Easing)? And what about asset price inflation targets to avoid bubbles driven by global capital flows (leaning against the wind)?

To deal with these questions, the cross-country element of the above goals is knowledge and capacity building. The CBK, through its Research Department, KSMS and the School of Economics at UoN, has already embarked on the cross-cutting dimension of a modern central bank.

3.4.3 Governance through Ownership: Should Central Banks Be Privatized?

Recent research suggests that ownership is an increasingly influential form of corporate governance.[45] This strand of literature may have important implications for future central banks. For example, after the outbreak of the global financial crisis in 2008, one eminent monetary economist delved into the history and the

[45] See Connelly, Hoskisson, Tihanyi, and Trevis Certo (2010) on ownership as a form of corporate governance.

desired future role of the Bank of England and concluded with a call for the UK central bank to be privatized.[46] The core argument was that the Bank of England had been unable to rise to the occasion and save Northern Rock, say via any lender-of-last-resort instruments, and to contain the subsequent instability in the UK financial system. So, a new structure was proposed, whereby the Bank of England would be privatized, with its capital provided by the commercial banks, which would provide the right incentive to regulate the banking system and also provide the banks with lender-of-last-resort facilities.

Broadly, the futurology of central banking cannot ignore the fact that there is some controversy about central bank ownership, including the call for some central banks to be privatized. True, many central banks are owned by governments (public owned). But, some non-conventional ownership structures of central banks do exist; for example, the Federal Reserve Bank is privately owned by its member banks; and the European Central Bank is owned by the national central banks. Nevertheless, it is useful to recall that before WWII, all European central banks were owned privately, which engendered many financial upheavals until the central banks were nationalized and controlled directly by governments. It's like déjà vu all over again![47]

3.4.4 Some Emerging Issues

There are four emerging issues, which we have side-stepped in this chapter, mainly because they feature prominently in the other presentations on the programme today:

Credit policy—modern central banks have played an important role in the formulation of credit policy, mainly through setting the central bank rate in such a way as to influence loan rates by commercial banks. Some Eastern and Southern African countries, including Kenya, feature persistently high loan interest rates and high spreads, but interestingly commercial banks in these countries also feature high loan default rates, as new research shows.[48] Tendencies towards financial repression in many African economies have been largely eliminated in the last 20–30 years, only to be revived, ironically, by national central banks through interest rate caps and by the major shareholders in the IMF and World Bank through Quantitative Easing. What are the policy options? How can central banks intervene, taking into account the relationship (in theory and empirical work) between different interest rates or bond yields and different terms or maturities (i.e. the term structure of interest rates)?

[46] See Congdon (2009) as the basis of the call: the Bank of England should be privatized.
[47] Taken from a famous quotation attributed to Yogi Berra; also the album by John Fogerty.
[48] A recent ESRC research project pins down these issues; see Griffith-Jones and Gottschalk (2016).

Inclusive finance—the financial inclusion revolution concerns the demand, access, use, and quality of financial services by disadvantaged and low-income social groups, segments of society, in order to bridge financial development gaps as well as financial inclusion gaps.[49] Broadly, policy and practice aims to address financial inclusion in a flow of funds framework (households, firms, governments, and capital markets) and to benefit from financial innovations such as mobile money banking and crowd-funding. FinScope surveys have been carried out to monitor national progress in many African countries including Kenya, Uganda, South Africa, Namibia, and Swaziland. The question is: what role should a modern central bank play, if any, on both the demand side and the supply side?

The 'new normal of monetary policy': Following the global financial crisis and quantitative easing (QE), central bank policy rates in industrial countries fell rapidly and have now hit the zero lower bound (ZLB), growth is slower and very low inflation rates actually pose a risk in maintaining price stability and financial stability.[50] Should the new normal include higher inflation targets? The experience in Eastern Africa and Kenya is not as bleak but these economies are highly vulnerable to the vagaries of the global financial weather conditions. The question is: what is the new normal of monetary policy in Kenya?

A single East Africa financial space: The CBK is already coordinating with other central banks in the region for greater regional financial integration, mainly under the EAC. The next question on the agenda is how quickly a single East Africa financial space can become a reality. This mimics a 'back to the future': from the common EACB, 1919–1966, to three separate central banks (Central Bank of Kenya, Bank of Uganda, and Bank of Tanzania, respectively) and then back in the future to integration of an EACB—East African Central Bank of Burundi, Kenya, South Sudan, Rwanda, Tanzania, and Uganda.

3.5 Conclusion and Some Key Take-away Highlights

There are many (stated and implied) important messages from this reflection on central banking, but we would like to highlight at least five key messages:

1. Central banks have evolved fairly smoothly and have made remarkable achievements of maintaining periods of price stability as well as promoting and sustaining global economic growth. Also, central banks have weathered a series of persistent economic and financial storms since 1668. They

[49] See Allen, Carletti, Cull, Qian, Senbet, and Valenzuela (2014) on financial inclusion gaps in Africa.

[50] With inflation expectations at the present 2 per cent, central banks are concerned that deflation might get out of control and unleash a long recession.

delivered the Great Moderation, right until the global financial crisis broke out in 2008. The Central Bank of Kenya stands tall in having shaped a strong and well-diversified financial system, with sustainable economic growth, over the last 50 years of its existence!

2. Price stability must remain mandate number 1 for central banks, but with the flexibility of the (*1+n*) rule, where central banks are flexible enough to prioritize any of the *n* elements when extraordinary circumstances arise. In the institutional design of a central bank, there is no 'one size fits all', so central banks have greater flexibility to fulfil their financial stability responsibilities and cope with the growing pressure to play a role in funding fiscal expansion to deliver faster growth—or more precisely promoting inclusive economic development rather than economic growth per se and paying more attention to inequality issues.
3. Central bank independence, in all its three forms, is a critical component of the architecture of a modern financial system: Personnel independence to limit the government's influence on the central bank board's membership or tenure; financial independence to restrict the government's use of central bank's loans to fund its expenditures (currently compromised in most OECD countries under QE and NIRP); and policy independence to select targets and instruments for monetary policy and to implement them. For example, the CBK is at the heart of Kenya's flow-of-funds, linked to households, companies, government, financial institutions and markets, and between the Kenyan economy and the rest of the world: If the CBK sneezes, these economic agents may catch a cold!
4. The architecture of Basel Accords is just moving away from the crossroads towards Basel III. Going forward, for many central banks, including the CBK, the three main aspects of Basel III (bank capital adequacy, stress testing, and market liquidity risk) are necessary but not sufficient: there is strong, incentive-compatible, imperative to integrate the role of peer monitoring and market discipline (for example, through the interbank market) into official bank regulation to safeguard financial stability.
5. Overall, the highlights in (1)–(4) above reflect the *good* of central banking. For the *unknown* of central banking, especially for the future, the knowledge component of central banks is critical in enabling central banks to keep pace with the quickly shifting economic and financial landscapes and to channel financial innovation to inclusive financial development and inclusive economic growth. As earlier noted, the CBK has a competent team in its Research Department, the KSMS and the School of Economics at the University of Nairobi. Given this huge battery of research expertise, it appears worthwhile for the CBK to invest in a suite of new model vintages, with each tailored to a special purpose, but offering the advantage of comparing outputs: the flow-of-funds model for macro and micro policy;

the BVAR for forecasting and the DSGE for dealing with specific monetary policy questions. This call goes beyond standard macroeconomic policy modelling work, in order to generate new models which fully reflect roles of the financial sector, money transmission, and financial contagion channels so that the central bank can help prevent (or at least mitigate the adverse effects of) another global financial crisis. The new models should also encompass studies on financial inclusion and randomized controlled experiments with household portfolio decisions, among other areas.[51]

References

Al-Deehani, T., Karim, R. A. A., and Murinde, V. (1999), 'The capital structure of Islamic banks under the contractual obligation of profit sharing', *International Journal of Theoretical and Applied Finance,* Vol. 2, No. 3, pp. 1–39.

Allen, F., Carletti, E., Cull, R., Qian, J., Senbet, L. W., and Valenzuela, P. (2014), 'The African financial development and financial inclusion gaps', *Journal of African Economies,* Vol. 23, No. 5, pp. 614–42.

Bahra, P., Green, C. J., and Murinde, V. (1999), 'Financial reform simulation experiments for Estonia and Poland', in C. J. Green and A. W. Mullineux (eds), *Financial Sector Reform in Central and Eastern Europe: Capital Flows, Bank and Enterprise Restructuring,* Cheltenham: Edward Elgar, pp. 227–304.

Barro, R. J. and Gordon, D. (1983), 'Rules, discretion and reputation in a model of monetary policy', *Journal of Political Economy,* Vol. 91, pp. 101–21.

Bernhard, W. (2002), *Banking on Reform, Political Parties and Central Bank Independence in the Industrial Democracies.* Ann Arbor, MI: University of Michigan Press.

Bernhard, W., Broz, J. L., and Clark, W. R. (2002), 'The political economy of monetary institutions', *International Organization,* Vol. 56, pp. 693–723.

Bodea, C. and Hicks, R. (2015), 'Price stability and central bank independence: Discipline, credibility, and democratic institutions', *International Organization,* Vol. 69, pp. 35–61.

Bordo, M. A. (2007), 'A brief history of central banks', Federal Reserve Bank of Cleveland.

Brainard, W. C. and Tobin, J. (1968), 'Pitfalls in financial model building', *American Economic Review,* Vol. 58, No. 2, pp. 99–122.

[51] For example, experimental work, through randomized controlled trials, is highly recommended for the CBK, mainly to understand the behaviour and incentives of heterogeneous households, including their demand for financial assets. See Sayinzoga et al. (2016). On household portfolio decisions, see Moore, Green, and Murinde (2005, 2006).

Brambila-Macias, J., Massa, I., and Murinde, V. (2011), 'Cross-border bank lending versus FDI in Africa's growth story', *Applied Financial Economics*, Vol. 21, No. 16, pp. 1205–13.

Caballero, J. (2015), 'Banking crises and financial integration: Insights from networks science', *Journal of International Financial Markets, Institutions and Money*, Vol. 34, pp. 127–46.

Congdon, T. (2009), *Central Banking in a Free Society*, London: Institute of Economic Affairs.

Connelly, B. L., Hoskisson, R. E., Tihanyi, L., and Trevis Certo, S. (2010), 'Ownership as a form of corporate governance', *Journal of Management Studies*, Vol. 47, No. 8, pp. 1561–89.

Cressy, R. (2006), 'Why do most firms die young?', *Small Business Economics*, Vol. 26, No. 2, pp. 103–16.

de Haan, J. and Berger, H. (2003), 'How to tie your hands: A currency board versus an independent central bank', in A. W. Mullineux and V. Murinde (eds), *Handbook of International Banking*, Cheltenham: Edward Elgar, Chapter 6.

Eijffinger, S. C. W. and de Haan, J. (1996), 'The political economy of central bank independence', Princeton Special Papers in International Economics, No. 19.

Elbahnasawy, N. G. and Ellis, M. A. (2015), 'Economic structure and seigniorage: A dynamic panel data analysis', *Economic Inquiry*, Vol. 54, No. 2, pp. 940–65.

Garriga, A. C. (2016), 'Central bank independence in the world: A new data set', *International Interactions*, Vol. 42, No. 5, pp. 849–68.

Green, C., Bai, Y., Murinde, V., Ngoka, K., Maana, I., and Tiriongo, S. (2016), 'Overnight interbank markets and the determination of the interbank rate: A selective survey', *International Review of Financial Analysis*, Vol. 44, March, pp. 149–61.

Green, C. J. and Murinde, V. (1993), 'The potency of stabilisation policy in developing economies: Kenya, Tanzania and Uganda', *Journal of Policy Modelling*, Vol. 15, No. 4, pp. 427–62.

Green, C. J. and Murinde, V. (1998), 'Modelling the macroeconomic policy framework for an emerging market economy', *The Manchester School*, Vol. 66, No. 3, June, pp. 302–30.

Green, C. J. and Murinde, V. (2003), 'Flow of funds: Implications for research on financial sector development and the real economy', *Journal of International Development*, Vol. 15, pp. 1015–36.

Green, C. J. and Murinde, V. (2005), 'Flow of funds: the relationship between finance and the macroeconomy', in C. J. Green, C. H. Kirkpatrick, and V. Murinde (eds), *Finance and Development: Surveys of Theory, Evidence and Policy*, Cheltenham: Edward Elgar, 2005, Chapter 3, pp. 62–89.

Green, C. J., Kimuyu, P., Manos, R., and Murinde, V. (2008), 'How do small firms in developing countries raise capital? Evidence from a large-scale survey of Kenyan micro and small scale enterprises', *Advances in Financial Economics*, Vol. 12, pp. 379–404.

Green, C. J., Maggioni, P., and Murinde, V. (2000), 'Regulatory lessons for emerging stock markets from a century of evidence on transactions costs and share price volatility in the London Stock Exchange', *Journal of Banking and Finance*, Vol. 24, pp. 577–601.

Griffith-Jones, S. and Gottschalk, R. (2016), *Achieving Financial Stability and Growth in Africa*. London and New York: Routledge.

Griffith-Jones, S., Ocampo, J. A., and Stiglitz, J. (2010), *Time for a Visible Hand: Lessons from the 2008 World Financial Crisis*. Oxford: Oxford University Press.

International Monetary Fund (1999), Code of Good Practices on Transparency in Monetary and Financial Policies: Declaration of Principles. Washington, DC: IMF.

Kamgnia, B., and Murinde, V. (2015), 'Employment creation for the youth in Africa: The role of extractive industries', in G. Kararach, H. Besada, and T. M. Shaw (eds), *Development in Africa: Refocusing the Lens after the Millennium Development Goals*. Bristol: Policy Press (chapter 6, pp. 169–91).

Kanga, D., Murinde, V., and Soumare, I. (2016), 'Capital, risk and profitability of WAEMU banks: Do foreign ownership and cross-border banking matter?', Mimeo.

Kirkpatrick, C. H., Murinde, V., and Tefula, M. (2008), 'The measurement and determinants of x-inefficiency in commercial banks in Sub-Saharan Africa', *European Journal of Finance*, Vol. 14, No. 7 (October), pp. 625–39.

Klein, L. R. (2000), 'Preface', in A. E. Fleming and M. M. Guigale (eds), *Financial Systems in Transition*, Singapore: World Scientific, pp. ix–xii.

Klein, L. R. (2003), 'Some potential linkages for input–output analysis with flow-of-funds', *Economic Systems Research*, Vol. 15, No. 3, pp. 269–77.

Kodongo, O., Natto, D. M. and Biekpe, N. (2015), 'Explaining cross-border bank expansion in East Africa', *Journal of International Financial Markets, Institutions and Money*, Vol. 36, pp. 71–84.

Kydland, F. E. and Prescott, E. C. (1977), 'Rules rather than discretion: The inconsistency for optimal plans', *Journal of Political Economy*, Vol. 85, pp. 473–91.

Law, S. H., Azmani-Saini, W. N. W. and Mansor, H. I. (2013), 'Institutional quality thresholds and the finance-growth nexus', *Journal of Banking and Finance*, Vol. 37, No. 12, pp. 5373–81.

Law, S. H. and Singh, N. (2014), 'Does too much finance harm economic growth?', *Journal of Banking and Finance*, Vol. 41, pp. 36–44.

Lensink, R. and Murinde, V. (2006), 'The inverted-U hypothesis for the effect of uncertainty on investment: Evidence from UK firms', *European Journal of Finance*, Vol. 12, No. 2 (February), pp. 95–107.

Lensink, R. and Meesters, A. (2014), 'Institutions and bank performance: A stochastic frontier analysis', *Oxford Bulletin of Economics and Statistics*, Vol. 76, No. 1, pp. 67–92.

Lensink, R., Hermes, N., and Murinde, V. (2000), 'Capital flight and political risk', *Journal of International Money and Finance*, Vol. 19, No. 1, pp. 73–92.

Llewellyn, D. T. (2013), 'A strategic approach to post-crisis regulation: The need for Pillar 4', in A. Dombret and O. Lucius (eds), *Stability of the Financial System*, Cheltenham: Edward Elgar.

Matthews, K., Murinde, V., and Zhao, T. (2007), 'Competitive conditions among the major British banks', *Journal of Banking & Finance*, Vol. 31, No. 7 (July), pp. 2025–42.

Moore, T., Green, C. J., and Murinde, V. (2005), 'Portfolio behaviour in a flow-of-funds model of the household sector in India', *Journal of Development Studies*, Vol. 41, No. 4, pp. 675–702.

Moore, T., Green, C. J., and Murinde, V (2006), 'Financial sector reforms and stochastic policy simulations: A flow-of-funds model', *Journal of Policy Modelling*, Vol. 28, pp. 319–33.

Murinde, V. (1992), 'The application of stochastic simulation and policy sensitivity techniques to a macroeconomic model of Uganda', *Applied Economics*, Vol. 17, January, pp. 1–17.

Murinde, V. (1993), 'Budgetary and financial policy potency amid structural bottlenecks: Evidence from Uganda', *World Development*, Vol. 21, No. 5, May, pp. 841–59.

Murinde, V. (2011), 'Bank regulation in Africa: From Basel I to Basel II and now at a crossroads', in Bradford, C. and Lim, W. (eds), *Towards the Consolidation of G20: From Crisis Committee to Global Steering Committee*, Washington, DC: Brookings Institution Press.

Murinde, V. (2012), (ed.), *Bank Regulatory Reforms in Africa*, London: Palgrave Macmillan.

Murinde, V. (2012), 'Financial development and economic growth: Global and African evidence', *Journal of African Economies*, Vol. 21, No. 1, pp. 10–56.

Murinde, V. and Ryan, C. (2003), 'The implications of WTO and GATS for the banking sector in Africa', *The World Economy*, Vol. 26, No. 2 (February), pp. 181–207.

Murinde, V., Agung, J., and Mullineux, A. W. (2004), 'Patterns of corporate financing and financial system convergence in Europe', *Review of International Economics*, Vol. 12, No. 4, pp. 693–705.

Murinde, V., Bai, Y., Maana, I., Ngoka-Kisinguh, K., Tiriongo, S., and Green, C. J. (2016), 'Peer monitoring role of the interbank market in Kenya: Implications for bank regulation', Mimeo.

Murinde, V., Mullineux, A. W., and Pinijkulviwat, A. (2003), 'Reforming the traditional structure of a central bank to cope with the Asian financial crisis: Lessons from the Bank of Thailand', in A. W. Mullineux and V. Murinde (eds), *The Handbook of International Banking*, Cheltenham: Edward Elgar, 2003, pp. 486–515.

Murinde, V., Ochieng, C. S., and Meng, Q. (2015), 'Capital flight and flow of funds'. In: I. Ajayi and L. Ndikumana (eds), *Capital Flight in Africa*. Oxford: Oxford University Press, Chapter 7.

Rogoff, K. S. (1985), 'The optimal degree of commitment to an intermediate monetary target', *Quarterly Journal of Economics*, Vol. 100, pp. 1169–89.

Sayinzoga, A., Bulte, E. H. and Lensink, R. (2016), 'Financial literacy and financial behaviour: Experimental evidence from rural Rwanda'. *The Economic Journal*, Vol. 126, Issue 594, pp. 1571–99.

Stone, R. (1984), 'The accounts of society', in *Les Prix Nobel* (Stockholm, Almqvist & Wiksell), pp. 263–87.

Symes, P. (2004), The East African Currency Board, Mimeo.

World Bank (1992), 'How the independence of central banks affects policy outcomes', *World Bank Policy Research Bulletin*, Vol. 3, Washington, DC: World Bank.

Zhao, T. and Murinde, V. (2011), 'Bank performance and deregulation in Nigeria', *African Development Review*, Vol. 23, Issue 1, pp. 30–43.

Zhao, T., Matthews, K., and Murinde, V. (2013), 'Cross-selling, switching costs and imperfect competition in British banks', *Journal of Banking & Finance*, Vol. 37, No. 12, pp. 5452–462.

4
Central Bank Independence
What Are the Key Issues?

Patrick Njoroge, Désiré Kanga, and Victor Murinde

4.1 Introduction

The concept of an independent central bank arises from the underlying idea that the central bank should be institutionally designed to be independent from political interference that may emanate from the Ministry of Finance or Treasury or the executive arm of the government in power. Precisely, by design, the central bank should be insulated from political pressure in undertaking the main roles of managing the country's currency,[1] money supply, and interest rates, as well as the ability to act as 'lender of last resort' to the banking sector whenever such a need arises. The central bank directly (or indirectly through a quasi-autonomous agency) also exercises independence in the supervision and regulation of commercial banks in order to ensure the solvency of banks, prevent bank runs, and discourage reckless or fraudulent behaviour by banks and other financial institutions and maintain financial stability. Hence, under central bank independence, the political authority of the country delegates monetary policy to the central bank, which effectively gives strong incentives to the central bank to manage inflation. It means that the executive's influence on monetary policy is restricted.

The idea of central bank independence is as old as the initial configuration of a central bank. The first central bank was created in 1668 (*Sveriges Riksbank*)[2] to enhance the financial power of governments. For example, the creation of the central bank reassured creditors and made it easier and cheaper for the government to borrow during the nine years' war (1688–1697). In the 1800s, central banks were forced to manage crises resulting from financial panics triggered by lenders who lost confidence in the creditworthiness of private banks. The central bank, namely Bank of England, acted as 'lender of last resort', consisting of central

[1] This means independence by the central bank in exercising its monopoly to issue the monetary base in the country, or to control the production of notes and coins of the national currency—the country's legal tender.

[2] It is worth noting that the template of the first central bank was set by Bank of England created in 1694.

Patrick Njoroge, Désiré Kanga, and Victor Murinde, *Central Bank Independence: What Are the Key Issues?* In: *50 Years of Central Banking in Kenya: Regional and Global Perspectives.* Edited by: Patrick Njoroge and Victor Murinde, Oxford University Press (2021). © The Central Bank of Kenya. DOI: 10.1093/oso/9780198851820.003.0004

bank lending to solvent banks, which could provide collateral, at high rates.[3] Already at this stage, a potential conflict is emerging: provide liquidity during the crisis (i.e. increase money supply) which can coincide with a need to restrict the money supply to safeguard the currency.

During the two world wars and aftermath of the Second World War (WWII), central banks played various roles: managing gold reserves, money supply, stabilization of currencies (exchange rate management), and interest rates. Central banks supported governments during the war by keeping interest rates low and ensuring that governments could borrow to finance military spending.[4] However, conflict emerged after WWII between politicians (government or president) and central bank governors. The United States is a typical example to illustrate this conflict. After experiencing the benefits of low interest rate during the war, government had no desire to see monetary policy tighten again. Harry Truman (President) pressed William McChesney Martin (who ran the Federal Reserve of the United States from 1951 to 1970), to keep rates low despite the inflationary consequences of the Korean war. Despite the Governor's refusal, the government maintained the pressure under him even after Truman left office. Outside the United States, finance ministries played the dominant role in deciding on interest rates, leaving central banks responsible for financial stability and maintaining exchange rates (fixed under the Bretton Woods regime).

After the collapse of the Bretton Woods system, currencies floated, inflation soared, and worse still, many countries suffered high unemployment at the same time. This crisis has paved the way for the current power of central banks since politicians had shown they could not be trusted with monetary discipline. Typically, politicians faced time inconsistency problems described by Kydland and Prescott (1977), and Barro and Gordon (1983): they worried that tightening policy to head off inflation would alienate voters, and hence could not stick to the stated policy for long. There is often an incentive to deviate from the stated policy. At this point in time, central banks had begun to enjoy independence to conduct monetary policy. An independent central bank could give full priority to low levels of inflation whereas other considerations (re-election perspectives of politicians and a low level of unemployment) may interfere with the objective of price stability in a country where the central bank lacks independence.

By following Milton Friedman's advice to control the growth rate of money supply to keep inflation low (*rules* instead of *discretions*), Paul Volcker was able to break the inflationary spiral in the United States in the mid-1980s. In the wake of Volcker's success, other countries moved towards making central banks more

[3] This is the original idea as defined by Bagehot in 1873. This concept changed during the recent financial crisis. Central banks have provided liquidity to the banking system as a whole and not only to solvent banks because of the systemic nature of the crisis.

[4] The Economist (2017), https://www.economist.com/briefing/2017/04/27/the-history-of-central-banks

independent, and central bankers were asked to target inflation. To put it differently, monetary policy was delegated to an independent and 'conservative' central banker (Rogoff, 1985). 'Conservative' means that the central banker is more averse to inflation than the government, in the sense that he places a greater weight on price stability than the government does (Berger et al., 2001). Now, it is widely believed that a high level of central bank independence coupled with some explicit mandate for the bank to restrain inflation are important institutional devices to assure price stability (Berger et al., 2001).

There are two major types of independence or autonomy: *instrument* independence and *goal* independence (see Table 4.1). Instrument independence is the ability of the central bank to decide on the use of its instruments without political interference. Goal independence is the ability of the central bank to set its own goals for monetary policy. This may be the case when the government gives a broad mandate to the central bank and the central bank then interprets and prioritizes these goals (Crowe and Meade, 2007), as in the United States. For instance, the Federal Reserve Act assigns the United States central bank to seek 'maximum employment, stable prices, and moderate long-term interest rates'. There is a strong case for instrument independence as opposed to goal independence because a 'broad consensus has emerged among policymakers, academics, and other informed observers around the world that the goals of monetary policy should be established by the political authorities, but that the

Table 4.1 Various configurations of central bank independence

Type of autonomy	Description
Goal autonomy	The central bank is responsible for determining the monetary policy and exchange rate regime. In principle, goal autonomy gives the central bank authority to determine its primary objective from among several objectives included in the central bank law or, rarely, to determine the objective if there is no clearly defined objective.
Target autonomy	The central bank is responsible for determining monetary policy and the exchange rate regime. Here, the primary objective is clearly defined and stipulated in the law; only the target can be fixed by the central bank.
Instrument autonomy	It implies that the government or the legislature decides the monetary policy target, in agreement with the central bank, or the exchange rate regime, but the central bank retains sufficient authority to implement the monetary policy target using the instruments it sees fit.
Limited (no) autonomy	It means that the central bank is basically a government agency. The government determines the policies (objectives and targets) as well as influences the implementation.

Source: Compiled by the authors from Lybek and Morris (2004).

conduct of monetary policy in pursuit of those goals should be free from political control' (Bernanke, 2010)[5]. Therefore, central banks have a delegated authority to achieve their legally mandated objectives with the available instruments in an independent manner. Some central banks, such as the European Central Bank (ECB), enjoy also 'target independence' or 'target autonomy', which means that the central bank determines the target of the overall goal. For example, the ECB has an overriding goal of price stability and attempts to keep inflation close to or below 2 per cent.

Some political scientists suggest that governments may choose to delegate monetary policy to detach it from political debates and power struggles (de Haan and Eijffinger, 2016) or central bank independence may be interpreted as an attempt to tie the hands of the future government by the current one (Goodman, 1991). Other scholars argue that the federal structures or political diversity of countries are associated with more politically independent central banks (Lohmann, 1998; Farvaque, 2002; Hallerberg, 2002; Gilardi, 2007). In addition to showing that central bank independence is endogenous to the political system, these studies emphasize that it is difficult to follow a strict policy rule. In the real world, monetary authorities do enjoy discretion because it is impossible to predict all potential contingencies that a central bank will confront (Fernández-Albertos, 2015). The most prominent evidence is the response of central banks to the recent crisis by deviating from rules to conduct 'unconventional' monetary policies (quantitative easing and forward guidance).

In this chapter, we discuss the key issues surrounding central bank independence. We examine the key ideas in the existing literature relating to the measurement of central bank independence and the implications for the main role of central banks, namely to deliver price stability (low and stable inflation). The remainder of this chapter is organized as follows. The next section reviews the measures of central bank independence and central bank conservatism. Section 4.3 examines the benefits of central bank independence. The governance of central banks is highlighted in Section 4.4. Section 4.5 presents observations about independence of the Central Bank of Kenya while Section 4.6 offers some concluding remarks. Within this chapter, examples and relevant data are drawn from all African countries as well as a number of emerging market economies and some developed countries, so there is a rich base of evidence and practices from Kenya, Africa, and around the world.

[5] This consensus is debatable since it could be interpreted as a loss of central bank's independence (Alesina and Stella, 2010).

4.2 Central Bank Independence and Central Bank Conservatism

Despite the large literature on the measure and the effects of central bank independence on inflation,[6] independence is often not distinguished carefully from conservativeness. The independence is the extent to which the central bank can freely decide about the use of monetary policy instruments whereas the conservativeness represents the preferences of the central bank regarding the stabilization of inflation relative to the stabilization of the output gap. A conservative central bank may be more inclined to put more weight on inflation. That is the more the preference for price stability the more the central bank is conservative. In practice, independence and conservativeness matter for optimal monetary policy (Eijffinger and Hoeberichts, 2008; Hefeker and Zimmer, 2011).

4.2.1 Central Bank Independence

The determinants of central bank governors' tenure show that central banks work together with elected governments and do not operate in a political vacuum (Fernández-Albertos, 2015). The independence of central banks is underpinned by time-inconsistency issue raised in the macro-literature in 1970s (Kydland and Prescott, 1977). However, Bernhard et al. (2002) argue that the time-inconsistency framework does not always capture how political actors evaluate the benefits and costs of different monetary arrangements. This may well be the case if political actors are interested in income redistribution rather than controlling inflation.

Nevertheless, some questions remain unanswered. For example: Why is central bank independence so attractive? Which institutional framework favours central bank independence? We summarize key contributions from excellent surveys by de Haan and Eijffinger (2016) and Fernández-Albertos (2015), among others.

According to Bernhard (1998), central bank independence is a way to facilitate the coexistence of actors with heterogeneous policy preferences within the executive. It is tentative answer to information asymmetries that create potential conflicts between different political actors. In particular, delegation of monetary policy to independent central banks alleviates the conflicts derived from the existence of informational asymmetries between ministers—who have greater information about the policy process—and coalition partners—who have less. Therefore, politically heterogeneous contexts (federal systems, strong systems of checks and balances, coalition governments) should be more welcoming to the

[6] See Berger et al. (2001) and Banaian (2008) for a review of the literature on the measure of central bank independence, and the references cited therein.

emergence of independent monetary authorities as shown in the literature (Farvaque, 2002; Hallerberg, 2002; Gilardi, 2007; Pistoresi et al., 2011). However, without a political coalition that wishes to have monetary stability, legal independence of the central bank would not be granted.

Another strand of the literature argues that a large number of veto players leads to more autonomous bureaucracies. The more veto players, the more difficult it will be for the government to overturn the independence of the central bank (Keefer and Stasavage, 2003).

Economic freedom of the countries has been found to be positively correlated with the choice of central bank with greater independence (Banaian and Luksetich, 2001). In this vein, Iversen (1999) argues that changes in the economic and institutional context since 1980s have increased the political and economic appeal of independent central banks. Some scholars suggest that exchange rate pegs—adopted usually after hyperinflation episode in some countries—justify the choice of independent central bank (Frieden and Stein, 2001; Broz, 2002). Indeed, exchange rate commitment is an alternative way to solve the credibility problem of monetary policy. The political system's degree of openness and transparency indicate how credible the delegation to an independent monetary authority will be perceived by markets (Broz, 2002).

In open and democratic contexts, delegation to an independent central bank will be seen as credible while in less transparent domestic political context, the only way for governments to gain monetary credibility is by tying monetary policy to an exchange rate commitment. Exchange rate commitment and central bank independence are substitutes in this perspective (Copelovitch and Singer, 2008). This is supported by O'Mahony (2007) who suggests that governments who dislike the distributive consequences of a conservative monetary policy might consider the adoption of an exchange rate peg to take monetary policy away from the central bank. This perspective is not entirely true as there is room for some overlap between these two institutional choices (Bodea, 2010). Further investigations pointed out that internationally exposed firms tend to be more favourable toward fixed exchange rates when central banks are more independent (Fernández-Albertos, 2012).

4.2.2 Key Measures of Central Bank Independence

The first measures of central bank independence initiated by Bade and Parkin (1982) were centred on two legal characteristics, namely, the appointment process for the central bank's board, and whether the central bank maintained autonomy for monetary policy or the government held a veto on central bank policy decisions. These authors considered three main questions:

- Who has the final authority for monetary policy?
- Are a majority of the members of the central banks appointed independently of the government?
- Is there a government official on the central bank board?

This pioneering work by Bade and Parkin (1982) has been improved by Alesina (1988) who adds a fiscal dimension to this list by asking whether or not central banks are required to purchase Treasury bills. Following Alesina (1998), central bank independence index benefits from the work by Cukierman (Cukierman, 1993; Cukierman, Webb, and Neyapti, 1992; Cukierman and Webb, 1995) and others (Eijffinger and Schaling, 1992; Grilli, Masciandaro, and Tabellini, 1991). Table 4.2 gives a summary of the central bank independence indices. Grilli, Masciandaro, and Tabellini (1991) or GMT index is a count type index that uses a yes/no choice for some institutional feature. Cukierman, Webb, and Neyapti (1992) improved the existing measures by allowing a richer set of possible institutional arrangements and a variety of scales (2/3 to 7-point scale compared to yes/no scale in GMT).

Although, they have been used in the empirical literature, the questions underlying these measures is that they do not include any reference to price stability. How does price stability fits in this arrangement? In addition, linear scale averaging used to compute the indices introduces the notion that the gap between each type of institutional arrangement within a certain measure, such as term of office, has an equal effect on independence or inflation fighting (Banaian, 2008). Further analysis show that a simple measure of central bank autonomy (i.e. the central bank is given final authority over issues clearly defined in the law as central bank objectives) is as useful a measure of central bank independence.

Other researchers have used turnover rates (TOR) as an alternative measure of central bank independence. This measure has two pitfalls. Firstly, is this a measure of independence or accountability? Secondly, this measure may be endogenous to economic performance (de Haan and Kooi, 2000; Dreher et al., 2006). For example, CEOs are replaced more often when inflation or political instability is high (Dreher et al., 2006). Adolph (2013) reports that central bank tenures are shorter when inflation (unemployment) is high under right (left)-wing governments. However, the implementation of reforms which strengthens central bank independence tends to lower governor turnover (Klomp and de Haan, 2010a).

Cukierman and Webb (1995) refined the turnover rate by distinguishing political and non-political turnover rates. Political (non-political) turnover is the likelihood that the central bank governor will be removed from office before (after) six months following a political transition. Despite this improvement, Keefer and Stasavage (2003) find that only multiple constitutional checks and balances and political polarization reduce the bank governor's risk of being fired within six months after elections took place. Dreher et al. (2010) show that

Table 4.2 Various measures of central bank independence

Measure	Definition
The Legal Variable Autonomy Weighted (LVAW) index and the Legal Variable Autonomy Unweighted (LVAU) index developed by Cukierman et al. (1992)	Based on 16 legal variables, the authors define four indexes (appointment and term of office of the governor of the central bank or CEO, policy formulation, objectives of the Central Bank, limits on lending to the government) and one aggregate index.
The Questionnaire-based Variable for Autonomy Weighted (QVAW) index measure developed by Cukierman (1993)	The questionnaire-based indices, which are based on the responses of experts in various central banks, are useful for identifying informal practices and other dimensions of independence that are not captured by the legal indices.
The Turn Over Rate (TOR) measure, by Cukierman, et al. (1992) for actual turnover of the central bank Governor	The likelihood that the governor will be removed from office following a political transition.
The Non-Political Turnover Rate(NTOR) developed by (Cukierman and Webb, 1995)	Probability of change of central bank governor more than nine months after a political transition.
The Grilli, Masciandaro and Tabellini (GMT) index, developed by Grilli, Masciandaro and Tabellini (1991)	The legal independence is a combination of political and economic independence.**
The Alesina-Summers (AL) measure, by Alesina and Summers (1993)	Central bank independence is measured by 'political independence'.***
The Eijffinger and Schaling (ES) index, developed by Eijffinger and Schaling (1992)	In fact, the ES index is more than a purely legal index of central bank independence. The central bank laws are examined against the background of monetary policy-making. This indicator tries to grab some of the actual independence.
The vulnerability (VUL) measure, developed by Cukierman and Webb (1995)	Political instability (Cukierman and Webb, 1995) is measured by counting political transitions of various types. Political vulnerability of the bank is the fraction of political transitions that are followed within six months by a replacement of the central bank governor.
The Latent index (LI), developed by de Haan et al. (2003)	A composite index based on AL, ES, LVAW, LVAU, GMT. The authors used a latent variables approach: the extent the above indicators describe the same unobservable phenomenon.

Note: ** Political independence includes: (i) the procedure for appointing the members of the central bank governing bodies; (ii) the relationship between these bodies and the government; and (iii) the formal responsibilities of the central bank. The economic independence of the central bank refers to the autonomy of a central bank in choosing the instruments of monetary policy and is described by: (i) the influence of the government in determining how much to borrow from the central bank; and (ii) the nature of the monetary instruments under the control of the central bank.

*** Political independence is taken to depend on the institutional relationship between the central bank and the executive, the procedure to nominate and dismiss the head of the central bank, the role of government officials on the central bank board, and the frequency of contacts between the executive and the bank. The index is based on the prior idea by Bade and Parkin (1982) and amended by Alesina (1988).

Source: Compiled by the authors from a survey of existing research.

political and regime instability and the occurrence of elections increase the probability of a turnover and Artha and de Haan (2015) find that financial crises increase the probability of a turnover.

Other scholars such as de Haan et al. (2003) proposed another way to aggregate the existing indices by using other computation techniques.

The main measures of central bank independence, developed by the above researchers, are summarized in Table 4.2.

4.2.3 Evidence on Central Bank Independence

All these measures encompass the legal dimension of the central bank independence or legal independence, which reflects, in the first place, the level of independence that legislators seek to confer on the central bank. In the empirical literature, central bank independence is measured by Cukierman et al. (1992) index and GMT index.

Table 4.3 reports these two indices by region. All indices are measured on a scale of 0 (lowest level of independence) and 1 (highest level of independence). We can see an overall increase in these two indices from 1995 to 2010 (2015 for LVAU index). This indicates an increase in central bank independence around the world. It is worth noting that South Asia and Middle East and North Africa regions have experienced the lowest level of central bank independence in the world from 1995 to 2015.

In order to shed light on the evolution of the central bank independence in Kenya and in the neighbouring countries, we plot in Figure 4.1 the LVAU indices for Kenya, Ethiopia, South Africa, Tanzania, Uganda, and Zambia. Over the mid of 1990s, Kenya and Tanzania have experienced the highest central bank independence compared to the other countries. The independence index in Ethiopia has dropped from 0.47 in 1972 to 0.39 in 2014, meaning that the central bank independence has worsened in this country.

4.2.4 Key Measures of Central Bank Conservatism

The main measure of the conservativeness of the central bank is defined by $(1-\lambda)/\lambda)$ where L is a solution of the central bank's loss function:

$$L = E_t[\lambda(\pi_t - \bar{\pi}_t)^2 + (1-\lambda)(y_t - \bar{y}_t)^2] \tag{4.1}$$

λ is the preferences of central bank regarding the stabilization of inflation (π_t) around its target $(\bar{\pi}_t)$, relative to the weight assigned to the stabilization of the output gap $(y_t - \bar{y}_t)$; t is a time subscript; and E is an expectations operator.

Table 4.3 Evolution of central bank independence indices around the world

	LVAU index			GMT (political)		GMT (economic)		GMT (overall)	
	1995–2007	2008–2010	2011–2015	1995–2007	2008–2010	1995–2007	2008–2010	1995–2007	2008–2010
East Asia & Pacific	0.45	0.50	0.52	0.21	0.21	0.67	0.71	0.44	0.46
Europe & Central Asia	0.64	0.74	0.75	0.76	0.83	0.80	0.83	0.78	0.83
Latin America & Caribbean	0.60	0.62	0.62						
Middle East & North Africa	0.42	0.47	0.48						
North America	0.49	0.49	0.49	0.50	0.50	0.88	0.88	0.69	0.69
South Asia	0.39	0.41	0.41						
Sub-Saharan Africa	0.47	0.52	0.52						
All region	0.54	0.58	0.59	0.54	0.58	0.78	0.80	0.66	0.69

Source: LVAU is Cukierman et al. (1992) index calculated by Bodea and Hicks (2015). GMT stands for Grilli, Masciandaro and Tabellini. The dataset is made available by Masciandaro and Roelli (2015).

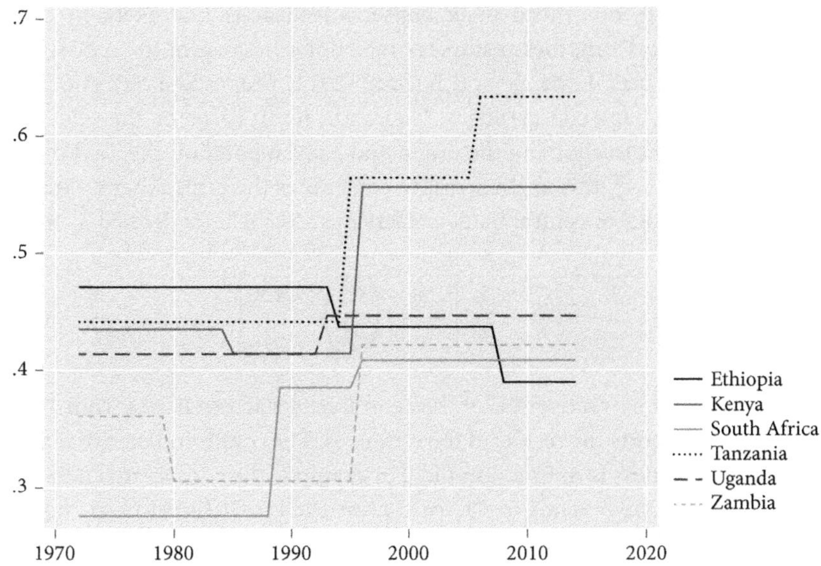

Figure 4.1 Evolution of the LVAU index for selected African countries

Table 4.4 Measures of the conservativeness of the Federal Reserve

References	$(1 - \lambda)/\lambda$	Period of the study
Ozlale (2003)	0.49	1979Q3–1999Q1
Cecchetti and Ehrmann (2002)	0.35	1981Q1–1997Q4
Krause and Mendez (2005)	0.17	1978Q1–2000Q4
Dennis (2006)	0.00	1982Q1–2000Q2
Favero and Rovelli (2003)	0.00	1980Q3–1998Q3
Castelnuovo and Surico (2003, 2004)	0.00	1987Q3–2001Q1
Tachibana (2004)	0.00	1980Q1–2000Q4

Source: Levieuge and Lucotte (2014).

Table 4.4 gives different measures of the Federal Reserve degree of conservativeness based on Equation (4.1). It reports the weight on output relative to inflation stabilization $(1 - \lambda)/\lambda$. Ozlale (2003), Cecchetti and Ehrmann (2002) and Krause and Mendez (2005) highlight the importance of inflation stabilization in the United States. In contrast, Dennis (2006), Favero and Rovelli (2003), Castelnuovo and Surico (2003, 2004), and Tachibana (2004) find that the weight assigned to output stabilization is insignificant. As shown in Table 4.4, the Federal Reserve Bank's degree of conservativeness varies over time.

Since the degree of central bank conservativeness is not likely to change radically in the short run, these estimates may differ because of the model used.[7] To overcome this bias, Levieuge and Lucotte (2014) proposed a new model-free measure of central bank conservatism. Their indicator is based on the value of the angle of the straight line joining the origin and a given point on the Taylor curve. Once rescaled to [0,1], this angle measure constitutes the central bank's inflation aversion. Their index of central bank conservatism (CONS) is defined as follows:

$$CONS = \frac{1}{90}\left[a, tan\left(\frac{\sigma_y^2}{\sigma_\pi^2}\right) \times \frac{180}{pi}\right] \tag{4.2}$$

We estimate the conservativeness of the central banks across Africa from 1980 to 2018. Table 4.5 reports the results of the estimates. The results indicate that central bank conservativeness is not monotonic. For example, the conservativeness of the Central Bank of Kenya seems to decrease from 1980 to 2010 before rising again between 2015 and 2018. Indeed, this decrease in conservativeness is due to a less volatile output gap compared to inflation. Between 2000 and 2004, the volatility—measured by the standard deviation—of the inflation was 3.9 per cent while that of the output gap was 1.5 per cent. Between 2015 and 2018, the values of these volatilities were 1.4 per cent (inflation) and 1.1 per cent (output gap).

In a stable environment, such as in Kenya, where inflation and output are both under control, the central may seem less conservative. This is also true in highly volatile environment like in Democratic Republic of Congo (DRC). During 2000–2004, the value of CONS was 0.000 because inflation was too volatile (237 per cent) compared to the output gap (4.3 per cent). Low values of CONS should be related to the underlying values of inflation and output gap volatilities for better interpretation.

4.3 Benefits of Central Bank Independence

The first benefit of central bank independence is low inflation. There is evidence from a negative and significant relationship between central bank independence measures and inflation. To put it differently, countries with an independent central bank, on average, have lower inflation than countries where the central bank is controlled by the government (Grilli et al. 1991; Alesina and Summers, 1993). But, there is a debate regarding the significant effect of central bank independence on inflation. This debate comes from an identification issue (Mas,

[7] Levieuge and Lucotte (2014) noted that the methodologies of the estimates are quite similar. Table 4.2 does not indicate a large variation in the time covered by the studies.

Table 4.5 Measure of central bank conservativeness for African countries estimated by using Equation (4.2)

	1980–1984	1985–1989	1990–1994	1995–1999	2000–2004	2005–2009	2010–2014	2015–2018
Algeria	0.240	0.763	0.327	0.008	0.831	0.360	0.009	0.720
Angola			0.001	0.000	0.001	0.690	0.108	0.427
Benin			0.001	0.022	0.072	0.080	0.307	0.867
Botswana	0.089	0.973	0.886	0.599	0.806	0.857	0.910	0.900
Burkina Faso	0.530	0.113	0.047	0.595	0.082	0.034	0.077	0.235
Burundi	0.252	0.406	0.540	0.093	0.033	0.122	0.213	0.069
Cameroon	0.919	0.702	0.193	0.693	0.775	0.096	0.870	0.105
Cape Verde		0.718	0.695	0.879	0.758	0.780	0.939	0.060
Central African Republic	0.164	0.084	0.094	0.096	0.542	0.794	0.868	
Chad		0.156	0.118	0.095	0.853	0.336	0.069	
Comoros					0.326	0.319	0.039	
Congo, Dem. Rep.	0.041	0.021	0.000	0.000	0.000	0.136	0.360	0.562
Congo, Rep.		0.919	0.044	0.369	0.120	0.736	0.241	0.967
Cote d'Ivoire	0.708	0.038	0.020	0.444	0.955	0.078	0.949	0.996
Djibouti							0.262	0.691
Egypt	0.296	0.071	0.265	0.034	0.195	0.253	0.841	0.002
Equatorial Guinea		0.798	0.171	0.985	0.987	0.965	0.984	1.000
Eswatini	0.533	0.665	0.781	0.443	0.053	0.182	0.595	0.590
Ethiopia	0.341	0.260	0.222	0.247	0.264	0.035	0.008	0.329
Gabon	0.306	0.685	0.008	0.504	0.341	0.644	0.925	0.411
Gambia	0.105	0.002	0.102	0.288	0.110	0.796	0.973	0.924
Ghana	0.019	0.072	0.006	0.000	0.009	0.046	0.657	0.062
Guinea						0.023	0.040	0.994
Guinea-Bissau		0.016	0.002	0.256	0.084	0.054	0.468	0.999
Kenya	**0.475**	**0.331**	**0.079**	**0.075**	**0.093**	**0.053**	**0.066**	**0.365**
Lesotho	0.585	0.293	0.190	1.000	0.009	0.277	0.854	0.918
Liberia					0.986	0.742	0.963	0.175

Continued

Table 4.5 *Continued*

	1980–1984	1985–1989	1990–1994	1995–1999	2000–2004	2005–2009	2010–2014	2015–2018
Libya					0.837	0.842	0.984	
Madagascar	0.230	0.087	0.056	0.011	0.409	0.453	0.106	0.888
Malawi	0.454	0.032	0.320	0.003	0.159	0.705	0.011	0.058
Mali			0.060	0.128	0.609	0.026	0.789	0.138
Mauritania		0.108	0.382	0.836	0.250	0.758	0.749	0.896
Mauritius	0.012	0.346	0.017	0.908	0.777	0.087	0.182	0.036
Morocco	0.496	0.544	0.941	0.701	0.872	0.698	0.705	0.946
Namibia					0.754	0.338	0.872	0.951
Niger	0.589	0.815	0.034	0.323	0.389	0.106	0.879	0.013
Nigeria	0.886	0.013	0.016	0.004	0.766	0.068	0.068	0.834
Rwanda	0.421	0.425	0.979	0.802	0.509	0.453	0.052	0.067
Sao Tome and Principe					0.321	0.052	0.083	0.716
Senegal	0.339	0.041	0.017	0.309	0.644	0.056	0.391	0.979
Seychelles	0.809	0.954	0.844	0.863	0.954	0.044	0.209	0.054
Sierra Leone						0.335	0.995	0.021
South Africa	0.744	0.251	0.563	0.319	0.060	0.319	0.293	0.880
South Sudan							0.396	0.000
Sudan	0.477	0.042	0.006	0.002	0.476	0.797	0.139	
Tanzania		0.008	0.363	0.014	0.974	0.027	0.014	0.171
Togo	0.457	0.630	0.231	0.509	0.773	0.034	0.886	0.033
Tunisia		0.977	0.383	0.781	0.885	0.897	0.013	0.547
Uganda				0.077	0.033	0.493	0.118	0.699
Zambia		0.004	0.005	0.032	0.211	0.477	0.592	0.246
Zimbabwe							0.989	0.818

Note: Inflation is measure by the growth rate of the consumer price index and the output gap is the cyclical component of the HP filter of the log of the gross domestic product at constant local currency.

1995). Indeed, the low inflation observed in countries with independent central banks could have less to do with the institutional innovation itself than with more profound and structural social and political factors. Oatley (1999) shows that many results of the literature are not robust to the inclusion of institutional variables in the estimation. This issue has not been resolved in the empirical literature (see Crowe and Meade, 2007; de Haan et al. 2008; Alesina and Stella 2010). However, recent meta-analysis by Klomp and de Haan (2010b) corroborates the negative relationship between central bank independence and inflation after controlling for publication bias as well as labour market characteristics.

We check the relationship between inflation (measured by consumer price index) and central bank independence by using robust regression.[8] The results of the estimates are presented in Table 4.6. We consider four central bank independence indices earlier reported in Table 4.3. We test the effects of the first lag and the second lag of each index on inflation (each at a time). Lag values help to reduce the reverse causality bias. We also control for time (common potential shocks) and country effects (potential unobservable variables). In the panel B, we control for employment—measured by the employment to population ratio—and composite risk index—which encompassed economic, political, and financial risk—in addition to time and country fixed effects. R-squares of the regression (not reported) vary from 0.695 to 0.920. Central bank independence reduces inflation rate. One-unit increase in central bank independence reduces inflation up to 6 percentage points. The effect of central bank independence on inflation decreases when we control for additional variables (institutions and labour market), but is still significant.

Other studies conclude that delegating monetary policy to an independent central bank increases debt sustainability (Giordano and Tommasino, 2011) and fosters fiscal discipline (Bodea, 2013; Bodea and Higashijima, 2017). If a central bank is sufficiently independent and conservative, the incentives for the government to default are lower.

[8] The following countries have been used in the regressions for the first dependent variables (LVAU): Albania, Algeria, Angola, Armenia, Australia, Austria, Azerbaijan, Bahrain, Bangladesh, Barbados, Belarus, Belgium, Bolivia, Bosnia, Botswana, Brazil, Brunei, Bulgaria, Burundi, Cambodia, Canada, Cape Verde, Chile, China, Colombia, Costa Rica, Croatia, Cyprus, Czech Republic, Denmark, Djibouti, Dominican Republic, Egypt, El Salvador, Estonia, Ethiopia, Fiji, Finland, France, Gambia, Germany, Ghana, Greece, Guatemala, Guinea, Guyana, Honduras, Hungary, Iceland, India, Indonesia, Iran, Ireland, Israel, Italy, Jamaica, Japan, Jordan, Kazakhstan, Kenya, Kuwait, Kyrgyz Republic, Laos, Latvia, Lebanon, Lesotho, Liberia, Lithuania, Macedonia, Madagascar, Malawi, Malaysia, Mauritania, Mauritius, Mexico, Moldova, Mongolia, Montenegro, Morocco, Namibia, Nepal, Netherlands, New Zealand, Nicaragua, Nigeria, Norway, Oman, Pakistan, Panama, Papua New Guinea, Paraguay, Peru, Philippines, Poland, Portugal, Qatar, Romania, Russia, Rwanda, Samoa, Serbia, Seychelles, Sierra Leone, Singapore, Slovakia, Slovenia, Solomon Islands, South Africa, South Korea, Spain, Sri Lanka, Sweden, Switzerland, Tajikistan, Tanzania, Thailand, Timor-Leste, Tonga, Trinidad And Tobago, Tunisia, Turkey, Uganda, Ukraine, United Arab Emirates, United Kingdom, United States, Uruguay, Vanuatu, Venezuela, Vietnam, Yemen, Zambia, Zimbabwe. For the other dependent variables (GMT), the sample is limited to Australia, Canada, France, Germany, Italy, Japan, New Zealand, Switzerland, United Kingdom, and United States.

Table 4.6 Effect of central bank independence on inflation

	LVAU	GMT political	GMT economic	GMT overall
A: With time and country fixed effects only				
First lag	−5.883***	−2.456***	−4.424***	−4.245***
	(0.558)	(0.588)	(0.644)	(0.699)
Second lag	−6.294***	−2.218***	−4.473***	−4.065***
	(0.540)	(0.566)	(0.654)	(0.688)
B: With employment, composite risk index, time and country fixed effects only				
First lag	−1.355**	−1.611***	−1.391***	−2.187***
	(0.626)	(0.512)	(0.612)	(0.705)
Second lag	−1.932***	−1.369***	−1.568***	−1.958***
	(0.584)	(0.498)	(0.579)	(0.641)

Note: This table reports the estimates of inflation on central bank independence indices by using robust regression. We control for time (common potential shocks) and country effects (potential unobservable variables). Each regression uses the level, the first lag or the second lag of each index (in column) as independent variable. Therefore, each cell is one regression. *, ** and *** indicate the parameter is statistically significant at 10 per cent, 5 per cent and 1 per cent levels, respectively. Robust standard errors are in parentheses below the estimated coefficients.

In addition, Eichler and Littke (2018) showed that an increase in the availability of information about monetary policy objectives decreases exchange rate volatility. This effect is more pronounced for countries with a lower level of central bank conservatism.

Nevertheless, price stability may not be enough to ensure financial stability. According to the Schwartz's conventional wisdom, by focusing on the objective of price stability, policy-makers contribute not only to achieving high levels of economic activity and employment, but also foster financial stability. This is the so-called 'divine coincidence' (Blanchard and Gali, 2007). But, because real imperfection matters in practice, a single inflation goal is not enough. Recent analysis shows that the more conservative the central bank, the higher the financial instability (Levieuge et al., 2019).

4.4 The Governance of Central Banks

Almost all the central banks make decisions through a committee. How are these committees structured? And what is the optimal size of each committee? The answers to these questions differ according to the type of central bank autonomy (see earlier discussion around Table 4.1) and the number of committees.

Each central bank has one or more boards. Based on a survey, Lybek and Morris (2004) found that 63 per cent of the surveyed laws of central bank charters provided for one board and the remaining provided for two to three boards. The Bank for International Settlements found that around one-third of the central banks have a single board, with a significant proportion of boards having multiple functions (BIS, 2009). Lybek and Morris (2004) identified six types of boards, namely policy board, implementation board, advisory board, supervisory board, audit committee, and management board (see Table 4.7).

Before presenting the types of boards, it is appropriate to present the central governance body of central banks which is the Board of Directors. As indicated in Table 4.8, the Board of Directors of the central bank typically include the

Table 4.7 Governing board and management

Type of boards	Description
Board of directors	The board of directors of a central bank is the overall authority in which all the power of the bank is vested. It is responsible for formulation of the policy that shapes the vision and mission of the central bank.
Monetary policy board	It determines the monetary policy and exchange rate policy (if applicable) to be followed by the central bank. In the case of goal autonomy, a policy board determines which objective to give priority. In the case of target autonomy, it specifies the target within a defined primary objective. A country with instrument autonomy would not have a policy board, as the policy is set by the government. However, in a few low-income countries, the governor plays a strong role in both the formulation and implementation of monetary policy.
Implementation board	It makes decisions on how to implement the target(s). In the case of goal and target autonomy, the implementation board is often the same as the policy board. It might also be the management board. The governor is often the chairman of the implementation board. In the case of instrument autonomy, the decisions of the implementation board are the highest priority of the central bank.
Advisory board	It advises the policy boards, implementation boards, or even management.
Supervisory board	It is responsible for overseeing and addressing any problems regarding the following conditions: (i) achieving objectives, tasks, and functions, (ii) the financial condition of the central bank, (iii) effective internal controls, and, in some cases, also (iv) efficient use of its resources. The composition of the supervisory board can help depoliticize the supervisory process, provided its tasks and powers are clearly defined.
Audit committee	It assists in performing the supervisory function.
Management	The primary responsibility of the management is the day-to-day operations of the central bank. This responsibility is delegated to one person usually named as governor, chairman, president, or general manager. The governor is assisted by one or more deputy or vice governors, a general manager, or a board comprising directors of various departments of the bank.

Source: Compiled by the authors from Lybek and Morris (2004).

Table 4.8 Who chairs the Board of Directors of the Central Bank?

Country/Institution	Governor	Independent	Country/Institution	Governor	Independent
Afghanistan	✓		Macedonia	✓	
Albania	✓		Madagascar	✓	
Algeria	✓		Malawi	✓	
European Central Bank	✓		Malaysia	✓	
Angola		✓	Maldives	✓	
Eastern Caribbean Central Bank	✓		Mauritania	✓	
Argentina	✓		Mauritius	✓	
Armenia	✓		Mexico	✓	
Australia	✓		Micronesia	✓	
Azerbaijan	✓		Moldova	✓	
Bahamas	✓		Mongolia	✓	
Bahrain		✓	Montenegro	✓	
Bangladesh	✓		Morocco	✓	
Barbados	✓		Mozambique	✓	
Belarus	✓		Myanmar	✓	
Belize		✓	Namibia	✓	
BCEAO	✓		Nepal	✓	
Bhutan	✓		New Zealand		✓
Bolivia	✓		Nicaragua	✓	
Bosnia and Herzegovina	✓		Nigeria	✓	
Botswana	✓		Norway	✓	
Brazil	✓		Oman	✓	
Brunei	✓		Pakistan	✓	
Bulgaria	✓		Palestine	✓	
Burundi	✓		Panama		✓
Cabo Verde	✓		Papua New Guinea	✓	
Cambodia	✓		Paraguay		✓
BEAC	✓		Peru	✓	

Canada	✓	
Chile	✓	
China	✓	
Colombia	✓	
Comoros	✓	
Democratic Republic of the Congo	✓	
Costa Rica	✓	
Croatia	✓	
Cuba	✓	
Czech Republic	✓	
Denmark	✓	
Djibouti	✓	
Dominican Republic	✓	
Ecuador	✓	
Egypt	✓	
El Salvador	✓	
Eritrea	✓	
Eswatini (former Swaziland)	✓	
Ethiopia		✓
Fiji	✓	
Gambia	✓	
Georgia	✓	
Ghana	✓	
Guatemala	✓	
Guinea	✓	
Guyana	✓	
Haiti	✓	
Honduras	✓	
Hungary	✓	
Philippines	✓	
Poland	✓	
Qatar	✓	
Romania	✓	
Russia	✓	
Rwanda	✓	
Samoa	✓	
Sao Tome and Principe	✓	
Saudi Arabia	✓	
Serbia	✓	
Seychelles	✓	
Sierra Leone	✓	
Singapore		✓
Solomon Islands	✓	
Somalia	✓	
South Africa	✓	
South Korea	✓	
South Sudan	✓	
Sri Lanka	✓	
Sudan	✓	
Suriname	✓	
Sweden	✓	
Switzerland	✓	
Syria		✓
Taiwan		✓
Tajikistan	✓	
Tanzania	✓	
Thailand	✓	
Timor-Leste	✓	

Continued

Table 4.8 *Continued*

Country/Institution	Governor	Independent	Country/Institution	Governor	Independent
Iceland	✓		Tonga		✓
India		✓	Trinidad and Tobago	✓	
Indonesia	✓		Tunisia	✓	
Iran	✓		Turkey	✓	
Iraq	✓		Uganda	✓	
Israel	✓		Ukraine	✓	
Jamaica	✓		United Arab Emirates (UAE)		✓
Japan	✓		United Kingdom (UK)	✓	
Jordan	✓		United States of America (USA)	✓	
Kazakhstan ✓	Uruguay	✓			
Kenya	✓ Uzbekistan	✓			
Kosovo ✓	Vanuatu	✓			
Kuwait ✓	Venezuela	✓			
Kyrgyzstan ✓	Vietnam	✓			
Lebanon ✓	Yemen	✓			
Lesotho ✓	Zambia	✓			
Liberia ✓	Zimbabwe	✓			
Libya ✓					

Note: Governor means that the Central Bank Governor also chairs the board and Independent is an independent chair of the Board. European Central Bank covers 22 countries including Monaco, Vatican City and San Marino. Eastern Caribbean Central Bank and BCEAO (*Banque Centrale des États de l'Afrique de l'Ouest* or Central Bank of West African States) cover eight countries respectively. BEAC (*Banque des États de l'Afrique Centrale* or Bank of Central African States) covers six countries. It is worth noting that the Federal Reserve (United States of America) controls three tools of monetary policy—open market operations, the discount rate, and reserve requirements. The Board of Governors of the Federal Reserve System is responsible for the discount rate and reserve requirements, and the Federal Open Market Committee (FOMC) is responsible for open market operations. The chairperson of the Board of Governors is different from that of FOMC. We were not able to classify the following countries due to lack of information: Turkmenistan, Tuvalu, North Korea, Marshall Islands, and Laos. The following countries use foreign currencies: Australian dollar (AUD) is used in Kiribati and in Nauru; Palau uses United States Dollar (USD); and Liechtenstein uses Swiss franc (CHF).

chairperson (who may be or may not be the Governor of the Central Bank—and this is one important issue[9]), other directors (mainly non-executive directors) appointed by the Minister of Finance, or the Treasury, or the executive head of government, from among persons with professional or academic experience in business or financial matters and who are not officials or employees of the Bank. In most countries, a high rank official from the Treasury is an ex-officio member of the Board and without power to vote.

The Policy Board determines the monetary policy and exchange rate policy (if applicable) to be followed by the central bank. It may comprise of management representatives and qualified external members. The presence of external members may alleviate concerns of so-called democratic deficit which arises from the fact that policy decisions have been delegated to a non-elected central banker.

The implementation board makes decisions on how to implement the target(s). In the case of goal and target autonomy, the implementation board is often the same as the policy board. It might also be the management board. In the case of instrument autonomy, the decisions of the implementation board are the highest priority of the central bank. This decision can be delegated to a board, but can be taken by one person, as in New Zealand. The governor is often the chairman of the implementation board.

The role of the advisory board is to advise the policy boards, implementation boards, or even management. Such board can contribute by providing a more balanced view. It can be composed of regional representatives, representatives from different economic sectors, or include former governors. This may also include experts without any right to vote.

The supervisory board is responsible for overseeing and addressing any problems regarding the following conditions: (i) achieving objectives, tasks, and functions; (ii) the financial condition of the central bank; (iii) effective internal controls, and, in some cases; also (iv) efficient use of its resources. The composition of the supervisory board can help depoliticize the supervisory process, provided its tasks and powers are clearly defined. The supervisory board may be composed of the government officers, legislators or politicians.

The audit committee assists in performing the supervisory function. It is mainly an Anglo-Saxon tradition for corporations to have only one board. These boards are usually large and seek for special expertise to address issues of internal control and financial disclosure.

The management is responsible for the day-to-day operations of the central bank. This responsibility is delegated to one person, usually named as governor, chairman, president, or general manager. He is always the chairman of the management board, usually the chairman of an implementation board, and in

[9] Table 4.8 gives the list of countries (or central banks) and the chairperson of the Board of Directors.

most cases the chairman of a policy board. In principle, the governor should not be chairman of the supervisory board to avoid conflicts of interest. However, in practice, the governor also chairs the supervisory board. The governor is assisted by one or more deputy or vice governors, a general manager, or a board comprising directors of various departments of the bank.

The optimal size of each board remains an open question. Blinder and Morgan (2005) determined that each committee should be composed of five individuals based on an artificial monetary policy experiment. This was supported by Sibert (2006). In practice, however, the size of the committees exceeds five members: 19 policymakers participate in meeting of the Federal Open Market Committee of the Federal Reserve (Crowe and Meade, 2007), 50 per cent of the central banks have seven to nine members (Lybek and Morris, 2004) and the actual Governing Council of the European Central Bank comprises 25 officials.

4.5 Observations about Central Bank Independence in Kenya

The Central Bank of Kenya (CBK) derives its autonomy from the Constitution of the Republic of Kenya 2010 and the Central Bank Act of 1966. The Constitution of Kenya 2010, Article 231 establishes the CBK and further specifies that the Bank shall not be under the direction or control of any person or authority in the exercise of its powers or in the performance of its functions. An Act of Parliament provides institutional arrangement of the CBK in terms of the composition, powers, functionism, and operations, giving Board members strong mandate to effectively play their oversight role. In particular, the *Central Bank of Kenya Act (Cap. 491)* provides the Board and Governor with the responsibility for determining the policy of the Bank, with later having the additional role of monetary policy formulation and implementation.

Reforms in the last decade have seen considerable improvements in the autonomy of the CBK from the National Treasury. The key developments are as follows:

- Establishment of Monetary Policy Committee (MPC) under an Act of Parliament in 2008 induced autonomy of the CBK on price stability.
- Anchoring the CBK in the constitution in 2010 strengthened her independence.
- Limiting of government overdraft utilization at the Central Bank to 5 per cent of the latest government audited revenues contributes to goal independence of the CBK.
- Non-voting rights by the National Treasury in MPC or the CBK Board ensures collaboration and independence.
- The National Treasury sets inflation targets with growth objective as secondary to the CBK, and the latter is held accountable in achieving this target.

- The CBK's reporting to the National Assembly through the Cabinet Secretary to the National Treasury ensures accountability and independence.
- Recruitment and appointment process of the executive team and the Board at the CBK has been strengthened, thus contributing to more independence.

In terms of operational autonomy, the CBK has instrument independence. The CBK has discretion in the deployment of its tools for monetary policy management as well as formulation of new tools in order to meet its mandate. Firstly, the CBK Act allows direct advances to the Government for the purpose of accommodating temporary shortfalls. Kenyan law allows the Bank to provide overdraft facility to Government to meet short term obligations, but it is limited to 5 per cent of the previous year's Government audited revenues, and by law, should be cleared within 12 months of borrowing. Despite the legal provision, there are instances when the government has not settled the outstanding balances by the end of the fiscal year as is required. Secondly, the role of the Bank as fiscal agent has in some instances compromised monetary policy operations. The bank issues securities on behalf of the Government to meet budget requirements (at a low cost) which may conflict with a tightening policy stance as an example. Thirdly, functions pertaining to licensing, regulating, and supervising banking institutions are subject to the laws enforced by the Bank versus other regulators of financial institutions in the market. The CBK regulates the banking sector and deposit taking Micro Finance Institutions. Since multiple agencies are charged with the responsibility of regulating and supervising the financial sector (SACCOs, pensions, insurance, and the capital market), a crisis afflicting the part not regulated by the Bank may pose systemic risks.

The CBK has some financial autonomy in its ability to adopt internal budget in accordance with defined law. However, ownership and control of capital and reserves is the prerogative of National Treasury. The depletion of bank capital may require capital injection from the National Treasury which compromises its autonomy and credibility. Where structural excess liquidity persists, central banks can incur high costs of open market operations, weakening their balance sheet. In the absence of systematic recapitalization, ongoing sterilization costs can undermine central bank independence to the point where the monetary policy objectives are compromised.

With respect to institutional autonomy, it is useful to consider the governance versus monetary policy mandate of the CBK. Even though the chairperson of the board and the governor are appointed by the President through transparent and competitive process and with the approval of Parliament, the ultimate goal of the central bank mandate falls on the Governor. Therefore, separating the ultimate decision-making entities at the Bank level and the Board level may hinder certain operations, in case the Board and Governor do not agree on the policy choices to be adopted.

The introduction of interest rate capping law, in September 2016 (with intention to reduce cost of borrowing and expand access to credit) has undermined central bank independence by severely constraining the formulation, conduct and effectiveness of monetary policy. In addition, there have been attempts by the National Assembly to water down some provisions in the Banking Law, with significant implications on Anti-Money Laundering/Combating the Financing of Terrorism (AML/CFT) Law.

4.6 Conclusion

Central bank independence means that monetary policy is delegated to officials (central banks) other than government and that the government has a limited influence on monetary policy implementation.

Measurement of central bank independence focused on a set of legal characteristics. The legal indices are related to four dimensions of central bank independence. Firstly, a secure tenure and independent appointment of central bank's management protect central bank from political pressure and increase its independence. Secondly, the lower the government's participation in decision-making, the higher the independence of the central bank. Thirdly, an increase in the central bank independence goes hand-in-hand with a restriction on the direct lending to governments. Fourthly, the independence is greater when a clear defined objective for monetary policy has been specified in the legal mandate of the central bank. Based on these aspects of a central bank's independence, Arnone et al. (2009) draw four consensus views of monetary policy-makers from global trend as follows[10]:

- Set price stability as the primary objective of monetary policy;
- Curtail direct lending to governments;
- Ensure full autonomy for setting the policy rate;
- Ensure non-government involvement in policy formulation.

Although the government's influence on monetary policy is restricted, it does not mean that independent central banks operate in a political vacuum. In one way or another, politicians or governments put pressure on central banks especially when they disagree with the central bank's policy (Ehrmann and Fratzscher, 2011). Therefore, the political economy of the central bank is an important dimension.

Central bank independence is associated with positive economic outcomes. First, the greater the independence of the central bank, the lower the level and the volatility of inflation. While, there is a controversial debate regarding this

[10] This section heavily draws on Banaian (2008, 42–3).

relationship in the literature, the evolution of central banking (reforms) in the world can be seen as a testimony of the positive effects of central bank independence and inflation. Second, independent central bank increases debt sustainability and may foster fiscal discipline which are useful for gaining credibility in the domestic and international markets.

Nevertheless, greater central bank independence needs to be reconciled with the requirements of institutional and personal accountability (Crowe and Meade, 2007)[11]. In addition, financial regulation should be strengthened in the mandate of the central bank and the setting of monetary policy should take into account price developments, the evolution of credit, and the emergence of bubbles (Fernández-Albertos, 2015). Indeed, in practice, the Schwartz's conventional wisdom does not work and the objective of price stability does not necessarily foster financial stability.

References

Adolph, C. (2013), *Bankers, Bureaucrats, and Central Bank Politics: The Myth of Neutrality*. Cambridge: Cambridge University Press.

Alesina, A. (1988), 'Macroeconomics and politics', *NBER Macroeconomics Annual*, Vol. 3, pp. 13–52.

Alesina, A. and Stella, A. (2010), 'The politics of monetary policy', in B. M. Friedman and M. Woodford (eds), *Handbook of Monetary Economics*, 1st edn, Vol. 3. New York: Elsevier, pp. 1001–54.

Alesina, A. and Summers, L. H. (1993), 'Central bank independence and macroeconomic performance: some comparative evidence', *Journal of Money, Credit and Banking*, Vol. 25, No. 2, pp. 151–62.

Arnone, M., Laurens, B. J., Segalotto, J. F., and Sommer, M. (2009), 'Central bank autonomy: Lessons from global trends', *IMF Staff Papers*, Vol. 56, No. 2, pp. 263–96.

Artha, I. K. D. S. and de Haan, J. (2015), 'Financial crises and the dismissal of central bank governors: New evidence', *International Journal of Finance and Economics*, Vol. 20, No. 1, pp. 80–95.

Bade R. and Parkin, M. (1982), 'Central bank laws and monetary policy', University of Western Ontario Working Paper, No. 10.

Banaian, K. (2008), 'Measuring central bank independence: Ordering, ranking, or scoring?', in *The Design and Use of Political Economy Indicators*, New York: Palgrave Macmillan, pp. 33–55.

Banaian, K. and Luksetich, W. A. (2001), 'Central bank independence, economic freedom, and inflation rates', *Economic Inquiry*, 39(1): 149–61.

[11] In 2005, the Governor of the Central Bank of Italy was under investigation for improprieties associated with a bank merger.

Barro, R. J. and Gordon, D. B. (1983), 'Rules, discretion and reputation in a model of monetary policy', *Journal of Monetary Economics*, Vol. 12, No. 1, pp. 101–21.

Berger, H., de Haan, J., and Eijffinger, S. C. (2001), 'Central bank independence: An update of theory and evidence', *Journal of Economic Surveys*, Vol. 15, No. 1, pp. 3–40.

Bernanke, B. S. (2010), 'Central bank independence, transparency, and accountability'. Speech of Chairman Ben S. Bernanke at the Institute for Monetary and Economic Studies International Conference, Bank of Japan, Tokyo, Japan, 25 May 2010.

Bernhard, W. (1998), 'A political explanation of variations in central bank independence', *American Political Science Review*, Vol. 92, No. 2, pp. 311–27.

Bernhard, W., Broz, J. L., and Clark, W. R. (2002), 'The political economy of monetary institutions', *International Organization*, Vol. 56, No. 4, pp. 693–723.

BIS (2009), *Issues in the Governance of Central Banks: A Report from the Central Bank Governance Group*. Switzerland: Bank for International Settlements Press & Communications.

Blanchard, O. and Galí, J. (2007), 'Real wage rigidities and the New Keynesian model', *Journal of Money, Credit and Banking*, Vol. 39, No. 1, pp. 35–65.

Blinder, A. S. and Morgan, J. (2005), 'Are two heads better than one? Monetary policy by committee', *Journal of Money, Credit and Banking*, Vol. 37, No. 5, pp. 789–811.

Bodea, C. (2010), 'Exchange rate regimes and independent central banks: A correlated choice of imperfectly credible institutions', *International Organization*, Vol. 64, No. 3, pp. 411–42.

Bodea, C. (2013), 'Independent central banks, regime type, and fiscal performance: The case of post-communist countries', *Public Choice*, Vol. 155, Nos 1–2, pp. 81–107.

Bodea, C. and Hicks, R. (2015), 'Price stability and central bank independence: Discipline, credibility, and democratic institutions', *International Organization*, Vol. 69, No. 1, pp. 35–61.

Bodea, C. and Higashijima, M. (2017), 'Central bank independence and fiscal policy: Can the central bank restrain deficit spending', *British Journal of Political Science*, Vol. 47, No. 1, pp. 47–70.

Broz, J. L. (2002), 'Political system transparency and monetary commitment regimes', *International Organization*, Vol. 56, No. 4, pp. 861–87.

Castelnuovo, E. and Surico, P. (2003), 'What does monetary policy reveal about a central bank's preferences?', *Economic Notes*, Vol. 32, pp. 335–59.

Castelnuovo, E. and Surico, P. (2004), 'Model uncertainty, optimal monetary policy and the preferences of the Fed', *Scottish Journal of Political Economy*, Vol. 51, No. 1, pp. 105–26.

Cecchetti, S. G. and Ehrmann, M. (2002), Does inflation targeting increase output volatility?: An international comparison of policymakers' preferences and outcomes, in N. Loayza, K. Schmidt-Hebbel, and N. Loayza, eds, 'Monetary Policy: Rules and Transmission Mechanisms', Vol. 4, Central Bank of Chile, Chapter 9, pp. 247–74.

Copelovitch, M. S. and Singer, D. A. (2008), 'Financial regulation, monetary policy, and inflation in the industrialized world', *The Journal of Politics*, Vol. 70, No. 3, pp. 663–80.

Crowe, C. and Meade, E. E. (2007), 'The evolution of central bank governance around the world', *Journal of Economic Perspectives*, 21(4): 69–90.

Cukierman, A. (1993), 'Central bank independence, political influence and macroeconomic performance: A survey of recent developments', *Cuadernos de Economía*, Vol. 30, No. 91, pp. 271–91.

Cukierman, A. and Webb, S. B. (1995), 'Political influence on the central bank: international evidence', *World Bank Economic Review*, Vol. 9, No. 3, pp. 397–423.

Cukierman, A., Web, S. B., and Neyapti, B. (1992), 'Measuring the independence of central banks and its effect on policy outcomes', *World Bank Economic Review*, Vol. 6, No. 3, pp. 353–98.

de Haan, J. and Eijffinger, S. C. W. (2016), 'The politics of central bank independence'. De Nederlandsche Bank Working Paper No. 539.

de Haan, J. and Kooi, W. J. (2000), 'Does central bank independence really matter?: New evidence for developing countries using a new indicator', *Journal of Banking & Finance*, Vol. 24, No. 4, pp. 643–64.

de Haan, J., Leertouwer, E., Meijer, E., and Wansbeek, T. (2003), 'Measuring central bank independence: A latent variables approach', *Scottish Journal of Political Economy*, Vol. 50, No. 3, pp. 326–40.

de Haan, J., Masciandaro, D., and Quintyn, M. (2008), 'Does central bank independence still matter?', *European Journal of Political Economy*, Vol. 24, No. 4, pp. 717–21.

Dennis, R. (2006), 'The policy preferences of the us federal reserve', *Journal of Applied Econometrics*, Vol. 21, No. 1, pp. 55–77.

Dreher, A., de Haan, J., and Sturm, J. E. (2006), 'When is a central bank governor fired? Evidence based on a new data set'. Working Paper 06-143. KOF Swiss Economic Institute, ETH Zurich.

Dreher, A., Sturm, J. E., and de Haan, J. (2010), 'When is a central bank governor replaced? Evidence based on a new data set', *Journal of Macroeconomics*, Vol. 32, No. 3, pp. 766–81.

Ehrmann, M. and M. Fratzscher (2011), 'Politics and monetary policy', *The Review of Economics and Statistics*, Vol. 93, No. 3, pp. 941–60.

Eichler, S. and Littke, H. C. (2018), 'Central bank transparency and the volatility of exchange rates', *Journal of International Money and Finance*, Vol. 89, pp. 23–49.

Eijffinger, S. C. and Hoeberichts, M. M. (2008), 'The trade-off between central bank independence and conservatism in a New Keynesian framework', *European Journal of Political Economy*, Vol. 24, No. 4, pp. 742–47.

Eijffinger, S. C. W. and Schaling, E. (1992), *Central Bank Independence: Criteria and indices.* Research Memorandum No. 548. Department of Economics, Tilburg University, processed.

Farvaque, E. (2002), 'Political determinants of central bank independence', *Economics Letters*, Vol. 77, No. 1, pp. 131–5.

Favero, C. A. and Rovelli, R. (2003), 'Macroeconomic stability and the preferences of the Fed: A formal analysis, 1961-98', *Journal of Money, Credit and Banking*, Vol. 35, No. 4, pp. 545–56.

Fernández-Albertos, J. (2012), 'Exchange rate regime preferences of the international sector. Firm-level evidence', *Economics Letters*, Vol. 116, No. 1, pp. 26–30.

Fernández-Albertos, J. (2015), 'The politics of central bank independence', *Annual Review of Political Science*, Vol. 18, No. 1, pp. 217–37.

Frieden, J. A. and Stein, E. (2001), *The Currency Game: Exchange Rate Politics in Latin America*. Washington, DC: Inter-American Development Bank.

Gilardi, F. (2007), 'The same, but different: Central banks, regulatory agencies, and the politics of delegation to independent authorities', *Comparative European Politics*, Vol. 5, No. 3, pp. 303–27.

Giordano, R. and Tommasino, P. (2011). 'What determines debt intolerance? The role of political and monetary institutions', *European Journal of Political Economy*, Vol. 27, No. 3, pp. 471–84.

Goodman, J. B. (1991), 'The politics of central bank independence', *Comparative Politics*, Vol. 23, No. 3, pp. 329–49.

Grilli, V., Masciandaro, D., and Tabellini, G. (1991), 'Political and monetary institutions and public financial policies in the industrial countries', *Economic Policy*, Vol. 6, No. 13, pp. 341–92.

Hallerberg, M. (2002), 'Veto players and the choice of monetary institutions', *International Organization*, Vol. 56, No. 4, pp. 775–802.

Hefeker, C. and Zimmer, B. (2011), 'The optimal choice of central bank independence and conservatism under uncertainty', *Journal of Macroeconomics*, Vol. 33, No. 4, pp. 595–606.

Iversen, T. (1999), 'Political economy of inflation: bargaining structure or central bank independence?', *Public Choice*, Vol. 101, Nos 3–4, pp. 285–306.

Keefer, P. and Stasavage, D. (2003), 'The limits of delegation: Veto players, central bank independence, and the credibility of monetary policy', *American Political Science Review*, Vol. 97, No. 3, pp. 407–23.

Klomp, J. and de Haan, J. (2010a), 'Do central bank law reforms affect the term in office of central bank governors?', *Economics Letters*, Vol. 106, No. 3, pp. 219–22.

Klomp, J. and de Haan, J. (2010b), 'Inflation and central bank independence: a meta-regression analysis', *Journal of Economic Surveys*, Vol. 24, (4): 593–621.

Krause, S. and Mendez, F. (2005), 'Policy makers' preferences, party ideology and the political business cycle', *Southern Economic Journal*, Vol. 71, No. 4, pp. 752–67.

Kydland, F. E. and Prescott, E. C. (1977), 'Rules rather than discretion: The inconsistency of optimal plans', *Journal of Political Economy*, Vol. 85, No. 3, pp. 473–91.

Levieuge, G. and Lucotte, Y. (2014), 'A simple empirical measure of central banks' conservatism', *Southern Economic Journal*, Vol. 81, No. 2, pp. 409–34.

Levieuge, G., Lucotte, Y. and Pradines-Jobet, F. (2019), 'Central banks' preferences and banking sector vulnerability', *Journal of Financial Stability*, Vol. 40, pp. 110–31.

Lohmann, S. (1998), 'Federalism and central bank independence: The politics of German monetary policy, 1957–92', *World Politics*, Vol. 50, No. 3, pp. 401–46.

Lybek, M. T. and Morris, M. J. (2004), 'Central bank governance: A survey of boards and management'. Working Paper No. 4–226. International Monetary Fund.

Mas, I. (1995), 'Central bank independence: A critical view from a developing country perspective', *World Development*, Vol. 23, No. 10, pp. 1639–52.

Masciandaro, D. and Romelli, D. (2015), 'Ups and downs of central bank independence from the Great Inflation to the Great Recession: Theory, institutions and empirics', *Financial History Review*, Vol. 22, No. 3, pp. 259–89.

Oatley, T. (1999), 'Central bank independence and inflation: Corporatism, partisanship, and alternative indices of central bank independence', *Public Choice*, Vol. 98, Nos 3–4, pp. 399–413.

O'Mahony, A. (2007), 'Escaping the ties that bind: Exchange rate choice under central bank independence', *Comparative Political Studies*, Vol. 40, No. 7, pp. 808–31.

Ozlale, U. (2003), 'Price stability vs. output stability: Tales of Federal Reserve administrations', *Journal of Economic Dynamics & Control*, Vol. 27, No. 3, pp. 1595–610.

Pistoresi, B., Salsano, F., and Ferrari, D. (2011), 'Political institutions and central bank independence revisited', *Applied Economics Letters*, Vol. 18, No. 7, pp. 679–82.

Rogoff, K. (1985), 'The optimal degree of commitment to an intermediate monetary target', *Quarterly Journal of Economics*, Vol. 100, No. 4, pp. 1169–89.

Sibert, A. (2006), 'Central banking by committee', *International Finance*, Vol. 9, No. 2, pp. 145–68.

Tachibana, M. (2004), 'Central bank's preferences in Japan, the UK, and the US', *Japan and the World Economy*, Vol. 16, Issue 1, pp. 81–93.

The Economist (2017), 'The battle of three centuries, the history of central banks: Contemporary criticisms of central banks echo debates from times past', *The Economist*, 27 April 2017.

5

Evolution of Central Banking

Some Observations

Federica Branca, Ixart Miquel-Flores, and Francesco Paolo Mongelli

5.1 Introduction

The 50th Anniversary of the Central Bank of Kenya (CBK) calls for celebrations. It is a moment of pride for all citizens and especially the staff of the Central Bank. It is also a moment to reflect upon the past, assess the present, as well as to look ahead to future challenges and endeavours. In fact, a lot has happened over these 50 years in Kenya and around Kenya. At the same time, the practice of monetary policy and the scope of central banks have also changed.

Kenya is strengthening economic and monetary integration with several neighbouring countries. Together with Uganda, Tanzania, Rwanda, and Burundi it has already established an East Africa Community (EAC). In fact, a Customs Union as well as a Common Market protocol was already put in place among these five countries, respectively, in 2005 and 2010. The East Africa Community intends to form a Monetary Union by 2024. A common currency is envisaged to replace the national currencies. Therefore, there will be a central banking system comprising the central banks of these partner countries.

The foregoing discussion means that these countries are contemplating an *East African Economic and Monetary Union* (i.e., EA-EMU). For convenience we shall call it in this chapter, the '*Shilling-EMU*'. The common market established by the East Africa Community will be an important pillar of the Shilling EMU, but it cannot be its only pillar. We know from past experiences in Europe that, in the case of new monetary unions, the role of central banks expands from harmonizing and coordinating monetary policy to supporting the building of shared monetary policy frameworks and strengthening of integrated financial infrastructures (such as for payments, supervision, and clearing). In other words, central banking systems support regional integration and institution building. At the same time, regional integration originates from political choices and the

Federica Branca, Ixart Miquel-Flores, and Francesco Paolo Mongelli, *Evolution of Central Banking: Some Observations* In: *50 Years of Central Banking in Kenya: Regional and Global Perspectives*. Edited by: Patrick Njoroge and Victor Murinde, Oxford University Press (2021). DOI: 10.1093/oso/9780198851820.003.0005

coming together of several processes and has various dimensions which are not addressed here.[1]

The aim of this chapter is to offer some snapshots for reflection on the path to a Shilling-EMU. The snapshots are based on the European experience with economic and monetary integration and reflect the difficulties encountered in recent years. These reflections are neither complete, nor may they encompass all challenges specifically relevant to the East African experience.

The chapter is guided by a series of questions. First, how does East Africa stand in terms of economic and financial convergence (Section 5.2)? Second, what are the milestones of central banking that all central banks of the EA-System/Shilling-System should master (Section 5.3)? Which monetary lessons could the euro area offer to East Africa that is contemplating a shared currency (Section 5.4)? What worked in the euro area, what hasn't worked and what is being fixed (Section 5.5)? Section 5.6 provides some final remarks.

5.2 Snapshot of Economic Convergence

In order to highlight the starting point for any plan of regional convergence, in this section we investigate some indicators of convergence often used in the literature. We find evidence of income divergence, particularly in the last decade, among Kenya, Uganda, Tanzania, Rwanda, and Burundi (Figure 5.1). This process started already in the 1960s, albeit with wide fluctuations, and has continued in

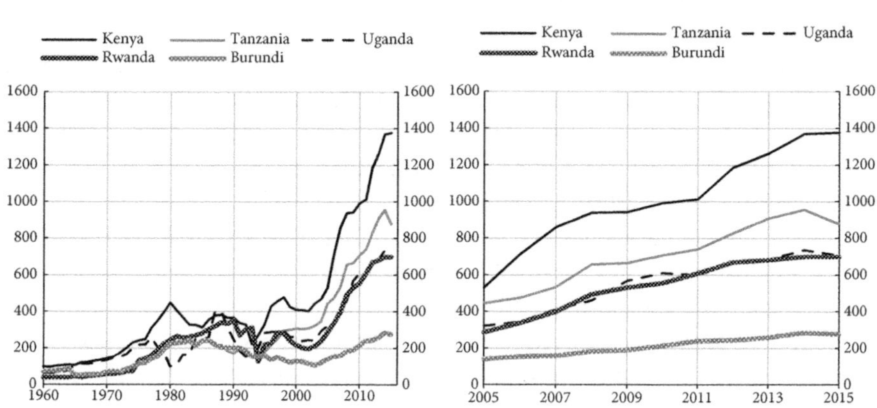

Figure 5.1 GDP per capita (current US$)
Source: World Bank (2017a), World Development Indicators.

[1] Bela Balassa described the following stages of regional integration: Free Trade Area, Custom Union, Common Market, Coordination of Monetary and Exchange Rate Policy, and Supranational

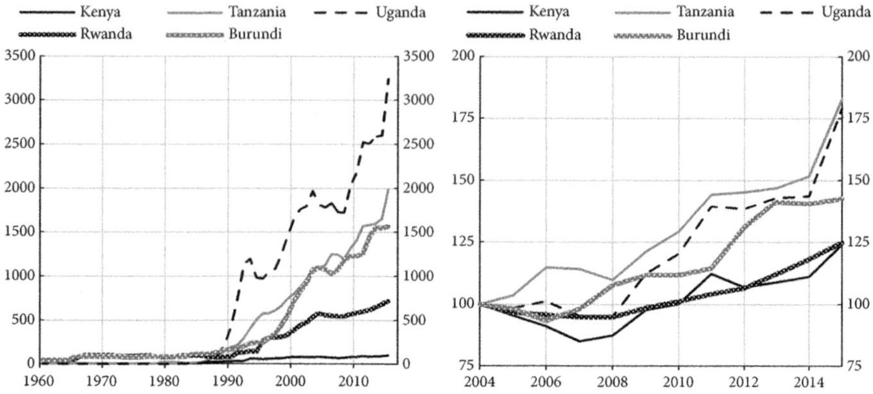

Figure 5.2 Official exchange rate (LCU per US$, period average)
Source: World Bank (2017a), World Development Indicators.

the 2006 to 2016 period. Today, income per capita are quite different among the five EAC countries.

When we examine the official exchange rate as measured in local currency units (LCU) per US dollar (see Figure 5.2) we observe that divergence in exchange rates started in earnest in the mid-1980s. At the bottom of the chart, the exchange rate of the Kenyan shilling remained pegged/anchored to the US dollar, whereas the other currencies devalued albeit with wide variations: a process that continued on a smaller scale over the 2006–16 period. The decline in exchange rate variance is captured by Figure 5.3, which shows the standard deviation of the exchange rates of the five EACs.

A different and yet complementary perspective is provided by actual exchange rate changes from 1985 onwards (Figure 5.4). Volatility has fallen dramatically since the higher levels in the 1980s and 1990s: however, fluctuations remain persistent over the past two decades. This will remain an important 'thermometer' of the progress toward EAC convergence.

Hence, there is evidence of divergence in income per capita across EAC countries. Domestic price levels also remain quite far apart. At the same time there are signs of incipient nominal convergence across Kenya, Uganda, Tanzania, Rwanda, and Burundi. A concern is that, in case of a process of economic regional integration a 'Balassa-Samuelson effect' might ensue, sustaining regional inflation differentials until price and income levels are more similar. This is often referred to as 'catching-up' process: in this case the benchmark would be Kenya. The transition burden on monetary policy coordination and exchange rate cooperation would be equally challenging until convergence is more advanced.

Institutions and Decision-Making (Balassa (1961); Dorrucci et al. (2002, 2004, 2005, 2015) provide several applications to Europe and Latin America.

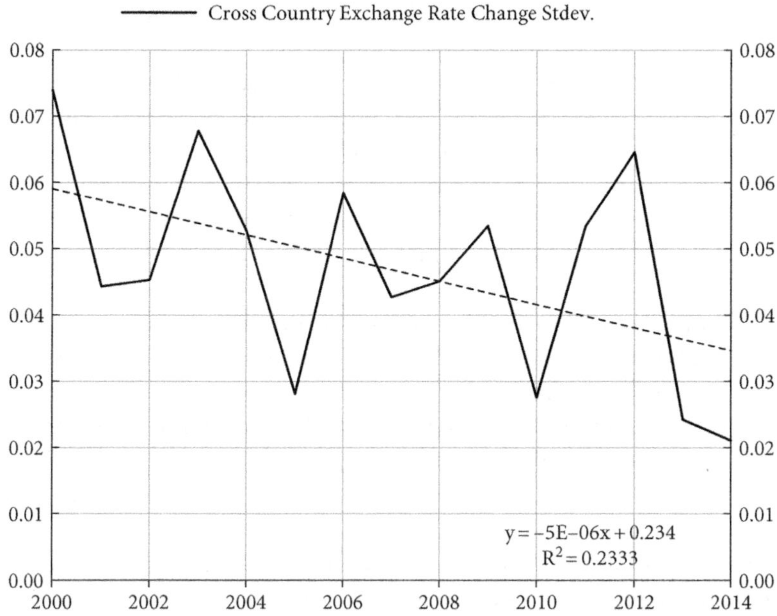

Figure 5.3 Variance in official exchange rate (LCU per US$, period average)
Source: World Bank (2017a), World Development Indicators, own elaboration.

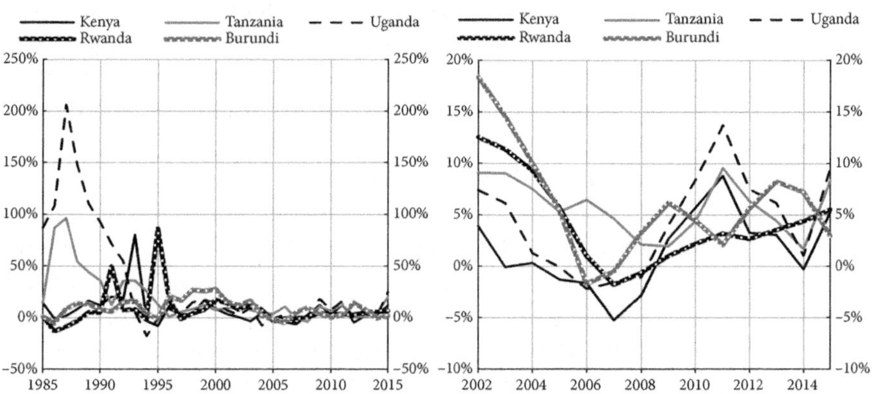

Figure 5.4 Official exchange rate (LCU per US$, period average) change YoY
Source: World Bank (2017a), World Development Indicators.

Moreover, a lesson from the euro area crisis has been the need to investigate changes in competitiveness and terms-of-trade among partner countries (thus, the real exchange rate). This aspect is not further discussed here.

At the same time, today's heterogeneity should not deter the integration of central banking practices and harmonization of monetary policy frameworks that would become one of the propellers of East African integration over time.

5.3 The Evolving Role of Central Banks

In order to support a sustainable convergence process, central banks of the partner countries need to align their monetary policy frameworks. This alignment of toolkits, mindset and preferences, as it might be called, has several components. The initial one is to share a similar conceptual framework and have common objectives (see Angeloni et al. (2005). For this, the partner central banks must embrace the key approaches to central banking over the last 30 years such as:

- Separation between central banking and national governments;
- Recognition of central bank independence in its mandate (see Maersch, 2017 and references therein);
- Importance of transparency and accountability by central bankers (see Praet, 2017 and references therein);
- Realization of the benefits of pursuing sustained low inflation (price stability) (ECB, 2011);
- Attention to financial stability and systemic risks, thus micro- and macro-prudential dimension (see Constâncio, 2016); and
- A 'quiet revolution', recognizing the role of committees work (see Blinder et al., 2016).

Modern central banks must score highly on all these approaches. In the case of the Central Bank of Kenya, it should be reassured that its neighbouring partner central banks are also committed to these approaches. An indirect gauge of monetary convergence is provided by the recent paths of inflation and the real interest rate in the economy.[2]

Figure 5.5 compares the path of inflation for Kenya, Uganda, Tanzania, Rwanda, and Burundi. The chart on the left illustrates relatively similar price level developments in the 1960s, 1970s, and 1980s. Thus, this region has known relative price stability and similar price developments for a number of decades. However, clear and rapid divergence in price levels starting in the 1990s. But when we zoom-in into the 2006–16 period we also see that both inflation and inflation differentials have been on a declining path albeit with fluctuations.

On the monetary policy side, we observe that in recent years the cross-country dispersion of real interest rates has fallen albeit with some fluctuations (Figure 5.6).

It would appear therefore that price convergence has not really happened; price levels are rather different across EAC countries. Although inflation is on a declining path, the price level gap to fill to render a single monetary policy more effective is still substantial.

[2] For more indicators, see Angeloni et al. (2007). However, we are constrained by data availability.

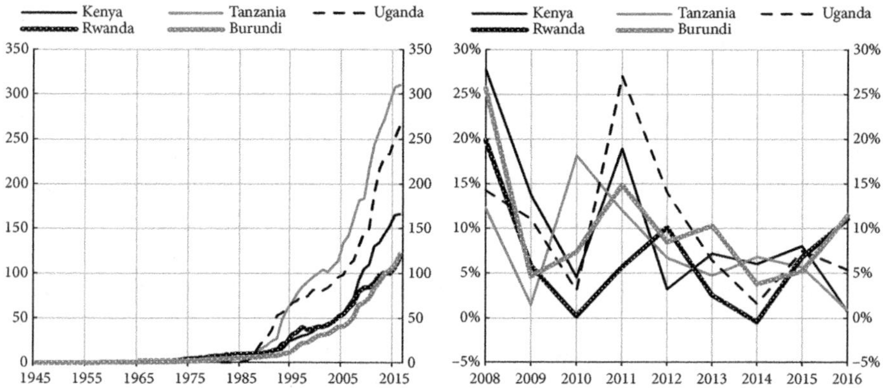

Figure 5.5 Consumer Price Index inflation rate
Source: Global Financial Data, Consumer Price Index.

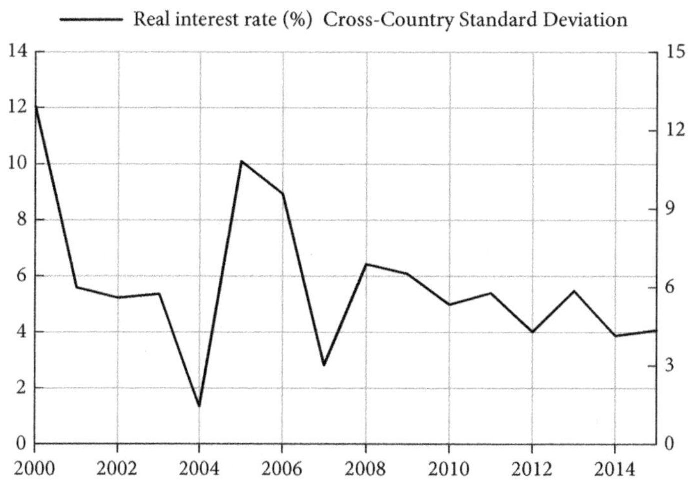

Figure 5.6 Real interest rate (%) cross-country standard deviation
Source: World Bank (2017a), World Development Indicators.

5.4 General Lessons from the Euro Area Crisis

As you are aware, the European economic and monetary union has endured a mutating hybrid and mutating crisis since mid-2007.[3] The causes were both exogenous and endogenous: i.e., they were linked to global shocks but also to flaws in the institutional framework of the euro area and weaknesses in its governance. In this section we discuss some lessons for the Shilling-EMU. In

[3] See Mongelli (2013) and Mongelli and van Riet (2013) and references therein.

our view, the euro per se was not directly responsible for the euro area crisis. Actually the ECB Eurosystem prevented worst outcomes. Thus, in the next section we discuss some supportive developments.[4]

First general lesson. EAC countries are likely to establish a joint monetary institution—call it the EA-System or the Shilling System—which will interface with several independent national governments. Managing such an arrangement has proven to be a very contentious hurdle in Europe. In the euro area, national governments have been bound by the Stability and Growth Pact which has failed to secure fiscal discipline and convergence. The fiscal governance of the euro area has been revamped in 2010 and 2011 with a renewed 'fiscal compact' (i.e., the 6-Pack, Fiscal Compact-proper and 2-Pack). EMU is also discussing the main features of a *Fiscal Union* (see Dorrucci et al. (2015)).

A solid fiscal arrangement among Kenya, Uganda, Tanzania, Rwanda, and Burundi is essential for the success of the EA-EMU (see also Thomas et al. (2015)). Moreover, given the sharp differences in income per capita among EAC countries earlier shown in Figure 5.1, there will need to be provisions for cohesion and convergence policies and also to stabilize the economy and risk-sharing in case of asymmetric shocks.

An interesting question here is: how will the EAC secure the necessary fiscal discipline, and how far apart are the countries? Figure 5.7 compares the fiscal developments in East Africa in recent years. Fiscal data coverage is uneven and we find evidence indicative of rising deficits (for Kenya, Uganda, and Burundi) and rising dispersion in government expenditures (Figure 5.8, only for Kenya, Uganda, and Burundi). No comparable data on public debt either held domestically or abroad, in local currency or foreign currency is available. A cautionary analysis is in Thomas et al. (2015).[5]

Second general lesson. EMU's financial crisis stems also from persistent and cumulative imbalances and weaknesses in market-based adjustment mechanisms (see ECB (2008), European Commission (2008), and Mongelli and Wyplosz (2009)). This is synonymous with lack of sound economic policies and policy coordination, but also a lack of flexibility, adaptability, and vitality in some countries. A similar flaw has been addressed in the euro area with the European Semester and the Macroeconomic Imbalances Procedure (MIP). Advancements in this area will be slow but rewarding. As an example, the EU Single Market is still not 100 per cent completed, and we recently celebrated the 60th anniversary of the

[4] As a background, creating an economic and monetary union is a political decision outside the remit of central banks. Still, EMUs: require a process to build and strengthen the necessary institutions and should be grounded on sound economics and genuine integration.

[5] Thomas et al. (2015) surveys the main fiscal risks facing the EAC, including: macroeconomic shocks and specific risks, such as the financial performance of the public enterprises, large infrastructure projects, PPPs, and pension funds. In addition, weaknesses in the institutional framework are reviewed.

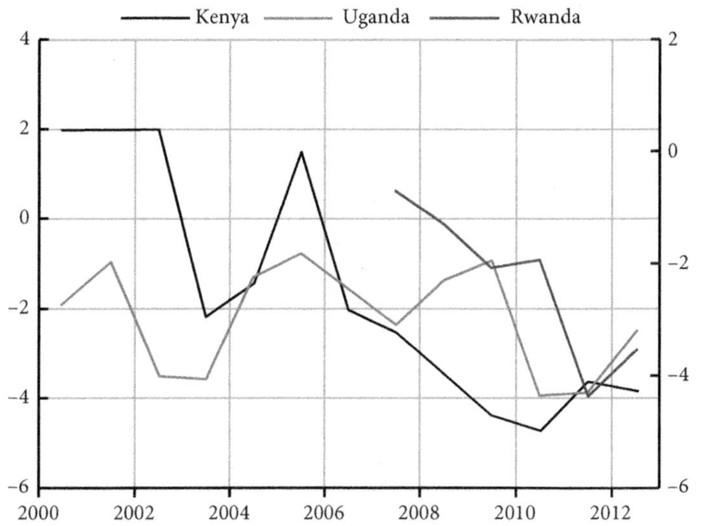

Figure 5.7 Central Government cash surplus/deficit (% of GDP)
Source: International Monetary Fund, World Bank (2017b).

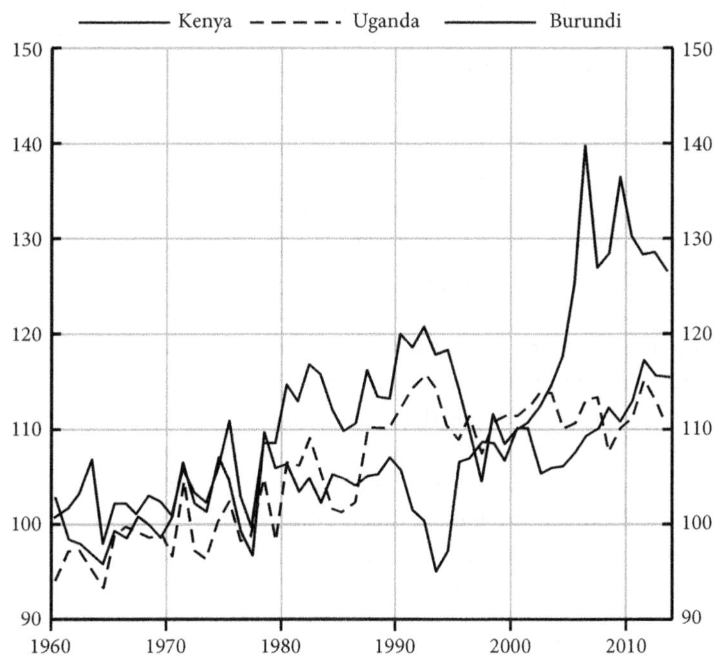

Figure 5.8 National accounts—expenditures
Source: World Bank (2017b), national accounts data, OECD national accounts data files.

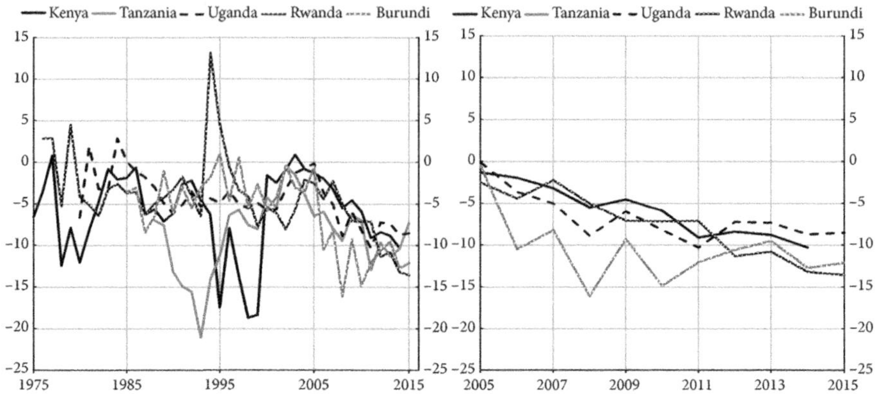

Figure 5.9 Current account balance (% of GDP)
Source: World Bank (2017a), World Development Indicators.

Treaty of Rome. Looking ahead, the Economic Union envisaged in the 5-Year Presidents' Report will push for progress in this area.[6]

By a similar token, the EA Common Market will also have to promote genuine economic integration across East Africa. This entails securing the four freedoms: i.e., freedom of movement of people, goods, services, and capital. Over time this is bound to promote economic integration and convergence. At the moment, on the external side, these five countries also exhibit rather different current account balances (Figure 5.9), and developments in various competitiveness indicators (Figures 5.10 and 5.11).

Third general lesson. The euro lacked the safeguard of a *political union*. There were no financial backstops for sovereigns and banks, and there was no crisis management and resolution framework either. Financial decisions were slow and agonizing at times (see Mongelli, 2013). We have them now. An EA-EMU among countries that are still quite heterogeneous will require some forms of political integration and risk-sharing arrangement.

Fourth general lesson. The euro lacked genuine and complete financial integration and joint financial supervision. There was no genuine financial union. These flaws have been remedied by, amongst others, the Single Supervisory Mechanism, and there are talks about a Capital Market Union.

On the financial side, domestic credit to the private sector has risen in all EA countries, albeit with some fluctuations (Figure 5.12). While financial deepening remains uneven among them, there are signs of lower dispersion of domestic credit to the private sector by banks (Figure 5.13).

[6] The 5-Year Presidents' Report is postulating four unions in the coming decades: a Financial Union (banking union and capital market union), a Fiscal Union, an Economic Union, and a Political Union (see European Commission (2015)).

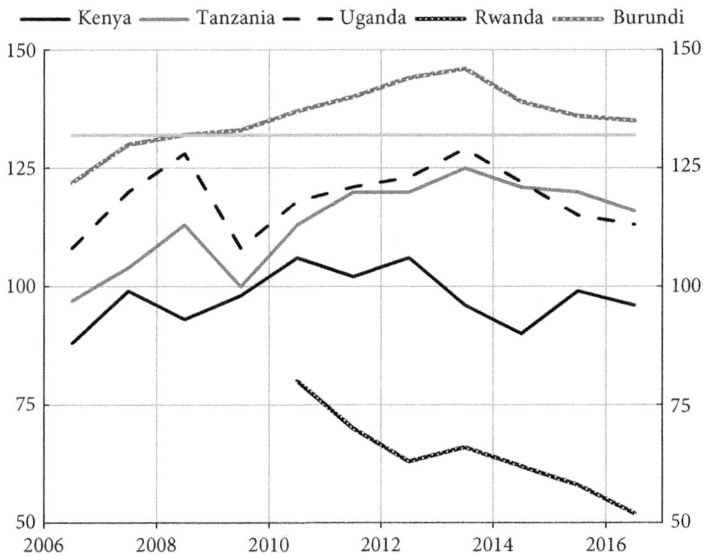

Figure 5.10 The World Economic Forum Global Competitiveness Index
Source: World Economic Forum, Bloomberg.

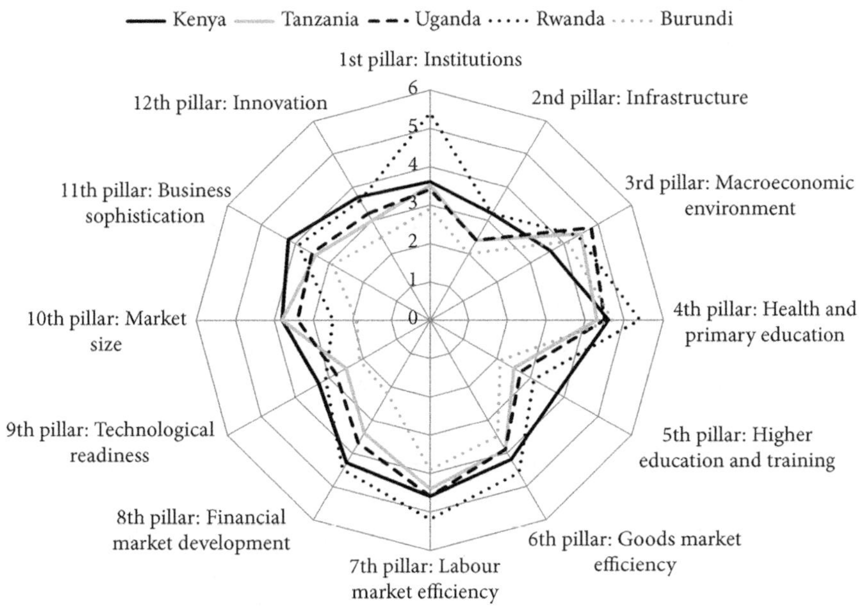

Figure 5.11 The World Economic Forum Global Competitiveness 12 Pillar Indicators
Source: World Economic Forum.

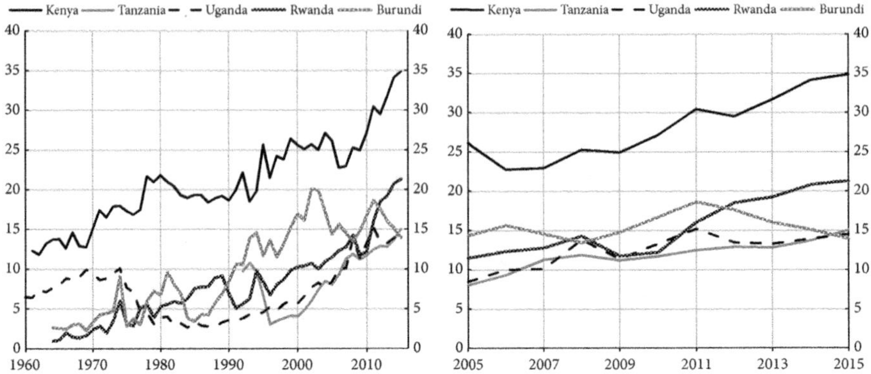

Figure 5.12 Domestic credit to private sector by banks (% of GDP)
Source: World Bank (2017a), World Development Indicators.

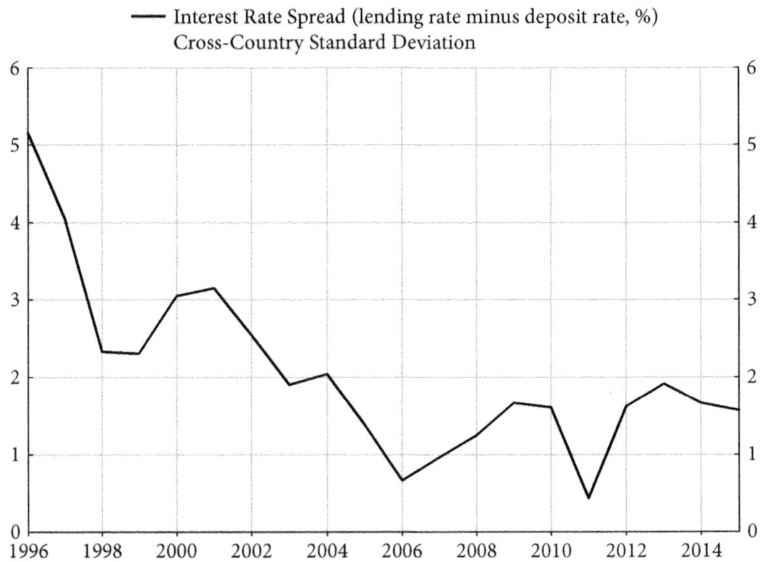

Figure 5.13 Domestic credit to private sector by banks (% of GDP)
Source: World Bank (2017a), World Development Indicators.

The EA-EMU might need to move on this front as well in order to enable financial institutions to thrive across East Africa.

To sum-up, EMU's founders had placed emphasis on achieving high nominal convergence prior to the launch of the euro. Yet, upon the launch of the euro in 1999 a gradual but persistent process of real divergence started: it was exacerbated by the Global Financial Crisis and the ensuing Great Recession that started in the US. Even worse, when the sovereign crisis hit in May 2010 there were no financial backstops for sovereign or banks, nor were there crisis management and resolution procedures. The EAC can learn these lessons, and build institutions to prevent such shocks and reduce their impact if they occur.

5.5 Blueprint for Designing the East African Monetary Union

We now turn to some of the building blocks of the Eurosystem. These are among the things that worked in Europe throughout the euro area crisis and gave it some resilience. Time and planning do matter (see Jung et al., 2010 and Moutot et al., 2008).

The path to European monetary union gathered pace over time (see Dorrucci et al., 2004):

- Early experiments in monetary cooperation go back to the former Committee of Governors (CoG), founded in 1964 and based in Basel.
- The Werner Report in 1970 formulated the European governments' aim to establish a common currency in Europe.
- After the demise of the Bretton Woods system, there was the 'Snake' in the mid-1970s.
- With the establishment of the European Monetary System (EMS) in 1979—and the Exchange Rate Mechanism (ERM)—monetary cooperation among several European countries became closer, and links between several national central banks were strengthened.
- A big impulse came in 1988 with the work of the Delors Committee that was asked to formulate a timetable and lay out the key elements for the Eurosystem.
- The Maastricht Treaty established the legal elements guaranteeing the independence of the Eurosystem (goal and instruments!), and defined price stability as its primary objective. The Treaty also reflected the principle of decentralization to the extent possible for the implementation of monetary policy.
- The treaty arranged that the European economic and monetary union (EMU) would be achieved along three stages touching upon all spheres of European integration and governance (see Figure 5.14).

In the context of the blueprint for designing the East African monetary System, let us now turn to the institutional provisions and organizational arrangements which have shaped the monetary policy decision-making process of the Eurosystem (see Moutot et al., 2008 and Jung et al., 2010).

- In 1990 the Committee of Governors (CoG) drafted the Statute of the ECB: based on its working arrangements since 1964.
- After the ratification of the Maastricht Treaty, links between national central banks became more systematic.

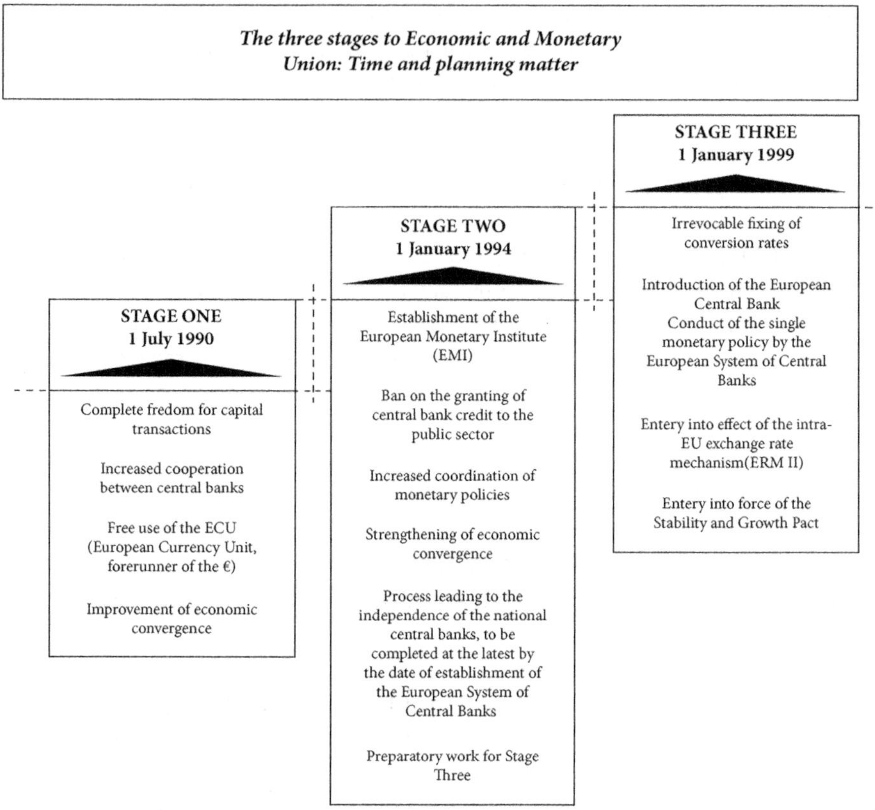

Figure 5.14 The three stages to Economic and Monetary Union

- Within this framework, committees, sub-committees, working groups, and task forces composed of national central banks experts were launched.
- The ECB decided to continue the organizational structure that had been established by the CoG (see Figure 5.15).
- Reasons for adopting this organizational structure:
  - Proven expertise easing coordinating tasks, processing input and building consensus.
  - Committees also took the lead in conceptual work, such as the design of the monetary policy framework.

'The ECB shall have recourse to the national central banks, to the extent deemed possible and appropriate, to carry out operations which form part of the Eurosystem' (Article 12.1 of the Statute of the ESCB).

Hence, the Eurosystem/ECB has to evaluate for each task the extent to which decentralization is feasible and desirable. This was done most recently at the time of the preparation and launch of the Single Supervisory Mechanism (SSM).

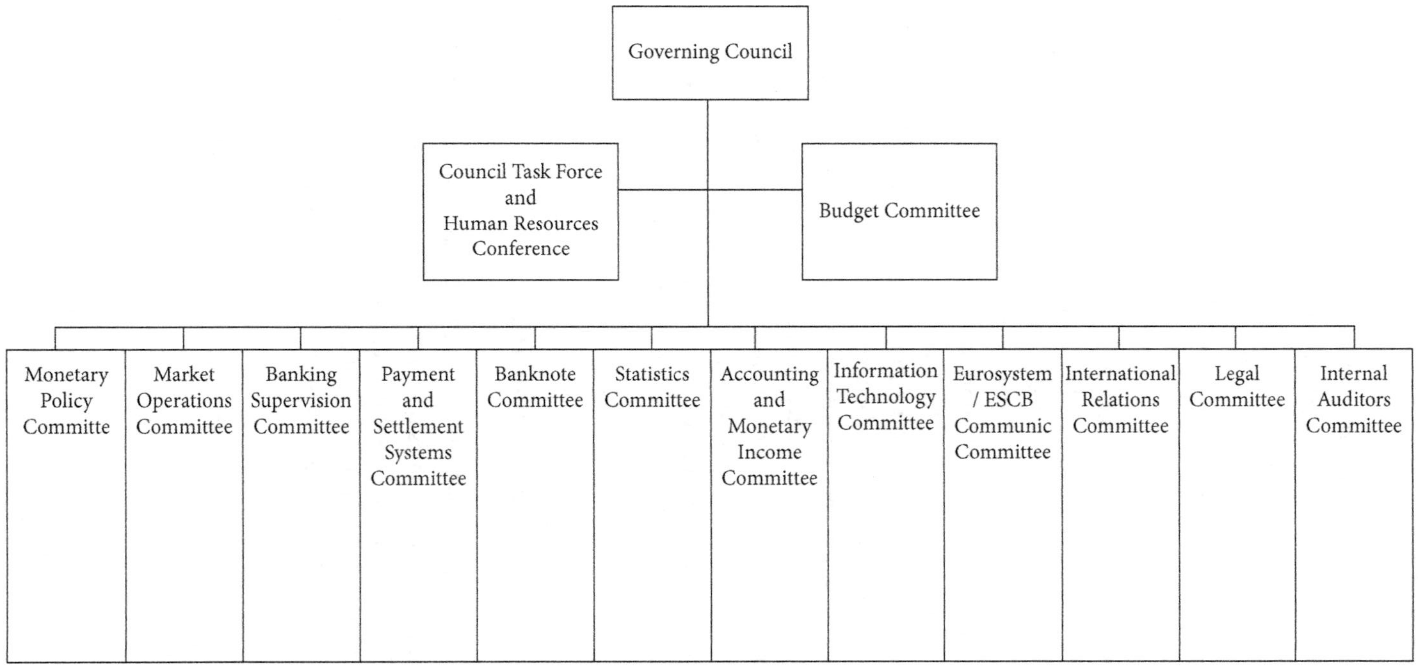

Figure 5.15 Who does what? A decentralized structure for a diverse set of tasks

It is relevant here to look at two cases:

1. Within the operational framework of the Eurosystem, national central banks perform almost all the Eurosystem's operational tasks. This is efficient as a number of ESCB tasks need an underlying regional and national infrastructure already established by NCBs
2. Monetary policy decision-making is conducted centrally by the Governing Council of the ECB.

Overall, the distribution of responsibilities and execution of tasks in the Eurosystem is more decentralized than in other central banks. Yet, the monetary policy decision-making process is centralized. Policy decisions are taken by the Governing Council, as highlighted in Figure 5.16. It would appear that the regional presence supports acquisition of information and policy communication, and adds to analytical diversity in committee work.

The strong ECB and Eurosystem paid off during the crisis. The ECB was able to implement a set of standard and non-standard monetary policy measures in order to safeguard piece stability and the integrity of the euro area (i.e., prevent the break-up of the euro).[7] It is to be noted that, in general, The ECB's and Eurosystem's credibility, structure, and clout allowed it to take these unconventional measures over the latter ten years (Mongelli, 2013).[8]

The EAC might consider undertaking a similar assessment about the degree of centralization in the decision-making process versus the degree of decentralization in the implementation of monetary policy tasks.

5.6 Final Remarks

This 50th Anniversary calls for celebrations, and it is also an occasion to look ahead at the challenges and opportunities from East-African integration. To some extent the Shilling-EMU and Shilling System might closely look at the framework of the ECB and the Eurosystem which was drafted in 1990 by the Committee of Governors based on its working arrangements since 1964. Within this framework,

[7] At the risk of oversimplifying, the ECB's non-standard measures enabled: credit easing which supported banks (pillar of the financial system); market making to fix some segments and support MP transmission: quantitative easing to provide further monetary stimulus at the zero lower bound; balance sheet effects (passive) to steer short-term rates and restore interbank financing; and balance sheet effects (active) to provide funding reassurances and reduce yields.

[8] The ECB's non-standard measures have: reverted financial fragmentation; fended break up and currency redenomination risks; lowered funding costs for banks, firms and households; and given the euro area and EU time to reform. Over time we have seen a number of important reforms and new institutions like the Single Supervisory Mechanism, the ESM, and the ESRB. Countries are adjusting and reforming, but it will take a bit more time to see the effects of those efforts.

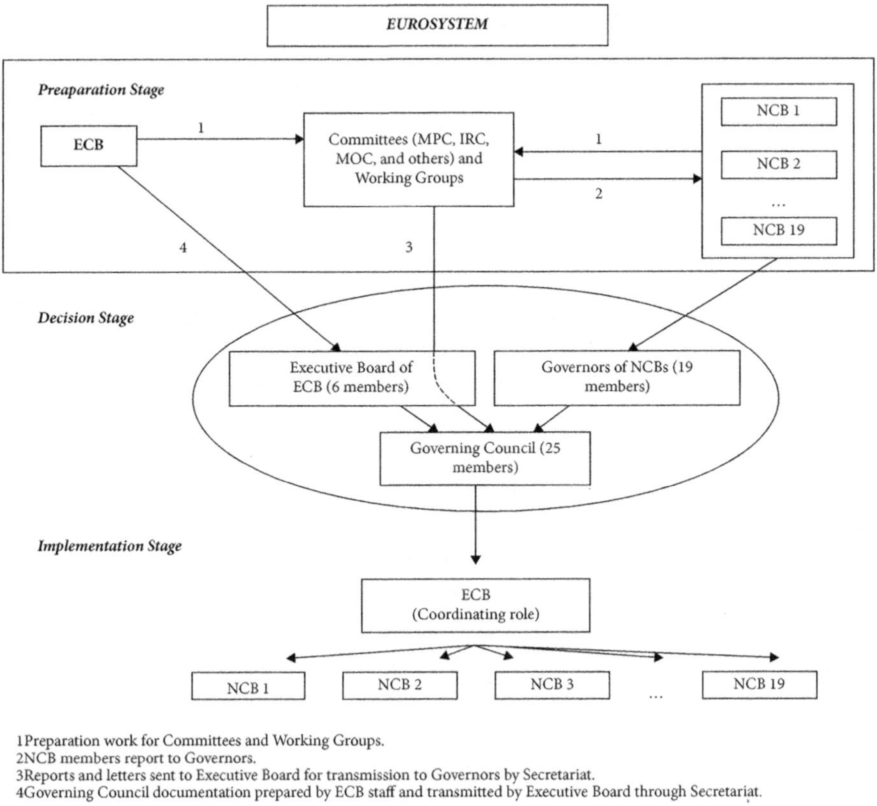

Figure 5.16 Policy decisions by the Governing Council
Note: NCB refers to the national central banks of the 19 euro area countries.

committees, sub-committees, working groups, and task forces composed of national central bank experts were launched. Such a network and the ECB's credibility greatly helped coping with the crisis in recent years.

Independently of when a monetary union might be launched, there is a lot that harmonized and coordinated central banks of the partner countries can already do. It is essential that the central banks of the countries that are going to share a single currency should share similar goals, monetary policy frameworks, and preferences (see Furusawa (2016) and IMF (2015)). Useful comments are also contained in Chapter 2. Thus, building a strong Shilling System is pivotal.

At the moment such a union would be rather imbalanced: Kenya is the relatively stronger economy and the others trail far behind. Tanzania is still in an economic transition [and the State apparently still owns 100 per cent of the land]. Uganda is benefitting from significant energy discoveries (thus it might be at risk of Dutch disease). Rwanda and Burundi are landlocked and still healing.

The main message of this chapter is that, independently from the speed of regional integration (both economic and financial), the steps towards a shared monetary policy framework and a 'Shilling System' (akin to the Eurosystem) will in any case support best practices and promote genuine integration, prosperity, and institutional resilience in the EAC region.

References

Angeloni I., Flad, M., and Mongelli, F. P. (2005), *Economic and Monetary Integration of the New Member States: Helping in Charting the Route,* ECB Occasional Paper No. 36.

Angeloni I., Flad, M., and Mongelli, F. P. (2007), 'Monetary integration of the new EU member states: What sets the pace of euro adoption?', *Journal of Common Market Studies (JCMS),* Vol. 45, No. 2, pp. 367–409.

Balassa, B. (1961), *The Theory of Economic Integration.* Homewood, IL: Richard Irwin.

Blinder A., M. Ehrmann, J.de Haan, and D. Jan Jansen (2016), *"Necessity as the Mother of Invention: Monetary Policy after the Crisis,"* NBER Working Papers 22735, National Bureau of Economic Research, Inc.

Constâncio V. (2016), "Principles of Macroprudential Policy", speech at the ECB-IMF Conference on Macroprudential Policy, Frankfurt am Main, 26 April 2016. See: https://www.ecb.europa.eu/press/key/date/2016/html/sp160426.en.html

Dorrucci, E., Firpo, S., Fratzscher, M., and Mongelli, F. (2002), *European Integration: What Lessons for Other Regions? The Case of Latin America.* ECB Working Paper No. 185 (October).

Dorrucci, E., Firpo, S., Fratzscher, M., and Mongelli, F. (2004), 'The link between institutional and economic integration: Insights for Latin America from the European experience', *Open Economies Review,* Vol. 15, pp. 239–60.

Dorrucci, E., Firpo, S., Fratzscher, M., and Mongelli, F. (2005), 'The path of institutional and financial integration', *Journal of Economic Integration,* Vol. 20, No. 2 (June).

Dorrucci, E., Ioannou, D., Mongelli, F. P., and Terzi, A. (2015), 'The four unions "PIE" on the Monetary Union "CHERRY": A new index of European Institutional Integration'. ECB Occasional Paper No. 160.

ECB (2008), 'The euro at ten: Special anniversary issue', *ECB Monthly Bulletin,* see ECB website.

ECB (2011), *The Monetary Policy of the ECB,* 3rd Edition. See ECB website.

European Commission (2008), 'EMU@10: successes and challenges after 10 years of Economic and Monetary Union', European Economy, No. 2, May.

European Commission (2014), 'A comprehensive EU response to the financial crisis: Substantial progress towards a strong financial framework for Europe and a banking union for the Eurozone'. European Commission memo/14/244, 28 March 2014.

Furusawa, M. (2016), 'Monetary policy and the future of central banking: Implications for Africa'. Remarks on the 50th Anniversary of the Central Bank of Kenya by the IMF Deputy Managing Director. http://www.imf.org/en/News/Articles/2016/09/13/sp091316-Monetary-Policy-and-the-Future-of-Central-Banking-Implications-for-Africa

IMF (2015), 'Evolving monetary policy frameworks in low-income and other developing countries—background paper—country experiences', 27 October 2015. http://www.imf.org/external/pp/longres.aspx?id=5001

Jung A., Mongelli, F. P., and Moutot, P. (2010), 'How are the Eurosystem's monetary policy decisions prepared?', *Journal of Common Market Studies*, Vol. 48, No. 2, pp. 319–45.

Maersch Y. (2017), 'Central bank independence revisited'. Speech at the *Symposium on Building the Financial System of the 21st Century: An Agenda for Europe and the United States*, Frankfurt am Main, 30 March. https://www.ecb.europa.eu/press/key/date/2017/html/sp170330.en.html

Mongelli, F. P. (2013), 'The mutating euro area crisis: Is the balance between "skeptics" and "advocates" shifting?' ECB Occasional Paper Series, No. 144.

Mongelli, F. P. and Riet, A. (2013), 'EMU in crisis: What's next?', in L. Paganetto (ed.), *Public Debt, Global Governance and Economic Dynamism*, Italia: Springer-Verlag, pp. 235–52.

Mongelli, F. P. and Wyplosz, C. (2009), 'The euro at ten—unfulfilled threats and unexpected challenges'. *Proceedings of 5th ECB Central Banking Conference*, European Central bank, Frankfurt am Main, Germany

Moutot, P., Jung, A., and Mongelli, F. P. (2008), 'The Eurosystem: Monetary policy preparation, decision-making, and enlargement—selected issues', ECB Occasional Paper No. 79.

Praet, P. (2017), 'Have unconventional policies overstretched central bank independence? Challenges for accountability and transparency in the wake of the crisis'. *Symposium on Building the Financial System of the 21st Century: An Agenda for Europe and the United States*, Frankfurt am Main, 29 March 2017. https://www.ecb.europa.eu/press/key/date/2017/html/sp170329.en.html

Thomas, A. H., Aisen, A., Mira, C., Alper, E., Yang, F., Boutin-Dufresne, F., Joly, H., Dridi, J., Gigineishvili, N., Mauro, P., Josephs, T., and Thakoor, V. (2015), 'Monitoring and managing fiscal risks in the East African community', IMF African Departmental Paper No. 15/7. http://www.imf.org/external/pubs/cat/longres.aspx?sk=43131.0

World Economic Forum (2017), 'Global Competitiveness Index'. See website.

World Bank (2017a), 'World Development Indicators'. See website.

World Bank (2017b), 'National Accounts Data'. See website.

6

Financial Stability and Bank Supervision in the Twenty-First Century

Babak Abbaszadeh

6.1 Introduction

This chapter focuses on the challenges and opportunities for financial stability and bank supervision in the twenty-first century. It is a contribution to the commemoration of Central Bank of Kenya's 50th Anniversary.

As the CEO of Toronto Centre for global leadership in financial supervision, I have the privilege to oversee our organization's efforts to achieve our vision of a world where financial systems are stable, reliable and accessible to all. Every year we offer training to nearly 2000 financial supervisors and regulators from developing countries in approximately 65 different weeklong capacity development programmes. Our programmes aim to strengthen institutions' effectiveness by helping them respond to particular local objectives and challenges, and implement the latest in international standards and best practices. We are grateful for the continued support from the governments of Canada and Sweden as well as the generosity of our key benefactors and friends at the International Monetary Fund and the World Bank, plus various national supervisory authorities, who altogether make it possible for us to achieve our mission.

The remainder of this chapter is structured into three parts. Section 6.2 examines the challenges of financial stability. Effective bank supervision is discussed in Section 6.3, while Section 6.4 provides some concluding remarks.

6.2 Financial Stability

Financial system supervisors have already faced down the first major challenge of the twenty-first century, namely the 2008 global financial crisis, whose effects are still with us. The financial stability board and the G20 quickly took up an agenda to improve regulation and supervision regimes globally. This has involved a multipronged regulatory agenda, including higher capital requirements and new liquidity regulations, to cite just two important initiatives. It also has involved a parallel effort to improve supervision, and I would note that this work was led by the

Babak Abbaszadeh, *Financial Stability and Bank Supervision in the Twenty-First Century* In: *50 Years of Central Banking in Kenya: Regional and Global Perspectives*. Edited by: Patrick Njoroge and Victor Murinde, Oxford University Press (2021).
 DOI: 10.1093/oso/9780198851820.003.0006

Financial Stability Board (FSB) Task Force on the intensity and effectiveness of supervision headed by Julie Dickson, then-head of Canada's Office of the Superintendent of Financial Institutions, and a Toronto Centre board member. This agenda will take years to implement and still presents many challenges to supervisors. The Basel Committee on Banking Supervision has also played a critical role under the leadership of its chair, Governor Stefan Ingves, another Toronto Centre board member.

But the challenges facing supervisors are constantly evolving and supervisors must evolve their approaches to respond to them. The global financial crisis made clear the threat that financial systems can pose to economies. Supervisors in developing economies in particular, face the challenge of how to ensure financial stability while at the same time promoting the development of the financial system so as to support the sustainable economic growth that will lift citizens out of poverty, and promote greater equality. While we celebrate the economic success of developing countries such as Kenya with their recent impressive growth rates of 6 per cent per annum, it is important to recognize that any lapses into financial instability could erode policy achievements in income distribution and poverty alleviation. So, key supervisory institutions, central banks in developing countries have a tremendous responsibility and the stakes can't be any higher.

At Toronto Centre, we have seen a lot of the progress that the Central Bank of Kenya has accomplished to strengthen the country's banking system, including through our recent training programmes on dealing with problem financial institutions and crisis preparedness. In 2015, the Central Bank of Kenya actively participated in various global and regional fora aimed at strengthening overall supervision both domestically and internationally. The Central Bank of Kenya tackled enhanced cross-border regulatory cooperation; macro-prudential surveillance; crisis management and resolution; anti-money laundering and combatting with the financing of terrorism, and capacity building and knowledge exchange on supervisory matters, the Central Bank of Kenya should be commended for their proactivity.

6.3 Effective Bank Supervision

Effective banking supervision is, in the international arena, no longer just a preoccupation of The Basel Committee or the FSB. In fact, it is actually discussed in the UN's sustainable development goals in its agenda 2030, and the Addis Ababa Action Agenda, which are influencing donor nations' priorities for reconfiguring international aid post-millennium development goals.

Policy-makers are increasingly aware of the central role that effective, sound, and accessible banking and financial services play in fostering growth that is sustainable and reduces poverty, by helping people save and plan for the future, insure against calamity, and access capital needed to start and expand businesses.

Access to financial services is an important method of empowering the poor and marginalized, in particular women and girls, who often face systemic barriers. A key challenge for supervisors going forward is how to close the gaps in access to financial services.

In some cases, creating access involves dismantling legislative or regulatory barriers to participation in finance. In other cases, what's needed is development and deployment of new services and technologies that meet the needs of women and the poor. For example, many of the world's disadvantaged live in rural areas or urban slums with limited access to financial services, but as is well recognized here in Kenya, I am sure, digital finance and branchless banking are emerging as important new paths to accessing financial services. Microfinance and micro-insurance sectors are helping small businesses get started and take root, offering a path to prosperity for many individuals who have found themselves shut out of the traditional financial sectors.

These innovations are important, but they raise challenges for supervisors. They need to take a proportionate and flexible approach to regulation and supervision as banks adapt their business models to incorporate these innovations. But they also need to protect consumers from abuse as banks reach less educated and even illiterate consumers, and as the delivery channels move from banks' own staff to, for example, agents, and mobile networks.

Indeed, Kenya has become a leader in the expansion of mobile banking, with, if I understand correctly, 26 million mobile money accounts as of 2014. Kenyan authorities have already dealt with some of the early growing pains related to the establishment of this new technology.

The G20's global partnership for financial inclusion has done excellent work in its recent white paper to elaborate on the need for our global standard-setting bodies to coordinate their responses to these new innovations. These bodies are working to provide policy-makers with a coherent set of frameworks and guidance to support the expansion of financial access while properly accounting for associated risks. Toronto Centre has long offered financial inclusion programmes to help develop the capacity of agencies to oversee microfinance and micro-insurance industries. We recently expanded our programming to cover digital finance and branchless banking, market conduct, and financial consumer protection.

In addition, supervisors are increasingly becoming aware of the need to incorporate risks related to climate change in their work. As Bank of England Governor Mark Carney noted in his speech to Lloyd's of London in September 2015, the climate change phenomenon poses substantial risks for whole swaths of financial systems. Climate change will increase insurance liabilities due to the physical risks as well as the consequences for businesses that may suffer due to extreme weather effects. There will be liability risks if those who have suffered loss related to climate change seek damage from those they hold responsible. And there will be transition risks related to the process of adjustment towards a lower-carbon economy such as new risks associated with 'green bonds', and the inclusion of environmental and sustainability criteria in credit risk management.

Supervisors must have the skills and judgement to ensure that climate risk is properly accounted for in their assessment of financial institutions. Toronto Centre has begun to address climate risk with a recent executive panel discussion at the spring meetings of the IMF and World Bank, and we are currently developing programming that examines climate risk and preparedness in financial supervisory agencies.

But advances in technology also present another major challenge for financial supervisors and regulators: cybercrime. I acknowledge Central Bank of Kenya's vigilance in this area, where the bank commissioned all external auditors of commercial banks and mortgage finance companies to conduct Information and Communications Technology (ICT) audits on the institutions. As an emerging issue, it will be important for supervisors to share information and learn from what other supervisors are doing. Resolving challenges like these is part of why Toronto Centre promotes cross-jurisdictional learning.

Supervisors also have an opportunity to play a leading role in promoting peace and security by combatting money-laundering, organized crime, corruption, and the financing of terrorism. Effective financial sector oversight is critical if supervisors are to rise to this challenge, and they must. Increased capacity of government bodies to supervise, investigate, and stop illicit flows of money makes people and states safer, which in turn promotes healthy investment climates and increased human development.

And traditional risks are still important, the likelihood of a prolonged period of slow growth and low commodity prices has the potential to place more stresses on banks. Credit risk has always been a key factor leading to bank failures. In our engagements with regulators and supervisors around the world, we know that many agencies still struggle to deal proactively with banks that make bad or mispriced lending decisions, which in turn plant the seeds of future problems. So a closer focus on credit risk, strong credit risk management and quality reviews by supervisors, and an attention to dealing with non-performing loans, are all warranted.

It seems that twenty-first century supervisors and regulators are adopting new methods to address these risks. They are making greater use of stress-testing to account for systemic risks. They are using thematic reviews to assess how well specific risks are managed across multiple institutions. They are relying on enhanced understanding and inclusion of macroeconomic and industry analysis in developing their understanding of the risk profiles of financial institutions. They are cooperating with other national and international authorities to coordinate and share information. They are issuing regular reports on risk outlook and financial stability in an effort to build a culture of risk preparedness and transparency.

Traditional risks are taking on new dimensions as the nature of the banking industry evolves. Banks are increasingly part of groups that include insurance providers, asset managers, and securities firms. The close ties between sectors and the tangible growth in importance of conglomerates, which have spread their tentacles in the banking sector, makes effective supervision more complex and demands that bank supervisors work cooperatively with other sectoral regulators and supervisors.

Toronto Centre has long offered cross-sectoral programmes that bring together supervisors from multiple sectors to explore common challenges and ways to work collaboratively to ensure financial markets remain stable. These courses explore topics such as how to minimize the risk of contagion from one sector or jurisdiction to another, how to reduce supervisory gaps, how to avoid unnecessary supervisory overlaps and duplication, and improve joint supervisory response.

Banks are also increasingly operating across jurisdictions, which presents challenges for national regulators and supervisors to ensure that financial contagion does not leak across borders. Effective supervision in the twenty-first century requires increasing cross-border cooperation, and ideally, cross-border harmonization of laws, regulations and supervisory policies. In many parts of the world, regional blocs are working to integrate and harmonize the laws and enforcement around financial services, including, as you know, here in east Africa.

A big focus of Toronto Centre's programming is on delivering regional programmes, which are customized to meet the needs of groups of countries in specific geographic areas and are offered in partnership with a local host organization. Participants share their experiences and discuss common challenges, with an eye toward solving cross-border issues. These programmes build financial sector knowledge, strengthen leadership skills, and help promote networking among peers and agencies in the region.

6.4 Conclusion

As financial system supervisors, you know that your work is never 'done.' There is no moment when we can say that we've completed the task of ensuring that financial systems are stable, inclusive and reliable. Financial system stability and soundness is an ever-shifting target. Supervisors must be prepared to constantly adjust their tactics and approaches, and update their training and knowledge, in order to effectively respond to the new challenges, risks, and opportunities that arise out of developing technologies, business trends, and global events.

The stakes are high: failure to effectively prepare for financial system risks will impact the lives of your constituents in profound ways, including exposing them to poverty and ruin, or, for the already poor, denying them the opportunity to escape poverty. Above all, twenty-first century supervisors must arm themselves with the wisdom to respond effectively to circumstances that are bound to evolve and change in ways that are impossible to predict.

We applaud the Central Bank of Kenya for convening this important forum.

7

Financial Innovation and Financial Inclusion

Insights from a Practitioner

Bob Collymore

7.1 Introduction

A decade ago, as the Central Bank of Kenya (CBK) turned 40, Safaricom launched M-PESA as a mobile money service.[1] It was a basic SMS-based service compared to what it would become. Even in those early years, it was clear that it was the boldest innovation in the history of Kenya's financial sector. As it evolved, M-PESA would grow to epitomize how the global mobile money revolution could enhance financial inclusion.

Before this revolution, the prevailing school of thought offered that financial deepening could only be 'savings-led' or 'credit-led' (Donovan, 2012). Mobile money, especially the success of M-PESA in Kenya, changed this by introducing a third element, that of an ecosystem that offers the platform on which other services could run. The opportunities for startups and other stakeholders are immense, especially in a country as tech savvy and innovation-hungry as Kenya.

Mobile money brings together many stakeholders across the telecommunications, finance, and governance sectors. It also ropes in innovators and entrepreneurs, as well as people who want to offer services critical to the sustainability of the network. This large group of stakeholders don't always have corresponding goals, and the interaction between such well-defined sectors may at times create unnecessary friction. Mobile money services are regulated primarily by the Communication Commission of Kenya (CCK) and the CBK, the regulators in telecommunications and finance respectively. The parley between these two regulators, especially the deep interest from the onset in expanding the Kenyan financial sector to encourage entrepreneurship and innovation, went a long way into driving the early uptake of the service.

[1] This chapter was written before the untimely death of Bob Collymore. In many ways, the chapter offers testimony to his great ideas and legacy. May his soul rest in peace (Editors).

Bob Collymore, *Financial Innovation and Financial Inclusion: Insights from a Practitioner* In: *50 Years of Central Banking in Kenya: Regional and Global Perspectives.* Edited by: Patrick Njoroge and Victor Murinde, Oxford University Press (2021).
 DOI: 10.1093/oso/9780198851820.003.0007

As stakeholders and regulators, the approach taken by Central Bank to mobile money is the primary reason why M-PESA is now hailed as the world's most successful mobile money deployment. Where interlocking regulators would traditionally have slowed such a process down by increasing the bureaucracy, both the CCK and the CBK worked seamlessly to reduce the regulatory burden while safeguarding customers from risk. There was a professional interest in reducing financial exclusion by encouraging financial innovation, as well as a much-needed laissez-faire approach to regulation.

Within a decade, M-PESA has moved 15 trillion shillings and inspired a global revolution in the financial sector. It has also done a lot more, especially in bringing financial services such as transaction accounts, savings, and credit services and payment services to the previously unbanked. Even for the banked, M-PESA has changed interactions with other financial services. It has improved the quality of life of many households, as well as facilitating broader social inclusion by offering payment services not just to merchants, but also to government institutions, services, and utility companies. The ripple effects are immense and long-term, but what is already clear is that M-PESA has revolutionized how we relate to financial services.

In Kenya today, M-PESA is no longer just a money service; it is a verb. It is a way of life.

This chapter offers the insights of a practitioner into financial innovation and financial inclusion in Kenya. The remainder of the chapter is structured into seven parts. Section 7.2 highlights the M-PESA journey, which has emerged as a major triumph in Kenya as well as globally. The partnerships that have underpinned the success of M-PESA are discussed in Section 7.3, while Section 7.4 explains how M-PESA has been able to fit into the regulatory environment in Kenya. Section 7.5 discusses the question of how and where mobile money services fit in the broader definitions of financial services in Kenya specifically but also in a broad sense. Section 7.6 introduces the concepts of M-PESA-powered financial inclusion; the concept is illustrated using the KPMG true value case study, Vision 2030 and savings and credit in mobile money. Section 7.7 discusses mobile money as a tool for financial deepening. The chapter concludes with Section 7.8, which charts the way forward by looking into the future of mobile money.

7.2 The M-PESA Journey: A Triumph

On Tuesday, 6 March 2007, Safaricom launched M-PESA with the tagline 'Send Money Home.' As a new service in a previously non-existent regulatory framework, M-PESA posed a challenge to regulators and potential customers alike. Even to Safaricom's customer base, this new service was quirky, and perhaps ambitious.

It sought to replace cash with money sent, as M-PESA at its most basic is, through text messages. It would grow to do a lot more than that, but it would also provide an unprecedented opportunity for innovation to shape regulation in the financial sector.

> Every second of the day, M-PESA processes a loan. Every minute, 3900 people buy airtime, while 1,500 people will receive money from their friends and family. Another 1700 will use to pay for bills and services, while 240 will deposit or withdraw from their banks. More than 15 businesses will make payments to other firms.[2]

In the age of M-PESA, a decade now feels like a lifetime. Many of its users can't remember a time before it existed, and the ecosystem now moves a quarter of Kenya's GDP. But it also does a lot more. It provides connections and has become an ecosystem that not only provides a critical service, but also creates jobs, alleviates poverty and boosts the economy. It is in every facet of Kenyan life, social, economic, and even political. Even today, a decade in, customers are still finding new and interesting ways to use it. M-PESA is not a product any more, it is a verb and a way of life.

When it was first launched in 2007, M-PESA's selling point was to allow people to send money back home. It was tapping into an age-old cultural connection where those who live and work in towns send money home, whether to help or to invest. Before 2007, this required either the postal service or putting it on the bus. Both were cumbersome to say the least, and added an expense and a risk to the process. In the political and social challenges that followed by the end of that year, the utility of M-PESA's initial tagline became even clearer. Since people couldn't move across towns, the ability to send each other money was essential.

Whatever we had envisioned M-PESA to be, even at that point, we quickly learnt that once it caught on, Kenyans would find new ways to use it. This actually predates the launch in 2007, and the six-month pilot phase in 2006. The curiosity that M-PESA tapped into and continues to became clear in the early Safaricom days, when people started using airtime as a currency. In 2006, with approval from the CBK, a small team from Safaricom and Vodafone piloted a system built by Sagentia. It was a microfinance loan repayment system where Faulu Kenya's customers could repay their loans through the phone. The idea was to ease the process by saving *chama*[3] treasurers the hustle of getting on a bus to physically deposit group loan repayments after getting all the contributions. All she had to do was send it to the microfinance and it would be recorded.

[2] Safaricom, March 2017. MPESA in 60 Seconds. #MPESAat10 #NiYanguNiYetu. https://www.youtube.com/watch?v=uygbfBWYMiE

[3] In Kenya, a *chama* is an informal cooperative society that works as a micro-savings group.

Something interesting started happening within this small pilot ecosystem. Members of the groups would help each other out with their contributions, sending each other money to forward to the treasurer. They would also exchange it for other things, such as airtime and even products and services. One lady sent it to her husband who had been mugged and freed of his bus fare home. Whatever we had originally thought M-PESA was going to be, the data and trends were showing that Kenyans were not just ready for such a service, they were actually ready to define it.

Cash carries a heavy burden of insecurity and cost. Seth Lumumba, M-PESA's first customer back in 2007, likes to give the story of how he recruited someone into it. He gave him a scenario where it was cheaper to lose his phone with its M-PESA balance than lose phone and cash. Lumumba's experience from 2007 also includes one of the challenges our first customers faced. One of the first transactions he tried to do, withdrawing money to give to his sister, failed when he put in the wrong agent number.

Among the first things we did, after getting the CBK's approval, was to train a network of agents. They would be akin to human ATMs, and earning their trust and participation was critical to the ecosystem we were building. As the core nodes in the network, their patience and understanding of M-PESA would also mean customers had a face they could trust on the ground. Our first agent was Patrick Macharia, the proprietor of Generation Insights Ltd. He had founded his business as a cyber café in 2006, and jumped onto the opportunity to try out what he calls 'the greatest risk I ever took'. Today, there are tens of thousands of agents like Macharia, many of whom have integrated M-PESA into other businesses as a secondary revenue stream.

Explaining exactly how M-PESA worked was perhaps the greatest challenge for my predecessor, Michael Joseph and the Safaricom team. Whether it was to agents, customers, and even legislators, the idea of giving cash for e-float,[4] although revolutionary, was a hard sell. To be effectively achieved, several things had to come into play. In the seven years that Safaricom had existed before M-PESA, we had built a solid brand that was now a household name. We already had millions of customers on the telecommunications side of things, and most of them were the early adopters of M-PESA. Another critical element was the regulatory attitude towards the environment we were essentially creating. The combination of regulators working to ensure M-PESA was a safe place for Kenyans to transact their money further built trust in the service.

By 2008, M-PESA was facing new challenges. The regulatory environment that the CBK had created for a new, ambitious, and fast-growing service had combined

[4] In Kenya, e-float is money that exists in an account that the account holder can access to make payments, transfer money, or undertake any other transaction on their mobile phone; also they can add to or exchange for cash by visiting an agent.

with a critical need to push the numbers through the roof within just a year after the launch. Initial assessments had pointed to the idea that it was a service for the unbanked, a way of bringing the majority of Kenyans into a formal financial service. This notion remains to date, but it is markedly untrue, or rather incomplete. Even from its earliest days, the appeal of M-PESA transcended the simple but pressing need of financial inclusiveness. It appealed to people who had one or even multiple bank accounts because it solved a basic need.

The CBK audit that begun in December 2008, instituted by the CBK and the acting Minister for Finance at the time, was essential to shaping M-PESA's future. While the service had caught on with customers, more than 3 million by then, there were still questions about how it actually worked. Where was Safaricom storing all the money? Who was actually responsible for monitoring it? Was it a pyramid scheme? Was Safaricom trying to stretch from being a telecom company to being a bank?

To the CBK representatives who first saw the system in 2006, these questions had already been answered. M-PESA was collaterized by a disciplined float management. Every e-float unit in circulation had a 'real' shilling in a trust account. It was a financial service not a bank. No Safaricom employee had access to the account at Commercial Bank of Africa (CBA), a fully licensed bank within the banking system.

The CBK audit report of January 2009 solved these questions in many ways. Since it was now clear that M-PESA was not trying to bank, and was a fast-evolving service, what was needed was an equally fast moving regulatory environment. Only the CBK had been providing this from as early as 2005 when the pilot phase was being formulated. A dynamic environment for a quirky product meant that feedback from users could allow Safaricom to continuously tinker with it to build something that addressed an actual need.

The fundamental reason for M-PESA's success was a conducive legal and regulatory environment. The 'market-led' approach to policy making meant that the mobile money revolution could thrive. As a key to financial development and inclusion, such an approach means that we have been able to continuously innovate with M-PESA as a service and an ecosystem. It was also a clear indication of how the Kenyan economy has come in allowing for innovations in the financial sector. Most efforts to open up the financial services sector had been hampered by perennial bank failures and insurmountable hurdles to opening an account or accessing formal financial services. With M-PESA's simplicity, backed in part by the fact that it was already attached to one's phone number and has a registration process, this hurdle was removed. It also triggered a revolution within the pre-existing financial services sector, especially because it preceded the smartphone revolution.

A decade in, we are working on making M-PESA a less clumsy service to enhance the user experience. In October 2017, we launched M-PESA 1Tap, a

NFC-based technology that reduces the number of steps it takes to complete a payment. While peer-to-peer (P2P) transactions and airtime purchases remain the primary uses of M-PESA, it is clear that the future of mobile money as a whole lie in payments as well. People are finding new and interesting ways to use digital financial services because they are safer and more convenient, but more needs to be done to ease the process of access and usage. M-PESA1 Tap does this by making it easier to use to make payments at critical pay points where time and efficiency are of the essence. This simplifies the process both for the user and for the merchant, and cuts down on the time it takes to pay for purchases and services.

7.3 M-PESA Partnerships and Successes

The early confidence in M-PESA also meant that aversion to M-PESA from banks thawed with time. It started with M-KESHO where Safaricom partnered with Equity Bank in March 2010. For the first time, instead of having to withdraw from one to deposit in the other, customers could integrate both. It might seem like a lifetime now since it is a must-have service today but at the time, it was revolutionary not just for M-PESA but also for Safaricom's greater vision. It was also perfect for Equity Bank, which had itself made it easy to open transaction accounts with no maintenance fee or minimum balance. For the bank, finding new ways for its customers to access their money meant they could transact more and reduce the strain on physical branches.

The first such partnership we had was with Grundfos International, a global water pump manufacturer in 2009. Their Corporate Social Responsibility (CSR) project was designed to solve the water access problem in rural areas, but they wanted to do more than that. They wanted the process to be sustainable, and to reduce the need to carry cash to pay each time someone went to buy water. In the two years we had been running M-PESA, we had never integrated it to another system of any kind.

What Safaricom and Grundfos eventually designed in between June and September 2009 was a water card system where customers prepaid for through M-PESA. Once the user got to the water pump, they simply placed the card in a slot in the dispenser and fetched water. The account number system may even seem simple today when M-PESA is the go-to payment method for everything from electricity bills to hotel bills, but in 2009 it was nothing short of a marvel. It was perhaps the true foundation of the *Lipa na M-PESA* service, which is now the default payment method in many Kenyan businesses.

Although some of the key issues that the CBK audited in late 2008 had already previously come up, it was also an opportunity to assess just how right their initial decision had been. For industry players, bankers, and customers, the audit was a much needed assurance that it was a legitimate financial service. This opened up an entirely new crop of stakeholders for us, and in many ways set the stage for the ecosystem we have today. Now, it is almost impossible to run a business without the *Lipa na M-PESA*. The service offers the same selling points that M-PESA was built on, that cash is expensive. M-PESA offers the convenience of carrying just a phone in one's pocket or bag instead of a huge and cumbersome wallet. With the same device that you use to connect to everything else, you can pay for your fuel, food, shopping, and almost anything else. You can even tip for service with it. Interestingly, its uptake was similar to that of M-PESA itself in that small traders discovered its utility and larger players followed.

In 2009, for example, Safaricom partnered with Kenya Power to allow people to pay their electricity bills through M-PESA. It was a simple solution but revolutionary in its own way because people didn't have to waste time queuing to pay their electricity bills any more. It was also the same year that we finally begun and scaled international remittances, and that insurance companies and microfinance institutions allowed their customers to pay via M-PESA. With an ever-expanding crop of stakeholders, the value added service that M-PESA was already becoming was thriving more than ever. It meant its millions of customers could now access an ever expanding array of services, both financial and non-financial, right from their phones.

The lessons that we had learnt as a company in our first seven years of operation came in handy in growing M-PESA. We learnt to listen to the customer and continually innovate, adding new services to the ecosystem and finding out new and interesting ways that our customers were using it. Within this ecosystem we could experiment with new ideas, some quirky even, to solve specific needs for both our individual and corporate customers.

That is one of the reasons why we brought M-PESA itself back home from its initial hub in Germany. From 2007 to 2015, the system had data from 25 million customers as well as hundreds of thousands of agents and merchants. While the process of migration and upgrade was itself akin to a complex operation, the reasons why we had to move it were worth the work. By this time, it had become so integral to Kenyan life that our preparations to transfer the system had to be preceded by an extensive awareness campaign. Any minute M-PESA is down, its millions of users are affected.

At the heart of it, M-PESA has grown around its initial goal of financial inclusiveness. People still use it to send money back home, and even that is no longer limited to Kenya's borders. It has become a verb, a social facilitator through which the Kenyan spirit thrives. It has embodied fundraising and disaster response, allowing individuals and groups to help each other by contributing to causes at their convenience. It has become a pillar of the economy as well, moving nearly half of Kenya's GDP.

In 2016 alone, M-PESA processed 6 billion transactions. It had 29.5 million active customers served by over 40,000 agents, collectively making an average 529 transactions per second.

On 8 January 2014, we upgraded our Application Programmable Interface (API). That allowed us to bring in even more partners into the M-PESA ecosystem, quickly growing to over 30 banks and 160 financial partners. With just a phone, M-PESA customers can now access their bank accounts and deposit or withdraw money as and when needed. The API upgrade facilitated this by allowing near real-time processing of transactions. As a payment platform, M-PESA's successes such as these create extensive ripple effects for both individuals and businesses.

A partnership with global money transfer service Western Union birthed M-PESA International Money Transfer (IMT). IMT has since expanded into a hub service with several other players, ensuring that our customers can receive money from over 100 countries today. Even regionally, our partnership with MTN in Rwanda has facilitated money transfer between the two countries. This is critical in the face of expanding trade opportunities, as well as the growth in trade volume and human traffic between the two countries.

The partnerships within those first few years showed that M-PESA was no longer just a service. It was no longer what we had started with to solve the need to send money back home. We had an ecosystem now where we needed to formulate solutions to emerging problems not just for our customers but for potential partners such as banks and companies in other sectors. Today, you can buy government bonds through M-PESA. You can do it without having to queue in a bank to withdraw the money, since it is connected to your bank, which most likely has an app. From a point where you would need to disrupt your day to do a bank visit, you can now do it while sitting comfortably at home or in the office. As an ecosystem, a lot more collaboration is necessary between players and stakeholders to drive partnerships as well as ensure a continuing dynamic approach to policy and regulation. As telecommunication companies, the challenge is in investing in infrastructure and technology, as well as extensive research into consumer habits to facilitate greater use of our mobile money services.

With 55 people from Telkom Kenya and five from Vodafone, this previously unknown entity holed up in a three-bedroom flat on Harry Thuku Road for most of 2000, building the foundations of what we know as Safaricom today. With just one competitor in the market, Safaricom needed to define itself differently. We needed a target customer base that could ideally push us to the top while allowing us to tap into the wider Kenyan market. To do this, we needed to push for cheaper phones, for lower rates across the board, and for as wide network coverage as possible.

Our approach to innovation was to make third party integration as seamless as possible, partially by opening up the M-PESA application programme interfaces

(APIs). The motivation for this was that seamless integration can and has triggered product development at an unprecedented rate. Expanding the M-PESA ecosystem has also triggered and driven most of the growth seen in internal transactions, meaning that more people are using the service as their primary wallet. With quicker product development, we can further tap into this and drive the next phase in financial innovation.

Millions of transactions take place within the M-PESA ecosystem daily. For example, the transaction may be undertaken by a lady paying her hairdresser, or a person paying a *matatu* (local bus) conductor. The transaction may also be undertaken by a young man paying for his shopping at the supermarket, or a lady buying government bonds. At *chama* meetings for mostly social gatherings, the participants send money in advance via M-PESA to the treasurer in order to settle their monthly contributions. It is usual practice for a Kenyan to check his/her bank balance at the end of the month or to check for their salary, and then move nearly all of it to M-PESA. The person can then pay for rent, utilities, soft loans from friends and family, shopping, luxuries, and then save a portion of what remains on M-Shwari or KCB-M-PESA.

7.4 How Does M-PESA Fit into the Regulatory Environment?

In his paper 'Regulatory Impact on Mobile Money and Financial Inclusion in African Countries', Ondiege (2015) rightly notes that for financial systems to become more inclusive, regulators will have to promote availability, accessibility, and affordability. When Kenya liberalized its telecommunications sector in 1999, it was unknown at the time that mobile technology would trigger such a significant disruption in how people access financial services. Mobile money wasn't the silver bullet, or at least not the only one, but it would trigger an unprecedented disruption in the financial services sector. In the early years of M-PESA, it was easy to see the potential of mobile money as a threat to the prevailing monetary policies. A telco-led approach further placed, at least to unknowing observers, a core part of a critical service outside the direct control of Central Bank. The difference in Kenya as opposed to other markets such as Nigeria was that we solved these things early enough by first realizing that liberalizing the financial sector was the only way to get real gains at the household level.

As a telco, Safaricom was directly under CCK but M-PESA, as a financial service, required approval and oversight from the CBK (Alliance for Financial Inclusion 2010). This regulatory tag team between the CCK and the Central Bank in formulating policies for M-PESA is a fundamental reason for its success. Although there was no pre-existing law on which to base policy on, the CBK team approached the new financial service with the same tenets that govern the sector. There was a continuing dialogue especially on risk management, expanding services and continuously improving the relationship between the service provider and the regulator (s). In context, the Kenyan market has a long history of non-bank financial services failing and customers losing billions of shillings. It had also had, in the years before and during M-PESA's first year, hundreds of pyramid schemes collapse in quick succession.

Despite this, and because of the leading brand status that Safaricom had already become, the new regulatory environment evolved with the service. The CBK's creation of this dynamic environment, where policy often worked hand in hand with innovation, is an important reason why M-PESA has succeeded. In the other nine countries it has been introduced in, it has not done as well as it has in Kenya. Where it had to be to be stopped in South Africa because of low numbers, in Kenya we were struggling to recruit and train enough agents to meet the growing customer base. Our original customer targets had been 350,000 by March 2008, but we had already crossed million within eight months. From a ratio of agent to customer ratio of 1:200 at first, we were at 1:1000 within a year. Ours was a unique problem of scaling fast enough to keep up.

In essence, the way M-PESA reshaped the regulatory environment and changed how regulators approach innovations because regulation was based on function rather than institutional form that addresses risk in a focused fashion.[5] A good example of the way the age of M-PESA has shaped regulation is the May 2017 directive from the Competition Authority of Kenya (CAK). The policy directive to inform customers on transaction costs in real-time enhanced the experience. It also brought a level of transparency on transaction charges that hadn't been there before. It was also a realization that we need to do more than disclosure—we should be seeking to build the experience based on informed choices. Essentially, we need to make sure the customer understands the modalities and pricing of each transaction.

Another example of a service along the same lines is *Hakikisha,* which shows the sender the name of the recipient to confirm before sending. The service was borne out of a constant complaint from customers, and it has since eased the pressure on customer care agents to rescind transactions sent to the wrong people. Such services are enhancing this experience by incorporating key tenets and best practices from other financial sector players.

In 2017, there are still many regulatory hurdles to cross as we try and set the stage for the next phase in the mobile money revolution. Interoperability is still on the table to further facilitate access to mobile money services while cutting the transaction costs. Although financial liberalization has led to increased financial inclusion, it also leaves the financial sector exposed to the risk of cyclical crisis. This was the background that banks and financial experts had at the onset of the

[5] https://www.sbs.ox.ac.uk/sites/default/files/research-projects/MiB/7-Safaricom-Presentation.pdf

mobile money revolution in early 2007 and late 2008. With few or no constraints, the flow of money increases but it also increases the chances that players will take unnecessary risks. But at the heart of this concern was a deep misunderstanding of what M-PESA was designed for, and how it fit into the larger frame of the financial sector. But some of these concerns are real issues. There is also the lingering concern of the security of mobile money wallets, as well as the need to continuously innovate to curb criminal and fraudulent activity. To do so, policy and regulation will need to work even more closely with market players to define the environment and its operations, as well as how to reduce the risk for the consumer.

There are many lessons here for the sector on how to approach the strengths and potential weaknesses of new financial innovations. For a telco offering a financial service, Safaricom was redefining how technology and solutions to other critical social problems interact and either boost or hamper each other. For example, M-PESA's would-be ancestors, Smart Money and GCASH, were launched in the Philippines in 2001 and 2004 respectively (Leishman, 2009). As basic mobile money deployments, the two services were designed to bring financial services to the previously unbanked, as well as simplifying a few telecom-related problems such as buying airtime. Research by GSMA shows that the two succeeded for almost the same reasons that M-PESA did in Kenya. Among these are widespread mobile coverage and a 'strong correlation between confidence in the mobile network and the likelihood of adopting mobile money' (Leishman, 2009). Because mobile phone penetration was already widespread, everything else fell into place when a new service changed the phone from a mere communication tool into a full interface to financial services.

The clean bill of health that the December 2008 audit of M-PESA gave in was an affirmation that we had the right product at the right time. Leveraging on our mobile phone customers, we were in the process of building an ecosystem that allowed each customer to access not just mobile services but money, and in future, loans and savings services. In 2009, the government went one step further and zero rated financial services, allowing the emerging sector to lower its transaction costs and reach even more people.

Today, the regulatory treatment of M-PESA from the onset has been the subject of many case studies. Other countries and regulators are looking to Kenya's experience and leading mobile money market status for lessons on how to approach their own. One recurring finding is that in countries that chose to approach mobile money from a traditional financial services perspective, penetration was low because of the high barriers to entry. It's easy to see why regulators in other markets chose that approach because mobile money is still an evolving concept. The underlying risk aversion, however, meant that those countries have lost one of the most important tools for financial inclusion today.

M-PESA is a product perfect for its time. It has not only changed how we relate to money but has also inspired at least seven competitors. From a point where we had to first win the trust of customers, agents, merchants, and regulators, we are now at a point where M-PESA is hailed as Kenya's greatest innovation yet. It is the world's most successful mobile money deployment, the subject of many case studies. Its success is seen as testament to the enduring ability of Kenyans to solve complex everyday problems with an agility that's the envy of other societies.

At the beginning of the M-PESA journey, we built a mostly P2P transaction service that didn't need much in the way of technological advancements. The Generation 1 (G1) servers, housed by IBM in Germany, were perfect for a nascent service with low growth projections. But the next few years showed that we needed to build a new and better system if we were going to create any increased value for our customers. M-PESA was evolving from just a service to somewhat of a way of life, as the social network effects spread across and along socio-economic layers. Our challenge by 2015 was how to store, mine, and process the data we had of our 25 million customers, over 100,000 agents and 200,000 Lipa na M-PESA merchants. Transferring the servers back home was just one of the challenges, the bigger one being how to do it without interfering with critical services, and to do it safely. Over 300 engineers in three continents had this arduous task, which culminated in a single week in mid-April 2015 after two years of preparations.

7.5 Is M-PESA a Banking Service?

One of the recurring questions in the age of mobile money is how and where mobile money services fit in the broader definitions of financial services. It was one of the first things that had to be defined in the approval process, because although there were laws governing financial institutions, there were none specifically for mobile money services. Because of the regulatory approach to M-PESA from its pilot days, even other players in the financial services sector were unsure whether Safaricom was launching a competitor or something else altogether. The initial friction between M-PESA and the banking sector revolved around the CBK's regulatory treatment of the former. To banking institutions, M-PESA as a financial service represented somewhat of a double-standard because it was not subjected to the same regulatory elements as they were. It was also raising their costs in some areas, especially in far-flung branches where mobile agents would need constant liquidity.

M-PESA is not a bank, and has never framed itself as one. When this question first publicly emerged in 2008, it was triggered in part by the events of the preceding year during which M-PESA had taken off and now had millions of customers. The CBK had already dealt with this question, by asking their research team to think beyond the original microfinance model. The legal question on the table of whether M-PESA was a bank by design or operation rose up then, in 2006, and was decided in 2007.

There is a core difference between the broader definition of a financial service and the legal definition of a bank. In January 2007, the CBK legal team found that M-PESA was not operating as a bank because there was no credit risk, the money was held in a trust account, and the service offered no interest on deposits. The question then became where exactly in the scheme of laws such a service would fall if it did not then fall under the Banking Act. It eventually fell on the CBK Act which broadly mandates the apex bank to formulate policies on financial services. The letter of no objection issued by the Governor of the CBK in February 2007 set the scene for many of the issues that had been discussed during the assessment phases. At the base of it, it included conditions such as security, proper accounting, integrity, and observance of the law.

From the outside, it was easy to claim that M-PESA had not undergone due diligence by the CBK, as well as other critical regulators. Both banks and our competitors at the time, Zain, claimed that Safaricom was getting preferential treatment. But this was never the case; the CBK team that first encountered M-PESA during its pilot phases did not have much experience with such a system, but quickly dived into its intricacies and continually assessed its health. By the time the idea evolved and caught on, there was official legal opinion as well as an operational risk audit. Add to that the September 2008 survey by Financial Sector Deepening (FSD) among thousands of M-PESA users, and there was more than sufficient reason to see why the service had obtained approval.

The financial sector M-PESA dove into had been evolving for at least three decades. From the late 1970s, the government opened up the Kenyan financial markets beyond banking institutions, allowing a flurry of new entrants into a hungry market. The next two decades were tumultuous, partly due to political waves, both domestically and internationally. But the Kenyan market that Safaricom was born in was evolving into a technology-driven twenty-first-century one where the need for financial and social inclusion was a primary concern for a fast-growing nation. The fast growth of Safaricom as Kenya's leading telco, trusted by tens of millions of users, provided the perfect breeding ground for a financial solution of M-PESA's nature to thrive. While almost 60 per cent of the population was outside the financial system in 2006, M-PESA's arrival and the ensuing ripples cut this down to just a quarter of the population within the next seven years (Manson, 2013).

A decade later, M-PESA's initial strengths have combined with other innovations such as banking applications and internet banking. Together, these systems are continuously reducing the need to carry or handle cash, as well as ease the cost of transaction and accounting. Kenya's handling of M-PESA epitomizes the merits of engineering financial development by encouraging investors and entrepreneurs to experiment with different models (Burns, 2016). Its slow growth in other markets shows that approaching mobile money as traditional banks can limit its growth and impact.

7.6 M-PESA-Powered Financial Inclusion

7.6.1 The Pilot Project for Financial Inclusion

At the launch of the M-PESA International Money Transfer in October 2009, the eighth governor of Central Bank of Kenya called M-PESA 'an extremely important tool for financial inclusion' (Ndung'u, 2009). The World Bank defines financial inclusion as when 'individuals and businesses have access to useful and affordable financial products and services that meet their needs-transactions, payments, savings, credit and insurance-delivered in a responsible and sustainable way'.[6] Financial inclusion is a key enabler to 7 of the 17 Sustainable Development Goals (SDGs), and to Kenya's own Vision 2030. The idea is to trigger financial stability by encouraging financial innovation, an area where M-PESA is often used as the poster child for how innovation can reduce exclusion. This is especially true for traditional marginalized groups and was in fact one of the original motivations for what we now know as M-PESA.

The original pilot project was designed to solve a problem affecting members of Faulu Kenya, a microfinance institution. The idea was to financial empower people by reducing travel and accounting time. Today, M-PESA's satisfies that goal and does more, especially by allowing people to save and borrow directly from their phones. For rural women, this is a critical area because it helps reduce wastage and encourages saving. According to Lucy Corkin (2016), in 'Kenya's Mobile Money Story and the Runaway Success of MPESA', this 'created financial independence and privacy' for many women by giving them a confidential way of transacting in a society that had previously marginalized them.

Until the mobile money revolution, financial inclusion was informally seen as having a bank account. The solution that the preceding telco revolution offered was access through affordable phones, reducing both the convenience and cost elements. While the initial form of M-PESA was rudimentary compared to what it is today, it still combined these elements in such a way that all stakeholders within it were benefitting in one way or the other. It was also tapping into the fact that Sub-Saharan Africa, not just Kenya, has one of the youngest populations in the world. This population has been the critical target of mobile and internet penetration, and has continually found ways to exploit both to their benefit.

[6] Financial Inclusion. World Bank. http://www.worldbank.org/en/topic/financialinclusion

For an older generation, a physical bank branch was the representation of financial access. It cost money to access it, and time to access its services. So, it had to be planned into a week and thought of to the detail. With the failures in the financial sector in Kenya in the late 1980s and the late 1990s, surviving banks raised the bar for who could operate a bank account. The idea was to weed out potential loan defaulters, but it ended up cutting off low income earners who could not justify consistently high income. A few banks did try in those years to reduce the requirements, but every reduction carried with it significant risk that seemed unjustifiable. The solution, which in the banking sector was spearheaded by banks such as Equity Bank, was to focus on providing financial services to the previously unbanked. This included allowing zero balance accounts as well as simplifying the account opening process. It still required a visit to a physical branch for the registration, and visits to ATMs to withdraw and later, deposit cash.

The mobile money revolution differs from this in how it approached access, especially in expanding the agent banking model. Bank branches are few and far between, while you can have hundreds of thousands of agents combining the money service with almost any other legal business. Our first agent started out as a cyber café, and the M-PESA business made sense to him as an extra income earner. With many agents across the country, and essentially the world, M-PESA solved the access problem. When you add the ecosystem element, where it is now possible to withdraw your salary from your bank account and pay most, if not all, your bills through M-PESA, then the access element becomes even clearer. There are more M-PESA accounts than Kenyan adults today (Corkin, 2016).

In the seven years of Safaricom's existence before M-PESA, it became clear that mobile phones were the next frontier. Where the barriers to entry to the formal banking system were high, the cost of mobile phones was falling with each passing year. Interest in the facets of owning a mobile phone was also driving subscription numbers up, and users were already using airtime as a currency to ease the costs of carrying cash. Mobile phone penetration was already soaring above bank account penetration in a way that seems unique to Sub-Saharan Africa (except for Paraguay).

At the end of the first year of its existence, we expanded M-PESA to allow employers to pay salaries through the service, and schools to accept fees (Alliance for Financial Inclusion 2010). With its burgeoning success at that point, it had become clear that its users were finding it convenient for an increasing number of services. The school fees problem was particularly interesting, because it meant that parents, guardians, and sponsors of school-going children were finding it inconvenient to have to withdraw money and buy banker's cheques to pay for fees. The cost of cash problem was perhaps clearest from the start here, because even banker's cheques and/or cash would get lost and create complexities in one of the most important facets of Kenyan life. It also created an accounting and logistical problem for accountants and auditors in learning institutions. M-PESA solved this by allowing parents to pay directly to institutions, and giving institutions a cashless way of handling the funds they received.

The low rate of financial inclusion in Kenya was one of the reasons why M-PESA took off fast, and has been growing still. The regulatory environment created by the government, specifically through the CBK and the Treasury, made M-PESA an integral component of a new digital financial revolution as well as an 'agent banking' model. While there had been some innovations targeting low income customers in the decades before, M-PESA combined the reach of Safaricom with a financial solution. The crux of the solution was that agents were independent contractors who would earn a commission on each transaction, and would essentially operate as M-PESA branches in whichever part of the country they were in.

Agents are a vital node between the technology and those it serves. While M-PESA is an ecosystem now that provides more than enough opportunities to use it as a primary mode of payment, the truth is that most transactions are still in cash. A majority of people still carry or deal in cash, hence the prevailing need for a large network of agents to convert it into and from e-float. The agent system has been successful because of a number of reasons. As 'physical branches' of a financial service, it costs a lot less to train and maintain an agent network than it does a physical branch network. Although the margins are considerably tight as they are commissions per transaction, agents are not limited to only providing the M-PESA service. The prevailing agent system of Automated Teller Machine (ATMs) was even lower than the bank branch network (1/1:5 per 100,000 people) because of security and cost concerns.

Because of the effect of this model, Central Bank also allowed banks to run agent banking services, reducing the need for full physical branches which are expensive to run and maintain. The agent network, whether it offers mobile money services or banking services, or both, has enhanced financial inclusion by spreading the distribution network. Other than creating direct employment for entrepreneurs, its enhancement has also created ripple effects at the base level, as well as simplifying financial services such as deposits and withdrawals.

7.6.2 KPMG True Value Case Study

It is impossible to assess the success of a mobile money service without assessing the mobile network within which it is built. The rapid growth of Safaricom has been the core backbone on which M-PESA has piggybacked, triggering a global disruption in a traditionally conservative sector. Already, the mobile revolution that begun in 2000 had, in many little ways, begun the process of financial inclusion we are seeing today. Data and anecdotal evidence had already shown, long before 2007, that Safaricom's customers were using airtime as a currency. This secondary use meant that there was a need, and perhaps a subconscious realization on their part, that mobile services would play a large part in the future of the financial services.

In October 2000, Kenyans woke up to the start of a new era in telecommunications. Nearly all of Nairobi's billboards bore a countdown with a backdrop of bold green colours. It was an announcement of a second player among Kenya's telecommunication companies, one that would eventually take off with the mobile revolution. The birth of Safaricom in 2000 was the end of a seven-year journey that begun as a government department, before being transformed into a company in 1997. Liberalization within the sector in the next two years provided the right ingredients for investment, roping in Vodafone through Vodafone Kenya, a local subsidiary that entered into a joint venture with the government.

Globally, there were nearly 300 million registered mobile money accounts by 2014. Sixty-one per cent of the world's developing countries had at least one service running, accounting for more than half of the available services. Still, this growth has not been as significant as it should have been because of several reasons, chief among them regulatory barriers in many countries as well as lethargic collaboration among players in the mobile money sector. With time, the number of new entrants into the mobile money services has fallen as the ones that exist scale up to meet customer demands and differentiate themselves from the competition. This market led approach has required many lessons from across the globe, as well as data-based design.

In 2015, we engaged KPMG's True Value Methodology to assess Safaricom's material socio-economic and environmental impacts.[7] The study found that Safaricom's operations generated a total of KShs. 144 billion in economic activity in the year 2015 (KPMG 2015). Considering the ripple effects of this direct and indirect economic activity, Safaricom contributed 6 per cent of Kenya's GDP. It also showed that Safaricom contributed 112,000 direct and indirect jobs, sustaining a network that has over 682,000 jobs. By just these, the assessment shows that Safaricom itself has created real value within the Kenyan economy, much of it trickling down to households. The numbers may not tell the entire story of what the mobile revolution has done in every home and every life, but it is a good place to start.

By these and other measures, such as the KShs. 54.8 billion contributed to government revenue in 2015, Safaricom has helped to alleviate poverty. KPMG's assessment found that 'Safaricom's capital expenditure has a poverty alleviation impact of the Kenyan economy, in that 6 per cent of the additional household income generated flows to low income households.' When Safaricom entered the market in October 2000, we set out to build a mobile platform that served the masses. The costs of operation were high in these early days, so even the services targeting lower socio-economic layers were still expensive and unreachable for

[7] https://home.kpmg.com/content/dam/kpmg/pdf/2016/07/case-study-safaricom-limited.pdf

many. Handsets and SIM cards were also costly, and one of our first challenges was to find and sell cheap enough phones to drive mobile penetration. Our initial customer projections were made in a time when the mobile market was young but promising. It took us three years to clock one million customers but as the price of handsets, SIM cards and mobile services fell, the customer base grew.

From being a purely telecommunications service, we are now at a point in our history when mobile money is the second biggest revenue earner. Its ripple effects are continuously being assessed but it is clear that it has vastly transformed how innovation drives actual change in the economy. By design, mobile money products have low direct overheads because of the agent system. This allows us to facilitate transactions as low as USD 10 which were previously considered too minute to warrant using a traditional bank. This is perhaps clearest in the comparison of national payments' throughput value compared to transactions by volume, as many of the tens of millions of customers transact small amounts. This isn't a revolution limited to Kenya, although no other country in the world epitomizes it like we do.

7.6.3 Financial Inclusion and Kenya's Vision 2030

One of the core pillars of Kenya's Vision 2030 is inclusive growth. While it is hard to conclusively define, inclusive growth aims at reducing inequality by bringing in the poorest into the formal economy and its many opportunities. The aim of Vision 2030 is to propel Kenya into a middle-income country on all facets, especially economic, social, and political. The proliferation of financial services is essential to this, especially as it is a key pillar to inclusive growth. From 2010, and triggered partially by the success of the agency model M-PESA pioneered, banks were allowed to expand their service offerings through third parties. Another key change was the return and expansion of credit reference bureaus (CRBs), which utilize information capital and use algorithms to calculate borrower's risk premium. This comes in handy for the savings and loan offerings we have, namely M-Shwari and KCB-M-PESA.

Over the decade of M-PESA, there has been a significant reduction in the barriers to entry for new players in the financial sector. There has also been an increasing interest in providing services to the bottom of the income pyramid, offering affordable solutions that require fast scaling to make economic sense.

At the base of the financial sector transformation within this economic are four core objectives:

- Curbing financial sector fragility through enhanced oversight.
- Enhancing deposits to 80 per cent of GDP.
- Efficiency, broadening and deepening.
- Increased investments from savings.

Other than promoting non-traditional players in the financial sector such as mobile money systems, Shariah-compliant banks and deposit taking MFIs, the CBK has also facilitated the growth of support infrastructure. For a budding, fast-growing financial sector like Kenya, such support infrastructure as CRBs and deposit/customer protection is essential for the trust between the supply and demand sides. Combine this with the benefits of consumer data from the telecommunications side and what you get is data-driven economic development.

From a point of friction and competition just eight years ago, the relationship between M-PESA and the traditional banking sector has grown into a collaborative one. There are now multiple interfaces between M-PESA and financial institutions. Such interfaces as Pesa-Pap, KCB-Mtaani, and M-Shwari promote financial deepening by easing access to financial services for existing customers. It also draws on the benefits of both sides of the partnership, resulting in an enhanced experience.

7.6.4 Savings and Credit in Mobile Money

After triggering a mobile money revolution at the end of the first decade of the twenty-first century, the next logical step was to find new and interesting ways to create value for our existing customers. At the helm of this was saving, a point that the then governor of the CBK made in an interview with the *Financial Times* (Manson, 2013). The idea is that if a service reduces the costs of accessing some financial services such as transactions, then it makes sense for it to also allow you to save and access credit. In much the same way we have approached mobile money as an innovation and solution for all stakeholders, allowing saving and borrowing services makes sense for banking institutions too. It reduces the demand for physical branches and makes data collection and processing easier. It also eliminates many of the complexities of credit approval for small loans, and gives customers a simple and convenient way to save without having to carry money to a physical branch.

In November 2012, we launched M-Shwari, a service available to our M-PESA customers that allows them to save and borrow. Since Safaricom is not a bank, we partnered with Commercial Bank of Africa (CBA) to raise the scale in providing higher value financial products. M-Shwari, the result of this partnership, offers M-PESA customers the opportunity to get small loans as well as save and earn interest (Kiiti and Hennink, 2016).As the operator of the transmission service through which this service runs, we have combined the strengths of client data to have a fully automated credit system. M-Shwari was the first product of its kind to provide such a revolutionary digital financial service.

By design, M-Shwari is an easy to use product which simplifies the process of credit access while giving the opportunity to save in the short term. The product offers an average 2 per cent interest, which is higher than the average weighted interest rate in the Kenyan banking sector. Yet research consistently show that the high interest isn't among the top reasons why people use M-Shwari. At the top of the allure of the product is the fact that it simplifies short-term saving and gives users the opportunity to access credit and improving their credit rating.

M-Survey[8] recently released the results of a survey where they tried to assess the true effect of M-PESA in fuelling financial inclusion for women. It was found that 96 per cent of the respondents had an M-PESA account, and 95 per cent of them were using it to send money to their relatives. The results also showed that of the 37 per cent who own or run a business, 80 per cent use M-PESA in the course of their work. The M-Survey research into the impact of mobile money showed that 20 per cent of business owners used M-Shwari to save profits from their enterprises.[9] In at least three other studies into the impact of M-Shwari, customers listed the benefits they get from the service as: accessibility, ease of use, privacy, and the separation from M-PESA.

Similar to our experience with Safaricom first and then M-PESA, our initial projections on M-Shwari uptake turned out to be modest. The original goal was a pilot test with at most 100,000 people, but there were 1 million enquiries on the very first day of the launch of the product (FSD 2016). Within the next 90 days, there were three million clients, meaning that the problem of scaling quickly was taking over a different form. The success of M-Shwari has altered social connections as well by reducing the need to borrow soft loans from family, friends, and loan sharks. Since it is private and easy to use, it facilitates a change in how we see social obligations to each other, especially in times of financial need.

A prevailing concern at the start of the age of M-PESA was that once the service reached the unbanked, they would see it as a long-term substitute for traditional banking institutions. This concern drove much of the initial aversion to the service, including from proponents who worried that since it was run by a telco in an emerging regulatory environment, it would not offer access to as wide a range of financial services as necessary. The entry point to financial inclusion is a transaction account. With the ability to store money and process transactions, people are more likely to access other financial services that improve their quality of life and facilitates planning. One of the core tenets of financial inclusion is not just physical access to financial services but also reducing the costs of doing such business.

World Bank statistics show that more than 2 billion adults don't have transaction accounts.[10] Mobile money accounts solve the physical access problem in

[8] An independent Nairobi-based startup that conducts research on the use of technology to improve communication. http://msurvey.co.ke/about-1/#about

[9] http://msurvey.co.ke/blog/2017/3/21/mobile-money-is-growing-womens-empires-in-kenya

[10] http://www.worldbank.org/en/topic/financialinclusion/overview

many ways, especially when the ecosystem is as inclusive as M-PESA. At the base of it, mobile money accounts tick many of the boxes that traditional bank accounts didn't. They are affordable and ride on the trust that the telco has built over the years. Initially, the costs of sending money through M-PESA reduced, as a proportion of the amount sent, on an escalating scale. We recently cut the cost of sending anything up to $1 to zero to encourage low income earners to utilize the service more even for smaller transactions. Withdrawals and deposits into savings accounts are not charged, as the partnerships make money through credit provision, while offering higher interest on deposit than one would obtain from a traditional banking or non-banking financial institutions.

With increased interfaces and the provision of savings and credit services, mobile money has promoted a new saving culture. It now offers two basic types of mobile financial savings, one within the individual M-PESA account and the other with bank integrated accounts. The privacy and convenience elements play a huge role here, as does the savings culture that has traditionally not seen banks as a good place to save small amounts of money. The continuing reduction of transaction costs within the mobile money ecosystem makes an even greater case here for the deepening of mobile financial savings.

There is still a long way to go. Although the 2016 FinAccess household survey showed that over three-quarters of Kenyans are formally included, it also showed a few missing bits of this win (CBK, KNBS, and FSD, 2016). The most significant were gender and location. Women, especially those living in rural areas, are still significantly less included than men in access to financial services. Similarly, people living in northern Kenya are more excluded. Financial exclusion has meant people go to bed hungry because they lack access to small loans if they do not borrow from friends or family. It has meant low access to water and services key to a humane quality of life that we all deserve.

The household survey also showed that although consumer habits in mobile money usage have evolved over the last decade, the core use remains sending to, as well as receiving money from, friends and family. In fact, this increased from 94.0 per cent positive responses in 2013 to 98.2 per cent in 2016. P2P transactions and airtime purchases remain the top two uses, followed by saving money for short-term goals and as a temporary travelling wallet. Uses with interfaces such as ATMs (for withdrawals) and transferring across other financial institutions remain low, which might point to some of the limitations of using mobile money today.

A key reason here is that although mobile money services do what cash does and does it better, Kenya remains a largely cash-centric economy. Most salaries are still paid in cash, with the only exception being in formal employment where bank transfers are more common, although not significantly so. Mobile money as the primary form of payment transfer is only highest in dependent relationships where it is still second to cash.

Although M-PESA remains an SMS-based service, the vast potential that the proliferation of smartphones has offered remains largely untapped. Smartphones are getting cheaper but access to them remains limited to a small proportion of mobile money users, as does access to the internet. This might explain why, for example, ATMs and physical bank visits remain the most frequently used channel to access bank services in a country where such a significant proportion of the adult population has access to a phone. Mobile banking is actually the least used channel, according to the 2016 FinAccess survey, although its use has increased in the last three years.

Another worrying finding in the survey was that, compared to a previous survey in 2013, more mobile money users reported an increase in loss of money and unexpected charges. While other financial players such as SACCOS seems to have figured out how to reduce such incidents, mobile money services haven't. The result may be due to increased usage especially of integrated services. Still, our research showed that not knowing how much a service was going to cost was reducing the trust our customers have for us. These charges now form a core part of the SMS confirmation, allowing users to properly account for their transaction costs. We have also enhanced our response time to consumer issues such as loss of money, although we need to do more to foment the security and privacy within the ecosystem.

7.7 Mobile Money as a Tool for Financial Deepening

While to most people poverty is mostly lack of money, financial deepening experts see it as more the lack of access to the tools you need to improve your status. While formal finance may not be present at the bottom of the pyramid, the situation created by poverty and the Kenyan spirit means that a complex informal system already existed. This is the system where the individual could borrow from the local *duka*[11] and repay at the end of the week or the month. The shopkeeper too has a credit system with suppliers, as well as a loose barter trade system with other nearby vendors. The financial fragility that poverty creates makes such informal structures exist and thrive. Mobile money simply plugged into this, meaning that the same structures could now expand and be slowly formalized.

A study by the Brookings Institution titled *Financial and Digital Inclusion Project* ranked Kenya number one among 26 countries (Lewis et al., 2017). With 75 per cent of Kenyans owning a financial account by August 2017, Kenya's leading status in offering affordable financial services to traditionally underserved groups are commendable but there's still a long way to go. Part of the current

[11] '*Duka*' is a Swahili word which translates into 'shop' in English.

success comes from the fact that M-PESA not only triggered a revolution in the mobile market but it also a ripple across the financial sector. Within the first three years of the mobile money service, the bank and agent branch also grew as the sector expanded to scale to new customers. The growing interest in financial services is a clear sign of moves towards deep financial inclusion. The proportion of banked Kenyans increased from 26 per cent in 2006 to 41 per cent in 2009. Still, its evolution and expansion as a mobile money service is only one part of a much larger story.

To be a financial deepening tool, mobile money needs to be more than just a money transfer service. At the heart of it, M-PESA remains a transfer service for most of its customers but it also offers other financial services and perks. Simply transferring money across social networks and economic units is essential but if the service doesn't do more, such as have specific ways to save and obtain credit, then it might not have a significant effort. A good example here is insurance, which was one of the earliest offerings of our first major partnership with a bank, Equity Bank, to offer M-KESHO. Insurance, especially outside mandatory services such as car insurance, has traditionally been unreachable for Kenya's poor. Finding a way to offer it, and to do so through the comfort of a phone, was a critical financial deepening effort.

The goal of financial deepening efforts should always be to enhance the welfare of both the individual and the household. It should offer higher value within social networks for as low transaction costs as possible. In the purely cash pre-M-PESA days, the risk and costs of carrying cash were tied to physical distribution channels. This not only spread the risk within small social networks but it was also costly and susceptible to unexpected shocks. M-PESA, as a mobile money service, eliminates this risk and provides social networks with the base they need to thrive. This was one of the quirks that researchers noticed in 2006; that within the social circles, people were finding new and interesting ways to help each other.

The numbers from the last decade show the vast potential of mobile money services like M-PESA, but it also points towards a shift in the future of financial deepening. By December 2016, there were nearly a hundred million more mobile money accounts than bank accounts in Sub-Saharan Africa.[12] In 7 of 39 countries assessed in the region, more than 40 per cent of the adult population had integrated mobile money into their daily life. Although there are income level patterns, most of these changes seemed to cross traditional socio-economic groupings. It also had a less significant gender gap.

Despite these successes, mobile money suffers some of the critical weaknesses that slowed down the uptake of banking. Universal access is impossible because even though phones are cheaper than they were a decade ago, they are still

[12] https://www.gsma.com/mobilefordevelopment/programme/mobile-money/mobile-money-driver-financial-inclusion-sub-saharan-africa

expensive for very poor people in society. M-PESA is an SMS-based service that can work with feature phones but some of the recent innovations and additions such as statements need internet access. There is also the cost element for infrastructure and networks that still limits connectivity and access especially in remote areas. There is still a lot more we can do as the leading players in a thriving ecosystem, as we move towards increasing the positive effects of M-PESA on the Kenyan economy and society.

An interesting relates to financial inclusion for rural women in Kenya. As a recent GSMA study showed,[13] there is a significant disparity in how men and women interact with mobile money. Women are more sensitive to transaction fees and are less likely to use mobile money, even where perception levels between them and men are almost at par. Another good example of this disparity is the fact that although there isn't a very significant disparity in phone ownership in the lower-income segment, women use mobile money a lot less than men. When they do, for most rural women at least, it is to make multiple small transactions. This was partially one of the reasons why we reduced the cost of sending anything up to 100 shillings, and are continuously finding ways to allow people to make small transactions for as cheap as possible. But we know we need to do more.

As the primary household managers, rural women need services that can either complement or even replace the traditional financial model. For example, one of the anecdotal reasons why mobile money has not been as successful among them is that it does not represent a viable option to the traditional *chama* setup. The *chama* has formed a core part of how Kenyan women in rural areas save and invest. But that setup is subject to the same complications that dogged financial services before M-PESA. Members have to be within physical proximity of each other to pool resources together, and normally carry cash which the treasurer has to go back with. Meetings normally happen on weekends, meaning banking services are not operational. The lingering question is why we have not created the right incentives within the mobile money sector to either enhance this by encouraging an affordable and cash-lite economy where rural women can transact within the ecosystem.

The risk aversion and price sensitivity points in how people use mobile money are a critical focus area not just for us, but also for how the regulatory environment in which we operate needs to evolve. As stakeholders in what has become a core part of the Kenyan economy, we need to design solutions that include rural women and other marginalized sections of society in the formal economy. We need to figure out how to bring in more women especially in the lower-income levels, even in urban areas, into the cash lite economy. The main areas that need to improvement are affordability and accessibility. An enabling regulatory

[13] https://www.gsma.com/mobilefordevelopment/wp-content/uploads/2016/02/Connected-Women-Women-and-Mobile-Money-Insights-from-Kenya-Nov15.pdf

environment, combined with political and social stability, would go a long way into giving us the right ingredients to design solutions to further drive financial inclusion.

7.8 Conclusion: The Future of Mobile Money

At just a little over a decade, M-PESA has revolutionized how Kenyans approach the financial system. It is no longer an impenetrable fort for most because of high transaction and account maintenance fees, or even over-complicated account opening requirements. What we now have is a situation where the success of mobile money has been more people not just sending and receiving money through their phones, but also interacting with other parts of the formal economy. M-PESA's future lies in payments, especially within the ecosystem.

From our initial experiment with Grundfos in 2009, we now have partnerships with everyone from banks, solar companies to government institutions. Essential platforms like E-Citizen now use M-PESA as a primary payment method, enhancing access to formal services for everyone. As such, the kind of ecosystem that M-PESA has become within the decade of existence has not just increased financial inclusion, it has also transformed Kenyan society in many subtle ways. The allure remains the same, that using the service is less costly than carrying cash, not just in real cost value but also because it eliminates the risks of carrying cash.

As the regulator with this critical sector, Central Bank has driven financial inclusion initiatives, combining dynamic regulation with policies that fuel growth within the sector. It has also partnered with other regulators to provide the seamless interaction necessary to ease licensing. Reduced bureaucracy and a liberal attitude towards investment in new financial services are just some of the things that have given us the right environment to continuously innovate and invest. Today, mobile financial services are the most used financial service across the country, transacting billions of shillings daily.

While mobile money is just one player in a much larger economy, its proliferation into Kenyan psyche and everyday life has created all the right ingredients for the achievement of Vision 2030. It has transformed how people view access to financial services, and how much it costs to use them. These successes have already reduced the proportion of excluded Kenyans from 41.3 per cent a decade ago to just 17.4 per cent in 2017. As future efforts seek to bring this down to zero, the next frontier is how to make the financial sector even more efficient and convenient. Access to formal financial services will broadly enhance the quality of life within Kenyan homes by reducing poverty. It will also increase income and hence facilitate better and easier access to services such as education and healthcare.

What will be most critical in these next phases of growth will be a continuing enabling policy and regulatory environment. Enabling here in a sense of both 'market-led' regulation as well as proactive measures to enhance growth as well as protect consumers. Such approaches should also encourage competition and facilitate financial innovation, as has been the case for the last decade. As a tool for financial inclusion and financial deepening, mobile money services will require even more risk-based approaches to regulation as they expand to serve marginalized and vulnerable sections of society.

As Central Bank turns 50, its experiences as well as enabling oversight are the only ways we can continue to innovate, affordably and quickly. As mentioned earlier, the key areas the future of mobile money needs to focus on is affordability, accessibility, and availability. While at least one of these is solved already, affordability and accessibility remain a challenge. Future laws governing the mobile money sector should seek to promote its growth instead of hampering it. They should seek to create an environment that is conducive to investment in research and product development. We still have a long way to go in penetration in rural areas, as well as expanding and improving the agent network to make the service more accessible. It is only by continuously innovating in an enabling environment that these and other improvements can be made, not just with the goal of formal inclusion for everyone, but also to create real value for users and the economy.

References

Alliance for Financial Inclusion (AFI) (2010), *Case Study: Enabling Mobile Money Transfer The Central Bank of Kenya's Treatment of M-Pesa.* AFI Report (February).

Burns, S. (2016), 'Finance for all: Kenya's M-PESA. Alt-M ideas for an alternative monetary future', available at <https://www.alt-m.org/2016/06/28/finance-for-all-kenyas-m-pesa/>, accessed 26 November 2018.

Central Bank of Kenya, Kenya National Bureau of Statistics and FSD Kenya (2016), *The 2016 FinAccess Household Survey on Financial Inclusion.* Nairobi, Kenya: FSD Kenya.

Corkin, L. (2016), 'Kenya's mobile money story and the runaway success of M-Pesa'. Available at <https://www.orfonline.org/expert-speak/kenyas-mobile-money-story-and-the-runaway-success-of-m-pesa/>, accessed 26 November 2018.

Donovan, K. (2012), 'Mobile money for financial inclusion', *Information and Communications for Development,* Vol. 61, No. 1, pp. 61–73.

FSD Africa (2016), 'The growth of M-Shwari in Kenya: A market development story'. Case Study Series (November).

Kiiti, N. and Hennink, M. (2016), *The Use and Impact of M-Shwari as a Financial Inclusion Banking Product in Urban and Rural Areas of Kenya.* Final Report Institute for Money, Technology, and Financial Inclusion (IMTFI).

Leishman, P. (2009), 'Mobile money in the Philippines—the market, the models and regulation'. GSMA Mobile Money for the Unbanked, 4 November. Available at <https://www.gsma.com/mobilefordevelopment/programme/mobile-money/mobile-money-in-the-philippines-the-market-the-models-and-regulation/>, accessed 26 November 2018.

Lewis, R. J., Villasenor, J. D., and West, D. M. (2017), 'The 2017 Brookings financial and digital inclusion project report: Building a secure and inclusive global financial ecosystem'. Center for Technology Innovation at Bookings, September.

Manson, K. (2013), 'Mobile phones are route to financial inclusion for Kenyans. Interview of the governor of the Central Bank of Kenya in Financial Times'. Available at <https://www.ft.com/content/6cd723d8-5049-11e3-9f0d-00144feabdc0>, accessed 26 November 2018.

Ndung'u, N. (2009), 'Official launch of M-PESA international money transfer service'. *'Address by Prof Njuguna Ndung'u, Governor of the Central Bank of Kenya, at the official launch of M-PESA International Money Transfer Service'*, Nairobi, 13 October 2009. https://www.bis.org/review/r091021b.pdf

Ondiege, P. (2015), 'Regulatory impact on mobile money and financial inclusion in African countries—Kenya, Nigeria, Tanzania and Uganda'. Background Paper. Center for Global Development. Available at <https://www.cgdev.org/sites/default/files/Background-Paper-Financial-Inclusion-Ondiege.pdf>, accessed 26 November 2018.

8

Do Central Banks Have a Role in Financial Inclusion?

David Ferrand and Ignacio Mas

8.1 Introduction

For more than a decade now, central banks have shown increasing interest in financial inclusion. Arguably, the genesis of the increased interest was to a large degree spurred on by the formation of the Alliance for Financial Inclusion (AFI) a decade ago, with funding from the Bill & Melinda Gates Foundation. AFI has created a global conversation among financial regulators and central banks on their role in financial inclusion.

Under AFI's auspices, 58 lower- and middle-income countries announced their own policy commitments to promote financial inclusion, through what is known as the Maya Declaration (AFI, 2015). As highlighted in Figure 8.1, almost two-thirds of AFI member national authorities have made some commitment, and interestingly four-fifths of these commitments were led by the country's central bank.

But is this level of interest justified? There is a strong global consensus that the primary function of modern central banking is around stability. Former Bank of England Governor Mervyn King expresses the core purpose of the central bank succinctly: 'In good times, ensure that the amount of money grows at a rate sufficient to maintain broad stability of the value of money. In bad times, ensure that the amount of money grows at a rate sufficient to provide the liquidity . . . to meet . . . the unpredictable swings in demand for it' (King, 2016). As events of the last ten years have shown, the stability of the financial system is at the heart of accomplishing this monetary policy objective, reflected in the objectives of many central banks. The Bank of England's stated mission is 'to promote the good of the people of the United Kingdom by maintaining monetary and financial stability'. But interestingly in some contexts the scope is broadened further. Thus, for example, the act which establishes the Central Bank of Kenya Act defines its purposes as:

David Ferrand and Ignacio Mas, *Do Central Banks Have a Role in Financial Inclusion?* In: *50 Years of Central Banking in Kenya: Regional and Global Perspectives*. Edited by: Patrick Njoroge and Victor Murinde, Oxford University Press (2021).
 DOI: 10.1093/oso/9780198851820.003.0008

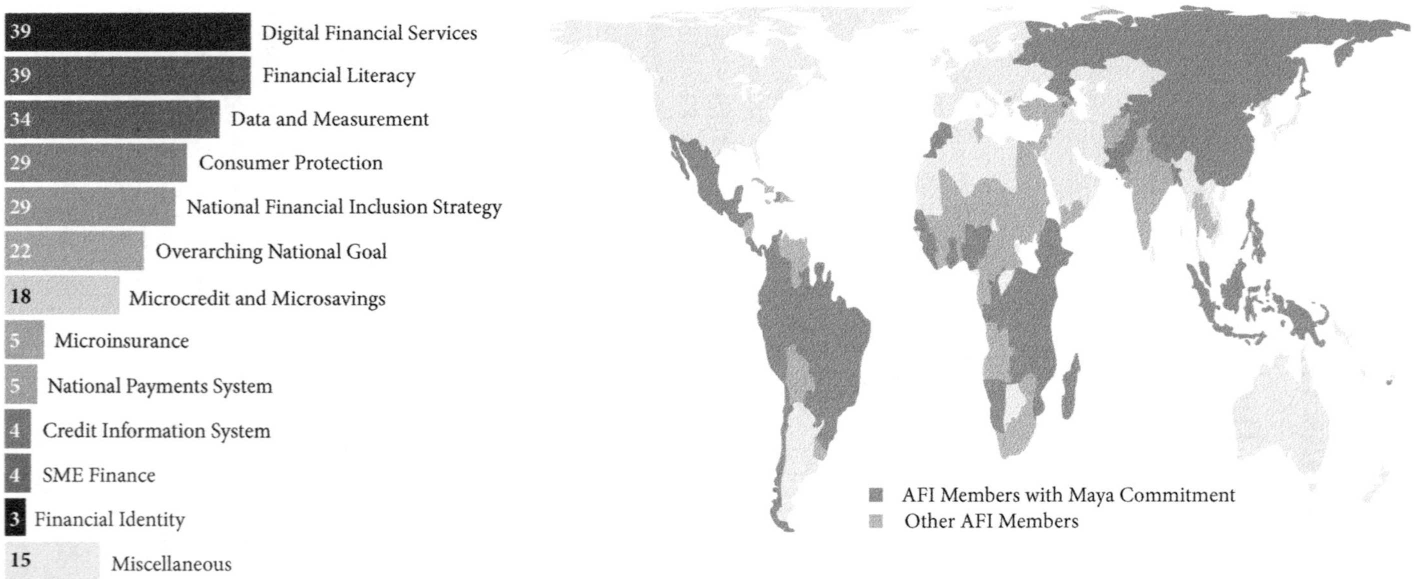

Figure 8.1 Policy commitments in financial inclusion, by thematic area and country

Source: AFI (2015).

> The principal object of the Bank shall be to formulate and implement monetary policy directed to achieving and maintaining stability in the general level of prices.
>
> The Bank shall foster the liquidity, solvency and proper functioning of a stable market-based financial system.
>
> Subject to subsections (1) and (2), the Bank shall support the economic policy of the Government, including its objectives for growth and employment.

While the primary agenda of the central bank is clearly one of financial stability, the final clause reflects the national priorities of a developing economy and explicitly suggests a significant broader remit.

The main question addressed by this chapter is: Do central banks have a role in financial inclusion? In seeking to address the question, the chapter first looks at the relationship between financial stability and financial inclusion before turning to the potential impact of financial inclusion on broader economic policy dimensions which some central banks regard as part of their remit. Kenya provides an interesting case study of central bank engagement in financial inclusion, motivated in large part by the desire to support economic development objectives.

But, before we delve into the issues highlighted above, we must first be clear about what financial inclusion actually means.

8.2 What Is Financial Inclusion All About?

People observing the flurry of conferences, papers, donor programmes, and commercial pilots relating to financial inclusion might see it as something of a new phenomenon, and particularly a new area of interest for policy-makers. But the fact is that modern financial markets have been developing for over three hundred years. In the industrialized economies the scale of activity in what we recognize as the financial sector has been increasing in both absolute terms and relative to the rest of the economy. Indeed some commentators, observing this expansion in recent decades, have suggested that it has become excessive (Kay, 2016). Alongside this growth in activity, in the world's wealthiest economies the financial sector has become pervasive reaching ever more businesses and people. Expanding financial inclusion has been a largely untold part of this story across today's industrialized countries, though it may not have been deliberate and it was certainly slow. Much of this expansion occurred without the direct engagement of policy-makers, albeit that early concerns over stability doubtless impacted on the way in which the sector developed at various points.

Equating financial inclusion with the market reach of the financial services industry has the appeal of simplicity. And it is a definition which is certainly useful from the perspective of the immediate concerns central banks have over stability as we shall explore shortly. At the very least it is a significant feature of the industry. However, it feels unsatisfactory for two reasons. First, it is actually rather less clear than it appears. Where are the perimeters of the financial services industry? Informal financial arrangements are ubiquitous and diverse, ranging from simply lending money to a friend or relative through informal group based intermediation to international money transfers through the *hawala* system. Second, it doesn't explain the recent level of policy interest in the topic. Looking at other sectors which have long attracted public policy attention—say healthcare and education—the concern is not with simply serving up more customers to the providers of these services. In the case of health and education there is little dissent on the importance of being healthy and educated both for the welfare of the individual and society. While debates may continue over how services should be best provided and paid for, there is nevertheless consensus that exclusion from healthcare and at least basic education presents a public policy problem.

This suggests we need to look at just what it is that finance does. The economist John Kay suggests four basic functions:

> First, the payments system is the means by which we receive wages and salaries, and buy the goods and services we need; the same payments system enables business to contribute to these purposes. Second, finance matches lenders with borrowers, helping to direct savings to their most effective uses. Third, finance enables us to manage our personal finances across our lifetimes and between generations. Fourth, finance helps both individuals and businesses to manage the risks inevitably associated with everyday life and economy activity.
>
> Kay (2016, p. 6)

These all matter for individuals, businesses and the wider economy. Evidence from detailed research shows that they are no less relevant to low-income households in developing economies than to the wealthy. How they are accomplished might vary but the need to do them does not. In fact, managing personal finance day-to-day is frequently more demanding the smaller and more unpredictable your income—the reality for many of the world's poor. Looked at from the perspective of the economy as a whole, empirical studies confirm that finance can be significant driver of growth. It is the strength of both theory and evidence which has led to current levels of policy interest and a growing concern over the implications of financial exclusion.

In the world's developed economies, formal finance—that it provided by specialized financial institutions—has become so pervasive that finance is simply equated with the services offered by this industry. However, all of the functions of finance can be accomplished with limited or no involvement of this specialized industry. Until recently in many developing economies people relied almost entirely on informal solutions. Often even where formal services become available we find that they are used as a complement to informal approaches.

This naturally raises the question of what drives the formalization of finance? The familiar gains to be made from specialization and economies of scale and scope certainly play a role. As in many other industries, these efficiencies help to drive down the costs of providing services and hence widen their efficient application. However in finance, it is the network effects associated with formalization which are frequently far most significant. Networked systems acquire a power way beyond that of their component elements. Payments, intermediation, and risk pooling are all far more useful the greater the number of participants. From the customer's point of view, the total is more than the sum of the parts; the value of the network is more than the value of any of the institutions on the network. Today formal finance is now indissociable from digitization. The network effects associated with modern finance are simply inconceivable without the connectivity, processing and storage capacity of digital information and communications technologies.

In the past the term *bankarization* was popularly used as a synonym for financial inclusion, especially in Latin America—simply equating inclusion with the use of a particular type of formal financial service. In hindsight the policy interest in inclusion understood in this way may seem questionable given that so few banks proved themselves able to offer services which were able to compete with the informal solutions which people already had. But the increasingly networked nature of finance driven by digitization sheds a different light on the concept of inclusion. Indeed the very concepts of inclusion and exclusion seem far more pertinent when we are talking about networks rather than a particular industry (or segments of an industry).

At its most basic financial inclusion is rapidly moving towards being about having a connection into digital money networks. Yes, you can only acquire that connection by becoming a customer of a regulated institution that is part of that network. The account is in fact your connection point with the digital money network. But the value that you derive from the network may be much more than the value that you derive from the specific services offered by that institution alone.

If you can send and receive money from anyone through the network, you may benefit from that connection or account in ways that the bank cannot even conceive. You can be receiving support from other people when your bank is not willing to lend you any (more) money. You may be sharing the benefits of your savings account or your bank borrowing capacity with your ageing mother, by sending her money when she needs it. Moreover, once you have a digital account, it becomes much easier to get services from other financial institutions, who may be much more distant from you. You can contract, and conveniently pay for, additional money market products, credit or insurance from more specialized institutions.

From the central bank perspective financial inclusion can be seen simply *descriptively*—it is an important feature of the financial market landscape and its evolution. Closely tied to this is the extent of formalization and participation in ever wider digital financial networks. The immediate concern for central banks will be the implications of these developments for their core stability objective. Addressing this stability issue is however complicated by an implicitly *normative* dimension to the conception of financial inclusion. We need to be concerned with both the implications of *exclusion* and the welfare impacts of the type of inclusion we do see. At the very least this suggests that the room for manoeuvre for a central bank which simply wants to focus solely on its stability mission may be constrained.

8.3 The Short-Term Threat to Stability

We can start by dispensing with the implications of financial inclusion for monetary policy. The direct impact on monetary stability issues seems unlikely to be significant. Other things equal, it can be expected to result in a modest increase in the monetary base as value previously stored in physical assets is monetized and deposited into bank accounts, as well as in a modest increase in the velocity of money as previously less liquid assets are replaced by more liquid banking deposits. On the other hand, financial inclusion may result in an increase in aggregate demand if, as we discuss further below, it has a positive effect on economic activity and growth. These effects on money supply and demand tend to offset each other, and any net effect is likely to be small relative to the total stock of money—nothing that the central bank cannot easily sterilize through the normal course of its monetary operations.

It is the potential impact of financial inclusion on financial sector stability where the concern arises. Take for instance the housing bubble fuelled by the booming subprime mortgage market in many developed countries such as the US, UK, Spain, and Ireland in the early to mid-2000s, which became one of the precursors to the global financial crisis (see Figure 8.3 for the US case). As illustrated in Figure 8.2, the development of the subprime mortgage market was fundamentally a financial inclusion play: finding ways for more people to be able to finance their homes. The motivation of the banks and financial institutions involved was largely commercial, but the outcome—for a period at least—was strongly in line with government policy objectives of increasing home ownership among lower-income groups. However, the risk management practices associated with the expansion into new markets were clearly woefully inadequate.

The developing world has not been immune from crises created by unsustainable financial inclusion practices. South Africa, for example, has experienced several over-indebtedness cycles, with the very rapid rise in micro-lending. Again targeting previously excluded segments, and again not adequately supported by

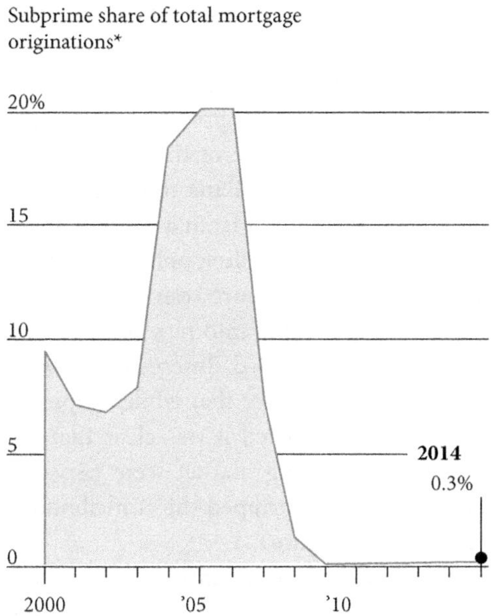

Figure 8.2 Subprime mortgage market boom and bust in the US

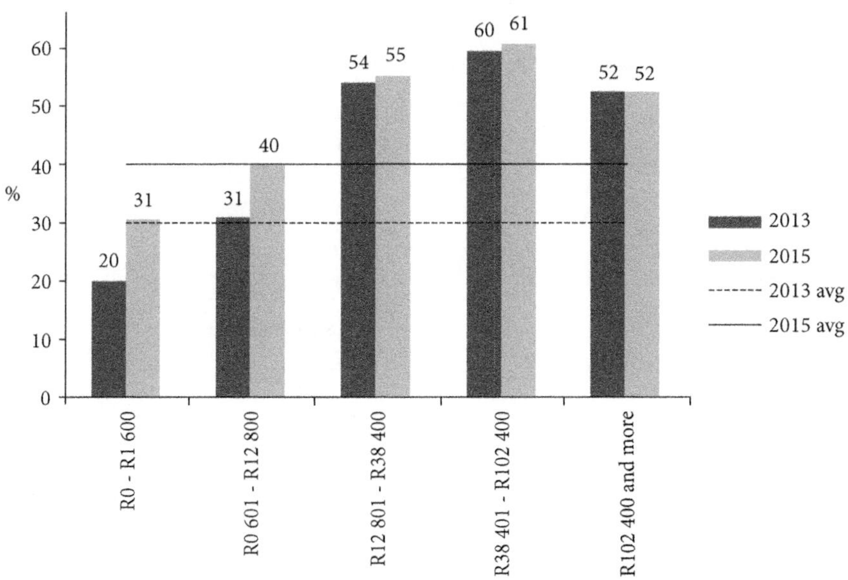

Figure 8.3 Evolution in the proportion of people in debt, by income group

Source: BusinessTech, 2016.

properly evolved risk management practices, as shown in Figure 8.3. The collapse of micro-lender Saambou in 2002 created a contagion problem resulting in a run on the sixth largest bank (BoE) which eventually had to be rescued in a takeover by Nedbank after receiving extensive support from the Reserve Bank of South Africa. Most recently, African Bank, one of the largest micro-lenders in South Africa, had to be rescued by the Reserve Bank to avoid contagion effects.

This might lead to the conclusion that from a narrow stability concern, central banks would in the absence of countervailing policy pressures, be inclined to take a more conservative approach. Had a more restrictive regulatory approach been taken towards the expansion of lending into new market segments then perhaps these problems could have been avoided. Interestingly looking at the evidence from the US housing market bust we see that while subprime lending was at the heart of the crisis, as the crisis unfolded it was clear that the problems of poor underwriting practices in the housing market were pervasive. Problems in the prime mortgage market quickly outstripped the contribution of subprime as the crisis unfolded, as illustrated in Figure 8.4.

Crucially however the unsustainable finance is not just or even primarily the preserve of formal solutions. Unsustainable growth, boom, and bust are in fact the hallmark of informal pyramid (or Ponzi) schemes, which tend to prey particularly on people who feel they have few attractive financial options. Ponzi schemes are a recurring feature in Kenya, as much as in most developing countries. The Central Bank of Kenya (CBK) felt obliged to become involved and regularly warned Kenyans not to invest in them, as it did (again) in early April 2017, as shown in Box 8.1.

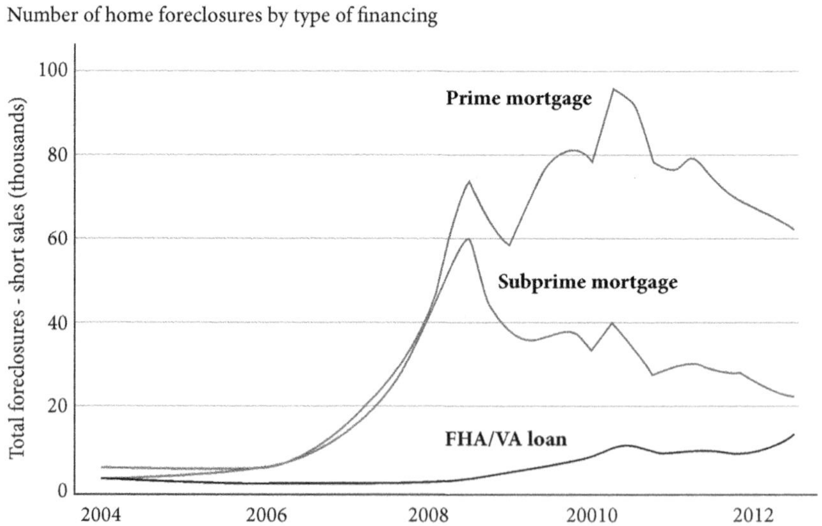

Figure 8.4 Contributions to the housing market bust in the US
Source: DataQuick.

Box 8.1 Public Notice on Unlicensed Deposit-Taking Entities and Pyramid Schemes

'The Central Bank of Kenya (CBK) and the Sacco Societies Regulatory Authority (SASRA) wish to draw the attention of members of the public to the re-emergence of unlicensed deposit-taking entities and Ponzi/pyramid schemes. Such entities entice members of the public to place money with them and promise quick and abnormally high returns on their money or acquisition of non-existent properties. CBK and SASRA advise members of the public not to place their money with such unlicensed entities.'

Source: https://www.centralbank.go.ke/2017/04/07/public-notice-unlicensed-deposit-taking-entities-pyramid-schemes/

There is a temptation to assume that this is purely a consumer protection issue. Surely a few informal pyramid schemes here and there cannot begin to do the kind of damage that the entirely formal subprime mortgage brought to millions of people. In Albania during the period 1996–97, a pyramid scheme developed rapidly across the country. At its peak it had two-thirds of the population invested in it, to a value equal to half the country's GDP. Following its inevitable collapse, there was extensive rioting and civil disorder in which it is estimated that 2000 people died and the government fell.

Reflecting the significance of finance to their lives, people will seek to find solutions. The wider financial system will develop as economies and societies evolve. Implicitly ignoring this pressure through prohibition does not solve the stability threat for central banks. It is difficult for the financial authorities to make a direct appeal to people who are outside the formal financial system, much less to intervene when one emerges in the financial shadows of a cash-based economy. Formal financial inclusion therefore at the very least offers a path for bringing all financial practices—the good ones as well as some unsavoury and unsustainable ones—into the purview of the central bank. That by itself does not ensure proper market development and good financial outcomes, but then these practices can begin to be addressable by the banking authorities.

8.4 The Longer-Term Perspective: Synergies

Having established that central banks certainly cannot afford to ignore the topic given the potential hazards for stability we now consider whether there may be a more positive angle. Rather than simply needing to navigate the perils, does inclusion matter for central banks because it can contribute positively to their core stability objectives?

The argument that stability is essential to meaningful financial inclusion seems hard to contest. It seems self-evident where finance is being used as a safe store of value. Whether this is about dealing with peaks and troughs in day-to-day liquidity, having resources to meet emergencies or putting aside the funds needed to live during retirement, if the store is not safe it is of little value. To drive the point home, let's return to the case of the sub-prime bubble in the United States circa 2008. It was a financial inclusion solution that led to unprecedented levels of home ownership. Yet all those gains are now gone, home ownership in the US is now *below* where it was 20 years ago, as shown in Figure 8.5. But the figure does not show the financial cost and distress suffered by millions of Americans who thought they had acquired a home and then lost it. Or the cost to taxpayers of salvaging the financial institutions that had underwritten the sub-prime mortgages.

Despite the evident risks associated with change there are nevertheless compelling reasons for arguing that effective inclusion could have a positive impact on longer-term market stability. We can posit a number of potential transmission paths, as illustrated in Figure 8.6:

> Greater participation and use leads to greater systemic scale, with benefits on both sides of intermediation. A diversified deposit base increases an institution´s funding options and reduces the concentration risk. Large numbers of small-scale deposits can be significantly more stable than a small number of large-scale depositors. A similar argument applies to credit. That inclusion is at least initially

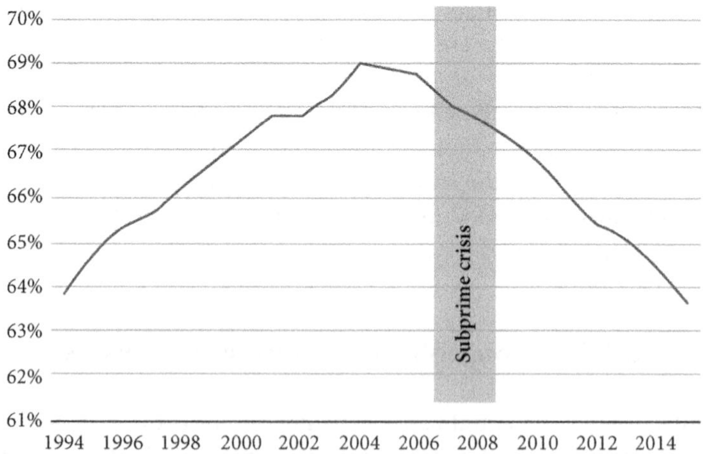

Figure 8.5 Home ownership rates in the US, before and after the subprime crisis

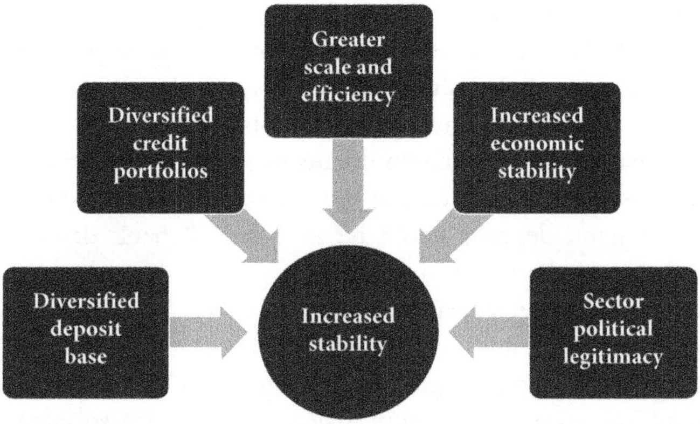

Figure 8.6 How inclusion may lead to financial stability

associated with broadening coverage to parts of the economy which are not strongly correlated with the modern formal sectors, the benefits from diversification may be amplified.

Expanding the financial system can of course lead to gains from greater scale and efficiency. Practically this can lead to improved institutional stability as a result of investment in enhanced risk management within institutions and more effective information systems. This can make for easier on and off-site surveillance by regulators. There are likely to be some scale economies in the activity of regulation itself. Finally, improved efficiency should be reflected in lower lending margins resulting in reduced pressure on end-clients and hence default rates.

There may be second-round effects. To the extent that inclusion enhances economic growth and stability (for which there is good evidence), it serves to create a more conducive general environment for banking.

Finally, a more inclusive financial sector can gain greater political legitimacy, which reduces political and policy pressures which can have adverse impacts on stability. Where the sector is seen to be simply serving the interests of a small group, there is a vulnerability to policy driven intervention.

There are of course potential counters to each of these arguments. The recent financial crisis invites scepticism towards the panglossian argument that increased financial sector sophistication will necessarily result in greater stability. There is as yet limited concrete empirical evidence to settle the question, in part because we don't have good long-term time series data on financial inclusion.

Roa-García (2016) reviewed several studies on the diverse possible links between financial inclusion and financial stability. She observed that in the short-term risks may rise from rapid credit growth associated with new financial inclusion institutions and instruments and from unregulated parts of the financial system. However, she also suggests that broader access to deposits that lead to a more diversified base of deposits could significantly improve resilience of the overall financial system and thus financial stability. Han and Melecky (2013) corroborates Roa-García's finding on the deposit side. By studying the dynamics of bank deposits prior to and during the 2008 crisis, they find that correlated withdrawals of bank deposits could be mitigated if bank deposits are more diversified, that is, held by more individuals.

Examining cross-country experiences to analyse the relationship between financial inclusion and financial stability policies, Cihak et al. (2016) again found both trade-offs and synergies, depending on the indicator of stability and inclusion used. But greater financial inclusion, particularly associated with extensive borrowing by individuals, may also increase the risk of extreme events, unexpected losses to the financial system, and ultimately more frequent banking crises. Morgan and Pontines (2014) suggest that policy measures to increase financial inclusion, at least by small and medium enterprises (SMEs), would have the side-benefit of contributing to financial stability as well. They find evidence that an increased share of lending to small and medium-sized enterprises (SMEs) aids financial stability, mainly by reducing non-performing loans and the probability of default by financial institutions.

The Global Partnership for Financial Inclusion looked more broadly at the relationship between financial inclusion and three other sets of financial policy objectives: financial stability, financial integrity, and financial consumer protection (GPFI, 2012). By looking at specific country examples, they concluded that careful policy-making can minimize the trade-offs, though that is not always an easy process.

In summary it is clear that in the long-term there is no necessary relationship between inclusion and stability but there are indeed good prospects for synergies between the two. There is no escaping the requirement for careful nuanced policy on financial market regulation with respect to financial inclusion. Central banks are necessarily drawn into concerns over how financial markets develop. Inclusion is evidently one key facet of that development. There will be judgement calls to be made on what new risks are presented by innovations to increase inclusion and how to best manage them. The interests of central banks here perhaps mirrors that in monetary policy—determining when there is need and opportunity to encourage growth and when it requires moderation.

8.5 Beyond Stability: Broader Economic Policy

Where central banks—as we saw for Kenya—also have an explicit responsibility beyond stability to support economic policy then we need to look further into the relationship between financial inclusion and common policy objectives.

It is useful to delve a little deeper into the role of inclusion in growth. Financial inclusion ought to lead to a greater digitalization of economic transactions. We can posit several potential channels through which this ought to translate into productivity gains, increased investment and economic growth:

With an enhanced ability to undertake remote payments reliably and securely, informal micro and small businesses should be in a position to source inputs and to sell their outputs further afield, resulting in more business and margin advantages.

With the possibility of more real-time access to information on the transactions conducted throughout their business, small-scale entrepreneurs should gain a greater sense of control over their business as it grows and they become less personally involved in all transactions; this level of confidence should push them to want to grow faster than otherwise.

With a greater digital record of their economic activities which can be shared with financial institutions, informal micro and small businesses ought to be able to attract more credit on better terms.

Digital payments have particular promise in integrating value chain players more efficiently. Corporate buyers would be able to create larger, more reliable and efficient supply networks reaching into small-holder farmers, artisanal producers, and piece work labourers.

With more financial options at their disposal with which to absorb economic shocks, inefficient worker practices such as moonlighting and job abandonment should diminish, and workers should have greater incentive to invest in job-specific skills.

Having all citizens connected and transacting regularly on a digital money network should help government across a range of other policies, beyond employment generation. Below are some examples:

Taxation: There would be greater visibility of economic transactions by the tax authority and hence less opportunities for tax avoidance. Also, tax and types of payments to the state could be done more efficiently by its citizens.

Social welfare: The state is generally the biggest micro-payer in any country, on account of all the social welfare, pension and teacher salary payments that it needs to undertake. So the state would be a direct beneficiary of a digital payment system that allows it to fulfil its payment obligations more efficiently.

Law enforcement: In economies with a greater preponderance of digitized transactions, enforcement authorities have more tools with which to trace illegal activities. Moreover, a culture sets in where large cash transactions become suspect, and making the task of operating illegal activities outside the financial system more difficult. This is an area in which central banks are frequently closely involved, in part simply because of involvement in oversight of the banking sector, but also because of the potential stability impacts.

8.6 Implications

If we accept that central banks do have a role in financial inclusion, then the obvious next question is: What exactly is that role? The preceding argument has already implied where the starting point is to be found. Central banks as regulators need to prioritize protection of the system, participants, and the wider economy. Rehearsing what is now orthodoxy in regulation a balanced, risk based approach is needed. Financial market change and expansion is inevitable. An overly enthusiastic policy seeking to simply throttle change through regulation is undesirable as we've seen leading to counterproductive results. Effective inclusion supports both stability and wider economic development goals. Restrictive regulation will simply increase demand for financial solutions which fall outside the regulatory perimeter potentially creating greater threats to the system. It is also probably politically untenable in many countries in any case. Failing to actively address the *specific* regulatory challenges of inclusion—relying on existing regulatory models or shifting towards an excessively laissez-faire approach seems equally problematic. On one hand it may simply preserve the status quo—relying on existing players to expand markets slowing inclusion advances. On the other it may allow certain instabilities to build up, as in the US subprime mortgage example.

But given the significance of financial inclusion, there is an argument for a more proactive approach. Rather than simply focusing on getting the right balance in conventional protective regulation, it can be argued that central banks should become more intentional in seeking to shape the development of markets. This doesn't mean to suggest that central banks should directly participate in markets to support financial inclusion. Where there is a role for state involvement—and that remains contested—institutionally it is hard to see that this would sit well with the central bank role. The performance of markets depends critically on the rules of the game and it is the core function of central banks as regulators to shape those rules. What is at issue here is rather the objective of those rules.

It is useful to reflect briefly on the economic function of regulation in financial markets. The creation of value through financial solutions is fundamentally based on the ability to credibly contract over time or space. This requires trust: trust that contracts will be fulfilled. This is central to the formalization of finance and hence the prospective gains in efficiency and functionality. Without the formal mechanisms to support trust, the scope of finance is limited to what can be accomplished through purely informal means. Effective regulation enables multiple parties who do not directly know one another to trust one another at far lower cost than could be achieved otherwise.

Central banks are centrally involved in the business of building trust. As markets change—whether driven by technology or expanding inclusion—the rules need to change with them. Who should be trusted? Who should not be trusted? How can the effective development and enforcement of rules create trust? But it has to be trust that is justified.

Working this out is not easy. It is perhaps necessarily an evolutionary process, and it requires making judgements, taking sensible risks, testing, and learning. Get it right and there are significant benefits for market development and financial inclusion. Get it wrong and the central banks' core stability mission is threatened.[1]

Earlier we looked at financial inclusion as being about access to a system rather than as merely being a customer of a service provider. Electronic payment systems exhibit strong network effects, since the value enjoyed by individual users grows with the number of users—potential payment counterparties—on it. This applies as much to end-users as to business customers: businesses will choose to distribute their payments and collect their bills through the system that reaches the largest number of their employees, suppliers, and customers. Larger systems are more likely to generate the viral effect that is characteristic of network businesses.

The economics of the business tends naturally towards a *winner takes all* market structure, which may be privately efficient but may lead to adverse longer-term consequences generally associated with monopolies: inefficient cost structures, slow innovation, dropping customer service levels. Therefore, one key area that central banks need to ponder is how to promote market contestability by a broader range of service providers, who may have different skills and perhaps a more specialized market segment focus—for instance, on lower-income customers. Interoperability standards and shared infrastructures can help make the digital money network more vibrant, more innovative, and more focused on customer services than if the market converges on a single dominant supplier that gains a lock on the market.

8.7 A Case Study of Central Bank Engagement: Kenya

Kenya is often touted as a global success case in financial inclusion. The statistics are certainly impressive: formal financial inclusion, understood as the share of the

[1] The 2007/08 financial crisis threated to turn into a global catastrophe as trust evaporated in financial markets and key institutions were therefore no longer able to readily transact with one another. Central banks were forced to intervene simply to maintain the basic trust necessary to allow markets to function at all. That the price of doing this had to be met by taxpayers and citizens gave rise to a different trust problem. Regulators had implicitly vouched for the stability of global financial institutions and markets, creating the necessary trust to support market function. But this was based on the premise that they both understood the risks and had in place the rules to manage them. Events revealed that neither was true.

adult population with an account at a formal financial institution, has increased from under 30 per cent to over 70 per cent within a decade.

Technology has received much of the credit for this success, and in particular the rise of mobile money enabled by the proliferation of mobile devices with real-time (albeit, low bandwidth) data communication capabilities. Mobile network operator (MNO) Safaricom has been at the forefront with its popular M-PESA mobile money service.

But in the background the CBK has been playing a key role in facilitating the development of this new market, and in particular in building the necessary trust in the new mobile money arrangements and providers. Figure 8.7 highlights some of the major regulatory initiatives that the CBK has undertaken to this effect in the last dozen years.

Throughout this period, the CBK has taken a very pragmatic, incremental stance when faced with proposed technical and business innovations that challenged existing regulatory thinking and practice. It adopted a *test and learn* approach (Ndung'u, 2017), granting enough room for new ideas to demonstrate their value rather than immediately encumbering them with onerous regulations. M-PESA started as a pilot initiative involving both Safaricom and its UK parent, Vodafone, with support from the UK's Department for International Development (DFID). The original conception was simply around providing a payments solution for microcredit programmes. The CBK gave its assent to the pilot to explore the viability of using mobile phones for value transfer. From a policy perspective, the CBK was already looking to encourage the expansion of financial inclusion. The first national survey on financial inclusion in Kenya had been completed at the same time. This provided the first clear evidence of just how limited access was in Kenya—only 19 per cent of adult Kenyans had a bank account in 2006.

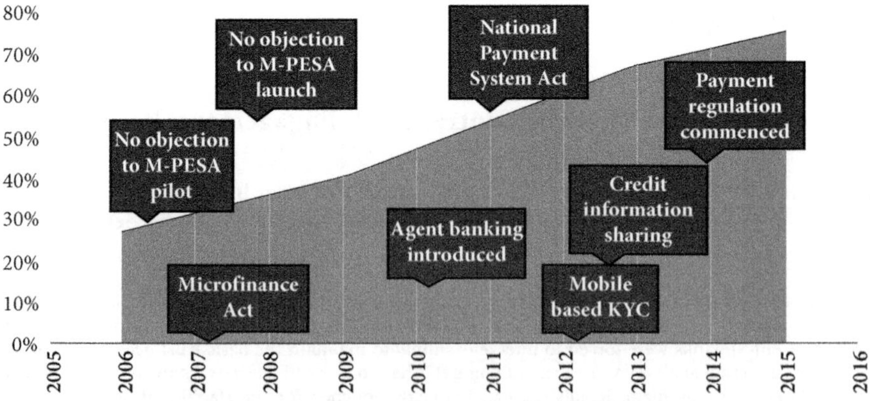

Figure 8.7 A timeline of CBK actions promoting financial inclusion

There was no specific legal framework in place to regulate the fast evolving electronic payments market in 2007 when Safaricom had developed the M-PESA mobile money-transfer solution. In marked contrast to the more conservative approach taken by regulators elsewhere, the CBK took a risk-based approach to the proposed structuring of M-PESA. Although the system was to be run by Safaricom, the electronic money created was actually held in a trust fund established to segregate funds from the MNO's balance sheet. With the funds held in a bank (the Commercial Bank of Africa) at the outset this avoided the problem of Safaricom—a non-bank entity—being deemed to be involved in deposit-taking. Other experiments were undertaken soon afterwards by various competing mobile money schemes though none with the same extraordinary success of M-PESA. Throughout, the CBK maintained its pragmatic stance, assessing each pilot proposition individually. A no objection was given only after the Central Bank was comfortable that what was proposed was consistent with existing legislation and wider stability and consumer protection concerns. In many respects the approach had many of the characteristics of the regulatory sandbox which is now being used by many regulators.

In taking a stance characterized by the governor at the time Njuguna Ndung'u as inductive, Kenya was able to make much more rapid progress in expanding financial inclusion. The legislation required to more formally regulate the expanding payments system was only finally operationalized in 2014. However, along the way many other regulatory changes were also introduced. The Microfinance Act—which had had a very long gestation period—was finally passed in 2007, allowing microfinance institutions (MFIs) to move into deposit-taking. Mindful of earlier crises created by the emergence of smaller deposit-taking institutions in the 1980s, the CBK took a cautious approach to opening up the regulatory space. Many of the nascent MFIs lacked the necessary capital, systems and capacity and a careful transformation period was warranted. Ultimately the contribution of microfinance to Kenya's dramatic improvement in inclusion has been largely through demonstrating ways to reach lower-income markets rather than building scale.

More impactful in terms of sheer numbers was the introduction of agent banking. In introducing the necessary regulation, the CBK looked to first learn from the experiences of others. A number of countries in Latin America had permitted commercial banks to use retail outlets to provide cash-in and cash-out and other basic banking services. The result has been to transform the economics of banking service provision. All Kenya's large network banks are now able to offer points of presence across rural areas which had been impossible to reach using the traditional 'bricks and mortar' channel of bank branches.

The convergence between mobile-phone financial services and banking took a further step forward with the evolution of regulatory practices on *know your customer* (KYC). Approval was given to a risk-based approach to KYC put forward by CBA which would allow 'over the air' account opening, creating mobile phone accessed bank accounts linked to M-PESA wallets. This has given rise to the rise of digital lending in Kenya, offering access to formal credit for millions who had previously been forced to rely on frequently unreliable and costly informal sources.

Throughout this period, the CBK did not see its stance as in anyway compromising its commitment to maintaining the stability of the financial system in Kenya. Rather it has sought to achieve long-term synergies between inclusion and stability while being mindful of the need to manage the risks associated with rapid change.

8.8 Conclusion

Central banks, like any other organization, work best when their mission is stated precisely, and that tends to be around the general theme of monetary and financial stability. We do not feel that it is necessary to encumber central banks with an additional explicit objective of financial inclusion. Their market stability objective leads to central banks necessarily having at least some role in financial inclusion.

There is a good case for positing a natural long-term virtuous relationship between financial stability and inclusion. Tensions may manifest themselves between these objectives in the short-term, as inclusion means changing current practices, and change can result in disruption and instability. But in the long term, sustainable inclusion supports stability, and inclusion without stability is illusory.

References

Alliance for Financial Inclusion (2015), *2015 Maya Declaration Progress Report: Commitments into Action*, December. https://www.afi-global.org/sites/default/files/publications/2015_maya_report_rev.1_low_res.pdf

BusinessTech (2016), 'One graph shows how bad South Africa's consumer debt is', 28 June. https://businesstech.co.za/news/business/128445/one-graph-shows-exactly-how-bad-south-africas-consumer-debt-crisis-has-become/

Cihak, M., Mare, D., and Melecky, M. (2016), 'The nexus of financial inclusion and financial stability: A study of trade-offs and synergies'. World Bank Policy Research Working Paper No. 7722, June.

Global Partnership for Financial Inclusion (2012), 'Issues paper for the plenary session on: financial inclusion—a pathway to financial stability? Understanding the linkages'. *GPFI 1st Annual Conference on Standard-Setting Bodies and Financial Inclusion: Promoting Financial Inclusion through Proportionate Standards and Guidance*, 29 October.

Han, R. and Melecky, M. (2013), 'Financial inclusion for financial stability: Access to bank deposits and the growth of deposits in the global financial crisis'. World Bank Policy Research Working Paper No. 6577, August.

Kay, J. (2016), *Other People's Money: Masters of the Universe of Servants of the People?* London: Profile Books.

King, M. (2016), *The End of Alchemy: Money, Banking and the Future of the Global Economy* UK: Abacus.

Morgan, P. J. and Pontines, V. (2014). 'Financial stability and financial inclusion'. Asian Development Bank Institute Working Paper Series No. 488, July.

Ndung'u, N. (2017), 'M-Pesa—a success story of digital financial inclusion'. Policy memo, Global Economic Governance Programme, Blavatnik School of Government, Oxford University, July 2017.

Roa-García, J. M. (2016), 'Can financial inclusion and financial stability go hand in hand?', *Economic Issues*, Vol. 21, No. 2, pp. 81–103.

9

Central Banking and Financial Inclusion

Some Key Issues

John Rwangombwa

9.1 Introduction

Financial inclusion[1] generally refers to individuals and businesses having access to useful and affordable financial products and services that meet their needs—transactions, payments, savings, credit, and insurance—delivered in a responsible, affordable, and sustainable way. Arguably, access to finance is a critical enabler to economic growth (see, for example, Abor et al., 2018; King and Levine, 1993a,1993b; Beck et al., 2000), poverty reduction, and sustainable economic development. In particular, as emphasized by Abor et al. (2018), the main transmission channel through which financial inclusion promotes economic growth is by enabling people to start and expand businesses, invest in education, manage risk, absorb financial shocks through insurance, increase consumption power (see also Dupas and Robinson, 2013), and expand employment opportunities (see, in particular, Ashraf et al., 2006).

This chapter identifies the key issues in the linkage between financial inclusion and monetary policy. It focuses on five main issues, namely: why financial inclusion matters for central banking in Section 9.2; the state of progress on financial inclusion in Africa in Section 9.3; what needs to be done to support further financial inclusion in Section 9.4; the critical role of central banks in embedding financial inclusion in Section 9.5; and some concluding observations and recommendations in Section 9.6.

9.2 Why Does Financial Inclusion Matter for Central Banking?

Financial Inclusion matters for the effectiveness of monetary policy, one of the core functions of central banks (Khan, 2011; Mehrotra and Yetman, 2014). Financial inclusion influences behaviours of firms and individuals, which affects

[1] Governor of the National Bank of Rwanda.

John Rwangombwa, *Central Banking and Financial Inclusion: Some Key Issues* In: *50 Years of Central Banking in Kenya: Regional and Global Perspectives*. Edited by: Patrick Njoroge and Victor Murinde, Oxford University Press (2021).
 DOI: 10.1093/oso/9780198851820.003.0009

the efficiency of monetary policy. It offers consumers opportunities to invest part of their income away from physical assets to deposits in banks. With low levels of financial inclusion, a large share of money stock is currency in circulation (outside the banking system), which the central bank has less control over, and the latter hinders monetary policy effectiveness. As financial inclusion increases, a growing share of reserve money is likely to be made up of interest bearing bank deposits. With more money in banks, central banks are capable of managing aggregate demand through both interest rate and reserve money alteration.

Financial inclusion also fosters quick monetary policy response, as households and firms can easily adjust their savings or borrowing patterns in line with central bank stance. In societies with high inclusion, households and firms will easily adjust their spending (because they can borrow and save) according to monetary policy orientation. Conversely, with financial exclusion, central bank requires stronger policy alteration to influence aggregate demand. It is actually not a surprise that monetary policy transmission mechanism has been strong in countries with relatively high financial inclusion.

Financial inclusion supports the central banking mission of safeguarding financial stability through facilitating banks to access a diversified pool of deposits. Access to formal financial institutions offers saving opportunities to households and firms, which increases banks' deposit base (Aportela, 1999). With more deposits, banks are able to increase their lending businesses. Increase of deposit stock also increases the resiliency muscles of banks, given the stability nature of deposit funding. Some banks, mostly in developing countries, face a problem of deposit concentration—a situation where a few depositors account for a big portion of bank deposits, and this is very risky. With increased access to finance, banks can tap into a diversified pool of depositors, which reduces the liquidity risk.

Financial inclusion further supports financial stability through enabling financial institutions to diversify their loan portfolio. With limited financial inclusion, banks lend to only few group of individuals and firms which increases the credit risk. High concentration of loans to a few sectors and single exposure are risks that central banks globally monitor. Financial inclusion opens up new investment opportunities for financial institutions. Moreover, lending to firms that were previously financially excluded may also lower the average credit risk of loan portfolios. Studies have proved that an increased number of borrowers from SMEs is associated with lower Non-Performing Loans and lower probability of defaults (Morgan and Pontines, 2014).

Despite the positive impacts of financial inclusion on financial stability outlined above, if misconceived, financial inclusion may compromise financial stability in the following manner: (i) If financial inclusion is associated with excessive credit growth, or the rapid expansion of unregulated parts of the financial sector, financial risks may rise; (ii) In some instances, where financial inclusion drives financial institutions to aggressively increase loans to the poor and other vulnerable segments of the population without due assessment of the repayment capacity, then financial stability may be compromised.

It is important that central banks strike the right balance between promoting financial inclusion and avoiding unhealthy or excessive credit growth. Balancing monetary policy objectives and financial stability objectives should be the driving principle in this effort. Financial stability aspects should be well weighed in the design of monetary policy targets. Central banks should clearly define financial inclusion as access to finance by more people and not credit growth. Credit can grow when it actually benefits a few portion of the population.

9.3 How Much Financial Inclusion Have We Achieved in Africa?

Despite the importance of financial inclusion mentioned above and great strides made recently, formal financial inclusion remains low in developing countries and concerted efforts are needed to increase it. For example, while account penetration is nearly universal in high-income OECD economies, with 94 per cent of adults reporting that they have an account at a formal financial institution, it is only 34 per cent in Sub-Saharan Africa (World Bank, 2015). It is therefore a mandate for all policy-makers (including central banks) in our countries to increase this access level. Recent achievements in financial inclusion in Africa are mainly attributed to technological advancements that have prompted innovations in financial services especially with regard to agency banking and mobile payments.

In terms of agent banking, policies that enable banks to contract with non-bank retail agents as outlets for financial services have proven highly successful in advancing financial inclusion where bank branches are not economically viable. Such policies leveraged existing retail infrastructure as delivery channels, and turned pharmacies, post offices, or supermarkets not only into agents of banks but agents of financial inclusion. Collaboration among banks and agents has become possible as technology has reduced the costs and risks of the remote exchange of information to carry out financial transactions. Coupled with simplified account opening procedures and other incentives to use this channel, such as the delivery of cash transfers, financial system outreach and numbers of users have amply increased.

In terms of mobile payments, high usage of mobile phones opened another delivery channel for basic financial services to unbanked and poor people. This new technology drastically reduced the costs of convenient and real-time financial transactions, expanded access points, lessened the need to carry cash by introducing e-money, and attracted previously unbanked customers. Several country cases illustrate the promise of mobile payments for financial inclusion. For example, in Kenya, the results of the 2016 FinAccess Households Survey revealed that M-PESA (SAFARICOM mobile financial service) has significantly contributed to increased financial inclusion, with 75.3 per cent of the adult population using formal financial services in 2016 from 26.7 per cent in 2006 (AFI, 2016).

9.4 What Needs to be Done to Support Further Financial Inclusion?

This section describes key challenges to pave the way for a greater inclusive finance.

Financial literacy: Measures are being taken in many jurisdictions to improve financial literacy as more households join the formal financial system. Financial education can help consumers to manage their financial risks by ensuring that they can better judge their capacity to spend, save, and borrow, as well as choose suitable financial services (Zeti, 2005). Financial literacy is first and foremost about empowering and educating consumers so that they are knowledgeable about finance in a way that is relevant to their lives and enables them to use this knowledge to evaluate products and make informed decisions. Mounting evidence shows that those who are less financially literate are more likely to have problems with debt, are less likely to save, are more likely to engage in high-cost credit, and are less likely to plan for the future.

Financial literacy enables people to make better financial decisions, to appreciate their rights and responsibilities as consumers of financial products, and to understand and manage risk. For poor and rich alike, financial literacy provides greater control of one's financial future, more effective use of financial products and services, and reduces vulnerability to overzealous retailers or fraudulent schemes. More financially literate consumers increase the demand for, and responsible use of financial services, help to underpin financial market stability, and contribute to wider economic growth and development. For example, consumers who are more financially literate are more likely to understand the importance of saving and to take action in that respect. Improved financial literacy could potentially play a positive role in boosting the low savings.

Consumer protection: Consumer protection is essential in promoting confidence in using digital financial services. As new customers enter financial markets, information asymmetry between consumers and banks regarding financial products and services puts these new customers at a disadvantage. This imbalance is greatest when customers are less experienced and the products are more sophisticated. Many financial institutions ensure that these customers are well served, but some have abused their information advantage to increase profits at the expense of consumers who found themselves over indebted, underinsured, or without a return on their investment (Mehrortra and Yetman, 2015). It is therefore important to treat new customers fairly, adequately disclose key product information, and establish safety and reliability standards to allow customers to make informed choices about products they select. Consumer protection regimes, including transparency and disclosure norms and market conduct rules, complement financial literacy efforts. For regulators of financial services, helping people to make informed financial decisions is central to protecting consumers, promoting public awareness, and maintaining market confidence.

Financially empower women: According to a global gender gap report of 2016, women in developing countries are 20 per cent less likely than men to have an account and 17 per cent less likely to have borrowed from a formal financial institution and they constitute 55 per cent of unbanked adults globally. In Kenya, women still have lower access to formal financial services such as banks: 34.6 per cent of women use banks compared to 50.3 per cent of men (AFI, 2016). To increase women access to finance, governments can establish specialized funds to support financial inclusion of women. Moreover, financial institutions must adapt financial products to suit women's needs and this can be done by enhancing ability of women to make basic financial decisions.

Institutional structure: Promoting financial inclusion is not the agenda of one institution. It calls for the participation and commitment of different stakeholders. Significantly improving and expanding financial inclusion requires a coordinated partnership and participation among regulators, government agencies, the private sector, and civil society. The responsibility of each and every stakeholder must be clearly identified.

Financial infrastructure development: Financial infrastructure underpins safe and efficient transactions and lowers the costs and risks to financial service providers. It supports greater transparency and efficiency of financial transactions in the financial system. Critical components of financial infrastructure include the secured transactions framework, credit reporting system, and payments system.

9.5 What Should Be the Role of Central Banks?

One mission of the central bank is to promote financial stability through regulation, supervision and licensing of financial institutions under its mandate.[2] Because financial inclusion supports the central bank mission of safeguarding financial stability (see Section 8.2), it is a public policy goal directly related to central banks' key objectives and activities (Mehrotra and Yetman, 2015). Therefore, this section highlights key actions to increase financial inclusion.

[2] See the mission of CBK (https://www.centralbank.go.ke/our-mission/, accessed 27 November 2018).

Financial inclusion strategy: In a bid to increase financial inclusion, central banks can put in place financial inclusion strategies devoted to promote a more effective and efficient process to achieve significant improvements in financial inclusion. The national financial inclusion strategy (NFIS) mainly indicates the plan of actions, main stakeholders, and responsibilities among them.

Financial inclusion monitoring: Central banks can monitor financial inclusion by conducting research to compile demand-side and supply-side, disaggregated informatory facts on the current status of financial inclusion in a particular place. Findings from the survey contribute in evaluation and appraisal of current schemes and in formulation of new master plan.

Regulation: No market can function without rules. The correct conduct of financial business requires competence and honesty on the part of financial intermediaries, both factors being decisive to ensure sound and prudent management in an effort to preserve public confidence. This necessity is intensified by the complexity of the external environment, the presence of large intermediaries, the economic, and reputational damage that can result from illegal behaviour. Central banks therefore have a role to draft laws and regulations that will oversee licensing and operations of financial institutions in a way that promotes, rather than hinders, financial inclusion in the broader sense of financial system integrity, soundness, and stability.

Supervision: Financial inclusion has resulted in the development of new products and services as well as new delivery channels often heavily dependent on technology. The number and type of financial services providers have expanded dramatically from the more traditional banks to now include many players and intermediaries such as bank agents, e-money issuers, and e-commerce providers of varying size and complexity. Central banks should supervise financial sector players to ensure that regulations are adhered to, risks are identified, and mitigating measures are put in place to ensure long-term sustainability. Given the sheer number, size, and complexity of today's financial sector players, central banks should fully adopt a risk-based approach to effectively supervise.

Advisory: Top government's economic entities (treasury and central bank) are main stakeholders in driving financial inclusion. Central bank plays a pivotal role of advising the government on economic affairs by providing timely information to the government on the ways to foster financial inclusion.

9.6 Conclusion

Financial inclusion matters for the effectiveness of monetary policy through the behaviour of firms and individuals. During the process of entrenching financial inclusion, monetary policy may be implemented through changes in interest rates (prices) or through changes in monetary aggregates (liquidity), which altogether may ultimately affect the flow of funds between households and firms or between the government and the private sector. For example, by increasing savings and investment opportunities, financial inclusion supports financial stability. In order to increase financial inclusion, a wide range of actions should be undertaken such as development of financial infrastructure, financial literacy, consumer protection, women empowerment, coordination among regulators, government agencies, the private sector, and civil society.

Despite the positive impacts of financial inclusion on financial stability, financial inclusion may compromise financial stability if it is associated with rapid credit growth and high non-performing loans.

The bottom line is that central banks should strike a careful balance between promoting financial inclusion and avoiding unhealthy credit growth.

References

Abor, J., Issahaku, H., Amidu, M., and Murinde, V. (2018). 'Financial inclusion and economic growth: What do we know?'. SOAS Centre for Global Finance Working Papers, No. 11/2018.

Alliance for Financial Inclusion (AFI) (2016), *2016 AFI Annual Report: Making Financial Services More Accessible to the World's Unbanked.* AFI Report (May).

Aportela, F. (1999), 'Effects of financial access on savings by low-income people'. Mimeo.

Ashraf, N., Karlan, D., and Yin, W. (2006), 'Tying Odysseus to the mast: Evidence from a commitment savings product in the Philippines', *Quarterly Journal of Economics*, Vol. 121, No. 2, pp. 635–72.

Beck, T., Levine, R., and Loayza, N. (2000), 'Finance and the sources of growth', *Journal of Financial Economics*, 58, Nos 1–2, pp. 261–300.

Dupas, P. and Robinson, J. (2013), 'Savings constraints and microenterprise development: Evidence from a field experiment in Kenya', *American Economic Journal: Applied Economics*, Vol. 5, pp. 163–92.

Khan, H. R. (2011), 'Financial inclusion and financial stability: Are they two sides of the same coin?'. Speech at BANCON.

King, R. G. and Levine, R. (1993a), 'Finance and growth: Schumpeter might be right', *Quarterly Journal of Economics*, Vol. 108, No. 3, pp. 717–37.

King, R. G. and Levine, R. (1993b), 'Finance, Entrepreneurship and Growth', *Journal of Monetary Economics*, Vol. 32, No. 3, pp. 513–42.

Mehrotra, A. and Yetman, J. (2014), 'Financial inclusion and optimal monetary policy'. BIS Working Paper.

Mehrortra, A and Yetman, J. (2015), 'Financial inclusion—issues for central banks'. BIS Quarterly Review (March).

Morgan, P and Pontines, V. (2014), 'Financial stability and financial inclusion'. ADBI Working Paper, no 488.

World Bank (2015), *The Little Data Book on Financial Inclusion 2015*. Washington, DC: World Bank.

Zeti, A. (2005), 'Enhancing financial literacy for sustained economic prosperity'. Dinner address at the Citigroup-INSEAD Financial Education Summit, Kuala Lumpur, 12 December.

10
Mobile Money

Tavneet Suri

10.1 Introduction

The mobile phone has been among the most rapidly adopted innovations in the world,[1] with SIM cards and airtime (prepaid phone minutes)[2] being ubiquitous now in many economies. This is particularly true in developing economies: As of 2015, India already had 1 billion[3] and Sub-Saharan Africa 747.4 million subscribers.[4] A large body of literature shows the benefits of mobile phones (see Aker and Mbiti (2010) for a review), with specific studies showing that communication via text can affect credit repayment (e.g., Karlan et al., 2012), savings behaviours (Karlan et al., 2016), adherence to medicinal treatments (for one example among many, see Lester et al., 2010), and voting behaviour (e.g., Marx et al., 2016). The expansion of mobile phone markets and networks has been accompanied by innovations that add substantial value for and provide beneficial services to customers, in particular, financial services that were previously inhibited by poor infrastructure and high transaction costs. This review focuses on one of the most celebrated innovations in the context of developing economies: mobile money.

The most prominent and best-known innovation adding service over the mobile phone has been mobile money. Mobile money enables mobile phone owners to deposit, transfer, and withdraw funds without owning a bank account. It is therefore distinct from mobile banking, which allows access to one's existing bank account via a mobile phone. Mobile money is an app in the true sense of the

[1] This chapter was previously published in the *Annual Review of Economics*, 2017, Vol. 9, pp. 497–520. Several studies cited in the chapter come from a long-running and extremely fruitful collaboration I have with William Jack at Georgetown. I am extremely grateful for his intellectual companionship. I am also indebted to Kamal Bhattacharya for numerous, lengthy discussions on the future of mobile money systems in Africa that have shaped a number of the ideas in this review. I thank Michael Boozer, Prashant Bharadwaj, Benjamin Marx, and Isaac Mbiti for comments and Layane El Hor, Shoan Jain, and Nikita Kohli for research assistance.

[2] About 95 per cent of connections in India are prepaid, as are 97 per cent in Kenya, 98 per cent in Tanzania, and 74 per cent in Brazil (Davidson and Leishman 2016).

[3] See https://www. gsmaintelligence.com/topics/3363/dashboard/

[4] World Development Indicators, available at http://data.worldbank.org/indicator/IT.CEL.SETS?year_high_desc = true

Tavneet Suri, *Mobile Money* In: *50 Years of Central Banking in Kenya: Regional and Global Perspectives.*
Edited by: Patrick Njoroge and Victor Murinde, Oxford University Press (2021).
DOI: 10.1093/oso/9780198851820.003.0010

word because it operates via software that is installed on a SIM card, although it is typically run on regular phones rather than smartphones.

Mobile money has been adopted widely and quickly across the developing world. Figure 10.1 shows the adoption of mobile phones worldwide in 2014, and Figure 10.2 shows the dramatic growth in their adoption between 1990 and 2014. Early deployments of mobile systems started in the mid-2000s, with the Philippines, Kenya, and Tanzania being among the first countries to use the service. Since then, this innovation has spread quickly across the developing world.

By the end of 2015, a total of 271 mobile money services were being offered in 93 countries (51 with regulatory frameworks), from Argentina to Zambia, with another 110 services planned in the near future (GSMA, 2015). In 19 of these countries, there were more mobile money accounts than bank accounts, and 37 of these countries had at least 10 times as many mobile money agents as bank branches. Sub-Saharan Africa accounts for 52 per cent of all live mobile money services. By the end of 2015, there were also 411 million registered mobile money accounts across the world (all in developing economies, 222.8 million in Sub-Saharan Africa alone), 134 million of which recorded at least one transaction in the 90 days preceding the collection of the data. On an average day, 32 million transactions were completed, more than twice the amount of PayPal transactions processed across the world. Similarly, as of 2015, there were a number of cross-border mobile money remittance initiatives across 29 corridors that connected 19 countries (GSMA, 2015). The most successful and well-known mobile money product was launched in 2007 in Kenya by one of the main telecommunications companies in the country, Safaricom. The product is called M-PESA, M referring to mobile and *pesa* being the word for money in Swahili. M-PESA has reached almost universal coverage in Kenya.

The aim of this chapter is not to provide a comprehensive review of all aspects of mobile money,[5] but rather to highlight the economics behind the product: What may have driven its adoption and what are its impacts. Given the success of M-PESA, a large volume of the research discussed in this review focuses on Kenya, although there are some more recent studies of mobile money systems in other countries that are now catching up. Towards the end of the review, I also discuss the more recent innovations that build on mobile money systems to deliver additional financial services and value. Although these innovations exist, they have not given rise to a thriving Fintech[6] sector. I therefore also discuss what the constraints to their growth have been, what this implies for the future of mobile

[5] Aron (2015) provides an excellent review that is more detailed, including on the macroeconomic impacts of mobile money and its regulation.

[6] Fintech refers to financial technology, encompassing all technologies that are related to the finance sector.

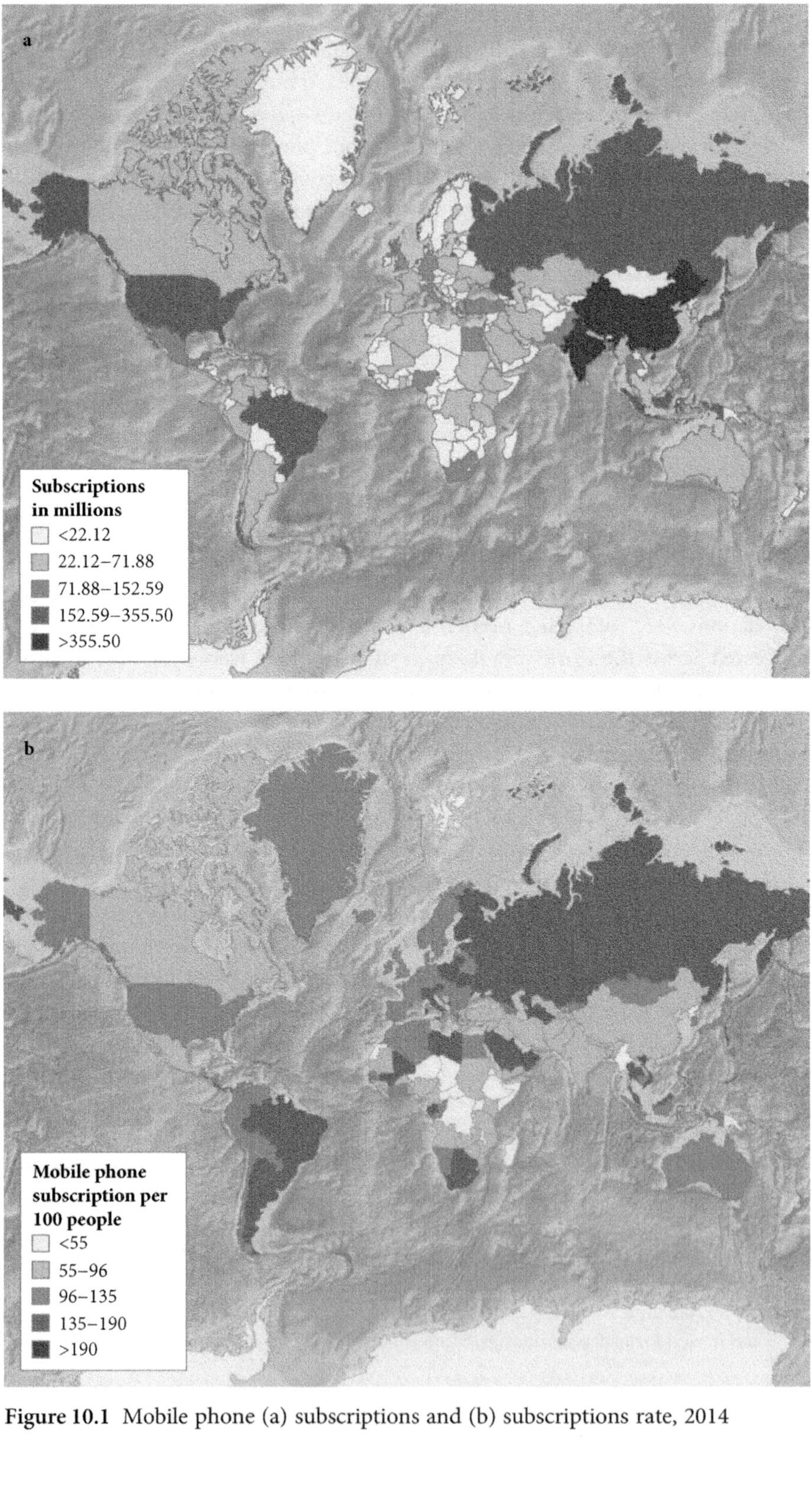

Figure 10.1 Mobile phone (a) subscriptions and (b) subscriptions rate, 2014

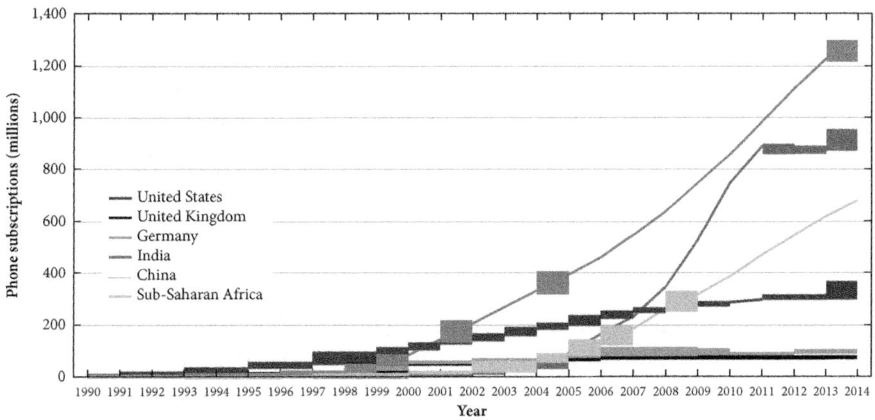

Figure 10.2 Mobile phone subscriptions, 1990–2014

money in developing economies, and where the most exciting opportunities for research may be.

The rest of this chapter is structured as follows. Section 10.2 describes how mobile money works in practice and provides a brief description of the regulatory innovations that have accompanied its expansion. In Section 10.3, I discuss the adoption of mobile money and outline the business models that have typically contributed to its success (or lack thereof). In Section 10.4, I discuss the impacts of mobile money, especially on financial resilience, and how the product's capacity to reduce transaction costs for internal remittances has contributed to these impacts. In Section 10.5, I describe the few innovations that have followed the initial expansion of mobile money, with a focus on East Africa, where adoption is almost universal. This section also discusses why few services have successfully built on mobile money—a phenomenon that highlights how mobile money systems remain very far from being true payment systems. I speculate on what may be needed to unleash further financial innovation.

10.2 How Mobile Money Works

10.2.1 Mobile Money as a Distinct Product

Mobile money is not mobile banking—it is a distinct product. It is most often provided by telecommunications companies, henceforth telcos (exceptions are B-Cash in Bangladesh and Splash in Sierra Leone[7]). Mobile money systems,

[7] These two implementations of mobile money are by private entrepreneurs that negotiated with all of the telcos in each country.

therefore, lie outside the formal banking system and have often been referred to as shadow banking systems (for a definition of a shadow banking system, see Bernanke, 2012). From the point of view of the consumer or user, the mobile money system is a payment account that sits on their mobile phone. It operates through a menu on their SIM card and allows them to engage in a variety of financial transactions.

In the initial stages of mobile money, the focus was largely on allowing consumers to make person-to-person (P2P) payments digitally without needing a bank account or a wire transfer. As mobile money expanded its purview, consumers were able to use it to pay their bills (including utilities), to store and hold money (i.e., save), to make person-to-business (P2B) payments, to receive payments from businesses (such as wages), and to receive government-to-person (G2P) payments.

Mobile money works very simply. On the consumer side, the consumer first shows up at a mobile money agent to register, the equivalent of Know Your Customer (KYC) banking rules. They register for the service with a government-issued ID (in some countries this is the ID used for voting).[8] This process takes a few minutes (as opposed to opening a bank account, which could take days or weeks). To be able to make any payments from their account, a consumer must deposit cash into it. They do this at any mobile money agent in the country. They give the agent the cash and immediately get a notification that cash has been deposited in their account. From there, they can use the menu on their mobile phone to transfer that money to anyone else in the country with a cell phone via their phone number. To get their cash back, they have to return to the agent. Each of these transactions (depositing is often an exception) incurs transaction fees; of course, the transaction fee schedule varies across countries. Figure 10.3 shows the transaction fees for transfers across a selection of different countries.[9] The consumer side is, therefore, quite simple—a mobile money account is superficially very similar to a bank account, allowing deposits, withdrawals (a number of banks in the developing world impose withdrawal fees, especially for low-balance accounts), holding money, and making transfers to other individuals. However, there is no interest paid on deposits, and the deposits and withdrawals are done through an agent for the mobile money service and not a bank branch.[10] In addition, other standard bank services, such as loans or standing order payments, are generally not available through mobile money.

[8] In many countries, one needs to show an ID to get a SIM card.

[9] I chose these countries because they have the most successful deployments of mobile money for which tariff charts were publicly available.

[10] In Kenya, withdrawals can also be made from an ATM, although this was added to the suite of services provided by M-PESA some time after the launch of the product.

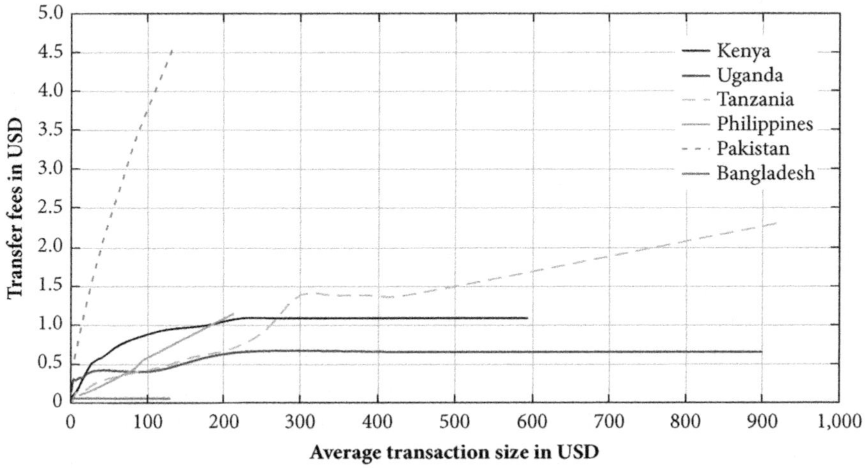

Figure 10.3 Transaction fees for Kenya, Uganda, Tanzania, the Philippines, Pakistan, and Bangladesh

Although the consumer side of mobile money feels similar to a bank account, it is not. The back end of the system and how it operates are quite different. The money in a mobile money account is called e-money (or electronic money) and always trades one for one with cash (minus the transaction costs for the particular transaction being conducted). When a consumer deposits money in their mobile money account, they are in fact purchasing the equivalent value in e-money from the agent. This means that the agent must hold a stock of e-money that they can then trade with the consumer. Similarly, if the consumer wants to withdraw money from their mobile money account, they are selling e-money to the agent for cash of the equivalent value (minus the transaction cost). The agent's primary role is, therefore, to manage their float or inventory of e-money as they would their inventory of any other commodity they stock.

Most of these agents are either existing businesses that sell airtime and phones or small retailers such as basic grocery stores, petrol stations, chemists, or tailors. As of December 2014, there were about 2.5 million agents globally, with the network growing at 25.2 per cent annually (GSMA, 2015). Agents always have an existing business and provide mobile money services as an addition to their regular business. The requirements to become an agent vary across countries. In Kenya, for example, potential agents need to apply to Safaricom, the operator of the country's main mobile money service, to become an agent (see Jack et al., 2010 for more details on the evolution of the agent system in Kenya). Applicants have to have a bank account and an Internet connection to be considered, and, if they are approved as agents, they have to purchase an initial quantity of e-money valued at USD1,000.[11] They can then trade this e-money as they would any other commodity of which they hold inventories. If they run out of e-money, they go back to Safaricom to purchase more, and if they run out of cash, they can sell e-money back to Safaricom. Since 2009, Safaricom has allowed banks to be agents to the agents, so that agents can trade cash and e-money back and forth with bank branches rather than only with Safaricom. Agents are a core part of the M-PESA model, as they provide consumer cash-in and cash-out services, i.e., they serve as the ATM equivalents for M-PESA. Therefore, the extent of the network of these agents is crucial. Aside from consumers and agents, there is a third component underlying the operation of mobile money: what happens to the money itself. The cash deposited in M-PESA accounts is ultimately held in trust accounts, which are administered by a small number of commercial banks in Kenya. The trust accounts are owned by the M-PESA account holders—think of each M-PESA account holder as having rights over a small sliver of one of these trust accounts. However, the account holder cannot deposit or withdraw money from their M-PESA account at the commercial bank that holds a trust account (unless the bank branches are themselves M-PESA agents). The accountholder can only deposit and withdraw money from an M-PESA agent. Similarly, an individual's M-PESA account is not considered to be a bank account—it does not earn interest, and loans are not available to users.[12] However, the trust accounts often earn interest, as they are accounts in the commercial banking system. Given this structure, the mobile operator with which the mobile money account is held is itself not subject to the same regulations under which commercial banks or other deposit-taking institutions conduct business.[13]

10.2.2 Regulation of Mobile Money

On the regulatory side, mobile money has required some innovation to build the necessary governance and institutions. For example, in the case of Kenya, when M-PESA started growing, a number of the commercial banks lobbied the Central Bank of Kenya to restrict and regulate it more heavily. These efforts were largely unsuccessful, as an audit by the Central Bank revealed few issues and user satisfaction surveys were extremely positive. However, this was soon followed by the Central Bank implementing agent banking regulations in 2010, which allowed

[11] More specifically, agents must be registered as a limited company and have traded for at least six months. The investment required is approximately USD1000 per outlet for float and USD1000 worth of SIM card replacements.

[12] As I discuss in Section 10.5, more recently, M-PESA has created partnerships with banks such that loans are available but come from the partner bank and not from Safaricom.

[13] In some countries, such as India, mobile money accounts must be delivered in partnership with a bank and are thus subject to the same regulatory requirements as traditional bank accounts.

banks and other financial institutions to offer some banking services (account opening, deposits, and withdrawals) at nonbank agents, the same agents targeted by M-PESA. Banking institutions, previously limited to expensive brick-and-mortar operations, were therefore allowed to compete more directly with mobile money.

Aron (2015) provides an excellent review of the regulatory side of mobile money systems, including how the regulation for mobile money may need to be unbundled at the level of the component systems and how regulation should be built around each of the components (such as customer registration, exchange and storage of e-money, foreign transfers, and interoperability). In this section, I touch on only the main innovations in the regulatory system that have emerged from the advent of mobile money.

Most countries have created their own regulatory frameworks around mobile money, but there are many common elements. The first is the requirement to report on aggregate transactions (and sometimes high-value individual transactions) to the regulator in charge (this is often the Central Bank but may also include the Communications Commission). Often, there are limits on transaction sizes and the amount that can be held in a mobile money account; for example, in Kenya, these limits are USD700 and USD1000 respectively, and in Uganda, USD1500 and USD1200, respectively. Similarly, there is often direct regulation around the trust or bank accounts that hold the float and rules on whether these can earn interest (as in Kenya, Malawi, Afghanistan, Sri Lanka, and several Pacific Island countries; see Greenacre and Buckley, 2014) or must be 100 per cent cash reserve accounts deposited at the Central Bank (as in the Philippines). When these accounts earn interest, rules regulate whether interest is to be disbursed to consumers and, if not, what happens to it. In Kenya, for example, the interest from the trust account has to go to charity; in Tanzania and Liberia, it can be disbursed back to consumers; and in India, the providers would pay out the interest earned on the value stored in the mobile account through payment banks (see below). Although there are variations in the exact regulatory framework across countries, these regulations are far less stringent than those for commercial banks.

A final regulatory issue that has been debated heavily in the policy sphere (see Camner, 2013; Davidson and Leishman, 2016) is the issue of interoperability, the ability to transact with mobile money across service providers. Interoperability can be at the platform level or the agent level (allowing customers or agents of different services to send mobile money to each other, respectively) or at the customer level (allowing customers to access their mobile money account through any SIM) (Davidson and Leishman, 2016). As mobile money systems come closer and closer to be- coming payment systems, the issue of whether transactions can cross different telcos has become relevant. In some countries, like Bangladesh and Sierra Leone, this is not an issue because, in both countries, at least one mobile money operator is an entrepreneur independent of a telco but with agreements with a number of different telcos. However, in most countries where a given product is launched by a single telco, policy-makers are debating their role in requiring interoperability. To date, Tanzania is the only country where this is operational. It was enabled by the industry leading the discussions and adopting common business standards to ease switching, working closely with the Bank of Tanzania, which oversaw the regulatory process.

A rather different approach to regulation that is worth mentioning is that of India. Starting in 2014, the Reserve Bank of India issued licences to several entities to function as payments banks, which remain separate from commercial banks with separate regulated functions. Unlike a regular small bank, this new financial institution is not permitted to extend credit. However, it can perform all the other functions of a banking institution, such as taking deposits, paying interest, enabling transfer and remittances, issuing debit and ATM cards, and offering Forex services.

The aim of setting up these payments banks was to boost financial inclusion across the country and enhance the use of mobile services in banking. In fact, some of the first payments bank licences in India were awarded to Aditya Birla Nuvo, Reliance Industries, Sun Pharmaceuticals, National Securities Depository, Vijay Shekhar Sharma (Paytm), Fino PayTech, Airtel M Commerce Services, Vodafone M-PESA, the Department of Posts, Cholamandalam Distribution Services, Dilip Sanghvi, and Tech Mahindra (the last three have since surrendered their licences).

In late 2016, the Indian economy was demonetized and the two largest notes withdrawn from circulation. Although much chaos ensued (for early opinions on demonetization, see Banerjee, 2016; Basu, 2016), payments banks and digital payment services like Paytm have made immense gains in the months post-demonetization as individuals switch from cash to digital payments where it is easy to do so (Chakravorti, 2017). Demonetization may prove to be the biggest push yet for digital payments in India.

10.3 The Success (or Lack Thereof) of Mobile Money

One of the most successful deployments of mobile money has been M-PESA in Kenya. M-PESA has been widely adopted, with 97 per cent of households having an account as of 2014 (see Suri and Jack, 2016). Although other countries are now catching up (for example, in Uganda, 35 per cent of individuals older than 15 years have an account, and in Tanzania, 32 per cent do (Demirgu¨c¸-Kunt et al., 2015), there are still many unsuccessful deployments of mobile money. Although it is hard to causally identify the reasons for the success (or lack thereof) of mobile money deployments, it is worth discussing some of the hypotheses for why mobile money has been a success in some economies but not others. It is important to understand how the business models and implementations of the various services may differ cross countries and what has correlated with success.

As a summary example, Vaughan et al. (2013), some of the actual implementers of M-PESA in Kenya,[14] describe their pilot, which started in October 2005 with a grant from the UK Department for International Development's innovation fund and with microfinance clients. The product was then changed and rebranded based on consumer feedback as an internal remittance product to send money to friends and family—this experimentation was important to the success of the product. Vaughan et al. (2013) also highlight some additional key factors that allowed mobile money to reach scale in Kenya, in particular, developing a strong network of agents, removing entry barriers for customers, investing in the infrastructure for scale at the very outset, and regulating the system after the innovation.

The success of mobile money systems is certainly underpinned by the rapid deployment and growth of the agent network, i.e., the end distributors of the service. This growth and reliability are associated with a network that is trustworthy, efficient, liquid, and profitable for the agents. As indicated by Camner et al. (2009) there were fewer than 1000 bank branches, just over 1000 ATMs, and 3000 M-PESA agents across Kenya in early 2008. At the time of writing there are 141,542 agents serving both M-PESA and other mobile money customers.[15] Table 10.1 shows data on the number of agents in some of the countries with mobile money deployments.[16] It is striking that the number of agents is at least triple the number of bank branches in Kenya, Uganda, Tanzania, and Bangladesh.[17] This is not the case in Nigeria because mobile money is both poorly deployed and poorly adopted there, with adoption rates of 2.3 per cent in 2015 (Demirgu¨c¸-Kunt et al., 2015).

As these agent networks grew and became denser, the distance between a household and an agent shrank. For example, Table 10.2 shows how the average distance to a mobile money agent changed in Kenya between 2007 and 2015 and how it compares to the average distance to a bank branch. These averages mask a lot of heterogeneity: in 2007, 32 per cent of households lived more than 10 km away from a bank branch, and 19 per cent lived more than 20 km away, whereas 46 per cent of households lived within 1 km of an agent, a number that rose to 68

[14] Pauline Vaughan ran M-PESA from 2007 to 2009, and Michael Joseph was the CEO of Safaricom from 2000 to 2010.

[15] Communications Commission of Kenya, Quarterly Sector Statistics Report for Quarter 2, 2015–2016 (October to December, 2015).

[16] The year of the data varies across countries because of the difficulty in finding recent data on the number of agents in each country.

[17] These numbers come from the FSP Maps data, which was collected in Kenya in 2015, in Nigeria in 2015, in Tanzania in 2014, in Bangladesh in 2013, and in Uganda (date unknown). The FSP maps data is available at http://fspmaps.org

Table 10.1 Number of agents in selected markets

Country	Number of agents by provider[a]		Number of agents[b]	Number of bank branches[b]
	Provider	Number of agents		
Pakistan	EasyPaisa	10,500	NA	NA
Philippines	GCash	18,000	NA	NA
Kenya	M-PESA	20,500	65,569	10,619
Uganda	NA	NA	41,794	477
Tanzania	NA	NA	45,429	579
Nigeria	NA	NA	3567	4989
Bangladesh	NA	NA	31,755	8641

[a] Data taken from Groupe Speciale Mobile Association data from the Agent Management toolkit, 2012.

[b] Data taken from Financial Services for the Poor maps data for Kenya from 2015, Nigeria from 2015, Tanzania from 2014, Bangladesh from 2013, and Uganda (date unknown).

Data available at http://fspmaps.org. Abbreviation: NA, not applicable.

Table 10.2 Average distance to the closest financial institutions, Kenya

Year	Bank branches	Bank agents	Mobile money agents
2007	9.2 km	NA	4.9 km
2011	7.0 km	5.2 km	1.9 km
2015	6.0 km	1.9 km	1.4 km

Data taken from Finaccess Geospatial Mapping 2016 https://dataverse.harvard.edu/dataset.xhtml?persistentId = doi:10.7910/DVN/SG589T.

per cent by 2015. In addition to a dense network of agents, successful deployments of mobile money had a network of agents that were efficient at managing their e-money and cash inventories, helped by consistent monitoring and liquidity management by the service operator. Eijkman et al. (2010) show that agents rebalanced their accounts almost daily, more frequently in urban areas. In addition, agents faced a lot of competition, as consumers favoured agents with better service and trading volumes.

Similarly, in a later study, Balasubramanian and Drake (2015) look at how the demand for mobile money in Kenya and Uganda is affected by agent quality (measured in terms of pricing transparency and expertise) and agent competition. They combine a survey of 3000 mobile money agents with location data on 68,000 financial access and transportation points, spatial census data, and population and poverty estimates. They find that greater agent competition is associated with a higher inventory of both cash and e-money, that more transparency in pricing and greater agent expertise are associated with higher demand, and that the return to expertise increases with competition.

Aside from the agent network, there are a number of other factors that may have driven the successful adoption of M-PESA and that have been described qualitatively. Mas and Morawczynski (2009) attribute some of the success of M-PESA to strong branding, an easy-to-use product, simple and transparent retail pricing, free deposit and no minimum balance feature, ability to send money to non-users, and ability to perform ATM withdrawals. Heyer and Mas (2009) highlight the importance of volume, momentum, and coverage, as well as the regulatory environment, the quality of the retail infrastructure, and the high telecom penetration. Mas and Ng'weno (2010) highlight brand management, channel management, and pricing as the major contributing factors behind M-PESA's massive success. Similarly, Mas and Radcliffe (2010) discuss the clever and easy-to-use design and Safaricom's business model. The authors suggest that the differentially wide spread of mobile money across countries could be partially attributed to differential regulations. M-PESA, in particular, benefited from a good working relationship between Safaricom and the Central Bank. Mas and Radcliffe (2011) also highlight how important network effects and trust are in scaling up a retail payment system. More recently, Lal and Sachdev (2015) compare five successful mobile money deployments[18] to five less successful ones.[19] In addition to the relationship with regulators and the agent networks mentioned above, they suggest that adoption is also driven by an underlying reliable mobile network with a successful and trusted brand and business.

One of the earliest quantitative studies of mobile money started in 2008 in Kenya around M-PESA. Jack and Suri (2011), in this and later work, document the patterns of adoption of M-PESA over 2008–14[20] using household surveys conducted across a large part of the country. They tracked the fast adoption of M-PESA in Kenya and traced the rollout of the agents in Kenya until 2010, recording the characteristics of the adopters and collecting data on access to the service. As expected, the initial users were richer and more educated; however, adoption of the product did reach down the income spectrum in the country, with

[18] These are Telesom ZAAD in Somaliland, Dialog eZ Cash in Sri Lanka, Econet EcoCash in Zimbabwe, SMART Communications SMART Money in the Philippines, and Globe Telecom GCASH in the Philippines.

[19] These are Vodacom M-PESA in South Africa, MTN money in Uganda, Eko Financial Services in India, and the broader situations in Nigeria and Brazil, although MTN money in Uganda is now growing rapidly.

[20] The surveys were conducted in 2008, 2009, 2010, 2011, and 2014. The sample was not national—it excluded sections of the North of the country, where households are seminomadic and therefore hard to track over time. The part of the country excluded from the sample covered about 8 per cent of the Kenyan population at the time. The sample was also weighted towards urban areas, as the initial sample drawn in 2008 was weighted by the number of agents in the administrative location (there were about 2500 locations in Kenya at the time). The reader is referred to Jack and Suri (2011, 2014) for more information on the sample.

over 90 per cent of households in their sample having an account by the time of their last survey in 2014.[21] Khan and Blumenstock (2016) study the adoption of mobile money more carefully in Ghana, Zambia, and Pakistan. They build a supervised machine-learning model of adoption using call record data and find this model does not distinguish very effectively between active and registered mobile money users, contrary to expectations that active users should be quite distinct in their patterns of phone use. Across countries, it is unlikely that any single set of characteristics will consistently predict mobile money adoption and use.

Beyond the household level, Banco de Moçambique (2015) survey firms in Maputo and Matola in Mozambique and show that financial illiteracy on the part of both the seller and the buyer restricts the use of financial services such as point of sale (POS) devices. Similarly, lack of trust and knowledge, coupled with technological issues, is a hindrance to business owners using mobile payments. Finally, they show that the adoption of POS devices is positively correlated with the size of business and the volume of transactions, whereas the use of mobile phone technologies for payments is related to the owner's age and whether they are a frequent cell phone user.

Although mobile money was a technological innovation, it was enabled by some creative regulation and, more importantly, a network to efficiently distribute and manage cash across vast distances. As we describe in Section 10.4, one of the most important uses of mobile money has been P2P remittances. Therefore, having a widespread agent network whose cash and e-money inventories are well managed is crucial to the success of the product. Of course, once adoption starts, there will be strong network effects, even stronger than for mobile phones themselves given that there is little interoperability in these markets. There has been surprisingly little work documenting network effects in the adoption of mobile money.[22]

10.4 Impacts of Basic Mobile Money

Since the launch and success of M-PESA and the launch of mobile money services across many countries in the developing world, there has been a lot of research around what role systems like M-PESA can play and what impacts they can have on economies.

What are the possible mechanisms through which mobile money systems can affect developing economies?[23] All mobile money systems have transaction fees

[21] Mbiti and Weil (2011) also document the characteristics of the users.

[22] An exception is Fafchamps et al. (2016), who study a precursor to mobile money, the P2P transfer of prepaid airtime credit in Rwanda.

[23] Maurer (2012a, b) and Donovan (2012) provide descriptions of similar mechanisms through which mobile money could affect economies.

and so do not really encourage cashless retail transactions in the way credit cards or debit cards have in the United States. Instead, they are largely used to make two types of transactions: (a) geographically disparate transactions, i.e., transactions across space, and (b) transactions where the opportunity cost of holding cash may be high, as in high-crime cities (see Economides and Jeziorski, 2015). For these types of transactions, mobile money provides a dramatic reduction in transaction costs, as well as improvements in convenience, security, and time taken for the transaction. For example, in Kenya, the average transaction travelled 200 km in 2008 (Jack and Suri, 2011), which would be an approximately USD5 bus ride; instead, consumers paid a USD0.35 fee (given the average transaction size). Also, the mobile money agents are much more easily accessible (see Table 10.2) than any other financial institution, so the money sent via this system can be easily deposited and withdrawn.

Given these reductions in transaction costs and improvements in safety, mobile money could simply facilitate trade both on the intensive margin (making existing transactions more efficient) and on the extensive margin (enabling transactions that would not have happened without mobile money). Such facilitation of trade could result in a better allocation of capital and, thus, increase savings. Similarly, there could be an improvement in the allocation of human capital as the returns to migration improve. In addition, mobile money accounts may provide safe storage of savings, thus potentially increasing total savings as well as improving the allocation of savings and risk (via increased and more efficient remittances) across households and firms.

Mobile money may also have effects on intrafamily dynamics, as these accounts are individually held. Finally, on the macroeconomic side, mobile money systems could increase the velocity of money and inflation (though the evidence is mixed on this, as discussed below). In economies with dual currencies, like that of Somaliland (see Iazzolino, 2015), mobile money could facilitate trade, remittances, and transactions in US dollars.

Economides and Jeziorski (2015) study the demand for mobile money, exploiting a natural experiment created by an exogenous and unanticipated increase in the transaction fees in Tanzania. They identify the slope of the demand curve and compute consumers' willingness to pay for risk amelioration using transportation and storage transactions. They find that consumers who execute large transactions are usually more price inelastic than consumers who execute smaller transactions and that demand for long-distance transfers is less elastic than that for short-distance transfers. Consumers use the mobile money network extensively for extremely short-term storage (less than 2 hours), probably due to high levels of street crime and burglaries, and are willing to pay up to 1 per cent of the transaction amount to avoid carrying money in the form of cash for each extra kilometre and up to 1.1 per cent to avoid keeping money at home for an extra day.

Looking at the impacts of mobile money in Kenya, Jack and Suri (2014) use the survey data described above to understand how M-PESA has improved the ability of households to share risk. Informal risk-sharing networks are used extensively to pool risk in developing economies,[24] including in Kenya (see Suri, 2014). Given the prevalence of such relationships, which involve transfers of money between households, and given the large transaction cost reductions afforded by M-PESA,[25] M-PESA could have important impacts on the efficiency with which individuals spread risk. As Jack and Suri (2014) show, these effects are sizeable—Panel (a) of Figure 10.4 illustrates their findings. Households with M-PESA are better able to smooth risks, and their consumption is less sensitive to shocks. When subject to a shock, households that have mobile money are more likely to receive a remittance from friends and family, receive more money in total, and receive it from a more diverse set of people in their network, all resulting in efficiency gains in risk sharing. This also explains why a large share of transactions on M-PESA are P2P remittances across long distances. Using similar empirical specifications, Riley (2016) finds that mobile money improves risk sharing in Tanzania.

In complementary work, Suri et al. (2012) look specifically at how M-PESA affects people's response to health shocks. They find that M-PESA users are able to spend more on medical expenses in the event of a health shock while also increasing expenses on food and maintaining their education expenditure. Non-user households or households far from agents are unable to increase expenditure on food after the shock, decrease their non-food subsistence expenditure, and might pull children out of school to finance health care costs. When hit by an illness shock, non-users substitute away from non-medical expenses, such as non-food subsistence, to finance the needed medical care expenditure. The authors find no evidence that non-users suffer significant food reductions, suggesting that both users and non-users do not cut back on necessary consumption. Non-users seem mostly to substitute away from their children's education to fund their health shocks. These results are illustrated in Panel (b) of Figure 10.4.

Finally, using the last round of their panel survey conducted in 2014, Suri and Jack (2016) measure the longer-term impacts of M-PESA. They find that better access to mobile money services has increased household consumption and savings and, thus, reduced poverty rates. They find that poverty rates declined by 2 percentage points as a result (196,000 households move out of extreme poverty), reductions that were larger among female-headed households. They also find significant changes in occupation choice, largely among women, who

[24] Kinnan (2014) provides an excellent review of the literature on informal risk sharing.

[25] The cost of sending money via M-PESA was almost 30 per cent of that of sending it via postal bank or via bus delivery through a driver and 46 per cent of the cost of sending it via Western Union (these percentages do not include transportation or time costs).

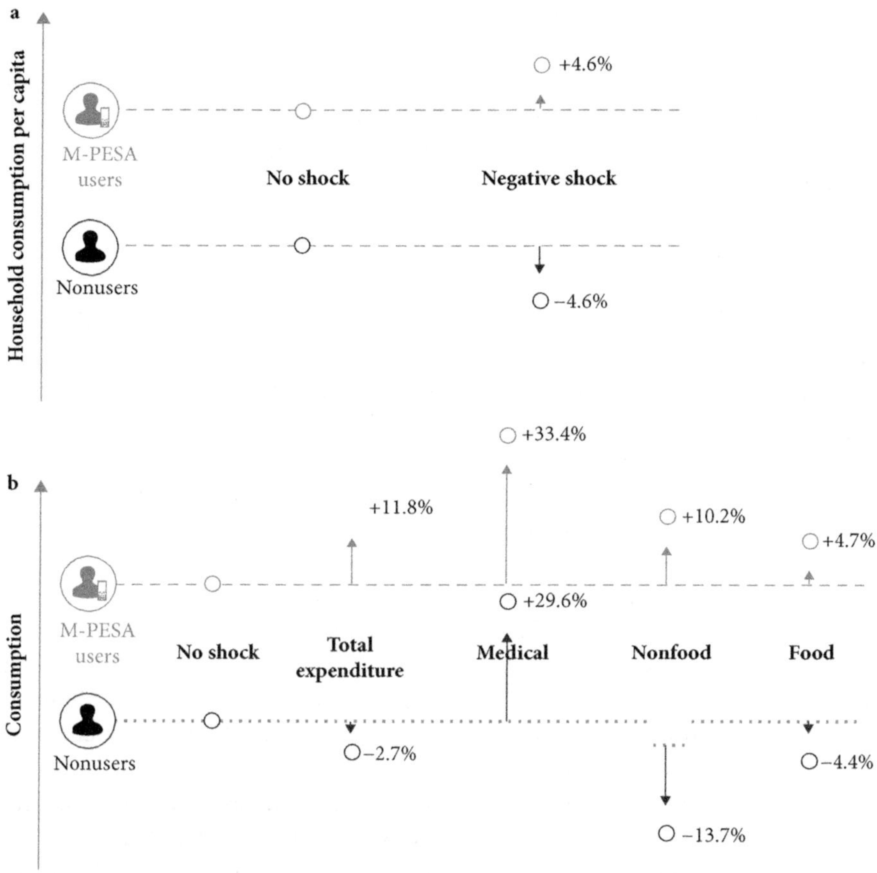

Figure 10.4 Resilience of M-PESA users and non-users to economic shocks. Panel *a* is based on data from Jack and Suri, 2014; panel *b* is based on data from Suri et al. (2012)

moved away from agriculture as their main occupation to business and retail. As a result of M-PESA, 186,000 women made this transition.

Blumenstock et al. (2016b) also study the response to shocks (in the context of an earthquake in Rwanda) using administrative data on mobile phone records, airtime purchases, and transfers of airtime. They find, as a result of the earthquake, a modest increase of USD84 in airtime transferred and an increase of USD16,959 in value of calls made, potentially indicative of indirect transfers as the caller bears the cost of the call in Rwanda. They also find that transfers were more likely to be sent to wealthier individuals and to individuals with a history of reciprocity with the sender. For Uganda, Munyegera and Matsumoto (2014) use panel survey data to show that using mobile money is associated with a 69 per cent increase in household per capita consumption, mobile money subscribers are 20 percentage points more likely to receive remittances from their family members in town, and the total annual value of remittances received is 33 per cent higher compared to non-user households.

Using survey and administrative data on M-PESA in Kenya, Jack et al. (2013) study the impact of mobile money on the volume, reach, direction, and type of internal remittances. They find that M-PESA users are more likely to receive and send remittances (by 37.4 and 34.3 percentage points, respectively). This includes an increase in the frequency (two more transactions per round) and amount of remittances. The reach of transactions is, on average, 100 km greater for M-PESA users, and reciprocity is also greater for M-PESA users (they are 13.2 percentage points more likely to engage in at least one reciprocal transfer). Finally, M-PESA users are more likely to transact for regular support, credit, and insurance purposes, and they change the composition of remittances by shifting from regular support purposes to credit arrangements.

Using qualitative methods, Morawczynski (2009) finds that M-PESA usage increased during periods of violence, like the postelection violence in 2007 in Kenya, and resulted in a reduced vulnerability to consumption shocks. Morawczynski and Pickens (2009) find that M-PESA increases savings for both the banked and unbanked, improves women's empowerment, and facilitates transfers within networks during bad events. Plyler et al. (2010) find community-level effects of M-PESA in terms of money circulation and local employment; physical, financial, and food security; greater financial, human, and social capital accumulation; and an improvement in the business environment, as transactions are easier.

Aside from these initial studies on mobile money, there has been one field experiment studying the impact of mobile money. Batista and Vicente (2013) study the initial rollout of a mobile money product, mKesh, in Mozambique. In the treatment areas, there was intense mobilization of agents and information dissemination (agents were recruited and trained and community theatre and community meetings were organized to describe mKesh). In addition, there was individual information dissemination to randomly chosen households in treatment areas. Using both survey and administrative data, the authors find that, in terms of take-up, 64 per cent of treated individuals conducted at least one transaction on the system. In terms of impact, financial literacy, the trust in local agents, and the usage of mCel (the accompanying telco), financial services were higher in treatment areas. In addition, the overall willingness to remit (independently of the money transfer mechanism) increased, though the overall willingness to save did not increase significantly. As with the studies on M-PESA, the remittance aspect of mobile money seems to be the most salient.

There has also been a growing body of literature that tries to understand the applications of mobile money, i.e., other aspects and circumstances where mobile money could play a role. For example, Aker et al. (2014) conduct the first randomized controlled trial (RCT) involving mobile money in the specific context of cash transfers. To reduce malnutrition during the drought and the 2009–10 food crisis, households in Niger were given monthly unconditional cash transfers, with women as the primary beneficiaries. The authors compared:

(a) a cash arm, where households received the transfer manually; (b) a Zap[26] arm, where transfers were received via mobile money and households were also given a service-enabled mobile phone; and (c) a mobile arm, where the transfers were received manually but households were also given a mobile phone. There was no pure control group.

Recipients of mobile money transfers had better nutrition, with a 10–16 per cent more diversified diet, including greater proportions of protein and energy-rich food, and their children ate 33 per cent more of a meal per day. The authors argue that these effects came from reduced time costs for the recipients, with mobile money transfer recipients saving, on average, two days over a five-month period. Despite the small magnitude of this effect, it could have had a significant opportunity cost because it occurred during the planting season. Another potential mechanism increasing bargaining power for women is the increase in privacy, given that the transfer was less observable to other household members. The electronic nature of the cash transfer did not, however, lead to significant use of mobile money beyond the programme. Finally, the authors also show that, although total costs were higher in mobile money villages (due to the distribution of phones), per-transaction costs were 20 per cent lower. With appropriate infrastructure, mobile money could, therefore, significantly reduce costs of cash transfers to disbursing agencies.

Blumenstock et al. (2015b) designed an experiment to study mobile salary payments in seven provinces across Afghanistan between August 2012 and March 2013. The intervention provided employees in a firm with a mobile phone and training on using M-Paisa, a mobile money service, and randomly assigned half of them to receive their salary through M-Paisa as opposed to cash. The authors used survey and administrative data and found significant cost reductions for the operating agency but no significant impacts of mobile money use on the recipients. Blumenstock et al. (2016a) conducted a field experiment with automatic payroll deductions towards savings through M-Paisa via a new salary platform called M-Pasandz. Employees were randomized into the following groups: (a) different default contribution rates from salary to a savings account (0 per cent or 5 per cent, which they could choose to change) and (b) different matching contribution rate from the firm (0 per cent, 25 per cent, or 50 per cent). These were cross-randomizations, creating a 2×3 design with a total of six treatment groups. The authors find that employees enrolled in the 5 per cent deduction rate were 40 percentage points more likely to save and that a 50 per cent

[26] Zap is a mobile money service operated by the mobile telecommunications company Zain.

matching rate had comparable results to the 5 per cent deduction for saving. The main explanation for this striking result seems to be present-bias preferences, where the employee procrastinates when making a non-default contribution.

Blumenstock et al. (2015c) study the relationship between violence and financial decisions in Afghanistan. Using data from an RCT administered to increase mobile money take-up and combining this with administrative data, a nationally representative household survey, and behavioural field experiments, the authors find that people increase their cash holdings when exposed to violence and that people experiencing violence are less likely to transact in mobile money and hold less funds in their mobile money accounts. They argue that the mechanism underlying these effects is a demand for liquidity that arises from the fear of future violence. In particular, a one standard-deviation increase in individual forecasts of violence is associated with holding 20 per cent less mobile money and 20 per cent more cash. This suggests that violence may play an important role in preventing the development of formal and digital financial networks.[27]

In an ongoing field experiment, Habyarimana and Jack (2016) study an innovative savings and credit product that layers over M-PESA, called M-Shwari (I discuss this innovation in more detail in Section 10.5). Habyarimana and Jack (2016) study M-Shwari in a set of schools in Kenya using a field experiment with two treatment arms: a commitment (locked) savings arm and a regular savings arm (with a cross-randomization of text message reminders to save for education). The intervention was targeted to the transition between primary and secondary school. The authors find an increase in savings and in secondary school enrolments for both groups relative to the control (though the effects are not significantly different across the two groups).

Finally, there has also been some work on the macroeconomic impact of mobile money systems. Weil et al. (2012) use survey data from Kenya, Tanzania, and Uganda to document the rapid adoption of mobile money between 2006 and 2009 and aggregate data from the Central Bank to look for structural breaks in monetary aggregates that would suggest macroeconomic effects of mobile money. They find evidence of these effects in Kenya, though the velocity of M-PESA, computed based on aggregate data provided by Safaricom, was no higher than that of cash or other monetary aggregates. Similarly, Mbiti and Weil (2011) start by showing that the transactions velocity of M-PESA was four transactions per month in 2008, not much higher than the velocity of cash. The calculated value of outstanding e-float was 3.3 billion shillings in August 2008, also a modest value in comparison to the 85.2 billion shillings of currency (M0) on average between January and June, 2008. Analysing transactions, they conclude

[27] In an accompanying policy white paper, Blumenstock et al. (2013) suggest that, when transactions are conducted in an unsafe or unstable environment, firms might benefit from shifting the costs of managing salary payments to mobile operators through mobile money.

that M-PESA is not used as a store of value, with the average account balance of users valued at less than $10 at any point in time. More importantly, they show an effect on the prices of competitors to M-PESA (such as Moneygram and Western Union), with competitors reducing prices on transaction sizes below M-PESA's thresholds.

Contrary to this, Mas and Klein (2012) find that the velocity of money increases considerably; however, it does not affect money supply base when e-money is based on a safe-deposit-box model. Aron et al. (2015) find little evidence of a link between mobile money and inflation using inflation forecasting models for Uganda. Simpasa et al. (2011) study the same question in Ethiopia, Kenya, Tanzania, and Uganda, highlighting the fact that mobile money could cause an increase in the velocity of money and, thus, the need for regulation to make sure such products do not undermine the effectiveness of monetary policy in these economies.

In a different vein, Jack et al. (2010) show how existing models of monetary theory can be used to think about the impact of mobile money on the operations of the financial system and the subsequent implications for monetary and regulatory policy decisions. Discussing results from household and agent surveys in late 2008, the authors show that the most common problems are agents' lack of cash and e-money, which would give rise to price discrimination if the price of cash to e-money was not fixed. However, they argue that there may be informal credit or debit relationships between the agents and their coordinating bodies, which can be welfare improving according to the theoretical models.

10.5 Conclusion: Is Mobile Money the Payment Infrastructure of the Future?

Although mobile money has been very successful in some countries (for example, by the end of 2014 in Kenya, 96 per cent of households outside Nairobi used M-PESA) and is expanding in a number of other economies, its use remains mostly limited to very specific P2P transactions: those that take place over long distances and those that are in places where holding cash is risky. Outside these applications, there has been less success, and the innovation ecosystem around mobile money is still in its early stages.[28] Even in Kenya, less than a third of households use the system for paying bills,[29] for receiving payments or wages from

[28] Mas and Mayer (2011) hypothesize that households need to manage their budgets, savings, and payments in order to better manage their livelihoods, and the services available to the poor rarely combine these needs. They suggest how mobile money may provide an avenue and set of products to do this.

[29] For the Safaricom product timeline, the reader is referred to http://www.safaricom.co.ke/mpesa_timeline/timeline.html. In April 2009, Safaricom partnered with Kenya Power to enable customers to

an organization, or for paying for other goods or services. Only 5 per cent use it to repay loans. As a result, few P2B, B2B, or G2P interactions take place over mobile money.[30] Although often referred to as a payment system, mobile money cannot fulfil its promise as a genuine payment system unless it can provide these other services at a sensible fee structure.

In the case of G2P transactions, it is important to mention innovations that are working toward delivering such services. In India, along with the universal ID, there has been a rollout of smartcards using a biometrically authenticated payments infrastructure through which government payments can be made to households. Muralidharan et al. (2016a) evaluate the impact of these smartcards on beneficiaries of the government's rural employment guarantee and pension programmes in Andhra Pradesh. They find that payments made using smartcards were faster and more predictable and involved less corruption and leakage than the existing system, especially for the employment programme. These effects resulted mostly from a reduction in over-reporting and quasi-ghost workers. These reductions in leakages, which do not involve any changes on the beneficiary side in receipts, make smartcards highly cost effective. In an accompanying study, Muralidharan et al. (2016b) look at the general equilibrium effects of the smartcards being used in the employment programme. They find an increase in income, 90 per cent of which came from private sector earnings (the remainder came from increases from the programme itself) through increased labour market competition, productivity, better credit access, and increases in demand.

Although the literature on mobile money is growing, research on the innovations that are already building on mobile money has been lagging. In the spirit of spurring new research ideas, I outline some of the more recent product innovations that have built on existing mobile money systems and encourage researchers to catch up with the innovations. Whether these innovations ultimately deliver improvements in livelihoods to households is still an open question.[31]

In 2011, Safaricom partnered with a local bank in Kenya, the Commercial Bank of Africa (CBA), to create a new banking product called M-Shwari. Since then, CBA has launched similar products in Tanzania (M-Pawa) and Uganda, Rwanda, and Cote d'Ivoire (MoKash). Similar platforms are provided by Equity Bank Kenya (Equitel) and Kenya Commercial Bank (KCB M-PESA). With M-Shwari, consumers can use their mobile phone to open a bank account at CBA, deposit money in it by transferring balances from M-PESA, withdraw from it via

pay electricity bills through M-PESA. Starting in October 2010, customers could pay at supermarkets using M-PESA. Similar bill payment services are now provided by many mobile money providers.

[30] One nongovernmental organization, Give Directly, operates in East Africa using mobile money to distribute cash transfers, though they do not yet reach anywhere near the scale of a G2P programme.

[31] Kendall et al. (2011) look at how some other market players use M-PESA as a platform to integrate more financial services using results from phone and Internet surveys.

M-PESA, and request a loan. Underlying the loan decision is a credit scoring rule or algorithm based on administrative data on airtime purchases and mobile money transactions (in Uganda, the product is based on a machine-learning credit scoring and credit limit assignment algorithm).[32] By April 2015, over 10 million Kenyans had an M-Shwari bank account, and some, for the first time, had access to formal financial services.[33] A company called Branch offers a slightly different form of mobile credit (with no savings component, as they are not a bank). To make a lending decision, the product asks for permission to scrape the applicant's phone for data on handset details, GPS info, call and SMS logs, social network data from Facebook, and contact lists. A machine-learning algorithm then uses these data to create a credit score and make a lending decision. Increased usage of the product results in lower interest fees and larger loans. The company Tala provides a very similar product to that of Branch. Similarly, M-KOPA and Angaza (two other systems in Kenya) offer asset-based financing for solar panels where payments on the loan are made from M-PESA.

In 2013, Safaricom launched Lipa-na-M-PESA, a product that encourages retail payments over the M-PESA platform. Before this, the transaction fees on M-PESA, as on all other mobile money systems (see Figure 10.3), were too high for basic retail payments, especially because the incidence of those fees falls on the end consumer and not on the retailer. Lipa was an attempt to lower these transaction fees to 1 per cent of the transaction size, which was then further lowered to 0.5 per cent in March 2017 for transactions above KShs 200 (USD2) and 0 per cent for transactions less than KShs 200. The retailer can choose to pay it or pass on the fee to the consumer.[34] In practice, there has been a mix of retailers choosing to pay it and choosing to pass it on. Regardless, given the size of many retail transactions, this fee was too high for both consumers and retailers, though the changes in March 2017 may make a marked difference.

In March 2017, the Kenyan Treasury launched a pilot version of a digital government bond called M-Akiba. It is a three-year infrastructure bond that is purchased over mobile phones. The back-end system is built to allow individuals to use the KYC behind their mobile money accounts to open a Central Depository System (CDS) account through their mobile phone in a few keystrokes.

[32] Although there is little research on the value of mobile money transaction data itself, the transaction data are being used in practice to create credit scores in Kenya. However, recent literature uses mobile phone call data records (CDRs), which are beyond the scope of this review. As an example, Blumenstock (2014) uses call records from Rwanda to predict wealth, and Blumenstock et al. (2015a) show that predictions from records match the Demographic and Health Survey in Rwanda fairly accurately.

[33] Cook & McKay (2015) provide more information on M-Shwari. In 2010, under a similar partnership between the mobile operator and a different bank, a bank account called M-KESHO was launched, focusing on promoting individual savings (kesho means tomorrow in Swahili). However, although heralded by many, that product was not widely adopted.

[34] This is in contrast to Visa and Mastercard, where the incidence of the fee is always entirely on the retailer.

Individuals can then actively purchase and trade these bonds on the underlying digital platform (which links to the bond exchange). These bonds come with a coupon rate payout of 10 per cent per annum, paid every six months. To make this happen, Kenya passed legislation that lowered the minimum investment in treasury bonds to KShs 3000 (USD30) from KShs 100,000. The government also allowed for a CDS account to be opened via a mobile phone and allowed individuals to use mobile money to purchase and trade treasury bonds over a mobile phone. M-Akiba will serve as a positive real return savings instrument for low-income households, hence the name: M for mobile and akiba meaning savings in Swahili. The March 2017 bond issue was only for KShs 150 million (USD1.5 million) because it is a pilot version, and it closed in just over two weeks. The Treasury plans another KShs 5 billion issue on M-Akiba in June 2017.

In late 2015, Safaricom made available an application programming interface (API) to allow for programmatic access to the M-PESA platform over the web, with a second generation expected to be launched in mid-2017.[35] APIs are a convenient approach for businesses to expose some of their core assets and to enable the emergence of a developer community around these assets. APIs come with instructions for developers on how to access them, but also with terms and conditions, a pricing model, and other business contractual agreements. Exposing APIs has become a standard approach to creating B2B interactions over the Internet without tedious human business development transactions in the way.

Given the popularity of M-PESA, one could assume significant uptake of the API in Kenya. However, there have been few integration efforts to date. This is most likely due to some design challenges for the API in terms of technology, as well as issues of business contracts for potential users. Whereas usage is encouraged in a sandbox model, production usage requires exactly those kinds of B2B negotiations that APIs should do away with.

It is fair to assume that these are teething challenges. The universal access to M-PESA presents a tremendous opportunity for an API model and could accelerate the fintech market in East Africa rapidly. The value of global fintech investment in 2015 was $22.3 billion (Skan et al., 2016), with the United States having the largest sector, receiving $4.5 billion in new funding in 2015. China had nearly $2 billion, India $1.65 billion, and Germany $770 million. Whereas the growth in investments in Asia-Pacific have been dramatic (a fourfold growth between 2014 and 2015), there has been little investment in Sub-Saharan Africa, where mobile money systems have no doubt been the most popular (Skan et al., 2016). Given

[35] For more on APIs and M-PESA's initial API, the reader is referred to the Bankable Frontiers Association (Bank. Front. Assoc., 2016) and Morawczynski (2015). For more on the operational aspects of M-PESA's API from Safaricom, the reader is referred to http://www.safaricom.co.ke/business/corporate/m-pesa-payments-services/m-pesa-api.

that Sub-Saharan Africa has some of the poorest economies in the world, it may also have the economies where the returns to fintech investments are the highest, as illustrated by the case of mobile money. Democratizing access to a payment system such as M-PESA might well be the missing link between the current situation and potential significant increases in investments in Fintech in the region.

The big question is: what can we learn from these nascent innovations that can change the gestalt of payments and financial markets in developing economies? Although mobile money may seem revolutionary, aside from the dramatic adoption, it is far from revolutionizing the role of financial markets or cash in these economies. Mobile money has been, in most cases, a cash-in-cash-out system, with the majority of transactions being the purchase of airtime and small P2P remittances, generally once a month. In the success cases, cash has come into the financial system, and the flow through the system has often amounted to a sizeable fraction of GDP. However, these economies are not to be mistaken for cashless when compared, for example, to Sweden, where cash makes up only 2 per cent of transactions (see Bank Int. Settl., 2015). Similarly, their financial flows are tiny when compared to the US financial system, which trades more than 60 times its GDP a day just through stocks, bonds, and derivatives. The benefits of cashless economies, especially in low-resource environments, remain an open question. Should these economies become cashless or close to cashless, and, if so, how will that be accomplished? Will the banking system be the primary venue for this transformation, and, if so, what sets of products and services will be needed to accomplish this? What will encourage financial market transformation in these economies? Will mobile money be the first stepping stone toward new financial markets and transactions in these economies? Will it encourage broader, better-integrated, secure platforms for transactions? There is a lot still to learn.

References

Aker, J. C. and Mbiti, I. M. (2010), 'Mobile phones and economic development in Africa', *Journal of Economic Perspectives,* Vol. 24, No. 3, pp. 207–32.

Aker, J. C., Boumnijel, R., McClelland, A., and Tierney, N. (2014), 'Payment mechanisms and anti-poverty programs: Evidence from a mobile money cash transfer experiment in Niger'. Working Paper 268, Centre Global Development, Washington, D.C.

Aron, J. (2015), 'Leapfrogging: A survey of the nature and economic implications of mobile money'. Working Paper, Centre for the Study of African Economies, Oxford University, Oxford, UK.

Aron, J., Muellbauer, J., and Sebudde, R. (2015). 'Inflation forecasting models for Uganda: Is mobile money relevant?' Working Paper, Centre for the Study of African Economies, Oxford University, Oxford, UK.

Balasubramanian, K. and Drake, D. (2015), 'Service quality, inventory and competition: an empirical analysis of mobile money agents in Africa'. Working Paper 15-059, Technology Operational Management Unit, Harvard Business School, Harvard University, Cambridge, MA.

Banco de Moçambique (2015), 'Electronic payments in Mozambique: a baseline on their adoption in Maputo and Matola'. Working Paper, International Growth Centre, London School of Economics, London.

Banerjee, A. (2016), 'Bad economics can bite', *Hindustan Times*, 22 December.

Bank for International Settlement (2015), *Statistics on Payment, Clearing and Settlement Systems in the CPMI Countries: Figures for 2014*. Report, Commission for Payment Market Infrastructure, Bank for International Settlement, Basel, Switzerland. https://www.bis.org/cpmi/publ/d135.pdf

Bank. Front. Assoc. (2016), *Implications, Insights and Guidance on Use of Open Application Programming Interfaces (APIs) by Financial Services Providers in Emerging Economies*. Report for FSD Kenya, Nairobi, Kenya.

Basu, K. (2016), 'In India, black money makes for bad policy', *The New York Times*, 27 November.

Batista, C. and Vicente, P. C. (2013), 'Introducing mobile money in rural Mozambique: evidence from a field experiment'. Working Paper, Nova School of Business and Economics, University Nova Lisboa, Lisbon.

Bernanke, B. S. (2012), 'Some reflections on the crisis and the policy response'. Presented at *Russell Sage Found. Century Found. Conference for Rethinking Finance*, New York, 13 April.

Blumenstock, J. (2014), 'Calling for better measurement: estimating an individual's wealth and well-being from mobile phone transaction records'. Presented at *Workshop on Data Science Social Good, 20th ACM Conference for Knowledge Discovery Ministry*, New York.

Blumenstock, J. E., Callen, M., and Ghani, T. (2013), 'Mobile salary payments in Afghanistan: Policy implications and lessons learned'. Policy Working Paper, Consortium for Financial System and Poverty, Chicago.

Blumenstock, J. E., Callen, M., Ghani, T., and Koepke, L. (2015c), 'Promises and pitfalls of mobile money in Afghanistan: Evidence from a randomized control trial'. *Proceedings of 7th International Conference on Information Communication Technology Development*, New York: ACM, p. 15.

Blumenstock, J., Callen, M. and Ghani, T. (2015a), *Violence and Financial Decisions: Evidence from Mobile Money in Afghanistan*. Seattle: University of Washington Press.

Blumenstock, J., Callen, M. and Ghani, T. (2015b), *Using mobile salary payment to improve Afghan frim performance*, Private enterprise development in low income countries, PEDL Research note.

Blumenstock, J., Callen, M., and Ghani, T. (2016a), 'Mobilizing savings with automatic contributions: Experimental evidence on dynamic inconsistency and the default effect in Afghanistan'. Discussion Paper 11400, Centre for Economic Policy Research, London.

Blumenstock, J., Eagle, N., and Fafchamps, M. (2016b), 'Airtime transfers and mobile communications: Evidence in the aftermath of natural disasters', *Journal of Development Economics,* Vol. 120, pp. 157–81.

Camner, G. (2013), *Snapshot: Implementing Mobile Money Interoperability in Indonesia.* Report, Groupe Special Mobile Association, London.

Camner, G., Pulver, C., and Sjoblom, E. (2009), *What Makes a Successful Mobile Money Implementation? Learnings from M-PESA in Kenya and Tanzania.* Report, Groupe Special Mobile Association, London.

Chakravorti, B. (2017), 'Early lessons from India's demonetization experiment', *Harvard Business Review,* 14 March.

Cook, T. and McKay, C. (2015), 'Top 10 things to know about M-Shwari'. *CGAP Blog,* 2 April. http://www.cgap.org/blog/top-10-things-know-about-m-shwari.

Davidson, N. and Leishman, P. (2016), *The Case for Interoperability: Assessing the Value that the Interconnection of Mobile Money Services Would Create for Customers and Operators.* Report, Groupe Spec. Mob. Assoc., London.

Demirgu¨c¸-Kunt, A., Klapper, L. F., Singer, D., and Van Oudheusden, P. (2015), 'The Global Findex Database 2014: Measuring financial inclusion around the world'. Working Paper, World Bank, Washington, DC.

Donovan, K. (2012), 'Mobile money for financial inclusion', *Information and Communications for Development,* Vol. 61, pp. 61–73.

Economides, N. and Jeziorski, P. (2015), Mobile money in Tanzania. Working Paper, New York University, New York.

Eijkman, F., Kendall, J., and Mas, I. (2010), 'Bridges to cash: The retail end of M-PESA', *Savings and Development,* Vol. 34, No. 2, pp. 219–52.

Fafchamps, M., Soderbom, M., and van den Boogaart, M. (2016), 'Adoption with social learning and network externalities'. Working Paper, Stanford University, Stanford, CA.

Greenacre J. and Buckley, R. P. (2014), 'Using trusts to protect mobile money customers', *Singapore Journal of Legal Studies,* Vol. 26, pp. 59–78.

GSMA (Groupe Spécial Mobile Association) (2015), *State of the Industry: Mobile Financial Services for the Unbanked,* Report, Groupe Special Mobile Association, London.

Habyarimana, J. and Jack, W. (2016), *Saving for High School with a Mobile-Money Lock-Box.* Working Paper, Georgetown University, Washington, DC.

Heyer A. and Mas, I. (2009), *Seeking Fertile Grounds for Mobile Money.* Unpublished manuscript, Financial Sector Deepening, Nairobi, Kenya.

Iazzolino, G. (2015), 'Following Mobile Money in Somaliland'. Research Paper 4, Rift Valley Forum, Rift Valley Institute, Nairobi, Kenya.

Jack, W. and Suri, T. (2011), 'Mobile money: The economics of M-PESA'. NBER Working Paper, 16721.

Jack, W. and Suri, T. (2014), 'Risk sharing and transactions costs: Evidence from Kenya's mobile money revolution', *American Economic Review,* Vol. 104, No. 1, pp. 183–223.

Jack, W., Ray, A., and Suri, T. (2013), 'Transaction networks: Evidence from mobile money in Kenya', *American Economic Review,* Vol. 103, No. 3, pp. 356–61.

Jack, W., Suri, T., and Townsend, R. M. (2010), 'Monetary theory and electronic money: Reflections on the Kenyan experience', *Federal Reserve Bank Richmond Economic Quarterly,* Vol. 96, No. 1, pp. 83–122.

Karlan D., Morten, M., and Zinman, J. (2012), 'A personal touch: Text messaging for loan repayment'. NBER Working Paper 17952.

Karlan, D., McConnell, M., Mullainathan, S., and Zinman, J. (2016), 'Getting to the top of mind: How reminders increase saving', *Management Science,* Vol. 62, No. 12, pp. 3393–3411.

Kendall, J., Maurer, B., Machoka, P., and Veniard, C. (2011), 'An emerging platform: From money transfer system to mobile money ecosystem', *Innovations,* Vol. 6, No. 4, pp. 49–64.

Khan, M. R. and Blumenstock, J. E. (2016), 'Predictors without borders: Behavioral modeling of product adoption in three developing countries'. *Proceedings of 22nd Conference Knowledge Discovery Data Ministry, Special Interest Group Knowledge Discovery Data Ministry, Association of Computing Machinery.* New York: ACM, pp. 145–54.

Kinnan, C. (2014), 'Distinguishing barriers to insurance in Thai villages'. Working Paper, Northwestern University, Evanston, IL.

Lal, R. and Sachdev, I. (2015), 'Mobile money services—design and development for financial inclusion'. Working Paper, Harvard Business School, Harvard University, Cambridge, MA.

Lester, R. T., Ritvo, P., Mills, E. J., Kariri, A., and Karanja, S. (2010), 'Effects of a mobile phone short message service on antiretroviral treatment adherence in Kenya (WelTel Kenya1): A randomised trial'. *Lancet,* Vol. 376, No. 9755, pp. 1838–45.

Marx, B., Pons, V., and Suri, T. (2016), 'Voter mobilization can backfire: Evidence from Kenya'. Working Paper, Massachusetts Institute of Technology, Cambridge, MA.

Mas, I. and Klein, M. (2012), 'A note on macro-financial implications of mobile money schemes'. Working Paper 188, Frankfurt School of Finance and Management, Frankfurt.

Mas, I. and Mayer, C. (2011), 'Savings as forward payments: Innovations on mobile money platforms', in E. Y. Mohammed and Z. B. Uraguchi (eds), *Financial Inclusion for Poverty Alleviation: Banking on the Unbanked.* London: Routledge.

Mas, I. and Morawczynski, O. (2009), 'Designing mobile money services: Lessons from M-PESA', *Innovations,* Vol. 4, No. 2, 77–91.

Mas, I. and Ng'weno, A. (2010), 'Three keys to M-PESA's success: Branding, channel management and pricing', *Journal of Payments Strategy & Systems,* Vol. 4, No. 4, 352–70.

Mas, I. and Radcliffe, D. (2010), 'Mobile payments go viral: M-PESA in Kenya'. Working Paper, Bill Melinda Gates Foundation, Seattle, WA.

Mas, I. and Radcliffe, D. (2011), 'Scaling mobile money', *Journal of Payments Strategy & Systems*, Vol. 5, No. 3, 298–315.

Maurer, B. (2012a), 'Mobile money: Communication, consumption and change in the payments space', *Journal of Development Studies*, Vol. 48, No. 5, pp. 589–604.

Maurer, B. (2012b), 'Regulation as retrospective ethnography: Mobile money and the arts of cash', *Banking and Finance Law Review*, Vol. 27, No. 2, pp. 299–313.

Mbiti, I. and Weil, D. N. (2011), 'Mobile banking: The impact of M-Pesa in Kenya'. NBER Working Paper, 17129.

Morawczynski, O. (2009), 'Exploring the usage and impact of "transformational" mobile financial services: The case of M-PESA in Kenya', *Journal of East African Studies*, Vol. 3, No. 3, pp. 509–25.

Morawczynski, O. (2015), 'Just how open is Safaricom's open API?', *CGAP*, 30 Oct.

Morawczynski, O. and Pickens, M. (2009), 'Poor people using mobile financial services: Observations on customer usage and impact from M-PESA'. Working Paper 9492, World Bank, Washington, DC.

Munyegera, G. K. and Matsumoto, T. (2014), *Mobile Money, Remittances and Rural Household Welfare: Panel Evidence from Uganda*. Tokyo: GRIPS.

Muralidharan, K., Niehaus, P., and Sukhtankar, S. (2016a), 'Building state capacity: Evidence from biometric smartcards in India', *American Economic Review*, Vol. 106, No. 10, pp. 2895–929.

Muralidharan, K., Niehaus, P., and Sukhtankar, S. (2016b), 'General equilibrium effects of (improving) public employment programs: Experimental evidence from India'. Working Paper, University of Califormia, San Diego, La Jolla, CA.

Plyler, M. G., Haas, S., and Nagarajan, G. (2010), 'Community-level economic effects of M-PESA in Kenya'. Working Paper, Iris Center, University of Maryland, College Park, MD.

Riley E. (2016), 'Mobile money and risk sharing against aggregate shocks'. Working Paper 2016-16, Centre for the Study of African Economies, University of Oxford, Oxford, UK.

Simpasa, A., Gurara, D., Shimeles, A., Vencatachellum, D., and Ncube, M. (2011), 'Inflation dynamics in selected East African countries: Ethiopia, Kenya, Tanzania and Uganda'. Policy Brief, African Development Bank, Abidjan, Côte d'Ivoire.

Skan, J., Dickerson, J., and Gagliardi, L. (2016), *Fintech and the Evolving Landscape: Landing Points for the Industry*. Report, Accenture Consultancy, Dublin.

Suri, T. (2014), 'Estimating the extent of local risk sharing between households'. Working Paper, Sloan School of Management, Massachusetts Institute of Technology, Cambridge, MA.

Suri, T. and Jack, W. (2016), 'The long run poverty and gender impacts of mobile money', *Science*, Vol. 354, No. 6317, pp. 1288–92.

Suri, T., Jack, W., and Stoker, T. M. (2012), 'Documenting the birth of a financial economy', *Proceedings of the National Academy of Sciences of the United States of America (PNAS)*, Vol. 109, No. 26, 10257–62.

Vaughan, P., Fengler, W., and Joseph, M. (2013), 'Scaling up through disruptive business models: The inside story of mobile money in Kenya', in L. Chandy, A. Hosono, H. Kharas, and J. Linn (eds), *Getting to Scale: How to Bring Development Solutions to Millions of Poor People*, Washington, DC: The Brookings Institution Press, pp. 189–219.

Weil, D. N., Mbiti, I., and Mwega, F. (2012), *The Implications of Innovations in the Financial Sector on the Conduct of Monetary Policy in East Africa*. Report, Tanzania Program, International Growth Centre, Dar es Salaam, Tanzania.

11

East African Monetary Union

What Lies Ahead?

Louis A. Kasekende

11.1 Introduction

In November 2013[1] the five East African Community (EAC) partner states, at that time, signed a protocol committing themselves to introducing the East African Monetary Union (EAMU) in 2024 and to implementing a series of preparatory measures in the years leading up to 2024.[2] Monetary unions potentially offer important benefits to economies which are closely integrated, but the problems experienced by some of the monetary unions already in existence around the world, including the European Monetary Union, indicate that they also entail serious risks.

The preparation for, and implementation of, EAMU, entails a huge agenda and work programme encompassing public policy and institutional change. Space does not allow all of these issues to be addressed in the detail that they merit in this chapter, hence the chapter confines its focus to what I judge are the key macroeconomic and fiscal policy challenges which must be tackled by the EAC partner states to ensure that the introduction of EAMU can be a success, leaving aside very important issues of institutional development, such as the creation of the East African Monetary Institute, the forerunner of the East African central bank.

The chapter focuses on four main issues. The first, in Section 11.2, is the imperative for extensive economic integration within the EAC if the establishment of EAMU is to deliver tangible benefits for the partner states. The second, in Section 11.3, is the need for strong, enforceable, but feasible rules to ensure the fiscal sustainability of each partner state, given that once EAMU has been established, they will no longer have the option of financing their public debt from their own central banks. The third issue, addressed in Section 11.4, is how to align the exchange rates of each partner state in the period prior to the introduction of the common currency, so that each partner state enters EAMU at an exchange rate

[1] Former Deputy Governor, Bank of Uganda.

[2] South Sudan joined the EAC in 2016.

Louis A. Kasekende, *East African Monetary Union: What Lies Ahead?* In: *50 Years of Central Banking in Kenya: Regional and Global Perspectives.* Edited by: Patrick Njoroge and Victor Murinde, Oxford University Press (2021).
 DOI: 10.1093/oso/9780198851820.003.0011

(a domestic price level relative to its partners) which is sustainable for its own economy. The fourth issue is how to mitigate the adverse impact of asymmetric macroeconomic shocks within the EAC, which is addressed in Section 11.5. Section 11.6 provides concluding remarks.

11.2 Strengthening Economic Integration within the EAC

The economic rationale for monetary union is to facilitate transactions within an integrated economic area, eliminating risks which might arise from unforeseen currency movements and the costs of exchanging currencies in order to complete transactions.[3] This implies that the benefits of EAMU can only be fully realized when there is comprehensive economic integration within the EAC, not just substantial trade in goods but also trade in services and movement of factors of production within the EAC. Without comprehensive economic integration in the EAC there is no more economic justification for its partner states sharing a common currency than there is for sharing a common currency with countries elsewhere in the world.

Unfortunately, economic integration in the EAC is still a long way short of that required to justify a common currency. Although the EAC partner states have implemented a customs union, trade in goods within the region comprised only 18 per cent of the total merchandise exports and 6 per cent of the imports of the (then) five partner states in 2014 and 2015 (Table 11.1). The five partner states had a combined GDP of approximately $147 billion, but their combined intra-EAC exports amount to only $2.4 billion in 2015, or 2 per cent of their combined GDP.[4] If South Sudan were included (it was not a member of the EAC in 2014 and 2015) intra-EAC exports would be higher, especially for Kenya and Uganda.

The low level of intra-regional trade is a result of two factors. The first is the structure of the region's economies, which do not have the capacities to produce a large share of their requirements for consumption, investment, and intermediate goods, which instead must be imported from outside of the EAC. Second, there are still numerous barriers to intra-regional trade. Although in almost all cases tariffs on intra-regional trade have been removed, trade is still impeded by ubiquitous trade distorting non-tariff measures or non-tariff barriers (NTBs). Many of these NTBs are not imposed specifically for protectionist purposes, but

[3] Another reason sometimes given for the creation of a monetary union is to improve macroeconomic policy in countries which have suffered from poor macroeconomic management at the national level, but this reason appears to have limited relevance for East Africa, where macroeconomic management at the national level has been generally good, as evidenced by relatively low inflation rates.

[4] The share of intra-regional exports in regional GDP would be higher if services were included but unfortunately comprehensive direction of trade statistics for services are not available.

Table 11.1 Exports and imports of EAC partner states to/from the world and to/from the EAC in 2014 and 2015 (millions of dollars)

	Exports fob		Imports cif	
	2014	2015	2014	2015
Burundi (total)	88	102	704	670
Intra-EAC	15	15	209	219
Intra-EAC as % of total	17	15	30	33
Kenya (total)	5769	6515	18,093	21,680
Intra-EAC	1392	1457	409	428
Intra-EAC as % of total	24	22	2	2
Rwanda (total)	441	384	1523	1574
Intra-EAC	30	31	497	520
Intra-EAC as % of total	7	8	33	33
Tanzania (total)	4197	4209	15,596	13,392
Intra-EAC	377	395	578	605
Intra-EAC as % of total	9	9	4	5
Uganda (total)	2926	1903	4639	4648
Intra-EAC	460	481	824	862
Intra-EAC as % of total	24	25	18	19
EAC (total)	12,411	13,114	40,555	41,964
Intra-EAC	2273	2379	2516	2533
Intra-EAC as % of total	18	18	6	6

Source: IMF Data Tables Direction of Trade Statistics (from IMF website accessed on 31/01/2017).

the manner in which they are implemented serves to discriminate against imports in favour of domestically produced goods. Examples of such NTBs include regulations pertaining to public health and product standards, non-recognition of EAC rules of origin and multiple road blocks and weighbridges (Kirk, 2012). World Bank (2013) reported that around 90 per cent of intra-EAC imports to Kenya and Uganda were affected by at least one NTB, roughly the same percentage as that which affected imports from outside the EAC.

The EAC has established a mechanism for identifying, reporting, and removing NTBs and to facilitate this it enacted, in 2015, the East African Community Elimination of Non-Tariff Barriers Act.[5] The EAC Secretariat compiles and publishes an inventory of NTBs and reported that, as of June 2016, 104 NTBs had been removed since the establishment of the NTB Reporting Mechanism in 2009, but that 25 NTBs remained in place (Calabrese and Eberhard-Ruiz, 2016). Hence progress is being made in tackling NTBs.

[5] The Act defines NTBs as 'laws, regulations, administrative and technical requirements other than tariffs imposed by a Partner State whose effect is to impede trade'.

Despite this, however, trading across borders in the region remains very problematic for businesses in the EAC. The World Bank conducts annual Doing Business Surveys which assess the extent to which the regulatory environment affects business in 190 countries around the world. The surveys cover various components of the business environment such as starting a business, access to credit, paying taxes, and trading across borders. Trading across borders is evaluated in terms of the hours taken with, and cost of, border compliance and compliance with trade-related documentary requirements. The Doing Business Surveys rank all of the countries in terms of both their overall indicator and each component of the overall indicator and also estimate the distance to the frontier, which is the extent to which each country's regulatory environment matches the best performing country (the frontier).

Table 11.2 reports the latest findings from the Doing Business Surveys for five of the EAC countries,[6] showing both the overall indicator and the indicator pertaining to trading across borders. There is a great deal of heterogeneity within the EAC, with Rwanda ranked relatively well in terms of its overall indicator while the rankings of Uganda, Tanzania, and especially Burundi are poor. In all five countries, the ranking pertaining to trading across borders is worse than the overall ranking and Tanzania and Burundi are in the bottom quintile of the rankings.

Free movement of capital and labour is crucial for economic integration for two reasons. First, if there is goods and services market integration within the EAC, specific industries are likely to cluster in specific locations, not only to exploit

Table 11.2 Doing business indicators, overall and trading across borders, rankings, and distance to frontier, 2017

Country	Overall Doing Business rank	Overall Doing Business distance to frontier (%)	Trading across borders rank	Trading across borders distance to frontier (%)
Burundi	157	47.4	160	47.4
Kenya	92	61.2	105	66.8
Rwanda	56	69.8	87	71.2
Tanzania	132	54.5	180	20.2
Uganda	115	57.8	136	58.9

Rankings are from 1 (best) to 190 (worst). The distance to the frontier is expressed as a percentage of the frontier, hence a higher percentage denotes a better performance.

Source: World Bank Doing Business Reports, World Bank website (accessed 1 February 2017).

[6] South Sudan was not covered by the surveys.

location specific advantages but also to realize the economies of scope which clustering provides, both of which should help to raise the efficiency of these industries, thereby not only benefitting consumers within the EAC but also helping to make these industries more competitive internationally. But the mobility of different industries within the EAC will only be possible if factors of production are also fully mobile within the EAC.

The EAC Common Market provides for, inter alia, the free movement of persons and labour, the right of residence, the right of establishment (of service providers), the free movement of services and capital. However, some of its key provisions have not been fully implemented. There are barriers to the free movement of capital, the free movement of services and especially to the free movement of labour. There are genuine reasons to oppose free movement of labour, capital, and services but they are not compatible with comprehensive economic integration and a monetary union.

11.3 Ensuring Fiscal Sustainability

The sustainability of a monetary union requires constraints on the fiscal policies of the partner states of the union. This is because membership of a monetary union could potentially allow a state to at least partially externalize the real cost of financing its fiscal deficit while fully internalizing the benefits, in terms of higher public spending or lower taxes. The real costs of financing the fiscal deficit can be externalized by borrowing from the common central bank or from integrated financial markets within the monetary union which raises borrowing costs for all partner states. This gives each partner state of the monetary union an incentive to incur larger fiscal deficits than is optimal, with the consequence that inflation within the monetary union will be higher than optimal, if the common central bank extends budgetary financing to the partner states and/or real interest rates will be higher, which will risk crowding out the private sector from credit markets.

To address these risks, a minimum requirement of a sustainable monetary union is that the common central bank should not finance the public sector borrowing requirements of the partner states, other than on a strictly limited and temporary basis. This is recognized in the EAMU Protocol, article 5 of which requires partner states to phase out government borrowing from their national central banks as a prerequisite for the monetary union.[7] However, a restriction on central bank financing of budgets is not sufficient by itself to avoid the dangers posed by excessive fiscal deficits, mainly for two reasons.

[7] The Schedule for the Realization of the Monetary Union states that this should be done by 2021.

First, central banks could face political pressure to accommodate the fiscal requirements of a partner state in ways other than by directly lending to that state, for example by reducing the policy interest rate to induce a fall in sovereign borrowing costs or by allowing higher inflation in order to deflate the real value of sovereign debt.

Second, a restriction on central bank financing of fiscal deficits is time inconsistent. Although it is optimal ex ante it may not be optimal ex post. If a partner state faces a fiscal crisis and risks defaulting on its sovereign debt, the costs of such a default could be very severe and would probably not be limited to that partner state alone. It is likely that, with integrated financial markets, the sovereign debt of the defaulting state is held by economic agents, including banks throughout the monetary union. A sovereign default could potentially threaten the systemic stability of the financial system throughout the monetary union. It would also damage public confidence in the monetary union and the stability of its currency. Consequently the optimal ex post response of the central bank might be to bail out the potential defaulter, to avert a sovereign default, as the lesser of two evils.[8]

As a consequence of the above, fiscal constraints in addition to restrictions on central bank financing of fiscal deficits are required to ensure that a monetary union is not undermined by the fiscal problems of one or more of its partner states. The primary motivation of these additional fiscal constraints is to ensure that national fiscal policies are managed on an ongoing basis in a manner which ensures fiscal sustainability, so that there is no risk of a partner state defaulting on its sovereign debt or having to seek accommodation from the common central bank to avoid a default. This is the motivation for the fiscal rules in the European Union's Stability and Growth Pact. Fiscal rules inevitably involve trade-offs between, on the one hand, the objective of aligning them with what is economically optimal for the monetary union and its partner states and, on the other hand, the need for rules which are transparent and enforceable and perceived as fair. What might be economically optimal might be far too complex to be transparent and enforceable. Buiter (2003) discusses these and other issues in the context of the desirable characteristics of fiscal rules.

The EAMU Protocol stipulates several quantitative fiscal criteria which partner States must comply with if they are to participate in the EAMU. The Protocol is silent on what, if any, fiscal rules will be applied to the participating partner States once the EAMU is actually implemented, but it would be logical if the same fiscal criteria which partner States have to meet in order to qualify for participating in the EAMU were also applied to those states on an ongoing basis once they become members of EAMU. The quantitative fiscal criteria in the EAMU Protocol are shown in Table 11.3. The Protocol also includes non-quantitative criteria

[8] Bovenberg et al. (1991) discuss these issues in relation to the European Monetary Union.

Table 11.3 Quantitative fiscal criteria in the EAMU Protocol

Article of Protocol	Quantitative Criteria
Article 5, indicative convergence criteria	Ceiling on fiscal deficits, excluding grants, of 6 per cent of GDP
	A tax to GDP ratio of 25 per cent
Article 6, macroeconomic convergence criteria	Ceiling on fiscal deficits, including grants, of 3% of GDP
	Ceiling on Gross Public Debt of 50% of GDP in NPV terms

Source: Protocol on the Establishment of the East African Community Monetary Union.

pertaining to fiscal policy, such as a requirement that partner States should harmonize and coordinate their fiscal policies and disclose information on fiscal policy to other partner states.

Unfortunately, applying fiscal rules in an optimal manner in the EAMU is likely to prove very challenging, not least because of heterogeneity among the six partner states in respect of borrowing capacities, economic growth rates, and volatility of revenues; a heterogeneity which may be intensified if more partner states become major oil or gas producers. Nevertheless, it would be very difficult to impose and enforce fiscal rules which are tailored to the specific requirements of each partner state, however optimal that might be in purely economic terms; fiscal rules which are uniform across the EAC are probably necessary to command political and public acceptance. However, the fiscal criteria in the EAMU Protocol may require some modification to strengthen their relevance to the challenges which are likely to face the monetary union and its partner states. These issues are discussed below.

11.3.1 The Debt Ceiling

Given that the primary motivation of fiscal rules is to ensure that public debt is sustainable, the debt ceiling is arguably the most important of the fiscal criteria in the EAMU Protocol. The ceiling is set at 50 per cent of GDP for the net present value (NPV) of total public debt, both external and domestic. Evaluating public debt sustainability in terms of its NPV is appropriate because, with the exception of Kenya, a large share of the external public debt of the EAC partner states is concessional and thus entails a lower debt burden than commercial debt. Using the nominal value of debt to evaluate the debt sustainability would overstate the actual debt burden, and thus overstate the risk of default, for countries which contract a substantial share of their external debt on concessional terms. Whether the 50 per cent of GDP threshold is set at a level low enough to ensure public debt sustainability for all of the partner states of the EAC is difficult to judge definitively, but it appears to be a reasonable benchmark, is consistent with some of the public debt strategies published by partner states,[9] and is in line with international benchmarks.[10]

11.3.2 Ceiling on the Fiscal Deficit Including Grants

The fiscal deficit including grants (revenue plus grants minus total expenditure), sometimes called the conventional fiscal deficit, is equivalent to the government's net financing requirement. The main reason for including this among the fiscal rules for a monetary union is that it supplements the public debt ceiling as a safeguard against unsustainable public debt.[11] There is a long-run relationship between the average level of the fiscal deficit as a per cent of GDP and the nominal public debt to GDP ratio, which depends on the long run average nominal growth of GDP. Given a nominal public debt to GDP ceiling of **B**, and a growth rate of nominal GDP of g, the long run average fiscal deficit to GDP ratio should be no larger than $B(g/(1+g))$. It thus makes sense to align the fiscal deficit rule with the public debt ceiling, using projections of long run nominal GDP growth.

Nominal GDP growth rates are the product of real GDP growth and the GDP deflator. Average real GDP growth rates among the EAC partner states over 2010–15 varied between 3.3 per cent for Burundi and 7.2 per cent for Rwanda.[12] With the exception of Burundi, which was affected by civil strife, all the other four countries achieved average real growth of at least 5 per cent. GDP deflators should be linked to inflation rates which, after the EAMU has been established, will be (at least in part) determined at the regional level by the common central bank. We don't know what numerical inflation target the future central bank will adopt, but 5 per cent would be a reasonable target and a figure lower than 5 per cent might not be feasible. Hence a projection of long-run average nominal GDP growth of around 10 per cent for each partner state appears plausible.

Using the formula noted above, with 10 per cent nominal GDP growth, a public debt (in nominal value) to GDP ceiling of 50 per cent allows an average fiscal deficit of up to 4.5 per cent of GDP, which is 1.5 percentage points higher than the target in the convergence criteria of the EAMU protocol. Furthermore, the public

[9] Uganda's Public Debt Management Framework, 2013, sets a benchmark for the NPV of public debt at under 50 per cent of GDP (Republic of Uganda, 2013).

[10] The Joint World Bank-IMF Debt Sustainability Framework for Low Income Countries applies thresholds for the NPV of external public debt which depend on the Country Policy and Institutional Assessments (CPIA) scores for the applicable country. The NPV of external debt to GDP threshold for a strong performer, with high CPIA ratings, is set at 50 per cent of GDP. As this threshold only applies to external debt, a country could meet this threshold but the NPV of its total public debt to GDP would be higher than 50 per cent if it also issues domestic debt.

[11] It is also relatively straightforward to estimate, not requiring complex technical judgments on the part of those making the estimates.

[12] Excluding South Sudan because data are not available for all of this period and growth rates for the years where data are available are very volatile because of the civil war.

debt ceiling is expressed in NPV terms rather than nominal terms, which allows a higher fiscal deficit to GDP ratio to be compatible with the debt ceiling for countries which contract part or all of their borrowing on concessional terms. For example, a country which contracts debt with an average 25 per cent grant element would be able to incur average fiscal deficits of 6 per cent of GDP over the long term without raising its public debt above the debt ceiling.

As such, it can be argued that the fiscal deficit including grants ceiling of 3 per cent of GDP in the macroeconomic convergence criteria of the EAMU Protocol isunnecessarily restrictive from the standpoint of ensuring public debt sustainability, especially for those countries in the EAC which contract part of their public debt on concessional terms. Furthermore, most of the EAC partner states have embarked on programmes to scale up public investment to improve public infrastructure, on roads, railways, electric power, etc. These objectives for public investment may not be compatible with a fiscal deficit ceiling of 3 per cent of GDP. Fiscal deficit targets which are not consistent with the fiscal objectives of governments will lack credibility because they are likely to be breached.

Buiter (2003) argues that, for a fiscal rule to be credible, governments must have strong internal incentives to comply with the rule and/or must be subject to an effective external disciplining mechanism. The internal incentives require that governments which breach the rule suffer adverse consequences, such as a rise in borrowing costs or a sovereign debt credit rating downgrade, because a breach of the rule signals a deterioration of public debt sustainability. But if the fiscal rule is set at a level which is excessively tight in terms of ensuring public debt sustainability, breaching the rule may not have adverse consequences, hence the internal incentives to comply with the rule will be weak. Furthermore, if all partner states have weak incentives to comply with the fiscal rule, the ability of a regional agency representing these partner states to enforce compliance by the partner states will be correspondingly weak; hence the external disciplining mechanism will be ineffective.

It would be better to set more feasible fiscal deficit ceilings while ensuring that they are consistent with long-run public debt sustainability, by setting a moderately higher deficit ceiling. In addition, it would be possible to accommodate better the interests of countries which contract concessional public debt by formulating the measure of the fiscal deficit which is subject to the ceiling in such a way as to include the grant element of concessional debt as an above the line budgetary resource, rather than as a financing item.

A major drawback with the use of a conventional fiscal deficit as a fiscal target is that it risks imparting a pro-cyclical bias to fiscal policy. If the fiscal deficit ceiling binds during normal economic conditions, a negative aggregate demand shock which adversely affects the tax base will widen the fiscal deficit, forcing the government, if it wants to remain compliant with the fiscal deficit ceiling, to cut its expenditure, thereby exacerbating the impact of the negative shock to demand.

Ideally the fiscal deficit ceiling should be expressed in terms of a structural (cyclically adjusted) fiscal deficit, which takes account of the impact of the economic cycle on public revenues and expenditures. This would at least allow the fiscal stance to be cyclically neutral, although it would not allow governments to run discretionary countercyclical fiscal policies in cases of economic downturns, unless they enter the downturn with the fiscal space to do so by running structural deficits which are smaller than those allowed by the fiscal rules.

Unfortunately there are major practical difficulties to estimating structural fiscal deficits in economies like those of the EAC; these include the difficulty in estimating potential output and, therefore, whether actual output is above or below potential (IMF, 2011). Estimates of structural fiscal deficits depend heavily on the judgements of those making the estimates; as such they are more vulnerable than the conventional measure of the deficit to being manipulated to accommodate the needs of governments. This is an issue where there is a clear trade-off between what is economically optimal (a structural measure of the fiscal deficit) and what is practical (a conventional measure). If a structural measure of the fiscal deficit is adopted by EAMU members, to replace or complement the conventional fiscal deficit, there would need to be some form of independent assessment, perhaps by a regional institution, of the estimates of cyclically adjusted deficits of each member state and whether they comply with the fiscal rules of the monetary union.

11.3.3 Fiscal Deficit Excluding Grants

The EAMU protocol includes, as an indicative target, a ceiling on the fiscal deficit excluding grants of 6 per cent of GDP. This implies that, if the ceiling on the fiscal deficit including grants of 3 per cent of GDP binds, grants can fund government spending of only 3 per cent of GDP at most. The importance of grants as a budgetary resource varies widely across the EAC. In the last three years grants averaged 6–8 per cent of GDP per annum in Burundi and Rwanda and over 10 per cent of GDP in South Sudan. In contrast budget grants have averaged less than 2 per cent of GDP in Kenya, Tanzania, and Uganda.

Given that the partner states are heterogeneous in terms of levels of development, per capita incomes and the magnitude of their tax bases, there are no inherent reasons for imposing a uniform ceiling, applicable to all partner states, on their fiscal deficits before grants. It is optimal for the less developed partner states of the EAC to utilize higher volumes of grants, as a share of their GDP, which should facilitate the convergence of their economies with those of the more developed partner states. Given that partner states already have to comply with a ceiling on the fiscal deficit including grants, which aims to address fiscal sustainability, the most compelling rationale for imposing a ceiling on the fiscal deficit excluding grants is that grant aid is more volatile than domestic revenues in aid dependent countries (Bulir and Hamann, 2003), hence an excessive reliance on grants might create vulnerabilities for the budget, forcing governments to resort to domestic borrowing in the event of unanticipated cutbacks in grant funding to avoid having to make disruptive expenditure cuts. However, the ceiling on the fiscal deficit excluding grants is a very crude instrument for mitigating these risks and is likely to prove over-restrictive for the poorer partner states of the EAC.

11.3.4 Tax to GDP Ceiling

The protocol imposes, as an indicative target, a tax to GDP ratio of 25 per cent. This is not a very credible target, as none of the partner states currently comes close to meeting it and three of the partner states are short of the target by more than 10 per cent of GDP. It is not obvious why a tax to GDP target should be necessary for a monetary union as there is no automatic link between the tax effort and public debt sustainability.

11.3.5 Fiscal Management in Oil Producing Economies

Ensuring long-term fiscal sustainability is particularly challenging for countries in which oil revenues comprise a substantial share of budget revenues. Currently only South Sudan falls into this category, but Uganda and Kenya are planning to begin production of oil over the medium term, although neither is likely to become as heavily dependent upon oil revenues as South Sudan. The volatility of global oil prices makes fiscal planning very difficult for two reasons. First, the real level of long-term global oil prices is very difficult to forecast, which means that oil producers face a great deal of uncertainty over the future magnitude of their oil revenues and thus the long-run sustainable level of public expenditure. Second, the short-term volatility in global oil prices can destabilize the domestic macroeconomy if volatility in public revenues is transmitted to volatility in public expenditures.[13] In a regional economic area such as the EAC, the volatility in the economy of an oil producer can be transmitted to its partner states through, for example, its demand for imports from those partner states, or demand for migrant labour from them.

For an economy dependent on oil revenues the fiscal deficit targets in the EAMU Protocol are not relevant for ensuring long-term fiscal sustainability. A country which can meet the fiscal deficit targets during an oil price boom

[13] As an example of the volatility in public revenues of economies dependent on oil revenues, the total public revenue of Chad fell from 23.2 per cent of GDP in 2011 to 8.7 per cent of GDP in 2016.

could find itself facing a fiscal crisis, with unsustainable borrowing, if oil prices slump. Furthermore, compliance with a conventional fiscal deficit target could jeopardize domestic macroeconomic stability if large falls in public revenue are matched by falls in public expenditure, and vice versa.

Instead of the conventional fiscal deficit, a more appropriate fiscal rule for an oil producer is a non-oil fiscal balance, which is defined as non-oil revenue plus grants minus total expenditure. A non-oil fiscal balance target would de-link government expenditure from the contemporaneous receipt of oil revenues, thereby helping to shield the macroeconomy from short term fluctuations in oil revenues. To ensure long-run fiscal sustainability, the non-oil fiscal deficit must be set at a level which can be funded from the long-term average sustainable level of oil revenues plus the sustainable rate of accumulation of public debt. For example, if, given average nominal GDP growth of 10 per cent, annual borrowing of 4.5 per cent of GDP is consistent with the public debt ceiling of 50 per cent of GDP (as discussed above), and the long-term average sustainable oil revenue amounts to 3 per cent of GDP, a non-oil fiscal deficit of 7.5 per cent of GDP would be consistent with long-term fiscal sustainability. However given the inherent uncertainty of future oil prices, it would be prudent to make very conservative estimates of long-term oil revenue inflows and to accumulate a substantial buffer of financial resources in the early years of oil production that can be drawn down if oil prices slump.

11.4 Aligning Exchange Rates Prior to the Introduction of the Single Currency

One of the most important prerequisites for EAMU is to align the bilateral exchange rates of the partner states so that they can be converted irrevocably into the common currency at rates which are sustainable for all partner states. The danger is that one or more countries will enter the common currency with an exchange rate that is overvalued or undervalued, which would jeopardize the internal and external balance of these countries, because its domestic price level relative to those of its partners would then be too high or too low to achieve sustainable macroeconomic balances.

Determining the optimal exchange rates at which to convert national currencies into the common currency is not a straightforward exercise. As shown in Figure 11.1, the exchange rates of the partner states over the last 10 years have been quite volatile, not just against the US dollar but against each other, as can be seen by the divergent trends of each county's exchange rate against the US dollar. The success of the EAMU will depend on reducing the volatility of bilateral exchange rates before the common currency is introduced, to lessen the probability that any individual country will join the common currency at an overvalued or

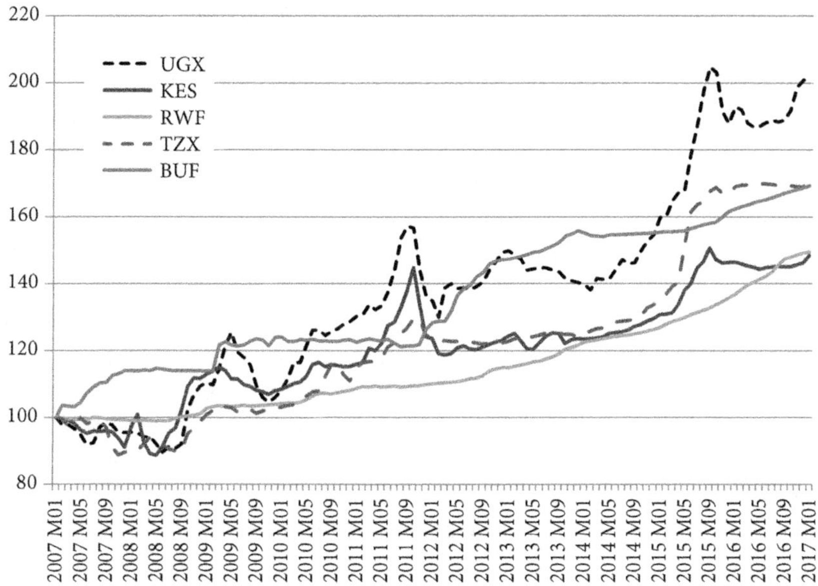

Figure 11.1 Exchange rate indices against the US dollar (January 2007 = 100) for the Burundi franc, Kenya shilling, Rwanda franc, Tanzania shilling, and Uganda shilling; January 2007–January 2017

Source: Bank of Uganda.

undervalued exchange rate; i.e. there must be exchange rate convergence within the EAC, which does not mean that the exchange rates of the partner states should be stable against third country currencies.

There are two complementary strategies for achieving exchange rate convergence within the EAC. The first is to align the inflation rates of the partner states on the grounds that differences in inflation rates are a major cause of divergence in bilateral exchange rates. Article 6 of the EAMU Protocol stipulates that all partner states should control their domestic inflation rates at 8 per cent or less. But convergence of inflation rates is unlikely to be sufficient to ensure sustainable exchange rate convergence, because real factors can also contribute to divergence of bilateral exchange rates. Hence the second leg of the strategy will involve an institutional mechanism for gradually aligning bilateral exchange rates in the run up to the introduction of the common currency.

The EAMU Protocol provides for the introduction of a mechanism for bringing about the conversion of the currencies of the partner states into a common currency but does not specify how this will be done in any detail.[14] Article 5 of

[14] Designing the common exchange rate mechanism will be the task of the East African Monetary Institute when it is established.

the EAMU Protocol states that, as a prerequisite for the monetary union, the partner states will 'introduce bands and gradually fix their bilateral exchange rates to facilitate the conversion of the currencies of the partner states to the East African currency unit'. The Schedule for the Realization of the Monetary Union which is an appendix to the Protocol, states that by 2022 the partner states will design and implement a common exchange rate mechanism which will include a phase of convergence during which the Partner States will implement managed float exchange rate regimes and then implement a phase of conversion during which the Council of Ministers will irrevocably fix the exchange rates among the partner states.

The conversion phase will involve each partner state managing its own exchange rate within bands against a common *numeraire*, which could be the currency of one of the partner states (the Deutschmark played this role in the European Exchange Rate Mechanism), or a basket of all the partner states' currencies. Bands would have to be set around the central rate, which would be progressively narrowed over time until each partner state's exchange rate with the common currency is irrevocably fixed. During this conversion period, the central banks of the partner states will confront the challenge of trying to meet two policy targets; their domestic target of inflation and an exchange rate target. If the exchange rate mechanism utilizes a basket of the partner states' currencies as *numeraire*, the monetary policies of the partner states could lose their nominal anchor, because there is no anchor to a third country currency such as the dollar or euro. This problem can be avoided if the EAC were to select one of the partner states to provide the *numeraire* for the exchange rate mechanism with its central bank then providing the nominal anchor (e.g. an inflation target) for all of the partner states, but this might not be politically acceptable to all the partner states.

As well as the choice of *numeraire* for the conversion period, key questions include the following. How should the bilateral exchange rates at which each partner state enters the common exchange rate mechanism be determined? How long should the conversion phase last? Should re-alignment of bilateral exchange rates be allowed during the conversion phase if the original alignment appears unsustainable? These questions are interrelated.

Adam et al. (2012) recommend that the conversion period should be short, lasting at most two quarters. They argue that a short conversion phase will 'reduce the scope for speculative attacks or asymmetric changes in real exchange rate fundamentals' (page 19) and also reduce the period under which the monetary policies of the partner states confront the inherent ambiguity of a dual anchor system. However, a short conversion period leaves little or no scope for re-alignment of bilateral exchange rates during the conversion period and, therefore, places a premium on the initial determination of bilateral exchange rates, at which each currency enters the common exchange rate mechanism, being appropriate. It runs the risk of locking one or more partner states into the common currency at a misaligned exchange rate.

A longer conversion phase could allow for some trial and error in determining bilateral exchange rates before they are irrevocably fixed. If a partner state cannot maintain its exchange rate within the bands around the central rate against the *numeraire*, or can only do so by running down its foreign currency reserves or raising domestic interest rates to levels which would jeopardize internal balance, the central rate could be adjusted (i.e. depreciated). A conversion phase lasting several years would allow each partner state to better understand how well its economy can adjust to asymmetric shocks without the benefit of nominal exchange rate flexibility, for example through wage and price flexibility. The drawback of a longer period, with the possibility of realignments, as noted by Adam et al. (2012), is that it would in effect entail each partner state operating an adjustable peg exchange rate regime, which is more vulnerable to speculative attacks than a credibly fixed exchange rate. If a longer conversion period were adopted, the EAC Partner States would have to decide how to provide a nominal anchor for their monetary policies which is consistent with both the exchange rate mechanism and the control of inflation.

11.5 The Challenge of Stabilization in the Face of Asymmetric Macroeconomic Shocks

Membership of a monetary union implies that each partner state irrevocably foregoes its own independent monetary and exchange rate policies. In addition, the fiscal policies of each partner state must unavoidably be constrained by the need for strict fiscal rules as discussed in Section 11.3. As a result, individual partner states will be highly circumscribed in their capacities to implement discretionary macroeconomic stabilization policies.

This lack of macroeconomic policy discretion might not matter if macroeconomic shocks are uniform across all six partner states. A uniform macroeconomic shock can be addressed by a common monetary policy and/or an adjustment in the common exchange rate. Unfortunately, there are no grounds for assuming that macroeconomic shocks within the EAC will be uniform, given that there are substantial differences between the individual economies of the partner states in terms of composition of production and exports, income levels, the magnitude of external capital flows, etc. The experience of the European Union since the global financial crisis should be salutary in this regard. While some economies have suffered severe and prolonged recession, others have operated at output levels close to their potential and the common monetary and exchange rate policy of the Eurozone has impeded the stabilization of some of these economies, especially those on the periphery, such as Greece, which need to restore their competitiveness.

Oil-related shocks are likely to be one potential cause of asymmetric shocks withe the EAC. A boom in oil prices would have opposite effects on the net oil exporters in the EAC and the net oil importers. The former would enjoy an increase in national income, principally through the channel of higher public revenues from oil, which will allow domestic spending to rise. A rise in domestic spending will require an appreciation of the real exchange rate to maintain internal balance. If the common nominal exchange rate does not appreciate, an appreciation of the real exchange rate can only be brought about by a rise in domestic inflation. To the extent that higher oil revenues are spent rather than being saved, the economy of the oil exporter will tend to overheat, unless the common central bank allows the nominal exchange rate to appreciate or tightens monetary policy. Conversely, the net oil importers will face a worsening of their external terms of trade (from higher oil prices) and a reduction in national income and, unless this is fully offset by increased demand for their exports from the booming oil economies within the EAC, their economies will require a depreciation of the common exchange rate and/or a loosening of monetary policy to restore internal and external balance. The optimal monetary and exchange rate combination for the oil exporters is appreciation or monetary tightening, while that for the oil importers is depreciation or monetary loosening. As noted in Section 11.3, the impact of oil price shocks on the economies of oil producers and the spill overs to other partner states, can be mitigated if the oil producers' fiscal policy is determined by targets for a non-oil fiscal deficit which insulates their public expenditures from volatility in oil revenues.

To some extent, adjustment to asymmetric shocks can be facilitated by wage and price flexibility. A high degree of wage and price flexibility (i.e. a steep aggregate supply curve) would facilitate economies to adjust to negative aggregate demand shocks with minimum loss of real output and employment, but that whether there is sufficient wage and price flexibility in each of the EAC partner states to allow this is not clear. Furthermore, wage and price flexibility would not prevent economies undergoing a boom in aggregate demand from overheating.

Given that a common monetary and exchange rate policy cannot be optimal for all economies in the event of an asymmetric shock, what options are available for mitigating the impact of asymmetric shocks within a monetary union? There are three potential options.

First, individual countries could use counter-cyclical fiscal policy. Tightening fiscal policy to offset a positive shock to aggregate demand would not be constrained by the fiscal targets discussed in Section 11.3, as these targets are ceilings on public debt and fiscal deficits. But if governments are to use fiscal policy to offset a negative shock to aggregate demand they would need to create the necessary fiscal space for more expansionary fiscal policies. To avoid breaching the fiscal targets of the monetary union, the fiscal stance in normal periods would have to be well within the EAMU fiscal ceilings. For example, the NPV of public debt prior to a negative shock would have to be much lower than the 50 per cent of GDP ceiling stipulated in article 6 of the EAMU Protocol and the conventional fiscal deficit would have to be less than 3 per cent of GDP.[15] It would be possible to allow partner states to breach the fiscal ceilings on a temporary basis when faced with temporary negative macroeconomic shocks, but this introduces elements of judgement into the implementation of the fiscal rules which makes them more vulnerable to abuse and could undermine their credibility.

Second, stabilization could be facilitated by the movement of factors of production within the EAC. For example, an economy experiencing a boom could attract migrant labour from other economies within the EAC which would facilitate output to be raised and inflation kept under control. At the same time the outflow of migrant labour from an economy experiencing a downturn will reduce unemployment and help to prevent deflation in that economy. The greater is the degree of factor mobility within the EAC, the more compatible will be a common monetary and exchange rate policy with the stabilization requirements of the individual economies of the EAC. As Robert Mundell argued more than 50 years ago, 'an essential ingredient of a common currency... is a high degree of factor mobility' (Mundell, 1961, p. 661).

Third, the EAC could establish a common stabilization fund, which will channel financial resources to those economies suffering from negative macroeconomic shocks. Article 10 of the EAMU Protocol provides for the establishment of 'a stabilisation facility to provide assistance to a Partner State experiencing or threatened with a severe exogenous economic shock'. Transfer payments from a stabilization facility would allow the recipients to expand the fiscal stance to offset a shock to private spending or to avoid the need to cut public expenditure in the event that the negative shock adversely affects government revenue. To accumulate resources in a stabilization facility, partner states would have to make regular payments into it during 'normal or good' periods. There will need to be strict rules covering payments into the fund (e.g. each government should pay x per cent of annual revenue) and very clear criteria for making payments from the fund to economies in need. However, as has been shown in the European Union, without political union and a strong sense of a shared identity among the populations of a monetary union, intra-regional financial transfers will face political opposition in some of the partner states if their populations feel that they are subsidizing other partner states.

11.6 Concluding Remarks

The preconditions for a successful monetary union in East Africa are very demanding. Economic integration is still relatively shallow in the EAC, with

[15] This means that governments would have to maintain structural fiscal deficits, after grants, which are less than 3 per cent of GDP.

intra-regional trade in goods and services amounting to a relatively small share of the region's total trade. Much more needs to be done to remove all policy induced obstacles to economic integration, including the still ubiquitous trade distorting non-tariff measures and barriers to free movement of labour and capital. Protection of national product and labour markets within the EAC will impede the growth of dynamic, internationally competitive, economies and obviate the rationale for a monetary union.

The key macroeconomic policy foundations for a successful monetary union include credible fiscal rules to ensure the fiscal sustainability of each partner state, a mechanism to ensure that each partner state enters the monetary union at a sustainable exchange rate relative to its partners and institutional mechanisms to facilitate the adjustment of individual economies within the monetary union to asymmetric macroeconomic shocks.

If the common monetary policy is to command public confidence, credible and enforceable fiscal rules are required to provide safeguards against unsustainable public debts of partner states. The fiscal rules should include quantitative ceilings on public debt and fiscal deficits as well as qualitative mechanisms to enhance sound fiscal management. The fiscal deficit targets should allow, to the extent that this is consistent with fiscal sustainability, member states to pursue their strategic fiscal objectives (e.g. for infrastructure spending). It will be necessary to allow some room for governments to accommodate negative shocks to public revenue without having to resort to pro-cyclical fiscal tightening. For those partner states which are, or will become, major oil producers, the fiscal rules should be complemented with targets for the non-oil fiscal deficit, to insulate public spending and thus aggregate demand from the volatility of oil revenues. This is not a problem for the oil producers alone, because volatility in their economies could have major spillovers for the economies of the non-oil producers.

A major technical challenge will be to design a common exchange rate mechanism for the conversion phase of the preparation of EAMU which can align the bilateral exchange rates of the partner states so that they can be converted irrevocably into a common currency without leaving any partner state with an unsustainable domestic price level relative to its partners. Key questions which need to be addressed are how to determine the exchange rates at which each partner state will enter the common exchange rate mechanism, how will the *numeraire* of the mechanism be determined, how long the conversion phase will last and what scope will exist for re-adjustment of the bilateral exchange rate of any partner state during the conversion phase if the initial exchange rate at which the partner state entered the mechanism appears unsustainable.

Unfortunately, the economies of the partner states are quite heterogeneous and are likely to be subject to asymmetric macroeconomic shocks which cannot be effectively addressed through common monetary and exchange rate policies. This potentially creates an element of time inconsistency in the macroeconomic framework of the EAMU. The principle that a monetary union should incorporate institutional mechanisms to mitigate the adverse impact of asymmetric shocks to partner states' economies is indisputable, but designing effective and politically acceptable ways to do this could prove difficult. There are essentially three main channels through which individual economies can adjust to asymmetric shocks.

The first is through fiscal policy to the extent that this is compatible with the fiscal rules of the monetary union, which provides an argument for allowing the fiscal rules to be sufficiently flexible to accommodate at least modestly countercyclical fiscal policies. However, if partner states are to be allowed room within the fiscal rules to implement countercyclical fiscal policies, there is a need for independent monitoring of their fiscal policies, ideally by a regional institution, to ensure that this room is not abused and puts long-term fiscal sustainability in jeopardy.

The second channel is through free movement of factors of production; one of the key rationales for a monetary union in a given region is that factors of production are fully mobile within that region but immobile across its external borders. Finally, adjustment to asymmetric shocks can be facilitated by a common stabilization fund, into which each partner state would pay a predetermined share of its revenues, with transparent criteria for making payments to a partner state in the event that its economy suffers an asymmetric negative macroeconomic shock.

The EAMU Protocol envisages that EAMU will begin in 2024. However the institutional and policy requirements for EAMU are very technically complex and very demanding of scarce public resources. The partner states are already behind the schedule set out in the annex attached to the Protocol. Given that it is imperative to establish EAMU on secure foundations, it may be necessary to accelerate the implementation of the measures needed to both ensure that all of the convergence criteria for the EAMU are met and that the requisite institutional structures are put in place.

References

Adam, C., Kessy, P., Kombe, C., and O'Connell, S.A. (2012), 'Exchange rate arrangements in the transition to East African Monetary Union', International Growth Centre.

Bovenberg, A. L., Kremers, J. J. M. and Masson, P. R. (1991), 'Economic and monetary union in Europe and constraints on national budgetary policies'. *IMF Staff Papers*, Vol. 38, No. 2, pp. 374–98.

Buiter, W. H. (2003), 'Ten commandments for a fiscal rule in the E(M)U', *Oxford Review of Economic Policy*, Vol. 19, No. 1, pp. 84–99.

Bulir, A. and Hamann, A. J. (2003), 'Aid volatility: An empirical assessment', *IMF Staff Papers*, Vol. 50, No. 1, pp. 64–89.

Calabrese, L. and Eberhard-Ruiz, A. (2016), 'What types of non-tariff barriers affect the East African Community?', Overseas Development Institute, London.

International Monetary Fund (2011), *Managing the Macroeconomic Convergence Process Ahead of Monetary Union.* Report prepared for the East African Community.

Kirk, R. (2012), 'Addressing trade restrictive non-tariff measures on goods trade in the East African Community', in Paul Brenton and Gozde Isik (eds), *De-fragmenting Africa: Deepening Regional Trade Integration in Goods and Services*, World Bank, pp. 99–14.

Mundell, R. A. (1961), 'A theory of optimal currency areas', *American Economic Review*, Vol. 51, No. 4, pp. 657–65.

Republic of Uganda (2013), Public Debt Management Framework, Kampala.

World Bank (2013), *Uganda Economic Update: Bridges across Borders*, Kampala.

PART II
THE CENTRAL BANK OF KENYA

12
The Early Days of the Central Bank of Kenya

Mahesh Gheewala

12.1 Introduction

In January 1962, I joined Government service as an economist/statistician in the Statistics Department of the Kenyan Treasury. In 1975, I retired as Deputy Secretary in Charge of the Monetary and Fiscal Division. Throughout my tenure, I handled many economic, monetary, fiscal, and other matters, and was instrumental in initiating and promoting major initiatives, and for their successful implementation. I happened to be Treasury Officer responsible for establishment of the Central Bank of Kenya.

This chapter aims to share with you my experience working at the frontier of policy and practice right from the first stages of the decision to establish a central bank of Kenya and to issue the Kenyan currency.

The narrative in the chapter is detailed and includes: Decision to establish a central bank in Kenya and issue Kenyan currency (12.2); discussions around the name of the new institution (12.3); independence of the central bank and relations with the treasury (12.4); capital and ownership of the central bank (12.5); government borrowings from the central bank (12.6); rudimentary monetary policy pre-central bank (12.7); monetary policy instruments in the Central Bank Act (12.8); foreign exchange reserves and its composition (12.9); location of the central bank (12.10); matters discussed in context of Kenya currency (12.11); revival of Nairobi Stock Exchange and government bonds' secondary market (12.12); my working relationship with Dr Baranski and decisions taken by us (12.13); establishment and strengthening of the commercial banking sector (12.14); establishment and strengthening of the re-insurance and insurance sector (12.15); devaluation of sterling, subsequent collapse of sterling area and related issues (12.16); establishment of structures to promote foreign private investments (12.17); the World Bank and IMF meetings in Kenya (12.18); other matters of interest I handled (12.19); and concluding remarks and honour (12.20).

Mahesh Gheewala, *The Early Days of the Central Bank of Kenya* In: *50 Years of Central Banking in Kenya: Regional and Global Perspectives*. Edited by: Patrick Njoroge and Victor Murinde, Oxford University Press (2021).
 DOI: 10.1093/oso/9780198851820.003.0012

12.2 Decision to Establish a Central Bank in Kenya and Issue Kenyan Currency

12.2.1 First News about the Decision

On his return in early 1965 from a routine inter state Budget meeting in Tanzania, the late Mr John Michuki, the Permanent Secretary to the Treasury, informed me that Tanzania had notified us that they had decided to establish their own Central Bank; to have a separate Tanzanian currency, and to impose exchange control against Sterling Area countries, and that they intended to announce these decisions during the June 1965 Budget Speech. He added that discussions between the Kenyan Government and Uganda to continue some form of monetary union were to be abandoned, because of practical considerations. Left with no alternative, both Kenya and Uganda also agreed to establish their own separate Central Banks, issue their own separate currencies and impose exchange control against Sterling Area countries. He further informed me that steps had been taken to secure technical assistance from the International Monetary Fund (IMF) for Central Bank matters, and from the Bank of England for Exchange Control matters. He cautioned me that these matters should be considered Top Secret. It was clear in my mind that these three decisions, and the split of one currency area, would bring a sea change not only in the fiscal and monetary policies and structure in Kenya, but also in future relations between Kenya, Uganda, and Tanzania, fondly known as East Africa.

Prior to these decisions, the East African Currency Board (EACB) was responsible for some Central Bank functions. Although the structure and legislation of EACB did not allow it to perform usual Central Bank functions, it performed some limited functions, such as currency issuance of the legal tender in Kenya, Uganda, and Tanzania; matters related to foreign exchange reserves; and even acting as a clearing house for commercial banks. It also provided short-term crop finance.

I was the Kenyan National Treasury Officer responsible for other Central Bank functions including monetary policy matters; public debt; foreign exchange; IMF matters; Special Drawing Rights; licensing of commercial banks and supervising and dealing with problems of commercial banks and other financial institutions. I was responsible for several Acts of Parliament that were anticipated to be part of Central Bank functions, including the General Loan and Stock Act, Foreign Exchange Control Act, Banking Act, Bill of Exchange Act, Cheque Act, Money Lenders Act, Hire Purchase Act, Unit Trusts Act, Trustee Act, etc.

Exchange control against the Sterling Area was imposed in June 1965. Legislation establishing the Central Bank of Kenya received Presidential Assent on 24 March 1965. The Central Bank of Kenya was inaugurated on 14 September 1966, and on the same day the Kenyan national currency was issued.

We successfully implemented each of these three decisions within a short time span which amazed many observers.

12.2.2 Dr Leon Baranski

One morning in mid-1965, the late Mr John Michuki called me to his office and introduced me to a tall smiling elderly gentleman, Dr Leon Baranski, as the IMF Advisor to the Kenya Government, on establishment of Central Bank, and told me that I should give him all the assistance he needed. An office in the Old Treasury building on the fourth floor, close to mine, was organized for him. He joked about the size of the office, and the lack of independent secretarial assistance. Subsequently, I came to view Dr Baranski as something of a father figure. Dr Baranski informed me that a delegation from the IMF, bringing with it a draft Central Bank Act, would arrive shortly. Mr Michuki had asked me fully to assist them, and to seek the Attorney General's advice on legislation. Thus, I became the main Treasury Officer responsible for Central Bank formation and legislation.

12.2.3 The Legislation

The IMF delegation promptly arrived, with a draft Act prepared by their Banking Division in Washington, titled the 'Currency and Bank of Kenya Act'. They informed me similar drafts had been submitted to Tanzania and Uganda, and that other IMF delegations were discussing them with Tanzanian and Ugandan authorities.

Because of my background in fiscal matters, monetary policy and its instruments, and financial institutions, I was familiar with the structure proposed by the IMF. I also reviewed materials held in the Treasury Library, detailing Central Bank Acts of several countries.

I prepared a comprehensive brief for Mr Michuki. We had detailed discussions on (amongst other things) the implications for the private banking and trading sector of the split of one EACB and one money market into three separate currencies; the future status of the erstwhile EACB, EACB's proposal to establish a Central Bank of East Africa, and short-term crop financing facility provided by them. Mr Michuki said the proposal to establish Central Bank of East Africa had been overtaken by events, and that discussions were taking place on the formation of a high-level Committee to consider and recommend ways of maintaining the advantages of a common market, despite the introduction of three separate national currencies. Mr Michuki unequivocally told me that we should give top priority to establishing a Central Bank in Kenya as Tanzania, having started earlier, was moving fast to establish its own Central Bank. He further informed me that it had now been decided to announce the decisions in the June Budget.

I started comprehensive discussions with the IMF Team and Dr Baranski on the draft Act, with the involvement of Mr Michuki, as required, and in consultation with the former Permanent Secretary and now Advisor to the Treasury John Butter and Oliver Knowles, Senior Deputy Secretary as needed. The Attorney General's Office was involved on drafting matters. After the principles were agreed the draft Act was sent to the Attorney General's Chambers (late 1965) for further necessary legal action to enact it.

12.3 Discussions Around the Name of the New Institution

12.3.1 The English Name

During initial discussions of the IMF Draft, the issue of the name of the new institution arose. Various options were discussed, and the IMF delegation informed me that the names suggested in the draft legislation sent to Tanzania and Uganda were 'Bank of Tanzania' and 'Bank of Uganda'. The IMF's view, accordingly, was that we should call the new institution 'Bank of Kenya', on the grounds of similarity to the Bank of Tanzania and the Bank of Uganda, and to the Bank of England (the Sterling Area Central Bank). Another option suggested was to call the new institution the 'Reserve Bank of Kenya', following the Reserve Bank of India. Dr Baranski, however, was firmly of the opinion that we should use the name the 'Central Bank of Kenya', on the grounds of simplicity, and that since the Bank would be operating internationally, this would be understood all over the world. He also advised that this name would correctly represent what the new institution was designed to do.

12.3.2 The Kiswahili Name

Mr Michuki and I discussed the possibility of using a Swahili name, and I suggested a translation for Central Bank of Kenya of 'Banki ya Katakati'. Mr Michuki asked me to speak to the late Tom Mboya, who at that time was the Minister for Economic Planning and Development. The Minister smiled at my translation, saying that it was a literal translation, but did not convey the true meaning. In his view, he said, the correct Swahili name was 'Banki Kuu ya Kenya'.

Dr Baranski was not in favour of two names, namely Central Bank of Kenya and Banki Ku ya Kenya. He advised that to 'avoid confusion' internationally we should only have the English name. I briefed Dr Baranski, however, on nationalistic feelings, and he accepted that the Swahili name could also be included in the legislation. It was agreed, accordingly, that the new institution would be called the 'Central Bank of Kenya', and that the Act establishing it would only be known as the 'Central Bank of Kenya Act'. It was further agreed, however, that the new institution would also be known as Banki Kuu ya Kenya, and that a suitable Clause to that effect would be included in the Act.

12.3.3 Which Name Should Take Precedence?

Subsequently, the issue arose as to whether the 'Central Bank of Kenya' or 'Banki Kuu ya Kenya' should be used first. Dr Baranski repeated his advice, that to avoid confusion internationally we should only use the English name. This was not, however, agreed to by Mr Michuki and myself—we felt that the institution should not have a Swahili name which was not used. Dr Baranski suggested that if both the names were to be used, the English name should appear first. We agreed, and thus, when the Central Bank stationery was first printed, it showed the English title first, and the Swahili second.

12.3.4 Which Name to be Used on Kenyan Currency?

The same issue arose in the case of currency. Mr Michuki was firmly of the view that, since Kenyan currency was for circulation in Kenya, there should be no objection to the Swahili name appearing first. Dr Baranski agreed, and accordingly it was decided that, on Kenyan currency notes, the name first appearing would be 'Banki Kuu ya Kenya', followed by 'Central Bank of Kenya'.

12.4 Independence of Central Bank and Relations with Treasury

12.4.1 Initial Discussions

A lot of discussions took place on powers of the Treasury, and Independence of the Central Bank. Dr Baranski and the IMF favoured considerable independence being given to the Central Bank from Treasury/Central Government control. Mr Michuki, however, favoured closer supervision and control. He argued that since any loss incurred by the Central Bank would represent a charge on the Government's Consolidated Fund, the Treasury should not abdicate its responsibility to the Consolidated Fund, and to Parliament. He also argued that since Treasury was responsible for all financial and monetary matters, it could not delegate a significant part of that responsibility to an institution that was unelected and unaccountable to Parliament. For the purposes of legislation, the issue revolved around two specific matters: first, the appointment of the Governor; Deputy Governor and Board of Directors, and second, whether the Central Bank should be subject to Treasury directions?

12.4.2 Powers to Appoint Governor, Deputy Governor and Board of Directors

The Treasury position was that the Governor, Deputy Governor, and Board of Directors should be appointed by the Minister of Finance. Dr Baranski insisted that not only the Governor and the Deputy Governor but also the Board of Directors of the Central Bank should be appointed by the highest political Office, being that of the President, as the Head of State. Dr Baranski also rejected our suggestion that the Governor and the Deputy Governor should be appointed by the President on the recommendations of the Minister. In separate discussions with the IMF delegation, I privately pointed out to them that the Bank of England, for example, was subject to directions from the UK Treasury, and that there could be times when the requirements of State policies were different from the requirements of strict monetary policies—and that in Kenya, State priorities shall prevail irrespective of any legal constraints. I also pointed out that though the Minister for Finance was the Chief Advisor to the President on all financial matters, but if Treasury was not involved in appointments, these were likely to take place without proper consultation. Accordingly, it would be better to have a system of checks and balances, and while it was appropriate for the Central Bank to be independent, there would be dangers inherent in it being too independent. We could not know who in the future would head the institution, and absolute power could be counterproductive. Other suggestions included that that Board of Directors could be appointed by the Minister, or on his recommendation—we confidentially understood that this was likely to be the position in both Uganda and Tanzania. However, this compromise suggestion was also not acceptable to Dr Baranski.

12.4.3 Relations between the Central Bank and the Treasury

Mr Michuki's position was that the Treasury was responsible for the country's financial and monetary matters, and that we could not allow the establishment of an independent, unaccountable, unelected parallel body to control financial and monetary matters. The Treasury view was that it should have supervision and control powers on the Central Bank, as it had with other Government institutions. This was to be achieved by Treasury retaining instruction and veto powers over the Central Bank. Dr Baranski and the IMF, however, objected to the Central Bank being treated as a Government institution under the control of the Treasury, even to the extent of considering that the remuneration of the Board of Directors or staff of the Central Bank should be fixed by the Treasury or subject to its approval. His view was that there should be no control or pressure by the Treasury on any staff or officers of the Central Bank, observing that this route had often been used in other countries to pressurize a central bank or its staff to tow a particular government line, which is usually driven primarily by political considerations. Dr Baranski gave examples of how government control over other countries' central bank and monetary policies had resulted in uncontrollable inflationary pressures, and declining living standards.

12.4.4 Dr Baranski Threatens to Resign

These discussions were spirited. At one-point Dr Baranski threatened to resign if any clause was included in the Central Bank Act that would give the Treasury control over the Central Bank, and clearly felt strongly on the issue. I had a long discussion with Mr Michuki. Dr Baranski's threat to resign had put the Treasury in a very difficult position—his resignation would delay the establishment of the Bank, which was inconceivable in view of the time table to which we were working. Subsequently, Mr Michuki informed me that he had inquired but was informed that a replacement could not be easily found.

12.4.5 Concessions by the Treasury

Mr Michuki conceded that the Governor, Deputy Governor and Board of Directors should be appointed by the President. It was also agreed that the Governor would be the Chief Executive Officer of the Bank, responsible for all staff and financial matters and only subject to policies laid down by the Board of the Central Bank. It was agreed Central Bank would determine its own procedures, and that the Central Bank could exercise all central banking functions without defining what these precisely were (although I was told these would include normal central bank functions such as acting as a clearing house, protection of depositors, etc.).

12.4.6 Concessions by Dr Baranski

In return, and in view of the strongly held Treasury position, Dr Baranski agreed the Governor of the Central Bank would not have absolute and unilateral powers on financial and monetary matters but would be subject to the governance and oversight of the Board of the Central Bank. Further Dr Baranski agreed that the Treasury representative on the Central Bank Board could request a Board meeting at any time; would form part of quorum i.e. no Board meeting could be held without the Treasury representative, and that the Treasury representative would have a right to suspend Board resolutions/vote and refer the matter to the Minister of Finance for a decision. However, to maintain the status of the Governor, it was agreed that he should also have the same right of veto. Further it was agreed that there would be communication channels between the Central Bank and the Treasury on all important monetary and other fiscal matters.

12.4.7 Other Matters Agreed between the Treasury and the IMF Delegation

After these issues had been agreed, most of the subsequent discussions were left to me and the IMF delegation, with the involvement of Dr Baranski only as and when required. I kept Mr Michuki informed of all important matters.

In subsequent discussions between me and the IMF delegates it was further agreed that the Central Bank could only appoint an auditor after prior approval of the Treasury; the Treasury could ask the Government Auditor General to audit the accounts of the Central Bank; the Governor and the Deputy Governor would not engage in business activities save with the permission of the President; that the Bank would not get involved in commercial activities as was the case in some developing countries; the President would have powers to terminate the appointments of the Governor, Deputy Governor or a Board Member if any of them became for any reason incapable of performing the functions of the Central Bank; and the licensing of commercial banks and financial institutions would be retained by the Treasury. Some currency matters were also reserved for approval by the Treasury.

The IMF delegates and myself considered various other provisions included in the draft Act, which were in the main procedural and not controversial, and were mostly adopted accordingly. Other provisions, on the winding up of the EACB, were the same as those contained in the Ugandan and Tanzanian Acts, and were approved by the EACB. There was some discussion on Objects related to Government's development effort, and on the Central Bank's financial year, which the Treasury preferred to be the same as Government's financial year, which was agreed.

All of the foregoing was included in the Central Bank Act.

12.5 Capital and Ownership of the Bank

The IMF delegation preferred the Bank to have substantial paid up capital, in order to assure it of the necessary standing both locally and internationally, and to meet the Bank's establishment costs. However, the Treasury was reluctant to allocate large sums. I informed Mr Michuki that I had been informed that the EACB was likely to provide substantial amounts to help fund the capitalization, as they had done in the case of contributions to the IMF; the World Bank and African Development Bank. Rough estimates of the cost of establishing the Central Bank were produced, and it was decided, for the purposes of the Attorney General's Office and Parliamentary requirements, to mention an initial cost figure of Shs.12 million. Finally, it was agreed that the Bank's authorized capital on establishment should be Shs.26 million, and the paid-up capital should be Shs.13 million, half the Bank's authorized capital. I was confidentially told by an IMF delegate the authorized capital was likely to be lower than that of the Central Bank of Uganda, but higher than that of Tanzania. The Treasury received from the EACB the bulk of its contributions to the Bank's capital.

It was also agreed that the paid-up capital of the Central Bank would be owned by the Permanent Secretary to the Treasury. Because of the position taken by the Treasury on cash contributions to the Central Bank, I had prepared a note for Mr Michuki, indicating the substantial returns Treasury would receive from the Central Bank. It was agreed to include a Clause in the Central Bank Act on transfer of profits of the Central Bank to the Treasury.

12.6 Government Borrowings from the Bank

12.6.1 The Flow of Funds

In the context of flow of funds, the Treasury view was that as a banker to the Government, the Central Bank should not only have a right to its deposits, but should also have an obligation to lend as and when the Treasury was short of funds. This was as per the position with the Government's then current banker. Treasury was also of the view that the Bank should help finance not only shortfalls in the Government's short term and seasonal needs but also its development plan. Dr Baranski and the IMF delegation agreed that advances to Treasury were a legitimate function of the Bank. However, they insisted that there must be a limit to direct and indirect borrowings by the Government, in order to ensure compliance with the Bank's Objects clause. He also repeated the dangers of reckless borrowing by a Government. Treasury did not object to this limitation.

I informed the IMF delegation that in Kenya the budgetary policy was prudent, and aimed for a balanced budget. Recurrent expenditure was financed by recurrent revenues (which we considered transfer of savings within the country); development expenditure was financed by foreign loans and grants (which we considered transfer of savings from foreign countries to Kenya); and local borrowings was mainly from the National Social Security Fund; pensions and provident funds; life assurance companies; the Post Office Savings Bank, etc. (which, again, we considered to be the transfer of savings within the country). I noted that we also tried to generate a surplus in the recurrent budget to be used for development expenditure. IMF Article IV Consultations had always been happy with our policies.

There was some discussion on what should be the limit of Government borrowings and period of advances. Should the limit be static or increase in line with Government revenues? I had confidentially been informed by the IMF delegation that the limit of Government borrowings in Tanzania and in Uganda was likely to be pegged to Government revenue. There was some discussion but no definite conclusion on the definition of 'Government revenue'. Treasury also asked what would be the position if the Government revenues fell. It was agreed a fixed amount would be simpler. The Treasury considered that they could always seek an increase to this fixed amount, by an amendment to the Act.

Accordingly, the relevant Clause in the Central Bank Act only stated that the Central Bank may make direct advances to the Government. No purpose was included. Thus, the direct advances could be to meet development needs, for general budgetary support, for revenue short fall, or for short-term crop financing.

Sometimes in late 1972, to accommodate expansionary policies adopted by the Treasury, and after an agreement was reached on definition of revenue, an amendment was made to this Section to enable the Government to borrow up to 25 per cent of its revenues as certified by the Auditor General.

12.6.2 First Direct Advance from the Central Bank to the Treasury

I arranged the first direct advance on an I-owe-you (IOU) basis without a fixed repayment date—it was considered that such an advance would support the weakening economy without risking unnecessary inflation. An interest rate of 3 per cent was fixed.

12.6.3 Short-Term Crop Financing

I briefed the IMF delegation about the Government-owned Cereals and Sugar Finance Corporation, of which I was Chairman. I appraised them that this Corporation was responsible for providing finance for guaranteed minimum returns, to maize farmers and sugar equalization funds. Maize farmers were mainly local farmers, and this was the most important source of credit for them. After crops had been harvested and sold, advances made by the Corporation were usually repaid. Thus, the finance facility provided by the Corporation was seasonal, and funds were revolving funds. The Corporation relied on short term borrowings. I briefed the delegation about crop finance under the EACB, and noted that commercial banks provided short-term crop finance by moving funds between East African countries or borrowing from their head offices as required. I had expected inter-territorial support would cease following a split of the currency union, and believed that in its role as banker to the Government, the Central Bank would have to take on this responsibility. It was agreed, accordingly, that the Central Bank could provide a short-term finance facility.

However, there was drought in two successive seasons. Most of the farmers were either unable or refused to repay advances made to them. Waiving of interest did not help. Fraudulent claims increased. I discussed the matter with Mr Michuki. Since the ultimate liability of the Corporation was with the Consolidated Fund, I persuaded Mr Michuki to agree that in future, the responsibility to finance minimum guaranteed returns should be of the Treasury, and not the Corporation.

12.7 Rudimentary Monetary Policy Pre-Central Bank

12.7.1 IMF Delegation

I briefed IMF delegation on the rudimentary monetary policy instruments available to me at the time. The EACB lacked Central Bank instruments of monetary policy. They had powers to issue currency, but the currency issued by them was not Kenya specific—it was legal tender in the whole of East Africa. They had no specific powers to control the credit system. The credit and issue of currency system was a passive reflection of the balance of payments position of each country. The EACB's legal structure provided no powers to control interest rates. Most of its operations were non-responsive to the economic and financial needs of Kenya, Uganda, and Tanzania. I mentioned to the IMF delegation that, nonetheless, within these constraints I, in Kenya, had been operating an indirect, rudimentary, pragmatic, and situation specific monetary policy. I said the need of the hour was to promote growth.

12.7.2 Interest Rates

First, we had a low interest rates policy. I informed them about some pre-Independence understanding between the Treasury and commercial banks which capped their deposit and lending interest rates. This was included in the Bankers' Agreement, and the maximum lending rate chargeable by a commercial bank was 9 per cent. My request for a copy was not accepted, and therefore, in the absence of details, I had agreed that the maximum interest rate should be 9 per cent. I told the IMF delegation that, as far as the market was concerned, we had used interest and yield rates on Government bonds to cap and maintain a general control of interest rates. Interest rates and gross yields on Government bonds were in single digits. The interest on deposits at the Post Office Savings Bank was kept tax free. This was especially because this represented the only savings and deposit and monetary contact facility available to local people.

12.7.3 Increase in Bank Deposits and Credit Base

Our second policy related to maintenance and expansion of the credit base. I briefed the IMF delegation that in apprehension of Kenya becoming independent, investment activities had declined. Substantial funds were transferred to sterling denominated countries by the expatriate community, reducing deposits with banks and financial institutions. The money supply contracted. Thus, the credit base became smaller. This was compounded by the British Government withdrawing their pre-Independence financial support to the Kenyan Budget. All these factors had had a negative effect on our foreign exchange, and banks' deposits and credit base. I appraised the IMF delegation that by following positive and friendly private investments policies, we had successfully managed to reverse this trend. The land transfer loans agreed by the British Government for former settler farmers was marginally positive for foreign exchange. Under the EACB system this automatically increased money supply in Kenya. Availability of credit also increased as the settler farmers repaid their bank loans. The Cereals and Sugar Finance Corporation also increased credit to maize farmers. Foreign private investments were actively promoted. I issued Foreign Investments Protection Certificates to commercial banks to encourage them to borrow from their head offices, thereby increasing the potential credit base. A new Division in the Treasury had been set up actively to secure foreign loans and grants to finance Development projects. We ensured there were minimum leakages in our foreign loans and grants agreements. I told the delegation that the basic objective was to promote investments and growth in Kenya, with the ancillary benefits of an increase in bank deposits and the credit base.

12.7.4 Protect Financial Institutions and Depositors

Thirdly, I briefed the delegation on our policy to protect financial institutions and depositors. We had successfully implemented policies to stabilise the banking sector following false rumours resulting in a run on an international branch bank in Kenya. Rumours had started to circulate in Nairobi that a bank was about to fail—this was in the early 1960s, before currencies and banking systems were split—after the bank's branch in a small town in Tanzania did not have enough cash to meet a large withdrawal that had been requested. The resulting rumours gave rise to large withdrawals from Kenya branches of the bank in 'trouble', and transfer of accounts to other banks. We persuaded other banks to organise credit lines for the bank concerned, and also secured their agreement that they would decline to accept deposits in cash or transfer of accounts from the bank in 'trouble'. Armed with credit lines the bank met all demands for withdrawals promptly. This restored confidence—after Treasury intervention, the rumours were proved to be false and stability returned in a few days.

12.7.5 Protection of Building Societies and Their Depositors

I also furnished the IMF delegation with examples of how we had protected building societies that experienced substantial withdrawals of deposits by expatriates. The UDI Rhodesian Crisis had affected the most important building society operating in Kenya, First Permanent Building Society. It had been split from Rhodesian Head Office with the help of the Commonwealth Development Corporation, and subsequently the Housing Finance Company took over the business of the First Permanent Building Society. Separately, the Savings and Loans Society ran into difficulties, and I organized for the Kenya Commercial Bank to acquire it. The East African Building Society (EABS) had also been on the verge of collapse until, in consultation with the Attorney General's Chambers, we drew up an agreement whereby National Assembly Members could open savings accounts with EABS, and the Society was encouraged to advance loans for house purchases to the Members of Parliament. On hearing of these ad hoc measures taken in the past, the IMF delegation advised me that protections of depositors and maintenance of a stable financial institutions structure would be one of the most important functions of the Central Bank.

12.7.6 Use of Exchange Control to Protect Foreign Exchange and Indirectly Bank Deposits

I mentioned to the IMF delegation that, although it was a bit early, I had already taken steps to use recently introduced exchange control to ensure external transfers were approved only for legitimate purposes. I had also issued instructions to control hidden capital transfers. I said that although the objective was to preserve foreign exchange, I expected that indirect results of these and other exchange control measures would be to increase bank deposits and the credit base.

In summary, in view of constraints of the EACB, and lack at the time of a Kenyan Central Bank, we had been forced to adopt these rudimentary policies to achieve specific objectives, as the need arose. In future, it was hoped, the newly formed Central Bank would take on the formulation, management, and implementation of these policies on a systematic basis.

12.8 Monetary Policy Instruments in the Central Bank Act

12.8.1 Instruments of Monetary Policy

Subsequently, I discussed in detail with the IMF delegation, the pros and cons of various Central Bank instruments of monetary policy and their suitability for inclusion in the Central Bank of Kenya Act. I also discussed with Dr Baranski, whether general qualitative or specific direct quantitative controls, including interest rates would be more appropriate for Kenya. I was concerned about ensuring maximum supply of funds for priority sectors and development purposes.

On instruments of Monetary Policy under a Central Bank, I relied on Dr Baranski and the IMF Delegation. It was the advice of Dr Baranski that direct control of interest rates on bank lending would not be a helpful monetary instrument. For it to be effective the interest rates would have to be very high, which might adversely affect priority sectors. In Dr Baranski's view, interest rate was a blunt instrument and not usually useful in developing countries. In his opinion changes in commercial banks' lending rates were not as effective as direct control instruments. It was agreed that the Central Bank would not have powers to control lending rates, although I understood confidentially that the Bank of Uganda was likely to have powers to control interest rates, and both Mr Michuki and myself believed lending rates by commercial banks should be controlled. Availability and costs of credit were important instruments to promote Kenyanization of the economy. Later Mr Michuki and I discussed this and agreed, instead, to use the Banking Act to control lending rates by the banks.

The IMF delegation informed me that other proposed monetary instruments contained in the draft legislation were the same as those included in the drafts supplied to Tanzania and Uganda. It was agreed that the Central Bank should have powers to discount credit instruments—I felt that besides providing credit this could also be used by the Central Bank to influence flow of finance to priority sectors. It was also agreed that the Central Bank should have power to provide short-term finance by rediscounting credit instruments but at interest rates and terms fixed by the Central Bank. It was the view of Dr Baranski and the IMF delegation that the Central Bank should have powers to impose variable reserve requirements on commercial banks. They considered that this would enable the Central Bank to either increase or decrease lending by the commercial banks as required by monetary policy. I agreed to variable reserve requirements as it was my opinion that variable reserve requirements could be used to finance priority sectors, including our Development Plan, and the Agricultural sector. Separately, Dr Baranski considered the Central Bank should have powers to control interest rates on deposits accepted by the banks, and this was also agreed to.

12.8.2 Par Value

It was agreed that the par value of the newly issued Kenyan currency would be as per our agreement with the IMF. It was agreed that this would be notified in the Gazette by the President acting on the advice of the Central Bank. Mr Michuki queried why this would not be done on the advice of Treasury, and I explained that the Central Bank could only act as per agreements entered into by the Treasury. Subsequently, when sterling was devalued, and the Bretton Woods fixed parity system collapsed, all issues related to par value and the IMF were dealt by the Central Bank in consultation with the Permanent Secretary to the Treasury, and the Minister of Finance.

12.9 Foreign Exchange Reserves and its Composition

12.9.1 Quantum of Foreign Exchange Reserves

I was responsible for the Foreign Exchange Control Act, and availability of foreign exchange for both the public and private sectors. I was not very much concerned about availability of foreign exchange under the EACB system—however, I was very much nervous about availability of foreign exchange under the new Central Bank setup. I asked the IMF delegation what would be the correct amount of foreign reserves for the Central Bank of Kenya, observing that the EACB had substantial external assets, and the currency cover by all assets was 100 per cent. The IMF delegation considered that a Currency Board system is very different from a Central Bank system, and that in the latter case, the quantum of foreign reserves to be held by a Central Bank is usually related to quantum of imports, which could vary between three and six months, as well as other criteria (such as reserves as a percentage of commercial banks' deposit liabilities). IMF delegates also considered there could be a requirement for a percentage of reserves always to be held in liquid or in near liquid assets.

Dr Baranski recommended that the Central Bank of Kenya should aim to maintain foreign currency reserves of not less than four months. In his opinion this would give both stability and flexibility to the Central Bank operations, and in his calculation, reserves covering four months' imports should be sufficient. However, there would be no binding requirement on the Central Bank to always maintain foreign reserves to cover four months' imports, and should foreign reserves continuously be significantly lower than the average four months' import bill, the Central Bank could formally advise the Government of the steps to be taken to correct the situation. It was agreed, accordingly, the Central Bank would use its best endeavours to maintain foreign currency reserves equal to no less than four months' imports. It was also agreed to transfer Kenya's share of surplus assets of the East African Currency Board to the new Central Bank, as and when they were distributed. It was agreed to transfer to the Central Bank all foreign currency held by the Government in international financial institutions, and to include all of these provisions in the Central Bank of Kenya Act.

12.9.2 Composition of Foreign Exchange Reserves

Consideration was also given to the form in which the foreign reserves should be held by the Central Bank. I observed that the foreign reserves by the EACB were usually held in liquid or near liquid form, as sterling deposits and sterling securities. Dr Baranski's advice was that there should be no restrictions on how the Central Bank was to hold foreign reserves—he observed this would be dictated by need to meet Kenya's obligations and to ensure confidence in the currency was not eroded. He felt that, especially now that foreign exchange controls had been introduced against the Sterling Area, there would be a need to open accounts with foreign banks in currencies other than sterling, to meet requirements in that currency. Furthermore, it might be necessary from time to time to maintain foreign exchange reserves in gold and different currencies, in order to maintain diversification and protect the value of Kenya Currency. It was agreed, therefore, that the foreign reserves would be maintained mainly in easily convertible form, but that the Central Bank would have flexibility to determine the content of reserves. It was agreed that the Central Bank could open accounts with foreign banks, and hold non-sterling in foreign reserves.

12.10 Location of Central Bank

Dr Baranski believed that urgent attention should be given to the location of the Central Bank. When we were considering office space, the Ministry of Works suggested we could rent space in a private office building. Dr Baranski was furious, and commented that most of the people do not seem to understand the significance and importance of a Central Bank.

I took him to see an old building used for Army pay and records known as 'archives'. Although the building was a little derelict, Dr Baranski immediately liked it. After considerable persuasion by me and pressure by Mr Michuki, and Minister of Finance James Gichuru, the Ministry of Works and other relevant

Ministries, including the Ministry of Defence and the Office of the President, agreed to find alternate accommodation for the archives and allocate the building for use by the Central Bank. Further, the Ministry of Works was instructed expeditiously to repair and upgrade the old building, as required by the Central Bank advisory team.

12.11 Matters Discussed in Context of Kenya Currency

It was agreed that only notes and coins issued by the Central Bank of Kenya would be legal tender in Kenya. At the request of the IMF delegation, it was agreed to include a Clause in the Central Bank Act prohibiting the issue of bearer securities. It had been agreed that the EACB would cease to have a right to issue legal tender as soon as separate Central Banks were established, and separate currencies issued.

12.11.1 Withdrawals of 'Lake Issues' or 'Lake Victoria' Notes

Transitional provisions related to the withdrawals of EACB Notes were to be made. These were mainly 'Lake Issues' or 'Lake Victoria' Currency Notes, which had been issued in 1964 to reflect the new political situation in Kenya, Uganda, and Tanzania. 'Kings' and 'Queens' Notes, issued earlier by the EACB, had already been redeemed. Problems arose because Kenya, Uganda, and Tanzania did not issue their new currency at the same time and these had to be resolved. Anecdotal evidence suggested that Tanzanian and Ugandan holders of Lake Victoria currency notes physically transferred them to Kenya, so that they could be exchanged for Kenyan currency, which was perceived as likely to be stronger in future than that of Tanzania and Uganda.

12.11.2 Share of Surplus of the EACB

There was also at this time an issue concerning the Redemption of 'Lake Victoria' currency notes in Aden. Although Lake Victoria notes were issued only in Kenya, Uganda, and Tanzania a large amount of these were surrendered in Aden—it was not known how these instruments had reached that country. This raised the question of whether Aden was entitled to a share of the surplus of the EACB related to the Lake Victoria Notes. Our opinion was that Aden was not so entitled, and we drew upon similar litigation before the British courts relating to the earlier withdrawal of 'Kings' and 'Queens' Notes, in establishing the Government's defence to the Aden claim.

12.11.3 Coins

Since Tanzania had much longer time to prepare themselves for the currency and coin change, Tanzanian coins were minted and ready for issue at the same time as their currency notes, in June 1966. However, Tanzania only issued its coins a month or so later. Both the Kenyan and Ugandan Central Banks were not ready to issue new coins at the same time as they issued their new currencies—in fact, the Central Bank of Kenya only issued new Kenyan coins in 1967, and EACB coins continued to be legal tender in Kenya until early 1969. This required special arrangements with the EACB, as their notes and coins otherwise stopped being legal tender as soon as one Central Bank issued its new national currency. In addition, some transitional arrangements had to be made for the exchange of EACB coins with the coins of Kenya, Uganda, and Tanzania. Although the issues related to storage, transport, conversion, etc. were handled by the Central Bank, I was kept informed.

12.11.4 Holes in Some Coins

On the subject of coins, I recall the late H.E. President Kenyatta's instructions that there should not be holes in any coins, as this was a 'colonial' relic. Holes were in only two coins, the third having been demonetized earlier. I recollect the abolition of holes being announced by the Minister of Finance, the Hon. Gichuru in his 1966 Budget Speech. I also recollect during the debate on Central Bank of Kenya Bill in March 1966, the successor Minister of Finance, Mwai Kibaki elaborated on what the President had meant by 'colonial' relic. He said that colonial opinion was that since Africans did not wear trousers or have pockets to put the coins, holes were needed for them to thread the coins with a string and wear around the neck or around the waist. Because of the alternate uses of coins, mainly due to the holes, a proportion of the EACB coins was never, in fact, surrendered for replacement by new Kenya, Uganda, and Tanzania coins.

12.11.5 Currency Notes or Coins?

Some discussions took place on the quantum of currency notes and coins that should be issued. Statistics produced indicated that the usage of coins was gradually being replaced by notes. It was opined, however, that coins have a much longer life span, and should be encouraged. It was agreed to issue a new note of Shs.50 and new coins of Shs.2 and 25 Cents. It was considered that a Shs.50 note would fill a gap that had risen because of price increases. Following suggestions by the EACB it was decided that introduction of Shs.2 coin would increase coin usage, and there was also discussion of the introduction of a Shs.5 coin.

Separately, a concern arose as to whether, since the new coins were thinner than the EACB coins, these would still be capable of being used in slot machines operated by the Post Office; Railways etc., although ultimately it was concluded that there was no need for the machines to be changed to accommodate the new coins. This assurance was given by the Minister of Finance Mr Gichuru to Parliament. Some time in 1973 a nine-sided coin of Shs.5 was issued and I was informed minting of 25 cents and Shs.2 had been discontinued.

12.11.6 Limits on Settlement of Debts using Coins

It was considered whether coins should be used to settle larger transactions, and it was decided that 50 cents could only be used to transactions up to Shs.20. It was also decided that smaller denomination coins could only be used to settle transaction up to Shs.5 and less.

12.11.7 Respect for Currency

Because of national feelings about Kenya's own currency, and to encourage people to show respect for coins and notes and discourage them from mishandling them, it was agreed that damaged notes and coins would only be exchanged by the Central Bank, and that too at its discretion. Further it was agreed that mishandling of notes and coins would be an offence. I recollect a trader had produced key chains with Kenya coins. There was a raid on his shop and all his stock confiscated.

12.11.8 First Drafts of Currency Notes

One day, Mr Michuki came to my office with a big package, containing first drafts of our new currency. He asked me to keep the package in my safe, and instructed that I should not show it to anyone. John Butter, former Permanent Secretary to the Treasury and now Advisor to the Treasury, came to my Office and asked to be shown the draft currency notes. I found myself now in great difficulty—Mr Butter was my first Permanent Secretary, and he and I had worked very closely on many matters. However, Mr Michuki's instructions were not to show the drafts to anyone, and so I told him that while I had no objections, Mr Michuki's instructions on the matter had been clear. He was not best pleased, although when I reported the matter to Mr Michuki, he told me not to worry.

Much later, when John Butter was appointed as financial adviser to the Abu Dhabi Government, he asked me if I would be interested to accompany him. I said that I did not speak Arabic—and he replied that neither did he!

12.11.9 Signature on Currency Notes

There was discussion on whether the new currency notes should be signed, and if so, by whom. Mr Michuki felt that the signature of the Permanent Secretary to the Treasury should appear on the Notes, as this would enhance the status of the currency. Dr Baranski felt the signature of the Governor alone should be sufficient, but accepted that the Permanent Secretary of Treasury's signature, as a Member of the Board, would be acceptable. This was the procedure adopted when the first Kenya currency notes were printed some time in mid-1966, and signed by both Dr Baranski as Governor, and Mr Michuki, not as Permanent Secretary to the Treasury, but as a Board Member of the Central Bank. However, in the view of Dr Baranski's opinion, it was provided in the Central Bank Act that the notes could, in fact, be signed by the Governor alone.

12.11.10 Kenya or Ethiopian Lion

Initially it was decided that the new Kenyan currency notes should have a portrait of His Excellency the President H.E. Mzee Jomo Kenyatta. It was also decided that the notes should depict various agricultural activities, and that Mount Kenya should be shown on all notes. Subsequently, it was decided that the word 'First' be inserted before 'President'.

Some time in 1974, new currency drafts were produced. On one of the notes, a picture of a lion family was shown, and I heard that H.E. the President was very upset about the picture, opining that 'this is not a Kenyan lion but an Ethiopian lion'. As a result, we all became busy looking for photographs of Ethiopian lions and Kenya lions, trying to pinpoint the differences!

12.11.11 Transportation of Currency Notes

It was decided that a military escort should be provided for all transportation of currency notes and coins.

12.12 Revival of Nairobi Stock Exchange and Government Bonds' Secondary Market

I was the Treasury official responsible for public debt. During the discussions on the Central Bank legislation it was agreed that following establishment of the Central Bank, as agent of the Government it would be responsible for administration of the public debt. I had used Government Bonds not only to fund Government development expenditure, but indirectly to cap interest rates in the country. I had also sought to revive the Nairobi Stock Exchange, and to attempt to create a bond market, with the intention of establishing a vibrant forum that could be used for future open market operations of Government Bonds as an instrument of debt policy.

12.12.1 Steps Taken to Create Active Market for Bonds

After Independence, I successfully arranged to issue the first Kenyan Currency Government Bond. The Bond issues became an integral part of financing Kenyan Government Development expenditure budgets, and I personally undertook to persuade insurance companies and pensions funds to invest in bond issues. Initially they were reluctant, viewing bonds as long-term investments. They observed that the current situation in Kenya was volatile, and that while they might need funds before the bonds matured, there was no market for these bonds in case they must sell. I undertook, therefore, to revive the bond market on the Nairobi Stock Exchange, and also assured them that the Treasury would repurchase bonds held by them in case they needed cash, under the 'Support Price Scheme'. Under this Scheme, every week, the Government Stock Broker and I would agree the purchase price for small amounts of bonds, and publish these prices on the Stock Exchange. If any investor wished to sell large amounts, it was agreed that they could discuss this with the Government Stock Broker. However, except in the case of one investor, who sought to sell his holdings (I arranged for this to be bought by the National Security Fund) the Bonds were generally held to maturity and rolled over.

12.12.2 Use of Exchange Control to Promote Bonds and Finance Development Expenditure

We used exchange control to reduce funds taken out by emigrants, and to delay repatriation of the balance of their funds, which were frozen for five years, with the aim of reducing foreign exchange leakage. I proposed a scheme to Mr Michuki, to put these dormant funds to active use. Accordingly, I persuaded Mr Michuki to authorize blocked funds to be invested in special low interest bearing Kenyan currency bonds, with five-year maturities. I also persuaded the Central Bank to agree that blocked funds could be invested in Government Bonds, and amended the bond prospectus accordingly. I organized special five-year bonds for these blocked funds. This enabled money, lying frozen in the Central Bank in blocked accounts, to be used for development projects. Demand for these bonds kept on increasing.

12.12.3 Promoting Confidence and the Market for Kenya Sterling Bonds in London

I was concerned about the repayment of substantial pre-Independence Kenyan bonds issued in sterling, and persuaded Mr Michuki to increase the Government's contributions to sinking funds for these Kenyan bonds issued in sterling in the UK. I was aware that this would, in the short run, be negative for foreign exchange. A special supplementary sinking fund was established, and Crown Agents recommended that we invest in non-Kenyan sterling stocks. Their opinion was that though returns on Kenyan Stocks were at the higher end of market, the discounts were substantial, which indicated a lack of confidence in Kenyan Government sterling stocks. John Butter thought we should accept Crown Agents advice—but I felt that we could not have such little confidence in ourselves, and that we should rather invest in Kenyan sterling stocks—and that the greater the discount, the better for the Government.

Thus, we ensured that the Supplementary Sinking Funds bought Kenya sterling stocks at a considerable discount, thus reducing the eventual debt burden. It so happened that the London Bond market perceived demand for Kenyan Stocks, a little confidence and interest returned in Kenyan sterling securities. Besides avoiding a possible default or unnecessary foreign exchange outflow, or a spike in budgetary allocation at maturity, this action meant that funds and foreign exchange required at redemption was much lower, and also created a 'market' for Kenyan sterling stocks in London.

12.13 My Working Relationship with Dr Baranski and Decisions Taken by Us

12.13.1 Before and After the Establishment of the Central Bank

I worked very closely with Dr Baranski, both before and after establishment of the Central Bank. A Clause was included in the Central Bank Act that would enable him as the first Governor of the Central Bank, and myself as representative of the Treasury to take implementation decisions without prior approval of the Central Bank Board of Directors. This procedure made it possible for large number of implementation decisions to be taken without undue bureaucratic procedures.

The Act also included a provision that retrospectively affirmed all actions taken to date in the establishment of the Central Bank, prior to the Act coming into force.

Dr Baranski congratulated me and my wife, Niti, when we got married in March 1967. He gave us a present. I miss him greatly to this day.

12.13.2 Dr Baranski's Offer to Me to Join Central Bank of Kenya as Bank Secretary

Dr Baranski organized for me to attend, a short IMF Seminar in Washington for Governors of newly formed Central Banks. On my return, Dr Baranski privately asked me if I would be interested in the Secretary's post at the Central Bank. He said that, since many matters I was handling in the Treasury would now be Central Bank functions, I could continue to perform these functions in my capacity as Secretary. He also recommended that I had been doing many jobs in the Treasury, but that I should now specialize. I thanked him for the confidence and advice, although following the death of my father in July 1965, I had become more involved in matters previously handled by him, and so I told Dr Baranski that I had not yet made up my mind about my future.

12.13.3 Bank General Manager

On management matters generally, Dr Baranski was assisted by a banking expert from the Bank of England. I discussed several implementations matters with him.

12.13.4 Information Received by Central Bank from Commercial Banks

As an economist statistician, my responsibility included compiling, developing, and refining statistics related to banking, insurance, GDP, and balance of payments, and to establish a basis for production of gross national product calculations. I also calculated the multiplier effect of various investments.

In view of this knowledge as a statistician, Dr Baranski involved me in the statistical information the Central Bank would be seeking from commercial banks. He advised me that the current statistics were very basic, and for the Central Bank to operate proper monetary policies, it would need much more detailed statistical information. He also guided me in what we should really be looking at from whatever information we had. I did look at this initially and discussed various matters with Central Bank staff. However, some time in mid-1967, my access was curtailed, on grounds of confidentiality.

12.13.5 Transfer of Government Accounts

As described above, it was agreed that the Central Bank of Kenya would be the banker to the Government. Accordingly, I took decisions to transfer numerous Government accounts and deposits to the Central Bank. There was, however, considerable opposition from commercial banks that held these deposits, and I had to ensure that when Government deposits moved from commercial banks to the Central Bank, there was no adverse impact on the commercial bank concerned.

I coordinated with Mr Sheen of the main Government Bank, the National and Grindlays Bank. I had also calculated that the Government balances in commercial banks were not large, and therefore there was unlikely to be any serious implications for the commercial banks in question. Since the Central Bank did not have offices outside Nairobi, services were required from commercial banks, and the impact of transfer of deposits was minimized. I did this with the assistance of the Chief Government Accountant, Mr Dennis—I remember him sitting in my office wondering and worrying about the transfer. I closely worked with him on Government accounts and budgetary estimates, and previously he had spoken to me about the advantages of computerizing Government Accounts. Despite considerable opposition to the use of technology and its adverse effects on employment, I persuaded Mr Michuki that we should computerize the Government Accounts, and that Mr Dennis should go to UK for training.

12.13.6 National Social Security Fund

I was Treasury representative and Secretary of the Finance Committee of the National Social Security Fund (NSSF). I organized an agreement at the NSSF to transfer its main account to the Central Bank. This was to avoid the large, short-term National Social Security Account distorting banks' operations. I would arrange for these funds quickly to be invested in Government bonds to finance the Government's Development budget, and to ensure that the NSSF did not lose valuable interest income. This would be achieved by shifting funds from one account at the Central Bank (the NSSF Account) to another Central Bank account (the Government Account). By this step we avoided a spike and sharp fluctuations in commercial banks' deposits. I remember I had discussed with the Central Bank to pay interest on the NSSF deposits but cannot remember what happened.

Originally in 1964, I had commented on a report produced by a British expert, Professor Turner, on the establishment of a Social Security Scheme in Kenya. I had recommended that instead of a full pension scheme, we should adopt a step-by-step approach, adopting a contributory provident fund scheme as a first step. This approach was finally agreed, and I subsequently participated in legislation and other matters to establish the NSSF. I had also secured formal approval of the Finance Committee that all surplus funds accumulated by the NSSF would be invested in Government bonds, to ensure that these funds would be used for development purposes and would be beneficial to the workers.

12.13.7 Use of NSSF Fund to Abolish Fee for Medical Treatment

Mr Michuki came to my office, and said that H.E. the President would like to offer something to the public in a forthcoming speech, notwithstanding strong opposition from the Supply/Advisory section of the Treasury, operating as it was on a very tight budget. Mr Michuki was of the view, however, that were Treasury not to suggest a positive announcement, one would be made anyway, without consultation, which Treasury would be required to implement.

There were at that time newspaper reports of people turned away from Government hospitals for lack of admission money. I looked at the accounts, and found the figures for the total amount collected by the Government for the past few years. I suggested to Mr Michuki that we could waive the admission charge and make admission to Government hospitals free, funded separately from the interest earned by National Social Security Fund. This was accepted and announced and very well received by the public as fruits of Uhuru. After the announcement, I recall the late Tom Mboya looking me in the eyes and nodding with approval.

12.13.8 International Monetary Fund

It was agreed that the Central Bank would be responsible for Kenya's relationship with the International Monetary Fund. Mr Duncan Ndegwa was appointed Alternate Director in place of Mr Michuki on the IMF Board. Thereafter most IMF matters were dealt with by the Central Bank. Because I had studied international financial institutions, I was asked in 1963 to assist in preparing legislation for Kenya's membership of the IMF under the Bretton Woods Agreements Act. In the Treasury, I had the overall responsibility for all IMF matters, including Kenya's legal relationship with IMF, our gold portion and its draw down.

I was the Kenyan Government officer designated to hold the top-secret communications code between Kenya and the IMF. Following the establishment of the Central Bank of Kenya, I passed this code to a designated officer of the Central Bank under strict IMF supervision. I fully participated in the 'Special

Drawing Rights' discussions, its acceptance by Kenya and subsequent legislation. There was fear that this 'paper foreign exchange' would increase inflation, and costs of Kenya's imports would further increase. The SDRs were passed on to the Central Bank.

12.13.9 IMF Article IV Consultations

I was responsible for hosting IMF Article IV delegations and ensuring they were properly briefed on Kenyan Government economic and monetary policy matters and the consultations were successfully concluded. I would brief various Ministries on IMF requirements, since the IMF delegation preferred to hold meetings with Ministries separately. I am glad to say that during my tenure, the IMF delegations expressed full support for the monetary and economic policies of the Kenyan Government, in the final meeting that was held with the Minister for Finance.

12.13.10 Tea Loan for Small-Scale Kenya Farmers

I would read IMF country reports of all important countries. I would also read directors' resolutions, and other reports of both IMF and World Bank. On one occasion, Kenya had applied for a World Bank loan to finance small-scale tea growers.

The World Bank rejected Kenya's application, saying that there was over supply of tea in the world. Hon. Mwai Kibaki asked me what shall we do, and since I was aware of a World Bank resolution agreeing to give loan for tea to Ceylon, I showed the World Bank resolution to the Minister, and drafted a protest letter for his signature. Subsequently, the World Bank relented and agreed loan for small-scale Kenyan tea growers.

12.13.11 Dr Baranski Appointed First Governor of the Central Bank

Sometimes in May 1966, the President appointed Dr Baranski as Governor of the Central Bank of Kenya, and four other Directors. I would be appointed Treasury Representative on the Board as and when required. I stopped attending Central Bank Board Meetings, because a question was raised on conflict of interest, as I was Chairman of the Cereals and Sugar Finance Corporation, and a Government employee. Mr Michuki and I agreed to amend the Act to exempt Government employees.

12.13.12 Requirement of Minimum Qualifications

During the discussions on appointments of the Governor, Deputy Governor, and the Board of Directors, Dr Baranski had advised that they should all be professionals, and preferably experienced bankers. This had been overlooked. After the appointment of the Board of Directors, Dr Baranski suggested to me that a Clause should have been included in the Act on minimum required qualifications for the Governor, Deputy Governor, and Board of Directors—whereas in fact we had only included provisions relating to grounds for disqualification, but not qualifications.

12.13.13 Exchange Control

Following the retirement of two expatriate Treasury Officers, I became the only Treasury Officer responsible for administering the Exchange Control Act. It was agreed that in future, the Central Bank would, instead, be responsible for administration of Exchange Control law, with the power to decide on policy matters being retained by the Treasury. I was informed by an IMF delegate that this was likely to be position in Tanzania. I was also the Gazetted Officer under the Exchange Control Act, Schedule V. The Minister of Finance had delegated enforcement powers to me.

I was not in favour of exchange control as, in my opinion, it distorts an economy. Subsequently I was in favour of lifting exchange control when Kenyan currency was issued, and I had suggested that we could negotiate funds from the IMF to underwrite Kenya's currency. This would take care of anticipated outwards flow. It was my opinion that in the long term this would increase the flow of inward funds for development. However, my view was rejected because of political pressures. In June 1965, it was decided to extend exchange control to the Sterling Area, except for Uganda and Tanzania. There was already an Exchange Control Act and exchange control applied to non-sterling countries. The Kenyan Treasury secured the assistance of Bank of England experts. I worked on several schedules that were issued to extend the Exchange Control to Sterling Area. During the Budget of June 1965, the imposition/extension of exchange control to Sterling Area countries was announced by Kenya, Uganda, and Tanzania. Subsequently I used exchange control powers as an indirect instrument of monetary policy, and restricted foreign exchange leakages and thereby increased banks deposits and credit base. I informed the IMF delegation that I had anecdotal evidence that after exchange control was imposed, bank deposits had shown an upward trend.

12.13.14 Enactment of New Banking Act: Powers to Licence Commercial Banks and Investments of Assigned Capital

During the discussions on the Central Bank of Kenya legislation, it was agreed that the Treasury will retain powers to issue banking licences but with the approval of the Central Bank. IMF had suggested that Kenya should have a modern Banking Law and sent to us a Model Draft and a Delegation. I handled the matter in Kenya Treasury. Subsequently lot of discussions took place between the Treasury and the Central Bank on the new Banking Act 1968. Questions were raised on the Treasury being licensing authority of commercial banks and financial institutions and not the Central Bank; on the Treasury having powers to revoke licences; on the Treasury having powers relating to inspection; on the use of the word 'bank'; on the Treasury having control on location of bank branches; on their mergers and consolidation; auditors etc. Provisions in the Act about maintaining minimum liquid assets and on control of certain types of operations were also queried by the Central Bank. There were objections to provisions relating to control of lending to their own employees. There were provisions to control maximum lending to one person. The most serious objection related to assigned capital and Treasury requirement that it be invested in Government Bonds.

The commercial banks affected by requirements of assigned capital and its investments in Government Bonds as a condition for issuing licences strongly protested and complained to the Central Bank; the Permanent Secretary to the Treasury Mr Michuki and to the Minister of Finance. They even involved their High Commission. I received several visits and threats of closure of Banks. The issue was: how should the assigned capital of some banks that were branches of overseas banks be held? Initially the commercial banks concerned suggested that the assigned capital should be part of their normal assets. The Treasury objected. Later they proposed that the assigned capital should be part of their assets held at the Central Bank. The Central Bank not only strongly supported this view but aggressively pushed it in Government circles. I had recommended that the assigned capital be held as Government Bond. The basis of my suggestion was that this would enable the Treasury to secure long-term finance from commercial banks to finance development and since the assigned capital would have to be transferred by their head offices this would also be a foreign exchange positive decision. Despite considerable opposition by the Central Bank and from the commercial banks concerned, the Treasury stayed firm. It was finally agreed that assigned capital had to be invested in Government Bonds before a licence would be issued. The Treasury agreed that the Bond would carry reasonable interest.

We had requested from the banks a copy of their agreement on interest rates and their charges but it was not forthcoming. The Treasury's intention was to issue instructions to them on interest and bank charges as Mr Michuki and I had discussed during the time of the Central Bank Act. In absence of information on bank charges, it was agreed that the banks could not increase their present charges without permission of the Minister. This matter was subsequently handled by the Central Bank.

12.13.15 Dr Baranski Not Happy at Initial Quantum of Foreign Exchange

Dr Baranski was not satisfied with the amount of foreign exchange the Central Bank must start life with. It was agreed that the currency board would allocate equal amounts of foreign exchange to Kenya, Uganda and Tanzania to enable their Central Banks to commence business. Subsequently foreign exchange allocation was to be made as per the quantum of withdrawal of East African currency in each country. Dr Baranski opined that the amount offered by the Currency Board was meagre, and he needed more reserves in order to issue the new Kenyan currency. In his view, the Kenyan economy was much bigger than that of Uganda or Tanzania, and furthermore felt that the Central Bank should have enough reserves to give the new Kenyan currency respect and standing.

It had already been agreed that the Treasury funds at the international institutions should be transferred to the new Central Bank. However, Dr Baranski believed that the Central Bank should start with a bigger pot of foreign exchange reserves. Dr Baranski and I discussed various options in detail.

12.13.16 Transfer of Sterling Funds Held by Provident and Pensions Funds

One option was to use exchange control legally to force provident and pensions funds to transfer foreign assets held by them to Kenya, thereby increasing the Central Bank's reserves. This would also be in accordance with the proposed establishment of the Workers Investment Trust and proposed prohibition for them to hold foreign assets. I was aware of the broad quantum of these funds, which was substantial.

12.13.17 Transfer of Commercial Banks' Foreign Exchange Reserves

A second option, I suggested, was to transfer foreign exchange reserves held by Kenyan commercial banks to the Central Bank. I was familiar with the statistics of commercial banks, and that these held significant foreign exchange reserves, and credit balances in their branches in Uganda and Tanzania. Dr Baranski, however, was not keen to disturb commercial banks foreign reserves, believing rather that they should only complement the Central Banks reserves. I mentioned to Dr Baranski that our actions on foreign exchange front were showing positive results—indications were that both the stock and the velocity of currency were improving. Estimates of foreign aid and grant showed these were rising. Confidence of the private sector was returning. All these would result in increases in bank deposits and foreign exchange. In Dr Baranski's view, however, this was still not sufficient.

12.13.18 Transfer of Life Insurance Companies Funds

The third option, I suggested, was to ask life insurance companies to transfer their assets to Kenya. Since I had responsibility for calculating for Kenya's Annual Budget the availability of funds from various local sources and to ensure funds from these flowed into bonds to finance planned development expenditure, I had statistics indicating foreign assets held by various local institutions including life insurance companies. I had calculated that a not insignificant amount of sterling bonds was held by Kenya by life insurance companies. These had matching Kenya currency liabilities. I suggested to Dr Baranski, that if need be, we could use our powers under the exchange control rules to release this sterling to support the Central Bank's foreign reserves.

12.13.19 Transfer of Supplementary Funds Assets

I briefed Dr Baranski on the supplementary sinking fund, denominated in sterling, and suggested the assets held by the supplementary sinking fund could be transferred to the Central Bank. This would be a simple transfer affected by the Crown Agents.

I informed Dr Baranski the sterling denominated assets held by all of the entities described above would be almost the same as total sterling assets held by the East African Currency Board. He smiled. However, none of the options was easy, or could be implemented with speed.

12.13.20 Transfer of Sterling Assets of Post Office Savings Bank to Central Bank of Kenya

Finally, I suggested that we could, subject to sorting out some technical matters, arrange for the foreign assets held by the Kenyan Post Office Savings Bank to be transferred to the Central Bank. This proposal excited Dr Baranski, who asked me how the transaction would be done.

I proposed a scheme, setting out two alternatives: first, the Post Office Savings Bank could sell the sterling stocks held by it. Proceeds would be deposited with their account with the Crown Agents. The Central Bank would open an account with the Crown Agents, who would transfer the proceeds of sterling bonds to the sterling account of the Central Bank. In return, the Central Bank would credit equivalent Kenyan currency to the Post Office Savings Bank's newly opened account with the Central Bank. Subsequently, the Post Office Savings Bank would re-invest the proceeds in Kenyan Currency Government bonds, giving the Government cash to help it finance its development expenditure. However, Dr Baranski had reservations about this scheme as this would result in a spike in Government finances.

The second way was to replace the sterling stocks of the Post Office Savings Bank with Kenya currency bonds. The sterling bonds, instead of being held on behalf of the Post Office Savings Bank by the Crown Agents, would be held on behalf of the Central Bank. In return, the Kenyan Government would issue Kenyan Currency Bonds to the Post Office Savings Bank with similar maturities and gross redemption yields. This procedure would not increase Government revenues, and not result in any spending spree by the Government. Dr Baranski was in favour of this approach.

I told Dr Baranski I had had some preliminary discussions with the Post Office Savings Bank. It had been agreed that the Kenyan currency denominated securities would be of almost the same maturity period as the sterling securities, while the Gross Redemption Yields on the Kenyan securities would be better than the sterling securities. I also said the Kenyan securities would be issued at a higher interest rate, but at a smaller discount. The Post Office Savings Bank was broadly in favour of this approach, subject to addressing legal and administrative technicalities.

Dr Baranski and I discussed this scheme with Mr Michuki, who gave authority to proceed. After further discussions with the East African Posts and Telecommunications, Kenya Post Office Savings Bank and Crown Agents, the UK assets held by the Kenya Post Office Savings Bank were transferred to a Central Bank account, and replaced by local Kenya currency Government bonds. This ensured that the Central Bank of Kenya had credible foreign exchange reserves in place from the outset.

The transfer of Kenya Post Office Savings Bank foreign assets to the Central Bank necessitated legal notices. In view of the timing, I issued instructions to the Post Office Savings Bank to instruct Crown Agents to transfer the assets forthwith. The Crown Agents needed to see legal notice signed by H.E. First President Jomo Kenyatta approving transaction. I had with Attorney General's Office drafted a suitable Gazette Notice. However, H.E. was on a working holiday in Mombasa and we were told he was returning to Nairobi but his return was delayed. We deliberated whether Hon. Gichuru and Mr Michuki should fly to Mombasa. Air transport was not, then, as efficient as it is today, and both had other pressing commitments in Nairobi. Further we were not given a definite date when H.E. was to return to Nairobi. H.E. usually travelled by train.

Because of time constraints, I had instructed the Government printer to print the legal notice in the Gazette. He had in good faith included the legal notice in the Gazette that was ready to be issued (the Gazette was issued every Thursday evening). H.E. returned on the same Thursday morning. At the railway station, Hon. Gichuru received him and, in the railway waiting room, presented the legal notice for signature. I was told H.E. was very annoyed but when the situation was explained he signed the notice. This legalized the entire transaction of transfer of assets to the Central Bank from the Post Office Savings Bank. Parliament was informed of this transaction by Hon. Gichuru as Minister for Finance, and assured that the sterling securities would remain part of Central Bank foreign exchange reserves.

12.13.21 Mr Duncan Ndegwa Appointed Governor

After one year, in mid-1967, Dr Baranski was replaced as Governor by Mr Duncan Ndegwa. I understood this was done under a clause in the Central Bank Act which allowed H.E. the President to terminate appointment of a Governor if he was not a Kenyan Citizen. After Dr Baranski was replaced as Governor he thanked me for all the help I had given him in setting up the Bank. I asked him who would handle monetary policy instruments in the Central Bank. He did not reply—and I noticed he had lost his usual smile.

12.13.22 Veto

I remember as Treasury Representative, on instructions, during Mr Duncan Ndegwa's Governorship, imposing the first 'Veto' by the Treasury on a Central Bank Board Resolution. I was conscious of an earlier discussion and 'threat' by Dr Baranski that he would resign. However, I pleaded with the Board that the issue was trivial and should be sorted out by discussion with the Permanent Secretary to the Treasury. This request was rejected by a 'hot' Board. The issue was whether the Governor should have a Mercedes car for personal use—the Treasury view being that all other senior civil servants, including the Head of the Civil Service, were only issued with Peugeots.

12.13.23 Post Establishment of Central Bank of Kenya

I was aware of a statement made by Mr Gichuru when I had just joined the Government in 1962. As was the practice at that time, Hon. Gichuru on being appointed Minister for Finance and Economic Planning, visited Senior Treasury Civil Servants in their offices. When he came to my office, accompanied by then Permanent Secretary John Butter, and on finding out that I was responsible for statistics of banks, insurance companies, and balance of payments, he said that when he had met President Nasser, he had advised that to be fully independent it was necessary to nationalize banks and insurance companies and impose exchange control. He was hurriedly taken away from my office!

After the establishment of the Central Bank my responsibility for several monetary matters, as foreseen by Dr Baranski, was transferred to the Central Bank, and I had more time to attend to my other responsibilities. I turned my attention to commercial banks; insurance companies; foreign exchange matters; ways and means of raising revenue; and the enactment of a legal structure to promote foreign private investment. I spoke to Mr Michuki, who agreed in principle but asked me to produce detailed proposals for each for his consideration.

12.14 Establishment and Strengthening of the Commercial Banking Sector

12.14.1 African Development Bank (1963)

When the proposal for African Development Bank was under discussion, I prepared briefs and calculations showing the best 'contribution' formula for Kenya, whereby we could have higher influence via our voting position, with a minimum financial contribution. I was subsequently told that this formula, with minor amendments, was adopted, and enshrined in the African Development Bank Act. Kenya's contribution to the African Development Bank was then financed by the East African Currency Board.

12.14.2 Commercial Bank of Africa (1967)

The Commercial Bank of Africa had its headquarters in Dar es Salaam, and a branch in Kenya. Following the nationalization of banks in Tanzania, Mr Michuki told me that instructions had been received that we should not allow a nationalized Tanzanian bank to operate in Kenya, and that we should find a way to protect our Kenya depositors.

A window of opportunity arose when, after the announcement of nationalization, it took a few days for Tanzania to pass the necessary legislation. We moved fast. With the assistance of the Attorney General's Chambers and foreign shareholders of the Commercial Bank of Africa, we managed to split its ownership, and made the Kenyan branch an unconnected independent bank owned directly by foreign shareholders. Thus, Commercial Bank of Africa's Kenyan branch did not become subject to nationalization in Tanzania.

12.14.3 Cooperative Bank of Kenya and Extension of Credit Base for Local Farmers (1968)

There was at this time significant political pressure for a fully fledged Cooperative Bank. Although there was a Cooperative Bank registered under the Co-operative Societies Act, it did not have a banking licence, nor authority to use the title 'bank'. A report on establishment of a Co-operative Bank had been prepared by an Israeli expert, and Dr Baranski and I considered it. I produced a brief for Mr Michuki on the conversion of the Co-operative Bank into a full bank. He agreed. We secured services of a banking expert from the Standard Bank, at that time considered to be leading provider of cooperative finance, and we successfully converted the existing Kenyan Cooperative Bank into a fully fledged and licensed bank.

All Kenyan cooperatives were directed to buy shares in the new bank, and directed to deposit their funds with it. Bigger cooperatives had misgivings over the safety and protection of their deposits, and we discussed the Government underwriting deposits as a charge on the Consolidated Fund, provided that the Treasury maintained absolute control over lending.

I was the Alternate Treasury Director on the Cooperative Bank's Board until 1975.

12.14.4 National Bank of Kenya and Extension of Credit Base for Local Entrepreneurs (1968)

I discussed with Mr Michuki the establishment of a fully Government owned commercial bank, and produced a brief. John Butter felt that this would take a long time to establish and still longer to be profitable, but I felt we could establish a fully Government owned commercial bank within one year, and make it profitable within 36 months. Given the experience of establishment of the Central Bank, Mr Michuki agreed, and authorized me to proceed.

We secured the assistance of an expert banker from National and Grindlays Bank, who was seconded to the Treasury for the purpose, and while in fact we were not quite able to establish the new bank within 12 months (there was a three months' delay in the strong room's arrival from the UK), it was nonetheless operationally profitable within 36 months. Eventually, the new bank would become one of the most important in Kenya, with several branches. Certain Government institutions were instructed to transfer funds to the National Bank and conduct all their banking matters through it.

There was a loan arrangement scheme, known as the Civil Servant Motor Car Hire purchase scheme, guaranteed by the Government for the purchase of cars by civil servants. I arranged to transfer this to the National Bank. The Bank also acquired banking business of Ottoman Bank.

There was lot of pressure from powerful politicians that the new National Bank should lend without proper security documents or collateral, in favour instead of letters of guarantee, in some instances signed by high-ranking politicians and Cabinet Ministers. With the help of Mr Michuki, however, we resisted unsecured and unviable lending.

I was the Alternate Treasury Director on the Board of the National Bank, which remained a profitable and sound institution until my eventual retirement from the Board.

12.14.5 Union Bank of Kenya

In the wake of more significant and widespread Government ownership and participation in the banking sector, Barclays Bank and the Standard Bank proposed formation of a bank with Government participation, and the Union Bank of Kenya was born (at least temporarily), its initial shareholders being the Kenyan Government, Barclays Bank, and Standard Bank. Unfortunately, Parliament objected and the new bank had to be wound up forthwith, with the entire amount invested by the Treasury returned to it.

12.14.6 Kenya Commercial Bank (1971)

In 1970, I participated in some of the discussions leading to a split of National and Grindlays Bank between local commercial banking operations and merchant banking operations. The discussions were headed by the Minster for Finance Hon. Mwai Kibaki. It was agreed that the initial share of Government would be 60 per cent of local banking operations and 40 per cent of the merchant bank, with the part dealing with the local commercial banking operations being called Kenya Commercial Bank, and the merchant bank called Grindlay's Bank.

After my retirement, I was appointed a director, in my personal capacity, to the Board of the Kenya Commercial Bank, until my eventual retirement in 1985.

12.14.7 Post Office Savings Bank (1978)

In 1972 I was invited to a conference in Berlin on the German savings bank system. At this time, the German savings banks were not only acting as pure savings institution, but also as a bank. On my return from Berlin, I discussed with the late Philip Ndegwa, the new Permanent Secretary to the Treasury, the idea of conversion of the Kenyan Post Office Savings Bank, so that instead of it discharging traditional Post Office savings services, it could also provide banking services. In 1977, after my retirement from the Government, this was eventually achieved.

I was appointed a director of the Kenyan Post Office Savings Bank in my personal capacity.

12.15 Establishment and Strengthening of the Re-insurance and Insurance Sector

12.15.1 Kenya National Assurance Company Limited

In 1964, I had ensured that the Kenya National Assurance Company (KNAC) had become a fully owned Government insurance company. KNAC had originally been formed by some foreign shareholders with a small participation by DFCK. It was projected as a Kenyan Government owned Company, but it was felt that it did not satisfy the requirement of Government ownership and that more needed to be done.

I studied the accounts of KNAC, which showed losses, and I felt that the Government could buy the entire foreign shareholding of the company at substantial discount. There was strong resistance. The foreign shareholders were agreeable, provided they were paid the full amount of their share subscriptions. Accordingly, Treasury became the owner of KNAC.

After analysing the reasons for losses at KNAC, I found that these mainly arose because of the way the re-insurance treaties were concluded with the foreign shareholder's parent companies. Despite considerable opposition, but with the assistance of Sir Ernest Vasey, we changed all re-insurance treaties, and were able to retain most profitable Kenyan business with KNAC. The outflow of foreign exchange was reduced, and I arranged for KNAC to enter the life insurance business, which it did successfully, with a fully African top management team. Between 1964 and 1975 the KNAC became the largest, and one of the most profitable, insurance companies in Kenya.

Following political fallout between the Chairman of the Board and the Government, Mr. Michuki entrusted me the task of ensuring that he did not continue as Chairman of a Government institution. I spoke to the Chairman, explained to him the Government's decision; the various options available were he to continue, and the likely course of action the Government would take were this to be the case. He asked for my advice, and upon being told that resignation was the only viable option, he asked me to draft a resignation letter, which he signed. Upon my giving the Chairman's resignation letter to Mr Michuki, he was very surprised and asked me how I had managed it. I just told him that it was done, as requested.

Subsequently, following the unilateral declaration of independence by Rhodesia, a Rhodesian Company (AAPCO) that operated in Kenya as a branch suffered serious losses and refused to honour commitments to Kenyan life policy-holders. I successfully arranged transfer of life policies to KNAC.

In 1964 I was appointed an Alternate Director to the Board of KNAC. In 1975 I was appointed a Director in my personal capacity.

12.15.2 Personal Accident Protection Scheme

Following the acquisition of the KNAC, I proposed to Mr Butter and Mr Michuki that we should have in place an insurance policy that would pay if a civil servant died in an accident. In consultation with KNAC I produced a scheme, which showed that the cost was not prohibitive. Mr Michuki agreed, with the proviso that the Scheme should also include Members of Parliament. I was asked to draft a circular. I recall that when Hon. Ronald Ngala tragically died in a car accident, his family was paid from this scheme.

12.15.3 Kenya Reinsurance Corporation (1970)

I was instrumental in the successful establishment of Kenya Reinsurance Company, known initially as the State Reinsurance Corporation. In the late 1960s, especially following nationalization by Tanzania of banks and insurance companies, there was clamour that Kenya should also try do the same. I persuaded Mr Michuki that the way to deflect this pressure was to adopt an alternative which we could present as partial nationalization of insurance business. He accepted, and legislation was drafted and approved by the Parliament. A re-insurance expert from India was recruited, and it was agreed that 25 per cent of all general insurance business in Kenya would have to be re-insured with the State Reinsurance Company. This was accepted as an alternative to full nationalization of the insurance sector. I carefully negotiated re-insurance treaties, which ultimately would make the State Reinsurance Company one of the most profitable Government owned companies. This also reduced the outflow of foreign exchange, and I persuaded the Board to invest in Government bonds to finance the Government's development effort.

I was appointed an Alternate Treasury Director on the Board of State Reinsurance Corporation.

12.15.4 Agreement with Lloyds of London (1972)

In 1972, I negotiated an agreement with Lloyds of London to ensure that profitable Kenyan insurance business was not excessively transferred to London market. This agreement ensured growth of KNAC, the State Re, and the insurance market in Kenya, and ensured reduced foreign exchange drainage.

12.15.5 Motor Pool

As a member of the Insurance Advisory Board, I was a key member in the formation of a Motor Insurance Pool, which ensured that all the vehicles in Kenya, including local passenger buses (locally known as *Matatus*), were adequately insured. I cancelled a previous agreement, which had resulted in substantial transfer of funds overseas.

12.16 Devaluation of Sterling, Subsequent Collapse of Sterling Area and Related Issues

12.16.1 Hon. Mwai Kibaki Appointed Minister of Finance (1969)

In 1964 Hon. Mwai Kibaki was appointed Assistant Minister of Finance, together with Hon. Okello Odongo. He was subsequently appointed Minister for Commerce. In 1969, he became Minister of Finance. Hon. Mwai Kibaki and I were students at the London School of Economics, and I had also worked with him when he was appointed the Assistant Minister of Finance.

12.16.2 Protection of Foreign Exchange Reserves

Although administration of the Foreign Exchange Act was transferred to the Central Bank, Treasury was inundated with very many matters. I was the Treasury officer responsible for foreign exchange matters. Two international events had considerable effects on the international monetary system, and the effects of these on the Kenyan economy and foreign exchange were considerable.

The first of these was the sterling crisis, which resulted in the de facto death of the Sterling Area, and the second was the delinking of the US dollar to gold, which resulted in the death of the Bretton Woods Fixed Parity Regime.

12.16.3 Devaluation of Sterling

In late 1967 the pound sterling was devalued, and its parity to the US dollar was changed. Kenya initially refused to follow suit, but subsequently the Kenyan currency was also devalued. However, Kenya's initial decision not to devalue meant that the Kenyan shilling was stronger than sterling—pre-sterling devaluation the Kenya pound and sterling pound were at par, but following devaluation this changed, with the Kenyan shilling appreciating in value significantly. Although I was kept informed, all matters on new parity were handled by the Central Bank, in consultation with the Minister Hon. Mwai Kibaki and Mr Michuki, and coordinated with Central Bank Governors and Finance Ministers of Uganda and Tanzania.

12.16.4 Rumours of Sterling Devaluation

Before sterling was devalued there was a strong feeling in the British press and radio (the two main communication channels at that time) that sterling was likely to be devalued. There were reports of some countries withdrawing large amounts from their sterling reserves and transferring them into US dollars and gold. There were also reports of discussions between the UK, IMF, USA, Germany, and some other countries on financial assistance to stabilize sterling reserves in view of significant outflows from sterling to other currencies, mainly US dollars.

I opened a top secret file on the subject and discussed the matter with Mr Brough, a colleague of mine since Statistics days, who had become an advisor to the Treasury in place of John Butter. I subsequently discussed the matter with John Michuki and Hon. Mwai Kibaki.

12.16.5 Assurance No Devaluation

I was told that both Mr Michuki and Minister Mwai Kibaki had discussed the matter with the Governor of the Central Bank, who was coordinating Kenya's policy with the Governors of the Ugandan and Tanzanian Central Banks. We had been assured that there was no risk of devaluation, we should not move our reserves from sterling, and there was no risk of change in parity between sterling and the US dollar. I suggested we should write a letter to the UK Chancellor of

Exchequer and include therein the confirmation we had received that there would not be devaluation, and that we are not moving our reserves in view of this assurance. I drafted a letter for the Minister's signature, and the letter was subsequently sent.

Following devaluation, I understand Kenya approached the UK for compensation because we had been misled, I was told this matter was being handled by the Governor of the Central Bank. I cannot recollect whether we received any compensation.

12.16.6 Collapse of the Sterling Area

Despite devaluation, there were many reports about loss of confidence in sterling, and transfer of sterling reserves held by many countries, including some Commonwealth countries, to US dollars. These reports also indicated that the US dollar had become the favourite reserve currency, and means of settling international transactions, worldwide. Thus, the importance of sterling had started to decline, and the UK decided to join a European currency system known as Snake.

There were reports that France had insisted that some sterling reserves held by some countries should be further reduced as a condition for admitting sterling to Snake arrangements. This resulted in de facto abandonment of the sterling area. I had discussed these matters and need to diversify as had been foreseen by Dr Baranski with Mr Michuki and the Minister Mwai Kibaki. I understood the Governor dealt with this matter.

12.16.7 Interim Costs Related to Decision Not to Devalue

There were interim costs arising from the hesitation and delay in devaluing the Kenyan shilling. There was an increase in pressure to declare and remit dividends by foreign investors. Requests for the transfer of foreign loan interest denominated in Kenyan shillings increased. There was pressure to repay foreign loans denominated in Kenyan shillings, and to pay for imports in advance. Requests to transfer salary paid to expatriates in Kenyan shillings increased, and inwards transfers declined. Tourism became more expensive. Our exports earned less in Kenyan shillings. Being responsible for exchange control policy matters, I was increasingly coordinating with Central Bank Exchange Control to delay the transfer applications.

12.16.8 Collapse of the Bretton Woods System

Post sterling devaluation the dollar convertibility into gold had already started to wobble. Finally, the US decision to abandon free convertibility of dollar to gold at a fixed price led to the collapse of the Bretton Woods System of fixed exchange rate system and affected Kenya. I was concerned about this and expressed the same to the Minister. I was told he was in touch with the Governor. One consequence of the US decision was a steep rise in oil prices. I calculated our foreign exchange reserves were not enough to meet normal payments including payments for higher oil prices.

12.16.9 Action to Protect Our Foreign Exchange

I discussed with Hon. Mwai Kibaki the above international economic and monetary matters that were adversely affecting our balance of payments and foreign exchange reserves. A task force was formed, of which I was a part, attempting to formulate suitable policies to ensure that adverse effects on Kenya were minimized. To ensure proper use of our limited foreign exchange, I persuaded Hon. Mwai Kibaki to establish two committees under the Exchange Control Act: first, a Foreign Exchange Allocation Committee, and second, a Capital Issues Committee. I also suggested that in order to control prices, we should form a Price Control Committee. This was also agreed.

Some time after I had retired, I was told by the Secretary of both Exchange Control Committees that Kenya had, in part as a result of the formation of those bodies, survived the foreign exchange crisis.

12.16.10 Foreign Exchange Allocation Committee

The Foreign Exchange Allocation Committee, of which I was appointed Chairman, was formed to ensure that the foreign exchange reserves were only used for essential imports. The committee consisted of representatives of several Ministries and the Central Bank. Though there was a suggestion that we should increase duty to restricted imports, I persuaded the Committee that the best way to achieve our objective would be to impose specific quantitative restrictions. Having made calculations of quantum of foreign exchange available for imports, for a six month period, these were agreed. I was conscious of the need for the Central Bank to maintain foreign exchange cover for at least four months of imports, as described above. Since it was not possible for the Committee to examine all applications for imports this was delegated to Ministry of Commerce.

However, I had drafted a priority list of imports. This included government and military imports; imports of essentials like agriculture imports, including fertilizers and chemicals; pharmaceuticals imports; imports of spare parts and raw material for our industries, etc. The Committee discussed the list, and a final priority list of imports was agreed.

12.16.11 Brief Case Importers

There was a great deal of pressure from ministers, senior civil servants and politicians to allocate foreign exchange to import items that did not fall within the Committee's priority list described above. These people were, typically, not genuine importers, but commission agents wishing to have foreign exchange allocated to them, who would sell the 'allocation' to mainly Indian traders. I discussed this matter with Minister Hon. Mwai Kibaki, and it was agreed that this practice would not be supported by the allocation of foreign exchange, at the expense of genuine traders.

12.16.12 Gold Imports

I like to give an example of the pressure I often operated under. One Minister approached Minister of Finance Hon. Mwai Kibaki and asked if foreign exchange could be issued to him to import gold. I was called by Hon. Mwai Kibaki to his office, and requested to discuss the matter with the Minister, and to be helpful. In my office, I spoke to the Minister in detail. I informed him that I was the Gazetted Officer to ensure that there was no fraud on exchange control matters. I told him about the dangers to Kenya's foreign exchange reserves if we were to permit gold imports, as he was requesting. I explained the risk of serious foreign exchange leakage, and that we had reports of illegal gold arriving into Kenya from neighbouring territories, especially Congo. Kenyan goldsmiths would not be short of gold to continue their business, and there was no likelihood of unemployment due to this measure. He was convinced and did not wish to pursue his request. He admitted he did not know what was happening, and thanked me for briefing him.

12.16.13 Export of Semi-Precious Stones

In a similar vein, certain semi-precious stone such as rubies, garnets, etc. were mined in Kenya and secured from neighbouring countries, mostly illegally. We received applications by these exporters to hold foreign exchange earned from exports of these offshore, in order to pay suppliers in neighbouring countries. This was not, however, agreed to.

12.16.14 Offers of Loans to Import Oil

Treasury was approached with offers to finance oil imports. Some offers were to supply oil to be repaid over an agreed period at low interest rates, while other offers were cash loans to purchase oil. These loans were proposed as a cushion on Kenya's foreign exchange, but with the condition of a Central Bank guarantee, supported by the deposit of reserves in the bank granting the loan. I advised against these loans, however.

Similar loan offers, effectively mortgaging Kenya's foreign exchange reserves, were received when the Central Bank was established. At that time, we were inundated with offers of loans to Government using foreign exchange reserves to finance its development programme. Very powerful and senior people had started canvassing for these very low interest rate loans, as a means to solve all of Kenya's development finance needs. There were several variations of the types of loans on offer, but a common theme was the presence of a Central Bank guarantee, backed by the Central Bank depositing its reserves at a foreign bank nominated by the prospective lender. I had said this was not possible, and also requested Dr Baranski to speak on the unsuitability of these proposals to Mr Michuki and the Minister of Finance Mr Gichuru. I was called to give evidence on this and other budget matters by a Parliamentary Committee Chaired by Hon. Martin Shikuku.

12.16.15 Capital Issues Committee

The Capital Issues Committee, of which I was again appointed Chairman, was established for the purpose of ensuring that Kenya's foreign exchange reserves were used for essential payments and transfer only. Whatever could be delayed was to be delayed, usually on the pretext that the matter was before the Capital Issues Committee for consideration. This Committee was comprised of representatives from several ministries and the Central Bank. The Committee considered all applications for the transfer of interest, dividends, repayment of loans, etc., and made policies to ensure that proceeds of Kenya's exports were not retained overseas. We also restricted local borrowing by foreign investors.

12.16.16 Price Control Committee

A Price Control Committee, under the Price Control Act, was established to control price rises arising from increased import costs and likely scarcity. It was felt that whilst some price rises would be needed, traders taking advantage of shortages that would arise because of import controls should not be allowed to make profits. However, due to the onerous nature of the Chairmanship of the Foreign Exchange Committee and the Capital Issues Committee and other matters, I declined to accept the Chairmanship of the Price Control Committee.

12.17 Establishment of Structures to Promote Foreign Private Investments

12.17.1 Foreign Investments Protection Act

There was increased political pressure, emanating from Tanzanian and Ugandan policies being pursued at the time, for Kenya to speed up Africanization. The Kenyan economic model was, by contrast, that of a mixed economy, encouraging private foreign investment in the country. I was the Treasury officer responsible for the administration of the Foreign Investments Protection Act, the implementation of which was designed to ensure maximum foreign investments in priority developments sectors. Over time, this was successfully achieved, in consultation with various ministries.

Prior to enactment of the Foreign Investments Protection Act, there was an agreement signed at the highest level protecting foreign investments. We successfully persuaded foreign investors, on a 'willing buyer, willing seller' basis, to sell shares to local people, and especially to newly Africanized management. In addition to other policies adopted by the Government, this helped reduce demands for nationalization.

12.17.2 Convention for Settlement of Investments Disputes

To give comfort to foreign investors we accepted to become a member of the International Convention for Settlement of Investments Disputes between States and Foreign Nationals. This was embodied in the Investments Protection Act.

12.17.3 Double Taxation Agreements

In line with our policies to promote external private investments I recommended that we should actively pursue Double Taxation Treaties to avoid double taxation that may deter foreign investments. This was agreed. Assisted by the Commissioner of Income Tax, I commenced Double Taxation Agreement discussions with several countries. I was appointed to head the Kenya negotiating team to several countries including the USA, UK, Switzerland, Norway, Denmark, and Sweden. These agreements, once concluded, resulted Kenya keeping a larger share of revenue, and also increased the prospects of foreign investments from those countries.

12.17.4 Tax and Foreign Exchange Concessions in Agreements Entered by Government with Private Investors

I was responsible for approving tax concessions to foreign investors with the assistance of an inter-Ministerial Committee that would examine the agreements and make recommendations. I was also responsible for foreign exchange concessions, foreign management fees, etc., in consultation with the Central Bank. I recall that in the case of Del Monte, we refused to agree to some tax and duty concessions they sought. It was my opinion that tax concessions should only be made to overseas investors where the technology they brought to Kenya was more labour friendly, although I was overruled in this view, and it was decided that the technology to be used would be a decision of the foreign investor. It was also my view that because our foreign exchange allocation system gave protection to local industries from competitive imports, we should not be generous with tax allowances—although this was also ultimately rejected. I attended several meetings where protection of industries and duty concessions to them were discussed.

12.17.5 Establishment of a Sound Revenue Structure

Since 1962, I had participated in some Budget matters, including economic survey, and the Budget speech. I had also attended budget and tax meetings in Mombasa (Customs and Excise Department) and Kampala (inter-territorial Budget meetings). In 1963, I had suggested the introduction of tax on second hand motor vehicles. This was agreed, and I participated in the preparation of second-hand motor vehicles tax legislation.

12.17.6 Graduated Personal Tax Abolition as a Political Decision

I was involved in discussions on the abolition of the Graduated Personal Tax (GPT), a colonial tax which replaced the hut tax. There was a great deal of political pressure to abolish GPT. Despite revenue from GPT being significant, ultimately the decision was taken to abolish it for political considerations—the Government political thinking favoured the centralization of power, and the abolition of GPT would result in withdrawal of revenue from the local authorities thereby weakening them, and forcing them to become more dependent on Central Government for revenue.

12.17.7 Tourism as an Instrument of Growth and Source of Foreign Exchange

Mr Oliver Knowles, a Senior Deputy Secretary in the Treasury, discussed with me the possibility of encouraging tourism in the country. His opinion was that there was some political resentment to tourists coming to Kenya, but that tourism was internationally a big industry, and a significant foreign exchange earner. He opined that if it were to be agreed that tourism should be promoted in Kenya, it would help our foreign exchange and balance of payments position. Meanwhile we had received an application to build Mount Kenya Safari Club from some leading Americans, including the Hollywood star William Holden, in partnership with Mr Ray Ryan, an oil magnate. Mr Knowles felt that we should support the application.

I discussed in detail with Mr Michuki the issue of tourists and the possibility of promoting the tourism industry to increase our foreign exchange earnings. He foresaw the advantages, and agreed that steps should be taken to promote tourism and the tourist industry. As a first step, I issued a protection Certificate under the Foreign Investments Protection Act to Mount Kenya Safari Club. A suggestion had also been made that we should give some tax concessions to builders of hotels, which was agreed and included in the tax laws.

12.17.8 Tax Suggestions on Insurance Pensions and Provident Funds

I had suggested that either the contributions to life insurance policies and to pensions and provident funds should be taxed or alternatively, the income of these funds should be taxed. It was my view that current tax exemptions were very generous, and a costly approach to generate and promote savings. This was, however, not agreed in view of considerable opposition from insurance companies, pensions, and provident funds, although I was subsequently able to implement the policy in part.

12.17.9 Capital Gains Tax

At a budget meeting Chaired by Mr Philip Ndegwa and attended by me, the Commissioner of Income Tax, Mr Ihiga, and Mr Brough, a proposal to introduce Capital Gains Tax was discussed. Mr Brough, who had replaced John Butter as an adviser, elaborated the pros and cons of the proposal, and produced estimates of the revenue that would be received. Mr Ihiga objected, however, on the grounds that the then on-going split with the East African Income Tax Department, and establishment of the Kenyan Income Tax Department, left no capacity for additional administrative responsibility at that stage. I proposed, instead, an increase in stamp duty, which would raise significant revenue without the associated administrative issues. Mr Ihiga supported my proposal, which was then adopted.

12.17.10 Tax Concessions to Promote Employment

Many discussions took place on tax concessions to promote employment. Professor Richard, the Head of the Planning Department, was very keen that this be done to promote employment and reduce unemployment. Several suggestions were made on how this concession could be introduced, but there was no clarity on revenue that would be foregone; what would happen to seasonal employment matters; and how to avoid the considerable risk of fraud. Further there was the issue of alternate uses of foregone revenue and this was raised. Should funds be used to raise educational standards of workers? Should they be used to reduce migration from rural areas to urban areas? Should they be used to control rapid growth of population? Policy to promote employment was felt to be a good and acceptable idea—however the idea of tax concession to promote employment was not pursued further.

12.17.11 Tax Concessions to Promote Savings

In late 1970, a paper on the promotion of savings had been prepared by an expert at the Ministry of Planning. Several proposals were included, all aimed at subsidizing savings by tax concessions. One proposal was to sharply increase interest rates on Post Office Saving Bank deposits. When I saw the paper, I asked for revenue cost of such a sharp increase in interest rates on the deposits at the Post Office Savings Bank and if it was worth subsidizing savings at that cost. I introduced the author to the Post Office Savings Bank, and after discussions with them, and armed with a better understanding of the facts, he withdrew his proposals. However, instead we introduced a Premium Bond that carried no interest but a chance of winning large sum. This became a popular instrument in the country.

12.17.12 Kenya Income Tax Act

I was the Treasury Officer responsible for Income Tax matters. In 1973, after the break-up of the East African Income Tax Department I, with the assistance of

Kenyan Designate Commissioner of Income Tax Department Mr Ihiga, and a British tax advisor, adapted the East African Income Tax Act into the new Kenya Income Tax Act, ensuring it was consistent with the needs of Kenya, a more foreign investor friendly jurisdiction compared with Uganda and Tanzania. We introduced PAYE, and reduced tax subsidies to savings for insurance, pensions and provident funds. Some income tax slabs were also altered. Aware of the mercantilist theory, I proposed 'transfer taxes' but this proposal evoked considerable opposition and was not adopted. Although the public were informed that the change from the East African to Kenya Act would be revenue neutral, we nevertheless made a number of changes which increased revenue, whilst, at the direction of Hon. Minister of Finance Mwai Kibaki, simplifying the Income Tax Act as much as we could.

12.17.13 Sales Tax (VAT) (1973)

I was the Treasury Officer responsible for imposition of sales tax. In view of the increase in demand for expenditure, the Treasury was keen to increase revenue from internal sources and widen the tax base. We had done the same in the case of income tax, and accordingly, I researched a report prepared by the IMF on the possibility of value added tax in Kenya, examining several options. However, none of the proposals were pursued because of implementation issues. I instead recommended that initially a simple system of sales tax should be introduced, levied at point of imports and at manufacturer's level. This would not give as much revenue as was initially hoped for, but could be developed further in due course, as the administrative machinery became established. With the assistance of the IMF and a Canadian tax advisor, an Act was drafted to establish the Sales Tax Department, as it was known at that time, and the measure enabled a gap in the Government revenues to be filled and widened the country's tax base.

12.17.14 Tax Suggestions

After Philip Ndegwa retired there was no immediate replacement. The Deputy Permanent Secretary, John Keriri had earlier moved to become Managing Director of the Development Finance Company of Kenya. The Acting Permanent Secretary requested me to prepare a note before my retirement on tax changes that I would recommend. Since I had dealt with tax matters and had also looked at the Annual Trade Report during my Chairmanship of the Foreign Exchange Allocation Committee, I was familiar with the trade and duty structure of our imports. I advised items where customs duty and sales tax could be imposed and or increased without disrupting the economy. I also produced some suggestions for other areas of revenue. Most of these measures were subsequently adopted in the June 1975 Budget.

12.18 World Bank and IMF Meetings in Kenya

It was decided that we should persuade the IMF and World Bank to hold their Annual Meetings in Kenya. A technical delegation from the IMF and World Bank was to come to Kenya to examine the feasibility of a conference in Nairobi, and in view of my connections with the IMF, I was given the responsibility to persuade the IMF and World Bank technical staff that Kenya could meet all their requirements for Annual Meetings. In the company of Hon. Mwai Kibaki I travelled to Copenhagen in 1970 to study specific requirements of the World Bank and the IMF for holding such large and important meetings outside Washington. The Kenyatta Conference Centre was under construction, and it was felt might be a suitable venue for the Annual Meetings. During discussions in Copenhagen, I was told a venue to accommodate at least 2500 would be required. The proposed Kenyatta Conference Centre was designed to accommodate only 600 delegates. The second requirement mentioned to me was the need to provide high level hotel/residential accommodation for 2500 Delegates and accompanying press. On my return, I informed the architect responsible for the Kenyatta Conference Centre at the Ministry of Works that we needed a large Plenary Hall to accommodate 2500 delegates before the IMF and World Bank would agree to meet in Kenya. Several options were discussed, including building a completely new conference centre. Finally, we agreed that the most viable option was to add a match box type conference hall to the plans for the Kenyatta Conference Centre. I was aware of controversy surrounding the shape of Kenyatta Conference Centre and its viability, and discussed the options and our view with Mr Michuki. Subsequently we were authorized to draw up plans for a rectangular conference hall. I instructed the Ministry of Works to draw up suitable plans to add a suitable plenary hall to the Kenyatta Conference Centre, notwithstanding any land or cost issues.

When the IMF and World Bank Delegation arrived in Kenya we showed them the proposed Plenary Hall plans. They were impressed by the size but wondered if it would be ready in time. We showed all details of hotel accommodation available and they considered there was need for increased higher class accommodation. They discussed transport and we said we had agreed to order the required number of Mercedes cars. The delegates and myself visited the Conference Centre that was under construction and noted any special requirements, including offices etc. It was agreed to add several floors to Kenyatta Conference Centre to provide additional office space that the IMF or World Bank would require.

The Head of IMF delegation informed me that their preliminary assessment was that Kenya could provide the necessary facilities. However, even if all facilities were adequate there were certain political requirements that would need to be cleared: for example, South African delegates must be permitted to attend, as well as delegates from Israel. These matters were referred to the Cabinet, accordingly, and clearance sought and secured. I successfully persuaded the IMF's technical delegation strongly to recommend that Kenya had the facilities to host the meetings, which, for the first time on the Continent of Africa, were successfully held in 1973.

At the meeting, I interacted with several bankers and Ministry of Finance officials whom I had met in Copenhagen. They congratulated me about the decision and shape of the Conference Hall. They foresaw many more international meetings in this plenary hall. I mentioned this to Mr Michuki. He said unwittingly we have become instrumental to making Nairobi a hub of international conferences.

12.19 Other Matters of Interest I Handled

When I joined the Government, I found most expatriate Officers were excellent administrators but did not comprehend what Independence meant or what it will entail. I was impressed that John Butter did. I found the returning Kenyan graduates were focussed and keen to progress Kenya. Two of these I handed over my statistical work to were Mr Masakhalia (who became a Minister) and Snr Obama.

I give here a few examples of the culture and climate of the times, and how these were affected by the arrival for Kenya of Independence:

12.19.1 Office for Minister of State for Constitutional Affairs and Economic Planning

When the National Government was formed in 1963, H.E. President Jomo Kenyatta was appointed the Minister of State for Constitutional Affair and Economic Planning. I participated in the selection of his office space. The Acting Permanent Secretary (one Mr Byron) to the Treasury who was also Acting Permanent Secretary the Ministry of State for Constitutional Affairs and Economic Planning, proposed a bigger office for himself and smaller office for the Minister. I suggested a bigger office for the Minister, saying that a smaller office would not be in keeping with the times. He accepted. On showing the office to the Minister he said 'Your office, sir.' This was printed with the photograph in the front page of the *East African Standard.*

12.19.2 Use of Treasury Lift

There was at that time in place a system regarding who could use the Treasury lift. Most African civil servants were not allowed to use the lift, while Asian civil servants could only use the lift in the absence of an expatriate officer (and were required to vacate the lift upon the arrival of an expatriate office). I refused to accept the discriminatory rule on the use of lift, and was confidentially informed that at least one expatriate civil servant had complained about that. However, nothing was ever mentioned to me officially.

12.19.3 Budgetary Names

John Butter came to my office. He mentioned that now Kenya had obtained Independence, the name of 'Colonial Budget' should no longer be used, and asked me for alternative suggestions. I recommended a change in name of the Government accounts to 'Recurrent Expenditure', and for the Capital Budget to 'Development Expenditure'—suggestions which were subsequently implemented.

12.19.4 Trade Agreement with China

I participated in Trade Agreement negotiations with China. The late Dr Kiano was the leader of Kenyan delegation, and I was in team that drafted our proposals for a Trade Agreement. China produced their proposals but written in Chinese. China was non-committal to our request to be treated as most favoured Nation. China stated that they were not able to amend the draft presented by them, without a special typewriter which they did not have in Kenya. Dr Kiano said he was prepared to sign the Kenyan draft, but not the draft submitted by China, and accordingly no agreement was signed.

Subsequently, I prepared briefs for initial Meetings of the OAU (now known as the AU). My brief for the Cairo meeting of 1964 caused a stir, since it stated that China was an important trading partner of apartheid South Africa, something which China denied. Our delegation, led by Dr Kiano, was asked to explain the source, and John Butter rushed to my office and asked me for it. I showed him an IMF document that was the basis of the brief, following which Dr Kiano was very happy to explain in Egypt the credible source as the IMF. The IMF decided thereafter not to print trading figures for certain countries.

12.19.5 Purchase of Planes

One day, John Butter came to my office. He told me of a proposal by the Kenyan national airline to buy either an American Boeing or a British aircraft. The prevailing advice was that Boeing was more economical to fly than the British plane, notwithstanding that if a British plane were to be bought there were good chances of securing finance from the UK on good terms, in addition to other projects the British Government would favourably consider to finance. He asked me for my opinion. I understood that the flying cost *per seat* of the Boeing was less than that of the British alternative, but asked John Butter if there was any evidence whether passengers would prefer to fly in the British plane or in the Boeing plane. He said that, of course, most of the traffic was to London, and people would be more inclined to fly a British plane to London. I said that, if this were the case, and if costs *per seat occupied* were taken as the appropriate measurement, which one would be more economical? He smiled and went away, and British planes were bought.

12.19.6 Nyali Bridge

At another time, Mr Michuki called me to his office, to say that the First President was going to Mombasa on a working holiday, and had received several complaints about the charges levied by the Nyali Bridge Company on crossings by pedestrians.

I had already been approached by Nyali Bridge Company representatives, as an agreement between them and the Government was coming to an end. They complained that they are not allowed to raise charges, and that the whole bridge needed repairs, and was turning into a loss.

I discussed with the Company their finances in detail, and pointed out how little net revenue they were receiving from pedestrians. I suggested, accordingly, that I would support a proposal to sell the bridge to the Government if they agreed to drop charges on pedestrians. I also told them there was a proposal to build another bridge which the Government is considering. The Company agreed to waive charges for the pedestrians. H.E. the First President announced the waiver of charges whilst in Mombasa, to great acclaim.

12.19.7 Mombasa Port and Containers

The late Mr Michuki informed me about a proposal to build a special berth at Mombasa Port suitable for containers and containers ships and asked for my opinion. I told him the international shipping was going the containers' route. If we do not provide facilities for containers our imports and exports will suffer excessive transport costs. I strongly recommended we adopt facilities for container ships and containers. I also produced some statistics and articles all showing the container trade was on the increase and that was the future of shipping transportation. Despite opposition that containers could be used for illegal international trade Mr Michuki accepted my advice.

12.19.8 Finance for Oil Pipeline

Hon. Mwai Kibaki asked my opinion on how to finance the Kenyan Oil Pipeline Company, as the finance for the project had got stuck. Mr Brough, the Treasury Advisor, was handling this matter. I spoke to him and obtained all the information and correspondence he had on the subject, and travelled to London to meet the pipeline advisors. They had made an application to the British Import Export Bank (Exim Bank) to provide finance for pipes, to which the Exim Bank had agreed, as the project would promote British industry. However, an application for finance of the Management Fees had been made to the World Bank, which was not agreeable, because its tendering procedures had not been followed. I spoke to Import Export Bank and to World Bank representatives who were in London, and asked Exim Bank whether it would finance Management Fees. They said yes, provided that the management team was British, which was the case. In turn, I asked the World Bank whether it would finance the pipes, to which they agreed provided we complied with their tender requirements. Thus the financial package was reorganized, with finance for Management Fees to be provided by Exim Bank, and finance for pipes to be provided by the World Bank as per its tendering procedure.

Exim Bank also asked for a guarantee by the Central Bank of Kenya, which we refused. On my return to Nairobi I briefed the Minister Mwai Kibaki on the re-arranged financial package, with which he was happy.

12.20 Concluding Remarks and Honour

There are many lessons that may be learned from this chapter on a long journey that involved the establishment of the Central Bank in Kenya, the relationship between the Central Bank and the Ministry of Finance, interactions with top Government officials and most importantly the architecture of the financial system in Kenya. I leave it to the readers to draw lessons after going through the chapter.

For rendering distinguished services to the nation in the field of finance and banking during independent Kenya's formative years, I was awarded the honour of Moran of the Order of the Burning Spear (MBS).

13

Central Banking in Kenya

Evolution, Challenges, and Future Prospects

Maureen Were, Charles Koori, and Julius Bett

13.1 Background

The history of central banking dates back to the seventeenth century, when the first institution recognized as a central bank—the Swedish Riksbank, was established in 1668 as *Riksens Ständers Bank* (the Estates of the Realm Bank).[1] The Bank of England followed in 1694. The two institutions, initially established as joint stock banks to purchase government debt, laid a foundation in defining the role of the first wave of central banks, which was basically orientated towards lending to government (Bordo, 2007). Initially they were not called central banks since the term 'central bank' only came to use in the late nineteenth century (Bordo and Siklos, 2017). By the beginning of the twentieth century there were only 18 central banks (Capie et al., 1994).

The role of central banks broadened in the nineteenth century to deal with management of financial crises.[2] 1873 remains a historic year since it marked the beginning of the period when the gold standard formally became established as the main exchange rate regime for much of the industrialized world (Capie et al., 1994). The primary focus of the central banks that emerged at the turn of the twentieth century was to consolidate the various instruments in use as currency and manage the gold standard that prevailed until 1914 (Bordo, 2007). Central banks were expected to adhere to the rule of maintaining gold convertibility, which served as the nominal anchor. Each country defined its currency in terms of a fixed weight of gold, and the amount of money banks could supply was constrained by the value of the gold they held in reserve, which in turn determined the price level. Maintaining price stability, stabilizing the business cycles, and

[1] The authors would like to thank Terry Ryan, Matu Mugo, and colleagues from the Research Department of the Central Bank of Kenya for helpful comments. However, the authors retain responsibility of any remaining errors.

[2] The nineteenth century witnessed a series of panic and bank failures in the US (1819, 1837, 1857, 1873, 1893), Belgium (1838, 1848), etc., which partly accounted for the rise in the pace of creation of central banks during the period, e.g. Norway (1816), Belgium (1850), Germany (1876), Japan (1882), Italy (1893), and US (1913).

Maureen Were, Charles Koori, and Julius Bett, *Central Banking in Kenya: Evolution, Challenges, and Future Prospects* In: *50 Years of Central Banking in Kenya: Regional and Global Perspectives.* Edited by: Patrick Njoroge and Victor Murinde, Oxford University Press (2021). © The Central Bank of Kenya. DOI: 10.1093/oso/9780198851820.003.0013

maintaining full employment became the key roles of central banks in the twentieth century (Bordo and Siklos, 2017).

Generally, the evolution of central banking over time has been largely shaped by developments and dynamics in the global economy. These include the events of World War I and II,[3] the Great Depression of the early 1930s, the creation of the Bretton Wood institutions (International Monetary Fund and the World Bank) in 1944, the collapse of the Bretton Wood System of fixed exchange rate regime in 1971[4] in favour of floating exchange rates, globalization and financial integration in the 1990s, and the global financial crisis of 2008. For instance, the emergence of stagflation in the early 1970s after the collapse of the fixed exchange rate regime posed a greater challenge to the foundations of the post-war confidence in the maintenance of full employment and the conventional wisdom of Phillips Curve, that is, inflation–unemployment trade-off. Consequently, efforts were directed towards controlling inflation that had risen globally in the wake of the first oil supply shock of 1973. Price stability became the primary objective of monetary policy. The concern with inflation management drew support from the monetarist school of thought[5] that advocated control of money supply to contain inflation, with a bias towards free markets. These led to an era of monetary targeting[6] until the mid-1980s when concerns about predictability of velocity and monetary stability intensified (Capie et al., 1994).

In terms of financial regulation, steps were taken towards international policy coordination with respect to prudential regulation and supervision, following episodes of financial distress, which impacted on central banking and led to renewed prominence for safeguarding the stability of the financial system. The move was rejuvenated by internationalization of finance and increased globalization following the ascendancy to free market philosophy that gathered momentum in the 1980s.

Overall, over time, the core mandates of central banks have become largely more focused on price stability, particularly as political environments have become more and more receptive to the idea of granting central banks a greater degree of autonomy from government. The attention and general shift towards inflation targeting as a modern monetary policy framework is partly underpinned by the understanding that an independent central bank is able to act promptly to head off inflation. Promoting the soundness of the financial sector through prudential regulation and supervision (micro-prudential level), as well as enhancing linkages across

[3] World War I: 1914–18; World War II: 1939–45. The number of central banks increased subsequently during the inter-war period as it became acceptable that any self-respecting independent country should have its own central bank and own currency (Capie et al., 1994). As the colonial period receded, more and more countries especially in Africa became independent and set up their own central banks.

[4] 1971 also marked the end of the Gold Standard.

[5] Led by Milton Friedman, an American economist and Nobel laureate.

[6] Beginning with West German in 1974. Other countries that adopted formal monetary targeting were USA, Switzerland, Canada, and UK.

institutions and markets (macro-prudential level) by upgrading payment and settlement systems is based on the need to safeguard financial stability. Whereas price and financial stability are commonly accepted as the two main objectives of modern central banks, the debate is far from concluded, particularly in the wake of the 2008 global financial crisis.[7] Some countries have de-linked the responsibilities of bank regulation and public-debt management from the central bank. However, for most African countries with less developed financial markets, these functions and even much more continue to be performed by the central banks.

The Central Bank of Kenya (CBK) celebrated its 50th anniversary on 14 September 2016. A lot has changed over the last 50 years. The CBK has sailed through various phases economically, politically, and globally over the years to be what it is. It has traversed a period of a largely state-controlled economy to a liberalized market economy. Politically, it has sailed through de facto one-party system regime to multi-party political democracy. Moreover, being a small open economy, Kenya has not been immune to the dynamics in the world economy.

The CBK has undoubtedly achieved several milestones over the years and remains steadily focused on discharging its mandate as enshrined in the Constitution of Kenya and the Central of Kenya Act upon which it was established. Nonetheless, from a global perspective and considering other central banks that have been in existence for over 200 years,[8] the CBK is relatively young and still evolving. In pursuance of its vision of a world-class modern central bank, there is ample scope to learn and adapt not only from other central banks, but also from the changing global dynamics. This chapter traces the evolution of central banking in Kenya over the last 50 years, including milestones, challenges, and future prospects.

The rest of the chapter is organized as follows. Section 13.2 traces the evolution of the CBK and key changes over time, starting from the formative years. Section 13.3 discusses the current developments, milestones, and challenges. Section 13.4 provides a highlight of some of the factors likely to shape the future of central banking in Kenya.

13.2 Evolution of the Central Bank of Kenya

13.2.1 The Formative Years

The history of the CBK closely parallels that of other central banks established around the same time in the East Africa region—specifically, in Uganda and Tanzania. Prior to the establishment of the three central banks in Kenya,

[7] The Bank of England, which had previously been stripped of these responsibilities in 1997, is back in charge of bank regulation. The Dodd-Frank act of 2010 gave the US Federal Reserve bank the authority to ensure financial stability.

[8] In 2018, the Riksbank will celebrate its 350th anniversary.

Uganda, and Tanzania, the traditional central banking functions in the East African Community (EAC) were performed by the East African Currency Board (EACB). The Board, established by the British Government in 1919, was mandated to promote and control the supply of currency to the East Africa Protectorate, namely the territories of Kenya, Uganda, and the then Tanganyika (currently Tanzania).[9] The Board was established on the 'Sterling Exchange Standard' system to issue and redeem its currency in exchange for an equivalent accumulation of sterling (CBK, 1972). It initially issued the East African Florin, which was replaced by the East African shilling in 1922.[10] In 1955, the EACB mandate was broadened from a purely automatic money changer, to encompass credit extension to the Governments of the constituent territories, by holding local Government securities (CBK, 2000a). In 1957, the maximum currency issue against local Government securities was increased from KSh 200 to KSh 400 million. The financial limit to short-term financing to Governments was later raised to KSh 500 million in 1963 and KSh 700 million in 1964. Whereas Uganda and Tanzania regularly used this facility, Kenya did not—an indication the three countries operated at different levels financially.

The need for central banking in East Africa emerged after the World War I, following the general price instability that ensued and the subsequent acceleration in establishment of central banks across Europe. Locally, the EACB encountered a myriad of challenges right from its inception. Foremost, it was difficult to coordinate monetary policy with other economic policies as each country pursued diverse economic policies. The failure of the proposed East African Federation that would have provided the framework for coordination of the area-wide socio-economic policies to take off made matters worse. Moreover, the monetary policy role of the Board was passive, as it lacked discretionary powers to regulate and influence the activities of commercial banks and non-bank financial institutions in the expansion of credit. The supply of credit was determined by commercial banks.

As the weaknesses of the EACB became apparent, a debate as to whether a common central bank or country specific central banks was the suitable replacement for the Board ensued. After the EAC countries attained independence (between 1961 and 1963), the Board ceased to issue notes with the image of the British Monarch and replaced them with new notes showing a dhow on Lake Victoria—a common territory to the three countries (CBK, 2016). On 25 November 1963, the EACB published a report advising the three countries (Kenya, Uganda, and Tanzania) to establish an East African Central Bank. The Kenya Government supported the idea of a regionally managed currency in East

[9] Kenya was a colony, Uganda was a Protectorate, and Tanganyika was a Trust Territory.

[10] Before the formation of the EACB, a Board of Currency Commissioners issued the Indian silver rupee in Kenya and Uganda, while in Tanganyika (Tanzania), which up to the end of the First World War was a German colony, a German silver rupee was in use.

Africa within the framework of an East African Federation, which, as a matter of fact, never materialized (CBK, 1972). Reconciling the concept of a regional central monetary institution with national sovereignty proved a challenge, particularly in the absence of political union. It then became imperative for each of the East African States to establish its own institution for monetary policy, particularly after it became apparent that the three countries did not have a unified view on a single currency and central bank. Attempts to establish one central bank for the region flopped when Tanzania decided to set up its own central bank in 1965, and announced it would issue its own currency. Uganda followed suit in August 1966.

The journey of the Central Bank of Kenya began on 24 March 1966, with the enactment of the Central Bank of Kenya Act, the legislation that established the CBK. However, it was not until 14 September 1966 that the Bank, also known as 'Banki Kuu ya Kenya' officially opened its doors for business, in Herufi House (an old building along Lt Tumbo Avenue). Upon its establishment, CBK issued Kenya's first currency (Kenya shillings) which was pegged to British sterling pound (£) at the rate of £1 = KSh 20. The Kenya shilling notes were initially issued in denominations of 5, 10, 20, 50, and 100, all bearing the portrait of the first President, Mzee Jomo Kenyatta, with other scenes of economic activities at the back. By 30 June 1966, the CBK had exchanged KSh 300 million of the East African currency notes, while its own notes in circulation amounted to KSh 360 million (CBK, 1986). The EACB notes ceased to be legal tender on 14 September 1967, while the coins remained legal tender until 1 April 1969.

The Central Bank of Kenya Act 1966 laid down the powers of the CBK. The principal objectives of the Bank were to: (i) regulate the issue of notes and coins, (ii) assist in the development and maintenance of a sound monetary, credit, and banking system, and (iii) serve as banker and financial adviser to the Government. The CBK Act also established a Board of Directors with the CBK Governor and the Deputy Governor as the chair and deputy chair, respectively.[11] The Bank had 60 members of staff comprising of 38 Kenyans and 22 expatriates (CBK, 1986). By the end of the first year, the number of staff had more than doubled to 148.

The CBK's functions and responsibilities quickly broadened as the Bank took over functions hitherto performed by the EACB and additional roles. On 16 November 1966, the CBK took over the running of the Bankers' Clearing House and opened accounts for commercial banks in Kenya.[12] These were the first steps towards the control and regulation of the banking system and the activities

[11] The first Governor, Dr Leon Baranski, was seconded to CBK by the IMF for a short period before the Government appointed in December 1966 Mr Duncan Ndegwa, who became the first African Governor in May 1967, while Mr A. Abdallah was appointed Deputy Governor.

[12] Commercial banking activities had begun much earlier in the late 1890s. These include National Bank of India which established a branch in Mombasa in 1896, followed by Standard Bank of South Africa (1910) and National Bank of South Africa which amalgamated with the Colonial Bank and the Anglo-Egyptian Bank Limited in 1926 to form Barclays Bank. The Chartered Bank of India, Australia and China is also believed to have existed along Kenya's coast.

of financial institutions. The Bank also took over the main accounts of the Government from the National and Grindlays Bank Ltd and began the collection of financial statistics on a regular basis. On 7 March 1967 the CBK took over management of the exchange rate control regime that had been set up under the Treasury in 1965. Less than two years later, CBK took over the responsibility for the issue and management of Government Treasury bills and the administration of government funded debt (CBK, 1986).

The regulatory scope of the CBK's function was entrenched in the Banking Act 1968, which replaced the Banking Act of 1956. The Act, which did not come into effect until 3 June 1969 gave the CBK comprehensive powers and responsibilities over commercial banks including licensing and inspection, and imposition of liquidity ratios as tool for monetary policy (minimum liquidity ratio of 1.5 per cent was applied on 1 December 1969). The amendments were aimed at harmonizing the Banking Act with the CBK Act, thereby laying the foundation for the future expansion of the banking industry (CBK, 1986). Whereas the CBK Act primarily aimed at facilitating the development and maintenance of a sound monetary policy, the Banking Act was designed to safeguard customers' deposits in banks and other financial institutions (CBK, 1972). The powers and operations of the CBK have since been governed by the CBK Act and the Banking Act. Both have gone through a series of amendments over time.

On the economic front, the first decade of independence recorded strong economic growth, with an average real GDP growth of 6.2 per cent in the period 1966–1970. Kenya was ranked among the few countries that achieved rapid economic growth with an enviable record of price stability[13] (Ikiara and Killick, 1981).

13.2.2 The Post-Independence Period: State Control Regime (1970s and 1980s)

After independence, the Government's development strategy focused on Africanization of business and promotion of local entrepreneurship. The economic policy framework which was anchored in the *Sessional Paper No. 10 of 1965 on African Socialism and its Application to Planning in Kenya* outlined the Government's intent to foster African socialism,[14] growth, and development. These goals were to be achieved largely through control of resources and state ownership, coupled with a wide range of price controls (interest rates, foreign exchange, prices of basic commodities). It was strongly felt that the financial sector

[13] Inflation was below 3 per cent in the 1960s.

[14] However unlike the African socialism of *Ujamaa* as formulated in Tanganyika, Kenya proposed a system embodying more or less market-based features embedded in *harambee* philosophy.

was not playing its role in addressing the developmental needs of the country. For instance, the foreign-owned banks that dominated the sector[15] were perceived to be biased against the small African businesses, and hence direct government intervention was viewed as a remedy. Consequently, there were deliberate efforts to set up state-owned banks. The first locally owned bank, the Cooperative Bank of Kenya, opened for business on 10 January 1968, followed closely by National Bank of Kenya and Kenya Commercial Bank (KCB). However, foreign-owned banks continued to dominate the banking business through most of the 1970s (CBK, 2000b). By 1972, the number of commercial banks had increased to 12, with three banks (Barclays, Standard, and KCB) controlling most of the operations. In January 1978, CBK opened its first branch in Mombasa.

Development Financial Institutions (DFIs) were set up to close the gap for long-term financing. With respect to agriculture for instance, these comprised the Agricultural Finance Corporation, Agricultural Development Corporation, and Cereals and Sugar Finance Corporation. Efforts to promote indigenous financial institutions led to rapid growth of Non-Bank Financial Institutions (NBFIs), particularly in view of the less stringent controls they were subjected to. The aim was mainly to mobilize private savings including small savers, and supply credit to enterprise and private households for financing a range of activities including mortgage lending, hire purchase financing, and merchant banking. As at 30 June 1971, the total assets/liabilities of NBFIs amounted to KSh 462 million—equivalent to 10.7 per cent of the total assets of commercial banks, while loans and advances as a proportion of commercial banks' was 14.4 per cent (CBK, 1972). Being in competition with banks for deposits, they offered high interest rates and more categories of term-deposit facilities than commercial banks. NBFIs increased rapidly in the 1980s as a number of commercial banks took advantage of the less stringent requirements[16] and higher interest rates to set up NBFIs.

However, the proliferation of NBFIs had regulatory implications, as they were not effectively under the supervision of the CBK. The rapid growth of banks and NBFIs was not marked by a corresponding effective prudential regulation (CBK, 1994). Imprudent lending practices led to a build-up in Non-Performing Loans (NPLs) which, coupled with liquidity and solvency challenges, led to the first banking crisis in 1984, after one bank and an NBFI collapsed.

In 1985, the Banking Act was comprehensively amended in a bid to address weaknesses in the legislation. The amendments gave more legal power to the CBK

[15] In 1965, Standard, Barclays, and National and Grindlays accounted for 80 per cent of total deposits.

[16] These included: lower minimal capital requirements compared to banks; NBFIs were not subjected to a minimum liquid assets requirement until 1971; whereas a minimal cash ratio was imposed on banks in December 1971, the requirement did not apply to NBFIs; administrative credit ceilings applied only to banks; and the differential regulation of interest rates favoured NBFIs (CBK, 1994).

to perform its regulatory function and broadened the responsibilities and the coverage of the institutions under the revised legislation. To ensure adequate capitalization and safeguard against mismanagement, minimal capital requirements were increased to 15 million for setting up a locally incorporated bank from KSh 10 million, and KSh 7.5 million for starting an NBFI.[17] To safeguard the interest of depositors, the Act prohibited banks and NBFIs from granting unsecured advances and credit facilities to its employees or their relatives amounts in excess of KSh 10000. The amended law also prohibited directors of banks and NBFIs from granting themselves, and their associated businesses, unsecured advances and credit facilities (CBK, 1986). A provision for the establishment of a Deposit Protection Fund was included to protect depositors, particularly small depositors in the event of insolvency and foster public confidence in the banking system (CBK, 1994). The Fund, which later converted to Kenya Deposit Insurance Corporation in 2012, is now an independent institution created through an Act of Parliament.

In general, central banking after independence was largely geared towards the development and expansion of the financial sector while safeguarding the interest of depositors, in an endeavour to maintain 'a sound monetary, credit and banking system' as envisaged at the establishment of the CBK. This necessitated review and amendments of laws to legally empower the CBK in performing regulatory functions in line with the broadened responsibilities. Over the first 20 years, the essential objectives of the CBK were to maintain the external and internal value of the currency and maintain financial stability (CBK, 1986). Monetary policy was generally passive, particularly in view of interest rate and foreign exchange controls, coupled with weak fiscal control and limited authority over monetary policy management. The formulation and pursuit of monetary policy largely focused on controlling the allocation and amount of credit in the economy, i.e. through quantitative monetary controls. This was implemented by setting targets for domestic credit of the banking system and control of growth in money supply to ensure consistence with the credit targets (monetary targeting). According to Honohan and O'Connell (2008), post-independence monetary policy frameworks in Africa were mainly geared towards the financing of government operations, extension of subsidized credit to preferred sectors and active pursuit of exchange rate target, rather than inflation control.

The Government's strategy of direct participation and intervention in the economy greatly impacted the nature and design of monetary policy in the post-independence period. The CBK embraced the Government's pursuit of a low interest rate regime, which was implemented through interest rate controls and quantitative credit restrictions. Consequently, the use of direct credit control measures became prevalent in the 1970s. Interest rate controls entailed fixing

[17] Both banks and NBFIs were given up to 16 May 1987 to increase their paid up or assigned capital.

minimum saving rates for all deposit taking institutions and maximum lending rates for all commercial banks, NBFIs and building societies. However, the deposit and savings rates were too low compared with the lending rates, leading to wide interest rate spreads that have continued to beleaguer the banking sector.

The economic shocks experienced in the early 1970s exposed the economy's vulnerability to external shocks and cracks in the control regime. In particular, the inflationary pressures that emerged following balance of payments (BOP) crisis in 1971–1972 and the international oil crisis of 1973 resulted in negative real savings rates. In mitigation, the CBK raised the interest rates on both deposits and loans for the first time since independence in June 1974. Minimum rates on deposits and lending were raised from 3 per cent and 7 per cent to 5 per cent and 8 per cent, respectively. In July 1974 a maximum lending rate of 10 per cent was introduced. A credit ceiling of 12 per cent with priority to agricultural sector, small African enterprises and exporters was issued in a bid to contain credit expansion to the private sector. Additionally, minimum liquidity requirement of 15 per cent which had previously applied only to commercial banks was extended to cover NBFIs. On the exchange rate front, in October 1975 the monetary authority switched the shilling peg from the US dollar to the SDR that was considered to be more stable, resulting in a devaluation of 10.8 per cent (CBK, 1981). Although domestic credit and growth in money supply considerably slowed down as a result of the various control measures undertaken by the CBK, inflation accelerated sharply to 15.8 per cent in 1974 from 5.4 per cent in 1972, while output growth slowed to 2.0 per cent from 6.4 per cent over the same period (Table A13.1).

The overall BOP improved substantially in 1976–77 as a result of the coffee boom, following a sharp rise in world coffee prices.[18] This was however short-lived, as it was accompanied by expansion of domestic credit, largely due to increased Government borrowing to finance expanded spending, including on imports. The rapid deterioration in foreign reserves prompted imposition of new restrictions on payments and transfers for international transactions.[19] The banks and NBFIs were awash with liquidity, and although the CBK took a raft of measures to avert possible worsening of the BOP and inflationary pressures, the impact was minimal as the BOP reverted to a deficit following a sharp drop in the coffee and tea world prices and increase in imports. By 1982, budget deficit as a ratio of GDP had risen to about 7 per cent. Inflation declined temporarily to 8.4 per cent in 1979 before hitting 22 per cent in 1982.[20] The remarkable

[18] Severe frost destroyed a significant production of Brazilian coffee, leading to a sharp reduction in world coffee production. Coffee prices increased by over 300 per cent from KSh 13, 420 per tonne in December 1975 to over KSh 61,000 per tonne by March 1977.

[19] These comprised an advance import deposit scheme, limitations on dividend remittances, restriction on the terms of trade, credit, and requirement of CBK approval for purchase of travel tickets (CBK, 1981).

[20] There was an attempted coup in August 1982.

economic growth witnessed after independence declined from an average of about 6.8 per cent in the period 1964–72 to 4.8 per cent in the period 1973–82 (Table A13.1). Real interest rates remained negative until the mid-1980s.

In general, the measures under the control regime were not adequate in offsetting the adverse effects of the external shocks and weak fiscal control. Moreover, the regime was marred with inefficiencies, distortions, high costs of enforcement, and lack of compliance. Academically, the scholarly work of McKinnon (1973) and Shaw (1973) regarding the financial liberalization thesis, which advocated for a rise in real interest rates to encourage saving had a far-reaching influence on the policy prescriptions adopted by many developing countries during the 1970s and 1980s. Their financial theories suggested that distortions in the financial systems such as controls on interest rates and credit were repressive and largely accountable for the poor economic performance of developing countries. Consequently, elimination of these distortions would significantly deepen the financial sector and stimulate growth. Internationally, the Bretton Woods multilateral financial institutions were ready with a reform recipe in the form of Structural Adjustment Programmes (SAPs), while at the same time the pressure to liberalize the economy was piling. The Government's commitment towards economic liberalization was eventually laid out in *Sessional Paper No. 1 of 1986 on Economic Management for Renewed Growth.*

With mounting pressure, particularly from the IMF on the need to attain positive real interest rates, Kenya gradually began liberalizing interest rates in the 1980s, through periodic reviews, with a view to allow commercial banks more room in meeting the demands of customers. The reviews were also aimed at making interest rates responsive to changes in international markets so as to mitigate against adverse movement of funds. In 1989 the ceilings on savings deposit rates for both commercial banks and NBFIs were progressively raised, while the ceilings on long-term bank loans were brought to the same level with the ceiling for NBFIs lending. In 1990 the lending institutions were allowed to include all lending related charges and fees, so that the effective rates on loans could exceed stipulated ceilings. The interest rates were eventually liberalized in July 1991 in tandem with the liberalization of the economy, paving the way to market-determined rates.

13.2.3 Economic Liberalization and Reform Period (1990s)

The 1990s were marked by extensive privatization and liberalization reform measures not just in the financial sector but the economy as a whole. These were mainly undertaken following immense pressure from multilateral financial institutions to implement structural reforms as part of conditionalities for donor funding.[21] The reforms entailed dismantling state controls to embrace free market economy, opening up the economy, as well as public sector reforms to improve efficiency and fiscal control. By early 2000s, a market-based economic system had been entrenched, notwithstanding the weak governance that still lingered. The push for economic reforms was accompanied by calls and clamour for political democracy, which saw the introduction of multi-party system in 1992 to enhance political governance.

Some of the reform measures undertaken in the financial sector in the early 1990s included establishment of Capital Markets Authority (CMA) in 1990, liberalization of interest rates in 1991 and foreign exchange market in 1993 (Were et al., 2006; Ngugi, 2002).[22] The reforms were targeted at addressing the institutional deficiencies, e.g. by restructuring distressed banks, reforming prudential legislation and the supervisory system, opening up financial markets, and developing money and capital markets.

Following the repeal of the Exchange Control Act, the CBK Act was amended in 1995 to equip CBK with residual regulatory powers of licensing and supervising foreign exchange dealers, and monitoring international payments. Consequently, forex bureaus were introduced in 1995 to serve the retail end of the forex market and increase competition in the foreign exchange market.[23]

The liberalization of the economy and subsequent shift to a market-based economy was accompanied by a shift in the conduct of monetary policy from direct to indirect monetary policy instruments with defined objectives. However, the major milestone and turning point in the history of central banking in Kenya was the fundamental review of the CBK Act in 1996, which, among other changes, granted the CBK operational autonomy. Moreover, the amendments also set out clear objectives of the Central Bank that currently govern the Bank's operations—the principal objective being 'to formulate and implement monetary policy directed at achieving and maintaining stability in the general level of prices'.

Additionally, every six months the Bank was expected to submit a Monetary Policy Statement (MPS) for the next twelve months to the Minister for Finance, specifying policies and means by which the Bank intended to achieve its policy targets, as well as a review of progress made in implementing the monetary policy of the preceding MPS. These changes were largely aimed at enhancing the efficiency of the financial system and effectiveness of the CBK in formulating and implementing monetary policy (CBK, 2000a). Implementation of monetary

[21] A standoff between the Government and IMF in 1992 and a hardened stance of donors towards corruption prompted the Government to hasten implementation of reforms such as fiscal control and dismantling the forex exchange controls (Adam et al., 2010), particularly following a freeze on quick-disbursing aid in November 1991. It is worth noting that after the collapse of the Berlin Wall in 1989, Kenya lost political mileage with the West. For a detailed discussion of reforms in Kenya see Were et al. (2006).

[22] For detailed analysis of the financial sector reform measures see Ngugi (2002).

[23] By December 1999, there were 48 licensed and operational forex bureaus.

policy was further strengthened by the liberalization of the foreign exchange market and capital account, which opened space for a floating exchange rate regime, as well as fiscal reforms that were undertaken to enhance fiscal discipline. From the mid-1990s, inflation became the main focus of monetary policy (Rotich et al., 2006).

Before the amendment of the CBK Act in 1996, the independence of the CBK and monetary policy had been grossly compromised. For instance, lack of maximum limit on the CBK advances to the government encouraged fiscal indiscipline in furtherance of political agenda. In a bid to reduce political interference, the responsibilities of the CBK management were transferred to a Board of Directors appointed by the President instead of direct appointment by the Minister for Finance.

The early 1990s had been rocked by fiscal indiscipline and governance issues some of which had direct implications on central bank independence (Were et al., 2006). The run up to the first multi-party general elections in 1992 saw heightened political meddling in the financial system—politically connected banks, most of which had links to the infamous *Goldenberg scandal,* flourished as part of a scheme to finance elections and reward cronies. There was heightened instability in the macro economy and the banking sector. The CBK had to put in place a moratorium on licensing of new banking institutions in 1993 in a bid to contain the situation. As a result of the excessive liquidity, inflation rose drastically to over 40 per cent, while the exchange rate depreciated sharply (Figure 13.1).

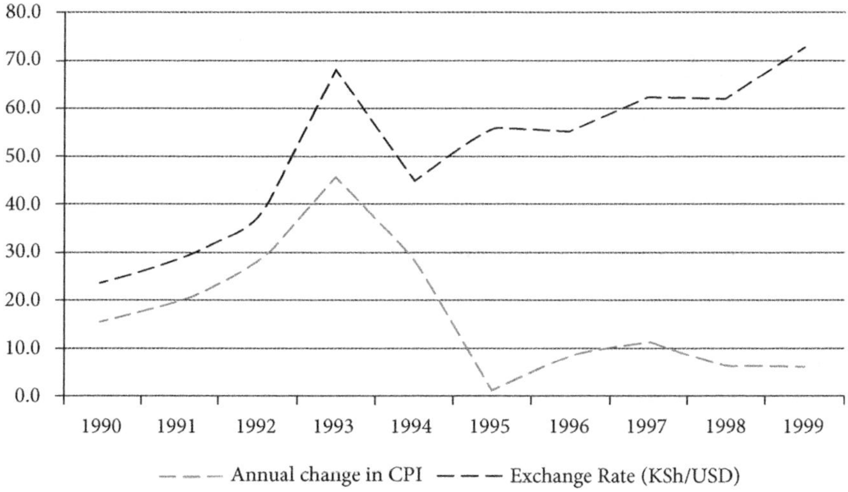

Figure 13.1 Trends in annual inflation and exchange rate in 1990s
Source: CBK and Kenya National Bureau of Statistics (KNBS).

The high NPLs associated with unsecured loans, especially by the state-owned banks and banks associated with the Goldenberg scandal sparked off bank failures and instability in the banking sector, necessitating five banks to be put under statutory management by the CBK in 1998.[24] The crisis was precipitated by imprudent practices such as reckless lending, mismanagement, and insider borrowing, as well as poor capitalization. To restore confidence in the banking sector, the Banking Act was amended to grant the CBK enhanced powers to censure non-compliant commercial banks and exert increased penalties for non-compliance. Other amendments included higher capital requirements and strict enforcement of the same, restrictions on insider lending, as well as guidelines on provisioning for NPLs and requirement for banks to publish their accounts in the national press.

Given the challenges experienced by the proliferation of NBFIs, the CBK also embraced a universal policy strategy that encouraged NBFIs to convert to banks. The number of banks and NBFIs had increased to over 80 by 1993 (CBK, 2000b). The liquidity ratio applicable to both banks and NBFIs was harmonized at 25 per cent in July 1995, hence removing the preferential treatment enjoyed by NBFIs. By end of 1996, 20 NBFIs had converted to banks while nine had merged with their parent banks. Consequently, the number of banks increased with corresponding fall in the number of NBFIs. In the period 1994 to 1997, the number of banks increased by 61 per cent, from 33 to 53 while the number of NBFIs declined by more than one-half from, 48 to 17 NBFIs over the same period. By end of 1999, the number of NBFIs had reduced to 8.

The reform measures bore fruit in restoring stability in the banking system. There was marked improvement in asset quality due to a fall in the proportion of NPLs, while profitability and liquidity remained strong. By April 2000, three[25] of the five banks put under statutory management in 1998 were restructured and reopened. The Banking Act was further amended to gradually raise capital from KSh 200 million to KSh 500 million for banks, and KSh 375 million for NBFIs by end of 2005, while the CBK continued to encourage bank mergers/acquisition and conversions of NFBIs to banks to strengthen the banking sector.

Stability in the macro economy was also restored following a raft of reforms towards economic management. Consequently, annual inflation fell sharply from the range of 46 per cent in 1993 to 1.6 per cent in 1995, while real GDP growth recovered from 1.6 per cent in the period 1990–93 to 3.8 per cent in the period 1994–96 (Table A13.1).

[24] The number of failed and restructured institutions between 1984 and 1997 rose to 30, out of which 87 per cent were due to insider abuse (CBK, 1996).

[25] Trust Bank, City Finance, and Bullion Bank.

13.2.4 Developments since 2000

At the turn of the millennium CBK took a keen interest in the micro-finance institutions (MFIs) sector, given the significant role of sector as an alternative source of financial services for Micro and Small Enterprises (MSEs), coupled with the need to enhance access to formal financial services by the majority of Kenyan households, particularly the low-income and the poor. It was noted that while over 100 organizations including non-governmental organizations (NGOs) practiced some form of micro financing, the sector lacked appropriate regulatory structure (CBK, 2001). Consequently, the CBK jointly with Association of Micro Finance Institutions (AMFI) developed a micro-finance policy that culminated in the enactment of Microfinance Act in 2006. The Act, which was operationalized by the CBK in 2008, sought to enhance the performance of the sector by putting in place the necessary regulatory framework for establishing, licensing, and supervising deposit-taking MFIs. By September 2015, there were 12 micro finance banks with an asset base of USD 3.4 billion. To date, the deposit-taking microfinance institutions (DTMs) are licensed and supervised by the CBK under the provisions of the Microfinance Act, while commercial banks are regulated under the provisions of the Banking Act.

In 2008, Kenya launched its national long-term development blue-print dubbed, the *Vision 2030*, with the objective of creating 'a globally competitive and prosperous nation with a high quality of life by 2030' through transformation of the economy into 'a newly industrializing, middle-income country....' For the financial sector, the aspiration under the *Vision 2030* is to 'create a vibrant and globally competitive financial sector promoting high-levels of savings and financing for Kenya's investment needs'. Thus, the financial policy thrust became strongly oriented towards increasing financial access to the growing population. The Government through financial sector institutions adopted outreach as a core objective of financial policy (FSD Kenya and Central Bank of Kenya, 2009). Most of the policies and reform measures implemented were shaped by the objective of promoting financial inclusion and widening access to formal financial sector services, all of which CBK had a key role to play. Among the measures and policy initiatives undertaken by the CBK were agency banking, embracing, and providing an enabling environment for financial innovations such as mobile money transfer and banking services, operationalization of the Microfinance Act by putting the deposit taking microfinance institutions under the regulatory purview of CBK, introduction of Credit Reference Bureaus (CRBs), increasing access to investments in government securities by small-scale investors, among others:

- *Agency banking*: The Banking Act was amended in 2009 to facilitate agency banking with the aim of increasing financial services outreach and promoting financial inclusion to the un-banked and under-banked population, without risking the safety and soundness of the banking system. The regulation allows commercial banks to offer services through third party agents approved by the CBK. Agents include telecommunication outlets, SMEs, retail chains, savings and credit co-operatives (SACCOs), post offices, security (courier) firms—essentially any profit-making entity that has been in business for at least 18 months and can afford to fund a float account to facilitate payments. Following the roll out of the agent banking model by the CBK in May 2010, eight commercial banks had contracted 9,748 active agents facilitating over 8 million transactions valued at KSh 43.6 billion (about 3 per cent of total deposit) by December 2011.
- *Mobile payments and mobile banking:* Introduction of mobile based funds transfer payments system was not only a notable innovation in Kenya's payments system but also a game changer. It provided greater access and increased convenience to many low income households and micro-enterprises in Kenya, including those in rural areas who do not have access to conventional banking. The growth in the transaction volumes and values following the rollout of the first mobile money transfer system (M-PESA) in 2007 was phenomenal, and a clear indication of the popularity in the usage of the mobile money transfer platforms. The number of customers nearly doubled, rising from 8.9 million in 2009 to 16.4 million in 2010. A total of KSh 732 billion was transacted in 2010, compared with KSh 473 billion in 2009, translating into 155 per cent rise in usage. The mobile payment platform has since become an integral part of the national payments system, and is the most widely used mode of payment in Kenya. The specific products include; M-PESA, Airtel Money, Orange Money, and Tangaza, among others.
- *Credit Reference Bureaus (CRBs):* The introduction of CRBs was prompted by the need to reduce information asymmetry within the financial sector, after it was established that the high cost of borrowing in the banking sector and loan defaults were partly associated with difficulties in gauging the quality of borrowers. The Banking (Credit Reference Bureaus) Regulations 2008 which became operational in February 2009 empowered the CBK to license and supervise the operations of CRBs. The mandate of CRBs is to collect, collate, and disseminate credit information to lenders in a bid to aid them in their credit decisions. This mode of establishing credit worthiness enables borrowers to use their credit repayment history as part of collateral, aids in building information capital, reducing information search costs, and making pricing decisions. The information enables commercial banks

ascertain information relating to a potential borrower's credibility based on assessment of credit history. By December 2011, there were over 1.3 million credit reports accessed by banks; and over 6000 credit reports accessed by individuals. Commercial banks are now permitted to share both positive and negative credit information with the credit reference bureaus.

- *Access to investment opportunities in government securities by small investors:* The CBK reduced the minimum investment in Treasury bill from KSh 1 million to KSh 100,000 in mid-2009, to encourage small investors to participate in the risk-free government debt market, which had been largely dominated by commercial banks.
- *The Proceeds of Crime and Anti-Money Act,* established in 2009 criminalized the offence of money laundering.

Both the Banking Act and CBK Act underwent a series of amendments in the 2000s and 2010s to reflect the dynamism in the local banking industry, as well as regional and global banking environment. For instance, the Banking Amendment Act of 2006 ceded substantial operational powers relating to the banking sector from the Minister of Finance to the CBK. These powers included licensing and closure of banks which the CBK could not do but had to recommend to the Minister for approval. Other changes included further enhancement of minimum capital requirements from KSh 250 million to KSh 1 billion by end of 2012. In November 2012, the CBK issued revised Prudential and Risk Management Guidelines in order to update the banking sector regulatory framework in line with the Basel Core Principles of Banking Supervision and the changes in the current constitution enacted in 2010.

Notable changes with respect to the CBK Act include the following:

- ***Central Bank objectives***: The CBK Act was amended to provide for the following additional CBK objectives:
  - √ *Promote the establishment, regulation and supervision of efficient and effective payment, clearing and settlement systems* (No. 15 of 2003 amendment of the CBK Act). The National Payment System Act was enacted in 2011 to enable the CBK to effectively deal with the challenges posed by rapid financial innovation such as the mobile money services and address associated risks such as fraud and money laundering. At present, the CBK has the oversight mandate of the national payment systems. The mobile phone money transfer service providers are regulated under the National Payment System Act, 2011 and National Payment System Regulations, 2014 that operationalized the Act.
  - √ *Support the economic policy of the Government, including its objectives for growth and employment,* subject to price and financial stability objectives (No. 9 of 2007 amendment of the CBK Act).

- ***Conduct of monetary policy:*** The most fundamental legislative changes with respect to the conduct of monetary policy were the following:
  - √ The introduction of the Central Bank Rate (CBR) in January 2004 and creation of the Monetary Policy Committee (MPC) in 2007. This set the stage for aligning the monetary policy conduct at the CBK in tandem with modern central bank practices. The formation of MPC was preceded by the Monetary Policy Advisory Committee. However, unlike its predecessor whose role was advisory, the MPC is executive and has the responsibility of formulating monetary policy. The MPC meets at least every two months to deliberate and make decisions on the monetary policy stance. It sets the CBR which has become the reference policy rate. The monetary policy decisions undertaken are communicated to the public through press releases and follow up meetings with chief executives of commercial banks. The Committee consists of both external and internal members, with the CBK Governor as the Chairperson and the Deputy Governor as the Deputy Chair.
  - √ In 2007 the Minister for Finance was given the powers to specify at least in every period of 12 months, the price stability target in consultation with the CBK and consistent with the economic policies to be taken by the Government. This is made at the beginning of the financial year. The current overall inflation target is 5 ± 2.5 per cent. The Bank formulates and conducts monetary policy aimed towards achieving the inflation objective, that is, contain overall inflation within the target range.
- ***CBK management and governance structure:*** In 2012 the law makers amended the law to create the position of the Chairperson of CBK Board of Directors. This change was motivated by the need to separate the powers of the Governor as both the chief executive officer of the Bank and the Chairman of Board in line with modern governance practices. In addition, an extra position of another Deputy Governor was created. The Chairperson, the Governor, the Deputy Governors, as well as the directors are appointed by the President through a competitive process but have to be vetted and approved by the National Assembly. The Board consists of the Chairperson, the Governor, Permanent Secretary to the Treasury or his/her representative (non-voting member) and eight other non-executive directors. In addition, CBK is now required by law to present to Parliament on a quarterly basis, a report on key economic and banking sector aggregates.

Economically, after a fairly smooth start at the turn of the millennium, there was marked turbulence towards the end of the first decade. Internationally,

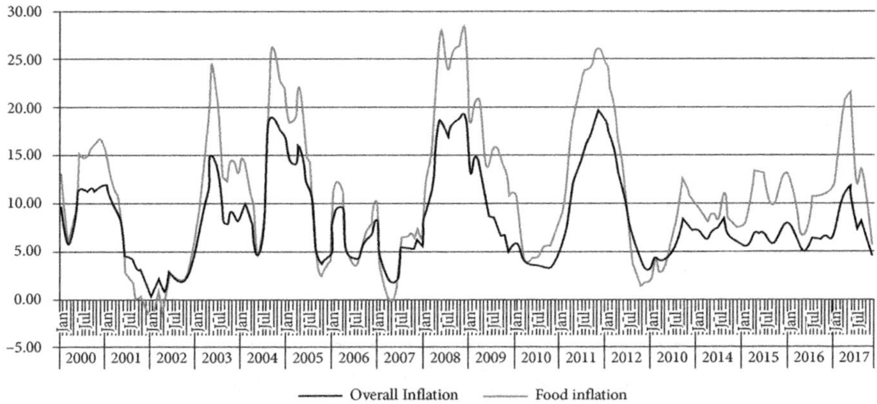

Figure 13.2 Trends in overall and food inflation

the key events that had direct implications on the Kenyan economy include global financial crisis of 2008, which came at the time when the economy was recovering from the aftermaths of the domestic crisis caused by the disputed general elections of December 2007. The displacements and disruptions of agricultural activities in the high potential agricultural areas occasioned an acute shortage of food supply, leading to a surge in inflation in 2008 (Figure 13.2). The inflationary pressures were further exacerbated by the supply-side constraints emanating from the increase in international oil prices and drought conditions in the first half of 2009. Growth of real GDP dropped substantially to about 0.2 per cent in 2008, thereby temporarily holding back the economy that was on a high growth path trajectory of 7 per cent in 2007. Nonetheless, with the political impasse having been resolved, fiscal stimulus complimented with counter-cyclical monetary policy helped in restoring confidence and resuscitating the economy.

Generally, the inflation episodes witnessed in the new millennium have largely been linked to supply-side shocks associated with adverse weather conditions, compounded with external shocks relating to global oil price changes. For instance, drought periods (2004–05, 2008–09, 2011, 2016–17) are often associated with inflation spikes due to the resultant shortages of staple food items (Figure 13.2). These factors are not easily amenable to monetary policy tools. Food has remained a key component in the consumer price index (CPI) basket, with a current weight of 32.9 per cent. Not surprisingly therefore, overall inflation is largely driven by food inflation (Figure 13.2). However, the inflationary pressures tend to dissipate fairly quickly once the weather conditions improve.

Overall, the management of the exogenous global shocks (including global financial crisis 2008/2009, Euro debt crisis 2011/12, and speculative reactions

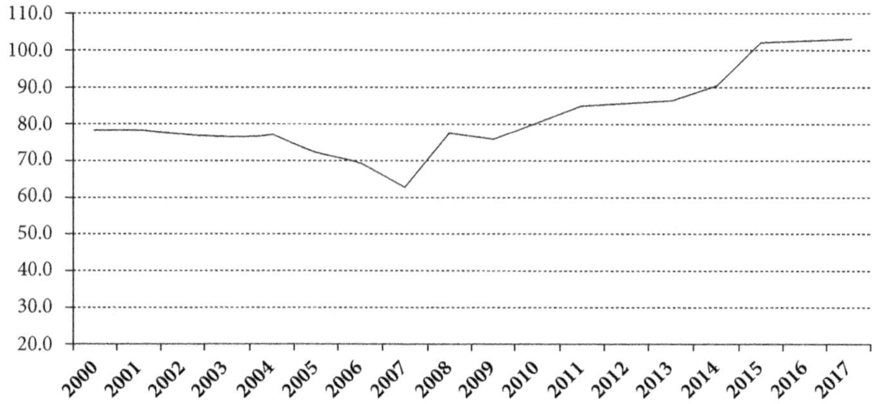

Figure 13.3 Trends in exchange rate (KSh/USD)
Source: CBK.

regarding reversal of quantitative easing US/Euro monetary policy) was quite successful, given the impact particularly on the exchange rate pressure was short-lived. This applies not only to Kenya but generally to the countries in the EAC region, which are basically vulnerable to the same global shocks. In general the exchange rate has remained fairly stable (Figure 13.3). An overview of CBK evolution vis-à-vis domestic economy and global environment is summarized in Figure A13.1.

13.3 Recent Developments, Milestones, and Challenges

13.3.1 Recent Developments

The CBK has come a long way—central banking in Kenya has been shaped and impacted by various factors, including political, economic, and social developments locally, regionally, and globally. The legal and regulatory framework has continually been reviewed in tandem with domestic and global dynamics to enhance the CBK's independence and effectiveness in performing its functions.

The liberalization of Kenya's economy from a controlled economy to a market-based economy necessitated a shift in the conduct of monetary policy. Globally, there has been a gradual shift from monetary targeting policy framework that predominantly prevailed till the 1980s to inflation targeting. The Bank is gradually transiting to inflation targeting framework, notwithstanding the structural challenges that still linger.

The banking industry has remained buoyant and vibrant despite challenges experienced by the sector in the past. Information, Communication and Technology (ICT), automation, and continued financial innovations such as the mobile money, coupled with the globally changing banking practices, have necessitated a continuous revision and amendment of the banking sector legal and regulatory framework. The banking sector is comprised of 38 commercial banks, 1 mortgage finance company, 14 microfinance banks, 9 representative offices of foreign banks, 68 foreign exchange bureaus, 19 money remittance providers, and 3 credit reference bureaus as of 30 June 2020. The regulation of the banking sector is currently guided by three pillars: greater transparency, enhanced governance and better business models in adaptation to the changing dynamics of the twenty-first century. Globally, banking regulations have evolved from Basel I to Basel III accord.

Regionally, the CBK is a key player in monetary and financial integration initiatives. Economic integration and the quest for monetary integration continue to impact on central banking in the region, particularly in view of the East African Community (EAC) Member States' objective of forming East African Monetary Union (EAMU) by 2024. Signed on 30 November 2013, the EAMU Protocol sets out the scope of monetary and financial cooperation. These include harmonization and coordination of fiscal policy, integration of financial, payment, and settlement systems, among others.

The existence and operational independence of CBK is anchored in the Constitution of Kenya 2010 under Article 231.[26] The current vision of the Bank is to be a world-class modern central bank. The objectives and functions of CBK have evolved over the years. The core mandate of the Bank is price and financial stability. Other objectives are management of foreign exchange policy and foreign exchange reserves; promotion of efficient and effective payment, clearing and settlement systems; banker, adviser, and fiscal agent of the Government and issuance of notes and coins. The current objectives of the CBK as outlined in the CBK Act are given in Box 13.1.

The CBK's mandate is discharged through the following core functions: monetary policy, financial markets, bank supervision, payment and settlement systems, banking and currency services. The departmental structure of the Bank is modelled along these functions that help deliver the mandates of the Bank, as well as the key support functions that facilitate efficient and effective delivery of the mandate in line with the CBK's vision of becoming a world-class modern central bank (Figure A13.3).

[26] Notwithstanding the operational independence, the CBK is under National Government.

Box 13.1 The Objectives of the Central Bank of Kenya

The principal objectives:

To formulate and implement monetary policy directed to achieving and maintaining stability in the general level of prices.

To foster the liquidity, solvency and proper functioning of a stable market-based financial system.

Subject to (1) and (2) above, to support the economic policy of the Government, including its objectives for growth and employment.

Without prejudice to the generality of the above, the Bank shall:

Formulate and implement foreign exchange policy.

Hold and manage its foreign exchange reserves.

License and supervise authorized dealers.

Formulate and implement such policies as best promote the establishment regulation and supervision of efficient and effective payment, clearing and settlement systems.

Act as banker and adviser to, and as fiscal agent of the Government.

Issue currency notes and coins.

Source: CBK Act.

13.3.2 Milestones

Over the last 50 years, the CBK has traversed through periods of turbulence and tranquillity, and remained focused on fulfilling its prescribed mandate. The CBK has undoubtedly achieved several milestones, including the following:

- The entrenchment of the operational autonomy of the CBK in the constitution following the enactment of the current Constitution of Kenya in August 2010 was a major milestone as it further safeguards the autonomy of the CBK.
- Transparency in the formulation and conduct of monetary policy has been greatly enhanced in line with modern central banks, particularly following the formation of the MPC, which is entrusted with the responsibility of monetary policy formulation. The clarity with which central banks are able to communicate monetary policy decisions cannot be overstated. The CBK's communication strategy has been significantly revamped and is continuously being enhanced to keep the market informed on the process and outcomes of the monetary policy. This is particularly important as the

Bank transitions to inflation targeting monetary policy. The constant update and communication with the public has been critical not only with regard to monetary policy but also in fostering stability of financial sector, especially during crises.

- The CBK has played a fundamental role in ensuring macroeconomic stability over the years, considering the various external and domestic shocks that continue to buffet the economy. Overall, inflation has largely been contained, particularly after granting the CBK operational independence and establishing price stability as a core mandate of the CBK. The inflationary episodes experienced in the past are mainly attributable to exogenous, supply-side constraints, especially adverse weather cycles, given the significance of food in the CPI basket and reliance on rain-fed agriculture. The Bank has maintained a flexible exchange rate regime with occasional interventions to tame excessive exchange rate volatility in the market and thereby protect the economy from associated adverse effects. The exchange rate remains stable, notwithstanding periods of turbulence that have been occasionally witnessed in the past. The Bank remains focused in fostering macroeconomic stability as a basis and foundation for achieving long-term economic growth and prosperity.
- Kenya's financial sector is fairly developed by regional standards. The sector has grown tremendously over the years, in line with the expanding economy and financial needs of the growing population. The banking sector, which is the dominant player in the financial sector, has weathered various financial and banking crises locally and globally, including the global financial crises of 2009, and remained steadily stable over the years. Besides the increase in number of commercial banks and branch network, the expansion of banking sector is exemplified by the growth in assets. Commercial banks' assets hit KSh 4.1 trillion by end of 2016 (57.2 per cent of GDP), from a meagre asset base of KSh 251.3 million (2.4 per cent of GDP) as at end of 1969. The number of bank branches nearly tripled from 512 branches in 2003 to 1443 in 2014, and stood at 1516 by September 2017. Kenya's banking sector continues to expand locally and across borders. The prudential regulation and supervision has been strengthened over the years.
- The CBK championed innovations in the financial sector by providing an enabling environment, particularly the advent of mobile money, which availed enormous opportunities. For example, through the mobile platform, the Bank in collaboration with the National Treasury has made access to and participation in government securities easier, thereby enhancing savings particularly by the low income and retail investors. Mobile banking and mobile money transfer platforms opened space for

increased financial inclusion, as Kenyans who were previously locked out of the formal financial sector have been able to access financial services, save and access credit. According to the *2016 FinAccess Household Survey*, 75.3 per cent of adult population in Kenya have access to formal financial services. Anchored on the Bank's pivotal role of promoting efficient, effective, payments and clearing settlement system, Kenya has become a leading regional hub for financial innovation, particularly the mobile banking and money transfer services. As a matter of fact, according to the Digital Planet Report 2017, Kenya was ranked fourth out of 60 countries on the digital finance momentum index.

- The various innovations in the payment systems and integration of information technology systems have significantly revamped efficiency in the payments, clearing, and settlement systems. These include the Real Time Gross Settlements (RTGS) Systems that allow settlements in real time; full automation of the Clearing House, mobile payments and internet banking among others.
- Macroeconomic modelling has made important advances over the years, including recent developments in forward-looking models to inform price or rule-based monetary policy frameworks. The CBK has not been left behind in this regard—the Bank has made major strides in developing and adopting a toolkit of appropriate modelling and forecasting frameworks as part of the fabric of the Bank's monetary policy modernization agenda to inform monetary policy decisions. These range from simple forecasting tools to economy wide semi-structural macroeconomic models.
- With respect to the government securities market, from 2000 there was a conscious effort to build up a yield curve by introducing Treasury bonds with maturities ranging from one to 30 years. Consequently, as a fiscal agent to the Government, the CBK in collaboration with the National Treasury spearheaded reforms in the domestic government securities market to broaden the investor base, promote secondary trading and develop an appropriate and reliable yield curve to guide pricing of securities and other financial products in the primary and secondary markets. Thanks to the domestic debt restructuring programme, the maturity profile of the domestic debt securities portfolio reversed from 30:70 ratio of Treasury bonds to Treasury bills to 70:30 ratio of Treasury bonds to Treasury bills following successful issuance of government securities with longer term tenor, leading to a reliable yield curve.
- The Kenya School of Monetary Studies (KSMS) whose principal shareholder is the CBK was established in 1997 to deliver international best practice capacity building programmes that are responsive to the needs of the financial sector in Kenya and the region.
- CBK asset base has grown from a mere KSh 427.56 million in 1966 to KSh 982,849 million for the financial year ending June 2016 (13.7 per cent of GDP). The structure of the CBK's real assets over time has evolved

in a fairly consistent fashion with other central banks in the region (Figure A13.2). Moreover, consistent with the growth of the economy, the CBK's operations have expanded greatly, from the head office in Nairobi to three branches (Mombasa, Kisumu, Eldoret) and four currency centres (Nyeri, Nakuru, Meru, Kisii), with an increase in staff establishment from 60 in 1966 to over 1300, in response to its expanded functions.

13.3.3 Challenges

Despite the milestones, the Bank is still confronted with a number of challenges, which include the following:

- Although the banking sector has grown tremendously, segmentation and market dominance still hamper the efficiency and operation of the sector, in line with the standard competitively determined market outcomes. The entrenched segmentation which is played out vividly in the interbank market impairs financial intermediation and leads to non-competitive market outcomes. This has implications on the efficiency of monetary policy, the operation of the sector as a whole, and the transition to inflation targeting framework.
- Whereas price stability still remains a core mandate of the Bank, the dominance of supply-side shocks continues to pose a challenge especially, to the transition and adoption of inflation targeting as a modern monetary policy framework.
- Globally, the rapid financial integration and technological revolution pose additional challenges. Being a small-open economy, Kenya is susceptible to external shocks, which directly and indirectly impacts on the CBK's efficacy in achieving the expected objectives. Recent examples include the global financial crisis of 2008, elevated trade tensions between the United States and China – the world's two largest economies and the uncertainties surrounding the United Kingdom's transitional arrangements with the European Union following Brexit. The continued innovations as well as increased financial integration in a highly globalized world present opportunities as well as risks, which calls for a continuous review of the banking sector legal and regulatory framework.
- The high cost of credit has continued to attract public debate, including legislative attempts to control interest rates in 2001 and 2013. The concern about the high interest rate spreads between the lending and deposit rates eventually culminated into passing of the Banking (Amendment) Bill 2015 that legislated the capping of interest rates in Kenya. The Banking

(Amendment) Act 2016 came into effect on 14 September 2016, the same date the CBK turned 50! It set the maximum lending rate at no more than four per cent above the Central Bank base rate, which was established as the policy rate; and the minimum interest rate granted on a deposit held in interest earning account to at least 70 per cent of the same rate. The capping of interest rates posed several challenges particularly with respect to the conduct of monetary policy as policy decisions produced perverse outcomes, and was not consistent with the free market economy ideology that Kenya embraces. Moreover, the strategy did not succeed in expanding credit to the majority of Kenyans as envisaged. Instead it resulted in reduced financial intermediation as banks rationed out small borrowers, and the micro, small and medium enterprises (MSMEs) leading to a decline in the rate of credit growth. Consequently, the interest rate caps were scrapped through the Banking (Amendment) Act, 2019. A better lasting solution to the high cost of credit is still needed.

- Given the fairly thin money market, there tends to be challenges associated with fiscal actions related to government spending and borrowing particularly if not well coordinated, with implications on liquidity distribution, interest rates, and monetary policy transmission.
- Like most African central banks, the CBK has multiple objectives, which are not always complementary. In some cases, the actions needed have conflicting effects and consequences that may drag the Bank into the political debate. Most modern central banks in advanced economies have just one or two objectives, price stability being the key.

13.4 The Future of Central Banking in Kenya

The 2008 global financial crisis, to a larger extent, impacted the future of central banking, with the adverse effects of the crisis and the subsequent (unconventional) monetary policy that ensued renewing the debate about central bank objectives. Should monetary policy be tied to real outcomes such as unemployment and growth, besides inflation? For nearly a decade after the crisis, key central banks around the world are still struggling to spur economic recovery, maintain price stability and ensure financial stability. Additionally, the post-financial crisis period has witnessed comprehensive reforms in the regulatory architecture targeted at the financial sector. The various regulations passed since 2008 have ignited debate regarding over-regulation of the financial industry.[27] To a certain

[27] Additionally, the latest accounting rules which include IFRS 9 and IFRS 16 have introduced fundamental changes in the way commercial banks operate. IFRS 9 requires an entity to recognize a financial asset or a financial liability in its statement of financial position when it becomes party to the

extent, all these make the future of central banking uncertain, or work in progress at best.

Whereas price stability remains a principal mandate of the CBK, the multiplicity of other functions still remains. Juggling between the various functions while keeping abreast with international standards is critical. As the Bank progresses into the future, there is need to review the functions of the CBK, with a view to delink some of the responsibilities such as public-debt management from the central bank in line with modern central banks. Additionally, further efforts towards strengthening the monetary policy transmission mechanism particularly in view of the transition to inflation targeting framework are critical.

The increasing accountability demands that continue to accompany operational central bank autonomy implies that the twenty-first-century central bank must meet external scrutiny and live within constraints (Mendzela, 2006). However, accountability is not only expected of the regulator, in this case the CBK, but also the banking sector. The CBK envisions a responsible and disciplined banking sector that will serve the needs of all Kenyans. To do so, the commercial banks must leverage on technology to adopt innovative, customer-centric business models to compete successfully in the future.

Whereas the heightened globalization (financial, trade, economic) and technological innovation continue to provide opportunities, they do pose new challenges. These include challenges associated with Fintech innovations such as cryptocurrencies. How does central bank deal with the increasingly complex global economy? The CBK will undoubtedly work towards strategies capable of optimizing opportunities provided by new technologies and innovation, while at the same time minimizing the risks associated with Fintech.

Other emerging issues likely to shape the future of central banking in Kenya include regional integration initiatives, particularly the monetary integration aspiration and cross-border banking. Additionally, debt sustainability concerns regarding the pace and cost of public debt accumulation have started attracting attention in policy discourses.

Overall, it is certainly becoming clear that national policies can no longer be designed in total disregard of the global economy. The CBK has to define its path for the next 50 years of central banking in the wider context of the evolving global dynamics. The Bank will have to think globally but act locally, taking into account the uniqueness of the Kenyan economy. The die is cast.

contractual provisions of the instrument. Changes introduced by IFRS 9 which became effective in January 2018 include expected credit loss model which require banks or entities to anticipate loan defaults and make provisions upon underwriting and not at the time of default.

Appendix Figures and Tables

	1960s	1970s–80s	1990s	2000s/2010s
CBK : Roles, functions, focus and challenges	Enactment of CBK Act establishing CBK in March 1966. CBK becomes operational Sep. 14, 1966. Consolidation of functions (note issuing, banker to Government, administration of exchange controls). Banking Act 1968. Set up of state-owned banks	Expansion of financial sector—local banks, IDFs and proliferation of NBFIs. First banking crisis 1984. Regulatory powers (Banking Act 1985). Fixed interest rates, foreign exchange and quantitative credit controls. Passive monetary policy. Limited independence.	Liberalization of interest rates and forex market. Shift from indirect to direct monetary policy tools. Mergers & conversions of NFBIs to banks. Re-definition and expansion of CBK objectives including price stability as core objective (CBK Act 1996). Operational autonomy 1996. Enhanced regulatory powers to deal with imprudent practices following heightened bank failures in early 1990s	Focus towards microfinance institutions, financial access and inclusion. Promotion financial innovation (mobile money) and effective payment system. Monetary policy—price based monetary instruments (CBR), creation of MPC, enhanced transparency. Banking—prudential supervision in line Basel core principles, enhanced governance and transparency
Domestic Economy	State-owned enterprises. Emphasis on Kenyanization. High rapid economic growth and economic stability.	State control regime (interest rates, forex, credit). Expanded public expenditure. BOP and inflation crisis in early 1970s Deterioration of economic growth. Structural Adjustment Programmes1980s	Price decontrols and liberalization of the economy. Heightened macroeconomic instability in the early 1990s. Macro stability restored from mid-1990s (inflation, exchange rate, interest rates)	Macroeconomic stability save for temporary spikes associated with exogenous shocks including weather related shocks. Stable economic growth. Increased financial inclusion associated with increased mobile money services
Global Economy	International gold crisis. Establishment of SDRs by IMF 1969	Oil crisis of 1973. Collapse of Bretton Wood system / floating of major currencies in early 1970s. Washington consensus Ascension to free market and trade liberalization. Collapse of Berlin Wall	Globalization. Financial and economic integration. Free trade/trade liberalization	Global financial crisis 2008/2009. Euro debt crisis 2011/12. Collapse of oil prices in 2014. Brexit debate and monetary policy normalization in advanced countries

Figure A13.1 Overview of CBK evolution vis-à-vis domestic economy and global environment

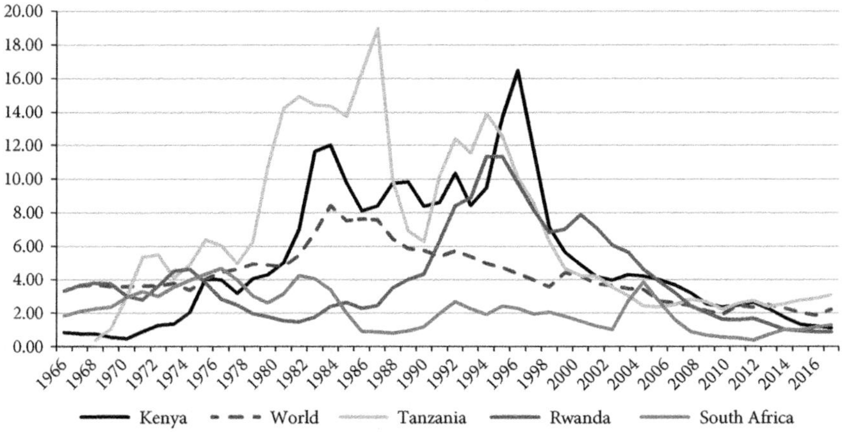

Figure A13.2 Selected central banks' assets to GDP (%)

Note: Central Bank assets measured as claims on domestic real non-financial sector by the Central Bank.

Source: World Bank, Central Bank assets to GDP retrieved from Federal Reserve Bank of St Loius.

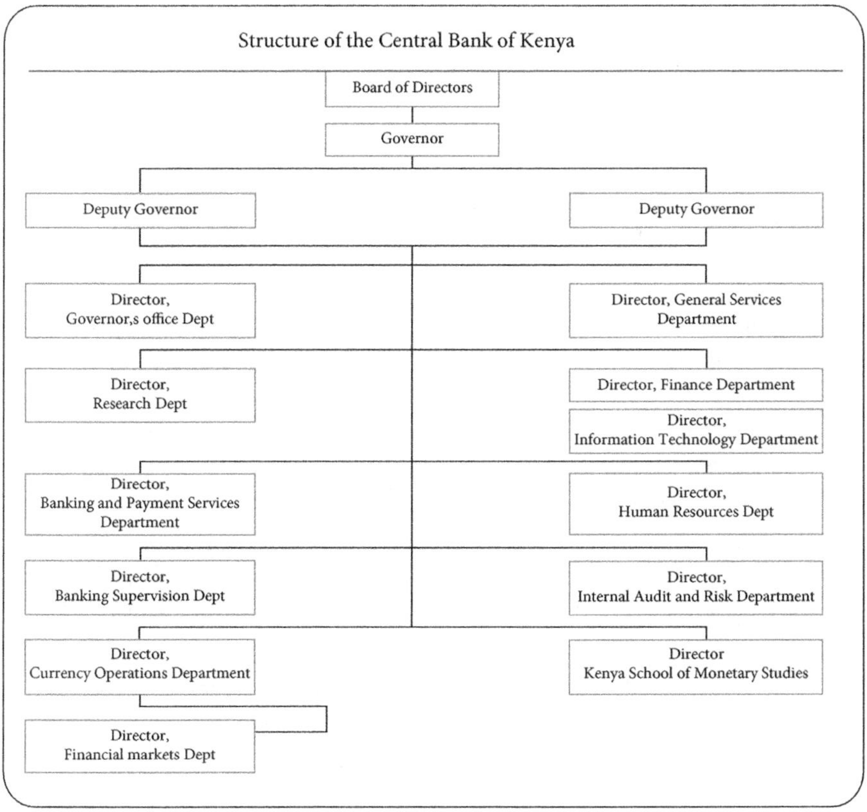

Figure A13.3 Organizational structure of the CBK

Table A13.1 Historical trends in selected macroeconomic indicators

	1968–70	1971–73	1974–75	1976–77	1978–79	1980–81	1982–83	1984–85	1986–87	1988–90	1991	1992	1993	1994	1995	1996	1997
Real GDP growth (%)	7.1	6.5	1.6	7.5	5.3	4.6	2.8	2.9	5.5	4.9	1.5	−0.3	0.8	4.5	3.5	3.4	0.3
Inflation (Annual change in CPI)	3.8	6.0	17.1	11.4	10.5	12.7	18.5	10.0	9.6	13.9	19.6	27.3	46.0	28.8	1.6	9.0	11.2
Money Supply growth (%)	19.8	15.4	12.9	35.5	14.9	6.1	10.5	9.8	21.8	13.6	19.7	42.9	25.7	30.4	18.6	15.9	11.9
Current Account/GDP (%)	−2.1	−5.1	−9.1	−8.1	−11.7	−10.6	−2.0	−1.7	−3.4	−6.0	−2.8	−1.2	1.7	1.5	−4.4	−0.8	−4.3
Budget Deficits/GDP (%)	3.6	5.7	5.1	6.0	6.0	6.9	4.9	4.8	4.8	−4.7	−4.6	−1.9	−5.3	−8.7	−0.4	−2.2	−2.0
Exchange Rate (Ksh/USD)	7.1	7.1	7.7	8.1	7.4	8.9	13.3	16.0	16.3	21.4	28.1	36.2	68.2	44.8	55.9	55.0	62.7
Lendigrates		9.0	9.8	10.0	10.0	11.5	15.2	14.2	14.0	17.0	19.0	21.1	30.0	36.2	28.8	33.8	30.3
TBR-91 days		2.3	5.4	3.8	5.2	6.4	13.4	13.6	13.0	14.2	17.2	18.2	55.7	25.2	19.0	23.0	22.

	1998	1999	2000	2001	2002	2003	2004	2005	2006	2007	2008	2009	2010	2011	2012	2013	2014	2015	2016	2017
Real GDP growth (%)	3.4	2.1	0.5	4.5	0.5	2.9	5.1	5.9	6.3	6.8	0.2	3.3	8.4	6.1	4.5	5.9	5.4	5.7	5.8	
Inflation (Annual change in CPI)	6.6	5.8	10.0	5.8	2.0	9.8	11.8	9.9	6.0	4.3	15.1	10.5	4.1	14.0	9.4	5.7	6.9	6.6	6.3	8.0
Money Supply growth (%)	3.55.1	4.2	2.4	10.0	11.5	13.4	9.1	17.0	19.1	15.9	16.0	21.	19.1	14.1	16.2	16.4	14.1	3.7	9.5	
Current Account/GDP (%)	−4.1	−0.7	−1.9	−3.0	−0.9	1.0	−0.8	−1.33	−1.9	−3.0	−5.5	−4.6	−6.0	−9.3	−8.7	−9.9	−10.4	−6.7	−5.2	−6.8
Budget Deficits/GDP (%)	−0.3	0.2	−1.6	−3.3	−3.6	−0.8	0.1	−2.3	−2.1	−3.5	−4.2	−7.6	−3.4	−4.2	−5.5	−5.6	−8.2	−7.7	−8.8	
Exchange Rate (Ksh/USD)	61.9	72.9	78.0	78.6	77.1	76.1	773.	72.4	69.4	62.7	77.7	75.8	80.8	85.1	86.0	86.3	90.6	102.3	102.5	103.2
Lendigrates	29.5	22.4	22.3	19.7	18.5	16.4	12.5	12.9	13.6	13.3	14.0	14.8	14.4	15.0	19.7	17.3	16.5	16.2	16.6	13.7
TBR-91 days	523.3	13.3	12.1	12.7	8.9	3.7	3.0	8.4	6.8	6.8	7.7	7.4	3.6	8.7	12.7	8.9	8.9	10.9	8.6	8.4

Source: Various Economic Surveys (Kenya Bureau of Statistics) and CBK Reports.

References

Bordo, M. D. (2007), 'A brief history of central banks: A commentary'. Federal Reserve Bank of Cleveland.

Bordo, M. D. and Siklos, P. L. (2017), 'Central banks: Evolution and innovation in historical perspective'. *Economics Working Paper 17,105*, Hoover Institution Economics Working Papers. Stanford University, Stanford.

Capie, F., Goodhart, C., and Schnadt, N. (1994), *The Development of Central Banking in the Future of Central Banking*. Cambridge: Cambridge University Press.

CBK (1972), *Money and Banking in Kenya*. Central Bank of Kenya, Nairobi.

CBK (1981), *Sources and Uses of Foreign Exchange in Kenya 1974–1979*. Central Bank of Kenya, Nairobi.

CBK (1986), *Central Bank of Kenya: Its Evolution, Responsibilities and Organization*. Central Bank of Kenya, Nairobi.

CBK (1994), *Bank Supervision Annual Report 1994*. Bank Supervision Department, Central Bank of Kenya, Nairobi.

CBK (1996), *Bank Supervision Annual Report 1996*. Bank Supervision Department, Central Bank of Kenya, Nairobi.

CBK (2000a), *Bank Supervision Annual Report 2000*. Bank Supervision Department, Central Bank of Kenya, Nairobi.

CBK (2000b), *The Practice of Monetary Policy in Kenya*. Central Bank of Kenya, Nairobi.

CBK (2001), *Bank Supervision Annual Report 2001*. Bank Supervision Department, Central Bank of Kenya, Nairobi.

CBK (2016), History and development of money in Kenya *A book published in commemoration of 50th anniversary: 1966–2016*, Central Bank of Kenya, Nairobi.

FSD Kenya; & Central Bank of Kenya. (2009). FinAccess National Survey 2009: Dynamics of Kenya's changing financial landscape. Central Bank of Kenya, Nairobi.

Ikiara, G. K. and Killick, T. (1981), *The Performance of the Economy since Independence in Papers on the Kenyan Economy: Performance, Problems and Policies*. London: Heinemann Educational Books Ltd.

McKinnon, R. I. (1973), *Money and Capital in Economic Development*. Washington: The Brookings Institution.

Mendzela, J. (2006), 'How to Manage the 21st Century Central Bank', Central Banking Publications, a reprint from *Central Banking Journal*, Vol. 16, No. 4, pp. 31–9.

Ngugi, R. W. (2002), 'Financial reform process in Kenya, 1986–1996', *African Development Review*, Vol. 12, No. 1, pp. 52–77.

Rotich, H., Kathanje, M. and Maana, I. (2006), 'A monetary policy reaction function for kenya'. *CBK Working Paper series WP/06/01*. Central Bank of Kenya: Nairobi.

Shaw, E. (1973), *Financial Deepening in Economic Development*. New York: Oxford University Press.

Were, M., Ngugi, R. W., and Makau, P. (2006), 'Understanding reform process in Kenya', in *Understanding Economic Reforms in Africa: A Tale of Seven Nations*. Hampshire: Palgrave Macmillan.

14
Dynamics of Monetary Policy in Kenya

Esman Nyamongo, Isaya Maana, and Anne Kamau

14.1 Introduction

The role of the Central Bank of Kenya (CBK) in formulating and implementing monetary policy is well anchored in the Constitution as well as in the CBK Act. However, the manner in which the CBK has conducted monetary policy since its inception in 1966 continues to elicit discussion and debate. A review of the monetary policy framework, institutional arrangements, and instruments of monetary policy reveals that the CBK has been dynamic since it was established. The purpose of this study, therefore, is twofold. Firstly, to analyse the conduct of monetary policy in Kenya in order to bring out the milestones, lessons, successes, and failures. Secondly, basing on the findings from the analysis, to shape current and future monetary policy.

It is useful to note that the evolution of monetary policy in Kenya, since the establishment of the CBK, was partly influenced by historical developments in monetary policy in the East African region and changes in monetary policy regimes at the global level, in particular due to the coordination role of the Bank for International Settlement (IBS) and oversight by the International Monetary Fund (IMF). In Chapter 3 of this book, Njoroge and Murinde (2021) examine the evolutionary forces involved in the development of monetary policy rules over time, at the global level, as well as developments in the theory of central banking and monetary policy. It is argued that when the Bank of England was created in 1694, the idea of monetary policy was established, whereby the early goals were to maintain the value of coinage, print notes, and prevent coins from leaving circulation. But, this was followed by a lot of experimentations and many pitfalls, including the debates about the function of a central bank and the cause of inflation, especially the disagreements between the British Currency School and the British Banking School, regarding the separation of money creation from bank intermediation.[1] Thereafter, especially during 1870–1920, industrial countries set

[1] The essence of the debate between the British Currency School and the British Banking School was the separation of money creation from bank intermediation, as incorporated in the 1844 Bank Act in the UK. The British Currency School argued that the excessive issuing of banknotes was a major cause of price inflation, hence issuers of new banknotes should be required to hold an equivalent value of gold as a reserve. On the contrary, the British Banking School argued that currency issue could be naturally

Esman Nyamongo, Isaya Maana, and Anne Kamau, *Dynamics of Monetary Policy in Kenya* In: *50 Years of Central Banking in Kenya: Regional and Global Perspectives*. Edited by: Patrick Njoroge and Victor Murinde, Oxford University Press (2021).
 DOI: 10.1093/oso/9780198851820.003.0014

up central banking systems, including the Federal Reserve System which was set up in 1913. As Sargent (2014) observes the evolution of monetary policy rules was gradual, but over time it was increasingly understood that interest rates had an effect on the entire economy, that the business cycle was important, and economic theory was helpful in highlighting the relationship between money and credit and the link between interest rates and business cycles. We side-step these global developments and refer the reader to Chapter 2 so that we can focus on the monetary policy developments in Kenya.

In order to explain the dynamics of monetary policy in Kenya, we partition the history of CBK's existence into five phases namely: (1) pre-1966, the Era of the East African Currency Board (EACB), which essentially covers the background to central banking and monetary policy in Kenya; (2) passive monetary policy phase, 1966–70; (3) active monetary policy phase with direct policy instruments, 1971–91; (4) active monetary policy phase with weak institutions, 1992–96; and (5) active monetary policy phase with indirect instruments and strong institutions, since 1997. In addition, the post interest rate capping regime since September 2016 is discussed.

The rest of this chapter is organized as follows. Section 14.2 documents developments during the era of the East African Currency Board, before the establishment of the CBK. The evolution of monetary policy during the existence of the CBK, through the various phases, is detailed in Section 14.3, including the status quo. Section 14.4 presents some concluding remarks.

14.2 Pre-1966 Period: The Era of the East African Currency Board

The East African Currency Board was the CBK's predecessor, with limited mandate for monetary policy. The EACB was based in London and issued notes and coins in exchange for equivalent values in pound sterling, hence serving as an equivalent of a money-changer.[2] However, its mandate was enhanced in 1955 when the EACB regulations were revised to allow the Board—subject to each territory's individual circumstances—to transfer a small portion of the investments held on behalf of colonial currency funds to locally issued securities. This way, the EACB was in a position to offer credit to the governments of

restricted by the desire of bank depositors to redeem their notes for gold, hence they opposed the reserve requirement on banknotes in the Bank Act of 1844. Interestingly, this debate is relevant to central banking and monetary policy today, albeit in a much more complex manner.

[2] The EACB, at the time, exchanged money at the exchange rate of East African shillings EASh20 being equivalent to one pound sterling. At the time the EACB served the three East African countries, Kenya, Uganda, and Tanzania.

the constituent territories by holding government or government-guaranteed securities, corresponding to a fiduciary issue, not exceeding £10 million.

Further enhancements to the limits on credit the EACB could extend to the constituent territories followed the 1957 amendment to the EACB regulations, increasing the limit to a maximum of £20 million. In 1959, the EACB was mandated to acquire local Treasury bills within specified limits of the fiduciary issues to the Government, thus being able to provide short-term funding.

Furthermore, in 1960, administrative changes were instituted at the EACB with the increase of its board members from four to seven and the transfer of its seat from London to East Africa—with its head office in Nairobi. Further amendments to the EACB Regulations anchored its ambition for a wider scope of activities, four of which stand out. Firstly, the EACB began exploring ways in which lending to governments would make the greatest contribution. Secondly, it began to provide seasonal credit facilities for crop exports, both as a way of promoting exports and to act as a banker of last resort to commercial banks. In the process, it became flexible on interest rates and commissions. Thirdly, in its endeavour to facilitate banking operations, it not only opened and maintained accounts for commercial banks but also introduced a multilateral clearing system between banks. Fourthly, it took measures to improve currency distribution by opening up new currency sub-centres and safe custody facilities in remote areas.

Although the EACB had fiduciary authority, it had limited powers and capacity to expand credit like central banks, as it did not have the authority to control credit except through fiduciary limits and moral suasion. During this time, commercial banks maintained accounts with the Board for settling payments; however, the Board had no legal mandate to enforce minimum reserves requirements and influence reserves through open market operations (OMO). Also, the Board was not mandated to act fully as a banker to the Government; it did not accept deposits from governments as the latter used the services of commercial banks. As a result, the Board did not have the tools to exercise or conduct monetary policy.

The Era of the EACB came to an end on June 10, 1965, when the Finance Ministers of the three East African governments announced simultaneously in their budget speeches the intention to liquidate the East African Currency Board and the establishment of three national central banks of each country and issue its own currency (Government of Kenya, 1965). The East African Currency Board ceased operations one year later, giving birth to the Central Bank of Kenya, Bank of Tanzania, and Bank of Uganda. The process for winding up the EACB was effectively kicked off with the budget announcements of the planned creation of a 'modern' central bank for each state. The 'modern' central bank was premised on the aspiration for an institutional set-up with greater flexibility in monetary, credit, and foreign exchange policies.

14.3 Evolution of Monetary Policy since 1966

In this section we conduct analysis for each specific phase outlined in Section 14.1, since the CBK was established in 1966. The discussion focuses on the nature of monetary policy and the macroeconomic outcomes associated with each phase.

14.3.1 The Birth of the Central Bank of Kenya and the Passive Monetary Policy Phase, 1966–1970

The Central Bank of Kenya was established in 1966 through *The Central Bank of Kenya Act No. 15 of 1966*. According to the Act, 'the principal objects of the Bank shall be to regulate the issue of notes and coins, to assist in the development and maintenance of a sound monetary, credit and banking system in Kenya conducive to the orderly and balanced economic development of the country and the external stability of the currency, and to serve as banker and financial adviser to the government'.

The CBK's principal objectives were complemented by a number of other provisions, which are relevant to some key elements of monetary policy. Notably, the main provisions were that the CBK was required to: (i) endeavour to maintain a reserve of external assets at a level not less than the value of four months of the recorded average imports over the preceding three years; (ii) administer any law to regulate the exchange rate; (iii) purchase from and sell to and on behalf of specified banks, re-discount bills of exchange, promissory notes and other credit instruments—the so-called re-discounting; (iv) exercise the authority to require banks to maintain minimum cash balances on deposits with it; (v) be responsible for determining and publishing the maximum rate that banks might pay on deposits and issuing instructions designed to control the volume and terms and conditions of credit.

In a bid to conduct monetary policy the Bank identified, interest rates, volume of credit expansion, and foreign exchange as its operational targets while growth of money supply was the intermediate target. A review of the macroeconomic outcomes during this phase shows that macroeconomic policies, namely fiscal, monetary, and exchange rate management, complimented by political stability, were largely successful as the period did not witness any unpleasant macroeconomic outcomes.

A review of selected macroeconomic indicators in Table 14.1, show that during the period 1966–70, economic growth averaged 7.2 per cent while growth of investment was largely at double digit and a measured growth of money supply. Consistent with these outcomes inflation remained below 2 per cent during the period. In view of all these outcomes the exchange rate remained fixed at

Table 14.1 Selected macroeconomic variables, 1966–70

	1966	1967	1968	1969	1970
Real GDP growth (%)	12.84	3.12	6.98	6.20	6.96
Growth of gross investment (%)	24.86	25.16	9.39	2.50	16.12
Growth of M2 (%)	12.75	10.78	10.29	19.40	27.61
Inflation rate	2.70	1.74	1.12	0.15	1.75
Exchange rate KSh/US$	7.17	7.14	7.14	7.14	7.14
Real interest rates	−0.53	1.92	2.99	3.66	1.44

Source: Central Bank of Kenya and Economic Survey, various issues.

US$1 = KSh7.14 from 1967 to 1970, as there were no macroeconomic imbalances which could warrant either a devaluation of the unit or otherwise. Although the interest rates were controlled, they remained largely positive in real terms during this period, suggesting that, on balance, the monetary and other related policies were successful and supportive of growth and development in line with the aspirations of the government during the first decade of independence.

14.3.2 The 1970s and 1980s: Active Monetary Policy Phase with Direct Policy Instruments

The 1970s and 1980s were more eventful as far as monetary policy is concerned. One of the milestones during this time was the 1972 amendment of the CBK Act to limit the Central Bank's direct advances to the Government to no more than 25 per cent of the latter's gross revenue according to its latest audited accounts.

This phase was characterized by abundant use of direct monetary policy instruments to address various imbalances in the economy. In some cases, CBK enforced the minimum cash ratio (the mandatory proportion of deposits that banks must maintain at the CBK) as well as the liquidity ratio (the proportion of the bank's assets, that include cash and others that can easily be converted to cash), with a view to containing credit expansion. In addition, to address the balance of payments (BOP) challenges, the CBK restricted commercial bank lending to foreign-controlled companies to no more than 60 per cent of the company's capital if Kenya citizens owned at least 50 per cent of the equity.

Over and above these monetary policy instruments, the government pursued a regime of interest rate controls and quantitative credit controls (credit ceilings) with the aim of encouraging investment and spurring economic development. Interest rate controls entailed fixing minimum saving rates for all deposit taking institutions and maximum lending rates for all commercial banks, Non-bank financial institutions (NBFIs), and building societies. Levying of extra charges on loans was not allowed.

Table 14.2 Evolution of inflation and interest rates in the 1970s and 1980s

	1973	1978	1979	1984	1985	1986	1987	1988
Spread	4	7	5	5	4	4.8	2.5	3
Saving rate	3	3	5	6	9.3	11.3	12.5	11
Lending rate	7	10	10	11	13.3	16	15	14
Inflation	0.23	20.14	16.19	13.02	11.3	18.7	11.99	9.99
Real interest rates	6.77	−10.14	−6.19	−2.02	2	−2.7	3.01	4.01

Source: Central Bank of Kenya and Economic Survey, various issues.

With the interest rate and credit allocation ceilings, the CBK attempted to offset the effect of large fiscal deficits on monetary expansion. However, selective enforcement of credit ceilings contributed to segmentation of the financial market and inflationary pressures. NBFIs were subjected to higher interest ceiling than commercial banks. This resulted in the government being unable to control inflationary pressures stemming from expansionary fiscal policy, expansion of lending by NBFIs, and government owned banks. At the same time, banks facing tight ceilings were unable to lend to high risky clients thus pushing them to lend to NBFIs.

Financial controls in place at the time led to financial repression characterized by negative real interest rates, especially in periods affected by shocks. For example, following the inflationary pressure associated with the economic shocks that hit the economy in the early 1970s, interest rates on both deposits and loans were raised for the first time since independence in June 1963. Nonetheless, as shown in Table 14.2, negative real interest rates persisted for a long time thus impacting adversely private savings mobilization and investment.

The Government had firm control over the allocation of credit to various sectors. Sectors which were perceived to be important were allocated a larger share of credit. However, such sectors were not necessarily profitable to repay the loans. In the allocation of credit, the government took a substantial and rising share of loanable funds to finance the budget deficit and finance state owned enterprises and agencies. As a result, the share of government domestic credit rose from an average of 18 per cent in 1970–74, to an average of approximately 45 per cent in 1990–93 (Figure 14.1). Funds were mobilized with the imposition of high liquidity requirements especially on banks. As the sector faced challenges, a number of banks and NBFIs were closed, mainly as a result of undercapitalization and non-performing loans.

The exchange rate policy was an integral part of the monetary policy, as such, the Exchange Control Act CAP 113 and its subsidiary legislation, rules, and regulations anchored activity in the foreign exchange market. The Act provided that all foreign exchange transactions (such as sale, purchase, borrowing or lending of foreign currency as well as maintenance of foreign balances, payment

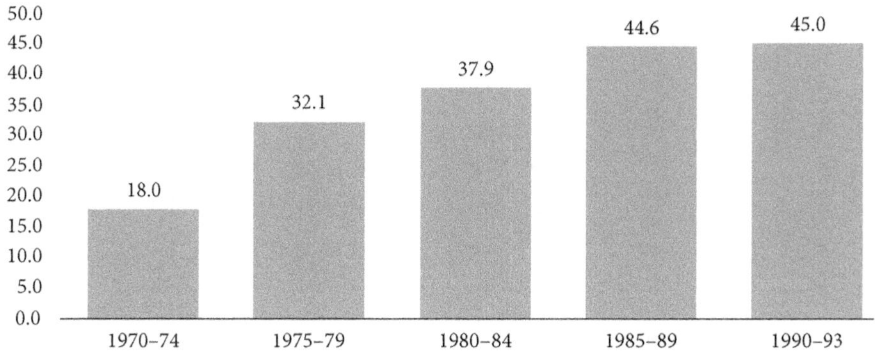

Figure 14.1 Share of credit of the banking sector to government (%)
Source: Economic Survey, various issues.

Table 14.3 Evolution of exchange rates and exports in 1970–89

	1970–74	1975–79	1980–84	1985–89
Official exchange rate	7.09	7.85	10.32	16.45
Parallel exchange rate	9.20	8.76	13.69	18.19
Parallel market premium (%)	29.90	11.78	32.81	10.41
Par. RER	0.96	1.01	1.03	1.05
Off. RER	1.20	1.16	1.52	1.48
Exch. Misalig. (%)	−15.40	−11.87	−28.38	−28.73
Export to GDP ratio (%)	28.00	32.00	17.00	13.60

Source: Central Bank of Kenya and Economic Survey, various issues.

to non-residents, export of any financial instrument or bill of exchange and transfer of securities between non-residents and residents) were prohibited unless directly permitted by the Central Bank of Kenya or directly through the authorized dealers.

As a result of the foreign exchange controls, rationing of the foreign exchange was common, with priority being given to importers of essential goods while tight restrictions were imposed on the non-essential imports. However, bureaucratic procedures made it difficult to access forex to import essential goods resulting in widespread rent seeking. As a market response, a parallel market for foreign exchange emerged to address the growing foreign exchange needs for non-essential imports, as highlighted in Table 14.3.

The parallel foreign exchange market manifested a high forex premium, ranging from 10.41 per cent to 32.81 per cent during 1970–1989 period.[3] The exchange rate in the parallel market fluctuated according to the forces of demand

[3] Data was obtained from Kidane (1994).

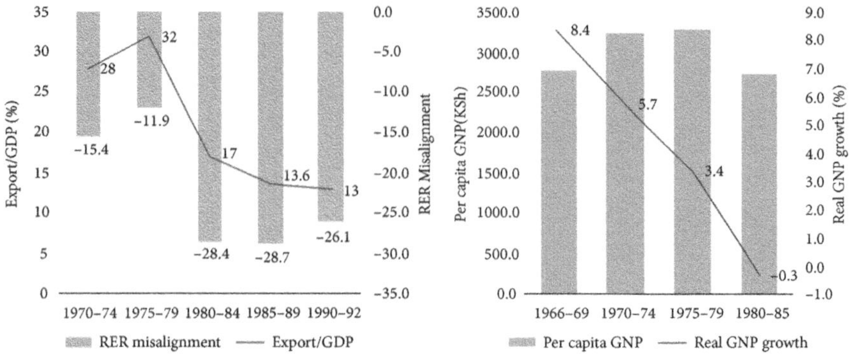

Figure 14.2 Evolution of exports, exchange rate misalignment and growth, 1966–85
Source: Central Bank of Kenya and Economic Survey, various issues.

and supply for the US dollar and other desired currencies. For instance, during the international oil crisis in 1973, and prolonged drought in 1981–84, which resulted in increased cost of importation of fuel and food, the parallel market premium was above 40 per cent of the official exchange rate, as shown in Table 14.3. The parallel market exchange rate was considered as a proxy for a floating exchange rate, thus reflecting the fundamentals of the Kenyan economy.

The fixed official exchange rates against all the major currencies was not reflective of the true value of the Kenyan currency.[4] Following the high inflation in the country relative to the rest of the world, during the mid-1970s and 1980s, the real exchange rate became overvalued. The magnitude of misalignment was moderate in the 1970s, averaging 13.6 per cent, rising to approx. 28.6 per cent in the 1980s (Table 14.3).

The overvalued exchange rate undermined exports performance. The exports to GDP ratio stood at approximately 28 per cent in 1970–74, rising to approximately 32 per cent in 1975–79. However, the various controls in the economy at the time, including overvalued real exchange rate, resulted in a decline in exports performance to 17 per cent in 1980–84, and remained at almost the same level for the remainder of the 1980s to early 1990s (Figure 14.2).

The many controls imposed on various sector resulted in significant contraction of the economy. At the inception of the controls, the real GNP growth average 8.4 per cent in 1966–69. Thereafter it declined to 5.7 per cent in 1970–74. Despite the coffee boom of 1976–77, the average growth during 1975–79 declined to 3.4 per cent. In 1980–84, the economy had contracted by 0.3 per cent. During this time the per capita real GNP stagnated (Figure 14.2). Following these unpleasant outcomes, the government commenced a comprehensive economic and

[4] The misalignment is calculated as per cent deviation of parallel real effective exchange rate from the official real effective exchange rate. Data extracted from Kidane (1994).

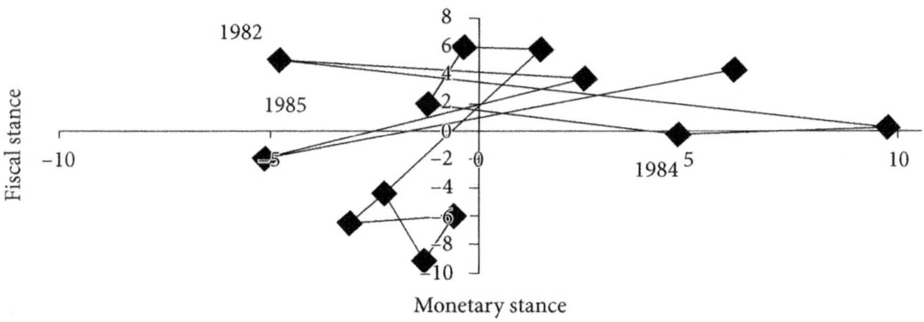

Figure 14.3 Fiscal and monetary policy mix in Kenya, 1978–89

financial programme, which are outlined in 'Sessional Paper No. 1 of 1986 on Economic Management for Renewed Growth' (Government of Kenya, 1986).

The overbearing role of fiscal policy[5] in influencing the efficacy of monetary policy was witnessed during this time. The relationship between monetary policy and the CBK's fiscal policy can be described as largely uncoordinated, that is, there are many instances when these policies were pulling in different directions to address the same macroeconomic problem. Here, we witnessed an expansionary fiscal policy that embodied the deficit bias versus a monetary policy with a tightening bias meant to either attain a monetary target or anchor macroeconomic stability (Figure 14.3). This was the case 1980s when the economy was facing stability challenges compounded by structural constraints that needed urgent attention.

14.3.3 Monetary Policy in the 1990s: Active Monetary Policy Phase with Weak Institutions

The 1990s had every attribute of a nightmare for the conduct of monetary policy in Kenya largely on account of the chaotic political environment which existed. As Alesina and Stella (2010) have shown, basing on global experiences and theoretical insight, the political economy of monetary policy is very important and raises questions of whether the political environment favours monetary policy rules or discretion, whether the central bank is independent or otherwise, both in normal times and in times of crisis, and the issue of electoral manipulation of monetary policy. In the context of monetary policy in Kenya, the highly charged political environment that characterized the period prior and subsequent to 1992 had

[5] Fiscal Stance (FS) is calculated as the residual between the cyclically neutral budget deficit (D_{CN}) and the actual budget deficit (D):. A cyclically neutral budget deficit is obtained using the following: where g_0 is the ratio of government expenditure to potential GDP (Yp) at the period while t_0 is the ratio of tax revenue to actual GDP during the base year.

contributed to the expansionary fiscal policy leading to the high inflation episode and significant depreciation of the Kenyan shilling, as shown in Table 14.4.

The money supply grew rapidly to 34 per cent in 1991 relative to the 9 per cent target at a time when the CBK was addressing distress in the banking sector (Table 14.4). The economy had to confront the double-digit fiscal deficit as a proportion of the GDP in the 1991/92 and 1992/93 fiscal years that were largely funded by printing money. This happened following the fiscal authority exploiting the existing CBK Act that allowed the Minister for Finance to override the CBK Board of Directors even on monetary policy. As a result, the inflation rate of 70 per cent and a real output growth of 0.2 per cent in 1993 were unprecedented. By July 1993, the 91-day Treasury bill rates had hit a high of 84.6 per cent. The loss of confidence in the economy saw a haemorrhage of foreign exchange reserves to a week's equivalent of imports cover. The Kenya shilling's value vis-à-vis other major currencies plunged to the extent that it lost the public's confidence as a preferred medium of exchange.

Following these unpleasant developments, it was imperative to retool the CBK's mandate as part of the comprehensive reform programme that the Government had adopted under an IMF monitored arrangement for financial support. An amendment of the CBK Act in 1995, removed the exchange control mandate.

However, the surge in inflation in the early 1990s to about 70 per cent (the time of first multiparty elections in 1992) led to amendment of the CBK Act in 1996 to give CBK more autonomy to manage monetary policy. The Act was amended substantially, narrowing the Central Bank's mandate to maintaining price stability and fostering liquidity, solvency and the proper functioning of a stable market-based financial system. In effect, it took nearly 30 years for the overall stability of the financial system including that of prices to become core mandates of the CBK. The operational independence necessitated clear provisions for accountability and transparency. The amended Act required the CBK to submit to the Minister for Finance, every six months, a monetary policy statement that: specified the policies and instruments to apply to achieve policy targets in the forthcoming 12 months; stated the rationale for the policies and the instruments; and provided an assessment of progress with the implementation of monetary policy in the immediate 12 months to which the previous statement related.

The minister was, in turn, required to table his monetary policy statement to the parliamentary committee on economic matters. Moreover, the Central Bank was required to disseminate to the public key financial data and information on monetary policy. The new monetary policy framework was hinged on a measure of the money supply, which was refined further with expectations that it would give the new amendments the required efficacy. The fine-tuning was meant to broaden the measure of the money supply to accommodate a wider class of deposits by both banks and non-bank financial institutions.

Table 14.4 Evolution of key economic indicators, 1990–99

	1990	1991	1992	1993	1994	1995	1996	1997	1998	1999
Growth of money supply (M3)	20.9	18.5	26.6	22.3	27.4	18.9	15.9	11.9	3.5	5.1
Growth of money supply (M2)	15.5	20.9	33.6	25.7	30.4	8.7	28.9	14.8	8.8	3.9
Growth of money supply (M1)	16.6	16.4	43.9	22.6	11.1	8.8	8.3	14.9	4.0	16.2
Exchange rate (KSh/U5$)	24.1	28.1	36.2	68.2	44.8	55.9	55	62.7	61.9	72.9
Exchange rate (change %)	11.6	16.6	28.8	88.4	−34.3	24.8	−1.6	14.0	−1.3	17.8
Inflation	20.1	14.5	33.7	54.7	6.7	6.8	10.8	8.3	2.5	8.0
Treasury bill rate-91 day	16.7	17.3	17.4	85.3	18.6	21.7	21.5	26.4	12.6	19.9
GDP growth (%)	4.2	1.4	−0.8	0.4	2.6	4.4	4.1	0.5	3.3	2.3

Source: Economic Survey, various issues.

Despite the severe macroeconomic challenges, the monetary targeting framework[6] continued to serve the country well with refinement of operations and procedures to enhance its effectiveness. The monetary policy framework was able to deliver single digit inflation in the latter part of the 1990s. However, financial innovations in the financial sector tended to weaken the anchor of monetary aggregates as policy targets.[7]

Econometric research by Mwega (1990) on monetary policy in Kenya, during 1967–88, uncovers evidence, which is mainly consistent with the main findings from the analysis above. In particular, the evidence emphasized the importance of monetary variables in explaining changes in inflation rates in Kenya during the sample period.

14.3.4 The 2000s: Active Monetary Policy Phase with Strong Institutions and Transitioning to a Modern Central Bank

Following the limitations on the conduct of monetary policy which were witnessed in the 1990s and coupled with the trends across the world, the CBK sought to improve its monetary policy regime from one largely driven by procedures to manage the money supply. The 2001[8] legislation required that the Monetary Policy Advisory Committee (MPAC) be established. In line with the amendment of the CBK Act in 2004, the MPAC, composed of CBK executives as well as independent members, was established and the Central Bank Rate (CBR)—the lowest rate that the CBK charges for loans to banks—was introduced.

With price stability as the CBK's primary objective, the CBK Act was further amended in 2007 to introduce a secondary objective that required the Central Bank to 'support the economic policy of the Government, including the objectives of growth and employment'. Such Government policy is communicated to the CBK by the Minister for Finance, a departure from what prevailed in 1990s when the CBK not only set the inflation target but had the independence to deploy any instrument at its disposal to reach that target. Deploying the monetary policy instruments at its disposal without any external influence meant that the CBK had instrument, and not goal, independence. This had the obvious limitation that it blurred accountability.

[6] The appropriateness of the monetary aggregates framework was given credence by studies conducted on Kenya in the 1980s and 1990s (see Killick and Mwega, 1990; Mwega, 1990; Adam et al., 2010) which showed the money demand was stable.

[7] See Sichei and Kamau (2012) who find money demand to be unstable following financial innovations.

[8] This same legislation re-introduced regulation of interest rates 'the Donde Act'. However, the CBK Act was amended in 2004, repealing the interest rates regulation.

The other milestone was the establishment the Monetary Policy Committee (MPC), which unlike the MPAC whose mandate was purely advisory, had the full responsibility to formulate monetary policy. In 2007, the Central Bank of Kenya Act was amended to allow the formation of the Monetary Policy Committee (MPC). The Committee is charged with the responsibility for formulating monetary policy. The MPC meets every sixty days, unless the macroeconomic environment necessitates more frequent meetings. The Committee meets to review the macroeconomic environment on the basis of which a decision is made on the monetary policy stance, mainly to review the Central Bank Rate.

During this time the country experienced many developments in the area of financial sector some which had implications for the conduct of monetary policy in Kenya.[9] These developments in financial access in Kenya during 2006–13 have positive and negative implications on the conduct of monetary policy. On a positive note, the currency outside banks (COB) has been on a downward trend since 2007. Figure 14.4, shows that while the ratio of COB to M3 was relatively

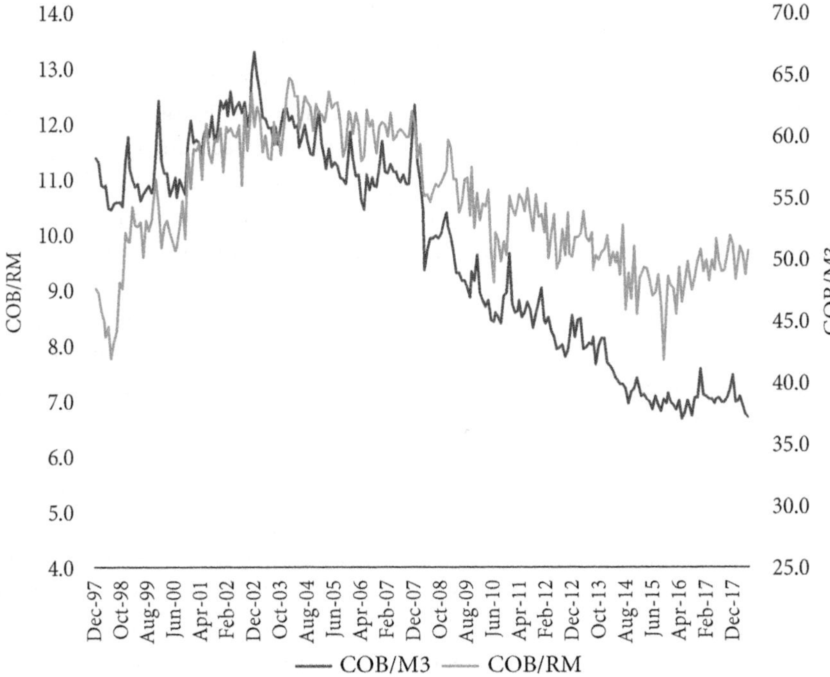

Figure 14.4 Evolution of currency outside banks
Source: Central Bank of Kenya.

[9] For example, MPesa was introduced in 2007, which marked a remarkable achievement of financial innovation and was followed by the diffusion of the MPESA innovative financial technology throughout the East African region and beyond (see Misati et al. 2010).

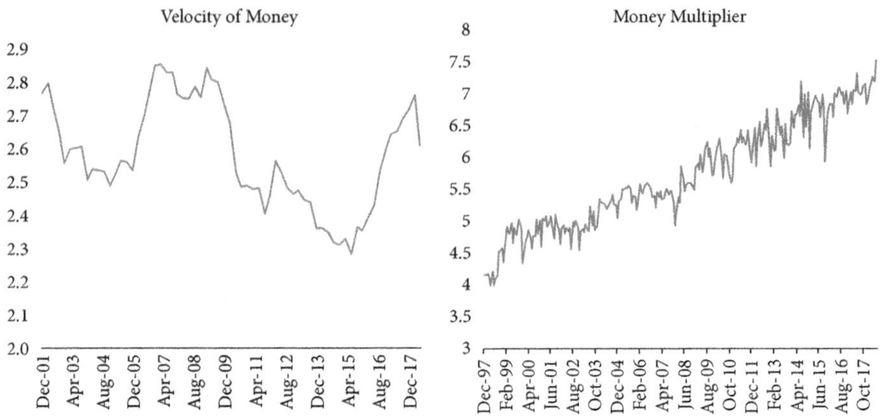

Figure 14.5 Evolution of velocity of money and money multiplier
Source: Central Bank of Kenya.

stable prior to 2007, it started to decline rapidly thereafter suggesting that the proportion of currency within the banking system has been increasing and therefore a greater control of the central bank on the economy.

In the first panel of Figure 14.5, it is shown that the velocity of money has also been on the decline. It stood at about 2.5 in January 2007 declining gradually until 2009 when it declined rapidly to stand at approximately 2.0 in 2010. Thereafter, the velocity of money has remained relatively stable. The money multiplier has been on an upward trend rising from 5.0 in 2007 to stand at approximately 6.5 in mid-2013.

These developments challenge the appropriateness of monetary policy framework in use in Kenya—the monetary aggregate targeting framework which is built around strict assumptions regarding the stability of the money multiplier and velocity of money. This called for a radical review of the monetary policy framework in order to enhance effectiveness of monetary policy. This evidence was not unique to Kenya, but rather, it was observed across many countries around the world[10] implementing monetary aggregates targeting framework.

Following these developments, the CBK has steadily moved to consolidate the gradual gains in monetary policy formulation to take its framework towards an inflation-targeting regime or forward-looking. Although, the CBK has not yet adopted the inflation targeting monetary policy framework—a forward-looking regime by which inflation is forecast as the intermediate target of policy and a short-term interest rate serves as the operational target—it has taken a deliberate decision to build its capacity to undertake forecasting and policy analysis as a

[10] For a detailed discussion, see IMF (2015) on evolving monetary policy frameworks in low-income and other developing countries.

means to disciplining and fine-tuning its policy formulation process. However, the challenges in the inter-bank market remain as the CBK strives to operationalize the interbank rate as the operational target.

Nonetheless, monetary policy conduct is now increasingly being centred on the CBR, the policy rate where other money market rates, such as the Treasury bill and the interbank rates, are expected to converge. In line with the goal independence instrument, the National Treasury sets the inflation target in consultation with the CBK at the beginning of every fiscal year. In the event that the inflation target, provided to the CBK by the Finance Minister at the beginning of every financial year, is missed, the CBK is expected to explain the deviation and offer the measures needed to address it, and also provide an indicative timeline for inflation to return to within target. An additional explanation is provided by the CBK if inflation remains above the target for three consecutive months after the first explanation.

The active monetary policy phase with indirect instruments and strong institutions, since 1997, was also characterized by ground-breaking technological financial innovation in Kenya, in the form of M-PESA. The discussion is fully covered by Mugo et al. (2021) in Chapter 16 of this book. With respect to implications of this innovation for monetary policy effectiveness, it is sufficient to note here that the effect of financial innovation on monetary policy transmission has been investigated, focusing on the interest rate channel through which the Central Bank implements monetary policy (see Misati et al., 2010). It was found that during the period 1996–2007, financial innovation dampened the interest rate channel of monetary transmission mechanism. One main implication of the evidence is that financial innovation may pose complex challenges to the conduct of monetary policy, such that the CBK may need to monitor and where necessary intervene in the use of monetary policy instruments, the targeting frameworks and operating procedures in order to enhance policy potency.

14.3.5 Monetary Policy under the Interest Rate Capping Regime

As the CBK celebrated its 50th anniversary in September 2016, debate on interest rate controls was raging in the National Assembly. The proponents of the interest rate controls had strong arguments regarding the cost of credit. The debate on interest rate capping started in the early 2000s. The high cost of credit and its attendant interest rate spreads, the interest rate capping debate began in 2001, when a bill was introduced in Parliament proposing to peg commercial banks interest rates to the 91-day Treasury bill rate as CBK did not have a base rate at the time. The second attempt in 2013 called for rates to be capped consistent with the Central Bank Rate—both attempts failed largely on the strength of the arguments for free market interest rate structure. In addition, the banks were given a chance to self-regulate in terms of designing measures towards lower cost of credit.

The Government initiated measures in a bid to lower the cost of credit and prevent capping of interest rates, with the following notable ones:

- The Credit Information Sharing. Credit Reference Bureaus (CRBs) were established to enhance credit information sharing mechanism and aid lenders in undertaking credit decisions based on credit history of borrowers.
- The Kenya Bankers Reference Rate (KBRR). The National Treasury constituted a Committee in January 2014 to explore ways of enhancing private sector credit and mortgage finance supply in Kenya. To enhance transparency in pricing of credit, the Committee recommended introduction of a transparent credit pricing framework known as the Kenya Banks' Reference Rate (KBRR). However, in practice, KBRR was less effective, owing to various challenges including the modalities of its computation and the limited flexibility of its review. Moreover, whereas the KBRR framework was duly implemented, it did not satisfactorily address the public concern regarding the high cost of credit.
- Establishment of currency centres to help lower transaction costs associated with transporting cash over long distances across the country.

Despite numerous efforts by the government, the banking sector continued to maintain high cost of credit with noticeable differences across bank tiers. Compared to its peers, Kenya's banks maintained high interest rate spreads (Table 14.5). Calls for capping interest rates were mainly anchored on the high spreads between lending rates and deposit rates compared to other developing peer economies, and the resulting high profitability in the sector. Although Kenya's average interest rate spread that stood at 14.2 per cent in 2000, it had declined to 8.14 per cent by 2014, however, it was still high compared to Kenya's comparators such as Mauritius, Namibia, and South Africa which had much lower interest rate spreads. As a result of high interest spreads Kenya's banking sector remained highly profitable compared to peers thus provoking debate on interest rate capping in the country.

The debate about the high cost of credit culminated into the Banking (Amendment) Act 2016, aimed at lowering the cost of credit. The Central Bank has continued to implement the new law. However, concerns were raised regarding the negative consequences of the amended law. The impact of this law may be witnessed in the short term, and the medium and long term. Globally, capping of interest rates has been declining over time.[11] International experience shows that interest rate caps generally have negative effects which tend to worsen with time.

[11] Maimbo and Gallegos (2014) on interest rate caps is one of the most widely cited papers as it provides a comprehensive review and general global landscape on interest rate caps. Overall, 76 countries around the world impose some form of interest rate caps on loans, most of which are in Sub Saharan Africa (SSA), and in Latin America and the Caribbean (LAC).

Table 14.5 Interest rate spreads across countries and regions

	2000	2004	2008	2009	2011	2012	2013	2014	2015	2016
Angola	6.4	6.7	6.0	8.1	12.4	13.1	12.7	12.9	13.6	10.2
Botswana	6.1	5.9	7.9	6.3	5.9	7.4	7.1	6.5	5.4	5.2
Algeria	2.5	4.4	6.3	6.3	6.3	6.3	6.3	6.3	6.3	6.3
Egypt. Arab Rep.	3.8	5.7	5.7	5.5	4.3	4.4	4.6	4.8	4.7	5.7
Kenya	**14.2**	**10.1**	**9.5**	**9.7**	**10.8**	**12.0**	**10.8**	**9.9**	**9.2**	**9.5**
Mauritius	11.2	12.9	1.4	0.8	1.8	2.4	1.7	1.7	2.4	3.3
Namibia	7.9	5.0	5.4	4.9	4.4	4.4	4.3	4.5	4.6	4.2
Nigeria	9.6	5.5	3.5	5.1	10.3	8.4	8.8	7.2	7.7	9.4
South Africa	5.3	4.7	3.5	3.2	3.3	3.3	3.3	3.3	3.3	3.3
World	7.4	6.0	5.7	5.7	5.8	5.4	5.8	5.5	5.3	5.5
East Asia and Pacific	5.0	5.4	4.6	5.0	5.0	5.0	5.0	4.9	5.0	4.8
Sub-Saharan Africa	13.6	12.9	6.7	6.7	8.0	7.1	7.1	7.2	6.8	6.1

Source: World Bank, World Development Indicators, and Central Bank of Kenya.

However, based on international experience and local reviews preceding the amendment of the law, the interest rate caps are expected to result in the following:

- *Increased demand for loans*: Following reduction in interest rates, demand for bank loans is expected to increase. This is mainly the case for those segments of the population which could not afford the high rates of interest prior to interest rate capping law, as well as top up by existing loan holders. Loan applications by the small borrowers were expected to increase.
- *Reduced access to financial services*: Interest rate capping results in banks changing their lending behaviour, viewing loans to small borrowers such as SMEs and individuals riskier and expensive to manage. Thus, they tend to offer less credit to these borrowers, preferring lending to government and large private borrowers.
- *Reduced transparency*: Interest rate caps, by restricting the ability of banks to make interest income, encourage banks to introduce or increase non-interest charges, such as fees, to compensate for lost income. As a result, it becomes difficult for customers to internalize the total cost of borrowing and also to make informed decisions on borrowing.
- *Elevated risks to financial stability*: the interest rate capping law is expected to impact the viability of the small banks compared to medium and large size banks. This may undermine the overall financial sector stability.
- *Reduced competition in the banking industry*: Following interest rate capping banks are expected to re-engineer their business models thus creating non-competitive tendencies in the industry— as a result there will be a tendency of concentration of business in a few banks. In addition, there will be a tendency for small banks to merge to survive resulting in furthering non-competitive practices.
- *Shifting to expensive loans*: The riskier borrowers rationed out resort to borrowing from alternative sources not regulated by the caps, which charge much higher rates.
- *Impairment of monetary policy transmission*: The Central Bank is charged with the mandate of conducting monetary policy aimed at ensuring price stability. To achieve this objective, the CBK uses a number of tools, including the CBR. In the interest rate capping environment, use of CBR will result in perverse outcomes. During the phase of monetary policy loosening to stimulate credit expansion to support growth, the interest rate cap will also adjust downward. As a result, those individuals with credit risk above the capped rate will be shunned by banks thereby leading to contraction in growth of credit to the private sector.
- *Impact on economic growth*: interest rate capping law is expected to impact access to credit by the SMEs. Considering that SMEs account for a large

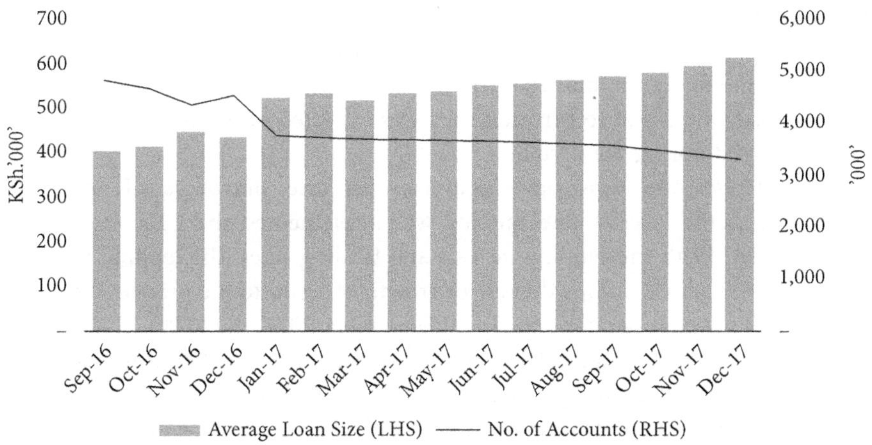

Figure 14.6 Evolution of number of loan accounts and average loan size
Source: Central Bank of Kenya.

share of enterprises, rationing out the SMEs by the banks will adversely impact their contribution to GDP and also compromise the overall real GDP growth prospects.

14.3.6 Interest Rates Caps and Financial Intermediation and Inclusion

Following interest rate capping a number of borrowers have been shunned by banks. Since the commencement of the interest rate capping law in September 2016, the number of loan accounts has continued to decline resulting in rising average loan size. The average loan size has increased by 36.7 per cent between October 2016 and June 2017, as shown in Figure 14.6. The rising value of loan size vis-à-vis reduced number of loan accounts reflects lower access to small borrowers and larger loans to more established firms after the imposition of the caps. This evidence is consistent with the experiences of Ecuador, Bolivia, South Africa, and Zambia, following implementation of interest rate capping in those countries.

14.3.7 The Impact of Interest Rate Controls on the Effectiveness of Monetary Policy

Available evidence suggests that under a normal environment monetary policy is effective. A change in the central bank rate will affect other rates and consequently impact on the growth of credit to the private sector. Analysis based on data for the period up to September 2016, show that a 1 per cent change in CBR results in a 0.4 per cent change in credit to the private sector in the opposite direction. Therefore, following the monetary policy stance which was implemented up to mid-last year, the credit to private sector was expected to decline at a slow pace than witnessed during the period.

The interest rate caps have delivered perverse outcomes of monetary policy. When the interest rate capping was implemented the CBR rate was at 10.5 per cent. With the binding deposit and lending rates, the lending rate was capped at 14.5 per cent while the rate of growth of credit to the private sector was at approx. 8 per cent per annum. On 20 September 2016, the MPC, in its regular meetings, noted that inflation was expected to decline but had concerns with the slowdown in credit to the private sector. Consequently, it decided to reduce the CBR by 50 basis points to 10.0 per cent with the anticipation of reversing the declining trend. However, credit to the private sector continued to decline leading one to conclude that the monetary policy action produced counter-intuitive results—a loosening on monetary policy yielding unexpected decline in credit to the private sector. The key question one would ask is why this could be the case. Perhaps the answer is found in the way monetary policy works under the Bank Lending Channel (BLC). The BLC, which focuses on how credit to the private sector behaves following a monetary policy stance is hinged on key balance sheet items: the level of liquidity, bank size (asset), and capitalization. An examination of these variables since the inception of interest rate caps in September 2016, show that they are trending in the direction that does not support effective monetary policy transmission, as highlighted in Figure 14.7.

Overall, the banking industry has remained liquid thus hurting extension of credit by commercial banks. The industry liquidity ratio averaged above 35 per cent against a prudential minimum requirement of 20 per cent throughout the period of this assessment, implying minimal liquidity risks even after interest rates caps. This high liquidity may be explained by increased holding of government securities by 40 banks, which rose by 40.4 per cent between June 2015 and June 2017 (Table 14.6). Government securities are not only safe assets for banks, but they are also considered as liquid instruments in the computation of the liquidity ratio. Therefore, banks can easily access additional liquidity in the event of potential risks using these securities as collateral if unencumbered, unlike other assets.

The commercial banks have diversified their revenue streams away from interest income (Table 14.7). Interest income is mainly centred on credit extension to the private sector, therefore less reliance on interest income to support growth of revenue implies that whatever signal the CBK sends to the market to influence credit growth, the banks may choose to ignore it as their focus is on streams that are not interest rate sensitive. As shown in Table 14.7, commercial

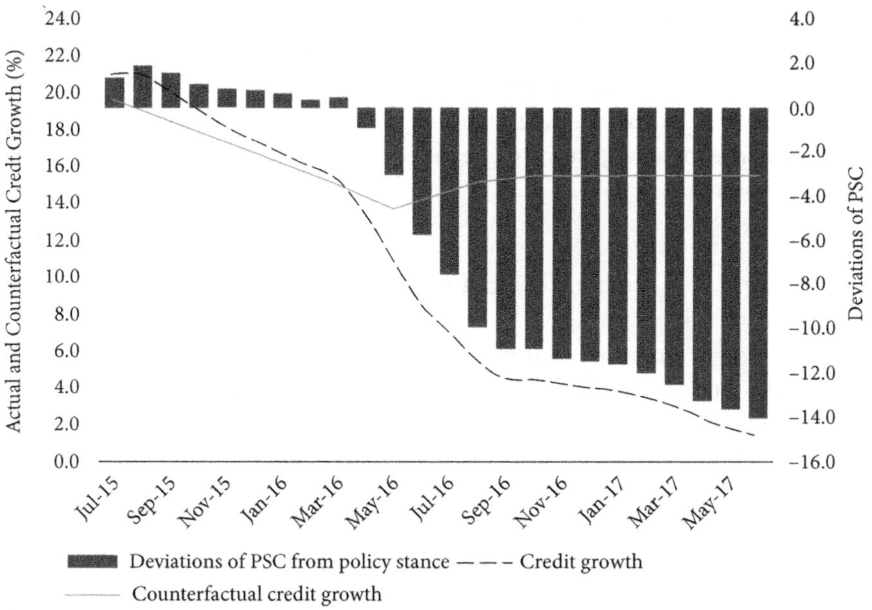

Figure 14.7 Evolution of credit to the private sector

Table 14.6 Evolution of bank liquidity by bank tier

	June 2015	Sep. 2015	Dec. 2015	Mar. 2016	June 2016	Sep. 2016	Dec. 2016	Mar. 2017	June 2017
Large	37.6	35.7	38.9	38.1	40.9	41.3	41.9	43.8	47.9
Medium	39.9	39.3	38.0	45.4	41.1	43.7	38.3	40.5	45.3
Small	39.5	38.1	33.5	36.3	33.6	36.4	35.5	35.4	37.6
All Banks	**38.7**	**37.4**	**38.1**	**40.3**	**40.4**	**41.7**	**40.4**	**42.2**	**46.3**

Source: Central Bank of Kenya.

Table 14.7 Evolution of structure of income of commercial banks

	June 2015	Sep. 2015	Dec. 2015	Mar. 2016	June 2016	Sep. 2016	Dec. 2016	Mar. 2017	June 2017
Interest on loans	60.6	63.4	62.5	62.1	61.1	61.2	55.7	56.0	54.8
Securities income	16.1	13.9	15.0	17.9	19.0	18.4	21.7	20.9	21.7
Fees and commisions	13.9	14.5	13.1	12.5	12.6	12.4	14.5	15.5	15.2
Other income	9.3	8.1	9.5	7.4	7.3	8.0	8.0	7.9	8.3

Source: Central Bank of Kenya.

banks have enhanced the share of their income from fees and commissions. The share of non-interest income stood at 12.4 per cent in September 2016 but it increased gradually to 15.2 per cent in June 2017.

These are preliminary findings regarding the impact of the interest rate caps. However, an enhanced picture will emerge in the medium to long-term, from ongoing research.

14.4 Concluding Remarks

The chronicle of monetary policy in Kenya has been dynamic over the past 50 years and continues to change as the economy and financial sector evolves. The policy has largely been supportive to economic growth and continues to deliver low and stable prices in the country. In the first two phases of pre-1966 and 1966–70, monetary policy remained passive to 1970. The setting up of the central bank in 1966, was to regulate the issue of notes and coins, maintain a sound monetary, credit, and banking system, and serve as a banker and financial advisor to the government. Remarkably, the macroeconomic outcomes during these phases were sound, with low inflation, high economic growth, and stable exchange rate.

The next two phases in the 1970s, '80s and '90s were characterized by domestic and external shocks that led to macroeconomic imbalances. In an effort to correct the imbalance, monetary policy become active in the economy, albeit in a controlling way. Direct monetary policy instruments were used leading to financial repression. In the 1990s improvements in the monetary policy frameworks were made, with the use of indirect instruments and adoption of monetary targeting framework. The role of the Central Bank was defined to price stability and was granted instrument independence via the CBK Act of 1996.

In the period 2000s to date, monetary policy has evolved in line with developments in the financial market brought about by financial innovations. The Central Bank's monetary policy is forward-looking aiming to contain inflation within a target band using interest rate instrument. The current monetary policy regime is operating under interest rates caps introduced in September 2016.

Going forward, monetary policy is expected to continue evolving, influenced by changes in the economy and developments in the financial sector. However, monetary policy developments within the Eastern Africa region and at the global level are likely to have spillover effects on domestic developments in Kenya. The implications of the developments in Eastern Africa towards a single monetary union are explored in Chapter 3 of this book while Chapter 2 considers the global developments.

References

Adam, C. S., Maturu, B. O., Ndung'u, S. N., and O'Connell, S. A. (2010), 'Building a monetary framework for the 21st century', in C. S. Adam, P. Collier, and N. Ndung'u (eds), *Kenya: Policies for Prosperity*. Oxford: Oxford University Press.

Alesina, A. and Stella, A. (2010), 'The politics of monetary policy', *Handbook of Monetary Economics,* Vol. 3, pp. 1001–54.

Government of Kenya (1965), 'African socialism and its application to planning in Kenya'. Sessional Paper No. 10. Nairobi: Government Printers.

Government of Kenya (1986), 'Economic management for renewed growth'. Sessional Paper No. 1. Nairobi: Government Printers.

International Monetary Fund (2015), *Evolving Monetary Policy Frameworks in Low-Income and other Developing Countries*. Washington, DC: International Monetary Fund.

Kidane A. (1994), 'Indices of effective exchange rates: A comparative study of Ethiopia, Kenya and the Sudan', AERC Research Paper No. 29, Africa Economic Research Consortium.

Killick, T. and Mwega, F. M. (1990), 'Monetary policy in Kenya, 1967–88', ODI Working Paper No. 39, Overseas Development Institute.

Maimbo, S. M. and Gallegos, C. A. H. (2014), 'Interest rate caps around the world: Still popular, but a blunt instrument'. World Bank Policy Research Working Paper 7070, The World Bank.

Misati, R. N., Njoroge, L., Kamau, A. W., and Ouma, S. (2010), 'Financial innovation and monetary policy transmission in Kenya', *International Research Journal of Finance and Economics*, Vol. 50, pp. 123–36.

Mugo, M., Kilonzo, E. K and Mariga, A.K (2021), Cross reference Chapter 16.

Mwega, F. M. (1990), 'An econometric study of monetary policy in Kenya'. ODI Working Paper No. 42, Overseas Development Institute.

Mwega, F. M., Ngola, S. M. and Mwangi, N. (1990), 'Real interest rates and mobilization of private savings in Africa: A case study of Kenya'. AERC Research Paper No. 2, Africa Economic Research Consortium.

Njoroge, P. and Murinde, V. (2021), Cross reference Chapter 3.

Sargent, T. J. (2014), 'The evolution of monetary policy rules', *Journal of Economic Dynamics and Control*, Vol. 49, pp. 147–50.

Sichei, M. and Kamau, A. W. (2012), 'Demand for money: Implications for the conduct of monetary policy in Kenya', *International Journal of Economics and Finance*, Vol. 4, No. 8, pp. 72–82.

15
Evolution of the Financial Sector in Kenya

Cappitus Chironga, Matu Mugo, and Daniel Tallam

15.1 Introduction

Kenya's financial sector is dualistic: formal[1] and informal[2] financial service providers exist simultaneously to satisfy the needs of consumers who increasingly prefer a portfolio of services drawn from both segments regardless of their level of financial literacy, wealth, age, or gender in the FinAccess Household Survey 2016 (see CBK, 2016). The findings indicate that 46.3 per cent of Kenya's adult population consumed both formal and informal financial services in 2015 up from 14.5 per cent in 2006. Only 29.1 per cent of adult population used formal financial services exclusively while 8.5 per cent relied solely on informal financial services in 2015 compared to 12 per cent and 32.2 per cent in 2006, respectively (Figure 15.1).

The consumption behaviour reflects the continued struggle to balance between safety (use of formal prudential channels) and convenience (use of informal channels) in accessing and usage of financial services. Access to informal financial services is much easier given minimal requirements and low value collateral required compared to formal financial services. However, informal services, especially the money lenders, are costly. Policy-makers therefore need to deal with consumer protection issues associated with this arrangement by instituting measures to bring the informal financial services into formal channels.

Kenya's financial sector comprises of banking,[3] capital markets, insurance, pensions, and savings credit cooperatives industries. Other players include microfinance institutions, hire purchase companies, money remittances companies,

[1] Formal financial services providers comprise of those financial institutions that are prudentially regulated and supervised by independent statutory regulators such as Central Bank, IRA, SASRA, RBA, and CMA. It also includes services under non-prudential oversight by regulatory agencies or government departments/ministries with focused legislation e.g. Post Bank, NSSF, NSE, NHIF. Moreover, they involve formal registered services, which are governed under a law or government direct intervention such as credit only MFIs, credit only SACCOs, hire purchase companies, etc.

[2] Financial services are not subject to regulation but have a relatively well-defined organizational structure. They include groups (ASCAs, ROSCAs, and Chamas), moneylenders/shylocks, employers, and shopkeepers/supply chain credit.

[3] Includes microfinance banks (deposit taking microfinance institutions) and building societies.

Cappitus Chironga, Matu Mugo, and Daniel Tallam, *Evolution of the Financial Sector in Kenya* In: *50 Years of Central Banking in Kenya: Regional and Global Perspectives.* Edited by: Patrick Njoroge and Victor Murinde, Oxford University Press (2021).
 DOI: 10.1093/oso/9780198851820.003.0015

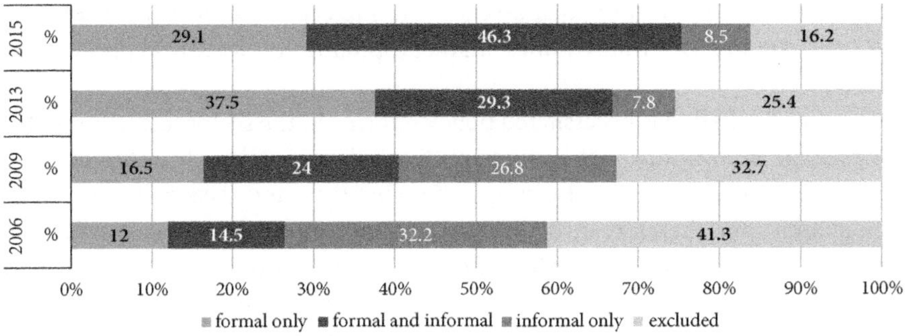

Figure 15.1 Overlaps in the use of financial services by consumers (%)
Source: CBK (2016) for FinAccess Household Survey 2016.

foreign exchange bureaus, and development finance institutions. There are also safety nets and resolution institutions such as the Kenya Deposits Insurance Corporation for commercial and microfinance banks; Investor Compensation Fund for Capital Markets; and the Insurance Policyholders' Compensation Fund for the insurance. These are supported by Credit Information Sharing (CIS) platforms through the Credit Reference Bureau and Financial Markets Infrastructure (FMI) comprising of trading, payments and settlements, and custodial services platforms. Informal players include: Rotating and Accumulating Savings and Credit Associations (ROSCAs and ASCAs); shopkeepers and moneylenders; friends and relatives; among many other informal financial service providers (see Figure A15.1).

The policy, regulatory, and supervisory oversight mandates fall in different Government ministries/departments and agencies. The National Treasury has the overall policy oversight on the Kenya's financial system, covering; banking, capital markets, insurance, and pensions industries, Kenya Post Office Savings Bank (KPOSB), Development Finance Institutions (DFIs) including Agricultural Finance Corporation (AFC), Kenya Industrial Estate (KIE), Industrial and Commercial Development Corporation (ICDC), and Kenya Tourism Development Corporation (KTDC). The Ministry of Industry, Trade and Cooperatives has oversight mandate of Savings and Credit Cooperatives Societies (SACCOs) and all other cooperatives in Kenya. Hire purchase companies and credit-only microfinance institutions (MFIs) fall under the Attorney General's Office while Ministry of Culture and Social Services handle informal financial service providers.

15.2 Financial Sector Development in Kenya

Kenya's financial sector has grown significantly in size, depth, inclusivity, players, and complexity (FSRF, 2017). As a proportion of nominal Gross Domestic

Product (GDP), the sector's total assets excluding capital markets accounted for 82.37 per cent in 2016 while equities' market capitalization was 26.98 per cent (see Figure 15.2).

The rapid growth has necessitated policy reforms in the sector to accommodate and manage innovations that leverage on technology to take advantage of emerging opportunities. Reforms also target emerging gaps and risks that may undermine stability and therefore instil public confidence. Being a key player in regional economies, reforms in the Kenya's financial sector also seek to align it with international best practices for competitiveness and compliance to the set standards (CBK, 2017).

The financial sector development journey in Kenya dates back to colonial times. The British Empire declared Kenya a British sphere of influence and established the East African Protectorate in 1895, Kenya officially becoming its colony in 1920. In the nineteenth century, the East African Protectorate, bringing together, Kenya, Uganda, Tanzania and Aden, engaged in trading activities. Since the times of the arrival of Greeks and Arabs sailors to the East African coast until the colonial era, merchant trading was central. This led to the need for use of various currencies including cowrie shells, Indian rupee, British currency, and the East African shilling, among others. Challenges arising from the use of these modes of payments, led to the development of financial sector.

To discuss the journey of the financial sector in Kenya, we break it down into five phases: pre-independence era; post-independence, 1963–80; financial sector development in the turbulent 1980s–90s; era of transformation, regionalization and take-off: 2002–14; and opportunities ahead in the banking, insurance, capital markets, pensions, and SACCO industries.

15.3 The Banking Industry

15.3.1 Banking in Kenya Prior to Independence

Banking business in Kenya dates back to 1896 when the National Bank of India opened its doors following establishment of the British Administration in Kenya.[4] It all started with Indian moneylenders operating quasi-bank services in the early eighteenth century. The entry point was when Jetha Lila Bankers from India opened a branch in Zanzibar in 1880s. In 1889, the National Bank of India appointed the trade house of Smith Mackenzie to be their agent in Zanzibar. Smith Mackenzie had a Mombasa branch in 1887, which was taken over by the Imperial British East Africa (IBEA) in 1888 to advance its trading activity.

[4] Development of banking in Kenya on https://www.centralbank.go.ke/banking-development/

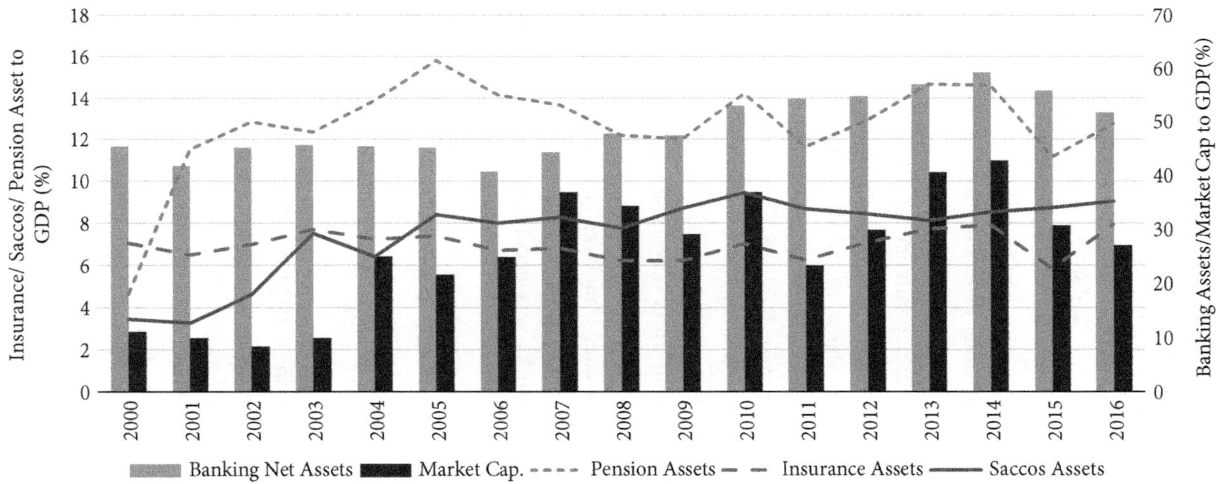

Figure 15.2 Proportion of financial sector assets and market capitalization to nominal GDP

Source: Bank Supervision annual reports, CBK/KNBS, IRA annual reports, RBA statistical reports, and WOCCU statistical reports.

Consequently, the National Bank of India opened its own office in Zanzibar in 1892 and in July 1896, it opened a branch in Mombasa, Kenya, renting premises from Sheriff Jaffer before extending to Nairobi in 1904.

Spread in the banking networks grew from one branch in Mombasa in 1896 to 8 branches in Nairobi, Nakuru, Kisumu, and Eldoret, before the First World War. The expansion was necessitated by the need to finance international trade along the Europe–South Africa–India axis before branching into other economic activities including a growing farming settler community and pioneer traders in the protectorate economy to whom they provided deposit and credit facilities. This proved profitable banking business, hence rapid expansion beyond the coastal region following the railway line extension to tap into farming business in highlands.

When Kenya attained her independence in 1963, there were more than ten banks operating 157 branches across the country. These included: National Bank of India in 1896; Standard Bank of South Africa in 1910; Kathlawad & Ahmedabad BC in 1911; National Bank of South Africa that merged with Anglo-Egyptian Bank Ltd to form Barclays Bank in 1916; Ismailia Corporation Limited, now Diamond Trust Bank in 1940; Exchange Bank of India & Africa in 1945; General Bank of Netherlands, later ABN Amro in 1951; Bank of India and Bank of Baroda in 1953; Habib Bank (Overseas) Ltd in 1956; National Bank of India merged with Grindlays Bank to form National and Grindlays Bank in 1956. National and Grindlays Bank later took over Ottoman Bank in 1958, and finally the Commercial Bank of Africa in 1962.

The rapid expansion of banks was accompanied by the need for regulatory framework to ensure orderly growth and stability. Consequently, the East Africa Post Office Savings Bank Ordinance was passed in April 1909 and a year later in April 1910, the Ordinance for the Regulation of Banks established or to be established in the East Africa Protectorate was passed. The former Ordinance established the first formal bank while the latter enabled the establishment of the National Bank of India.

During the Great Depression of 1929–39, there was a gold rush in Kakamega. This led to opening of two bank branches in 1934 in the town to serve the prospectors. These branches however did not last long and were closed during the Second World War. By 1948, three banks operated 18 branches in ten towns in Kenya—Mombasa, Nairobi, Nakuru, Kisumu, Nyeri, Nanyuki, Kitale, Kericho, Kakamega, and Thompson's Falls (Nyahururu). After independence, Kenya's first locally owned commercial bank, the Cooperative Bank of Kenya, opened doors on 10 January 1968, having begun as a cooperative society. It served the needs of growing farming communities given that cooperatives and banks that existed mainly served the white settlers. On 19 June 1968, the National Bank of Kenya was established as the first fully owned government bank to help indigenous Kenyans get access to credit and control their economy after independence. The need to serve more indigenous Kenyans for accelerated development, as envisaged in the Sessional Paper No. 1 of 1965, saw the establishment of Kenya Commercial Bank in 1971 following the merger of the National and Grindlays Bank, with the government owning a 60 per cent majority stake, becoming Kenya's largest bank by deposits and branch network.

The banking sector in Kenya has continued to grow in post-independence period, driven by policy desires towards accelerated economic prosperity. However, the industry faced many takeovers and mergers influenced by capital flight of 1950s and 60s following violence related to struggle for independence and economic hardships arising from domestic and global challenges. The era was also characterized by opening and closure or mergers of several non-bank financial institutions (NBFI) that include insurance companies, cooperative societies, and building societies.

15.3.2 Banking in Post-Independence Era, 1963–1980

The post-independence banking developments started with the establishment of the Central Bank of Kenya (CBK) in 1966 occasioned by the dissolution of the East African Currency Board as former colonies gained independence. At independence, Kenya's development policies targeted massive resource mobilization and Africanization of Kenyan economy as outlined in the Sessional Paper No. 10 of 1965: 'African socialism and its application to planning in Kenya' (Government of Kenya,1965). Financial institutions, which had been the preserve of the colonialists, became key instruments of this process and therefore ownership by the indigenous Africans was paramount to achieving this goal. Unlike most of other African countries, Kenya did not undertake wholesale nationalization of foreign banks. Instead, her three local banks, the Cooperative Bank of Kenya, the National Bank of Kenya (both set up in 1968) and the Kenya Commercial Bank operated alongside the foreign-owned banks, which dominated the banking industry through the 1970s. This negated the political reality that needed to be addressed—a need for visible ownership of the economy by indigenous Kenyans.

Establishment of the two indigenous banks did not satisfy the need for Africanization of the economy. As a result, several Development Financial Institutions, building societies and Non-Bank Financial Institutions fully owned by the government or indigenous banks were established to advance credit to indigenous Kenyans. In addition, significant changes took place in the structure and operations of National and Grindlays Bank following agreement with the government. Its commercial banking operations came under the control of the newly created Kenya Commercial Bank, which was 60 per cent government-owned. It remained the largest commercial bank in Kenya in terms of deposits and number of branches. The merchant banking operations of National and Grindlays Bank were taken up by a new bank, Grindlays Bank International (Kenya) Ltd, which was 40 per cent owned by the Kenya government. By 1972, there were 12 commercial banks operating in Kenya, three fully owned by the government and nine foreign-owned, including Barclays and Standard Chartered that later in 1980s sold some of their shares to the public to broaden Kenya's ownership.

Development of the banking industry in the country was not smooth. The petroleum crisis that hit many developing countries in early 1970s impacted the industry significantly. This followed significant scale down in oil supply by the Middle Eastern producers to protest against Israeli invasion of Arab lands. It triggered runaway inflation in most global economies and oil prices sky-rocketed. Some miracle, however, happened to Kenya. A devastating frost hit Brazil coffee farms, pushing global coffee prices through the roof. Kenya, then a major coffee producer and exporter, saw her coffee prices increase significantly, bringing in more hard currencies and therefore neutralizing the damage caused otherwise by high oil prices. The period witnessed a lot of coffee smuggling across the Uganda–Kenya border to satisfy global demand. This came infamously to be known in Kiswahili as '*Chebukube ni Soko ya Magendo*'—translated as 'Chebukube is a Market for Smugglers'.

Strong coffee exports saw Kenya record the highest annual economic growth rate of over 9 per cent in 1977–78, with coffee becoming the top foreign exchange earner for the country. To mitigate effects of coffee and oil crises, the CBK took measures to tighten capital outflows by introducing foreign currency controls, and restricting dividend repatriation by companies to cushion the balance of payments position. To dampen risks on credit market, the CBK introduced interest rate controls on lending and deposits and restricted credit expansion by banks at 15 per cent in 1979. The non-banks financial institutions, mainly owned by indigenous, had however less restrictions and relaxed regulatory framework, creating regulatory arbitrage. The increased cash in the economy led to a number of new non-bank players opening up as investors sought to cash on the 'coffee boom'. The banking industry was fairly stable through the 1970s underpinned by strong macroeconomic environment in the second half of the period. A total of 15 banks and 16 non-bank financial institutions operated 286 branches by the end of 1979.

15.3.3 Banking in the Turbulent 1980s and Reforms of 1990s

The period 1970s-80s experienced more participation in the banking industry by Africans. Between 1971 and 1980, one local private bank and nine NBFIs and building societies were licensed (Kariuki, P, 1995). The high number of NBFIs put pressure on the conservative lending practices that banks practised. Banks required substantial collateral above the value of the loans on top of a host of other conditions. NBFIs were less conservative in their lending practices though their interest rates were higher than those of banks because they were largely free from regulatory controls.[5] The resultant aggressive competition from NBFIs forced banks to change their lending attitudes especially to indigenous investors.

The 1980s witnessed rapid expansion of the banking industry following less stringent entry requirements for NBFIs. There were 53 NBFIs in 1990 up from 20 in 1980 while commercial banks increased to 20 from 17 during the period. In the meantime, regulatory oversight capacity was lagging behind. The rapid expansion of local banks and NBFIs were largely driven by several political and regulatory factors. There was a regulatory 'arbitrage' between banks and NBFIs, saw banks establish subsidiary NBFIs to take advantage of the regulatory loophole. In addition, strong political patronage and very little CBK capacity to supervise the rapid growth of NBFIs complicated the situation (CBK, 1993). Slowly, liquidity and solvency challenges started to emerge as non-performing loans began building up at a fast rate. The bubble finally burst in 1984 when the first banking crisis in Kenya broke out. One locally owned bank and a financial institution collapsed, causing major losses to depositors and greatly eroding public confidence in the financial system (CBK, 1985). This was followed by more failures and, in total, 12 institutions collapsed between 1984 and 1989. Besides regulatory weaknesses, the subdued economic growth prospects following a severe drought in 1984 made it difficult for banks to recover loans (CBK, 1985). A further banking crisis occurred in 1989 when nine indigenous financial institutions suffered liquidity strains leading to a near systemic crisis. To avert the crisis becoming contagious to the rest of industry, the CBK in collaboration with the Ministry of Finance facilitated a merger of the nine institutions into one bank, the Consolidated Bank of Kenya Ltd.

To restore public confidence and foster financial stability, the CBK embarked on strengthening regulatory framework, including amendment to the Banking Act (Chapter 488) in 1985 that brought on board an explicit deposit insurance scheme—Deposit Protection Fund Board (DPFB under section 22 (CBK, 1994)). Further amendments to the Act under section 37(3) allowed the Fund to receive premiums from member institutions and invest them to grow the Fund. Other amendments allowed DPFB to act as a receiver and liquidator of failed member institutions licensed under the Banking Act and membership to the Fund extended to cover building societies licensed under the Building Societies Act.

To address economic weaknesses experienced in 1980s, the Structural Adjustment Programmes (SAPs) of the 1980s by the International Monetary Fund targeted debt and budget reforms with little attention paid on financial sector reforms. The Kenya Government noted this shortcoming and embarked on full financial liberalization in the 1990s with support from the World Bank under

[5] For further details, see http://www.centralbank.go.ke/reports/bank-supervision-and-banking-sector-reports/

the Financial Sector Adjustment Credit (FSAC), approved in June 1989 (CBK, 1993). The outcomes were complete deregulation of interest rates in 1991, adoption of market determined exchange rate in 1993 and allowing banks to trade foreign exchange. Despite these reforms, disruptions in the banking system persisted, culminating in another round of banking crises in 1993/94, with 15 institutions failing in 1993. At this time, there were forty five NBFIs and thirty six commercial banks. Consequently, the CBK through DPFB either liquidated or took over management of the troubled institutions.

The most common causes of banking crises in 1990s were: poor asset quality; high insider lending to directors and associates; weak internal controls and corporate governance; lack of competent management; poor liquidity management; inadequate earning capacity; and weak legal, regulatory, and supervisory frameworks. These were manifested in huge non-performing loans. This fragility drove the Government and CBK to initiate comprehensive reforms including strengthening of DPFB; tight inspection programmes and enhanced prudential returns to collect data for off-site surveillance (CBK, 1994).

The CBK also adopted universal banking policy that required NBFIs to convert to banks, reduced the regulatory advantages they enjoyed and introduced more prudential regulations. This eliminated regulatory arbitrage that banks exploited by lending through NBFIs. A moratorium on licensing of new institutions was issued in 1996, further reducing the number of institutions in the industry. By end of 1996, twenty NBFIs had converted to banks, five were in the process of conversion while nine NBFIs had merged with their parent banks. To build capacity in the industry, the CBK in partnership with Ministry of Finance established the Kenya School of Monetary Studies (KSMS) in 1997 to address skills constraints cited in bank failures in the 1980s–90s. KSMS focused on building knowledge and skills gaps in banking and management. Despite many reforms, the industry remained fragile towards the end of the 1990s, with six more banks being placed under statutory management in 1998. This prompted the introduction of further regulatory and supervisory reforms including raising the minimum capital requirements and enhancing classification and provisioning requirements of asset quality. The reforms finally bore stability in the banking industry. Fewer institutions experienced challenges in late 1990s to early 2000s, with only two banks failing in 2003, due to high non-performing loans (NPLs) and weak governance.

Three common factors cited among bank failures in the late 1990s and early 2000s were: political interference, weak governance, and internal controls, all leading to serial defaulters. To mitigate these, the CBK introduced limits on insider lending, single borrower and related parties' exposure as well as limits on large exposures. In addition, credit information sharing mechanism was established to address serial defaulters' problem. This has however not borne much fruit as the NPLs issue persisted and good borrowers do not benefit on lower cost of credit, leading to the interest rates control debate.

Removal of foreign exchange controls in early 1990s enabled the CBK to license foreign exchange bureaus to serve the retail end of the market. The CBK licensed thirty two forex bureaus in 1995/96 under the provisions of the CBK Act (Cap 491). By December 2004, there were eighty nine Forex Bureaus from forty eight in June 1998. Increased competition in the foreign exchange market led to a narrow spot exchange rate spread.

15.3.4 Transformation, Regionalization and Take-Off Period: 2003–2015

The period, 2003–2015 is characterized by transformation and take-off in the banking industry on multiple fronts: legal, regulatory, and supervisory reforms; institutional developments and complexity involving increased interconnectedness and cross-border operations; rapid adoption of technology in payments and settlement; and innovations in products and delivery channels. This was based on the need for *Safety*, *Inclusion*, *Efficiency*, *Integrity*, and *Stability* pillars to create a vibrant and globally competitive financial sector. As a result, the number of institutions supervised by the CBK stood at 159 in 2017, with no NBFIs operational (see Table 15.1).

Increased competition caused a number of banks to adopt technology-led innovations in services and delivery channels. The rudimentary Automated Teller Machines (ATMs) introduced in October 1989 by the Standard Chartered Bank Kenya Limited at its Moi Avenue branch and Kenyatta Avenue branch to

Table 15.1 Number of CBK's supervised institutions, 2003–17

Year	Commercial Banks	MFCs	NBFIs	FXBs	MFBs	MRPs	CRBs	Rep. Offices	Total
2003	46	2	3	80	–	–	–	–	**131**
2004	49	2	2	89	–	–	–	–	**142**
2005	44	2	2	93	–	–	–	–	**141**
2006	44	2	2	95	–	–	–	–	**143**
2007	44	2	1	97	–	–	–	–	**144**
2008	45	2	–	120	–	–	–	1	**168**
2009	46	2	–	130	1	–	–	1	**180**
2010	45	2	–	126	5	–	1	2	**181**
2011	44	1	–	118	7	–	2	4	**176**
2012	43	1	–	112	8	–	2	5	**171**
2013	43	1	–	109	9	1	2	7	**172**
2014	43	1	–	87	9	13	2	8	**163**
2015	43	1	–	80	12	14	3	8	**161**
2016	42	1	–	77	13	17	3	8	**161**
2017	42	1	–	73	13	19	3	8	**159**

Source: Bank Supervision Reports on https://www.centralbank.go.ke/BankSupervision/Annual/Reports/

serve Kenyan elite with a collectors' item in the name of an ATM card, was quickly followed by other banks. Banks experienced long queues as customers struggled to make transactions. Cheque clearance took a minimum of three days. Adoption of information technology and networking of branches in 2000s changed all these.

There were also significant changes in policy, legal, regulatory, and supervisory framework governing banking industry in tandem with market developments, need to align the industry to international standards and innovations, and to forestall any possible risks and vulnerabilities. Key changes over time include: issuance of the Risk Management Guidelines in 2005 to cover wide range of risks (Strategic, Credit, Liquidity, Interest Rate, Foreign Exchange, Price, Operational, Reputation, and Compliance/Regulatory); ceding of the Minister's operational and supervisory powers to the CBK in 2006; enactment and operationalization of the Microfinance Act, 2006 and 2008 respectively; issuance of the Banking (Credit Reference Bureau) Regulations, 2008; and introduction of agency banking in 2009 through Banking Act amendment that allowed institutions to contract third parties (agents) for banking business on their behalf.

To align the industry to international standards, the Proceeds of Crime and Anti-Money Act 2009 was enacted by Parliament to criminalize offence of money laundering and proceeds of crime. This was institutionalized by the establishment of the Financial Reporting Centre, the Assets Recovery Agency, and the Anti-Money Laundering Advisory Board. This not only ensured enhanced integrity of Kenya's banking sector, but also shielded it from heavy penalties imposed by international communities for non-compliance, including de-risking by international banking corporations that disrupted correspondence banking.

The need for a more stable banking industry saw a move towards building strong capital buffers to absorb potential shocks, which may arise as banks expanded. Consequently, the minimum core capital requirements for commercial banks was increased from KSh 250 million in 2009 to KSh 1 billion by the end of 2012. In addition, the Kenya Deposit Insurance (KDI) Act was enacted in 2012 to replace the DPFB as the banking sector's resolution authority, under the Kenya Deposit Insurance Corporation (KDIC). The CBK was granted powers to supervise institutions and their associates on a consolidated basis and in liaison with other competent authorities in 2013. This was timely as the industry became more complex, following increased interconnectedness, cross-sector, and cross-border operations of financial institutions. The CBK entered into several bilateral or multilateral Memoranda of Associations with domestic or cross border regulators to facilitate information sharing and supervisory collaboration.

Adoption of technology moved a notch higher with the introduction of the mobile financial services through the Safaricom M-PESA innovation in 2007. Adoption of mobile phone technology in banking business started in 2007 as a partnership between the mobile phone operators and some banks for money transfer services. This has evolved into payments platform, encompassing all financial services and products including innovative delivery channels and methodologies overtime. Although the money transfer service still dominates, continued innovations have led to emergence of digital financial services and Fintech. These have enhanced financial inclusion, improved convenience, and reduced costs. Almost all banks are currently in partnership with a mobile phone operator to provide innovative digital financial services. Agency banking introduced in May 2010 by banks to expand outreach and cut cost of establishing physical branch offices has expanded rapidly, rising to 18 banks with 61,290 active agents in 2017 compared to 5 banks with 8,809 active agents as at December 2010 in the Bank Supervision Annual Report 2010 (see CBK, 2010). In addition, 5 out of 13 MFBs had contracted 2,191 active agents as at December 2017. These signify the role of agency banking model in driving efficiency and effectiveness in business delivery channel and methods.

The technological revolution has made banks no longer rely on their physical branches to mobilize deposits and expand their business. Banks are now reaching wider corners of the country and beyond to mobilize deposits and provide other services at minimal establishment costs. Therefore, technological transformation involving mobile banking, internet banking and agency banking are now complementing physical branches in driving business models and expansion plans.

The outcomes of transformative measures in the banking industry are phenomenal. Specifically, the bank branch network grew by 196.5 per cent in just 15 years, reflecting increased banking business, adoption of technology enabled products, increased financial inclusion and competition (see Table 15.2). More

Table 15.2 Commercial banks' expansion indicators, 2003–17

Year end	Number of branches	Total deposits (KSh billions)	Loans and advances (KSh billions)
2003	512	415	241
2004	532	465	302
2005	534	504	338
2006	575	598	396
2007	740	710	495
2008	887	864	631
2009	996	1006	722
2010	1100	1237	884
2011	1221	1488	1168
2012	1346	1708	1316
2013	1392	1980	1499
2014	1443	2292	1941
2015	1523	2486	2165
2016	1541	2618	2229
2017	1518	2900	2159

Source: CBK, from Bank Supervision Annual Reports and Financial Stability Reports.

banks ventured into previously underserved populations and remote areas. This was supported by availability of improved infrastructure such as electricity and internet connectivity (CBK, 2017).

The growing need to expend lending drove banks to mobilize more deposits, the largest funding source. Total deposits rose from KSh 415 billion in 2003 to KSh 2,900 billion in 2017 (see Table 15.2). Strong growth in deposits, a critical funding source of banks' assets has led to significant growth in total gross loans from KSh 241 billion in 2003 to KSh 2.16 trillion in 2017 (see Table 15.2). With expanding bank assets base, pre-tax profit grew to KSh 133.8 billion in 2017 from KSh 14 billion in 2003.

To tap the regional business opportunities as the East African Community (EAC) integration process progressed, Kenyan banks extended their operations across borders, with a total of nine Kenyan banks subsidiaries operating in the EAC region served by 297 branches in 2016.

Despite the rapid expansion, banks have been slow in passing the benefits of technological innovations and associated efficiency to the customers in terms of lower cost of credit. Even the implementation of Credit Reference Bureaus has not helped a lot. As a result, Parliament enacted interest rates capping law in 2016, which unfortunately has yielded undesired effects to the economy.

15.3.5 Opportunities and Innovations Ahead (Next 50 Years)

The continued reforms, innovations, and technology-enabled delivery channels and methodologies have made Kenya's banking sub-sector among the leading in Sub-Saharan Africa, especially in terms of mobile financial services, digital financial services, and Fintech. Going forward, Kenya will continue with reforms to mitigate any risks while allowing useful innovations to prosper. Reforms being implemented include the following:

- **Fostering greater transparency**, reflected in data accuracy to build public confidence. Financial statements released to the public should be credible and reflect a true and fair view to inform decisions. Transparency also extends to other disclosures by banks on their corporate governance and risk management structures.
- **Stronger governance** with clear demarcation of responsibilities, greater accountability, fair market conduct, and stronger supervision. When all stakeholders of banks (shareholders, board of directors, management, and external auditors) play their roles effectively, banks will operate sustainably and ethically. The CBK will strengthen its supervisory practices and processes to ensure that banks are truly practising effective corporate governance.

- **Effective business models**, aimed at strengthening the resilience of banks, reducing costs, and supporting innovation. Resilience of banks can only be realized under sound business models. The business models should be strengthened to accommodate new business lines and innovations. The CBK has asked banks to ensure that they maintain sufficient capital to cater for existing and potential risks they are exposed to and their market niche.
- **Implementation of Internal Capital Adequacy Assessment Process (ICAAP)** by banks is envisaged to enhance safety, integrity, access, soundness, and stability. This is expected to encourage increased savings needed in financing Kenya's investment needs.

15.3.6 The Insurance Industry

15.3.6.1 Insurance Globally

Insurance as a practice dates back to early human civilization where communities would come together to assist one other during times of calamities or in unfortunate events. The early traders using ships would redistribute their goods across many ships to mitigate gravity of loss if a single ship capsized. The Babylonians developed a system that was recorded in the famous Code of Hammurabi, 1750 BC, and practised by early Mediterranean sailing merchants. If a merchant received a loan to fund his shipment, he would pay the lender an additional sum in exchange for the lender's guarantee to cancel the loan should the shipment be stolen or lost at sea. The needs for insurance grew overtime, with Phoenicians and the Greeks favouring the same type of insurance with their seaborne commerce.

Property insurance as it is known today can be traced to the Great Fire of London, which destroyed more than 13,000 houses in 1666. Devastating effects of the fire caused for a rethinking of risk mitigation and the concept of pooling risks and insurance started taking shape. The Romans were the first to have burial insurance whereby people joined burial clubs, which paid funeral expenses to surviving family members. In medieval times, the guilds protected their members from loss by fire and shipwreck, paid ransoms to pirates, and provided respectable burials as well as support in times of sickness and poverty.

The first actual insurance contract signed in Genoa in 1347 provided policies for individuals or in a group. They each wrote their name and amount of risk they were willing to assume under the insurance proposal, hence emergence of the term underwriting. In 1681 the first fire insurance company, the 'Insurance Office for Houses', was established to insure brick and frame homes. About 5000 homes were insured and this model venture was a great success. What followed in succession was establishment of similar companies in the following decades and mainly in the areas of property and casualty. In 1688, Edward Lloyd opened a coffee house on Tower Street in London, which became a popular haunt for ship owners, merchants, and ships' captains, becoming a reliable source of the latest shipping news. It became the meeting place for parties in the shipping industry wishing to insure cargo and ships, and those willing to underwrite such ventures. These informal beginnings led to the establishment of the insurance company, Lloyd's of London in 1688 at Lloyd's Coffee House. Several related shipping and insurance businesses sprang up. In 1693, the astronomer Edmond Halley created a basis for underwriting life insurance by developing the first mortality table. However, its limitation of using the same rate for all ages, saw Joseph Dodson correct this error in 1756 by scaling the premium rate based on the age. By this time, the practice of insuring cargo in shipping was widespread throughout the maritime nations of Europe.

The first life insurance policies were taken out in the early eighteenth century, with Amicable Society for a Perpetual Assurance Office, founded in London in 1706 offering the first life policy. The first plan of life insurance was that each member paid a fixed annual payment per share from one to three shares. Membership age ranged between 12 and 55 years. At the end of the year, a portion of the 'amicable contribution' was divided among the wives and children of deceased members in proportion to the amount of shares the heirs owned. With these initiatives, insurance as known today started taking shape. The economic importance of the insurance sector has therefore grown over time across the globe, becoming more integrated to the rest of economy. Insurance companies have also become significant players in the international capital markets.

15.3.6.2 Insurance Industry in Kenya before Independence

The concept of insurance in Kenya, and particularly the 'social insurance programme' to address socio-economic problems, has existed for many years. Members of a community pooled together resources to create a 'social insurance fund'. The 'premiums' ranged from material to moral support or other payments in kind. From the fund, 'drawings were made out' to support the few unfortunate members exposed to perils. However, the history of commercial insurance in Kenya is closely related to colonialism in the early twentieth century. With the conquest of Kenya as a British colony, white settlers invested heavily in farming and extraction of agricultural products. Like the Italian merchants, these substantial investments by the British needed some form of protection against various risks. British insurers saw an opportunity and opened agency offices to provide cover to the colony's insurance needs.

In pre-independence era, several multinational insurers opened liaison offices in Kenya with parent companies being domiciled mainly in the United Kingdom and India. In 1904, the London and Lancashire Insurance Company appointed agents for fire business in Nairobi. In 1922, Royal Exchange Assurance opened a branch in Kenya and was followed by the Commercial Union in 1929 (Wachira, 2008). Prosperity in the colony soon justified expansion of these agencies to the branch networks with more autonomy and expertise to service the growing insurance needs. By 1963, most branches had been transformed to fully fledged insurance companies, mostly owned by British insurers. Other earlier insurance companies include: Pioneer Assurance Society (1930), Jubilee Insurance Company (1937), Pan Africa Insurance (1946), and Provincial Insurance Company Limited in 1949. Until the late 1970s, Kenya's insurance industry was stable, had low demand for services, offered standardized products, and minimal government supervision. The first insurance legislation in Kenya, the Insurance Ordinance, was promulgated in 1960. Prior to this, insurance companies complied with the UK legislation under the Companies Act 1960.

After independence, Kenya Government saw the need to have some control of the insurance sector but there was no competent authority to supervise the industry. The growing number of players in the sector to underwrite more risks, saw mushrooming of branch offices of international insurance companies and local companies. Many of them got involved in malpractices, culminating in several failures. This was compounded by increased competition for business, governance issues, and fraud.

15.3.6.3 Post-Independence Period, 1963–1980

At independence, the British insurance agencies in Kenya had been upgraded to full insurance companies to meet the needs of clients. They however continued to operate under the UK law, with several provisions scattered across different statutes. The industry had no sector-specific legislation. To address these legal and regulatory weaknesses, the Minister for Finance issued a directive in 1978, requiring all foreign insurance companies in Kenya to be incorporated in Kenya by 1980 under insurance sector specific laws. This culminated in the introduction of Insurance Act Cap 487 of the laws of Kenya. It ushered in the need to move towards a more market oriented and policy-based regulations of the insurance industry.

The Directive also required all imports into the country to be insured locally. In addition, reinsurance treaties arranged by local companies should be reviewed and approved by Kenya Reinsurance Corporation in the absence of a supervisory authority. By the early 1980s, Government initiated the drafting of laws to regulate the industry under the support of the United Nations Conference for Trade and Development (UNCTAD). And in 1984, the Insurance Act was enacted with the enforcement date being set for 1 January 1987.

Further reforms and transformations saw the establishment of Office of the Commissioner of Insurance in the Ministry of Finance in early 1987 under the Insurance Act, Cap 487 in 1986. As the sector grew in size, scope, complexity, and significance to the economy, it required an independent body to provide oversight.

This resulted in the establishment of the Insurance Regulatory Authority in 2006 under the Insurance Act (Amendment) 2006, Cap 487 of the Laws of Kenya to regulate, supervise, and develop the insurance industry. The act came into effect on 1 May 2007. It was charged with the duty of administering the Insurance Act Cap 487 and generally advising the government on policy matters regarding insurance. Of focus also was the duty of protecting interests of policyholders, especially for vulnerable groups. There are also two self-regulating Associations—Association of Kenya Insurers (AKI) and Association of Kenya Insurance Brokers of Kenya (AIBK).

15.3.6.4 Insurance Industry in the Turbulent 1980s and Reforms

Since the enactment of Insurance Act, the government continues to institute measures to address supply-side constraints, implementing effective financial and supervisory framework to ensure smooth functioning of the insurance sector, and identifying areas where the Government has a role as a provider of insurance services. This has resulted in initiatives towards enhancing the role of insurance in National Development. The level of insurance development and its contribution to national development is measured by insurance penetration and density.

Insurance industry plays commercial and infrastructural roles in the economy given its ability to mobilize long-term savings for development. In particular, insurance in Kenya has contributed to:

- Fostering financial stability for both households and firms through transfer and pooling risks. This enables individuals, households, and firms to venture into activities which they would hitherto not undertake.
- Savings mobilization through life insurance products that support faster growth.
- Reduced pressure on the government budget since life insurance reduces demands on government social security and health programmes.
- Enhanced trade, commerce, and entrepreneurial activity in manufacturing, shipping, aviation, medical, legal, accounting, and banking services, which rely on risk transfer.
- Improved investor confidence due to a promise of getting back to business if an undesired event occurs.
- Improved individuals' quality of life and increased social stability

To ensure good practices in the industry, stakeholders lobbied for the creation of an autonomous body to regulate and provide oversight to insurance industry as early as 2000. This led to the Insurance (Amendment) Act of 2006, establishing the Insurance Regulatory Authority (IRA) as a corporate body. The IRA was meant to make the regulatory environment more transparent, effective, flexible, and simplified. Under the Act, IRA was expected to:

- Ensure the effective administration, supervision, regulation, and control of insurance and reinsurance business in Kenya;
- Formulate and enforce standards for the conduct of insurance and reinsurance business in Kenya;
- Issue licences to all persons involved in or connected with insurance business, including insurance and reinsurance companies, insurance and reinsurance intermediaries, loss adjusters and motor assessors, risk surveyors and valuers;
- Protect the interests of insurance policy holders and insurance beneficiaries in any insurance contract;
- Promote the development of the insurance sector;
- Advise the Government on the national policy to be followed in order to ensure adequate insurance protection and security for national assets and national properties;
- Issue supervisory guidelines and prudential standards from time to time, for better administration of the insurance business of persons licensed under the Act;
- Share information with other regulatory authorities and to carry out any other related activities in furtherance of its supervisory role; and
- Undertake such other functions as may be conferred on it by the Act or by any other written law.

In 2004, the Government established the Policyholders Compensation Fund (PCF) under Section 179 of the Insurance Act via Legal Notice No. 105 of 2004 to handle resolutions of failed companies and instil public confidence. This followed the collapse of several insurance companies: Access Insurance Company Ltd, Kenya National Assurance Company Ltd, Stallion Insurance Company Ltd, and Lakestar Insurance Company Ltd. More companies were placed under statutory management, including; United Insurance Company, Liberty Insurance Company, Standard Assurance, Blue Shield Insurance, Invesco, and Concord Insurance Company. The Fund was meant to compensate policyholders of an insurer that has been declared insolvent and also increasing the general public's confidence in the industry. It was later encapsulated in the Act to strengthen the industry solvency.

Kenya's insurance companies have spread to the EAC region to benefit from emerging business opportunities. In 2016, Kenya had 52 insurance companies, with some operating 30 branches across the EAC region. These include; the APA Insurance, Insurance Company of East Africa, Jubilee Insurance, Phoenix of East Africa, Real Insurance, and UAP Insurance.

15.3.6.5 Insurance Industry Growth and Transformation

Growth of insurance in Kenya falls into three phases mimicking the level of economic development. The first phase is the initiation and restoration in

Table 15.3 Players in Kenya's insurance market

Year/player	2012	2013	2014	2015	2016
Insurance companies	47	48	50	51	52
Agents	4862	4631	5155	6424	7720
Brokers	170	187	198	144	204
Investigators	140	134	133	133	146
Medical IPs	24	29	29	29	32
Insurance surveyors	27	27	24	30	32
Risk managers	10	8	8	7	9
Loss adjustors	21	22	25	27	31
Motor assessors	92	105	108	114	121

Source: IRA annual reports (various).

1960–87, the second is market-oriented reform phase in 1987–97 and the third phase is opening-up and rapid growth phase of 1997 to date. Liberalization of the economy in early 1990s saw the registered insurance companies grew from 15 in 1978 to 39 in 2001 and 52 in 2016 (see Table 15.3).

In 2016, the industry had grown significantly in terms of number of licensees, products, and assets. The growth in business has been adequately supported by capital and other investments necessary for revenue generation and cushioning against losses (IRA, 2016). The asset base for the industry has grown tremendously, from KSh 125 billion in 2006 to KSh 525 billion in 2016, reflecting strong profitability in the industry. Similarly, investments grew from KSh 91 billion in 2006 to KSh 420 billion, highlighting the importance of investment income to the industry (see Figure 15.3).

There were also foreign reinsurance companies and reinsurance brokers operating liaison offices in Kenya in 2016. These include: Munich Reinsurance Company from Germany; Ghana Reinsurance Company from Ghana; CICA Re from Togo; and PTA Reinsurance Company and Africa Trade Insurance Agency (ATI) as regional insurance organizations operating under various regional charters. The foreign reinsurance brokers were J. B. Boda Reinsurance Broker and Afro Asia Reinsurance Broker from India. Other insurance industry players include The National Hospital Insurance Fund (NHIF), a state corporation under the NHIF Act No. 9 of 1998. NHIF is a social health insurance fund providing medical cover to its members and their dependants. It is not regulated by IRA.

Kenya ranks highly in terms of insurance industry development across the EAC region and is a key player in the Common Market for Eastern and Southern Africa (COMESA) as well as Sub-Saharan Africa. In the EAC, only Uganda's industry is closer to the level of Kenya's insurance landscape (see Table 15.4). However, following the opening up of the Uganda and Tanzania Insurance markets and increased emphasis on globalization and regionalization, the industry now faces stiffer competition from its neighbours.

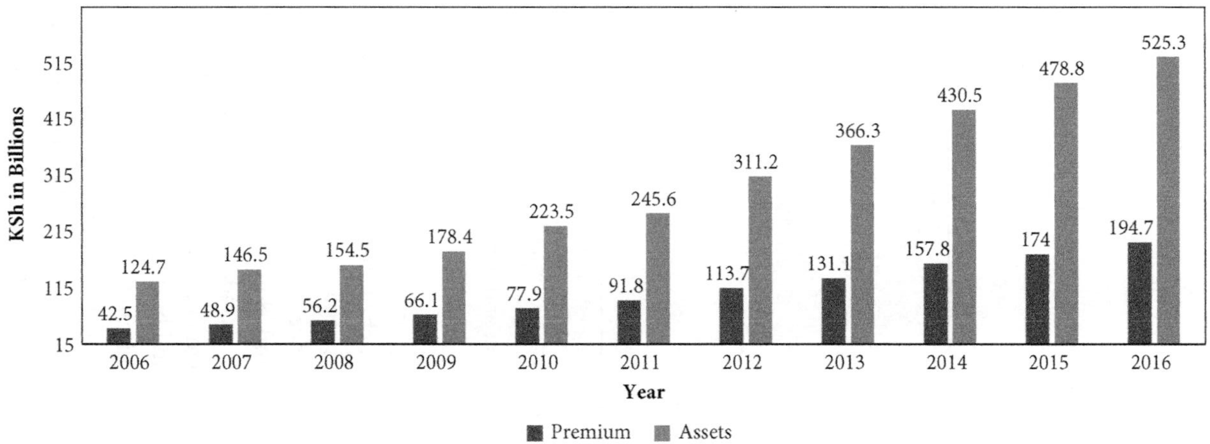

Figure 15.3 Growth in industry premiums and assets

Source: IRA annual reports (various).

Table 15.4 Insurance industry players in East Africa, 2016

Player/country in 2016	Kenya	Tanzania	Rwanda	Burundi***	Uganda
Insurance companies	52	31	14	6	29
Agents	7720	398	557	1	1296
Brokers	204	123	13	13	35
Investigators	146	–	12	–	–
Medical IPs	32	–	–	2	6
Insurance surveyors	32	–	–	–	10
Risk managers	9	–	5	–	–
Loss adjustors	31	45*	18	–	21***
Motor assessors	121	–	8	–	–

Source: AKI 2016 annual report.

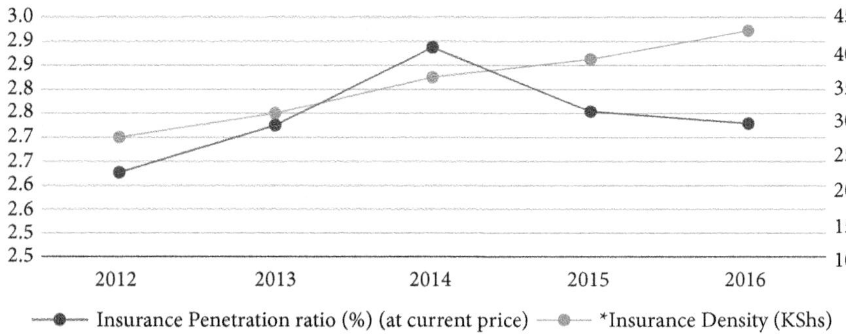

Figure 15.4 Insurance penetration and density
Source: IRA annual report, 2016.

Insurance industry has faced challenges but remains resilient. These are; weak corporate governance, low insurance awareness levels, negative perception of insurance, low uptake of insurance, capitalization of insurance companies, limited capacity for emerging risks and slow uptake of new technologies to enhance service delivery. Other issues include: complexity in contract/product design, sophistication in product design and the need to ensure proper market conduct for the benefit of individuals and businesses.

Despite significant growth in number and products, insurance penetration in Kenya remains way below the global average of 6.28 per cent (Swiss Re Sigma 2016). The insurance penetration, which is the ratio of Gross Direct Insurance Premiums to (GDP), declined from 2.88 per cent in 2015 to 2.73 per cent in 2016, despite several initiatives taken to enhance market access and inclusion in insurance (see Figure 15.4).

Further reforms are needed to address issues such as fragmentation and competition; low insurance literacy levels; customer service (customer treatment practices); limited distribution channels; insurance fraud; continued reliance on traditional product lines; cultural and religious beliefs and low utilization of technology. Consequently, IRA continues to institute measures to enhance insurance access and inclusion. These measures include; localization of marine insurance business, development of a micro-insurance policy (introduced as a new class of insurance business in 2015), capacity development through the actuarial and agents scholarship programmes, encouraging the use of technology (insureTech, RegTech, and SupTech) in insurance business and authorizing the use of new distribution channels and training of insurance agents under the Executive Certificate of Proficiency in Insurance (ECOP) programme.

Other measures include development of Islamic insurance; Takaful, Sharia-compliant insurance product; development of index-based regulations targeting crop and livestock insurance in Kenya and development of agricultural insurance policy in partnership with the State Departments of Agriculture and Livestock. The industry has also adopted bancassurance model for distribution of insurance products through banks. The IRA saw the introduction of new classes of long-term insurance; business Life Assurance; Annuities; Pensions (Personal Pensions and Deposit Administration); Group Life; Group Credit, and Investment (Unit Link and Linked Investments, and Non-Linked investments) (IRA Annual Report 2016). Measures such as simplification of products, tailor-made to customers' needs, adoption of more efficient distribution channels, and enhanced public education and awareness are crucial to increased access and usage of insurance services across the wider public.

The need to standardize insurance regulation in Kenya in line with standards setting body, the International Association of Insurance Supervisors (IAIS), has influenced changes in the country's insurance industry. It has seen several amendments to the Insurance Act to ensure compliance with international best practice. Also changes taken to accommodate the increased size and complexity of insurance market as more products come on board to meet growing insurance demand.

To transform the industry, the IRA in conformity with good practice as set by the IAIS, moved to market-oriented and policy-based regulations through adoption of risk-based supervision from the traditional rule-based regulatory regime, which was cumbersome and a burden to regulated entities.

15.3.7 The Savings and Credit Cooperatives (SACCOs) Industry

15.3.7.1 History of Cooperatives and SACCOs

The history of credit unionism is traced to a tradition of community-based cooperative banking in Germany in the middle of the nineteenth century. People have used these informal savings and lending associations to help each other through difficult times, to educate children, finance special events such as weddings or for development purposes such as land and construction. Individuals who join the organization make regular deposits and contributors can then borrow from the accumulated pool.

Credit unions, however, are also formal financial cooperatives. They are legal institutions, incorporated under provincial, state or national legislation. Their legal status distinguishes them from informal mutual institutions which have helped make organized human existence possible. It also helps differentiate them from other financial institutions and usually from other cooperatives. Credit unions have their origins in the 1840s, when the organized cooperative movement began to emerge. The movement's founding model emerged in 1844, when a group of workers opened a cooperative store in Rochdale, an industrial community near Manchester, England. The Equitable Society of Pioneers, as the Rochdale Association was formally called, dealt with providing good quality consumer goods at fair prices to its members and accumulation of capital. Rochdale Society reduced its objectives to focus on developing an integrated consumer cooperative system to include production in factories and on farms as well as sales in cooperative stores. These activities became so successful that many came to believe it would be possible to organize the entire economy through cooperative organizations. It profoundly affected the British movement, similar movements in Europe and the international movement generally when it took form at the end of the nineteenth century.[6] The Rochdale Pioneers are famous for designing the Rochdale Principles that provide the foundation for the principles on which cooperatives around the world operate to this day.[7]

The cooperative business model is based on internationally accepted cooperative principles and values—Self-help, Self-reliance, Self-responsibility, Democracy, Equality, Equity, and Solidarity. The cooperative principles are the universally accepted guidelines by which cooperatives put their values into practice: open and voluntary membership; democratic member control; member economic participation; autonomy and independence; education, training and information; cooperation amongst cooperative enterprises; and concern for the community. Cooperative members believe in ethical values of trust, honesty, openness, social responsibility, and caring for others. Cooperatives offer the institutional framework through which local communities gain control over the productive activities for their livelihoods. Members tap the energies of group effort and economies of scale to engage in economic activities that they would not have otherwise been able to carry out on their own, which hence improves their living

[6] See further details in Macpherson (1999), especially on the history of the international credit union movement and the role and development of World Council of Credit Unions.

[7] Ministry of Industrialization and Enterprise Development, History and Organization of the Cooperative Development and Marketing Subsector in Kenya

conditions. It is for this reason that cooperatives continue to be promoted in Africa and other parts of the developing world for poverty alleviation.[8]

15.3.7.2 Cooperatives in Kenya Prior to Independence

The modern cooperative movement in Kenya can be traced back to 1908 when cooperative production and marketing were first established by the European farmers at Lumbwa in Kericho. It was not however until 1930s that cooperatives organized by Africans were founded but remained low due to lack of support by the colonial Government. Initially the colonial Government neither encouraged nor supported the formation of cooperatives by Kenyans because it was considered too early to attempt anything of the kind. It was also thought impossible to find people among Africans who could command the trust of their fellow members in the keeping of accounts and business operations. It was however part of economic segregation.

In 1931, the colonial Government took the first step towards formal involvement in cooperatives when it enacted the first Cooperative Ordinance to regulate the operations of Cooperatives. In 1946, the colonial government acknowledged the need for inclusion of Africans to participate in the economy through cooperatives resulting in the enactment of a new Cooperative Societies' Ordinance and the establishment of the department of cooperatives development. Thereafter in 1955 there was a reinvigorated effort by Africans involvement in the growing of cash crops following the Swynnerton Plan that paved the way for the formation of more cooperatives. By 1960, there were only 19 SACCOs registered by the Ministry of Cooperative Development. All these reflected colonials hold on to economy and reluctance to allow Africans participate in economic development.

15.3.7.3 SACCOs in 1963 to the 1990s

After independence in 1963, the government recognized the critical role that cooperatives played in economic empowerment of its people. Cooperatives mobilized capital for the acquisition of businesses and farms, formally owned by colonialists. Creation of a Ministry of Cooperative Development was the climax of cooperative development in the country as it was to accelerate cooperative development in agriculture, rural financial services, and the business sectors of the economy. The government sessional paper No. 10 of 1965 on 'African Socialism' gave impetus to rapid Africanization of the Kenyan economy and poverty eradication. Additionally, the first post-independence Government Cooperative Development Policy contained in Sessional Paper No. 8 of 1970 articulated consolidation of the cooperative activities. The policy was reviewed in 1975

[8] See Wanyama, Develtere, and Pollet (2009) on African cooperatives in a liberalized economic environment.

wherein the government continued to recognize cooperatives as vital organs for mobilizing material, human, and financial resources for national development.

The Sessional Paper No. 1 of 1986 on 'Economic Management for Renewed Growth' emphasized the need for private sector-led economic development. This was refined through the Sessional Paper No. 4 of 1987 on 'Renewed Growth through the Co-operative Movement', which reiterated the government's commitment to enhance the participation of Kenyans in the economy through Cooperatives. The responsibility of organizing and managing cooperatives was left to the members and their management committees while the government played an advisory role. This led to huge growth in the cooperative enterprises and enhanced public confidence.

Cooperative development in Africa has generally traversed two main eras: the era of state control and that of liberalization. The first era saw the origin and substantial growth of cooperatives on the continent under state direction. Originating from government policy and directives rather than people's common interests and own motivation, these organizations were conditioned to emerge as dependent agents and/or clients of the state and other semi-public agencies in many countries, particularly in Kenya. As channels for implementing government socio-economic policies, cooperatives in many countries provided an avenue to promote economic agenda for the wider populace. However, institutions became a liability to the members when the Cooperatives became embroiled state in politics to the extent that the failures of state policies were manifested in the cooperative movement.[9]

Such failures partly triggered calls for a change in cooperative development in the early 1990s because state control was stifling cooperatives. In its Sessional Paper No. 1 of 1994 on 'Recovery and sustainable development to the year 2010', the government reaffirmed the need for a private sector-led economy to accelerate and sustain development (Kenya National Assembly, 1994). In addition, the Sessional Paper No. 6 of 1997, on 'Co-operatives in a liberalized economic environment', not only articulated less involvement of government in the management of cooperatives, but it also provided room for cooperatives to operate in a competitive economic environment (Kenya National Assembly, 1997). The envisaged legal and regulatory framework led to the enactment of Cooperative Societies Act No. 12 of 1997, thus removing the government's role in the affairs of cooperative societies. The first-round effects were a near collapse of the entire cooperative movement in the country.

To restore stability and confidence in the cooperatives sector, the government initiated legislative and institutional reforms by amending the Cooperative Societies' Act No. 12 of 1997 vide the Cooperative Societies (Amendment) Act

[9] For further details regarding the impact of liberalization on the Cooperative movement in Kenya, see Wanyama (2007).

No. 2 of 2004 and prepared new Cooperative Societies Rules, 2004. This also revamped the role of Cooperative Tribunal Court (a first in Africa), a specialized Cooperative Commercial Court, to fast track and speedily dispense the backlog of cases previously pending. The Tribunal model has attracted many countries to consult on how to establish similar Tribunals in their countries.[10]

From the mid-1990s, SACCOs started offering basic 'banking' services through Front Office Services Activity (FOSA). This was triggered by high account operating balances by commercial banks, which was unaffordable to many SACCO members. The first FOSA was opened by Muhigia Teachers SACCO in 1995 to facilitate payment of salaries from Teachers Services Commission. FOSA enabled diversification of savings and credit products including service delivery channels/facilities. FOSA operating SACCOs, also legally referred to as deposit taking SACCOs, account for 75 per cent of the assets and deposits for the SACCO industry. Table 15.5 summarizes trends in SACCOs in 1995–2002. The penetration rate was 7 per cent in 1996 and increased slightly to 8 per cent in 2002.

In 2004, the Cooperatives Societies Act was amended to introduce a regulatory body to provide oversight for the operations of SACCOs.[11] It also provided a definition of different types of cooperatives societies. Prior to 2008, the only type of Cooperative Societies that was officially recognized in the law was the 'savings and credit cooperative societies (SACCO Societies)'. But this provision was repealed by the SACCO Societies Act in 2008,[12] hence the regulation of 'savings and credit cooperative societies (SACCO Societies)' was removed from the Cooperative Societies Act, and brought under the SACCO Societies Act. Prior to the SACCOs Societies Act, there were deposit-taking SACCO Societies, and the non-deposit taking SACCO Societies.

The deposit-taking SACCOs are legally permitted to engage in savings mobilization, which is used as collateral for credit since savings are non-refundable (non-withdrawable deposits). There are also withdrawable deposits, similar to the savings accounts offered by banks, and can be withdrawn by the member at any time, without necessarily exiting the SACCO. Other activities of deposit-taking SACCOs include; quasi-banking services such as payment channels such as ATM services, debit (and credit) card facilities, mobile, and electronic transactions among others (under the concept of FOSA (Front Office Service Activity) services).

The non-deposit taking SACCOs offer non-withdrawable deposits, which are used as collateral for credit facilities. Deposits are not refundable, except when the

[10] Ministry of Industrialization and Enterprise Development, History and Organization of the Cooperative Development and Marketing Subsector in Kenya.

[11] It is also necessary to observe that the repealed section 91A of the Kenyan Cooperative Societies Act was itself an amendment that was introduced in 2004 vide Act No. 2 of 2004. This effectively means that before 2004, even SACCO Societies were not mentioned in the Cooperative Societies Act.

[12] Section 72 of the Kenyan Sacco Societies Act (Cap 490B).

Table 15.5 Growth of key SACCO indicators, 1995–2002

Item	YEAR								
	1995	1996	1997	1998	1999	2000	2001	2002	CAGR
Members	1,285,190	934,056	1,121,343	977,170	1,200,000	951,685	951,685	1,484,424	
% Growth		−27%	20%	−13%	23%	−21%	0%	56%	2%
Savings and Shares (Ksh. billion)	29,495	30,184	28,784	34,969	36,210	32,693	32,693	47,259	
% Growth		2%	−5%	21%	4%	−10%	0%	45%	7%
Loans (Ksh. billion)	20,400	25,643	15,211	27,059	28,305	30,827	30,827	53,551	
% Growth		26%	−41%	78%	5%	9%	0%	74%	15%
Assets (Ksh. billion)	30,855	31,797	NA	37,530	34,000	35,949	35,949	52,634	
% Growth		3%	#VALUE!	#VALUE!	−9%	6%	0%	46%	8%
Penetration	NA	7%	7%	16%	8%	6%	6%	8%	

Source: WOCCU statistical data, 1995–2002.

member is quitting the SACCOs. In recognition of the growing sophistication of SACCOs, a SACCO Societies' Act (SSA) was enacted in 2008 to facilitate the enforcement of prudential standards for SACCOs offering FOSAs. All deposit-taking SACCOs are now regulated under SSA and the non-deposit-taking SACCOs are supervised under the framework of the CSA.

SACCOs' membership grew by 13 per cent annually, Loan book expanded by 17 per cent annually, and total assets grew by 18 per cent annually in seven years to 2009. As at 31 December 2010, there were 6737 registered SACCO societies of which 3280 were active (annual accounts were audited and registered with the Commissioner for Cooperative Development (CCD)). By category, 215 active SACCOs were deposit taking while 3065 operated Back Office Savings Activity (BOSA) only, implying that 3457 SACCOs were dormant (see Table 15.6).

The SACCOs membership has grown faster, reaching 5.4 million in 2015 up from 3.9 million in 2010 and 1.3 million in 1995 (see Table 15.7). Similar trends have been recorded in savings, deposits, loans book, and total assets, translating into higher penetration rate of 21.3 per cent in 2015 from just 7 per cent in 1996. Increased competition among SACCOs, policy reforms, and general market developments have encouraged innovative developments in the industry other players tap into the market segments earlier presumed as captive for SACCOs. These include but are not limited to: agency banking; developments of mobile financial services, and mobile banking services; and innovations in information, communication, and technology (ICT).

15.3.7.4 Role of SACCOs under Vision 2030

The large FOSA operating SACCOs are now integrating mobile delivery services as a core service delivery channel to members, but huge costs involved against minimal returns has discouraged a majority of SACCOs. Under the country's Vision 2030 and Medium-Term Plan III, SACCOs are envisaged to play the following key functions:

- **The economic pillar**: The SACCOs are expected to mobilize savings and develop demand-driven financial products to encourage members to save more in line with economic pillar under Vision 2030. The government has focused on registration of Youth Cooperatives, transport, and *Jua Kali* SACCOs. It is also enhancing the management of existing SACCOs through adoption of best accounting, management, and governance practices. Cooperatives have also transformed *Jua Kali* informal sector involving transport, community-based interest groups, and youth groups into organized Cooperative enterprises. Cooperatives in agro-processing sector have also been revamped to process and market their products in Supermarkets.
- **Social pillar:** SACCOs contribute to the social pillar of Vision 2030 significantly by mobilizing resources to finance education from primary to

Table 15.6 Growth figures of key SACCO parameters, 2003–09

Item	YEAR							
	2003	2004	2005	2006	2007	2008	2009	CAGR
Members	1,800,000	2,106.000	2,708,316	3,265,545	4,000,000	3,682,272	3,835,250	
% Growth		17%	29%	21%	22%	−8%	4%	**13%**
Savings and shares (Ksh. billion)	82,889	96,193	97,873	116,011	142,348	156,611	212,742	
% Growth		16%	2%	19%	23%	10%	36%	**17%**
Loans (Ksh. billion)	76,258	84,900	113,913	115,724	153,830	136,548	194,698	
% Growth		11%	34%	2%	33%	−11%	43%	**17%**
Assets (Ksh. billion)	93,941	84,900	124,249	154,880	191,625	170,716	254,397	
% Growth		−10%	46%	25%	24%	−11%	49%	**18%**
Penetration	9.95%	11.28%	14.50%	16.0%	19.11%	17.1%	17.9%	

Source: WOCCU statistical data 2003–09.

Table 15.7 Growth figures of key SACCO parameters, 2010–15

Item	YEAR						
	2010	2011	2012	2013	2014	2015	CAGR
Members	3,918,490	4,183,220	4,722,126	4,722,127	5,103,231	5,432,009	
% Growth		7%	13%	0%	8%	6%	7%
Savings and shares (Ksh. billion)	221,490	225,242	251,262	229,074	287,179	349,984	
% Growth		2%	12%	−9%	25%	22%	**10%**
Loans (Ksh. billion)	257,229	238,013	287,194	321,492	377,013	444,838	
% Growth		−7%	21%	12%	17%	18%	**12%**
Assets (Ksh. billion)	293,544	337,490	353,389	384,665	445,689	528,065	
% Growth		15%	5%	9%	16%	18%	**12%**
Penetration	17.3%	18.5%	19.53%	19.02%	20.50%	21.30%	

Source: WOCCU statistical data, 2003–09.

university through affordable loans to the members. In housing, Cooperatives facilitate members to pool resources to construct rental and commercial properties. The National Cooperative Housing Union (NACHU) and Kenya Union of Savings and Credit Cooperative Society Ltd, through housing scheme are financing long-term mortgages for individuals and societies to put up houses. Cooperatives complement government efforts of building 150,000 houses in urban areas.

- **Political pillar:** Cooperatives bring people together irrespective of class, social status in life, ethnicity, or other considerations. They have institutionalized democratic culture through engagement in free and fair elections, hence form the basis for a cohesive society, and enhances political economy.

15.3.7.5 More Reforms and Innovations in SACCOs Industry

- **Participation in the National Payment Systems (NPS):** Full potential of SACCOs will further be realized by integrating SACCOs into the national payments platform and deposit insurance. Prudential regulation of Deposit Taking Sacco Societies (DTSs) is a step towards modalities for DT SACCOs to efficiently participate in the payment system to enhance the financial soundness of the SACCOs, improve governance and market discipline, and deepen financial inclusion through diversification of deposit and credit products.
- **Shared services for SACCOs:** to pool their resources together and create an autonomous agency. This includes business infrastructure such as member services centres, ICT, payment channels (ATM, mobile money services), research and development. This will help reduce costs associated with every financial cooperatives trying to invest in the services which would otherwise be provided in pooled resources.
- **Islamic (Sharia) compliant financial cooperative enterprises:** Islamic finance is an alternative mode of mobilization of resources to support economic development. Cooperatives are thus potential providers of Islamic financial services and products, to complement the conventional financial services.
- **Legal protection of the names of certain types of cooperatives:** Since the introduction of the prudential regulatory framework for DTS in Kenya in 2010, concerns have emerged on the use of the name 'SACCO' or 'SACCO Society'. In particular, concerns on how prudentially regulated DTSs can be separately distinguished from other cooperative societies, including non-deposit taking SACCO Societies (non-DTS), remain. This is because many cooperative societies have been invariably using the name 'SACCO' or 'SACCO Society'. Hence, the difficulty in differentiating between DTS and non-DTS.

- DTSs face losses because of the unique quasi-banking business they undertake and are the only ones under strict prudential regulations. This has made them more competitive than non-DTS. Hence more non-DTSs and other forms cooperative societies seek to use the name, 'SACCO' or 'SACCO Society' to attract more customers. The fact that both the SACCO Societies Act, and Cooperative Society Act did not secure the identities of the DTSs or use of the word 'SACCO' has exacerbated the confusion. Hence a call for change in legal and policy framework to secure the identities of DTSs, together with the unique regulatory framework that appertains to them.
- **Deposit Guarantee Fund (DGF):** The envisaged operationalization of the Deposit Guarantee Fund will enhance members' confidence.

15.3.8 The Pensions Sector Development in Kenya

Living standards and welfare of workers reduce significantly after exiting active workforce, not only as a result of loss of income, but also due to age. In order to ensure that retirees attain minimum standard of living and to protect them against low or declining living standards, the Government established Public Service Pension Schemes (PSPS) for civil servants and the armed forces. In addition, the National Social Security Fund (NSSF) established by an Act of parliament in 1965 was meant to insure living condition of workers and their households in the formal employment. Other than PSPS and the NSSF, the occupational pension schemes for some companies and individual trusts provide social insurance for the employees.

Generally, social insurance schemes can be categorized as either Pay As You Go, where the currently employed are taxed to pay benefits to those retiring, or fully funded wherebythe employee and the employer make defined contributions which are then invested to augment the benefits paid to the retirees. Despite the pension sector growing over the years, it faces challenges such as ability to timely pay benefits, loss of contributions, mismanagement, high administrative costs, unallocated contributions, and low rates of returns on investment, which reduce retirement benefits.

To address some of the challenges in the pension sector, the Retirement Benefits Act (1997) established the Retirements Benefits Authority (RBA) as the industry regulator. The NSSF act was also amended, transforming the NSSF from a provident fund to a pension fund regulated by RBA. The Retirement Benefits Act was enacted as part of the on-going reform process to bring the retirement benefits industry under harmonized legislation. The Act filled a regulatory vacuum created by highly fragmented legislations, mostly trust and income tax laws. RBA was thus established to facilitate industry reform and ensure members' interests are protected. Prior to this, sponsors (employers) dominated the operations of the industry including management of members' funds and assets to the extent that at the time of retirement, members' benefits could not easily be determined. In addition, sponsors treated members' contributions as their own money and ploughed back the money into their business. The majority of schemes lacked funds to pay their members on retirement.

15.3.8.1 Pensions Industry Structure

With the enactment of the Retirement Benefits Act (1997) and the Retirement Benefits Regulations (2000), the retirement benefits schemes are now distinctly separate entities from the sponsors, established under an irrevocable trust and administered by a legitimately appointed board of trustees. Retirement benefits industry comprises of: National Social Security Fund (NSSF), Occupational Retirement Benefits Schemes, Individual Retirement Benefits Schemes and Civil Service Pension Scheme.

- **The National Social Security Fund (NSSF):** All private sector employers and employees are mandated to make joint contributions to the NSSF on a monthly basis. The NSSF Act, Cap. 258, provides for a comprehensive social security for the members and their dependants for various contingencies. It further aims to convert the NSSF from a National Provident Fund into a pension fund for all persons in the formal sector who are above 18 years of age and a provident fund for all self-employed persons and voluntary registrations. Benefits remain locked/preserved until age 50. The Fund is run by a board of trustees, with Managing Trustee appointed by the government. The Board of Trustees is drawn from the various stakeholders (employee and workers' associations). The fund had a membership of 2.5 million with an asset value of KSh172 billion in 2016
- **Occupational retirement benefits schemes:** The schemes are voluntarily established by employers for the benefit of their employees. There were over 1400 active schemes in Kenya with assets value of KSh 651 billion and membership of 460,000 in 2016. Occupational schemes are funded through contributions from employers and employees, with amounts and rates varying across schemes. In some cases, however, either the employer or employees alone make the contributions. Occupational retirement benefits schemes vary in design, most of them are defined contribution pension schemes that enable members earn a stream of income in their retirement. The provident fund types of schemes are much fewer.
- **Individual retirement benefits schemes:** These schemes are established by corporate institutions, mainly insurance companies. They are open to the general public and are convenient channels of retirement benefits savings for those in employment but whose employers have not established occupational schemes for them, those in self-employment and those who wish to

make additional voluntary contributions. In cases where employers are not able to establish independent occupation schemes due to the small workforce, employers are encouraged to enjoin their employees to the individual schemes. All individual retirement benefits schemes must be registered by the RBA to operate and must also be funded. Contributions vary from one scheme to another with minimum contributions ranging from KSh 500 to KSh 2000 per month. Contributions amounts are flexible since members can make varying amounts depending on their income positions above the minimum. Employers who have employees as members of individual schemes can make contributions on behalf of the employees. The total fund value of the Individual Pension Plans was KSh 35 billion with 200,000 Members in 2016.

- **Umbrella schemes:** These schemes bring together several employers under one roof for the purposes of saving for retirement. The employers' and employees' contribution are paid into this fund. There were 13 umbrella funds with a total fund value of KSh 30 billion and 63,000 members in 2016.
- **Civil service pension scheme:** This scheme has existed since the colonial times to provide retirement benefits for all the civil servants employed by the government. It was established by an Act of parliament as a Pay-As-You-Go non-funded and non-contributory scheme. The scheme liabilities are funded from government revenue collections. The Public Service Superannuation Act 2012 was enacted to jump-start the conversion process and establish a pension programme based on a contribution of 7.5 per cent of the pensionable earnings by employees and a 15 per cent contribution by the government. The current scheme has a membership of over 500,000.

15.3.8.2 Key Developments in the Industry

15.3.8.2.1 Growth of the Retirement Benefits Sector

The pensions industry in Kenya has grown significantly, both in membership and assets. In 2016, there are over 1300 registered schemes with membership exceeding 2.2 million. The industry's assets rose more than tenfold, from about KSh 85 billion in 2001 to KSh 963.05 billion in June 2017. The phenomenal growth is largely attributable to improved regulatory environment and prudent management of the schemes (see Figure 15.5). The industry is a major contributor to the country's economic development through investment of its close to KSh 1 trillion assets. Investments are well-diversified, primarily targeting long-term assets that yield maximum economic linkages. The industry is the largest investor in longer-dated Government Securities including infrastructure bonds which enable the government to fund infrastructure projects.

The industry is the largest investor in infrastructure bonds issued by public institutions, such as the KenGen Bond, has over KSh 200 billion invested in real estate countrywide and invested heavily at the Nairobi Securities Exchange with

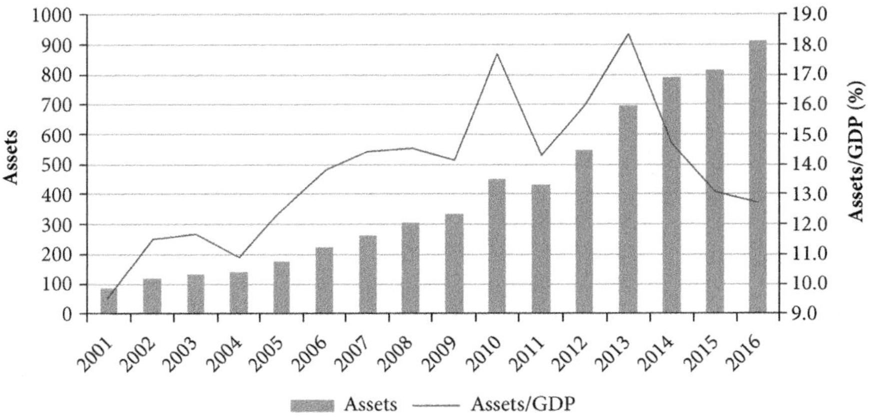

Figure 15.5 Retirement benefits assets in KSh billions
Source: Central Bank of Kenya.

over KSh 180 billion across different counters. In recent years, it has diversified investments into alternative asset classes such as Corporate Bonds, Real Estate Investment Trusts (REITS), and Private Equity further driving capital markets development (see Table 15.8).

15.3.8.2.2 Risk-Based Supervision and National Policy

Previously, RBA followed extensive review process in regulating pension plans, with few considerations of the risk profile of different plans. This wasted a lot of time on pension schemes and provident funds which are largely in compliant with the requirements under the legislation and the regulations. Adoption of risk-based approach enables RBA to concentrate her resources on supervising individual schemes to match the size and risk of each scheme. It is a more proactive approach that identifies cases requiring closer supervision on a timely basis for prompt corrective action The RBA also implemented an online portal that enables parties wishing to establish pension schemes to submit their applications electronically, thus hastening the process significantly. Schemes and their service providers also use this system to submit the statutory returns to RBA for continuous assessment of the scheme's health status and level of compliance with set regulations. RBA can therefore undertake quick interventions on schemes that do not meet requirements and, thus, protect scheme members' and sponsors' interests.

In order to build on the success of the Retirement Benefits Act, harmonize all the various sectors of the retirement benefits industry, and improve the life of all Kenyans after their retirement, RBA is developing a draft National Pensions Policy targeting the following areas of reform once adopted:

Table 15.8 Overall industry investment portfolio (KSh billions)

	Assetscategory	Dec. 2015		June 2016		Dec. 2016		June 2017	
		KSh	%	KSh	%	KSh	%	KSh	%
1	Government Securities	242.43	29.78	211.85	25.47	349.15	38.26	353.47	36.70
2	Quoted equities	186.81	22.95	129.68	15.59	159.07	17.43	180.35	18.73
3	Immovable property	150.78	18.52	126.52	15.21	178.42	19.55	204.60	21.25
4	Guaranteed funds	99.40	12.21	101.89	12.25	129.58	14.20	103.67	10.76
5	Listed corporate bonds	48.09	5.91	39.42	4.74	46.95	5.14	46.83	4.86
6	Fixed deposits	55.61	6.83	28.31	3.40	24.57	2.69	45.49	4.72
7	Offshore	7.16	0.88	5.27	0.63	6.96	0.76	9.68	1.00
8	Cash	11.26	1.38	8.71	1.05	12.93	1.42	13.91	1.44
9	Unquoted equities	2.77	0.38	62.57	7.52	3.95	0.43	3.91	0.41
10	Private Equity	0.17	0.02	0	0	0.22	0.02	0.25	0.03
11	REITS			0		0.84	0.09	0.888	0.09
12	U Classified/others*	9.62	1.18	117.56	14.13	0		0.002	0.00
	TOTAL	**814.11**	**100**	**831.78**	**100**	**912.66**	**100**	**963.05**	**100**

Source: RBA data.

Others* include: Commercial Paper, non-listed bonds by private companies.

- *The pension structure and legal framework*: The policy seeks to provide comprehensive pension system framework that follows a structure that recognizes the different level of needs, utilizes various sources of funding, and reflects the various roles of stakeholders. It therefore proposes the development and implementation of a harmonized pension legal and regulatory framework.
- *Pension coverage*: The policy seeks to have measures in place to broaden pension coverage in both formal and informal sectors to enhance social protection for all citizens.
- *Consumer protection*: The policy seeks to develop mechanisms of consumer protection of members and their beneficiaries of pension schemes and stakeholders.
- *Transferability and portability of retirement benefits*: The policy seeks to allow for portability of accrued benefits to another retirement savings arrangement in the country, EAC region, and in other countries with bilateral arrangements with Kenya.
- *Administration and management of pension funds*: The policy to come up with innovative ways to optimize administrative costs in relation to returns in order to grow members' pension savings.
- *Annuities and income drawdown*: To promote the development of the market for annuities and income drawdown in Kenya.
- *Indexation to promote indexation of pension benefits*: In order to avoid erosion of retirement benefits.
- *Mutual recognition*: The policy seeks to encourage pension supervisors to practise mutual recognition of service providers and share information pertaining to registration to allow pension players registered in one EAC.

15.3.8.2.3 Trustees Certification Programme

The Pension Trustee Certification Programme was officially launched on 29 August 2011 in collaboration with RBA, Association of Retirement Benefits Scheme (ARBS), and College of Insurance under the technical assistance from Humber Institute of Technology and Advanced Learning of Canada. The programme is part of efforts by the RBA to improve governance in the management of pension funds and responds to the requirement for every scheme or a corporate trust to have in the Board of Trustees, at least one member who has been vetted by RBA to provide trust services. All trustees of retirement benefits schemes and directors of corporate trustees of retirement benefit schemes in Kenya are required to undergo training in the programme for them to be certified by RBA to engage in the provision of trust services.

15.3.8.2.4 Preservation of Retirement Benefits

The Retirement Benefits Act (1997) and the Retirement Benefits Regulations (2000) were amended to allow for preservation of 50 per cent of the employers' accumulated benefits upon change of jobs. Members are now able to access their accumulated benefits and 50 per cent of the employers' accumulated benefits upon change of jobs. Through the pension education, a number of members are now opting to have their benefits preserved until retirement age, thus contributing further to the industry growth.

15.3.8.2.5 Pension Education Campaigns

RBA has continued to undertake research driven multi-faceted public education campaigns to educate Kenyans on the importance of saving for retirement and the channels available for saving, encourage employers to establish pension schemes for their employees, and urge Kenyans to sign up for pension. In addition, RBA also prepares Kenyans for old age pension saving. It hosts seminars for members of schemes to equip them with skills that enable them to participate actively in the management of their schemes.

15.3.8.2.6 Research Collaboration and Policy Formulation

RBA has continued to partner with universities and research institutions to conduct research to be used in influencing government policy.

15.3.8.2.7 Scheme Governance and Consumer Protection

RBA developing various policies to improve governance and prudent management of scheme funds. These include: The National Retirement Benefits Policy, Treating Customers Fairly (TCF) guidelines, and Scheme Good Governance Practices guideline. These initiatives are targeting to enhance consumer protection and better management of schemes.

15.3.8.2.8 Post-Retirement Medical Cover

The Retirement Benefits regulations were amended to allow for additional voluntary contributions by a member to fund a medical fund to be accessed at retirement. To this end, RBA has developed a draft prudential guideline to guide the amendment of schemes rules by trustees and sponsors to provide for post-retirement medical cover. It also seeks to provide regulation 19(6) of the Retirement Benefits (Occupational Retirement Benefits Schemes), which requires rules of schemes to allow members to transfer a portion of benefits to a medical-cover provider where the member has been unable to build a post-retirement medical fund from additional contributions.

15.3.8.3 Challenges Facing the Industry

- **Pension Coverage:** Kenya's employment is categorized into three sectors: formal, informal and agriculture. The labour market is skewed towards the informal, which accounts for nearly 83 per cent of the labour force. Coverage of the informal sector still remains as a major challenge. The coverage of the pension schemes is currently 15 per cent of the total workforce which constitutes the formal sector. The uncovered are in the informal and agricultural sectors.

- **Longevity Risk:** Life expectancy after retirement is rising, to average 17.79 years in 2015 for adults aged 60 in 2015 compared with 14.37 years in 1960. This poses the longevity risk since retirees may outlive their retirement savings.
- **Low Replacement Rates:** Replacement rate is the ratio of retirement benefits income a retiree earns in relation to the average salary earnings during working years. It secures an individual's standard of living in retirement. The higher the replacement rate the more able a person is to maintain their living standards in retirement thus avoiding deterioration in livelihood. Data from RBA surveys indicates low replacement rates.

15.3.9 The Capital Markets Development in Kenya

Regulation of Kenya's capital markets is not an end but a means to facilitative, effective, efficient, and responsive capital market infrastructure, characterized by diversified products and professional services to mobilize and allocate capital resources optimally for financing long-term productive investments. The Kenyan capital markets play important role in promoting economic activity by acting as a conduit for channelling funds to productive enterprises in the economy.

The history of capital markets in Kenya can be traced back to the emergence and growth of the Nairobi Stock Exchange, later named, Nairobi Securities Exchange (NSE). Founded in 1954, the NSE has a long heritage in listing equity and debt securities. In the 1920s to 1953, dealing in shares in Kenya commenced with trading taking place on a gentleman's agreement with no physical trading floor. London Stock Exchange (LSE) officials accepted to recognize the setting up of the Nairobi Stock Exchange as an overseas stock exchange in 1953. In 1954–62, the NSE was registered under the Societies Act (1954) as a voluntary association of stockbrokers, responsible for developing the securities market and regulating trading activities. Business was transacted by telephone and prices determined through negotiation.

The Government adopted a new policy with the primary goal of transferring economic and social control to citizens immediately after independence. By 1968, the number of listed public sector securities was 66 of which 45 per cent were for Government of Kenya, 23 per cent for Government of Tanzania, and 11 per cent for the Government of Uganda. This was just after independence and NSE was still operating as a regional market in East Africa. However, in 1975 when the EAC collapsed, Uganda compulsorily nationalized companies which were either quoted or subsidiaries of listed companies. Challenges in movement of capital across the region led to delisting of regional companies at the NSE.

15.3.9.1 Laying Foundations for Capital Markets Innovations and Growth

As the capital markets grew, the government established Capital Markets Authority (CMA) as an independent public agency under an Act of Parliament, Cap 485 A under the Ministry of Finance. CMA was established on 5 December 1989 when the Act was passed and was inaugurated in March 1990. It is responsible for supervising, licensing, and regulating activities of market intermediaries. These include the stock exchange, the central depository and settlement system, and all the other persons licensed under the Capital Markets Act.

As the regulator, CMA created an enabling environment for the efficient functioning and development of the capital markets, hence its efforts in deepening the capital markets in Kenya. Under the Act, it is expected to;

- License and supervise all the capital market intermediaries;
- Ensure proper conduct of all licensed persons and market institutions;
- Regulate the issuance of capital market products such as bonds and shares;
- Promote market development through provision of a conducive environment for product innovation, supporting institutional capacity development, and stimulating robust market infrastructure;
- Promote investor education and public awareness; and
- Protect investors' interests.

Reflecting the transformation, growth, and modernization of capital markets in Kenya, the NSE has recorded significant milestones. From the first successful privatization through the NSE in 1988 by selling a 20 per cent Government stake in Kenya Commercial Bank, the Government registered the NSE as a private company limited by shares in 1991 to increase trading activity. Consequently, share trading moved from being conducted over a cup of tea, to the floor based open outcry system, located at IPS Building, Kimathi Street, Nairobi. It later relocated to spacious Nation Centre in July 1994, which enabled it to set up a computerized delivery and settlement system (DASS). By June 1995, the total number of stockbrokers rose to twenty (20), which saw CMA establish Investor Compensation Fund to compensate investors for financial losses arising from the failure of a licensed broker or dealer to meet their contractual obligations (CMA Annual Reports).

To steer the capital markets to the global level, institutional arrangement of the NSE emerged an important issue. This included the ownership structure, corporate governance, and the overall management that meet international standards for a modern stock exchange. Consequently, the NSE received formal approval to operate as a demutualized entity in order to separate ownership and trading rights. As a result, it offered its shares to the public through an Initial Public Offer (IPO) and subsequently self-listed its shares on the Main Investment Market Segment (MIMS) on 9 September 2014 after recording 763.9 per cent subscription rate against the 66 million new shares offered at a price of KShs 9.50 per share. The NSE became the second African Exchange after the Johannesburg Stock Exchange to be listed.

Other institutional changes include: the split of the market at the Nairobi Stock Exchange into the Main Investment Market Segment (MIMS), Alternate Investment Market Segment (AIMS), and the Fixed Income Securities Market Segment (FISMS) in 2001. The Exchange also introduced Growth Enterprises Market Segment (GEMS) on 22 January 2013 to enable SMEs access capital markets for long-term funding. As part of efforts towards infrastructure modernization, the Central Depository and Settlement Corporation Ltd (CDSC) was incorporated under the Companies Act (Cap 486) of 2000 on 23 March 1999 and operationalized in June 2003. The commissioning of CDS on 10 November 2004 ensured automation of clearing and settlement of shares. The immobilization of securities cut down on inefficiencies and minimized risks, thus enhancing liquidity in the equities market. This strong growth momentum has been maintained into 2017 (see Table 15.9).

Further modernization of the trading and settlement infrastructure saw NSE implement live trading on its automated trading systems (ATS) for equities on 11 September 2006. The ATS also had the capability of trading immobilized corporate bonds and treasury bonds. Consequently, NSE extended trading hours from two hours (10:00 am–12:00 pm) to three hours (10:00 am–1:00 pm), thus providing more trading time. It also implemented Wide Area Network (WAN) platform on 17 December 2007, enabling brokers and investment banks to trade through terminals in their offices linked to the NSE trading engine. These cut settlement cycle from T+4 to T+3 on 4 July 2011. The NSE also launched automated trading of government bonds through the ATS on 7 December 2009,

Table 15.9 Key equities market indicators

Year	Equity turnover (KShs Bn)	Share volume (Mn)	End day NSE 20-Share Index	End day market capitalization (KSh Bn)
2008	97.52	5,856.54	3,521.18	853.88
2009	38.16	3,160.03	3,247.44	834.17
2010	110.32	7545.79	4,432.60	1,166.99
2011	78.06	5,721.83	3,205.02	868.24
2012	86.79	5,464.23	4,133.02	1,272.00
2013	155.75	7,665.92	4,926.97	1,920.72
2014	215.73	8,133.67	5,112.65	2,316.00
2015	209.38	6,812.14	4,040.75	2,053.52
2016	147.18	5,813.49	3,186.21	1,931.61
2017	171.61	7,065.36	3,711.94	2,521.77

Source: NSE/CMA.

Table 15.10 Key bond market indicators, 2008–17

	Treasury bond turnover (KSh Bn)	Corporate bond turnover (KSh Bn)	Total bond turnover (KSh Bn)	Corporate bond turnover to total bond turnover	Treasury bond turnover to total bond turnover
2008	95.36	0.00	95.36	0.00%	100.00%
2009	110.65	0.00	110.65	0.00%	100.00%
2010	466.89	12.47	479.36	2.60%	97.40%
2011	437.13	8.52	445.65	1.91%	98.09%
2012	563.82	1.86	565.68	0.33%	99.67%
2013	451.58	0.88	452.46	0.19%	99.81%
2014	504.30	1.95	506.25	0.39%	99.61%
2015	302.14	2.96	305.10	0.97%	99.03%
2016	431.59	1.53	433.12	0.35%	99.65%
2017	432.81	3.08	435.89	0.71%	99.29%

Source: NSE/CMA.

significantly contributing to vibrancy and liquidity in the secondary market for fixed income securities (see Table 15.10).

The launch of an online system for trading of all listed debt securities on 26 September 2014 is further deepening the fixed income market. The system is integrated with the settlement system at the CBK, making it more efficient, scalable, and flexible. It can also support trading in bonds issued in foreign currencies.

Perhaps the listing of Safaricom IPO at the NSE, the largest in Sub-Saharan Africa where KSh 50 billion was raised by the Government (oversubscribed by 363 per cent) in 2008. The Safaricom IPO increased the number of shares listed on the bourse to over 55 billion shares, from the previous 15 billion. On the fixed income segment, CMA facilitated the Government to issue a debut infrastructure bond to raise KSh 18.5 billion to fund projects in the water, energy, and roads sectors in 2009. The 12-year was oversubscribed by 45 per cent, paving way for more issuance of this asset class by both government and private sector.

To provide investors with a comprehensive measure of the performance of the stock market, the bourse introduced the NSE All-Share Index (NASI) on 25 February 2008 to complement the NSE 20 Share Index. On 8 November 2011, NSE together with FTSE International launched the FTSE NSE Kenya 15 and FTSE NSE Kenya 25 Indices. The NSE also launched the FTSE NSE Kenyan Shilling Government Bond Index on 3 October 2012, the first of its kind in Eastern Africa. This gave investors opportunity to access current information and provided a reliable valuation of Kenya's Government Bond market's performance.

Other innovations at the bourse include cross-listing of UMEME Holdings Limited from Uganda on the MIMS of NSE on 14 December 2012; listing of equity-linked note of KSh 4.19 billion for trading on the FISMS by Centum

Investment Company on 25 February 2013; the first reverse takeover transaction in East Africa by I&M Holdings of City Trust. This allowed City Trust, which was listed on AIMS to migrate to MIMS on 15 July 2013; listing of Home Afrika by introduction on the Growth Enterprise Market Segment (GEMS) on 25 June 2013; and listing of the first Income Real Estate Investment Trust, the Stanlib Fahari I-REIT in October 2015. The CMA also approved the secondary listing of the first Exchange Traded Fund (ETF) in Kenya in February 2017. The listing of 400,000 gold bullion debentures by New Gold Issuer (RF) Ltd on the MIMS to provide a wide menu of asset classes at the NSE commenced trading on 27 March 2017.

The NSE has also been active in regional and international cooperation, contributing to modernization of Kenya's capital markets. In 1997, East African Securities Regulatory Authority (EASRA) was established for the East African Capital markets regulators to develop a common market for members and to harmonize laws that would allow for seamless regional trading. On 30 November 1999, the EAC Treaty was signed in Arusha. Following the signing of an MOU between the Dar-es-Salaam Stock Exchange, the Uganda Securities Exchange, and the Nairobi Securities Exchange, the East African Securities Exchanges Association was formed in 2004.The CMA was admitted as a full signatory of the International Organization of Securities Commissions (IOSCO) Multilateral Memorandum of Understanding (MMOU) in 2009.

The CMA established a Capital Markets Master Plan (CMMP) Steering Committee in 2012 to formulate a ten-year Capital Markets Master Plan. The Plan sets to transform the Kenyan capital markets into the heart of capital markets financing in Africa with an emphasis on facilitating investment flows into Africa. The key target of this transformation consists of the players captioned in Table A15.1.

15.4 Conclusion

Kenya's financial sector has grown significantly since independence in terms of size, complexity, and operating environment, diversity in services and products. It has contributed significantly to the overall economy, with spillovers to the Eastern Africa region. The system has experienced tremendous innovations, especially on digital financial services, thus putting the country on the global map.

The journey has not been without many challenges. Instability episodes in the banking industry, insurance industry, and capital markets have had a negative socio-economic impact to the country. They have however provided opportunities for regulators to institute robust policy measures, adopt strong regulatory frameworks and come up with reforms not only to minimize occurrence of such episodes or minimized the impact whenever such crisis emerges, but also adopt transformative initiatives of propelling the financial system to global standards.

The resilience of the financial system and vibrancy in innovations therefore provides a strong base for take-off to the next level of making Kenya a financial hub in Sub-Saharan Africa as envisaged under the Economic Pillar of the country's long-term economic blue print, Vision 2030.

Annex

Table A15.1 Capital markets industry players in Kenya

Licensed entity/year	2012	2013	2014	2015	2016	2017
Securities Exchange (NSE)	1	1	1	1	1	1
Central Depositories (CDSC)	1	1	1	1	1	1
Investment banks	10	10	14	14	14	14
Stockbrokers	12	11	9	9	10	10
Investment advisers	18	18	17	17	13	14
Fund managers	21	25	24	25	28	26
Collective investment schemes	16	16	19	18	23	23
Authorized depositories/custodians	15	15	14	14	14	14
Credit rating agencies	1	2	3	3	3	3
Venture capital companies	1	1	1	1	1	0
REIT managers	–	–	6	6	8	8
REIT trustees	–	–	3	2	3	3
Employee Share Ownership Plans (ESOPS)	9	10	11	11	11	14
Authorized real estate investment trusts	–	–		3	3	1
Total	**105**	**110**	**123**	**125**	**133**	**132**

Source: Capital Markets Authority.

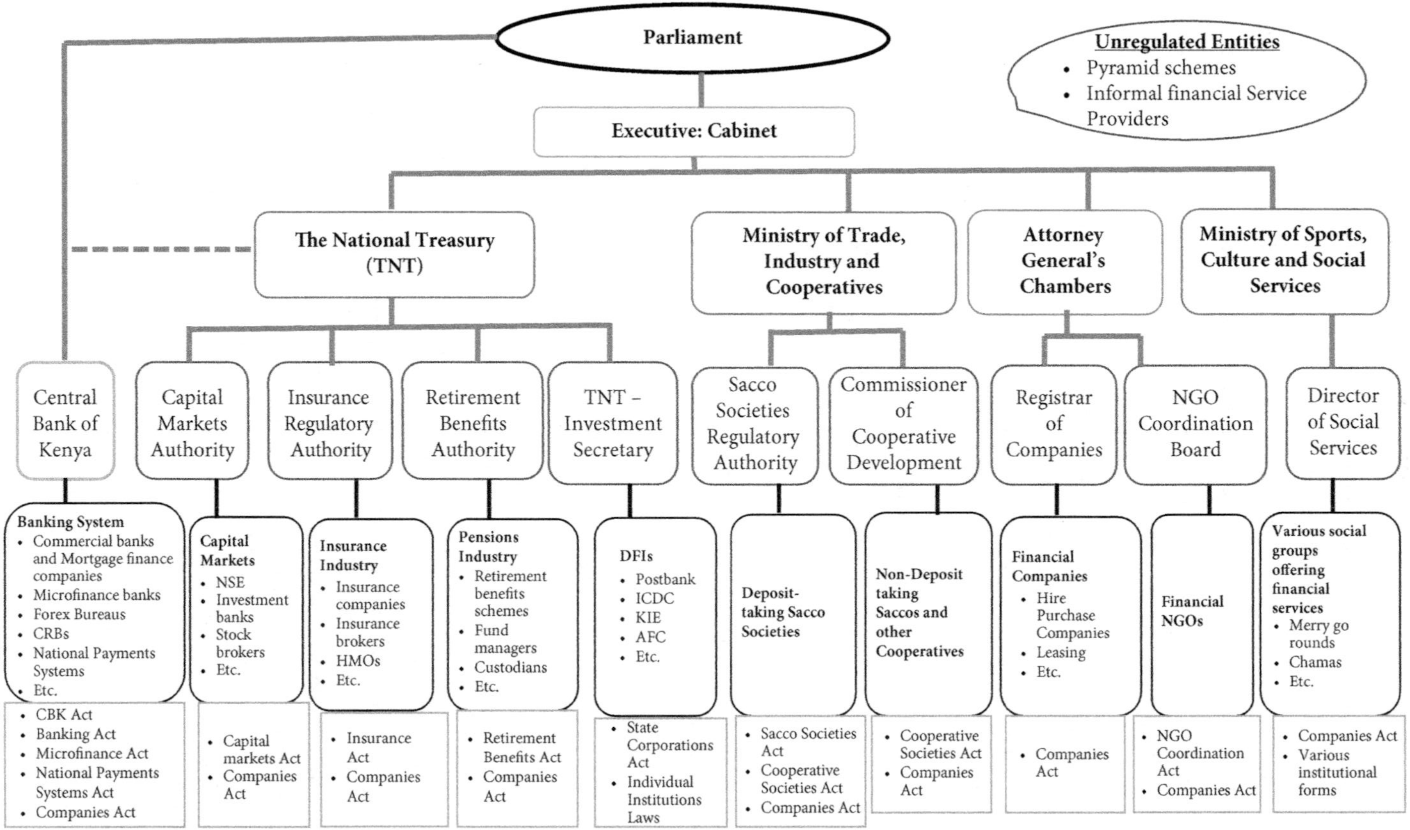

Figure A15.1 Kenya's financial system landscape

Source: Authors.

References

Central Bank of Kenya (CBK) (1985), *Bank Supervision Annual Report 1985.* CBK Report.

Central Bank of Kenya (CBK) (1993), *Bank Supervision Annual Report 1993.* CBK Report.

Central Bank of Kenya (CBK) (1994), *Bank Supervision Annual Report 1994.* CBK Report.

Central Bank of Kenya (CBK) (2010), Bank Supervision Annual Report 2010. CBK Report.

Central Bank of Kenya (CBK) (2016), *FinAccess Household Survey Report.* CBK Report.

Central Bank of Kenya (CBK) (2017), *Bank Supervision Annual Reports 2017.* CBK Report.

Financial Sector Regulators Forum (FSRF) (2017), *The Kenya Financial Sector Stability Report 2016.* FSRF Report (September).

Government of Kenya (1965), 'African socialism and its application to planning in Kenya'. Nairobi: Government Printer, Sessional Paper no. 10 of 1963/65, pp. 1–2, 49.

Insurance Regulatory Authority (IRA) (2016), *Insurance Industry Report for the Period January–December 2016.* IRA Report (February).

Kariuki, P. W. (1995), 'The impact of interest rate liberalization on financial savings: The case of Kenya.' *African Review of Money, Finance and Banking,* No.1/2, pp. 5–23.

MacPherson, I. (1999), *Hands Around the Globe: A History of the International Credit Union Movement and the Role and Development of World Council of Credit Unions.* Inc. Touchwood Ed.

Ministry of Industrialization & Enterprise Development (2020), 'History and organization of cooperative development and marketing sub sector in Kenya', available at: http://www.industrialization.go.ke/index.php/downloads/123-history-and-organization-of-cooperative-development-and-marketing-sub-sector-in-kenya

National Assembly, Kenya (1994), 'Recovery and sustainable development to the year 2010'. Sessional paper no. 1. National Assembly. Kenya.

National Assembly, Kenya (1997), 'Co-operatives in a liberalized economic environment'. Sessional Paper No. 6. National Assembly. Kenya.

Wachira, L. W. (2008), 'Assessment of the attractiveness of Kenya's insurance industry'. MBA Thesis, University of Nairobi. Accessed on 28 April 2020 at http://erepository.unobi.ac.ke:8080/xmlui/handle/123456789/12692

Wanyama, F. O. (2007), 'The impact of liberalization on the co-operative movement in Kenya'. In *First International CIRIEC Social Economy Conference on Strengthening and Building Communities: The Social Economy in a Changing World.* Victoria, British Columbia.

Wanyama, F. O., Patrick, D., and Ignace, P. (2009), 'Reinventing the wheel? African cooperatives in a liberalized economic environment'. *Annals of Public and Cooperative Economics,* Vol. 80, No. 3, pp. 361–92.

16
Powering Financial Inclusion through Innovative Payment Systems

Matu Mugo, Evelyne Kilonzo, and Anne W. Mariga

16.1 Introduction

Over the past half a century, Kenya's payments and banking systems have undergone both incremental and revolutionary modifications that have transformed Kenya's financial landscape.[1] From cash transactions to digital finance ecosystems, the most notable of these developments have taken place over the last two decades. These innovations include the reduction in clearing period for cheques, introduction of the Real Time Gross Settlement System for high-value payments, agency banking, and credit information sharing, among others. One of the most remarkable of these developments, M-PESA, rolled out in 2007, undoubtedly has earned its place in Kenya's Hall of Fame.

The developments in the payments system have culminated in a more accessible, effective, and efficient Kenyan payment system. This chapter tells the M-PESA story from the lens of a regulator. It details the fairly routine meeting that introduced the Central Bank of Kenya (CBK) to the product, review of the product, testing, the dilemma faced to the eventual launch in March 2007. More importantly, the chapter tells other understated stories of payments and related banking sector innovations that have seen the level of financial inclusion in Kenya triple from 26 per cent in 2006 to over 75 per cent in 2016 (Steadman Group Research Division, 2007; CBK and FSD, 2009; CBK et al., 2016). The chapter provides lessons that the CBK has learnt in this transformational journey. One of the most important lessons is the need for regulators to understand the business models underpinning innovations, risks thereon, and the mitigation of the risks.

[1] We acknowledge the support of colleagues in the Bank Supervision, Banking and Payments Services and Research Departments of the Central Bank of Kenya for providing input into the chapter. In particular, we acknowledge John Kipkirui, Lucy Kabethi, Harun Mahiạnyu, Reuben Chepng'ar, Richard Kioko, and Talaso Rasa of Bank Supervision Department; Maureen Were and Julienne Lauler of Research Department; and Madge Salat, Veska Kipsaina, Monica Oraro, Timothy Kimalel, Stephen Wambua, Simon Karemu, Enock Omweri, and Luka Plapan of Banking and Payment Department, who provided input into various sections of the chapter.

Matu Mugo, Evelyne Kilonzo, and Anne W. Mariga, *Powering Financial Inclusion through Innovative Payment Systems* In: *50 Years of Central Banking in Kenya: Regional and Global Perspectives.* Edited by: Patrick Njoroge and Victor Murinde, Oxford University Press (2021). © The Central Bank of Kenya. DOI: 10.1093/oso/9780198851820.003.0016

16.2 Background: Early Digital Evolution

Over the years, cash has been one of the most common payment mediums used across the world. Building from the premise that cash has certain disadvantages—high transaction costs, transactional inefficiencies, vulnerability to loss or theft and geographic restrictions, among others (McKinsey and Company, 2016), the reduction of the use of cash through the modernization of payments systems can be viewed as rather advantageous for populaces and economies.

The modernization of the Kenyan National Payment System, which has lowered transaction costs and improved efficiency and effectiveness of the payment, clearing, and settlement systems, is markedly one of the most remarkable developments in Kenya's banking sector. This modernization is marked by innovative technological advancements which have completely revolutionized financial service delivery and enabled millions of previously financially excluded Kenyans to access financial services.

The use of technology in banking in Kenya, in fact, dates back to the era of the National Bank of India in Kenya. Until 1965, the National Bank of India and its successors, National and Grindlays (and currently Kenya Commercial Bank), were the official government banker. Policy matters, however, were handled by the East African Currency Board, with its headquarters in London (CBK, 2018). The technology in use at that time, like manual weighing scales, was fairly rudimentary and mechanical. The weighing scales were manufactured in London and shipped in, already calibrated and ready for use. They came in varying sizes and used different weighing stones whose fixed weight was the equivalent of a certain amount of rupees. Huge volumes of books were used for purposes of keeping accounts as well as documents that constituted powers of attorney and wills. Customers were issued with passbooks in which all their transactions with the bank were entered by clerks.

Withdrawal of large sums of cash was rare, and one was required to notify the bank in advance. The notice duration was dependent on the sum one wished to withdraw but ranged from one to three weeks. Cheques were mostly the preserve of companies and individual clients who were very wealthy. And in the 1950s it took longer than a month for a cheque to clear. This improved to 21 days in the 1980s. Banks were generally open to clients for a half day, five days a week so as to give bank staff more time to balance the books and attend to other internal matters before closing. The fastest way of sending and receiving money at the time was through telegraphic transfer and money orders.

By the early 2000s, bank customers were able to access services from any branch of their bank unlike previously when one had to go to their specific branch. Automated Teller Machines (ATMs) were enhanced to offer a variety of services besides cash withdrawal. These included cash and cheque deposit, issuance of mini statements, and transfer of money directly to another account within the bank. Banks also interconnected their ATM networks thereby allowing customers to access the services on ATMs beyond those of their banks.

An even more innovative system of banking would come in 2004 when Co-operative Bank pioneered mobile-phone banking in Kenya. But although the service allowed customers to check their account balances, request for statements, and track the status of cheques, it did not facilitate the actual transfer of money. This only became a possibility with the launch of the M-PESA mobile-phone financial service (then money transfer system) by Safaricom in 2007.

The spread of mobile-phone financial services have drastically transformed the way the majority of Kenyans send and receive money. Currently, most banks have adopted and integrated mobile-phone financial services concept in their everyday services. Most banks are also offering internet banking, where customers can transact their business on personal computers or smartphones in the comforts of their homes or offices. This is being achieved by banks partnering with local telecommunication firms like Safaricom, Airtel, and Telkom, among others, to facilitate online financial services.

Besides the roll-out of M-PESA in 2007, over the last two decades, Kenya's payment and banking system has undergone other transformative developments that have not only reconfigured the nature of transactions but also enhanced the features and capabilities of the Kenyan banking and payment systems.

16.3 The Story of M-PESA from the Regulator's Lense

A fairly routine meeting in 2005 introduced the CBK to what was to become Kenya's financial inclusion 'poster child'.[2] The Commercial Bank of Africa (CBA) had requested for this meeting to brief the CBK on a pilot it intended to launch with Faulu Microfinance, Microsave, Vodafone, and Safaricom on a mechanism to facilitate repayment of microfinance loans through the mobile phone. Given that the CBA was a licensed bank, the CBK regarded the CBA's request as a normal application to roll out a new product, like any other bank would. Following a series of meetings, the CBK allowed the pilot to proceed with the expectation that periodic reports would be sent to the CBK within strict timelines.

The ground began shifting in 2006, however, when Safaricom indicated to the CBK that it intended to launch M-PESA (Mobile Money[3] as translated into English) as a commercial domestic money transfer service. The automatic reaction would have been for the CBK to respond that Safaricom was not one of its regulated entities; and that for Safaricom to move ahead with the proposal, it would need to partner with a regulated commercial bank. However, the CBK took

[2] This section draws extensively from internal CBK correspondences, briefs, and memos.

[3] M for mobile; Pesa is a Swahili word for money.

a chance and gave Safaricom an opportunity to present its proposal to the CBK Senior Management Team.

The presentation took place on 14 August 2006, and in retrospect, in today's world, it would have been akin to founders of a start-up Fintech presenting a funding proposal to the management team of a 'centuries-old' traditional bank. The Safaricom and Vodafone teams, however, gave a very persuasive presentation and demonstration to the CBK senior management team led by the (then) Acting Governor.[4] Although the CBK team was visibly impressed by the presentation, they still had the typical central bankers 'risk hat' on, and they raised quite a number of issues that required clarity. These issues revolved around the legal framework, product feasibility, concerns by other regulators, customer identification procedures, product security, and security of customers, agents, and their places of business. The CBK management, thereafter, constituted a technical committee comprising representatives from the Bank Supervision Department, National Payments Systems Division, and Legal Services Division to address these issues with Safaricom.

What followed were extensive consultations between the CBK technical committee and Safaricom between September and December 2006. Fundamental to these consultations were practical demonstrations of the product that were made to the CBK team. These entailed actual walkthroughs of the product, by Safaricom to the CBK team using phones provided to all team members in order to interact practically with a prototype of the M-PESA product. In today's world, this kind of approach would exotically be referred to as a 'regulatory sandbox'.

A typical central banker's dilemma then set in; that of balancing financial stability and financial inclusion. This dilemma is aptly captured in an internal brief prepared by the CBK technical committee to management in October 2006, an excerpt of which is highlighted here below.

> The vast majority of Kenyans remain unbanked, with the CBK records indicating that there are approximately 2.5 million accounts in the banking sector. This implies that the vast majority of the approximately 30 million Kenyan population is unbanked. An ongoing survey on Financial Services Access[5] is expected to provide a clearer picture of access to financial services and products by the Kenyan populace.
>
> It has been argued that expensive payment systems are one of the barriers to access to financial services in East Africa (Lovegrove, 2006). The use of mobile

[4] Jacinta Wanjala Mwatela was appointed the Deputy Governor of the Central Bank of Kenya on 12 May 2005. In March 2006 she was appointed the Acting Governor following the exit of former governor Andrew Mullei.

[5] The first National Financial Access (FinAccess) survey of 2006 (Steadman Group Research Division (2007), was ongoing to determine the extent of financial access in the country, from a demand perspective.

> phone networks has thus been proposed as one of the ways of reducing costs especially for low value payments. M-PESA would indeed play an invaluable role in extending access to financial services and products in Rural Kenya that is largely underserved by the formal banking sector. However, it has the potential especially if other mobile phone operators also join the bandwagon to grow to proportions that may even exceed the formal payment system posing a potential risk to financial system stability. This is particularly in view of the fact that there are approximately five million mobile phone subscribers as opposed to the approximately 2.5 million account holders in the formal banking system.

Even as consultations with Safaricom continued, the CBK continued to review practices on electronic money in other jurisdictions to inform its position on M-PESA. In a nutshell regulatory approaches to electronic money in 2006 could be categorized as follows:

- Definition of a special type of institution to provide electronic money in addition to licensed institutions, as in the European Union.
- Licensing of payment providers who may not necessarily be banks, as in the case of Australia.
- Issuance of e-money only by banks, such as in Singapore.
- No restrictions on the issuance of e-money by the depository or non-depository institutions, such as in the United States.

However, practices in the jurisdictions cited above were not seen as corresponding with the proposed M-PESA product. More emphasis was laid on the Philippines, which at the time, had two mobile-phone providers, SMART and Globe Telecom providing mobile financial services. Smart's product, SMART Money, had been introduced in 2000 while G-Cash by Globe had been introduced in 2004. But there was still a catch as these two products were not exactly similar to the proposed M-PESA. SMART Money was a bank-led product rolled out by Banco de Oro of the Philippines with SMART providing the technological back end. G-Cash was more similar to M-PESA as it was led by Globe Telecom with the cash float being held by its usual business bank.

Where G-Cash diverted from M-PESA was in its regulatory framework. It was regulated and overseen by the Central Bank of Philippines as a remittance agent. The Central Bank of the Philippines had in January 2005 issued rules and regulations to govern the registration and operations of foreign exchange dealers/money changers and remittance agents (Bangko Sentral ng Pilipina (2005).[6]

[6] Circular 471, Bangko Sentral ng Pilipina, https://www.bsp.gov.ph, January 2005.

At this juncture, the regulatory framework required for M-PESA remained unclear. Granted, the Central Bank of Kenya Act had, in 2003, been amended to empower the CBK to oversee payment systems. However, the enabling legislation and regulations were yet to be enacted and would take time to be put in place. The CBK had also, in early 2006, been involved in a project to lay the ground for an enabling legal and regulatory framework for mobile-phone banking.

Given the potential of mobile phones to become the 'next frontier' innovation in enhancing access to financial services, the United Kingdom's Department for International Development (DFID), the Financial Sector Deepening (FSD) Trust Kenya and the FinMark Trust of South Africa financed a project to review the regulatory framework for mobile banking in Africa early in 2006 (Porteous, 2006). Kenya and South Africa were the focus of the study given that in both countries there were serious expressions of interest in the use of mobile phones to enhance access to financial services. The CBK participated in this project through a project team with representatives from the Bank Supervision Department, National Payments Systems Division and the Rural Finance Development Department.

The project report concluded that the field of mobile payments (m-payments) and mobile banking (m-banking) was not only new and fast-evolving, but it also sat at the overlap of several regulatory domains—those of banking, telecommunication, and payment system supervisors, and anti-money laundering agencies.[7] The overlap substantially raised the risk of coordination failure, where legislation or regulatory approaches were inconsistent or contradictory. In this regard, a framework of two-tier principles which was necessary, although not sufficient, for m-payments and m-banking to be enabled in a country, was identified.

It was determined that the following **first tier principles** are necessary for m-banking to develop to scale:

- There should be sufficient certainty around electronic contracting.
- Customers should be adequately protected against fraud and abuse in the m-banking environment.
- Interoperability should be encouraged, through ensuring that providers can access payment platforms and that consumers are able to switch to and from financial providers with ease.

These **second-tier principles** are also critical for m-banking to enable access to financial services by the unbanked.

[7] Refer to the Alliance for Financial Inclusion Guideline Note No. 19 on Digital financial services basic terminology from https://www.afi-global.org/sites/default/files/publications/2016-08/Guideline%20Note-19%20DFS-Terminology.pdf (Alliance for Financial Inclusion, 2016)

- Customer due diligence procedures for account opening should be risk-based and should not unduly prejudice remote account openings by small customers.
- Customers should be able to, at least, make deposits and withdraw cash through agents and remote points outside of bank branches.
- Adequate provision must be made for the issuance of e-money by appropriately capitalized and supervised entities which are not necessarily banks.

Putting in place a legal and regulatory framework to satisfy these principles in Kenya could only be a long-term initiative that could not address the current M-PESA application. The CBK, therefore, proceeded to address what it considered to be the key issues arising from the M-PESA application:

- Was the product constituted as a 'deposit' for purposes of the Banking Act and therefore requiring the CBK licensing?
- Did the CBK have a mandate over payment products such as M-PESA?
- How would risks arising from money laundering, fraud, loss of service, Information Technology (IT) Security, loss of money, data confidentiality, and broader consumer protection concerns be addressed?
- Was the trust company that held the M-PESA funds a 'shell' that could lead to customers losing their money if it became bankrupt?

On the deposit-taking question, internal and external legal opinions settled the matter conclusively. In a nutshell, the M-PESA product was not construed to be a 'deposit' as it did not have the 'terms' attached to a deposit as to when it would be repaid and the interest payable. In addition, Safaricom or Vodafone could not use the funds transacted through the product to finance their operations to any material extent. This was a reassuring position, particularly to the CBK bank supervisors. The Basel Core Principles on Effective Banking Supervision require prudential regulation of deposit-taking entities. By these definitions and terms, M-PESA did not, therefore, require prudential regulation.

On the CBK mandate, it was noted that the CBK's ambit had been extended to include the oversight of payment systems in 2003. However specific legislation, in particular, the National Payments Systems Bill and regulations were still under development.

On the risks, Safaricom and Vodafone provided detailed procedures and manuals on money laundering and consumer protection that were well aligned with international practices in these areas. On IT security, an independent vulnerability assessment and penetration report was presented to the CBK to address its concerns.

A legal review of the M-PESA holding company provided comfort to the CBK that it was duly constituted under the trustee's act. In this regard, funds generated by M-PESA were 'ring-fenced' from usage by Safaricom or even Vodafone and could only be used for purposes of meeting obligations arising from M-PESA transactions.

Having addressed its core concerns and following consultations with various stakeholders, including the (then) Ministry of Finance and the Ministry of Information and Communication, the CBK was, in early 2007, in a position to advise Safaricom on its application. Of importance to the CBK was that M-PESA would not be in breach of any existing laws given that relevant legislation was yet to be enacted. The CBK, therefore, advised Safaricom in February 2007 that for M-PESA to be launched, it was necessary to ensure that:

- Appropriate measures were put in place to safeguard the integrity of the system in order to protect customers against fraud, loss of money, and loss of privacy and quality of service.
- The system would provide for adequate measures to guard against money laundering in matters such as account opening procedures, transactions limits and monitoring, and warning systems.
- Proper records were kept and availed to regulatory authorities in agreed formats as may be required from time to time.
- M-PESA would observe all existing laws governing its relationship with its agents and customers.

In setting these conditions, the CBK was informed by the fact that there were inherent potential systemic implications from M-PESA's use by the wider general public. And that was how M-PESA came to be launched in March 2007.

16.4 Why Was M-PESA Such a Game Changer?

The premise that drove the development of M-PESA was based on the potential of the mobile phone to enable Kenyans to safely, cheaply, and efficiently remit cash locally, particularly for workers in urban areas to send money home to their families in rural areas (AFI, 2010).

In the past, remitting money was not only expensive but it was also cumbersome. The majority of Kenyans sent money locally through friends (43 per cent), public transportation (20 per cent), or the local post office (18 per cent) as highlighted in Figure 16.1. These options were hardly secure, efficient, or convenient modes of transfers.

M-PESA thus presented an opportunity to dramatically reduce time and costs and transfer funds in a cheaper, safer, and more convenient manner.

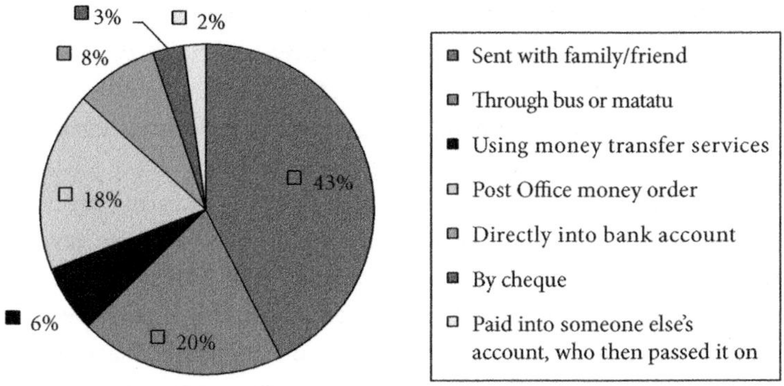

Figure 16.1 Mode of local money transfers
Source: FinAccess Household Survey, 2006.

16.5 Expansion of Digital Finance through Mobile-Phone Financial Services

Over the years, Kenya has witnessed an unprecedented increase in the uptake of digital finance in the country. This digital revolution has allowed people to make financial transactions remotely at the comfort of their localities and without disrupting their business operations. They are able to manage time as they no longer have to travel long distances to bank outlets and avoid the risks of transporting physical cash from one place to another. More significantly, digital finance has opened up new avenues for those who did not have access to cheap and convenient finance to have the opportunity to interact with financial services.

Kenya's mobile-phone financial services platform has since grown from a money transfer system in 2007 to a fully accessorized digital finance ecosystem. This ecosystem is quite a complex and dynamic one. It hosts a motley of diverse players and fascinating partnerships across sectors, all built on the mobile money 'rails'. For instance, over the years, the country has seen the entry and exit of six mobile-money PSPs,[8] with four still in existence as of September 2017, Safaricom's M-PESA (2007), Airtel's Airtel Money (2009), (2011), Finserve's Equitel (2014), and Telkom Kenya's T-Cash[9] (2017). Tangaza also operates in this space as a super-agent that offers mobile money services, Tangaza Pesa, in conjunction with other Mobile Network Operators (MNOs) (CBK, 2018).

It has grown exponentially, giving the opportunity to individuals and businesses that were left out of the traditional banking system to access financial services. Besides the growth in number and values of customers and transactions, there is

[8] Yu Mobile's Yu Cash and Mobikash exited the market in 2014 and 2016, respectively.

[9] Telkom Kenya rebranded in June 2017 by dropping its initial brand name, 'Orange'. In 2010, Orange had been given an approval as an MNO to launch 'Iko Pesa'.

an increased fusion and integration of payment and banking services to form a robust digital finance ecosystem. The digital ecosystem hosts varied value-added products and services, like credit and saving platforms and e-commerce intertwined through linkages between both financial and non-financial institutions.

For instance, telecommunications companies are increasingly partnering with banks to allow their customers to link the mobile platform directly to their accounts leveraging on mobile-phone technology. These linkages have given rise to innovative products such as M-Shwari, and KCB M-PESA, among others, which continue to bring convenient, safe, accessible, and cheaper financial services to the Kenyan populace. A new emerging trend is banks also acquiring Mobile Virtual Network Operator (MVNO) licences from the communications regulator. MVNOs, like Equity Bank's Equitel, leverage on the infrastructure of mobile network operators to roll out telecommunication services.

Digital innovations have even surpassed existing payment and credit solutions, and support other financial services such as the provision of savings, investment, insurance, and pension products. In 2017, a mobile-based government issued a retail bond, named M-Akiba, was rolled out. The aim of the Bond is to promote a savings and investment culture, raise debt, and enhance financial inclusion for economic development (Government of Kenya, 2018).

The digital finance ecosystem has also grown to accommodate financial services for goods and services outside the financial sector. This service has driven partnerships with other industries in the broader economy in the health, water and sanitation, education, energy, insurance, and agriculture sub-sector. All these linkages and resultant interactions are modernizing the economy to serve the Kenyan populace better.

16.6 Outcome: Unprecedented Growth in Mobile-Phone Financial Services

The uptake of mobile-phone financial services has gained great traction in providing an alternative platform for retail payments. In terms of growth, the use of mobile phone financial services has more than doubled from 23.4 per cent in 2009 to 71.4 per cent in 2016 (CBK et al., 2016). As of September 2017,[10] the number of mobile subscriptions had increased exponentially to 41.0 million moving mobile penetration rate to 90.4 per cent. There were a growing number of 184,537 agents who had handled over 28.19 million customers and had processed 537.24 million transactions valued at KShs. 1.65 trillion (USD 16.02 billion)[11] for the period

[10] https://ca.go.ke/wp-content/uploads/2018/02/Sector-Statistics-Report-Q1-2017-18.pdf

[11] The Applicable exchange rate used is KShs 103/USD, being the average annual rate for the year 2017.

between July and September 2017 (Communications Authority, 2017) compared to 1.5 million transactions valued at KShs. 4.71 billion (USD 45.73 million) for the period between July and September 2007.[12]

Table 16.1 and Figure 16.2 provide detailed indicators mapping the development of mobile-phone financial services in Kenya over the last decade.

Table 16.1 Summary of Kenya's digital finance landscape over the last decade

	September 2007	September 2017
Mobile phone subscribers	10.8 million Penetration rate of 28.97 per cent	41 million Penetration rate of 90.4 per cent
Mobile money subscriptions	640,000	28.1 million
Number of transactions	1.5 million (July–September 2007)	537.2 million (July–September 2017)
Value of transactions	Ksh 4.71 billion (USD 45.73 million) (July–September 2007)	Ksh 1.65 trillion (USD 16.02 billion) (July–September 2017)
Active agents	1582 mobile money agents	184,537 mobile money agents

Source: Communications Authority Sector Statistics Report, 2017.

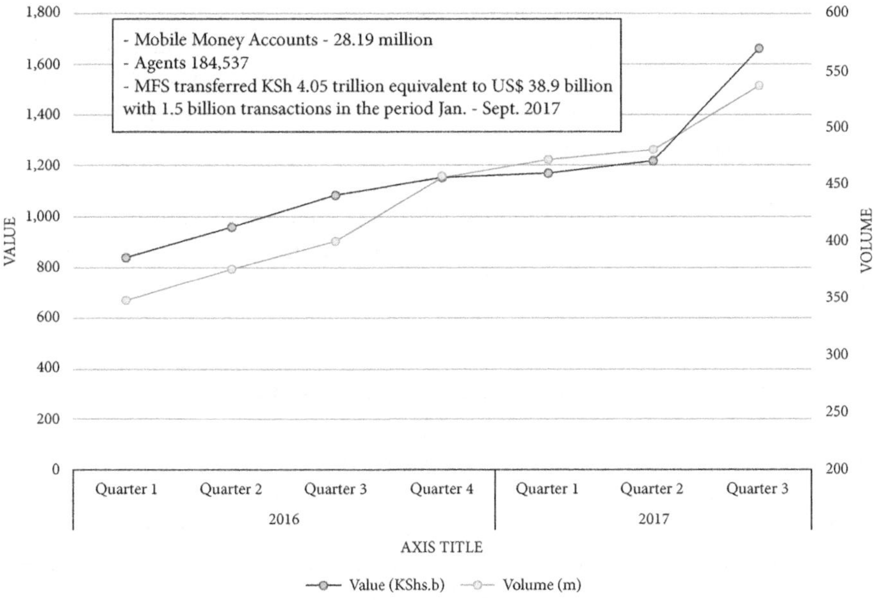

Figure 16.2 Mobile money growth

Source: Communications Authority Sector Statistics Report, 2017.

[12] From data collated by the CBK.

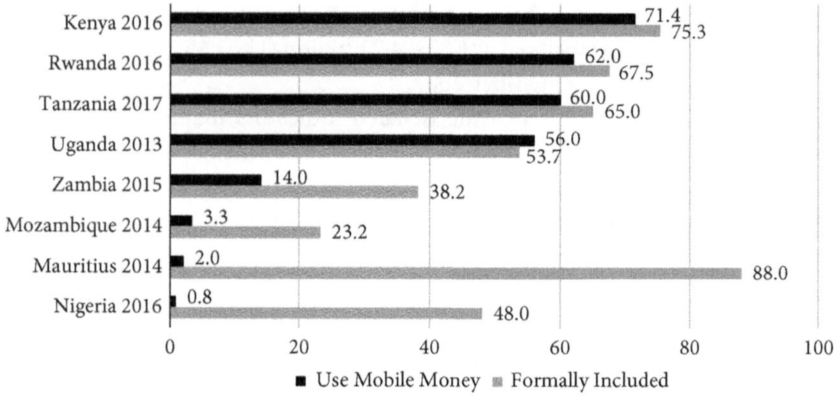

Figure 16.3 Regional comparison of use of mobile money and financial inclusion strands

Source: Kenya FinAccess 2016/i2i Data Portal/FinScope SA 2015/EFInA Nigeria 2014/FinScope Mauritius 2014.

It is worth noting that the mobile phone platform is a high-volume, low-value retail payments platform. Although the mobile transactions represent *over 86 per cent* of the total number of transactions in the payment system, they represent about *10 per cent* of the total value of transactions (as of September 2017).

Kenya has also become a regional leader in financial inclusion and mobile-phone financial services as seen in Figure 16.3.

As illustrated in Figure 16.3, out of the 75 per cent financially included in Kenya, 71 per cent use mobile money. This is in contrast to Mauritius where in 2014, out of the 88 per cent financially included adult populace, only 2 per cent used mobile money.

16.7 From Manual to Automated Payment Processes

In the 1990s, bank services and transactions were predominantly manual and paper-based. Consequently, it took quite a lot of time and effort for transactions to be completed. It was, therefore, not uncommon to see banking halls filled with large crowds of people in long winding queues, patronizing the service counters for their transactions to be processed. Completing a transaction, especially at bank branches, was, by and large, a whole day operation for the customer.

To give a practical example, the manual clearing and settlement of cheques took not less than 14 days; and in the case of up-country cheques up to 21 days, from the point of depositing the cheque to the point of payment

(CBK, 2013).[13] Why? Physical cheques from all banks countrywide were collected at a central clearing house in Nairobi to be sorted manually, perused, exchanged, and accepted by the various banks for processing. This required that the cheques be physically moved from the collecting bank to the paying bank as part of the clearing process. The Settlement was only done after physically and manually confirming availability of funds in the drawers' account, and values were then duly transferred.

There were many risks associated with the manual system which notably included; fraud, theft, and loss of cheques in transit. The credit risk compounded in the manual clearing house was also huge considering that there were no limits to the amount that could be drawn on a cheque. To mitigate these risks, the CBK, in collaboration with the banking sector, proactively took to modernizing the payments system.

16.8 Automation of the Kenyan Payment Systems

16.8.1 Establishment of the Automated Clearing House (ACH)

These efforts to modernize the payments system began with the automation of the Nairobi Clearing House in May 1998 in order to enhance the clearing of cheques between banks. This automation was facilitated by the adoption of the Magnetic Ink Character Recognition (MICR) technology and in 2002 Electronic Funds Transfer (EFT) payments were introduced. MICR enabled cheque numbers, bank codes, and account numbers to be electronically read at the bank they were deposited instead of being manually keyed in (CBK, 2018).

The result of these efforts was the reduction of the cheque clearing period from a high of 14 days to 3 days. The automation also inevitably reduced operational costs by introducing efficiency in cheque processing; reduced the cheque clearing cycles; facilitated the quick detection of fraud and enabled customers to access their funds earlier. Remote towns were an exception due to challenges posed by the need for physical movement of cheques to Nairobi for clearing. In these regions, the clearing cycle could only be reduced to 10 days (CBK, 2016).

16.8.2 Securing Large Payments through the Real Time Gross Settlement System

Although clearing was now automated, the interbank settlement was under an arrangement called deferred net settlement. Banks would prepare electronic journal files of all the transactions received, then present them at the clearing

[13] Adapted from the CBK archived speeches, retrieved from https://www.bis.org/review/r130805a.pdf and https://www.centralbank.go.ke/images/Launch_of_Kenya50_Commemorative_Coin_.pdf.

house, on the following business day for clearing and settlement. This system presented a challenge in that payments could not be settled on the same day but had to wait for the clearing cycle to be completed. Additionally, the Automated Clearing House (ACH) was exposed to settlement risk where a bank fails to honour the settlement obligations of another bank. This challenging situation led to the introduction of the Kenya Electronic Payments and Settlement System (KEPSS), Kenya's local Real Time Gross Settlement System (RTGS) in July 2005. KEPSS, which is wholly owned and managed by CBK, facilitates the settlement of high-value critical payments. KEPSS relies on credit push as opposed to ACH which is a debit push. This means that an RTGS transaction can only be initiated by a participant bank that has a credit balance. The system is classified as a Systemically Important Payment System (SIPS)[14] due to the high value of transactions it processes and its critical role in the economy (Bank for International Settlements, 2005).

The implementation of KEPSS has mitigated the risks associated with the paper-based inter-bank settlement system, transformed the management of liquidity in the banking industry, reduced the systemic importance of the ACH and enhanced financial stability; while providing an efficient mechanism for monetary policy transmission (CBK, 2018).

KEPSS, over the years, has achieved these gains and has continued to register remarkable growth in both volume and value of transactions as depicted in Figure 16.4.

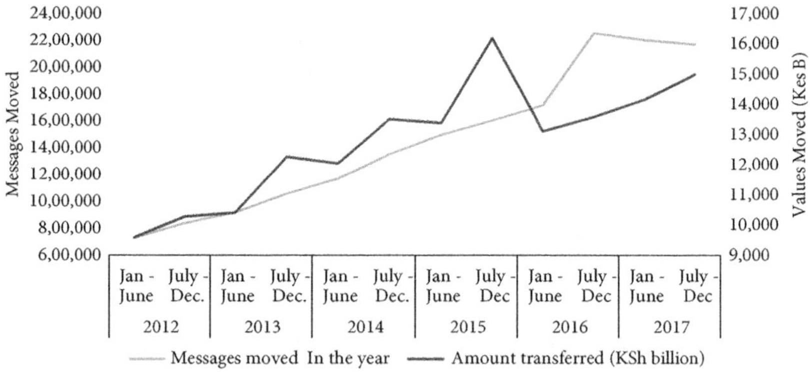

Figure 16.4 Volumes and values of transactions in KEPSS
Source: Central Bank of Kenya, 2018.

[14] A SIP is a 'payment system which has the potential to trigger or transmit systemic disruptions.... systems that are the sole payment system in a jurisdiction or the principal system in terms of the aggregate value of payments, and systems that mainly handle time-critical, high value payments...' (Source: https://www.bis.org/dcms/glossary/glossary.pdf?scope=CPMI&base=term).

Amounts transferred through the RTGS (KEPSS) have gradually increased over the years, with October 2015 processing 273,487 transactions worth Ksh 3070 billion (USD 29.81 billion), an all-time high in the value of transactions (CBK, 2018). In 2016, due to tight liquidity in the market, the value processed decreased with the volumes recording growth, an indication of continued usage of the RTGS services by the industry. However, the upward trajectory of the volume and value of transactions recorded is an indication of the confidence and significance of the RTGS in the economy's financial infrastructure.

16.8.3 Implementation of the Value Capping Policy

The introduction of KEPSS, as an avenue for facilitating high-value critical payments, was expected to reduce the systemic importance of the ACH and increase the stability and soundness of the payment systems. However, there was no significant change in the volumes and values of payment instruments going through the clearinghouse by 2009. Therefore, the ACH still has remained as a Systemically Important Payment System as opposed to the intended low-risk retail payment system (CBK, 2016).

The Central Bank of Kenya, in conjunction with the Kenya Bankers' Association and the (then) Ministry of Finance, therefore, saw it necessary to introduce a value capping policy in October 2009. The policy halted the processing of high-value payments using cheques and EFTs of above KSh.1 million and above through the ACH. Payments through the ACH were capped at less than Ksh 1 million in local currency and USD 35,000, EUR 30,000 and GBP 15,000 in foreign currency transactions. The value cap for foreign currencies was reduced further in October 2016 to USD 15,000, EUR 10,000 and GBP 8000.

This policy shift was in line with international best practice of transforming automated cheque clearing houses from high-risk into low-risk retail payment systems. The automated clearinghouse now automatically blocks cheques over the stipulated amounts from entering the clearing and settlement streams. It has reduced the risk of settlement and increased KEPSS usage.

Figure 16.5 illustrates the performance of the ACH, since 2007, demonstrating that the introduction of value capping managed to transfer the high value of transactions to KEPSS. This lowered settlement risks at the ACH. It is also shown that the value of transactions between 2007 and 2010 significantly reduced; this reflects the impact of value capping introduced at the ACH in October 2009. The volume of transactions has seen a slow but steady rise over the period. What was driving the value at the ACH were large value cheque transactions which were low in volume, representing only 5 per cent of transactions, but made up majority of the transactional value in the ACH. These transactions were transferred to the RTGS once the value capping mechanism was implemented.

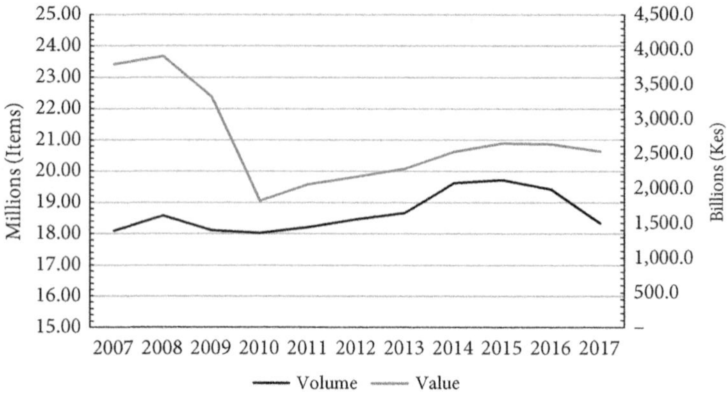

Figure 16.5 Automatic clearinghouse throughput
Source: Central Bank of Kenya, 2018.

16.8.4 Cheque Truncation

In its continuing efforts to modernize the payment and settlement systems, CBK, in partnership with KBA, implemented the Cheque Truncation System in October 2011. Cheque truncation is defined in the Bills of Exchange Act No. Cap 27 as 'a system of cheque clearing and settlement between banks based on either electronic data or images or both, without the conventional physical exchange of instruments' (Government of Kenya, 2017).

The cheque truncation system not only saw the introduction of a new, more secure cheque format but also improved the efficiency of the clearing process. Cheque truncation removed the need to send bank representatives to the clearinghouse to physically exchange cheques; meaning that all cheques deposited are stored at the point of deposit, and only electronic images are used for clearing purposes. The image of the physical cheque is captured at the deposit point and electronically truncated before being transmitted to the clearinghouse for clearing and settlement.

Truncation of cheques greatly improved the cheques clearing cycle increasing efficiency, reducing the cost associated with handling physical cheques and mitigating fraud related risk in the ACH (CBK, 2013).[15] On go-live date, October 2011, the whole country moved to one clearing zone with a three-day clearing period (T+3). The clearing period was further reduced to one clearing day (T+1) in October 2013. The truncation of cheques and faster clearing times greatly benefitted remote areas of the country where clearing took T+10 days due to the

[15] Also accessible on https://www.bis.org/review/r130805a.pdf

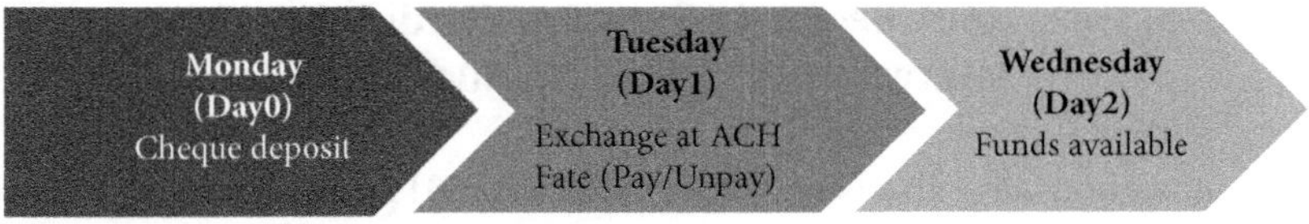

Figure 16.6 Current clearing period T+1
Source: Central Bank of Kenya.

Table 16.2 Pesalink in numbers

No. of approved banks	27 banks (being 51 per cent)
No. of registered customers	3 million
Total number of transactions (YTD Nov. 2017)	7.25 billion
Market share	1.00 per cent of retail value Person to Person (P2P) transfers

Source: Integrated Payment Services Ltd, 2018.

need to move physical cheques. Figure 16.6 demonstrates the current clearing period T+1 under the cheque truncation system (CBK, 2013).

16.8.5 Roll-Out of the Pesalink Payment System: The Kenyan Banking Sector Catches Up with Payments Innovations

The Central Bank of Kenya encourages innovation in the financial services and continues to support and guide the banking industry in various initiatives.

One such initiative is the Pesalink system which went live in February 2017 (CBK, 2017). Pesalink is an innovative technological platform intended to facilitate real-time retail Person-to-Person (P2P) payments of KSh.1.00—999,999.99 between customers of banks round-the-clock (24/7). It offers customers an attractive and cost-effective payment services channel. The system has the following benefits:

- It facilitates interoperability between the Kenyan banks to enhance safety, efficiency, effectiveness, and reduce the cost of offering retail financial services to bank customers.
- It has the potential to help the banking sector meet the shared objective of promoting lower cost, efficiency, effectiveness, and financial inclusion through enhanced interoperability.

The performance of Pesalink since its rollout is highlighted in Table 16.2.

16.9 Securing Payment Cards via Migration to EMV (Pin and Chip)

Many innovations have also been witnessed in the card payments arena. Payment cards hold a strong foothold not only in Kenya but globally, offering customers better and easier access to their money. However, as commercial banks issued more credit and debit cards to their customers, in Kenya, like most countries across the globe, it became increasingly apparent that the cards in circulation were susceptible to fraud (IhuB, 2014), for instance, the cloning of cards used in suspicious transactions or skimming of customers' credentials. The magnetic strip technology had been 'cracked' by fraudsters globally.

The need to adopt a more secure, convenient, and safe technology to curb the rising insecurity in the card payment system thus necessitated the migration to a more secure system in 2014.

The EMV migration project saw the payment card industry in Kenya shift from magnetic strip based cards to EMV chip-enabled cards. EMV chip technology is a global standard for inter-operation of integrated circuit cards and IC card capable point of sale (POS) terminals and automated teller machines (ATMs), for authenticating credit and debit card transactions. Named after its original developers (Europay, MasterCard®, and Visa®), this technology features payment instruments (cards, mobile phones, etc.) with embedded microprocessor chips that store and protect cardholder data.

This programme was rolled out in phases ending in March 2014 with all instruments being certified EMV compliant. The modernization process improved the security of cards and ensured they were globally interoperable. As seen in Figure 16.7, transactions facilitated by payment card instruments have increased gradually over the years.

16.10 Catalysing Regional Trade through Cross-Border Payment Systems

The wave of innovation has not been elusive to other nations within the African continent with the spread of regional trade and investments. The CBK has participated in the implementation of two regional payment systems which were developed within the East African Community (EAC) and Common Market for East and South Africa (COMESA) regions, respectively, to facilitate cross border payments and settlement. These initiatives were developed to enhance regional cross-border payments efficiencies and promote regional trade and economic integration within the two trade blocs.

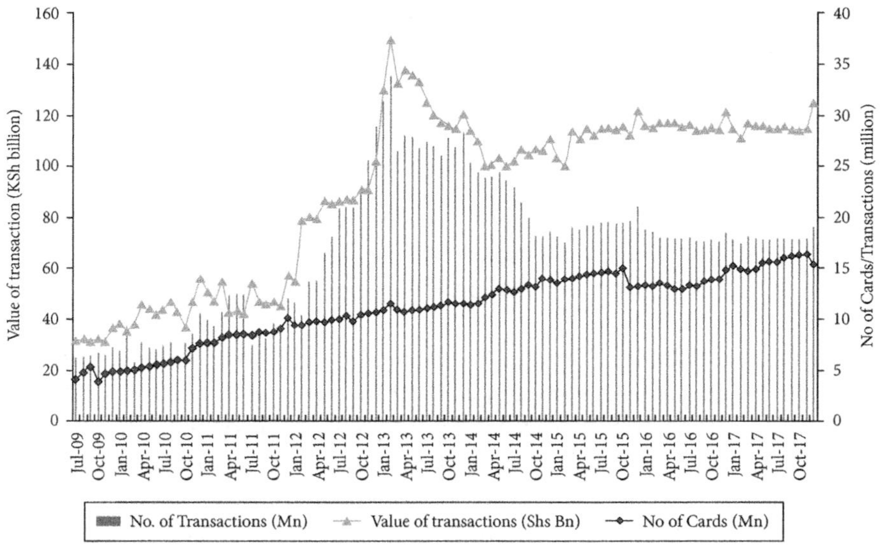

Figure 16.7 Payments card performance in Kenya
Source: Central Bank of Kenya.

16.10.1 Implementation of the East African Payments System (EAPS)

The implementation of the East Africa Payment System (EAPS) was spearheaded by the East African Community (EAC) Central Banks to enhance cross-border payment systems across the EAC region in November 2013. EAPS is a funds transfer mechanism used to transfer money from one bank to another across the borders of the EAC countries of Kenya, Rwanda, Burundi,[16] Tanzania, and Uganda.

Officially launched in May 2014, the purpose of the system is to facilitate trade and to enable the public to pay and receive payments across the EAC using any of the five East African currencies. EAPS is currently integrated into the respective RTGSs of Kenya, Uganda, Tanzania, and Rwanda via SWIFT and all their commercial banks are participants.

The benefits attributed to implementing EAPS include: transfer of large value funds in a secure environment, enhanced safety through the use of SWIFT interfaces, increased reliability due to the integration of the EAC country RTGS and reduced cost of transactions since the transactions are charged at local costs.

[16] Burundi is in the process of implementing their local RTGS system and is expected to join EAPS once the system is in place.

More fundamentally, it overcomes the long circuitous routes that intra-EAC payments had to go through European and American bank correspondents.

The number of transactions through this cross-border payments system has been on an upward trend since 'go live' in 2013 which indicates that EAC citizens have embraced this regional payments system to send money within the region.

16.10.2 Implementation of the Regional Payment and Settlement System (REPSS)

Kenya further joined the Common Market for East and South Africa (COMESA) Regional Payment and Settlement System (REPSS) in November 2014. REPSS is a multilateral netting system managed by the Common Market for Eastern and Southern Africa (COMESA) Clearing House situated in Zimbabwe. The project commenced in 1997 after approval was received from Bureau of Governors in Harare in November 2002 and started operations on 3 October 2012, with the Bank of Mauritius as the settlement bank. Kenya went live on 14 November 2014.

Over the three and half-year period to April 2018, the value of transactions processed through REPSS reached nearly USD. 43.7 million and €1 million, with the Central Bank of Kenya accounting for 91 per cent of the total value of USD transactions while the Bank of Uganda accounted for 81 per cent of the value of Euro transactions. Other Central Banks actively using the system include National Bank of Rwanda, Central Bank of Egypt, Bank of Mauritius, and Reserve Bank of Malawi.

In Table 16.3 and Figure 16.8 the growth of the volume of transaction is correlated with the value of transactions using the USD transactions, for purposes of illustration. The trend of transactions is growing. The growth rate for the period between July and December 2015 was the highest compared with other periods. This was the period of growth for REPSS as the countries that joined the system (Kenya, Uganda, Mauritius, and Rwanda) were eager to push transactions through the system. The Central Bank of Kenya, as the main user of the system, made payments to Bank of Mauritius totalling USD 5.7 million to fund its settlement account at Bank of Mauritius in order to support Kenyan banks funding imports from Uganda, Mauritius, and Rwanda.

Table 16.3 REPSS transactions (in USD), 2014–18

	Dec. 2014	June 2015	Dec. 2015	June 2016	Dec. 2016	June 2017	Dec. 2017	Apr. 2018
Value (US$ M)	327	1,690	8,648	2,384	3,587	4,190	10,105	12,710
Volume	11	54	235	70	83	101	170	209

Source: Central Bank of Kenya, 2018.

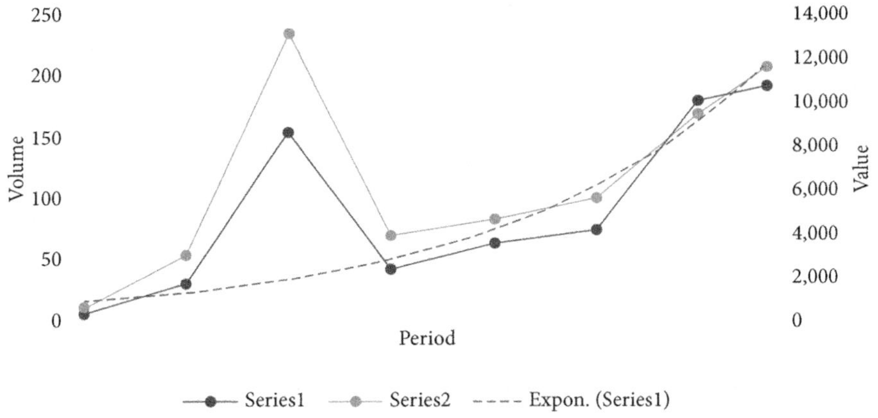

Figure 16.8 REPSS transactions (in USD) 2014–18
Source: Central Bank of Kenya, 2018.

The REPSS system eliminated the need for each commercial bank to use off-shore correspondent banks for inter-country settlements among COMESA member Central Banks in US Dollars. It adopted a multilateral netting system that converts all payments in local currencies to a 'settlement currency' based on a fixed daily rate for transfers among the member-countries, which make or receive US dollar and Euro payments in the region with same-day value. The purpose of the system is to facilitate trade among the 19 member states in the COMESA region. However, only five of the 19 COMESA member-countries are currently linked to the system. REPSS is in its nascent stage but holds great promise to support trade in the COMESA region.

16.11 Laying the Legal and Regulatory Payments System Rails

Safe and effective financial market infrastructures support a regulators' objective of ensuring financial stability while encouraging innovation. Enabling and sound financial market infrastructures also require appropriate regulation, supervision, and oversight. Regulatory authorities should, therefore, adopt relevant regulations and apply them appropriately. Cooperation with other regulatory authorities is also crucial for central banks, in undertaking these tasks (BIS, 2005).

In discharging its role and responsibilities, the CBK has taken positive steps in formulating appropriate laws and regulations for the payment systems, working closely with stakeholders to promote a sound financial system. This collaborative environment has grown the potential of Kenya as a global payments innovator and shows the strong desire of the CBK to work with market participants to improve the payments market in Kenya (CBK, 2018).

The legal framework for the National Payments System in Kenya vests in the CBK the responsibility to oversee the country's payment systems (CBK, 2018). The discharge of this function is guided by various legal tools which include:

- The Central Bank of Kenya Act, which was amended to include Section 4 A (i)d mandating the CBK to formulate and implement such policies as to best promote the establishment, regulation, and supervision of efficient, effective payment, clearing, and settlement systems. This mandate requires the CBK to provide regulatory oversight over the country's National Payments System (CBK, 2015).
- Subsequently, the Central Bank developed laws and regulations to guide the conduct and operations of Payment Service Providers.
- The National Payment System (NPS) Act, which was assented into law in 2011. It provided a comprehensive legal framework for National Payment Systems in Kenya. This Act of Parliament specifically provided for the regulation and supervision of payment systems and payment service providers.
- National Payment System Regulations, which were gazetted in August 2014 to operationalize the NPS Act. The Regulations empower the Central Bank of Kenya to issue guidelines for the better carrying into effect the provision of the Act and were issued under Section 31 of the NPS Act, 2011.

In line with the emerging developments and innovation taking place globally in the payment industry, the CBK continuously holds consultations with the stakeholders towards the development of a responsive regulatory framework. Such a framework supports payment system initiatives that enhance financial inclusion, interoperability, and security of the payment systems in the country.

Besides setting up an appropriate oversight framework for the existing and new systems and enhancing the data reporting mechanisms, various standards adopted vis-à-vis the existing international standards/best practices will be assessed to strengthen the effectiveness of oversight mechanisms. In this context, boosting the resilience of the Financial Market Infrastructures (FMIs) and the System-Wide Important Payment System (SWIPS) in the country is very significant. The CBK oversight focus is on all systems that are likely to be exposed to systemic risk such as RTGS–KEPSS system and also SWIPS, such as the ACH and M-PESA system.

16.12 Other Innovations Riding on the Payments Platform

There are several number of banking sector innovations also riding on the payment platforms.

16.12.1 The Agent Banking Model

In the 1990s, Kenya's banking sector began to experience a slowdown in the expansion of brick and mortar branches. This impacted the reach of the banking sector to the Kenyan populace. The under-banked and unbanked Kenyans were not inclined to access banking services as they perceived them to be rather 'elitist', targeting the more sophisticated and employed segments of the population. The CBK thus sought to develop expansive and more customer friendly, convenient and lower cost delivery channels for Kenyan consumers.

The Guidelines allow commercial banks and microfinance banks to partner with third-party enterprises (undertaking a legally recognized business activity) to offer specified banking services on their behalf. The agent banking model, which leveraged on digitally enabled channels, has enabled commercial and microfinance banks to expand their reach to areas they would otherwise have not, due to such limitations as the viability of establishing a brick and mortar branch, establishment costs, and lack of infrastructure. Agent banking also takes banking services to the convenience of consumers who can now save on transport costs and time taken to visit bank outlets. It also ensures greater efficiency in the delivery of financial services (CBK, 2010).

Since the rollout of agent banking in 2010, 18 commercial banks and five microfinance banks (MFBs) had contracted 61,290 and 2203 agents respectively. These agents have managed over 162 billion transactions (cumulatively from 2010 to December 2017) worth over KShs. 3.3 trillion (USD 32.04 billion) over the same period. Figure 16.9 illustrates the growth over this period.

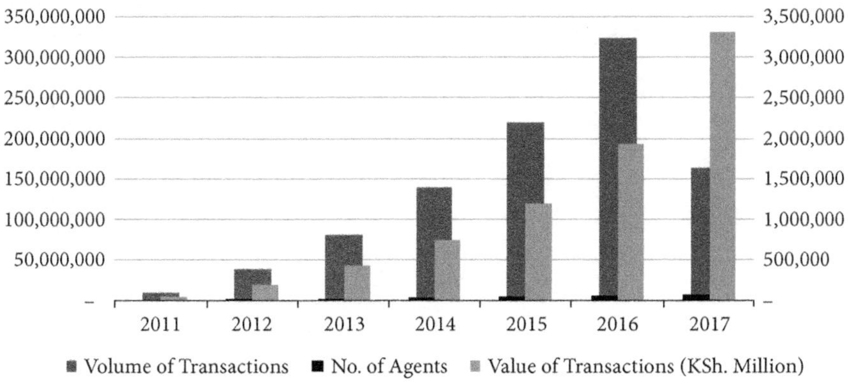

Figure 16.9 Growth of agent banking business
Source: Central Bank of Kenya, 2018.

16.12.2 Expanding Access to Credit Using Alternative Collateral Technology

Prior to 2010, Kenyan banks were faced by the dual problems of information asymmetry and huge search costs as they appraised credit applications. These problems arose as banks were not sharing credit histories of their customers among themselves. The problem with this is that high-risk premiums were placed on consumers, consequently increasing their cost of credit. The development of Credit Reference Bureau Regulations in 2008 and licensing of credit reference bureaus from 2010 thus provided an opportunity for individuals and businesses to rely on good credit history as an alternative form of collateral, to secure cheaper credit facilities from banks. This was especially useful for those who were locked out of the formal financial system for lacking traditional physical collateral (CBK, 2018).

The Credit Information Sharing Mechanism (CIS) requires banks to share both positive and negative credit information through licensed credit reference bureaus (CRBs). Other than enabling banks to enhance the soundness of their credit appraisals based on the readily available credit histories, the CIS mechanism also enables the borrowing public to negotiate for better credit terms and conditions based on their good credit histories. The borrowers are also able to use their good credit history as information collateral, including transactional data on their mobile phones, which serves as a substitute for physical collateral. In order for the CIS mechanism to achieve the optimum desired benefits, efforts are on-going to bring on board all credit providers to ensure that the borrowers' credit histories are sufficiently comprehensive; reflecting all their borrowing history.

As of December 2017, three credit reference bureaus (CRBs) had been licensed by the CBK to collate credit histories and avail credit reports to the lenders. Since the introduction of the credit information sharing mechanism in July 2010, a cumulative number of credit reports requested by commercial banks and microfinance banks from the three CRBs as of December 2017 was 19.6 million while those requested by customers were over 355,000 (CBK, 2018). Figure 16.10 shows this growth trajectory.

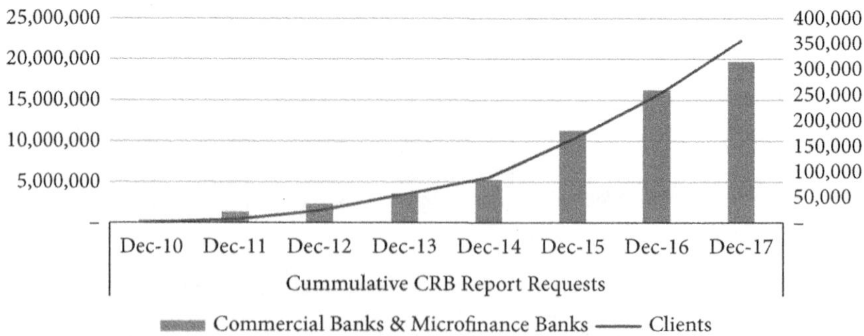

Figure 16.10 CRB reporting trajectory
Source: Central Bank of Kenya, 2018.

16.13 Outcomes of the Payments and Related Banking Sector Innovations

The payments and banking system innovations and initiatives have contributed to the expansive delivery of innovative and inclusive finance. These have had a great impact on enhancing the efficiency of the payment and banking systems. Consequently, they have promoted financial inclusion efforts which have contributed to the socio-economic development of the Kenyan citizenry at different levels. Some of the key outcomes are highlighted below.

16.13.1 Increasing Level of Financial Access in Kenya

There has been an increase in the level of financial inclusion through formal financial institutions, while the population with access to informal financial services, as well as those excluded from any financial services, has decreased. The impact of financial service provision is being felt more, in terms of reach and depth, and with regard to expanding the supply of affordable and appropriate financial services and products to more Kenyans, including the poor.

Overall, 75.3 per cent of Kenyans are now formally included from 26.7 per cent in 2006; an over 50 per cent increase in the last ten years. These developments are highlighted in Figure 16.11.

There has been increased demand for:

- Payments—consumers are increasingly accessing financial services that are instantaneous, secure, reliable, and accessible from anywhere and at any time.
- Credit—consumers are increasingly able to access digital credit through integrated payments and banking platforms.

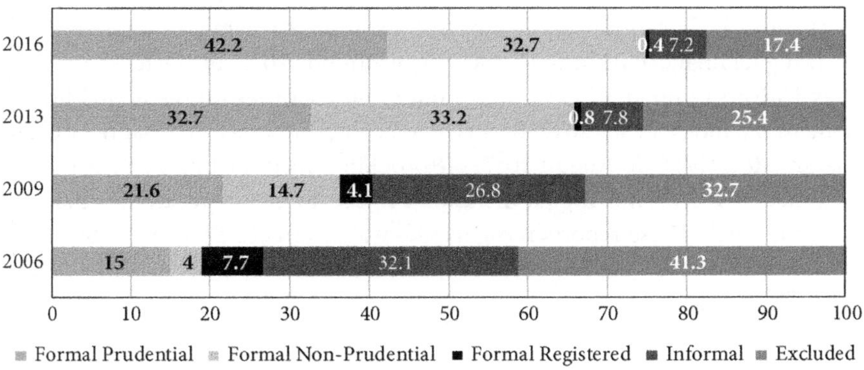

Figure 16.11 Increased access to financial services

Source: FinAccess reports, 2006, 2009, 2013, 2016.

- Insurance—Digital finance is increasingly making the provision of micro-insurance possible.
- And other financial services such as capital markets and pensions products accessed through digital platforms.

16.13.2 Increased Supply of Financial Services to Majority of Kenyans

There has also been an increase in the number of financial access service points reaching larger segments of the Kenyan populace. A GIS Spatial Mapping of financial access touch points in Kenya was conducted in 2015 to digitally map out the financial access touch points in the country. It established that financial services access touch points per 100,000 people had increased in 2015 to 218 compared to 161.7 in 2013.

The percentage of the population living within a 3 kilometre distance of a financial services access touch point was 73 per cent in 2015 compared to 58.7 per cent in 2013 and 86 per cent of the population was within 5 kilometres of a mobile money agent (Taylor, 2015).[17] Further, it showed that 60 per cent and 73 per cent of the population accessed bank and mobile money agents in 2015, respectively, compared to 53 per cent and 69 per cent, in 2015, respectively. Figure 16.12 provides an illustration of the changes.

Although there are great gains that have been reached in expanding access to financial services, it is noted that the greatest beneficiaries in the financial developments have not been the poorest customers but rather clients in the middle and lower middle-class groups. We, however, continue to put efforts into developing even more inclusive financial systems to ensure the poor and low income are served with appropriate financial services.

Kenya's success in financial inclusion has been widely acclaimed, locally, and internationally. For instance, two eminent institutions recently recognized Kenya for its digital financial inclusion achievements. In July 2017, the Fletcher School at Tufts University ranked Kenya fourth out of 60 countries on the digital finance momentum index in its 2017 Digital Planet Report (Bhaskar Chakravorti and Chaturvedi, 2017).[18] In August 2017, the Brookings Institute ranked Kenya first in its annual Financial and Digital Inclusion Project (FDIP) scorecard, for the third year in a row.[19] These reports recognize Kenya's efforts to develop robust policy environments and regulatory infrastructure for the development of digital finance (Lewis et al, 2017).

[17] FinAccess Geospatial Mapping Survey, FSD Kenya, 2015.
[18] https://sites.tufts.edu/digitalplanet/files/2017/05/Digital_Planet_2017_FINAL.pdf
[19] https://www.brookings.edu/wp-content/uploads/2017/08/fdip_20170831_project_report.pdf

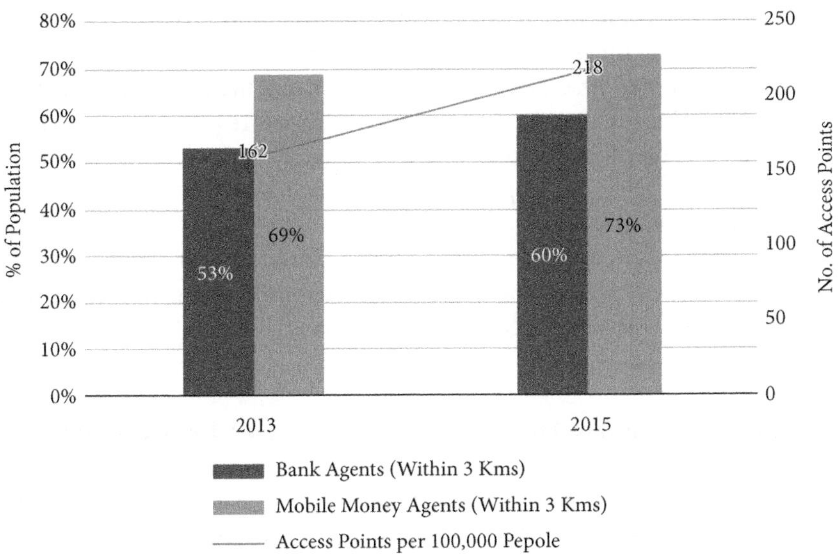

Figure 16.12 Increased access points
Source: FinAccess Geospatial Mapping Survey, 2013 and 2015.

16.14 Lessons from the Transformative Payments Journey?

Innovative technology has played a critical role in enhancing efficient and effective payment and settlement systems. There are clear lessons to be learnt from the journey towards modernizing the payment systems. We learnt that:

- Regulators must proactively seek to understand emerging innovations, potential risks and how to regulate them. This way they are able to carefully consider new approaches to regulating technology and ensure the necessary safeguards are applied to mitigate the potential risks of innovative financial models and solutions without stifling them.
- Kenya's financial sector embraced technological innovations through a test and learn approach. This approach enables innovations to take place while ensuring sufficient risk safeguards. It works hand in hand with the use of appropriate and proportionate regulation as opposed to stringent and more regulation. Close monitoring and supervision are also being applied to every new innovation to ensure that the stability and integrity of the financial system are maintained at all times. This approach has helped spur various innovations and notable developments within the digital financial services ecosystem.
- Some of Kenya's innovations were successfully implemented on the basis of the lessons learnt from other countries. We have learnt the importance of

learning from others rather than reinventing the wheel. We have also learnt that there were times we needed to be brave enough to blaze the trail and be the one that tried first, made mistakes, and shared these lessons with others.
- Realizing the full potential of inclusive finance requires innovative and proactive leadership, coordination, and sustained effort from governments, the private sector, development partners, and even consumers. Working together achieves much.
- Banking and payment services providers must seek to adopt customer-centric business models; with products, channels, and above all, pricing, informed by customers' needs, preferences, and affordability.

16.15 There Are However Risks That Must be Mitigated

All innovative developments are not without risks. There are emerging concerns that increased access to innovative and transformative payments instruments and financial products bring in new emerging risks, which if not well mitigated and managed, may pose vulnerabilities to the financial system. The payment systems can be exposed to a wide range of risks including and not limited to legal risk, credit risk, liquidity risk, cyber risk, and operational risk that may have implications on the financial infrastructure. Some of the key risks noted as payments systems evolve are:

- *Cybercrime and cyber-attacks* continue to be a concern with the increased use of innovative technologies and increased financial sector interconnectivity. In the payments arena, there has been an increase of cyber-attacks, with 54 per cent of global fraud in payment systems attributable to 'card-not-present' transactions such as those facilitated by mobile money platforms[20]. Regulators must be proactive in identifying and addressing these risks.
- *Credit risks:* While digital credit channels expand inclusion by reducing borrowing constraints, research has shown that financial stability risks increase when access to credit is expanded without proper supervision. For example, Dabla-Norris[21] (2015) shows that higher access to credit could raise non-performing loans in credit providers such as banks, thus demonstrating a trade-off between inclusion and stability. Therefore, as more and more people gain access to financial services for the first time, many using digital platforms, it is important that we remain cautious and ensure that we protect

[20] See relevant discussion in Sarma and Efenure (2017) and some useful references therein.

[21] See also the identification of constraints to financial inclusion and their implications for economic welfare in Dabla-Norris et al. (2015).

consumers, mitigate emerging risks, and do not endanger the stability of the financial system.

- *Anti-Money Laundering/Combatting Financing of Terrorism (AML/CFT) risks:* As the size and systemic relevance of Fintechs increases, it becomes a viable conduit to channel proceeds of crime and terror finances. Given the increasing volumes of payments, there will be an increasing need to understand the extent of AML/CFT risks and mitigate them proportionally. A National Risk Assessment for AML/CFT thus becomes a critical aspect of understanding these risks.
- *Operational risks like fraud,* which is increasingly becoming a widespread global problem. Although it is a concept that is generally understood, the characteristics of fraud are often not recognized until it is too late. Regulators will need to remain vigilant on the various forms of fraud infiltrating financial systems.
- *Financial stability concerns:* As payments systems introduce innovative products and infrastructure and platforms, this opens a gateway for more technology-based, unregulated or less-regulated non-bank players to enter into the formal financial sector. This increases the threat of regulatory arbitrage by non-banks operating within the formal financial sector. The impact on the safety and soundness of existing regulated institutions as well as likely disruptions to systemically important markets must also be taken into consideration.
- *Vulnerability of the poor consumers to the financial system:* As innovative finance takes its place on the dais of finance; poor first-time consumers may not be aware of the complexities of the new financial systems or their consumer rights. Financial service providers may not accord them fair treatment and quality service to meet their needs. It is important that they are empowered with knowledge to abate these challenges.

16.16 The Way Forward

As technologies, innovations, economic, and public policy continue to change, it is inevitable that the payment system and the existing regulatory frameworks shall continue to evolve. The CBK will ensure that this is line with its mandate to safeguard the stability, integrity, and safety of the Kenyan payment system as entrusted.

Dynamic, sophisticated, and persistent risks such as cybersecurity and money laundering will require the CBK to remain adaptive, innovative, and vigilant. The CBK is committed towards the provision of a safer, secure, and more efficient payment system in compliance with the National Payment System Act (2011), and its attendant Regulations (2014), as well as global best practices.

Cognizant of the above opportunities and challenges presented by technological innovations (Fintech) and in pursuit of the Bank's vision of being a modern, world-class Central Bank, the CBK, in collaboration with the payment industry stakeholders, has embarked on the development of a National Payment System Framework and Strategy Document.

The NPS Strategy document overarching vision is aligning the National Payment System to support a twenty-first-century economy in line with Vision 2030. Among the flagship projects under the current Third Medium Term Plan 2018–22 (MTP III) of Vision 2030, is Digital Finance. This is a major cross-government initiative to create a 'digital money grid' as a form of national infrastructure that will unleash a new wave of innovation to provide financial solutions across all parts of the economy. Multiple layers will be required to create the required functionality including building upon existing digital identity cards and passports, real-time money transfer, cash conversion, and payment interfaces and applications.

The NPS Strategy will also focus on other key areas such as the enabling legal and regulatory framework, market structure and competition, governance and risk management, and market conduct among others. The future envisaged NPS will promote competition and innovation, respond to customer demands and competitive pressures, allow full interoperability of payment systems, and increase flexibility, security, and adaptability.

References

Alliance for Financial Inclusion (2010), 'Case study: Enabling mobile money transfer the Central Bank of Kenya's Treatment of Mpesa'. Retrieved from https://www.afi-global.org/sites/default/files/publications/afi_casestudy_mpesa_en.pdf.

Alliance for Financial Inclusion (2016),. 'Digital financial services basic terminology, Guideline Note No. 19'. Retrieved from https://www.afi-global.org/sites/default/files/publications/2016-08/Guideline%20Note-19%20DFS-Terminology.pdf.

Bangko Sentral ng Pilipina (2005), Circular 471. Retrieved from http://www.bsp.gov.ph, January 2005.

Bank for International Settlements (2005), 'Central bank oversight of payment and settlement systems'. Retrieved from https://www.bis.org/cpmi/publ/d68.pdf.

Bank for International Settlements (2016),. 'Committee on payment and settlement systems: A glossary of terms used in payments and settlement systems'. Retrieved from https://www.bis.org/cpmi/publ/d00b.htm?&selection=24&scope=CPMI&c=a&base=term

Bhaskar Chakravorti, B. and Chaturvedi, R. S. (2017), 'Digital planet 2017: How competitiveness and trust in digital economies vary across the world'. Retrieved from https://sites.tufts.edu/digitalplanet/files/2017/05/Digital_Planet_2017_FINAL.pdf. Boston, USA. The Fletcher School, Tufts University.

Central Bank of Kenya and FSD Kenya (2009), *FinAccess National Survey 2009: Dynamics of Kenya's Changing Financial Landscape*. Nairobi, Kenya: FSD Kenya.

Central Bank of Kenya (2010), Bank Supervision Annual Report 2010. Retrieved from https://www.centralbank.go.ke/images/docs/Bank%20Supervision%20Reports/Annual%20Reports/bsd2010(2).pdf . Nairobi, Kenya.

Central Bank of Kenya, Kenya National Bureau of Statistics, and FSD Kenya (2016), *The 2016 FinAccess Household Survey on Financial Inclusion*. Nairobi, Kenya: FSD Kenya.

Central Bank of Kenya (2013), Speech by Professor Njuguna Ndungu, 'The announcement of the T+1 cheque clearing cycle'. Retrieved from https://www.centralbank.go.ke/images/docs/speeches/2013/New%20Cheque%20%20Clearing%20Cycle.pdf.

Central Bank of Kenya (2015), 'Act title: The Central Bank of Kenya Act Chapter 491'. Retrieved from https://www.centralbank.go.ke/wp-content/uploads/2016/08/CBKAct1stOct2015.pdf. Nairobi, Kenya.

Central Bank of Kenya (2017), Bank Supervision Annual Report 2017. Retrieved from https://www.centralbank.go.ke/uploads/banking_sector_annual_reports/873911276_2017%20Annual%20Report.pdf . Nairobi, Kenya.

Central Bank of Kenya (2018), 'Bank history'. Retrieved from https://www.centralbank.go.ke/bank-history/. Nairobi, Kenya.

Central Bank of Kenya (2016), Circular: 'Value capping: The issues'. Retrieved from https://www.centralbank.go.ke/wp-content/uploads/2016/08/Value_capping.pdf. Nairobi, Kenya.

Central Bank of Kenya (2018), 'National Payment System'. Retrieved in 2018 from https://www.centralbank.go.ke/national-payments-system/. Nairobi, Kenya.

Communications Authority Sector Statistics Reports (2017). Retrieved from https://ca.go.ke/wp-content/uploads/2018/02/Sector-Statistics-Report-Q1-2017-18.pdf. Nairobi, Kenya.

Dabla-Norris, E., Ji, Y., Townsend, R., and Unsal, D. U. (2015), 'Identifying constraints to financial inclusion and their impact on GDP and inequality: A structural framework for policy'. IMF Working Paper. Washington, DC.

Government of Kenya (2017), 'Act title: Bills of exchange: An Act of Parliament relating to bills of exchange, cheques and promissory notes'. Retrieved from http://www.kenyalaw.org/lex/actview.xql?actid=CAP.%2027, Nairobi, Kenya.

IhuB (2014), 'Review of Kenya's move to EMV credit cards'. Retrieved from https://ihub.co.ke/blogs/20279/review-of-kenya-s-move-to-emv-credit-cards

Kenya FinAccess 2016/i2i Data Portal/FinScope SA 2015/EFInA Nigeria 2014/FinScope Mauritius 2014.

Lewis, R. J., Villasenor, J. D. and West, D. M. (2017), 'The 2017 Brookings Financial and Digital Inclusion Project Report: Building a secure and inclusive global financial ecosystem'. Retrieved from https://www.Brookings.Edu/Wp-Content/Uploads/2017/08/Fdip_20170831_Project_Report.Pdf. Washington DC, USA. Brookings Institute.

Lovegrove, A. (2006), *Financial sector integration in Sub-Saharan Africa: How Creating Scale in Financial Markets Support Growth and Development.* Washington, DC, USA: World Bank.

McKinsey & Company (2016), *Digital Finance for All: Powering Inclusive Growth in Emerging Economies.* New York: McKinsey Global Institute.

Porteous, D. (2006), *The Enabling Environment for Mobile Banking in Africa, Report Commissioned by Department for International Development.* Boston, USA: Bankable Frontiers Associates.

Sarma, V. and Efenure, E. (2017), *Safety and Security Briefing Presentation for Central Bank of Kenya on Card Payments.* Nairobi, Kenya: MasterCard.

Taylor, D. (2015), *FinAccess Geospatial Mapping Survey: Analysis and Use Cases.* Nairobi, Kenya: FSD Kenya.

The Steadman Group Research Division (2007), *Financial Access in Kenya: Results of the 2006 National Survey.* Nairobi, Kenya: FSD Kenya.

17

Development of the Government Securities Market in Kenya

Leonard Thotho, Caroline Wanjiku, and Daniel Amanja

17.1 Background

This chapter evaluates developments in the domestic Government securities market in Kenya during the period 1966–2016, a 50-year period since the Central Bank of Kenya (CBK) was established. A well-functioning domestic government securities market is not only a key determinant of a country's economic growth but also acts as a ready fall back for the government to meet its budget financing needs at optimal cost and risk. It promotes a strong market-oriented economy with a robust financial system which is resilient to external shocks. Governments that do not support deliberate measures to boost liquidity and efficiency of the domestic capital market risk overdependence on external sources of financing which is subject to exchange rate vulnerabilities and stringent lending conditionalities.

Therefore, the need for a developed domestic government securities market cannot be overemphasized. The market helps governments to meet growing financing needs. Most countries in Africa have been experiencing increased development financing needs (in addition to growing recurrent expenditure), as they seek to expand key economic sectors, social infrastructure, and stimulate economic activity (Bhattacharyay, 2011).

Overreliance on external financing sources reduces a country's independence in the management of public finance and financing needs. Foreign sources of finance attach stringent conditions and unfavourable covenants affecting sovereignty of countries. There is a double mismatch risk, in terms of currency risk when value of foreign currency in which the debt is denominated appreciates, and refinancing risk associated with the maturity of the loans. Short maturity loans are riskier to the borrowing government as obligations are due sooner than later (Christensen, 2005). In an open economy, foreign financing sources increase vulnerability to external or global shocks significantly reducing a country's resilience.

The cost and risk of Government borrowing in the domestic market are largely reduced as the market develops and demand for securities increases. Short maturities of bonds increase refinancing risk to the issuer (Yibin, Phelps, and

Leonard Thotho, Caroline Wanjiku, and Daniel Amanja, *Development of the Government Securities Market in Kenya* In: *50 Years of Central Banking in Kenya: Regional and Global Perspectives.* Edited by: Patrick Njoroge and Victor Murinde, Oxford University Press (2021). © The Central Bank of Kenya. DOI: 10.1093/oso/9780198851820.003.0017

Table 17.1 Kenya's national debt, 1970–2016

	1970	1980	1990	2000	2010	2011	2012	2013	2014	2015	2016
Domestic debt (% GDP)	0.23	0.39	8.19	3.70	21.77	22.29	21.29	23.34	25.29	24.38	27.04
External debt (% GDP)	14.25	19.17	34.80	41.34	18.64	21.22	18.95	18.74	21.38	24.40	26.80
Total public debt (% GDP)	14.48	19.56	42.98	45.03	40.41	43.51	40.25	42.08	46.66	48.78	53.S4

Source: KNBS, Statistical Bulletin, various publications.

Stotsky, 2013). A liquid bond market is competitive and offers lower prices for securities informed by market fundamentals, thus creating investor confidence.

Government reliance on banking sector financing is reduced as markets develop and investor base is diversified. Where a government depends too much on bank finance as a captive financing source there will be increased borrowing costs and risks as banks exploit the government by overpricing the securities. Most commercial banks in Africa are affiliates of foreign parent banks thus exposing the financial sector to global market swings resulting from market sentiments and negative risk perception by foreign investors (Thupayagale, 2015). In addition, financial crisis or bank failures may largely impact on government financing needs as banks' financial capabilities are limited.

As can be seen in Table 17.1, domestic debt issuance was very low in the first three decades of Independence rising from 0.23 and 0.38 per cent of GDP in 1970 and 1980 to 21.8 per cent of GDP in 2010 before peaking at 27 per cent in 2016 reflecting the growing importance of domestic primary market for government securities. On the other hand, external debt has been relatively stable accounting for 14.3 and 19.2 per cent of GDP in 1970 and 1980, respectively, increasing to 26.8 per cent in 2016 (Kenya National Bureau of Statistics, Economic Survey (various years)).

A developed domestic Government debt market provides a benchmark for risk free investment and the corporate market. Government bond investment is regarded as risk free and is the basis on which other products are priced with a liquidity and credit risk premium (World Bank, 2007). To improve liquidity and efficiency of the domestic Government bond markets, specific market development reforms have been under implementation in Kenya with the aim of eliminating structural and operational inefficiencies through competition and increasing demand for securities.

Assessment of the development of the domestic Government securities market in Kenya in this chapter focuses on the domestic debt and domestic government securities market. Domestic debt dynamics include: (a) developments in the fiscal policy framework, (b) legal framework for public debt management, (c) the Medium-Term Debt Strategy (MTDS), (d) the Debt Sustainability analysis (DSA), and (e) trends in public domestic debt. Domestic government securities market dynamics covers trends and developments at the primary and secondary markets for government securities. In addition, a future outlook on the trends and reforms described above is provided.

In studying developments during the period from 1966 to 2016, the chapter focuses on times when key reforms for public debt management and market development were muted and begun to be implemented. We observe that the domestic government securities market in Kenya was largely shallow and under-developed during the period from 1966 to 2000. Deliberate reforms to develop the market were first put in place in 2001 when the restructuring of the domestic public debt began to be undertaken to reduce the share of Treasury bills in favour of Treasury bonds. The implementation of key market development initiatives such as the benchmark bond programme and automation of market infrastructure and operations were started in 2007. Throughout this chapter, we shall refer to the period between 2001 and 2007 as the pre-reform period while the period from 2008 to 2016 will be the post-reform period, where we attempt to assess the outcomes of reforms aimed at developing the domestic government securities market. The rest of the chapter is organized as follows: Section 17.2 outlines the legal and regulatory framework for government securities. This is followed in Section 17.3 by a discussion on institutional arrangements for government securities in Kenya. Issuance policy, strategy, and debt management framework, developments in the primary and secondary markets for government securities are covered in Sections 17.4, 17.5, and 17.6 in that order. Sections 17.7 and 17.8 end the chapter by discussing milestones and outlook for the government securities markets, respectively.

17.2 Legal and Regulatory Framework for Government Securities Market

A proper functioning and efficient securities market must operate within a legal and regulatory framework. In Kenya, this has been guided by the internal and external loans Acts, the Public Finance Management Act, and the Central Bank Act. To reflect the dynamic nature of a liberalized market, these legal statutes have undergone amendments over the years. In this section, we focus on key statutes which have regulated securities market in Kenya for the last 50 years. These include the Internal Loans Act, External Loans Act, Credit Act and National Government Loans Guarantee Act, Public Finance Management Act and the Central Bank of Kenya Act.

17.2.1 Internal Loans Act

The first legislation governing the issuance of debt securities was the Central Bank of Kenya Act. On 1 July 1968, the Central Bank was mandated to officially administer government debt in line with the Central Bank of Kenya Act. This mandate entailed maintenance of the Government securities register including details of investors, transfer of ownership of securities, payment of interest and redemption of securities and assisting in management of the sinking fund. The overall National debt policy remained in the custody of the National Treasury (Ministry of Finance) but the terms of issuance of new stock such as amount, price, interest rate, redemption date, and commissions was carried out in consultations with the Central Bank.

In 1979, the Internal Loans Act came into force to complement other pre-existing legislation on management of public debt (Republic of Kenya, 1979). This Act was amended in 2009 with some sections and subsections repealed in 1994 and 2007. The Act guided the undertaking of borrowing in domestic currency through the issuance of government securities. The Act recognized government securities as valid and binding to the government, and registered in the register as a debt security. The Act also provided a reporting framework for government securities, payment of expenses incurred in the issuance securities, and payment of the principal and interest on government securities. The registrar of Government securities was responsible for establishing and maintaining a domestic debt register. The Internal Loans Act also provided for secondary trading of government securities by permitting the minister for finance to impose conditions on the price and the interest rate of government securities, the form and denominations in which the government securities are issued or transferred, and the time and place of the repayment of principal and interest.

17.2.2 Public Finance Management Act (PFMA)

The Public Finance Management Act (PFMA) of 2012 consolidated all the pre-existing laws on public debt management. The law provides the legal basis for issuance of local and external government securities and loans and the basis of government guarantees to public entities. The PFM Act repealed the Internal Loans Act, External Loans Act, Credit Act, and National Government Loans Guarantee Act. The PFM Act provides for the issuance of securities by the National Government, exemption of National Government securities from stamp duty, establishment of the office of Registrar of National Government securities and issuance of debt securities by county governments. The Public Debt Management Office (PDMO) is established to act as the principal in the issuance and management of national public debt on behalf of the National

Treasury with the role of promoting the development of market institutions for Government debt securities. The Act also provides for secondary trading of National Government securities (Republic of Kenya, 2012).

17.2.3 The Central Bank of Kenya Act and Fiscal Agent Role

The Central Bank Kenya Act defines the fiscal agency role between the Central Bank of Kenya and the National Government. According to the Act, the Bank, shall administer the public debt including the issuance of, payment of a return on, and redemption of, bonds and other securities of the Government. The Act also mandates the Bank to purchase, sell, transfer, or accept for custody of government securities and to collect the proceeds, whether principal or interest, resulting from the sale of securities (Central Bank of Kenya, 2012).

An agency agreement between the National Treasury and the Central Bank as the fiscal agent of the Government guides the working relationship between the two institutions in public debt and cash management operations. Under the mandate as a fiscal agent, the CBK has been managing the Central Depository for Securities (CDS) (or the national debt registry) since January 1997 when it was first set up. The CDS is an electronic book entry system that keeps custody of ownership of Treasury bills and bonds issued by the Government. Before the introduction of the CBK-CDS in 1997, Government securities were issued in paper form. Investors of government securities can open and maintain CDS accounts at the CBK directly or indirectly through authorized agents of the CBK, mainly commercial and investment banks on behalf of their clients. Domestic and foreign investors, retail or institutional, can open and maintain CDS accounts at the CBK provided they have a local commercial bank account.

Trading of government securities takes place at the Nairobi Securities Exchange's system which is linked to the CBK-CDS through the Automated Trading System (ATS). The trading system is interfaced to the real time gross settlement (RTGS) also known as the Kenya Electronic Payment and Settlement System (KEPSS). As securities in the CDS were dematerialised,[1] settlement of cash and delivery of securities takes place on a Delivery versus Payment (DvP) basis with settlement cycle of T+3. Under this system, investors are able to transfer or move securities and use them as collateral (liens) to access credit facilities from banks as well as for Repo and Intraday Liquidity Facility (ILF) transactions. These legal statutes have provided the framework through which trading in government securities has evolved.

[1] Ownership of securities is in electronic holdings maintained in the CDS, eliminating risks associated with physical certificates, reducing the transaction clearing time, easier and faster transfer or sale of securities, and lower cost of issuing new securities.

17.3 Institutional Arrangements for Government Securities Market

The institutional arrangement for the management and development of the government securities market comprises the National Treasury, the Capital Markets Authority (CMA), the Central Depository of Securities Corporation (CDSC), and the Nairobi Securities Exchange (NSE). We briefly discuss the role played by these institutions in the development of the government securities in Kenya.

17.3.1 The National Treasury

The current arrangement in the management of public debt is set out in the PFMA which establishes the National Treasury headed by a Cabinet Secretary (Minister for Finance) responsible for fiscal policy and managing public finances. The authority for borrowing by the National Government is vested on the Cabinet Secretary for Finance who may raise loans on behalf of the National Government, in line with the fiscal responsibility principles and the financial objectives set out in the Budget Policy Statement and the public debt management strategy. The office of the registrar of National Government Securities is established under the Public Debt Management Office.

The PDMO is established within the National Treasury with the mandate of minimizing the cost of public debt management and borrowing over the long-term taking account of risk, promoting the development of the market institutions for Government debt securities and ensuring the sharing of the benefits and costs of public debt between the current and future generations among others. The PDMO is also mandated to assist County Government Treasuries on debt management and borrowing.

17.3.2 The Capital Markets Authority (CMA)

Approval of issuance and listing of Government securities is granted by the CMA which was established under the Capital Markets Act. The Capital Markets Act mandates the CMA to promote, regulate, and facilitate the development of an orderly, fair, and efficient capital market in Kenya (Capital Markets Authority, 2012).

The need for policy reforms to foster efficiency and stability of the financial system for sustainable economic development was conceived in the 1980s, with particular focus on enhancing the role of the private sector in economic development and rationalizing public sector operations to promote the development of the capital market and provide access to long-term finance.

In 1984, the Central Bank and the International Finance Corporation (IFC) conducted a joint study on the Development of Money and Capital Markets in Kenya, and provided recommendations on measures to promote active strengthening and development of the financial sector. The 1986 Sessional Paper no. 1 on 'Economic management for renewed growth' supported the creation of a capital markets regulatory body. The Capital Markets Development Advisory Council was set up in November 1988 to draft a bill for establishment of the Capital Markets Authority, among other roles. The bill was passed in November 1989 and the CMA was constituted in January 1990 through the Capital Markets Authority Act (Cap 495A) and inaugurated in March 1990 (Capital Markets Authority, 1990).

Over the years, there has been several changes to the CMA Act to guide the conduct of capital markets, including amendment to allow establishment of a securities exchange (Nairobi Stock Exchange) as a company limited by guarantee under regulation by the CMA. Other changes included new guidelines on the disclosure standards for listed companies introduced in 1998 on public offerings of securities and reporting obligations among others; guidelines to promote good corporate governance practices by listed companies in 1999.

17.3.3 The Central Depository of Securities Corporation (CDSC)

The idea of establishing a Central Depository for non-government securities was mooted in 1995. The Central Depositories Act was passed in 2000 with operations[2] commencing in 2004, with full delivery versus payment (DVP) settlement at the NSE and market education activities begun in 2005. The first major operation for the CDSC that saw the number of CDS accounts shoot up was the KenGen Initial Public Offer (IPO) in 2006. Following the listing of Safaricom Ltd shares, there was a further rise in the number of CDS accounts to 1.7 million from 0.8 million before the IPO. The process of dematerialization of securities begun in 2012 and was finalized in 2013 with shares of listed firms at the NSE converted to electronic form while dematerialization of corporate bonds took place in 2014. Dematerialization has led to increased market liquidity provided a platform for new market development initiatives products such as short selling and securities lending and borrowing (www.cdsckenya.com).

[2] Operations included the process of immobilization of securities—converting shares from physical certificates to electronic form and Delivery Verses Payment (DVP) Settlement.

17.3.4 The Nairobi Securities Exchange (NSE)

In the secondary market, Government bonds are traded at the NSE which was registered under the Societies Act (1954) between 1954 and 1962 as a voluntary association of stockbrokers and charged with the responsibility of developing the securities market and regulating trading activities. The business at the exchange was conducted through telephone and prices determined through negotiation system. The NSE was registered under the Companies Act in 1991 as private company limited by shares and phased out the 'call over' trading system in favour of the floor-based 'Open Outcry System'. Subsequently the stock exchange embarked on an extensive modernization exercise including a modern information centre. With the incorporation of the Central Depository and Settlement Corporation, trading of shares was conducted on an electronic platform contributing to increased turnover.

17.4 Issuance Policy, Strategy and Debt Management Framework

17.4.1 Government Borrowing Strategy (Medium Term Debt Strategy—MTDS)

Kenya's MTDS is a plan aimed at achieving the desired debt portfolio and is prepared utilizing a set of analytical tools and procedures in accordance with international best practice. The type of borrowing and the attendant risks or shocks that may impact on the government's ability to meet its debt obligations are taken into account. The MTDS therefore enhances the Government's commitment to developing and designing a strategy that is evidence based and feasible in ensuring that public debt remains sustainable and support broad-based and inclusive growth which is consistent with Kenya's Constitution and relevant legislation in terms of transparency and accountability.

The Debt Management Strategy is published in accordance with Articles 25 and 33 of the PFM Act which requires the National Treasury to prepare and submit to the Cabinet the Budget Policy Statement (BPS) and Debt Management Strategy by 15 February each year. Thereafter, Parliament discusses the BPS and MTDS within two weeks and the NT publish the same within 15 days. The Cabinet Secretary ensures that the medium-term debt management strategy is aligned to the broad strategic priorities and policy goals set out in the BPS.

In June 2009, the Government published the first official Medium-Term Debt Strategy (2009 MTDS) covering three financial years 2009/10, 2010/11, and 2011/12. The key objectives of the strategy were to minimize refinancing risk by lengthening the maturity of domestic debt and to develop the domestic debt market. The need to minimize foreign exchange rate risk exposure associated with the external debt is an important consideration for the MTDS. The 2009 MTDS envisaged a significant reliance on domestic borrowing to meet the central Government budget financing requirement. Government considered substituting external with domestic sources of financing, this strategy was however to be pursued with caution given the risk of crowding out of private sector (MTDS, 2009).

In 2010, the principal objective of the MTDS was to meet the net financing of the Central Government in the following manner: 25 per cent through official concessional external financing and 75 per cent domestic financing. Domestic borrowing strategy sought to lengthen the maturity profile of domestic debt to 30:70 ratio in Treasury bills to bonds (MTDS, 2010). Treasury bond issues were limited to benchmark bonds with maturities of 2, 5, 10, 15, and 20 years in order to build bond liquidity and accelerate domestic debt market development.

The 2011 MTDS entailed 70 per cent net domestic financing mainly medium-term instruments and 30 per cent external financing while the 2012 MTDS accounted for both cost and risk considerations and the need to develop the domestic debt market. The strategy involved 65 per cent net domestic borrowing, mainly medium-term instruments and 35 per cent net external borrowing to finance the central government budget (MTDS, 2011).

The 2014 strategy assumed that 40 per cent of the gross financing needs would be met by external borrowing, mainly from concessional creditors, and 60 per cent from the domestic market, mainly through medium tenor Treasury bonds to reduce the cost of domestic debt associated with longer dated securities (MTDS, 2014). The 2015 MTDS emphasized financing from non-concessional window limited to projects with high-expected risk-adjusted rates of return including critical infrastructure projects. External and domestic borrowing accounted for 45 per cent and 55 per cent of gross financing needs, respectively (MTDS, 2015).

In terms of forecast, the 2017 MTDS was the ninth MTDS tabled in Parliament and the fourth under the requirement of the PFM Act (2012). The optimal strategy was 60 per cent external borrowing and 40 per cent domestic borrowing and considered both risk and cost trade-offs, the implied quantity of gross borrowing, the need to develop the domestic debt market, the need to diversify the funding sources and ability to implement the strategy over the medium term. Of the 60 per cent allocated to external borrowing, 20 per cent was concessional, 30 per cent semi-concessional, and 10 per cent commercial.

With the coordination and collaboration of all agencies involved, the implementation of the MTDS through the Government Borrowing Programme has been closely monitored. The implementation of the MTDS is closely coordinated with cash management to enable management of liquidity around set targets on a regular basis.

17.4.2 The Public Debt Sustainability Framework (DSF)

Debt sustainability framework (DSF), developed jointly by IMF and World Bank, is an analytical tool used to assess a country's debt burden. It guides borrowers and donors in mobilising financing development needs without compromising recipient countries' future debt-carrying capacities (IMF, 2003). Kenya's debt sustainability is assessed using the Low Income Countries Debt Sustainability Framework (LIC DSF) operationalised in 2005. The framework was revised in 2006 to incorporate implications of debt relief under Multilateral Debt Relief Initiative and reviewed again in 2009 and 2012 to incorporate policy reforms of the Fund facilities and country-specific factors (IMF, 2005, 2006 and 2012).

Debt sustainability is assessed in relation to policy-dependent debt burden thresholds and benchmarks. Kenya was rated a strong policy performer (World Bank, 2015) in terms of quality of policies and institutions as measured by a three-year average score on the World Bank's Country Policy and Institutional Assessment (CPIA) index. The inaugural Debt Sustainability Analysis (DSA) on Kenya's public debt in 2008 showed that Kenya's public debt was sustainable with low risk of debt distress though sensitive to sharp increases in borrowing. Subsequent DSAs (2009, 2011, 2013, 2014 and 2015) made similar conclusions on Kenya's public debt sustainability.

The March 2016 DSA further affirmed that Kenya's public debt was sustainable in the medium term. However, this assessment revealed rising risks to the outlook with near breach scenarios in case of lower exports growth and currency depreciation. The assessment associated with the rising risk to debt distress to the structure of external debt where bunched maturities on Eurobonds could lead to a liquidity pressure and subsequent breaching of the policy dependent thresholds. .

17.4.3 Public Debt Reporting

The requirements for public debt reporting are set out in the PFM Act where every four months, the Cabinet Secretary to the National Treasury submits to Parliament a report of all loans made to the national government, national government entities, and county governments, as well as a record of all guarantees given by the national government, not later than seven days after receiving a request to do so from either House of Parliament—the National Assembly and the Senate. This is in addition to the requirement under the PFMA for the CS National Treasury to submit to Parliament, on or before 15 February each year, a statement setting out the debt management strategy of the national government over the medium term with respect to its actual liability and potential liability in respect of loans and guarantees and its plans for dealing with those liabilities. Every financial year, the National Treasury publishes the Annual Public Debt Report covering immediate preceding financial year's debt management operations as part of public debt reporting.

17.4.4 Domestic Government Borrowing Process

Every financial year, the Government of Kenya through the National Treasury presents the national budget to Parliament in which the level of deficit is defined and how the deficit would be financed. The budget deficit (difference between revenues and expenditures) is financed from both domestic and external sources. Domestic borrowing is financed through issuance of Government securities (Treasury bills and bonds) to institutional and retail investors. This is supplemented by syndicated borrowing arrangements and direct borrowing from banks and the Central Bank. External financing comes from bilateral, multilateral, as well as commercial creditors and consists of different currencies, dominated by the USD. The Central Bank, as the fiscal agent of the Government, manages the domestic debt component of the budget deficit.

The borrowing programme is a plan of realizing the target domestic borrowing amount through issuance and redemption of Government securities and is prepared in line with annual cash plan issued by the National Treasury. The offer amounts on securities are determined by the amount of maturities of Treasury bills and bonds, government cash requirements, and the absorption capacity of the market at the auctions. In recent years, Treasury bills have been issued on a weekly basis and bonds on monthly basis. The main method of issuance of government securities has been the auction system.

Kenya's post-colonial government experienced the first budget deficit in 1968 during the FY 1968/69. The administration of domestic national debt was handed over to the Central Bank of Kenya by the Ministry of Finance (now the National Treasury) in July 1968. The Bank begun with the determination of the terms of issuance of government securities including amount to issue, pricing, rate of interest, features of instruments, commissions earned by authorized agents among others. The Central Bank Act was amended in 1972 to limit government's overdraft facility (previously at KSh 12 million) at 25 per cent of gross revenues received into the exchequer recurrent account, which included all forms of recurrent receipts—taxes, customs, excise, fees, rent, export and other duties, profits and income from any investment or undertaking but would exclude proceeds from grants or loans or any form of borrowing. The key justification for this amendment was the growing size of government and to provide flexibility for the Central Bank to carry out rediscount of the Treasury bills.

17.4.5 Domestic Government Borrowing Programme (GBP)

The Government Borrowing Programme is prepared and implemented every financial year running from July to June during the period under review. The targets for domestic borrowing grew significantly from 2002 as the need for financing in the national budget increased over the years. The performance of the borrowing programme improved gradually as the market evolved and the uptake of government securities at the auctions continued to rise. The increased absorption capacity for government securities by the market had resulted in reasonable pricing and lower cost and risk of borrowing to the government as a result of competition at the auction.

17.5 Developments in the Primary Market for Government Securities

17.5.1 Government Securities Portfolio by Instrument

Figure 17.1 shows the composition of Treasury bills and bonds in the debt portfolio since 1964. Prior to the first issuance of Treasury bills in March 1969, domestic government debt portfolio was dominated by long-term stocks by over 50 per cent up to mid-1980s. In 1994 issuance of long-term stocks was suspended in line with a plan to gradually introduce marketable securities. Treasury bonds were issued with the aim of supporting budgetary financing as well as mop up liquidity in the market (CBK Annual Report, June 1990).

In 1990s, Treasury bills became popular instruments leading to high refinancing risk as a large size of the portfolio was due for refinancing within one year. To minimize the refinancing risk and accommodate investor preferences, the 180 days Treasury bill was introduced but investors still preferred the 91-days over the 180 days Treasury bill. Just as in other Sub-Saharan Africa countries, Kenya undertook restructuring of public debt due to debt crisis experienced in the 1990s. Domestic debt restructuring entailed retiring the existing stock of Treasury bills and conversion into Treasury bonds to lengthen the average maturity of the portfolio and of individual securities (Figure 17.1 and Figure A17.1).

Figures 17.2 show the growth of the stock of government securities from the year 2000. Evidently, the stock increased from KSh 170.98 billion in 2000 to KSh 1,869.5 billion in 2016 (a growth of 993.4 per cent), with increased growth momentum from 2009 to 2016 (289.6 per cent increase), reflecting increased market demand for government securities. The stock of Treasury bonds compared to Treasury bills was highest in 2011 at 85.5 per cent compared to its lowest level of 17.0 per cent in 2001. The growth in stock of Government securities over the

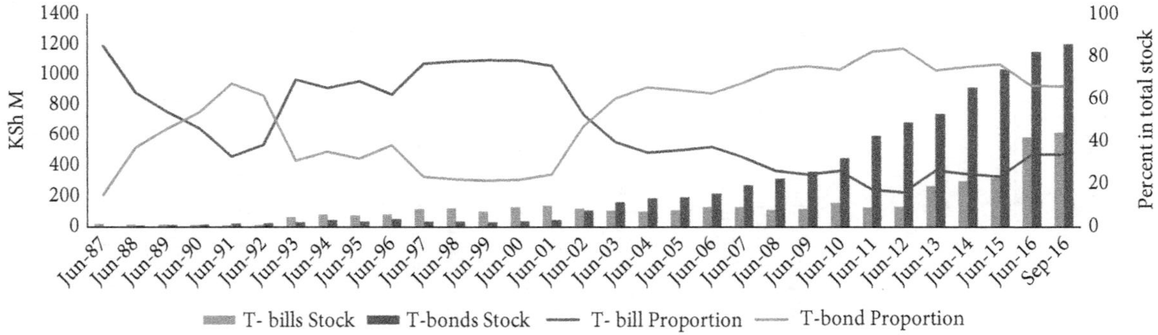

Figure 17.1 Composition of Treasury bills and bonds, 1987–2012

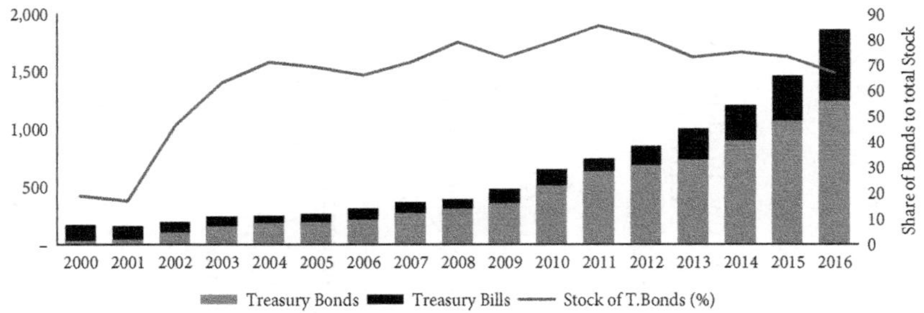

Figure 17.2 Stock of domestic government securities by instrument, 2000–16

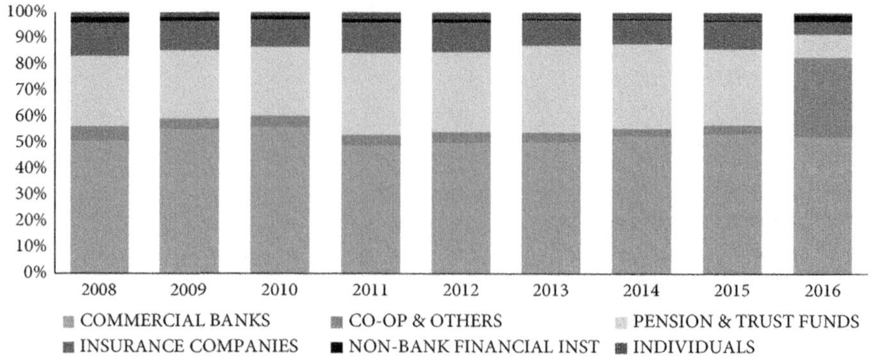

Figure 17.3 Holders of government securities, 2008–16

years was partly due to increased need for government to borrow arising from growing national budgets and deficits, and increased reforms for market development, particularly from the year 2000, enabling greater uptake of securities.

17.5.2 Holders of Government Securities

In terms of holders of government securities during the period 2008–16 which is the post-reform period, commercial banks dominated the stock of Government securities, holding more than 50 per cent while pension or trust fund firms held between 25 per cent and 30 per cent of the portfolio (Figure 17.3).

As reforms for market development continued to be undertaken, the investor base has broadened over the years with the pension and insurance sectors accounting for over 30 per cent and 20 per cent of portfolio holdings, respectively.

17.5.3 Government Securities by Maturity

In May 2001, the Central Bank implemented a debt restructuring programme to reduce the pressure on interest rates arising from frequent rollover of maturing Treasury bills. The borrowing programme concentrated on issuance of fixed and floating rate bonds to increase the proportion of medium- to long-term bonds and reduce dominance of 91-day Treasury bill (Figure 17.1). Consequently, the maturity profile of the domestic debt securities portfolio reversed from 30:70 Treasury bonds to bills back in 2001 to 70:30 Treasury bonds to bills by 2007. The second objective of the restructuring programme was to develop a reliable yield curve to guide pricing of securities and other financial products at the primary and secondary markets.

Average maturity of domestic debt continued to increase (Figures 17.4 and 17.5) following successful issuance of long tenor bonds of maturities of 7, 8, 9, and 10 years in March 2003 (earlier in Figure 17.1). The stock of Treasury bills (including Repo bills) continued to reduce with the zero-coupon Treasury bonds also introduced in 2003. A longer dated portfolio of government securities was also intended to help reduce rollover risk and borrowing costs associated with short-term debt. There was demand for longer dated bonds from pension fund and insurance companies seeking to match their long-term liabilities with bond assets. Arising from increased demand for long term bonds, a debut 20-year bond was issued in June 2008 attracting KSh 7.5 billion out of KSh 15 billion advertised (subscription of 50.26 per cent), with just KSh 1.9 billion accepted at a weighted average yield (WAY) of 14.741 per cent against a coupon rate of 13.750 per cent. This bond has since been reopened four different times netting a total face value of KSh 38.15 billion. In 2007, the benchmark bond programme was established, beginning with the identification of benchmark tenors of 2, 5, 10, 15, and 20 years. The aim of this programme was to create liquidity on benchmark tenors by issuing large volumes and helping to reduce fragmentation of small and illiquid bonds in the secondary market. This initiative was intended to result in more liquid bonds and a reliable and firm benchmark yield curve.

At less than 0.5 years in 2001, average maturity of Government securities increased to more than 2 years by June 2004, dropped slightly to between 1.5 years and 2 years in June 2005 and continued to rise to between 3.5 years to 4 years by June 2009 (Figure 17.4). According to Figure 17.5, average maturity of government securities peaked to 5.75 years by June 2011 but declined steadily to 4.3 years by September 2016, due to unfavourable market conditions such as tight liquidity that led to increased issuance of short-term instruments. Average maturity of bonds alone was highest in 2015 at 7.91 years compared to 7.87 years in 2011, 6.35 years in 2016 and 5.27 years in 2008 when implementation of reforms to lengthen the maturity of the debt portfolio begun to be fast tracked.

The medium-term objective set in the 2016 MTDS and by the market stakeholder forum[3] has been to achieve a bonds portfolio maturity of ten years through issuance of long-term large size bonds under the benchmark bonds programme. Given that average maturity of Government securities had been shortening since 2015, there was potential for higher rollover or refinancing risk going forward and strategies to further lengthen the maturity of the debt needed to be implemented. There was need to consider an optimization of cost and risk as long-term bonds attract higher cost of borrowing but lower refinancing risk while short-term debt

[3] Since 2001, this forum was known as Market Leaders Forum (MLF) until 2015 when it was restructured to the Consultative Forum for Domestic Debt Market (CFDDM) and the Bond Market Stakeholders Forum (BMSF) which are currently chaired by the Governor, CBK and Deputy Governor, CBK respectively.

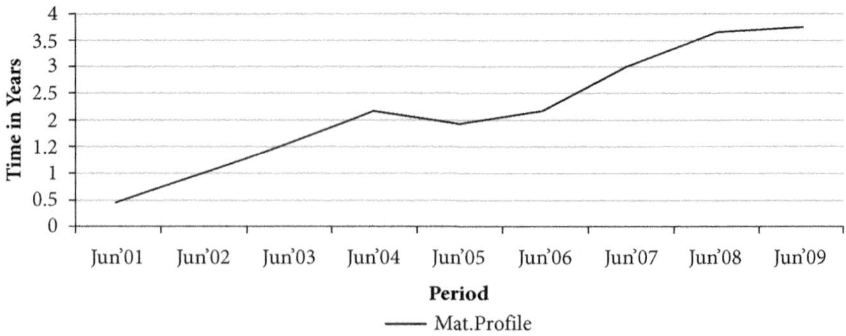

Figure 17.4 Average maturity of government securities, 2001–09

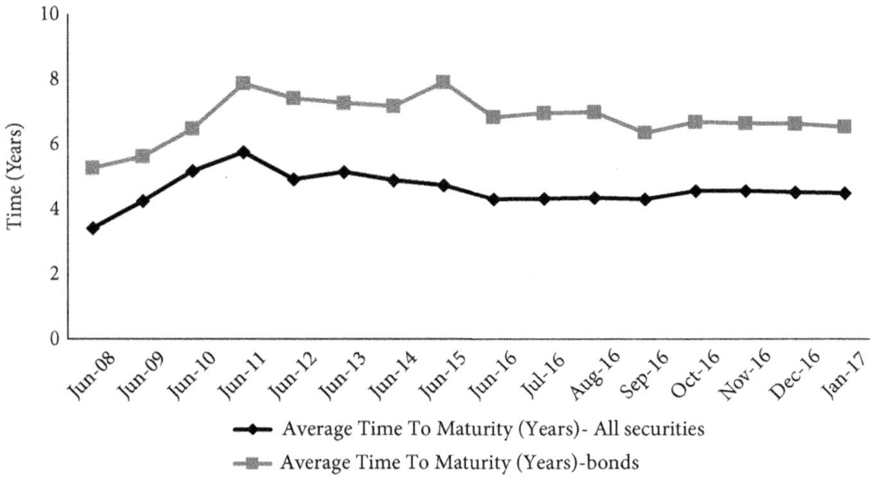

Figure 17.5 Average time to maturity of government securities, June 2008 to January 2017

attracts lower cost and higher refinancing risk. To achieve this, there was need to support market development initiatives that would result in an appropriately priced, firm, and reliable benchmark yield curve, as this would promote liquidity of bonds at the secondary market and translate to lower debt cost resulting from increased demand and better pricing of securities at the primary market.

17.5.4 Treasury Bills

Kenya Treasury bills are short-term (up to 1 year) Government securities issued by the Central Bank of Kenya as part of financing of the budget deficit. Issuance of Treasury bills started with maturities of 30, 60, and 91 days but at the moment, they are in maturities of 19, 182, and 364 days. Treasury bills are sold at a discounted price and redeemed at face (par) value, the difference of which reflects return to the investors. The purchase amount of Treasury bills is usually lower than the face value redeemed at maturity.

The CBK issued the maiden Treasury bills of 30, 60, and 91 days with an offer amount of KSh 20 million each, on 21 March 1969 in the FY 1968/69. This debut auction was oversubscribed at 208 per cent. In recent years up to 2016, 91-days, 182-days, and 364-days Treasury bills have been on offer every week. Beginning January 2009, the CBK lowered the minimum threshold for investment in Treasury bills from KSh 1,000,000 to KSh 100,000 with an aim to promote participation by the retail market and increase national savings. Additional amounts above KSh 100,000 have been in multiples of KSh 50,000. In addition, the CBK relaxed the requirements for opening and maintaining CDS accounts for investment in Government securities.

Treasury bills are not listed at the NSE and therefore have not been tradable at the exchange. However, plans are underway to establish an Over the Counter (OTC) platform to trade Treasury bills and increase liquidity. Treasury bills may be transferred from one holder to another and investors may pledge them as collateral (or for lien) security against credit facilities (loans). Commercial banks also use Treasury bills as collateral for liquidity management through Repurchase Agreements (Repos) and Intraday Liquidity Facility (ILF). Investors who do not wish to hold their Treasury bill investments until maturity are allowed to sell back (rediscount) to the Central Bank as a last resort, but at a punitive interest rate is applied to discourage the practice.

17.5.4.1 Treasury Bills by Tenor

Figure 17.6a shows Treasury bills issued in the period 1969 to 1993, with a concentration of 91-day Treasury bills between 1969 and 1978 and the 90-day Treasury bills from 1979 to 1993. The 30-day and the 60-day Treasury bills were suspended due to challenges of refinancing risk but were reintroduced in July 1972.[4] Issuance of Treasury bills during the next three years majorly comprised the 91 days Treasury bill resulting in lower rollover risk. The 85-days Treasury bill was introduced in June 1978 to cater for investor preferences. New Treasury bills issued were however used to redeem maturities of earlier issued bills (Figures 17.6 and 17.7). Over time, there was increased issuance of Treasury bills with offer amount per issuance increasing to KSh 100 million in 1972 from KSh 20 million in 1968.

In 1997 the stock of outstanding Treasury bills increased significantly due to conversion of part of the government overdraft at the Central Bank to Treasury

[4] In 1972 Kenya experienced economic prosperity from recovery in agricultural production and improved external trade.

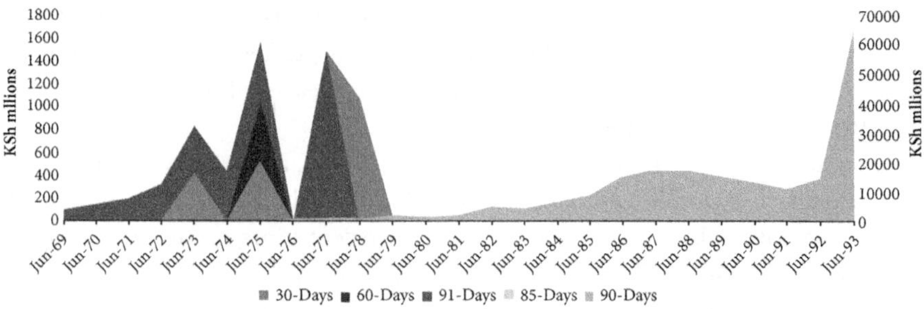

Figure 17.6 Treasury bills by tenor

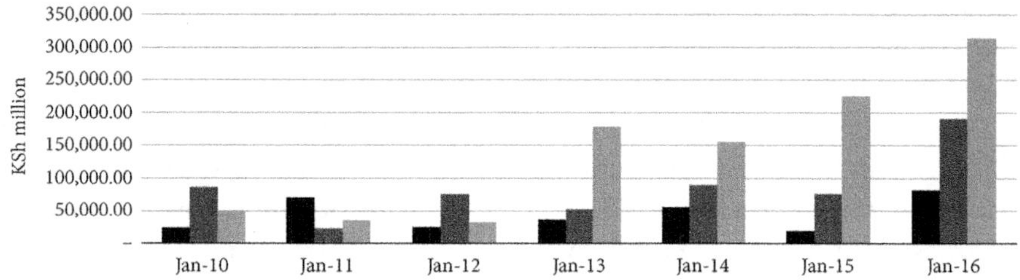

	Jan-10	Jan-11	Jan-12	Jan-13	Jan-14	Jan-15	Jan-16
91 day	23,663.45	69,134.85	24,322.65	36,203.35	54,659.95	18,554.25	81,783.65
182 day	85,337.45	22,528.10	75,669.25	52,167.30	88,948.80	75,251.35	191,840.55
364 day	49,493.65	34,942.15	32,055.65	178,840.10	155,797.40	225,122.55	314,463.50

Figure 17.7 Treasury bills by tenor

bills. This move was to help mop up excess liquidity arising from the purchase of foreign exchange in the interbank market by the Central Bank. However, this trend was reversed after the rollout of the May 2001 domestic debt restructuring programme. As the government yield curve normalized,[5] the 182-day Treasury bill was preferred over the 91-day Treasury bills (with a 3:1 ratio by June 2008) especially by the shorter end of the market.

Following the introduction of the 364 days Treasury bills in 2009 due to increased preference for longer maturities by investors, the Treasury bills portfolio shifted and the domestic debt maturity profile improved. The government goals were towards mitigation of the refinancing risk therefore the issuance of longer maturity Treasury bills.

17.5.4.2 Treasury Bill Interest Rates

The average discount rate declined to 0.4 per cent in January 1974 from 1.9 per cent in July 1973 due to increased demand for Treasury bills. However, the discount rate

[5] The development of the yield curve was mainly boosted by domestic debt restructuring and implementation of a predictable borrowing that increased participation by a wider investor base.

shot to 5.6 per cent by June 1974 due to liquidity constraints in the banking sector which persisted into 1975[6] resulting in under subscriptions and rise and volatility in the discount rate. With improvement in the balance of payment position, liquidity tightening eased in the second half of 1975. Treasury bills demand was supported by the requirement by the CBK in August 1974, for licensed Non-Bank Financial institutions to maintain a liquidity ratio of 15 per cent.

During FY 1977/78, the government ran down its deposits at the Central Bank due to growing budget deficit. New taxation measures were introduced to increase tax revenue and help bridge the deficit gap. Banks' liquidity increased sharply to 35 per cent compared to the legal requirement of 18 per cent with most banks' liquid assets being held in Treasury bills. Consequently, there was an increase in the issuance of Treasury bills and in liquidity driving the average discount rate to 1.5 per cent in June 1977.

The Treasury bill discount rate increased to 6.8 per cent in 1979 from 2.7 per cent in 1978, increasing further during 1980s due to tight liquidity, drought crisis, and delayed disbursements of aid. Political uncertainty in 1992 surrounding transition from single party rule to multi-party democracy led to capital flight, decline of economic growth to 0.4 per cent in 1992 from 2.3 per cent in 1991. Budget deficit increased to 7.3 per cent of GDP in 1992 from 2.9 per cent in 1991. As a result of this economic downturn coupled with the liberalization of the Treasury bill market in November 1990, the Treasury bills discount rate increased to a high of 70.6 per cent in June 1993 from 14.9 per cent in 1990 (Figure 17.8).

In 1997, part of the government overdraft at the Central Bank was converted into Treasury bills significantly increasing the stock of Treasury bills. This move

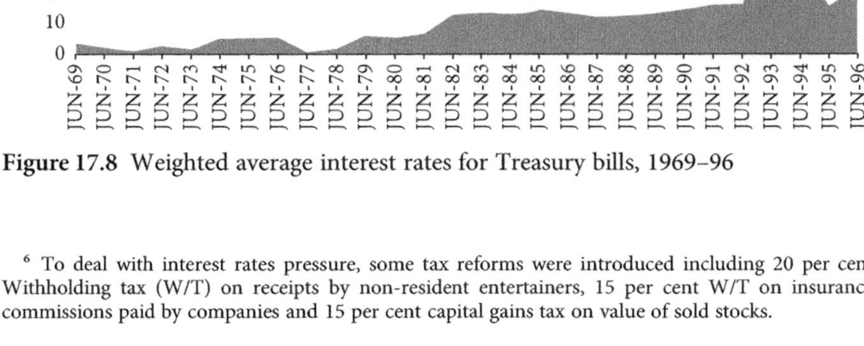

Figure 17.8 Weighted average interest rates for Treasury bills, 1969–96

[6] To deal with interest rates pressure, some tax reforms were introduced including 20 per cent Withholding tax (W/T) on receipts by non-resident entertainers, 15 per cent W/T on insurance commissions paid by companies and 15 per cent capital gains tax on value of sold stocks.

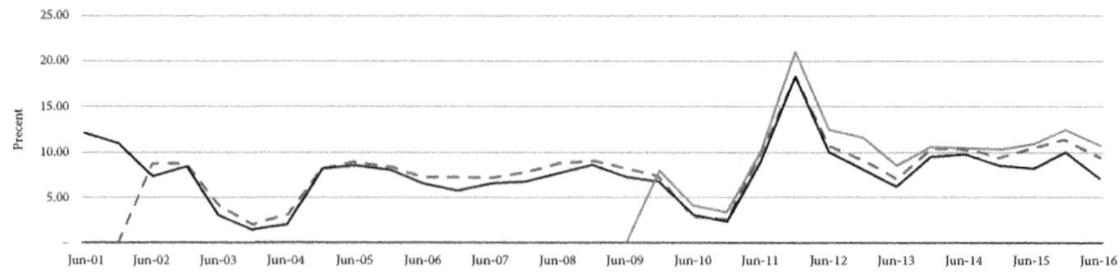

	Jun-01	Dec-01	Jun-02	Dec-02	Jun-03	Dec-03	Jun-04	Dec-04	Jun-05	Dec-05	Jun-06	Dec-06	Jun-07	Dec-07	Jun-08
91 day	12.0	11.0	7.34	8.34	3.00	1.46	2.01	8.04	8.50	8.07	8.60	5.73	6.53	6.87	7.73
182 day	-	-	8.80	8.79	4.12	2.09	3.15	8.19	8.96	8.49	7.32	7.32	7.19	7.87	8.84
364 day	-	-	-	-	-	-	-	-	-	-	-	-	-	-	-

	Dec-08	Jun-09	Dec-09	Jun-10	Dec-10	Jun-11	Dec-11	Jun-12	Dec-12	Jun-13	Dec-13	Jun-14	Dec-14	Jun-15	Dec-15	Jun-16
91 day	8.59	7.33	6.82	2.98	2.28	8.95	18.3	10.0	8.30	6.21	9.52	9.81	8.58	8.26	9.81	7.25
182 day	9.08	8.28	7.38	2.86	2.59	9.93	18.3	10.6	9.25	7.12	10.4	10.5	9.49	10.5	11.4	9.56
364 day	-	-	8.01	4.14	3.36	10.2	20.9	12.4	11.7	8.57	10.6	10.5	10.3	10.9	12.5	10.8

Figure 17.9 Treasury bills interest rates

was to help mop up excess liquidity arising from the purchase of foreign exchange in the interbank market by the Central Bank. But with restructuring of domestic debt in May 2001, this trend was reversed. The Government securities yield curve begun to normalize[7] with the 182-day Treasury bills preferred by short-term investors over the 91-day Treasury bills (ratio of 3:1 by June 2008).

During 2011, interest rates on shorter dated securities doubled from their previous positions in 2010 due to liquidity constraints. Swift management of the liquidity conditions and stabilization exchange rate saw the rates bounce back to their previous position in 2010 (Figure 17.9).

17.5.4.3 Treasury Bill Holders

Figure 17.10 shows the holders of Treasury bills during the period 1997 to 2016 where the dominant investors were banks, followed by pension funds, and insurance firms. Retail investors were included in the 'other' category. Banks' holdings increased significantly between 2009 and 2016 (over 50 per cent of Treasury bills stock) compared to the period between 1997 and 2009. Pension firms upped their holdings from 2011 (at between 10 and 20 per cent of the stock of Treasury bills) and remained the second largest holders of Treasury bills after banks up to 2016.

Holdings of Treasury bills by retail and other unclassified investors decreased significantly to less than 10 per cent during the period 2010 to 2016, partly due to competition from institutional investors.

17.5.5 Treasury Bonds

Kenya Treasury bonds are medium to long-term Government debt securities with maturities longer than one year. Investors buying Treasury bonds lend the

[7] The development of the yield curve was mainly boosted by domestic debt restructuring and implementation of a predictable borrowing that increased participation by a wider investor base.

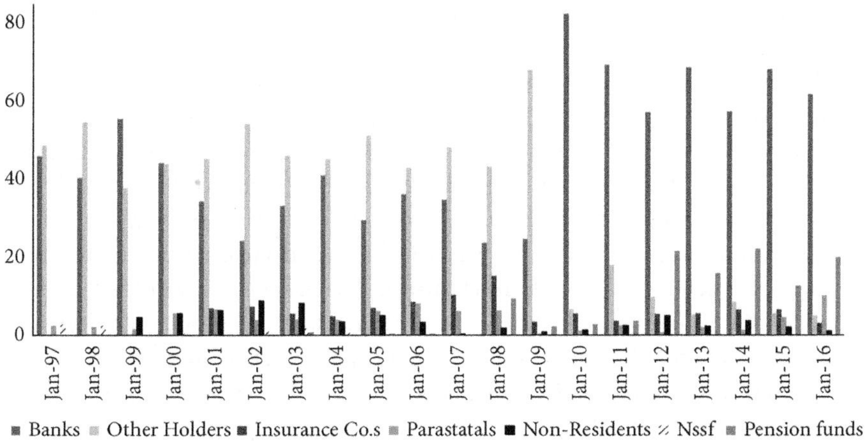

Figure 17.10 Holders of Treasury bills

government money for a specific period of time (referred to as tenor), which is the life of the bond before its maturity date. The Government of Kenya has been issuing fixed coupon bonds where investors receive fixed interest (coupons) every six months (semi-annual) throughout the life of the bond and face value on maturity date. Infrastructure bonds and savings bonds have also been issued. Other types of bonds that the government issued in the past but were discontinued in recent years include bearer bonds, non-bearer bonds, floating rate bonds, and special bonds.

The first Kenyan Treasury bonds were two- and five-year maturities issued in February 1986. For a span of eight months thereafter, issuance of bonds stalled, but resumed with one year and six-month maturities issued in September and December 1987. The average yields on the six-month and one-year bonds were 18 per cent and 14 per cent, respectively, while the Treasury bill rate was at 13 per cent. If the six-month bond was allowed to trade in the market, the outcome would have been a negatively sloping yield curve, thus the bond was stopped from trading. From February 1988, new Treasury bond maturities were launched with rates for the various maturities set in a way to achieve a positively sloped yield curve. The interest rate for the one-year bond was set at 14.5 per cent, while two-year and five-year rates were set at 15.5 per cent and 16.5 per cent respectively (Mbewa, Ngugi, and Kithinji, 2007; Ngugi and Agoti, 2007).

Despite the government efforts to introduce different tenors of bonds to cater for investor preferences, auctions were still undersubscribed. The auction method of issuance was suspended and fixed pricing (interest rates) adopted to attract demand in bonds and stimulate development of the government securities market. In March 1990, the rates were revised to 15 per cent, 16.5 per cent, and 17 per cent for the one-, two- and five-year maturities, respectively. Attractive returns in the Treasury bill market in mid 1990s led to a stagnated Treasury bond market. This was to be achieved through deliberate measures to market the bonds. In May 2001, deliberate reforms to develop the Government bond market were put in place with different types of bonds issued such as fixed coupon rate, floating rate bonds, zero coupon bonds, and special bonds. The reforms were targeted at restructuring the domestic debt portfolio with a view to increase long-term bonds and reduce short-term instruments. Efforts were made to develop the money market with a number of policy reforms which affected Treasury bill interest rates in ways that encouraged bond market growth. For instance, within the first eight months of the 2003/04 fiscal year, interest payments on domestic debt decreased to Ksh 16.4 billion (10.2 per cent of revenue) from Ksh 18.0 billion (12.7 per cent of revenue) in the same period the previous year (Mbewa, Ngugi, and Kithinji, 2007; Ngugi and Agoti, 2007).

Returns (discount and periodic interest/coupon) earned on Treasury bonds attract Withholding Tax of 15 per cent on Treasury bonds of nine years or shorter and 10 per cent for Treasury bonds of ten years or more, unless an investor is tax exempt, in which case a tax exemption certificate from the tax authority is required. However, discount and interest earnings from infrastructure bonds are exempt from all types of taxes as provided for in the Income Tax Act.

Treasury bonds are listed and traded at the NSE and can be pledged as collateral (or for lien) security against credit facilities (loans), and may also be transferred among holders of CDS accounts. Commercial banks also use bonds as collateral for liquidity management through Repurchase Agreements (Repos) and Intraday Liquidity Facility (ILF). T-bonds can also be rediscounted (at a punitive interest rate or yield) at the Central Bank, it there is proof of lack of buy-side at the NSE.

17.5.5.1 Stock of Treasury Bonds

The stock of bonds has been increasing at a fast rate since 2001 when deliberate reforms were put in place to restructure the debt portfolio and develop the domestic market for Government securities. As shown in Figure 17.9, the stock of bonds grew to KSh 1249 billion by 2016 from KSh 36.85 billion in 2000, representing an increase by 32.89 times. The increase in the stock of bonds took a much faster pace from 2009 (the post-reform period), rising from KSh 360.7 billion to KSh 1249 billion in 2016. In terms of ratio of bonds in the portfolio of government securities, bonds dominated (more than 50 per cent) the portfolio from 2003 when the proportion moved to 63 per cent from 46 per cent in 2002, rising to the highest level of 85.54 per cent in 2011 then to 73.29 per cent in 2015 (Table A17.1).

Between 1997 and 2016, fixed coupon bonds dominated the portfolio increasing to KSh 905 billion in 2016 from KSh 66.06 billion in 2002, a 12.70 times growth rate (Table A17.1). Bearer bonds existed in 1997 and paid off by 1999 while the last issuance of floating rate bonds was on 2001 with the last outstanding bonds worth KSh 0.74 billion redeemed in 2007. Special bonds worth KSh 0.94 billion were first issued in 1999 with the last issuance in 2008 and KSh 11 billion outstanding by 2016. Zero coupon bonds were first issued in 2003 with outstanding balances of KSh 5.41 billion and were last issued in 2009 with outstanding value of KSh 14.79 billion. Infrastructure bonds (IFB) were first issued in 2009 and became very popular attracting increasing demand due to special features such as tax exemption and amortization. IFB issuance grew from KSh 19.73 billion in 2009 to KSh 257.54 billion in 2016. The longest bond ever issued in Kenya was the 30-year savings bond in 2011, accumulating an outstanding volume of KSh 28.24 billion by 2016 through reopening auctions and issuance by tap sales (Table A17.1).

17.5.5.2 Holders of Treasury Bonds

Unlike the trend in the holding of Treasury bills, Figure 17.11 shows that banks dominated the holdings in Treasury bonds since 2001, rising above 40 per cent, remaining between 40 per cent and 50 per cent from 2002 to 2016. Holding by pension firms was subdued during the period between 1997 and 2007 but rose up in 2007 from below 10 per cent to a high of 30 per cent in 2013 which was maintained up to 2016.

Holding by insurance firms peaked in 2000 to about 20 per cent declining to levels of 10 per cent from 2002 which was maintained consistently up to 2016. Non-resident investors invested decimally in Treasury bonds during the period under review.

17.5.5.3 Auctions of Treasury Bonds

In recent years, the Central Bank has been issuing Treasury bonds on a monthly basis. The Bank uses the auction method of issuance, although sometimes this has been supplemented by tap issuance occasionally used immediately after an auction if market conditions are favourable to the issuer. To invest in Treasury bonds, the first step is to open a CDS account at the Central Bank of Kenya, correctly fill in the Treasury bonds application form available at the CBK website and submit to the CBK (head office or branches or currency centres). The minimum amount required to invest in a Treasury bonds is KSh 50,000 with additional amounts in multiples of KSh 50,000.

Domestic Government bonds issued during the period 1995–96 and 2001–16 were largely fixed coupon bonds with floating rate bonds (mainly 1–3 years and referenced on the 91-day Treasury bill rate) issued from 1997 to 2002 and discontinued in 2003. Zero coupon bonds, mainly one year in tenor, were also issued between 2001 and 2008, and withdrawn from 2009 when the 364-day Treasury bill was introduced. According to Figure A17.2 there was general stability of interest rates (coupon rate and yield to maturity (WAY)) of bonds issued at the primary market in the period between 2002 and 2016.

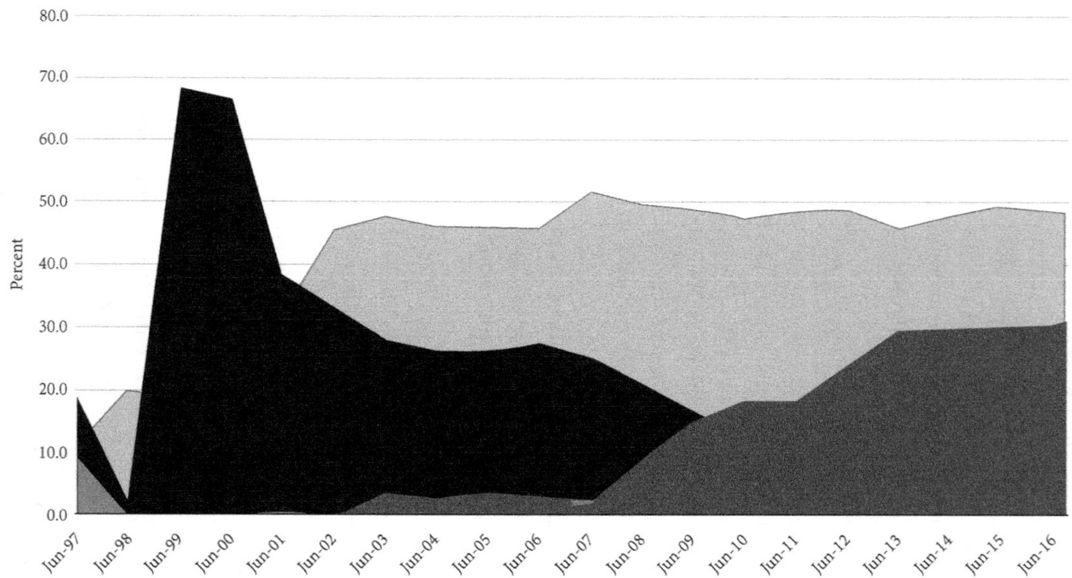

	Jun-97	Jun-98	Jun-99	Jun-00	Jun-01	Jun-02	Jun-03	Jun-04	Jun-05	Jun-06	Jun-07	Jun-08	Jun-09	Jun-10	Jun-11	Jun-12	Jun-13	Jun-14	Jun-15	Jun-16	Sep-16
Banks	11.0	19.9	17.8	23.2	32.2	45.4	47.6	46.1	45.8	45.9	50.7	49.5	48.8	47.4	48.4	48.6	45.8	47.7	49.3	48.7	48.5
Insurance Co.s	0.0	3.5	0.0	0.0	22.7	16.4	13.9	13.6	13.4	12.1	10.1	10.1	10.6	12.2	12.5	12.4	12.6	11.1	10.3	10.1	10.0
Parastatals	4.6	0.0	9.1	5.6	5.5	3.5	3.6	6.8	8.5	8.4	7.5	5.8	4.3	4.0	4.0	3.1	2.7	3.8	3.2	3.2	3.2
Non-Residents	0.0	0.0	4.6	4.4	0.6	0.3	0.3	0.3	0.5	0.3	0.2	0.2	0.1	0.2	0.8	0.6	0.5	4.1	0.4	0.6	0.6
Other Holders	19.2	2.4	68.5	66.8	38.3	32.9	28.0	26.3	26.2	27.5	25.3	20.5	16.5	13.3	11.9	7.1	5.7	1.8	5.3	5.9	5.7
NSSF	9.2	0.0	0.0	0.0	0.4	0.0	0.5	1.5	1.5	2.2	2.5	3.6	4.4	4.4	3.8	3.6	3.1	1.8	1.3	1.1	1.0
Pension funds	0.0	0.0	0.0	0.0	0.0	0.0	3.8	2.7	3.7	3.0	2.2	9.1	15.1	18.4	18.5	24.0	29.6	29.8	30.1	30.5	31.1

Figure 17.11 Holders of Treasury bonds, 1998–2016

However, volatility was observed in 2002, 2003, and 2011. The average tenor of bonds issued during the period under review was 7.7 years while average coupon rate and WAY was 10.914 per cent and 11.582 per cent respectively.

In 2007, there were deliberate efforts to fast track the implementation of reforms for developing the Government bond market, some of which had first been muted in 2001. Such reforms included among others, the benchmark bond programme, product diversification through instruments such as infrastructure bonds and the horizontal repo (HRT), electronic platforms for government securities both at primary and secondary market levels. The reforms were aimed at helping to meet the objectives of domestic government borrowing (achieve financing requirements of the government at optimal cost and risk) and promote the growth of the secondary market for government securities.

The implementation of these reforms resulted in positive outcomes as shown in Figure A17.2. Average tenor of bonds issued at the primary market increased to 9.3 years in the period between 2008 and 2016 (post-reform period) compared with 5.3 years (growth of 73.76 per cent) in the period between 2001 and 2007 (pre-reform period) while median tenor remained unchanged at 5 years both in the pre- and post-reform periods. Average coupon rate and WAY in the post-reform period increased to 11.426 per cent and 12.487 per cent compared to 10.148 per cent and 10.224 per cent in the pre-reform period, respectively. Median coupon rate and WAY in the post-reform period increased to 11.934 per cent and 12.531 per cent compared to 11.250 per cent and 10.943 per cent in the pre-reform period respectively. With continued implementation of reforms and as the liquidity of bonds at the secondary market continues to improve, it is expected that the levels of coupon rates and WAY at the primary market will decline as more medium-longer term bonds are issued, resulting in lower cost and risk of debt.

Figure 17.12 shows that auctions of Treasury bonds were generally oversubscribed during the period 2001 and 2016, indicating sustained demand. However,

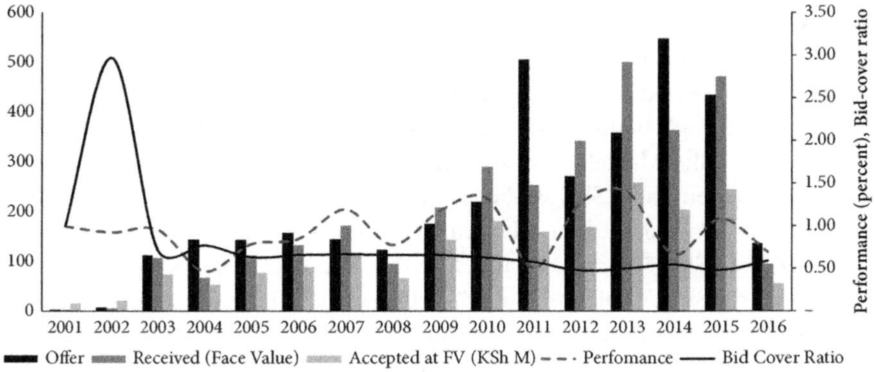

Figure 17.12 Auctions of Treasury bonds

Table 17.2 Auctions of Treasury bonds in the period, 2001–16 (KSh billion)

	Offer	Received (Face Value)	Accepted at FV (KSh M)	Accepted at cost (KSh M)	Performance (per cent)	Bid Cover Ratio (Times)
Average	217.70	201.50	120.61	115.52	0.94	0.78
Median	150.86	152.66	102.75	101.42	0.94	0.64
Pre-2007 Average	101.50	85.92	63.83	60.82	0.88	1.06
Post-2007 Average	308.08	291.39	164.77	158.06	0.99	0.57
Pre-2007 Median	143.00	107.13	73.99	71.00	0.92	0.72
Post-2007 Median	271.12	290.38	169.59	163.27	1.09	0.58
Minimum	3.00	2.98	15.30	2.98	0.47	0.48
Maximum	547.82	501.28	258.58	250.99	1.40	2.97

2011 and 2014 recorded significant undersubscriptions partly due to unfavorable market conditions at the time.

Table 17.2 shows that the average annual offer size of bonds issued during the period 2001 and 2016 was KSh 217.70 billion while average annual received and accepted amounts were KSh 201.50 billion and KSh 120.61 billion respectively. Annual average and median subscription rates and bid to cover ratios during the period was 94 per cent (similar for average and median), 0.78 times and 0.64 times, respectively.

Annual average and median offer amounts of bonds issued in the post-reform period increased to KSh 308.08 billion and KSh 271.12 billion compared to KSh 101.50 billion (203.52 per cent growth) and KSh 143 billion (87.50 per cent growth) during the pre-reform period respectively. Annual average amount received and accepted in the post-reform period increased to KSh 291.39 billion and KSh 164.77 billion compared with KSh 85.92 billion (139.13 per cent growth) and KSh 63.83 billion (158.15 per cent growth) in the pre-reform period respectively. Median amount received and accepted in the post-reform period increased to KSh 290.38 billion and KSh 169.59 billion compared to KSh 107.13 billion (171.06 per cent growth) and KSh 73.99 billion (129.19 per cent growth) in the pre-reform period respectively (Table 17.2).

In terms of single bond issuances, average offer size of bonds during the period 2001–16 was KSh 12.85 billion while average amounts received and accepted were KSh 11.73 billion and KSh 7.32 billion, respectively. Average and median offer amounts of bonds issued at the primary market in the post-reform period increased to KSh 15.96 billion and KSh 15 billion (116.08 per cent growth) compared to KSh 7.39 billion and KSh 8 billion (87.50 per cent growth) during the pre-reform period respectively. Average amount received and accepted in the post-reform period increased to KSh 15.21 billion and KSh 9.73 billion compared with KSh 5.81 billion (161.68 per cent growth) and KSh 3.70 billion (162.99 per cent growth) in the pre-reform period, respectively. Median amount received and accepted in the post-reform period increased to KSh 13.11 billion and KSh 9.36 billion compared to KSh 5.07 billion (158.49 per cent growth) and KSh 3.34 billion (179.39 per cent growth) in the pre-reform period, respectively.

With sustained reforms to develop the primary market for government securities and as the liquidity of bonds at the secondary market increases, it is expected that subscriptions and demand for bonds at the primary market will continue to improve resulting in lower cost and risk of debt and success of the government borrowing programme every financial year.

17.6 Developments in the Secondary Market for Government Securities

17.6.1 Trading of Government Bonds

Before 2007, Kenya's government bond market was characterized by many small bonds of the similar or different maturities scattered along the yield curve. This bond fragmentation phenomenon led to an illiquid secondary market (Figure 17.13), reflected by infrequent trades and wide yield spreads. The net result was an unstable and unreliable yield curve, with most investors pursuing buy-hold rather than buy-trade strategies due to lack of reliable pricing mechanism. Bond market fragmentation discouraged the development of a yield curve and a bond index. To develop a robust domestic bond market, deliberate measures through the benchmark bond programme were put in place with an aim to achieve a reliable yield curve as a reference pricing tool and a bond index as a portfolio valuation tool. A benchmark bond is a bond against which other bonds, securities or interest rate products are priced or referenced. Benchmark bonds have the following key features; most liquid, most actively traded, deep i.e. widely held by different investors, narrowest bid-offer spreads, and lower yield compared to non-benchmark bonds.

As shown in Figures 17.13 and 17.14, annual bond trading turnover at the Nairobi Securities Exchange (NSE) improved significantly from 2010 to 2016

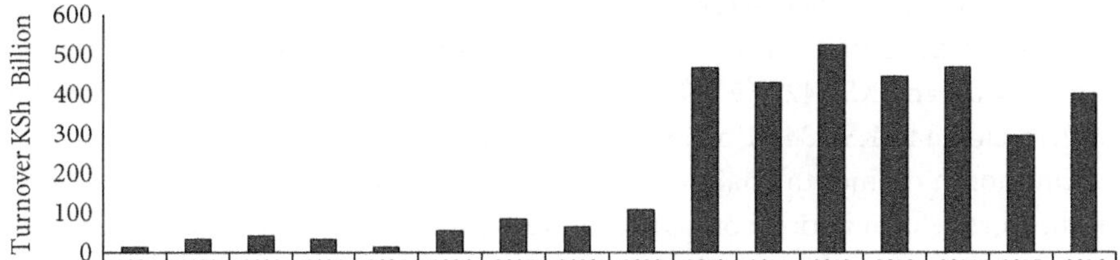

	2001	2002	2003	2004	2005	2006	2007	2008	2009	2010	2011	2012	2013	2014	2015	2016
■Turnover	14.08	33.63	41.13	34.11	13.63	54.16	84.14	63.21	107.85	466.07	427.69	522.89	442.40	467.40	294.32	399.90

Figure 17.13 Annual trading turnover of Treasury bonds

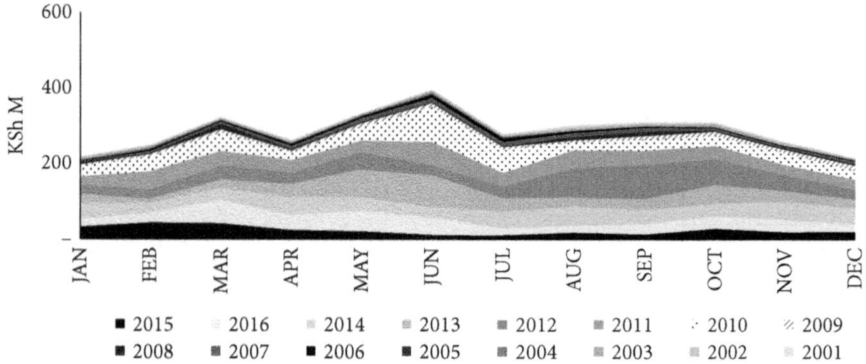

Figure 17.14 Monthly Treasury bonds trading turnover

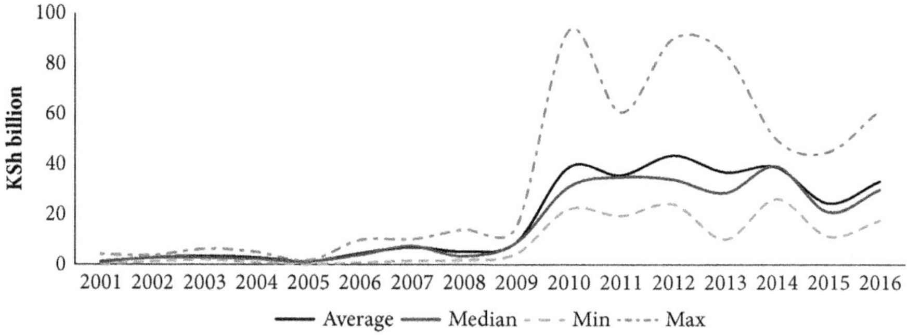

Figure 17.15 Annual Treasury bonds turnover

which was the post-reform period compared to 2001 to 2009, the pre-reform period. As indicated earlier, deliberate reforms to develop the government securities market were first muted in 2001, with implementation fast tracked from 2007. During the period under review, trading turnover was at its highest point in 2012 at KSh 522.89 billion (an increase by 36.14 times) compared to KSh 14.08 billion back in 2001. Annual average turnover during the period 2001 to 2016 was KSh 216.66 billion while annual median turnover KSh 95.99 billion. Annual average and median turnover in the post-reform period (2008–16) was KSh 354.64 billion (803.08 per cent growth) and KSh 427.69 billion (growth by 1,153.86 per cent) compared to KSh 39.27 billion and KSh 34.11 billion, respectively.

On month on month analysis, 17.14 shows increased monthly trading activity in the post-reform period compared to pre-reform period. For instance, turnover in June 2010 rose to KSh 93.38 billion compared to KSh 0.14 billion in June 2001 and KSh 11.10 billion in June 2009, representing an increase by 666 times and 7.41 times, respectively.

Table 17.3 Descriptive statistics on Treasury bonds turnover (KSh billion)

Annual average	Annual median	pre-reform annual average turnover	Post-reform annual average turnover	Pre-reform annual median turnover	Post-reform annual median turnover
216.66	95.99	39.27	354.64	34.11	427.69

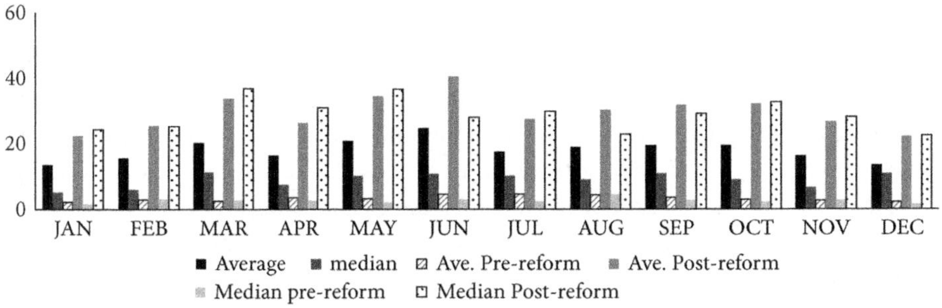

Figure 17.16 Monthly bonds turnover in the period, 2001–16

According to Figure 17.15 and Table 17.3, there was significant improvement in average, median, minimum, and maximum turnover levels from 2009 to 2016 compared to 2001 to 2008. The highest average and median annual turnover was KSh 43.57 billion in 2012 and KSh 39.24 billion in 2014 compared to lowest levels of KSh 1.14 billion in 2005 and 0.90 billion in 2001. Maximum turnover declined significantly to KSh 60.73 billion in 2011 from KSh 93.28 billion in 2010, partly due to tight liquidity and high interest rates in 2011. The monetary policy was tight as the Central Bank Rate (CBR) was gradually raised from 5.75 per cent in June 2011 to 18 per cent in December 2011.

Figure 17.16 shows that bond trading turnover peaked in the months of March, May, and June during the entire period under review, with highest observations during the post-reform period from 2008 to 2016. Average turnover for the entire period was KSh 20.21 billion, KSh 20.86 billion and KSh 24.77 billion while average turnover during post-reform period was KSh 33.94 billion, KSh 34.57 billion and KSh 40.48 billion in the months of March, May, and June.

17.7 Milestones in the Government Securities Market

Since 2001, there has been great success in the implementation of different initiatives aimed at developing the primary market for Government securities, helping to meet Government's domestic financing requirements at optimal cost and risk every financial year. This has been possible through collaboration between the National Treasury and the Central Bank and market stakeholders. The Market Leaders Forum (MLF)[8] for instance, was one stakeholder forum that has been instrumental in contributing significantly to the success of the bond market in Kenya. We briefly discuss below some of the key milestones.

17.7.1 Benchmark Bonds Programme (BBP)

Before 2007, Kenya's bond market was characterized by many small bonds of the similar and/or different maturities scattered along the yield curve. This bond fragmentation phenomenon led to an illiquid secondary market, reflected by infrequent trades and wide spreads on the yields. The net result was an unstable and unreliable yield curve, with most investors pursuing buy-hold rather than buy-trade strategies due to lack of reliable pricing mechanism. Imperative to developing a robust domestic bond market is a reliable yield curve as a pricing tool and the bond index as portfolio valuation tool. Bond market fragmentation discourages the development of the yield curve and bond index.

Since 2007 when the implementation of the benchmark bond programme began, the problem of fragmentation of the bond market has been reduced through increased liquidity of fewer bond series. The benchmark bonds programme started with the identification and adoption of benchmark tenors of 2-, 5-, 10-, 15-, 20-, and 25-years along the yield curve. Cap or ceiling sizes per tenor were initially set at KSh 30 billion and KSh 40 billion for 2-, 5-year and 10-, 15-, 20-, and 25-year, respectively, and regular bond issuance has been restricted to these benchmark tenors with a view to building liquidity through strategies such as reopening, tap sales, switching, or bond exchanges. In April 2009, the CBK successfully reopened the first benchmark series, a 5-year bond which was 4.5 years to maturity at the time. The outstanding amount on the bond rose from KSh 4.4 billion to KSh 10 billion as a result of the reopening exercise. By 2016, 24 more bond series had been reopened raising additional financing in excess of KSh 643.750 billion in face value. Average outstanding size of reopened series in the portfolio range of KSh 20 billion to KSh 40 billion.

The process of building benchmark bonds as entrenched in the Government's Medium Term Debt Strategy was initially conceived to involve two stages. The first phase entailed actions by the issuer to build large volumes in benchmark tenors through large offerings and reopening with the aim of realizing few but large size bonds to spur trading and deepen the bond market. As a result, the

[8] MLF was reconstituted into consultative forum for domestic debt market (CFDDM) and Bond market stakeholders forum (BMSF) in 2015 and 2016 respectively

maturity profile of bonds would consist of large maturities for government to refinance in future, which could present a key challenge in terms of large redemptions in the absence of a sinking fund. The second phase was intended to address debt refinancing through strategies aimed at smoothening the maturity profile.

In terms of the main Characteristics of the Benchmark Portfolio by June 2016, the features of the benchmark bonds portfolio are summarized as follows:

i. As at June 2016, there were 55 outstanding bonds (including benchmark and non-benchmark tenors, infrastructure bonds but excluding special bonds—KSh 11 billion) worth KSh 1141.04 billion in face value (Figure 17.17).
ii. Of these, 38 were benchmark series worth KSh 794.588 billion representing 70.00 per cent of the portfolio (Figures 17.17 and 17.18).
iii. Of the 38 benchmark series, 25 had been re-opened raising financing worth KSh 643.750 billion in face value (Figures 17.17, 17.18, and 17.19).

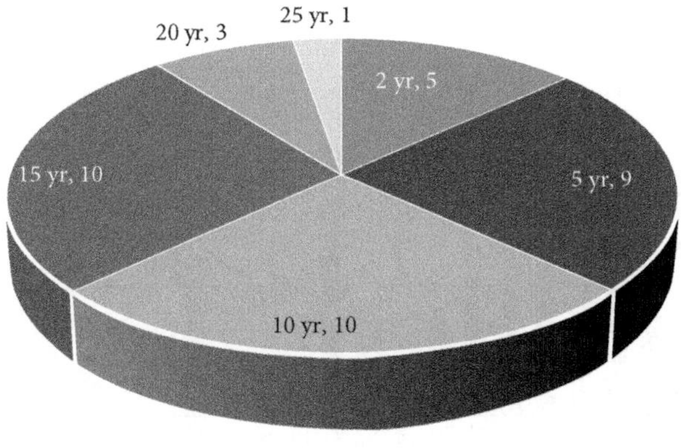

Figure 17.17 Number of bond series per tenor

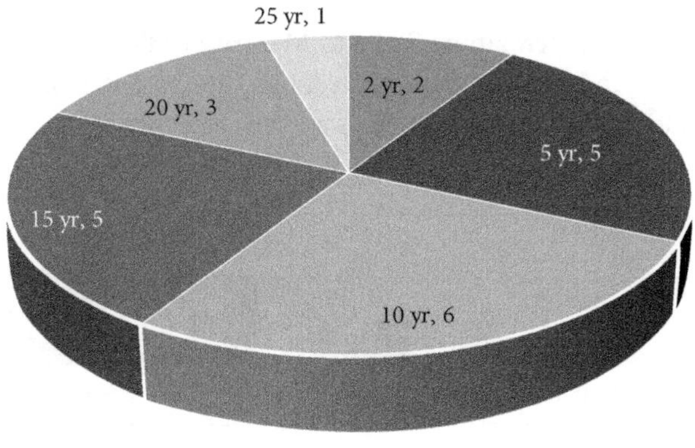

Figure 17.18 Number of bonds reopened per tenor

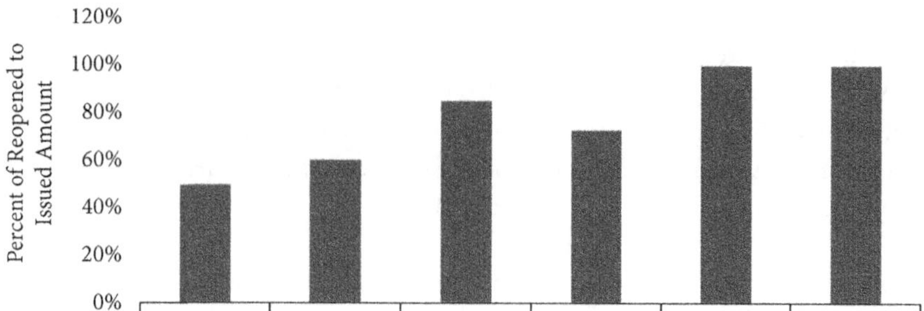

	2 yr	5 yr	10 yr	15 yr	20 yr	25 yr
■ Proportion Reopened	49.82%	60.45%	85.27%	72.89%	100.00%	100.00%

Figure 17.19 Reopened bonds by tenor

iv. The maturities of benchmark tenors were highly skewed to the short-medium term as shown in Figure 17.20.

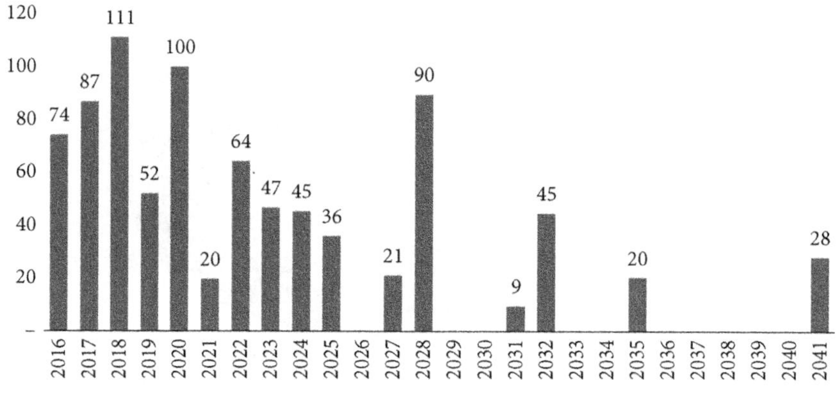

Figure 17.20 Benchmark portfolio maturity profile (KSh billion)

v. In terms of average Remaining Time to Maturity (RTM), bond series of 2-, 5-10-, 15-, 20-, and 25-year were on average 0.76, 1.94, 4.2, 9.59, 14.92, and 18.98 years to maturity respectively as shown in Figure 17.21.

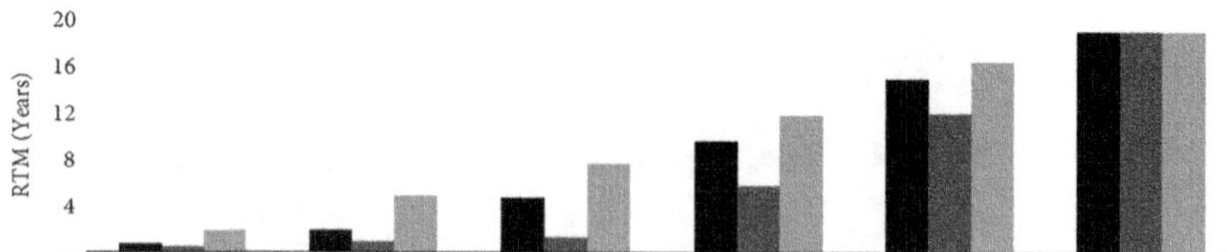

	2 yr	5 yr	10 yr	15 yr	20 yr	25 yr
■ Ave. RTM	0.76	1.94	4.72	9.59	14.92	18.98
■ RTM short	0.48	0.90	1.31	5.71	11.98	18.98
■ RTM Long	1.90	4.83	7.58	11.83	16.40	18.98

Figure 17.21 Benchmark portfolio by remaining time to maturity (RTM)

vi. The proportions of bonds of original tenors of 2-, 5-, 10-, 15-, 20-, and 25-year were in maturity baskets of less than 1 year, between 1–2 years and 2–5 years, 5–10 years, 10–15 years, and 15–20 years as shown in Figures 17.22 and 17.23.

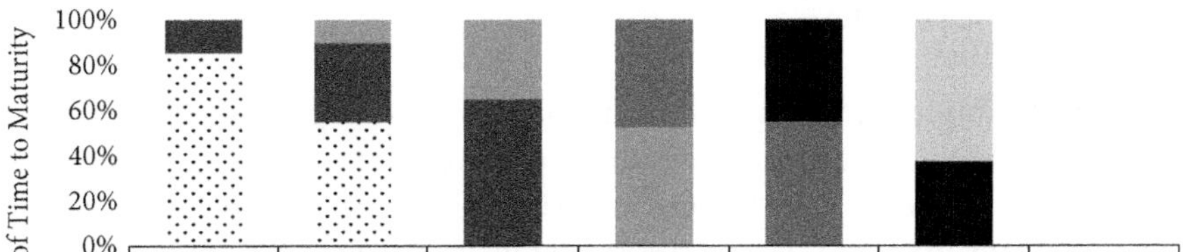

	<1 yr	>1 - <2 yr	>2 - <5yr	>5 - <10 yr	>10 - <15 yr	>15 - <20 yr	>20 - <25 yr
25 yr	-	-	-	-	-	100.00%	-
20 yr	-	-	-	-	40.00%	60.00%	-
15 yr	-	-	-	51.50%	48.50%	-	-
10 yr	-	5.94%	37.06%	57.00%	-	-	-
5 yr	11.53%	20.09%	68.38%	-	-	-	-
2 yr	68.12%	31.88%	-	-	-	-	-

Figure 17.22 Proportion of bonds by remaining time to maturity

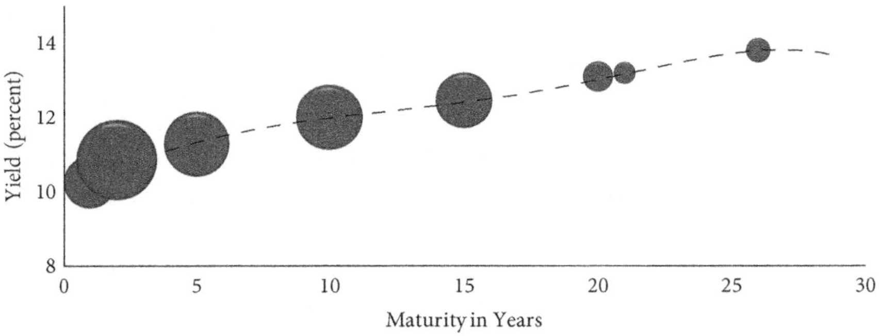

Figure 17.23 Stock of bonds along the yield curve

vii. As shown in Figure 17.24, average coupon rates for the benchmark maturities was 11.766 per cent with minimum and maximum at 8.79 per cent and 15.760 per cent respectively.

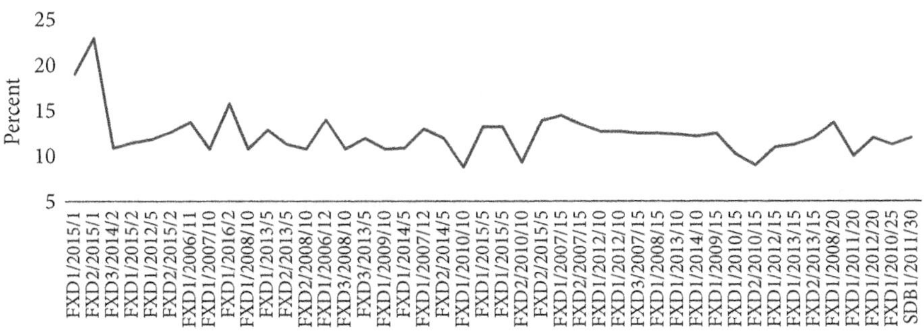

Figure 17.24 Coupon rates on benchmark issues

viii. Outside the benchmark portfolio, there were ten outstanding infrastructure bonds valued at KSh 271.737 billion in face value or 23.81 per cent of the portfolio and two special bonds valued at KSh 11 billion. There were three outstanding non-benchmark series worth KSh 7.932 billion or 0.7 per cent of the portfolio.

By 2016, the implementation of the benchmark bonds programme was largely in phase I with a number of milestones achieved. The average maturity of Government securities had lengthened rising to 3 years 9 months in 2009, 5 years 1 month (or ratio 23:77 in Treasury bills to bonds) in 2010, then to 4.31 years in 2016 from just 8 months in 2001 (virtually 100 per cent Treasury bills financing). For bonds only, average maturity was 6.84 years in 2016 compared to 7.9 years in 2015, due to a market environment that occasioned increased issuance of short-term bonds and Treasury bills in 2016. With a further lengthening of the maturity of bonds (preferred at 10 years) and proper functioning of the secondary market, the Government will benefit from lower rollover risk usually associated with short-term debt.

A number of other outcomes that may be attributed to the benchmark bond programme include; less fragmentation of bonds in the market; increased bond trading turnover in the secondary market; lower bond yields; firmed up the yield curve and lower debt cost as a result of narrow bond yield spreads. Following these developments, the NSE launched FTSE NSE Kenya Shilling Government Bond Index in 2012 which has played a key role as a benchmark tool for measuring the performance of the bond market, facilitating diversification through emergence of new financial products and market participants thereby encouraging foreign investors. Bond market indicators such as the yield curve and the index have potential to open up the market to the rest of the world and increase Kenya's financial sector competitiveness. Further, the successful issuance of debut Euro bond by the Government in 2014 was a reflection of maturity of the domestic market and confidence for Kenya by the international market. This success was supported by the fact that Kenya's bond market is one of the best in Africa while the country's credit rating has been an incentive for investors.

17.7.2 The Kenya Government Bond Yield Curve

A yield is the annual return on a bond investment and is based on both the purchase price and coupon payments and maturity value. The current yield (CY) is the annual return earned on the bond's price. The yield to maturity (YTM) is the total return an investor receives by holding the bond until maturity. YTM is preferable to investors than current yield as it represents total return during the life of the bond and offers comparison of bonds with different features—credit quality, maturity, and coupon rates.

A yield curve (also the term structure of interest rates) represents the relationship between yield to maturity and time to maturity of bonds of similar asset class and credit quality. It reflects the sentiments of investors and traders on the direction of future interest rates. The shape (slope, level, and curvature) of the yield curve is affected by changes in interest rates, supply and demand, maturity, and credit quality of bonds.

Following volatility of the market in 2005, the Central Bank embarked on strategies to develop a stable and vibrant secondary market in order to support development of a reliable yield curve. With stable interest rates on Treasury bills which were perceived by the market as benchmark rates, the Government begun implementation of the benchmark bonds programme with identification of 2-, 5-, 10-, 15-, and 20-year maturities as benchmark tenors with the first coupon rates of 8.75 per cent, 9.50 per cent, 10.75 per cent, 12.50 per cent, and 13.75 per cent, respectively. Specific ceiling volumes were also set on these benchmark tenors to provide adequate liquidity for trading of the bonds at the secondary market. In the absence of a sinking fund, capping of the maximum size per benchmark tenor was based on available overdraft limit to mitigate redemption risk (Chironga, Wambua, and Ngugi, 2010).

Before 2007, the secondary bond market was characterized by many small short term bonds leading to market fragmentation and a highly illiquid market reflected by infrequent trades and wide yield spreads. Increased issuance of benchmark tenors and consistent reopening of bonds attempted to address the market fragmentation, increased turnover in the secondary market, lowered interest rates, firmed up the yield curve (Figures 17.25 and 17.26) and also minimized issuance costs as a result of narrower bond yield spreads

	91 days	182 days	1 yr	2yr	3yr	4yr	5yr	6yr	7yr	8yr	9yr	10yr	11yr	12yr	13yr	14yr	15yr	20yr	25yr	29yr
2010 YC	2.313	2.631	3.283	4.586	5.405	6.223	6.980	6.987	7.223	7.769	8.172	8.577	8.989	9.361	9.914	10.41	10.92	10.77	10.51	
2011 YC	18.94	18.58	21.40	22.00	18.40	15.67	14.92	14.37	14.02	13.75	13.58	13.37	13.28	13.36	13.51	13.59	13.69	14.00	15.16	16.00
2012 YC	10.31	10.60	12.67	12.90	12.93	12.97	12.97	12.99	13.00	13.06	13.17	13.22	13.28	13.32	13.36	13.40	13.43	13.57	13.67	13.70
2013 YC	9.400	10.38	10.50	11.28	11.38	11.80	11.88	11.95	11.97	11.99	12.85	12.93	12.95	13.02	13.05	13.10	13.35	13.54	13.78	13.85
2014 YC	8.571	9.855	10.57	10.89	11.30	11.40	11.56	11.64	11.68	11.72	12.22	12.36	12.44	12.53	12.62	12.72	12.84	13.24	13.45	
2015 YC	10.41	12.34	12.75	13.56	13.9	14.06	14.14	14.1	14.09	14.07	14.06	14.05	14.04	14.03	14.03	14.02	14.02	14	13.99	
2016 YC	8.607	11.18	11.98	13.39	13.83	14.12	14.15	14.42	14.46	14.52	14.56	14.6	14.62	14.64	14.7	14.73	14.74	14.85	14.9	

Figure 17.25 Evolution of Kenya Government bond yield curve

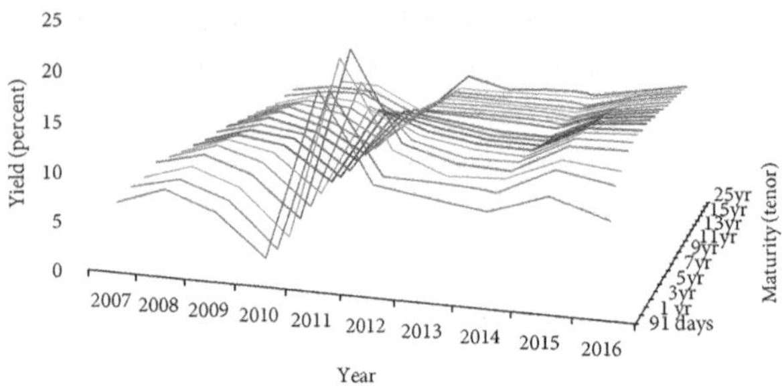

Figure 17.26 Evolution of Kenya Government bond yield curve

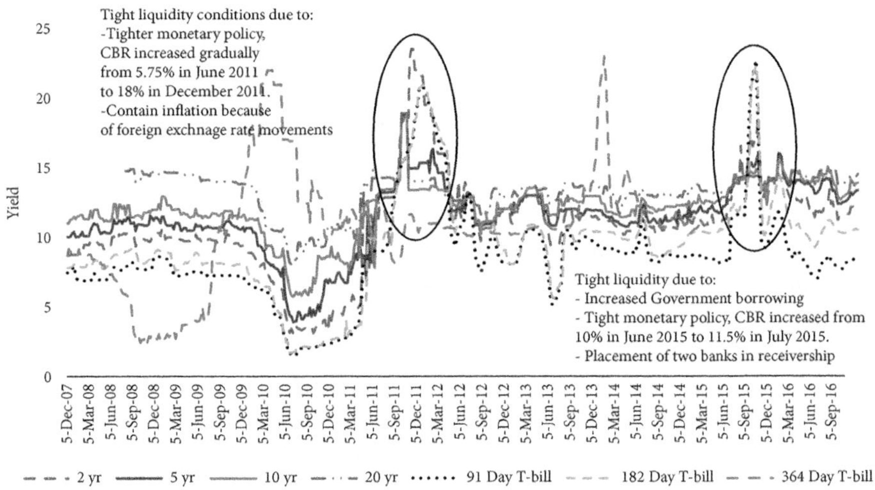

Figure 17.27 Benchmark bonds yields and Treasury bills rates

in the secondary market (Figure 17.27). In addition, there was improved subscription for bonds at the primary market auctions and enhanced market confidence.

The Kenyan government bond yield curve has been estimated purely using the prevailing yields of traded Treasury bonds at the NSE. It excludes yields from small value trades (less than KSh 10 million) of fixed rate Treasury bonds, traded yields from other types of bonds such as government infrastructure bonds and corporate bonds. Corporate bonds are few both in value and number, mostly restricted to institutional investors due to higher entry threshold of KSh 1 million, implying illiquidity (Chironga, Wambua, and Ngugi, 2010).

17.7.3 Market Infrastructure: Trading, Clearing Settlement Arrangements

Market infrastructures such as the Central Securities Depositories (CBK-CSD, CDSC), trading systems (Electronic Trading System—ETS), and clearing and settlement systems (RTGS) have evolved from manual to electronic processes over the years.

In September 2006, the NSE implemented live trading of equities on an automated trading system which had capability of trading immobilized corporate bonds and Treasury bonds. Following this development, the trading hours were increased from two hours (10:00 am – 12:00 pm) to three hours (10:00 am–1:00 pm) due to increased activity. The Electronic Trading System (ETS) implemented through a Wide Area Network (WAN) was launched in 2007 enabling participants (brokers and investment banks) to trade financial instruments remotely through terminals in their offices linked to the trading engine at the NSE without physical presence on the trading floor. The settlement cycle for equities was reduced to T+3 from the previous T+4 in July 2011.

In November 2009, the CBK together with NSE and market stakeholders through the MLF put in place an automated bonds trading system known as the Automated Trading System (ATS) with settlement of cash and securities at the CBK-CSD. The ATS enabled same day transactions on a Delivery versus Payment basis where deals were initiated and settled within a business day even though settlement was allowed to take place within T+3. This development helped to increase efficiency of Treasury bonds trading operations, contributed to increased bond turnover as well as enhanced market confidence and transparency. In September 2012, NSE broker back office started operations with a system capable of facilitating internet trading, improving the integrity of the exchange trading systems.

In September 2014, the CBK together with CMA, CDSC and NSE incorporated enhancements to the trading and settlement infrastructure to allow the CBK become the settlement bank for cash transactions on trading of corporate instruments including bonds and equities executed at the NSE. Settlement of transactions is executed through the CBK's Real Time Gross Settlement (RTGS) system known as KEPSS. This framework works on DVP within T+3 such that the CBK concludes execution of settlement and notifies CDSC through a secure electronic link in order to facilitate immediate transfer of securities. Corporate securities are listed at the NSE with custody at the CDSC.

The growth of Digital Financial Services (DFS) in Kenya has also facilitated greater access to Government securities through mobile phone based products such as the 'M-Akiba', a mobile-phone based government debt product developed by the National Treasury together with market stakeholders which was aimed at providing opportunity for the vast majority of the public to invest small amounts in Government securities using their mobile phones. This product was transformational and did not only deepen financial inclusion, but also broadened the investor base for government securities and improved the national savings culture.

At the Central Bank, the Treasury Mobile Direct (TMD) is aimed at improving efficiency in the existing issuance operations of domestic debt by providing a channel to access small denomination government securities through the mobile phone has been under development. TMD began as a joint initiative of the CBK and the World Bank targeted to allow investors in government securities to open central depository securities (CDS) accounts and check status of investments; receive information on Government securities; buy and sell, pledge and transfer securities and settle investments in Government securities within allowed limits on mobile money platforms. In addition to promoting financial inclusion, the project was aimed at supporting market development by increasing outreach to retail investors, broadening the investor base and improving the national savings rate.

17.7.4 Rollout of Horizontal (Interbank) REPO

In September 2008, the CBK rolled out the Interbank (Horizontal) Repo facility, a product aimed at providing a platform for better liquidity distribution among banks and help individual banks meet their daily liquidity needs at a reasonable cost using Government securities as collateral. To utilize this facility, banks sign Master Repurchase Agreements (MRAs). This product is being reviewed in consultation with the market players to improve its uptake and liquidity in the money market.

17.7.5 Infrastructure Bonds (IFB) Issuance

The debut IFB in February 2009 attracted impressive demand with KSh 26.88 billion received compared to KSh 18.5 billion offered which was a 145.32 per cent subscription rate, and a WAY of 13.505 per cent against a coupon rate of 12.500 per cent (Table 17.4). Building on this success, the Government has been allocating significant proportions of the budget deficit financing to infrastructure bonds. By 2016, ten (10) IFBs worth KSh 258.58 billion had successfully been issued, attracting significant demand both at the primary and secondary markets. At the NSE, IFBs account for a significant portion of

Table 17.4 Performance of infrastructure bond auctions (KSh M)

Bond	Date of issue	Offer amount	Bids received	Successful bids		Coupon rate (per cent)	Successful average rate (per cent)
Issue number			**F.V.**	**Cost**	**F.V.**		
IFB 1/2009/12	23-02-09	18,500	26,884	10,588	11,244	12.5	13.505
IFB 2/2009/12	7-12-2009	18,500	44,121	9448	9704	12	12.537
IFB 1/2010/8	1-3-2010	14,500	35,273	7192	7132	9.75	9.579
IFB 2/2010/9	30-08-10	31,600	37,362	17,422	18,672	6	7.293
IFB1/2011/12	3-10-11[1]	35,850	38,999	37,190	24,326	12	16.64
IFB1/2013/12	30-09-13[2]	36,000	37,629	35,941	38,364	11	12.363
IFB1/2014/12	27-10-14[3]	35,000	41,003	35,015	35,481	11	11.263
IFB1/2015/12	30-03-15[4]	50,000	76,394	49,712	51,192	11	11.556
IFB1/2015/09	14-12-15	30,000		21,178	25,120	11	14.753
IFB1/2016/09	23-05-16	30,000	39,429	34,898	36,303	12.5	13.339
Grand Total				**258,584**	**257,537**		

[1] This bond was reissued on tap on 7 Nov. 2011, 5 Dec. 2011, 2 Jan. 2012, 6 Feb. 2012, and 27 Feb. 2012. The bond will be amortized on 28 Sep. 2015, 23 Sep. 2019, and 18 Sep. 2023.

[2] This bond was reissued on tap on 28 Oct. 2013. The bond will be amortized on 25 Sep. 2017, 20 Sep. 2021, and 15 Sep. 2025.

[3] This bond was reissued on tap on 3 Nov. 2014, 10 Nov. 2014, and 17 Nov. 2014. The bond will be amortized on 22 Oct. 2018, 17 Oct. 2022, and 12 Oct. 2026.

[4] This bond was reissued on tap on 13 Apr. 2015. The bond will be amortized on 22 Mar. 2021, 18 Mar. 2024, and 15 Mar. 2027.

government bond trading with buy/sell demand largely from institutional investors.

17.7.6 Reduced Moratorium Period for Trading New or Reopened Bonds

To improve trading of Treasury bonds at the NSE, the CBK in 2009 reduced to one day, the number of days that investors waited to trade their bonds after primary market purchase, from one week that was the practice earlier. This was facilitated through provision of a functionality in the bond auction system to update the CSD on real time basis rather than on batch processing. This change helped to improve operational efficiency and liquidity of bonds at the secondary market.

17.8 Outlook on Development of Government Securities Market

Going forward, enhancement of the benchmark bond programme will entail continued building of liquidity on bonds through reopening and issuance of large size bonds. This is important to address debt refinancing, undertake liability management operations to optimize the benchmark portfolio which will entail use of strategies such as switching, exchanges, and bond swaps. Liability management operations will aim at achieving the following purposes: increase liquidity in the bonds market around benchmark bonds by retiring illiquid bonds from the market); minimize risks (refinancing and interest rate) in debt portfolio; minimize the cost of debt service through bond refinancing and to take advantage of favourable market environment to undertake bond refinancing or raise cash for the sinking fund.

Some of the considerations important when making choices on an appropriate bond exchange programme include legal and regulatory provisions; pricing—determination of exchange ratio; cost savings—compute net present value of bond refinancing decision and communication to the market and timing through the issuance calendar. Conducive market conditions to undertake bond refinancing include when interest rates in the market are sufficiently lower than the coupon rate on the candidate bonds and price of the candidate bonds is lower than par. Countries that have implemented bond switches, swaps, and buy backs include Turkey, Brazil Colombia, Indonesia, Hungary, Malaysia, Poland, Sri Lanka, and South Africa. Common issuance method is the auction with pre-announced bond exchange calendar and market consultations.

In terms of electronic platforms for Government securities market operations, the CBK has progressed implementation of a range of electronic platforms such as Internet Banking (IB), Treasury Mobile Direct (TMD) and CSD-based securities system. Over The Counter (OTC) trading for Treasury bill on a non-electronic deal matching platform (and an automated settlement process at the CBK) has been operational since 2014. To enhance trading efficiency, the CBK is progressing the implementation of a fully electronic OTC platform for trading Treasury bills.

Other market development initiatives being undertaken in consultation with industry stakeholders include (i) launch of new products such as financial derivatives, Global Depository Receipts/Notes (GDRs/GDNs), securities lending and borrowing, Exchange Traded Funds (ETFs), which are collective investment vehicles that track market indicators such as indices or a basket of securities or commodities; (ii) Establishment of Over The Counter (OTC) market for trading Government securities and privately issued securities. These initiatives will deepen the market for government securities and the overall capital market to enable it to play its rightful role as the financial hub in the region as envisaged in the Vision 2030 development blueprint (Republic of Kenya, 2007).

Appendix

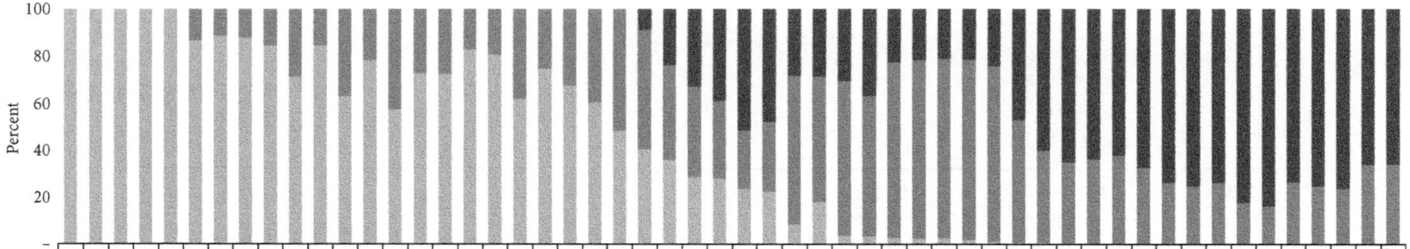

	1964	1965	1966	1967	1968	1969	1970	1971	1972	1973	1974	1975	1976	1977	1978	1979	1980	1981	1982	1983	1984	1985	1986	1987	1988	1989	1990
T-bonds	-	-	-	-	-	-	-	-	-	-	-	-	-	-	-	-	-	-	-	-	-	-	-	8.9	23.	32.	38.
T-bills	-	-	-	-	-	13.	11.	12.	15.	28.	15.	36.	21.	42.	27.	27.	17.	19.	37.	25.	32.	39.	51.	50.	40.	38.	33.
Stocks	100	100	100	100	100	86.	88.	87.	84.	71.	84.	63.	78.	57.	72.	72.	82.	80.	62.	74.	67.	60.	48.	40.	36.	28.	27.

	1991	1992	1993	1994	1995	1996	1997	1998	1999	2000	2001	2002	2003	2004	2005	2006	2007	2008	2009	2010	2011	2012	2013	2014	2015	2016	Sep-16
T-bonds	51.	47.	28.	28.	30.	36.	22.	21.	21.	21.	24.	47.	60.	65.	63.	62.	67.	73.	75.	73.	82.	83.	73.	75.	76.	66.	66.
T-bills	25.	29.	63.	53.	65.	60.	74.	75.	76.	76.	74.	52.	39.	34.	35.	37.	32.	26.	24.	26.	17.	16.	26.	24.	23.	33.	33.
Stocks	23.	22.	8.5	17.	3.7	3.1	2.5	2.3	2.5	1.7	0.8	0.6	0.3	0.3	0.3	0.3	0.1	0.1	0.1	0.1	-	-	-	-	-	-	-

Figure A17.1 Composition of Treasury bills, bonds, and government stocks, 1964–2016

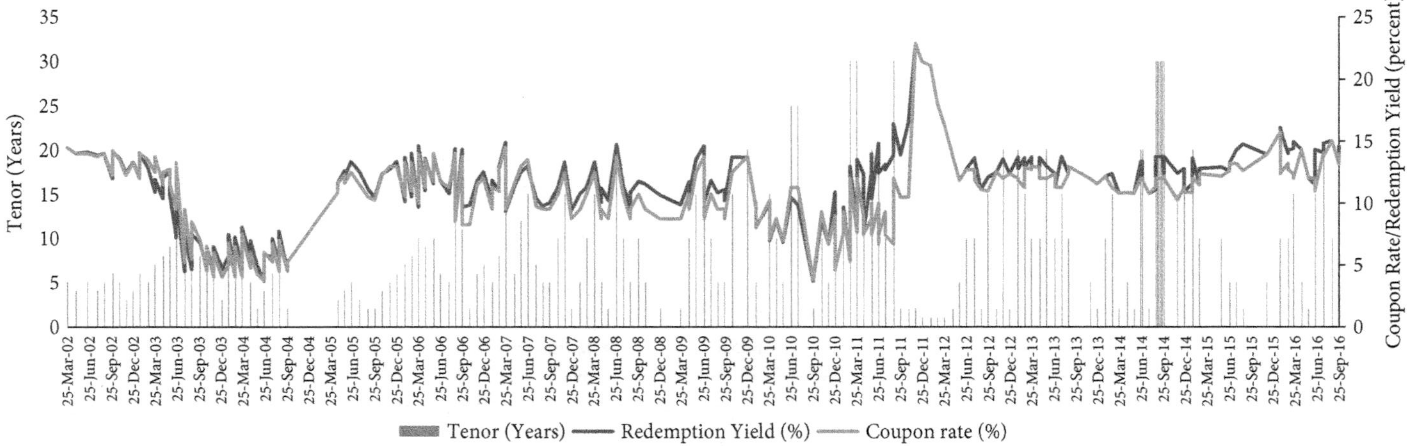

Figure A17.2 Kenya Government bond yield, coupon rate, and tenor

Table A17.1 Outstanding Treasury bonds by type of bond (KSh million)

Date	Bearer	Non-bearer	Floating rate	Special	FXD	Zero coupon	IFB	SBD
June 97	671	4407	30,536	–	–	–	–	–
June 98	–	315	34,372	–	–	–	–	–
June 99	7	256	26,983	940	–	–	–	–
June 00	–	77	32,645	4129	–	–	–	–
June 01	–	–	38,173	6273	54	–	–	–
June 02	–	–	33,909	6362	66,062	–	–	–
June 03	–	–	28,559	7473	120,104	5413	–	–
June 04	–	–	20,476	4320	156,131	7699	–	–
June 05	–	–	7129	1906	147,802	36,522	–	–
June 06	–	–	2232	3553	206,822	5750	–	–
June 07	–	–	744	22,553	240,175	8728	–	–
June 08	–	–	–	31,275	276,224	7691	–	–
June 09	–	–	–	24,531	301,697	14,789	19,727	–
June 10	–	–	–	17,781	376,302	–	54,533	–
June 11	–	–	–	16,000	492,257	–	87,404	–
June 12	–	–	–	16,000	517,870	–	130,851	22,229
June 13	–	–	–	11,000	580,093	–	130,851	22,229
June 14	–	–	–	11,000	712,318	–	169,215	22,229
June 15	–	–	–	11,000	749,064	–	247,406	28,237
June 16	–	–	–	11,000	841,066	–	271,738	28,237
Sep. 16	–	–	–	11,000	905,002	–	257,538	28,237

References

Bhattacharyay, B. (2011), 'Bond market development in Asia: An empirical analysis of major determinants'. ADBI Working Paper 300. Tokyo: Asian Development Bank Institute. <http://www.adbi.org/working-paper/2011/07/28/4659.bond.market.development.asia/>

Capital Markets Authority (1990, 2012) The Capital Markets Act, http://www.cma.or.ke/

CBK Annual Report, June 1990.

Central Bank of Kenya (2012) The Central Bank of Kenya Act, https://www.centralbank.go.ke

Chironga, C., Wambua, J., and Ngugi, R. (2010), 'Term structure of interest rates—recent developments in Kenya'. Central Bank of Kenya Working Paper Series.

Christensen, J. (2005), 'Domestic debt markets in Sub-Saharan Africa'. IMF working papers, Vol. 52, No. 3, p. 521.

IMF, 2003, Debt Sustainability in Low-Income Countries – Towards a Forward-looking Strategy.

IMF, 2005, Operational Framework for Debt Sustainability Assessment in Low-Income Countries – Further Considerations.

IMF, 2006, Review of Low-Income Country Debt Sustainability Framework and Implications of the multilateral Debt Relief Initiative (MDRI).

IMF, 2012, Revisiting the Debt Sustainability Framework for Low-Income Countries.

Kenya National Bureau of Statistics, Economic Survey (various years).

Mbewa, M., Ngugi, R. W., and Kithinji, A. (2007), 'Development of bonds market: Kenya's experience'. KIPPRA, Working Paper No. 15.

Medium term debt strategy (MTDS) (2009, 2010, 2011, 2012, 2013, 2014, 2015, 2016), Retrieved from www.treasury.go.ke

Ngugi, R. W. and Agoti, J. (2007), 'Microstructure elements of bonds in Kenya'. *African Economic Conference Globalization, Institutions and Economic Development in Africa Public Finance Management Act 2012.*

Republic of Kenya (2007), Kenya Vision 2030.

Republic of Kenya (2012) The Public Finance Management Act.

Thupayagale, P. (2015), 'Fixed income market efficiency: Evidence from Kenya's 10-year local currency bond', *Botswana Journal of Economics*, Vol. 12, No. 2.

World Bank (2007), *Developing the Domestic Government Debt Market: From Diagnostics to Reform Implementation*. Washington DC, World Bank Publications, Vol. 2, p. 16. http://www8.iadb.org/res/laresnetwork/files/pr268finaldraft.pdf

Yibin M., Phelps P., and Stotsky J. G. (2013), 'Bond markets in Africa'. *IMF* WP/13/12. <http://www.imf.org/external/pubs/cat/longres.aspx?sk=40239>

18

The Structure of the Interbank Market in Kenya

Prospects and Challenges

Lydia Ndirangu, Kethi Ngoka-Kisinguh, and Esther Kariuki

18.1 Introduction

There is a general agreement among central bankers regarding the benefits to the economy of market-based instruments for the implementation of monetary policy. Most central banks have therefore attempted to regulate overall liquidity conditions in the economy through financial operations in the domestic money markets. The objective is to influence the underlying demand and supply conditions for money supply. But for the interbank market to successfully play this role in the transmission of monetary policy, the interbank market needs to be deep. Deep markets allow variations in interbank rates to be rapidly transmitted to the entire term structure, thus affecting borrowing conditions for households and firms (Green et al., 2016). Deep markets also make possible smooth distribution of liquidity between participants, thereby allowing a central bank to rely on money market operations for liquidity management for the system as a whole, as opposed to managing a specific bank's liquidity position.

However, as shown by the global financial crisis a decade ago, exposures through the interbank market also provide a potentially important channel for contagion, as the market is driven by relationship lending (Bräuning and Fecht, 2017). Often, collateral requirements are waived. The risk posed by such contagion in turn depends on the exact structure (e.g. level of interconnectedness, completeness, concentration, etc.) of the interbank market network. This is because the pattern of connection, particularly the pattern of interaction among the players in a network, affects both the route through which the information (funds) flow, and the efficiency with which the market transmits such information (Newman, 2010). Since the structure of the interbank network is so important for resilience of the market and the economy, policymakers need information on its actual topology, including clear analysis of how and why the market changes.

Lydia Ndirangu, Kethi Ngoka-Kisinguh, and Esther Kariuki, *The Structure of the Interbank Market in Kenya: Prospects and Challenges* In: *50 Years of Central Banking in Kenya: Regional and Global Perspectives*. Edited by: Patrick Njoroge and Victor Murinde, Oxford University Press (2021). © The Central Bank of Kenya. DOI: 10.1093/oso/9780198851820.003.0018

It is interesting to note, therefore, that although Kenya has an active interbank market, which accounts for approximately 10 per cent of total banking assets, with the overnight market constituting about a third of the interbank assets, documentation of the structure of interbank market in Kenya is quite limited as of now. The exceptions include Mwega (2012) who study the overnight interbank microstructure for the period 2003–11; and Oduor et al. (2014) who examine the segmentation of the interbank market from 2008 to 2011. However, the above existing studies do not trace the intrinsic structure of the market since its origins in 1995 in order to map the important milestones in the evolution of the interbank market in Kenya.

Hence, the purpose of the chapter is to document how the network structure of the interbank market in Kenya has evolved over time, by invoking several measurements derived from network theory to uncover several microstructure characteristics, including the nature of segmentation and associated asymmetric information in the interbank market. This has an impact on effectiveness of the flow of funds. We add to existing knowledge by introducing the topology of the network itself. The network analysis is based on an exploration of 123,282 overnight interbank transactions from 2008:q4 to 2017:q2. Continuous data on detailed bank transactions is only available from September 2008. We exploit the notion of community detection in complex networks to identify cliques within the interbank market over time. Banks in one cluster are more connected to each other than to other banks in other clusters. Liquidity is likely to flow better within a community and so is the propagation of a shock. Identifying these communities is thus meaningful as it can allow an assessment of the impact of shocks to the interbank market with more precision, and can aid in design of better-targeted policy measures to increase network resilience. To the best of our knowledge, this chapter is the first to uncover the evolution of the intrinsic structure of the overnight interbank market in Kenya since its first operations to the present using network theory.

We highlight three main findings. First, it is noted that interbank market grew over time in terms of volume, number of deals, and participating banks, reaching a peak around 2009–10. A notable decline is observed thereafter, especially in the number of deals and participating banks. The average level of interbank rate and its volatility also rose post 2010. A slight increase in concentration of contracts and volume is also noted. Measures derived from the topology of the interbank network point to a decline in interconnections since 2012. This is demonstrated by lower levels of the network density, clustering, and closeness. The analysis of centrality measures points to an increase in importance of some banks overtime. Using the notion of community detection in complex networks, we find that interbank network is fragmented into sub networks, with each sub network constituting a complete network. This decentralized structure has some banks with a relatively higher degree of connectivity than others, leading to an overall topology that consists of local clusters with hub-like banks and periphery ones. These features seem to become more prominent with time.

Second, although the interbank structure is largely incomplete, with a density of about 0.25, each bank can be linked to all other banks in the network in no more than three steps (two banks in between). While this may imply that the core potentially provides an efficient shortcut for most peripheral banks for accessing and/or providing liquidity in the network, the short-path length between the banks suggests that contagion can also spread with ease. Exposure is about two banks away. Furthermore, although the observed core–periphery structure may confer some stability to the network with respect to the random breakdown of an individual bank, it also means that the system is vulnerable to removal of the very few well connected banks in the network. The use of the network measures allows us to identify some of the most central banks in the network at each point in time; and whose disruption would destabilize the flow of funds. Knowledge of the banks through which liquidity can be circulated most effectively is an important consideration in the design of measures for central bank's supply of liquidity, especially when the interbank money market is under stress.

Third, notwithstanding the above, the Kenyan interbank market can be described as shallow based on the level of segmentation and concentration of liquidity in a few banks. Money market operations would only be effective if the central bank can expect its liquidity providing or withdrawing operations to be disseminated to all financial institutions in need. The kind of segmentation in some periods may not guarantee such an even distribution and therefore, a reliable price formation process. This limits the ability of the Central Bank to use price-based indicators as intermediate targets for monetary policy. Development in the fiscal space, especially a substantial rise in volatility of the net position of the government from 2013, may also have limited advancement towards smooth functioning of the interbank market.

The remainder of this chapter is organized as follows. Section 18.2 describes the evolution of the interbank market from year 2000. This is followed in Section 18.3 by a brief introduction into network analysis, as applied to the interbank market. Section 18.4 describes the structural features using the network statistics and visual representation of the interbank network. Section 18.5 concludes.

18.2 Evolution of the Overnight Interbank Market

We chart the evolution of the transactions and participating banks in the interbank market. The analysis is performed on all the available overnight interbank exposures from January 2000 to June 2017. There exist data gaps for the detailed bank level transactions from January 2006 to September 2008. Analysis on bank level transactions therefore starts from October 2008.

The overnight interbank's non-collateralized assets have, on average, accounted for about 33 per cent of total interbank assets. Figures 18.1 to 18.3 show the evolution of the interbank volume, the number of transactions and the number of participating banks, respectively. More banks participate in the market as lenders

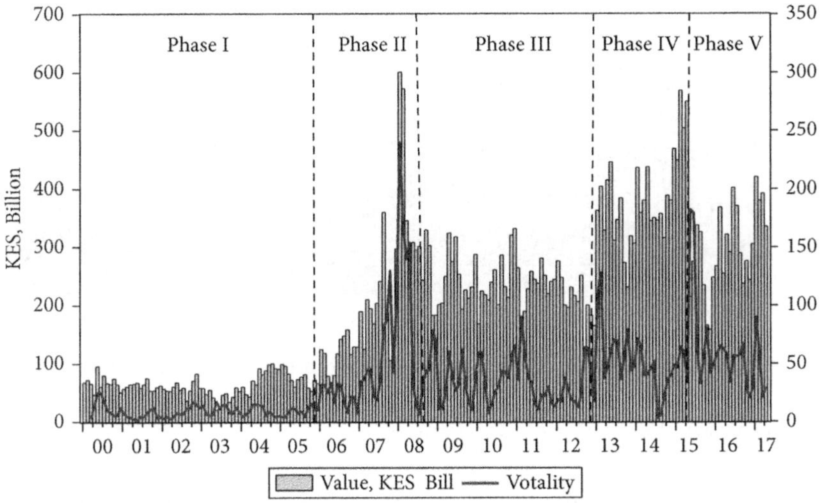

Figure 18.1 Monthly value and volatility of the overnight interbank transactions, 2000–June 2017
Source: Central Bank of Kenya.

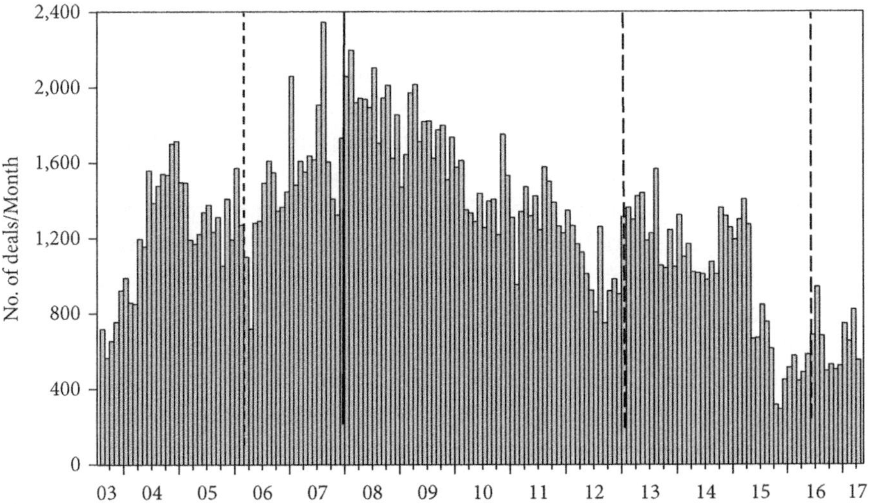

Figure 18.2 Number of overnight deals per month
Source: Central Bank of Kenya.

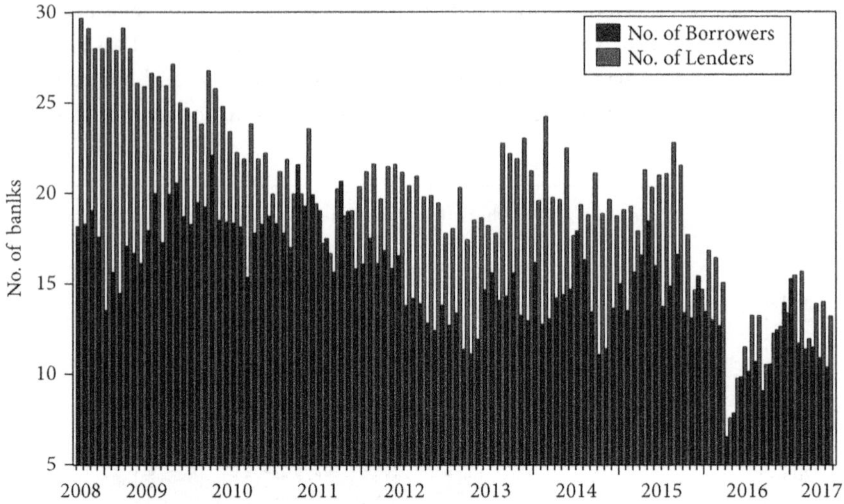

Figure 18.3 Average number of banks participating in the interbank market, 2008–June 2017
Source: Central Bank of Kenya.

than borrowers. The exemption are periods of intense market volatility when there are as many borrowing banks as they are lenders; for example, 2011:q4 and between 2016:q2 to 2016:q4.

From Figure 18.1, the study period can be divided into five distinct phases which are largely related to evolvement of the operating mechanisms of monetary policy. This can be summarized as follows:

- Phase I: This marks the period before the establishment of the Monetary Policy Advisory Committee (MPAC). The MPAC was established in July 2005 for the purpose of advising on monetary policy issues. Before this, the Central Bank of Kenya (hereafter CBK) monetary policy was anchored by targets for the money supply. The targets were determined within a consultative framework between the National Treasury and the CBK.
- Phase II: This represented a growth phase in the interbank market.[1] The Central Bank Rate (CBR) was introduced on 31 May 2006 in accordance with Section 36(4) of the CBK Act. The CBR was supposed to signal the intended direction of monetary policy and was operationalized through the open market operations (OMO). Consequently, various modifications were made to the repo arrangements and cash reserve requirements from mid-2006

[1] The pick in volume from early 2006 also follows the introduction of the Real Time Gross Settlement (RTGS) System which went live end July 2005.

to improve liquidity management (see Table A18.1). The Monetary Policy Committee (MPC) was established in April 2008 to replace MPAC.

- Phase III: Number of deals and interbank rates declined after the global financial crisis in 2007-2008 and Kenya's post-election violence. The monthly value of the transactions also dropped from a high of KES 500 billion to about KES 250-300 billion. The interbank rates rose sharply towards the end of 2010 and through 2011 despite a high presence of excess reserves in the market (Figure 18.4). This may point to distortions in the market which can arise due to skewed distribution of liquidity in the market. The volatility of the interbank rate and the spreads also increased from mid-2011 through 2012 (Figure 18.5).
- Phase IV: The market seemed to have achieved some stability between 2012 and 2014. However, the level of interest rate volatility remained higher than it was before 2011. The high interest rate volatility may also be partly attributed to variations in liquidity supply arising from instability in the net position of the government. Figure 18.6 shows that this increasingly became volatile from 2013.
- In this phase, CBK was implementing a modified monetary programme which was introduced in March 2010. A new monetary operations framework was introduced in November 2011. All Central Bank market operations were based on the CBR as the reference rate. The operational targets in this period were the net domestic assets (NDA) and the net international reserves (NIR). As part of the daily liquidity management, NDA was supported by the monitoring of reserve money, interbank rates, liquidity distribution in the banking sector and deviations of broad money from target. CBK started experimenting with an interest rate corridor from April 2012 of CBR$\pm$2.5. This phase thus represented a move towards the use of market based instruments for monetary policy. However, the ruled-based instruments retained their central role.
- Phase V: A fiscal cash crunch and exchange rate instability interrupted the interbank market in mid-2015. The interbank rate deviated substantially from the CBR and the CBK had to abandon the corridor due to the high volatility of interest rates. There were clear signs of fiscal dominance then and inversion of the yield curve (Figure 18.7).The instability was soon followed by a financial sector shock following the placement of the Imperial Bank under receivership in October 2015 and Chase bank in April 2016, resulting in a further increase in segmentation of the interbank market as demonstrated by the rise in rate spreads (Figure 18.5).

A major deduction from the foregoing, i.e. the evolution of the volumes, interest rate, and number of contracts, given the shocks, is that the interbank market may not have developed deep enough to enable the interbank market rate to sustainably act as an effective operational target. Development in the fiscal space may have played a role given the substantial increase in volatility of the net position of the government. Such high variations in a major component of liquidity supply limits the ability of the Central Bank to make effective decisions on timing and size of its liquidity providing and absorbing operations; and hence the development of conditions for smooth functioning of the interbank market.

It is useful here to show some insight to the distribution of interbank assets and liabilities, during the evolution of the market. Complementary to the information on volumes and number of deals is how much the volume and number of contracts are concentrated across the market.

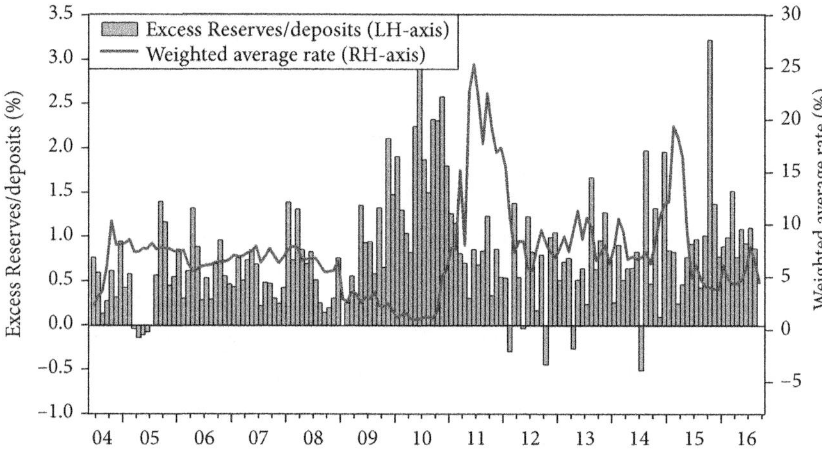

Figure 18.4 Trends of the interbank rate and excess reserves
Source: Central Bank of Kenya.

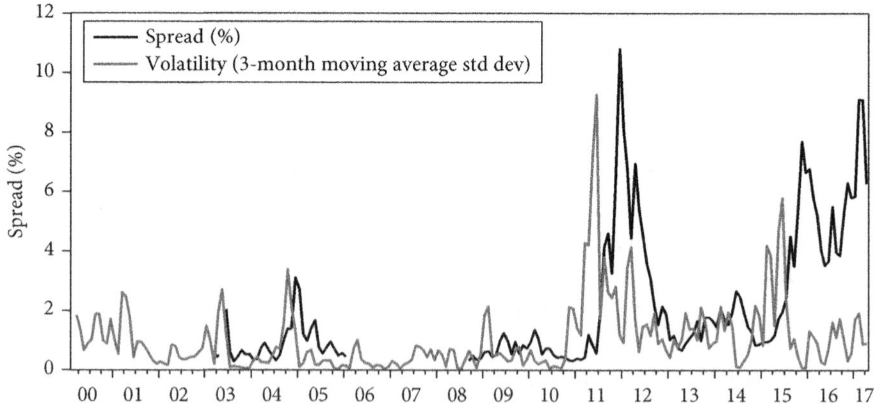

Figure 18.5 Volatility and spread of interbank interest rate, 2000–June 2017
Source: Central Bank of Kenya.

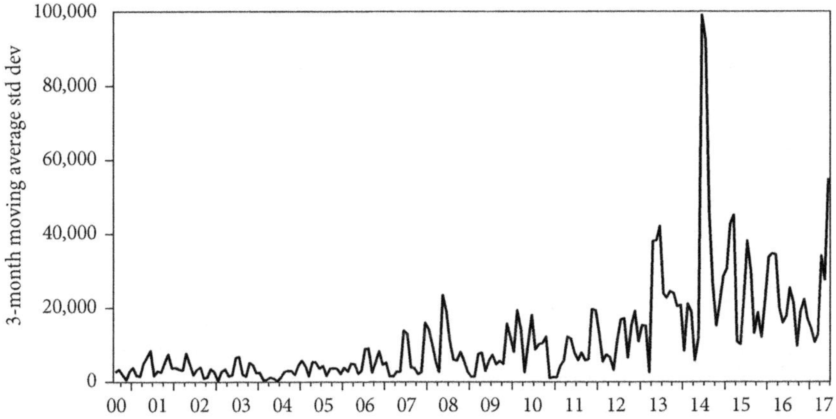

Figure 18.6 Volatility of the net position of the Government
Source: Central Bank of Kenya.

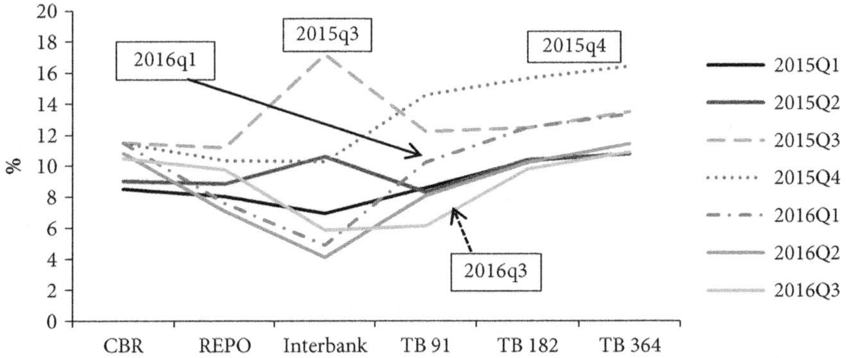

Figure 18.7 Liquidity conditions and the term structure, 2015–16
Source: Central Bank of Kenya.

Figure 18.8 shows the distribution of the interbank assets and liabilities from 2008q4 to 2017q2. About 80 per cent of the interbank liabilities and 77 per cent of the assets are concentrated in the respective top 20 per cent of the banks over the study period. Very few assets and liabilities are recorded for the lowest 20 per cent of the banks. The proportion of assets held by the bottom 40 per cent declines from about 6 per cent to about 1 per cent over time. This points to an increase in concentration in the interbank trading. Figure 18.9 shows this to be the case.

Concentration as measured by the Herfindal-Hirschman Index (HHI), show a rising trend especially for the interbank assets from 2012q4 (Figure 18.9(a)). The inverse of the HHI gives a proxy of the number of leading banks in the market. The number of leading banks in asset holding gradually declines from 16 to about 10 by

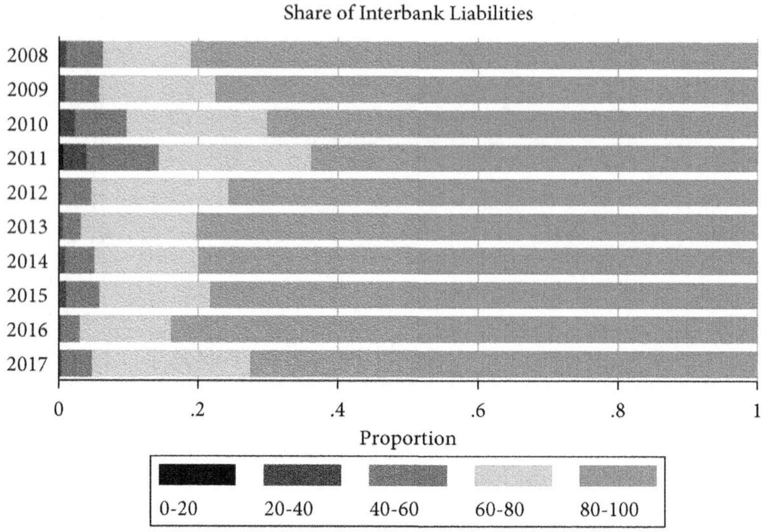

Figure 18.8 Distribution of interbank assets and liabilities, 2008q4–2017Q2
Source: Central Bank of Kenya.

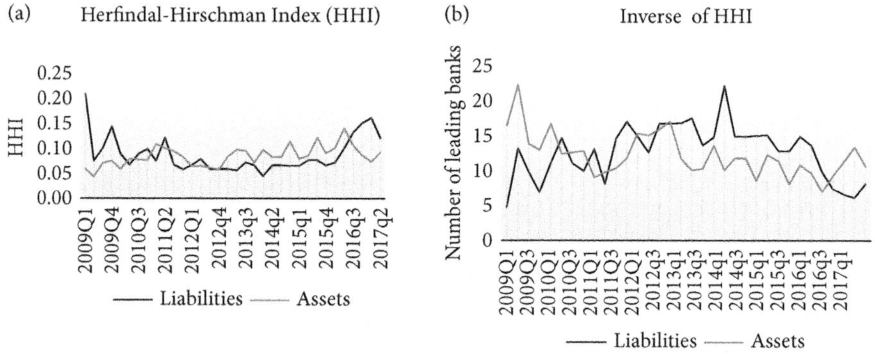

Figure 18.9 Evolution of concentration of assets and liabilities
Source: Central Bank of Kenya.

mid-2015 (Figure 18.9(b)). That is, even if there were more than 40 banks in each year, the market behaves as if it has only 10 banks supplying liquidity by mid-2015.

18.3 Indicators of Topology of the Interbank Network

In this section, we present the network measurements that are used to characterize the role of banks in the interbank market. The measures are extracted from classical network theory, often applied in natural and physical sciences describing, for example, how diseases or information spread (Newman, 2010; Albert and Barabási, 2002). This analysis follows an increasing number of studies in central banks that have used this approach to describe the topology of financial systems e.g. Brazil (Silva et al., 2015), ECB (Peltonen et al., 2013), South Africa (Brink and Georg, 2011), Italy (Iazzetta and Manna, 2009); Bank of England (Becher et al., 2008); the Fed (Bech and Atala, 2008) and Austria (Boss et al., 2004), among others. The analysis is performed on data from 2008q4 to 2017q2.

18.3.1 The Network

A network consists of a set of N nodes that are connected by M edges (links). In the language of the network theory, each bank in the interbank market represents a node and the interbank exposure and payments define the links between the banks. It is such simple quantities that are used to express many other network metrics, which allow a deeper understanding of the dynamics of the interbank system. We consider a range of commonly used indicators used to assess the span and completeness/connectivity of the network; and centrality. These indicators are used to investigate the statistical and structural properties of the interbank system.

18.3.1.1 Network Completeness and Span Measures

18.3.1.1.1 Density/Completeness

The density of a network is the ratio of the number of existing links and the number of the maximum possible links. It is a measure of completeness of a network, where for a complete network, all possible links are present. The closer the density is to 1, the more complete the network is.

18.3.1.1.2 Shortest Path Length/Distance and Diameter

Distance measures offer insight into the span of the network and how different types of information may flow through the interbank market. Distance measures are expressed in terms paths and length of the path. A path is defined as any connection between two nodes, and the length of the path between any two nodes is the number of links passed to get from one node to the other along this path. In the interbank network, the path length is then the number of connections that is needed to transfer liquidity from one bank to another.

The shortest path length (distance) is the minimum number of nodes it takes to get from any node A to another node B. The maximum distance of a node is the longest path to any other node. The diameter of a network is the maximum of all distances between pairs. Higher density networks tend to yield smaller average shortest path length (ASPL). In normal times a small ASPL implies liquidity can easily be transferred from one bank to another. In times of crises, however, a short ASPL may mean faster spread of contagion through the system.

18.3.1.1.3 Small World Property

Related to the concept of the ASPL is the notion of the small world property. According to Watts and Strogatz (2001), small world networks are distinguished from other networks by two specific properties; namely, high clustering among nodes and short path lengths. Small path lengths ensure that information or resources easily spreads throughout the network. This property implies that most nodes can be reached from any other node via a few number of links.[2]

In the context of the interbank market, the attribute of a small world would reflect that the interbank network comprises of a core or a number of hubs (because of the high nodal clustering) and the presence of shortcut links with distant nodes. In such a small-world network, it is possible for a shock originating in one bank in the system to easily spread to the entire network. Thus, the financial system's small-world property suggests the potential presence of systemic risk.

In this chapter, we measure the maximum number of steps (links) between any two banks within the network, and the average shortest path length. We then assess how this has evolved over time.

18.3.1.2 Network Centrality Measures

Centrality deals with the question: 'which are the most important or central nodes in a network?' (Newman, 2010). For the interbank networks, measures of centrality summarize a bank's involvement in or contribution to the cohesiveness of the interbank network. The larger the centrality measure, the greater the importance such a node/bank has in the network. According to Henggeler-Muller (2006), quoted in Martinez-Jaramillo et al. (2012), a financial institution is considered important in a network if it has the following characteristics:

- Possesses many linkages to other members of the network (degree);
- The total amount of its assets, liabilities in the network is very large (strength);
- There are many paths which pass through it (betweenness).
- Its failure could transmit contagion in a few steps (closeness);
- Its counterparts are also considered relevant (eigenvector and PageRank)

18.3.1.2.1 Degree

The degree of a bank (node) measures the number of links it has with other banks or the number of counterparties as a lender or as a borrower. It represents the simplest characterization of a bank in the interbank market. For networks such as the interbank one, for which the direction of the interaction matter, the degree can

[2] In the context of social networks, the small world phenomenon results in a network of strangers being linked by a short chain of acquaintances.

be decomposed into in- and out-degree. The in-degree is the number of creditors a bank has at a given time, while the out-degree is the number of debtors. If a bank has many interbank creditors (exposures), it is said to have a high in-degree (out-degree). The banks that have higher in-degree measures are the most systemically relevant, while those with higher out-degree measures are the most important sources of funds (or money centres).

18.3.1.2.2 Strength

The strength measure is an extension of the degree by taking the size of the liabilities and exposures into account. It can be interpreted as a measure of intensity of the interaction. The in-strength represents the sum of the interbank liabilities; or borrowing dependency for each bank, and the out-strength, the sum of the assets. The out-strength can also be seen as a measure of activeness from the investment perspective. Banks with high degree and strength are considered to be closer to the centre of the debit/credit network, and therefore more important players within the financial system.

However, the degree and strength are local measures, i.e. they do not take into account the whole network, but only the local neighbourhood of the node. Thus, while the degree is a sensible centrality measure for small networks, it can miss important global characteristics of the importance of the node in large networks.

18.3.1.2.3 Betweenness Centrality

This is one of the most popular global centrality measures. It quantifies how frequently a node lies on the shortest path between two unconnected nodes (Newman, 2010). This measure of centrality is particularly important in a payment system network. This is because a bank with a high betweenness centrality would have an important influence on other banks, as it can stop the flow of funds/information that passes through it. For instance, consider two banks A and B with the same degree, but bank A has a higher betweenness centrality. It means that, relative to bank B, it is located on a more important path in the network. It is more likely to be involved in the transmission of a liquidity shock if it is unable to pay a transaction, and more likely to also have a larger impact on the network. The more important a bank is as a debtor, the greater is its tendency to have a high betweenness centrality, and thus occupy an important position within the network.

18.3.1.2.4 Closeness

Closeness centrality is a measure of the degree to which a node is near all other nodes in a network. It is the inverse of the sum of the shortest distances between each node and every other node reachable from it. The higher the value, the lower the distance separating the bank from the counterparties. A bank with higher closeness centrality is directly connected to more banks in the network. It can therefore facilitate the efficient spread of liquidity, as well as the rapid spread of shocks.

18.3.1.2.5 Eigenvector and PageRank Centrality

Like degree centrality, Eigen centrality measures a node's influence by counting the number of links it has to other nodes within the network, but goes a step further. We can think of degree centrality as awarding one 'central point' for every network neighbour a bank has. But not all neighbours are equal. In many instances, a bank's importance in a network is increased by having connections to other banks that are themselves important. The concept of Eigenvector centrality therefore emphasizes that power is not an individual attribute but is inherently relational. Instead of awarding to a node just one point for each neighbour, Eigenvector centrality gives each node a score proportional to the sum of the scores of its neighbours.

A high Eigen centrality score indicates a strong influence over other nodes in the network. It indicates not just direct influence, but also implied influence over nodes more than one 'hop' away. A node may have a high degree score (i.e. many connections) but a relatively low Eigen centrality score if many of those connections are with similarly low-scored nodes. Also, a node may have a high betweenness score (indicating it connects disparate parts of a network) but a low Eigen centrality score because it is still some distance from the centre of power in the network.

Like Eigen centrality, PageRank can help uncover influential or important nodes whose reach extends beyond just their direct connections. The main difference to Eigen centrality is that PageRank takes link direction and weight into account. We examine the PageRank of the Kenyan banks and compare it with other centrality measures.

18.3.1.2.6 Clustering Coefficient

The clustering coefficient ($c_{i,}$) is a measure of the probability that two nodes which are neighbours of the same node, themselves share a link (i.e. the three nodes form a triangle). The local $c_{i,}$ of node i is the ratio of therefore the fraction of triangles present in the network out of all the possible triangles that could be formed. It is thus a measure of connection density around a node. The closer the local c_i is to 1, the more likely it is for the network to form clusters.

The higher the $c_{i,}$ of a bank the higher the chances that its counterparties are engaging in trading together. In order to have a triangle in the payments system, at least one bank must lend to one counterparty and borrow from another. The $c_{i,}$ provides a way to assess the extent of this kind of intermediary trading. It also quantifies how close the particular bank and its neighbours are to being a clique. From a lending perspective, a high c_i means that bank i is easily substitutable because its neighbourhood has other nearby options to invest in. Conversely, a low c_i means that few options are available for the neighbours of i suggesting that bank i is important in its neighbourhood because its removal would significantly reduce the trading options in the nearby surroundings. Hence, c_i can be viewed as a measure of diversification of the counterparties of i.

18.3.1.2.7 Degree Correlation/Affinity

Affinity or the concept of assortative mixing represents the extent to which banks in a network associate with similar ones. The likelihood that a bank interacts with another bank depends on the characteristics of the two banks. One characteristic of a node that is endogenous to the structure of the network is its degree. A network is said to be assortative if high (low) degree nodes form links with other high (low) degree ones (Newman, 2003). The Pearson's correlation (r) of degree of the node in each connected pair is used to measure this dependency. When $r=1$, the interbank market has perfect assortative mixing, while it is completely disassortative when $r=-1$. Negative assortativity is often correlated with the existence of hubs. There is also the case where $r\approx 0$. In this case, banks on average, may not indicate preferential attachment, and the network may have a slight mixture of assortative and disassortative trends.

The question as to whether the banking network is assortative or disassortative is crucial to the stability of the whole network. For instance, Newman (2003) found that assortative networks are more resilient, whereas disassortative networks are particularly vulnerable against directed attacks on high degree nodes (hubs).

Empirical evidence shows that interbank networks very frequently display disassortative mixing patterns in terms of degree (Soramäki et al., 2007 for the Fedwire settlement system; Imakubo and Soejima, 2006 for Japan; and Silva et al., 2015 for Brazil). As such, they are closer to technological and biological networks than social networks. Social networks tend to be assortative. All these studies are on relatively well developed interbank networks compared to Kenya.

18.4 Kenya Interbank Network Topology and Centrality Measures

18.4.1 Network Topology and Centrality Measures

As mentioned earlier, the most easily understood statistics for measuring the centrality of a node within a network are its degree and strength. Figure 18.10 (a&b) present the average in- and out-degree of the banks by size. The in-degree represents the number of banks that have funded bank i in the market, and the out-degree denotes the number of banks i has lent to. In a sense, the in- and out-degree represents funding and investment diversification. The large banks are

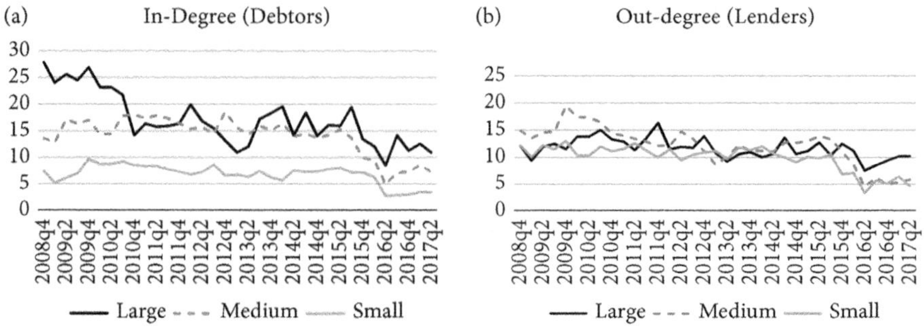

Figure 18.10 Evolution of the degree measures by tier group

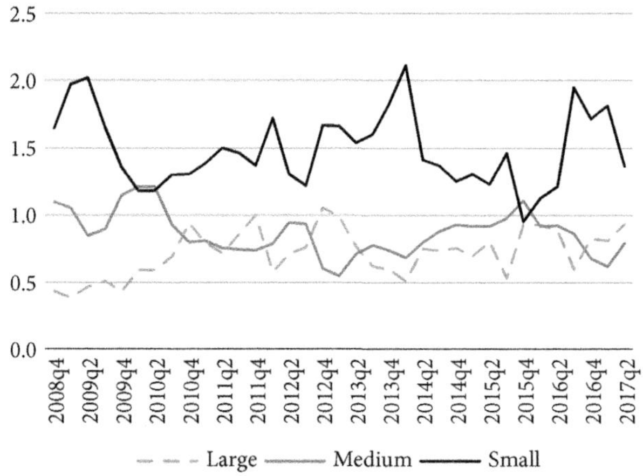

Figure 18.11 Ratio of out- to in-degree

the most connected as debtors while the small banks have the least funding diversification. On average, only 7 banks were exposed to small banks between 2009 and 2015 compared to 18 and 16 banks for large and medium banks. However, on the lending side, small banks were on average, just as diversified as the large banks before the drop from 2015q4.

Figure 18.11 shows the ratio of the out-to in-degree. The out-degree for small banks is on average about 1.5 times higher than their in-degree. This means that they trade with more counterparties when leading liquidity that when buying. This could point to possible lack of power in choosing their lenders. Medium banks tend to have the same number of creditors and debtors since their ratio is close to one most of the time. In general, we find a negative and significant correlation between the in-and out-degree, implying that banks with a large number of credit counterparties have a low number of debtors (Figure 18.12). This may suggest that banks tend to specialize as either lenders or borrowers in the

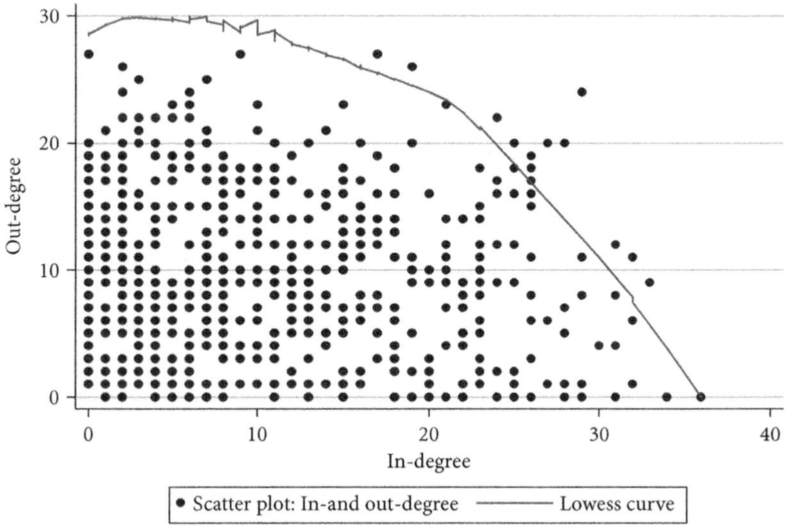

Figure 18.12 Correlation between in- and out-degree*
*Spearman's coefficient = –0.09; p-value = 0.017.

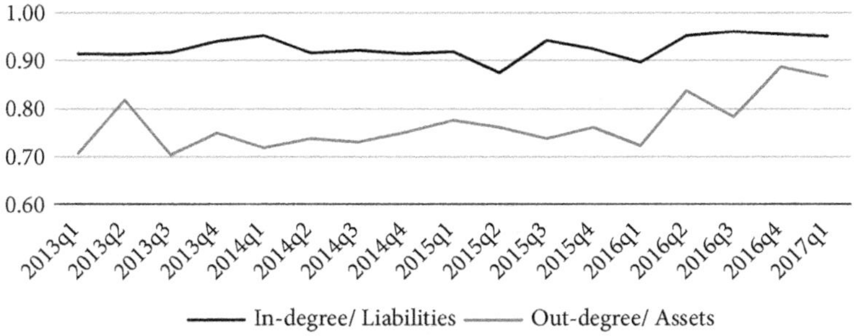

Figure 18.13 Comparison between the degrees and strength

interbank market. Such a finding would be consistent with other studies that show that interbank markets typically have natural lenders and borrowers, with the small banks tending to turn over their surplus funds to large banks that distribute or invest the funds in other ways (Bech andAtalay, 2010; Craig and Peter, 2014).

Considerable information can also be obtained based on the relationship between degree and strength. Figure 18.13 depict a high correlation between the out-degree and the out-strength and in-strength and the in-degree. Both correlations are quite high (over 0.7), with the in-measures being much higher. The very high correlation (> 0.9) between in-degree and in-strength suggest that banks with large value of interbank liabilities have these liabilities with many counterparties. The risk of default of one of these banks would thus be divided among many.

However, the contagion effects can be large if the non-repayment by such a bank jeopardizes the ability of its creditor banks to meet their interbank obligations.

The analysis of this market microstructure can be enriched by looking at the distribution function of the in- and out-degree and the in- and out-strength. Figure 18.14 (a&b) shows substantial asymmetry in the degree's distribution especially for the borrowing transactions (Figure 18.14a). The skewness seems to have increased over time, especially from 2012. While on average 14–17 banks have less than five connections per year, the right tail of the distribution has few banks (1–2) connected to almost 40 banks, especially before the shock in 2015q3. The out-degree tends to be more evenly distributed but becomes more right-skewed towards the end of the study period. The distribution of funds flow, both in and out values (strength), is shown in Figure 18.15. Both the in- and the out-strength have long right tails.

This right-skewed distribution is a common feature for networks characterized by the presence of hubs (Clauset et al., 2009; Barabási, 2009). The concentration of links on a smaller number of nodes gives rise to hub-like nodes in the network. Several studies have shown that many interbank networks have similar degree

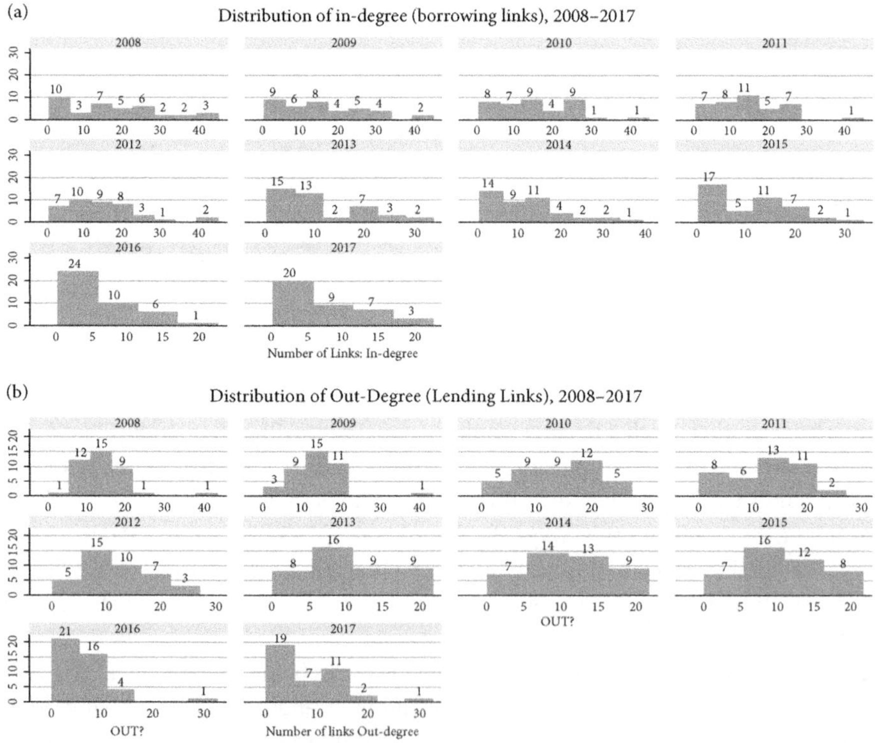

Figure 18.14 Distribution of the degrees by direction of flow

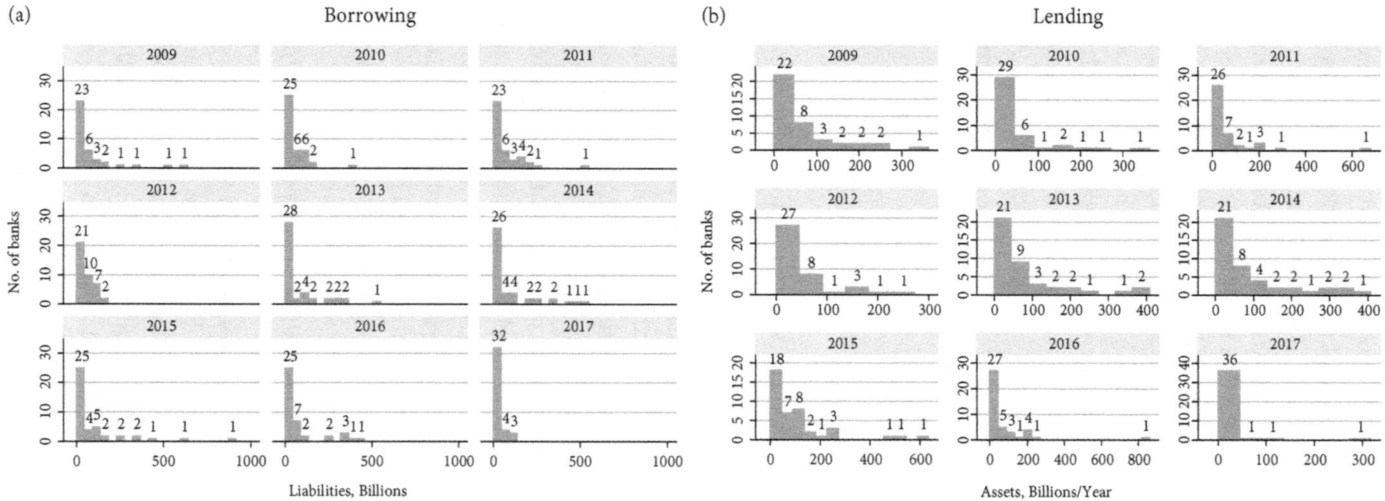

Figure 18.15 Distribution of value, 2013–2017q2

distribution (e.g. Boss et al., 2004 for Austria; Soramäki et al., (2006) for the Fed; Imakubo and Soejima (2006) for Japan; and Cajueiro and Tabak (2008) for Brazil). One important feature of such networks is that they can be described as robust, yet fragile (Albert et al., 2000; Newman, 2003). This is because random disturbances are easily absorbed (robust) whereas targeted attacks on the hub-like nodes have a significant effect on the entire network (fragile).

This feature has important policy implication. While such a network might experience long stable periods during which disruptions are confined to peripheral banks, and can thus be absorbed easily within the entire system, such periods could be a misleading indicator of the overall stability of the system. This is because it is only when a hub (a bank with many connections) is subject to stress that the true network dynamics emerge (Haldane, 2009). We now turn to the detailed visualization and characterization of the interbank market network to be able to identify such hub-like banks.

18.4.2 The Network Structure

Figure A18.1 provides graphical depiction of the network of transactions in the interbank market for each complete year from 2009 to 2016; and up to June for year 2017. Each node represents a bank, and each link denotes the presence of a transactional relationship observed during the year. To reduce visual complexity of the network and to be able to extract meaning from the hairballs of the node-link diagrams, we try to identify common patterns of nodes and links. We exploit the notion of community/clique detection in complex networks (Newman and Girvan, 2004). As defined above in calculation of the clustering coefficient, we use the probability that two banks which are neighbours of the same bank themselves share a link. The algorithm used to extract the clusters identifies communities of banks which have at least four members linked to them. Each clique is defined as a sub-graph whose nodes almost completely connect with each other, but may be sparsely connected with the rest of the network. The revealed patterns can uncover hidden relationships within the network.

The graphs in column 1 of Figure A18.1 show the cliques extracted from the transactional relations. Each cluster is marked in a different colour. Knowledge of the cliques can help predict behaviour and the 'structural signatures' or roles of individual banks in the network. For instance, further analysis shows that the cliques roughly reflect known characteristics/behaviour sometimes as predicted by the balance sheet. The charts presented in Figure A18.2 show the grouping by bank tier group (we restrict the charts to start in 2013). The grouping also reviews the nature of segmentation of the interbank market. Previous studies have shown that the interbank market is segmented but the nature of this segmentation has not been consistently unravelled.

The diagrams in Figure A18.1 depict a decentralized network.[3] The graphs point to a network which is characterized by several core banks and peripheral ones. A core is defined as a subset of nodes (banks) which are maximally connected with other core members, while the periphery banks tend to have very few links with the rest of the market. These are the 'wildcards' in column 1. Column 2 shows the expanded cliques but with the inter-group links omitted. The generally scanty graphs in column 2 become a hairball of links in column 3 once the links between the various clusters and the peripheral banks are included. The peripheral banks are coloured black. Almost every bank in a hub is linked to at least one bank in the periphery, but the converse is not the case (column 3).

The graphs in column 2 also highlight the important actors in the network as revealed by the betweenness centrality (strategically linked banks). The size of the nodes reflects this centrality. It is possible to identify in each clique the particular bank around which others in the clique cluster. Such banks were found to have the highest betweenness centrality and the lowest clustering coefficient in each clique. Removal of such a bank from the network would significantly reduce the trading options for other banks in its sub-network. We also find a high betweenness centrality in some of the periphery banks because their removal would cut off some other periphery members from the network e.g. in 2013, bank number 26 is very central to bank 22 since it is only through it that bank 22 connects to the rest of the market.

The evolution of the cliques between 2009 and 2015 shows that the bank clustering has been quite stable. There are 4–5 cliques in each year, constituting of one large clique (about 17–14 banks) and 3 smaller ones of about 4–7 banks each (Figure A18.1, column 2). Although some banks move between the cliques over the period, the tendency is for most banks to stick and move between the cliques together. While the financial instability of 2015q3 disturbs the trading patterns as new clustering starts to emerge, the overall structure of the sub-networks remain almost the same. Other studies have shown that while the structure of the banking networks varies overtime in response to economic and financial shocks (e.g. Hale, 2012), the strength of core–periphery structures in national interbank markets tends to be stable overtime (Craig and von Peter, 2014; Fricke and Lux, 2015; Puhr et al., 2012).

The evolution of the network density over time can also inform on stability/cohesion of the network (Figure 18.16). The estimated density exhibit phases similar to that depicted in Figure 18.1 above, and it is quite stable over each phase. However, a declining trend is observed. The major drops are largely in response to the instability related to global financial crisis about 2009, the 2011 forex shock and after 2015q3.

[3] A decentralized network is one without any overall dominant central hub. But instead, the network has some nodes with a higher degree of connectivity than others, giving the overall topology local clusters with local hubs. Although there may be some overall centre to it, the network is still defined largely by what is happening at the local level (Baran, 1964).

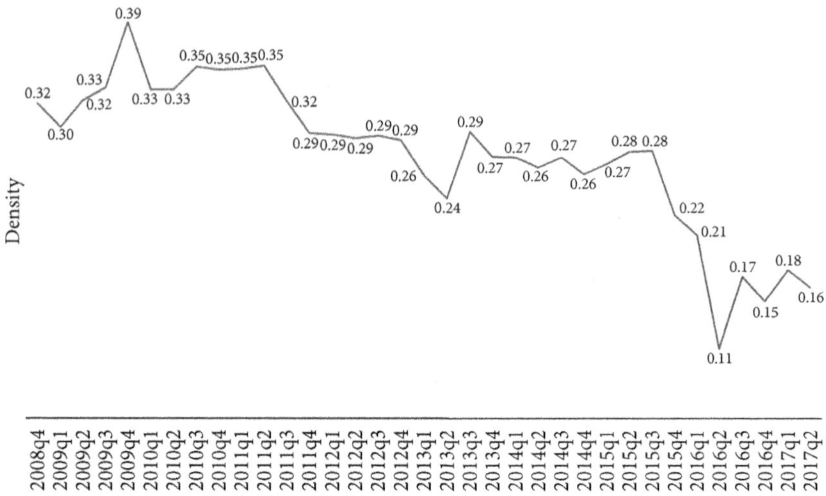

Figure 18.16 Density of the interbank network

18.4.3 Affinity of the Interbank Network

From the literature, networks exhibiting a core-periphery character tend to be disassortative (affinity for dissimilar banks to link with each other). However, Noldus and Mieghem (2015) observe that it is still possible to observe high affinity for similar banks to link with each other if the network is fragmented into sub networks, whereby each sub network itself constitutes a complete network. This is the case for each of the identified cluster shown in Figure A18.1. Every bank in each cluster is connected to every other bank in the clique (column 2). The periphery banks have either mutual links among some of them, or have links to a member of one or more within the cliques (depicted in column 3).

Figure 18.17 shows the trends for in-and-out affinity for each quarter between 2009q1 and 2017q2. Although the interbank network tends to oscillate between assortativeness (positive *r*) and disassortativeness (negative *r*), the market seems to have, on average, positive affinity i.e. Kenyan banks most of the times tend to behave like social networks rather than technological ones. This tendency for banks to trade with those like them declines slightly from 2013.

In general, the network tends to be disassortative during stressful periods as marked in the chart. These periods tend to be associated with tightness in the interbank market and presence of high government deposits (see Figure A18.3). The tendency for the interbank network to become disassortative during stressful times can be explained by the fact that, the need to get funding (for example to meet reserve requirements) may take precedence over counterparty selection. This would result in an increase in transactions with banks not

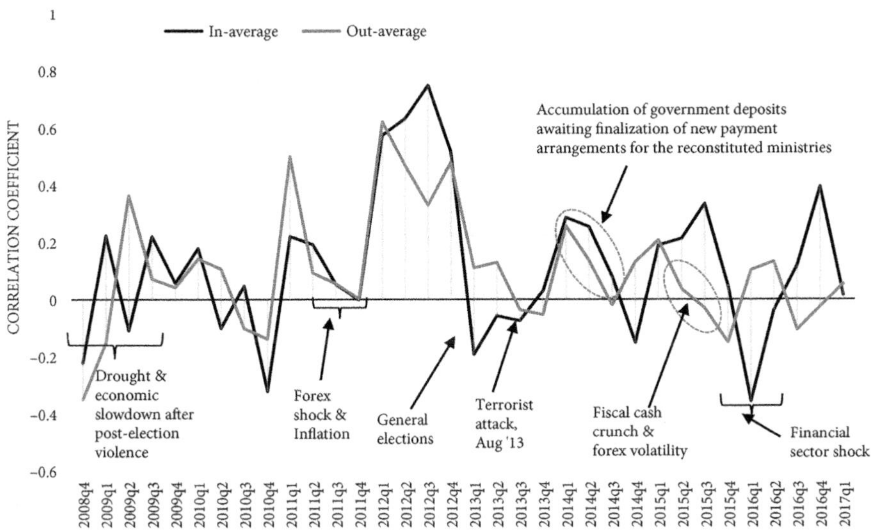

Figure 18.17 Affinity in the interbank market

normally transacted with. Puhr et al. (2012) presents similar changes in trading patterns for the Austrian interbank market. They showed that core banks tended to rely on the liquidity of periphery banks during the global financial crises, whereas in normal times they were net providers of liquidity to the system.

The rise in disassortativeness during stressful times is more so for the borrowing affinity. It may be possible to foretell when the market is approaching such stressful episodes by studying the trend of the lending affinity. From Figure 18.17, out-affinity seems to lead the in-affinity especially after 2012 (from Phase IV as per Figure 18.1).

18.4.4 The Small World Property of the Interbank Network

This attribute of a number of hubs and the presence of links with distant nodes is a characteristic often associated with small-world networks.

Figure 18.18 shows the estimated average shortest and maximum path (diameter) connecting two banks. The estimated average shortest path is about 2 links (circa one bank in-between); and each bank is linked to all other banks in the network in no more than 3 steps (maximum average distance). That is with the exception of q2 and q3 of 2016, where the maximum average distance (diameter) increases to 4 and 5 links respectively. The short-path length means that even if two given peripheral banks are not linked to the same hub, they can be linked via 2 or 3 steps, particularly because the hubs/core form nearly a complete network. While this

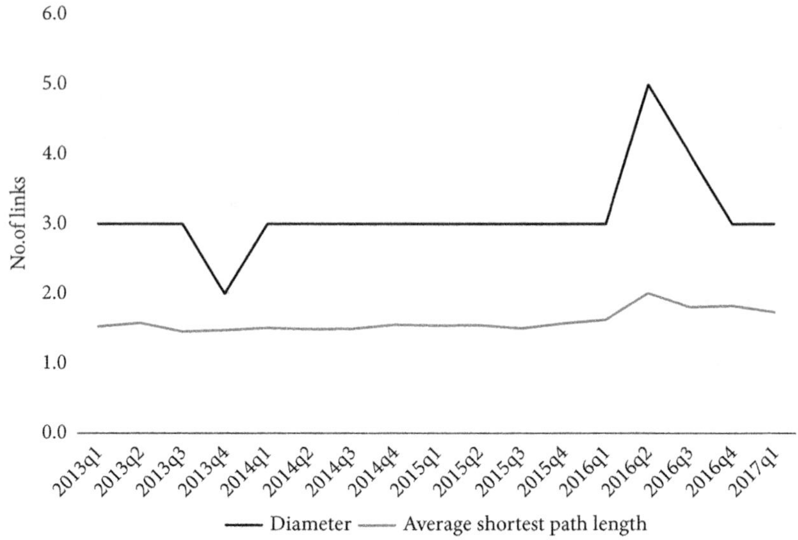

Figure 18.18 Network diameter and average shortest path length

means that the core provides an efficient shortcut for most peripheral banks for accessing/providing liquidity in the network; the short-path length suggests that contagion can also spread with ease.

18.4.5 Clustering Coefficient, Closeness and Betweenness Centralities

The trends of the clustering coefficient (c_i), closeness and betweenness also provides additional information about the evolvement of the network representation. These are provided in Figure A18.5(a–c). As noted in Section 18.2, clustering coefficient measures the local density of a sub-network comprising all nodes linked to a given target node. The average clustering of the network has fallen over time (Figure A18.4(a)). This is in line with the network density shown above, and closeness in Figure A18.4(b). The trend of average betweenness centrality (Figure A18.4(c)) suggests that some banks have become very central to the network over the study period. We try to identify some of these banks by examining the relationship between clustering, betweenness, and PageRank centralities below.

Figure 18.19 (a&b) shows the relationship between the local clustering and the in- and out-degree for each bank. Banks located in region A transact with a small number of institutions (low degree), but tend to have counterparties that are more connected to each other as the c_i is relatively high. Most of the very small banks

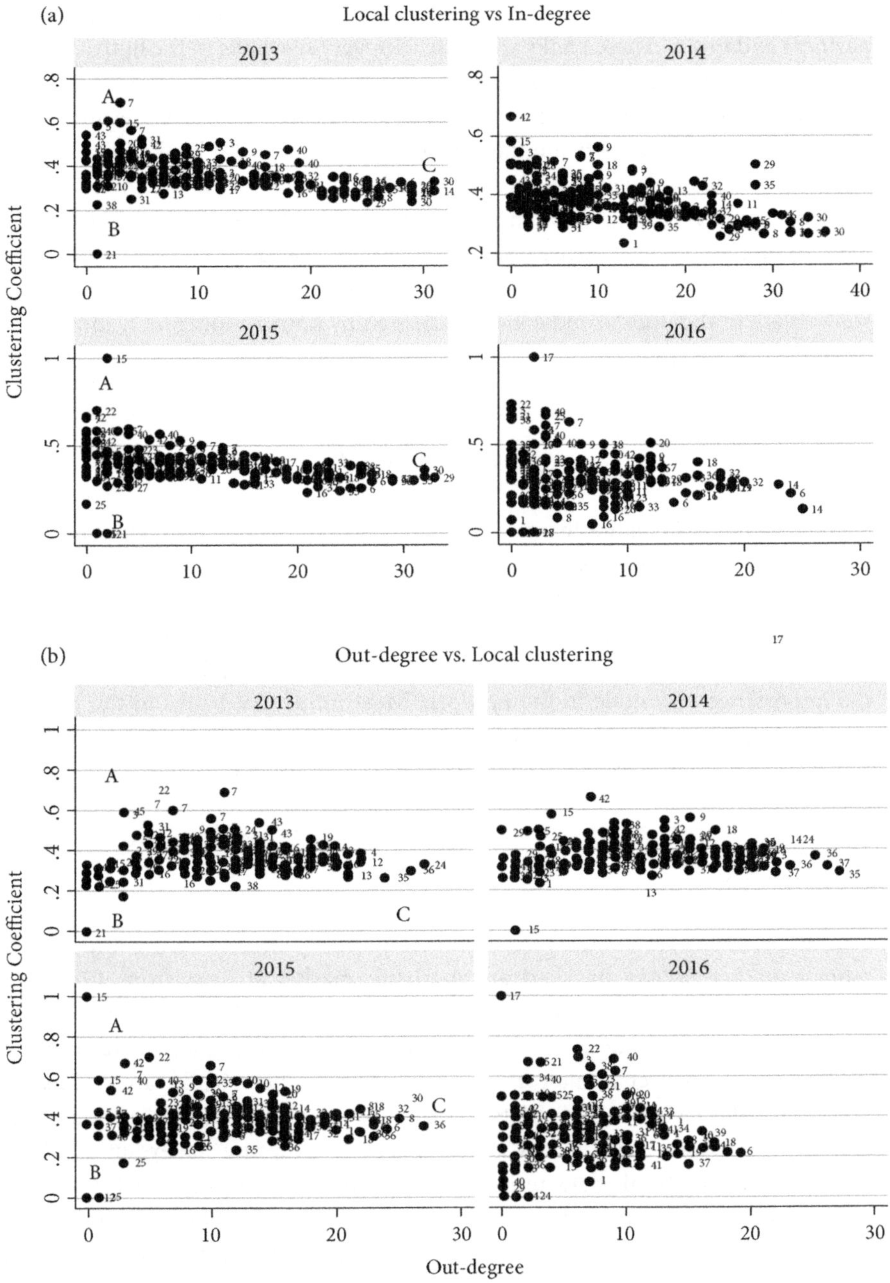

Figure 18.19 Clustering coefficient and the degree

appear in this region. Banks located in area B have a small number of transaction partners and low c_i. These banks are those with very few links to the hub or form a local small-scale fragmented network in the periphery. Banks located in area C seem to contain some of the most centrally located banks in the interbank market. These have a high number of links but low c_i. The banks identified in Figure A18.1 around which other banks cluster in each clique are found in this area. In Figure 18.19(a), banks in area C largely constitute the major borrowers while in Figure 18.19(b), the banks in area C are the liquidity suppliers. Areas A, B, and C, however, constitutes a minority, as most of the banks are concentrated somewhere in the middle and are characterized by both a moderate c_i and degree level most of the times.

18.4.6 PageRank

The centrality of the banks in area C above is also demonstrated by a plot between the PageRank centrality and betweenness centrality (circled banks in Figure 18.20) and the degree measures in Appendix (Figures A18.6–A18.8). The importance of the PageRank measure lies in the fact that, unlike other centrality measures (e.g. degree, betweenness, etc.) it considers the relevance of neighbours to determine the importance of a node in the network. Most influential banks in the Kenyan interbank market, i.e. those with high PageRank, also have a high betweenness centrality. They also tend to have high liabilities (Figure A18.7).

18.5 Conclusion

The chapter explores the network of interconnections in the overnight interbank money market. Kenya has had an interbank market at least from 1995. We examine its evolution from year 2000 to June 2017. Several metrics derived from network theory are applied to uncover a number of microstructure characteristics. The interbank market is interpreted as a network where banks are defined as nodes and the claims and liabilities between banks as links. An advantage of employing network-based theory is that it is able to capture the evolution of the topology and structural characteristics of the data relationships. Knowledge of the network structure can provide valuable input into the design of the Central Bank's systems to supply liquidity into the market and to improve the resilience of the banking system.

The interbank market grew overtime in terms of volume, number of deals, and participating banks to reach a pick around 2009–10. Thereafter, there is a notable decline especially in the number of deals and a general increase in the level, spread and volatility of the interbank rate. Measures derived from the topology of the

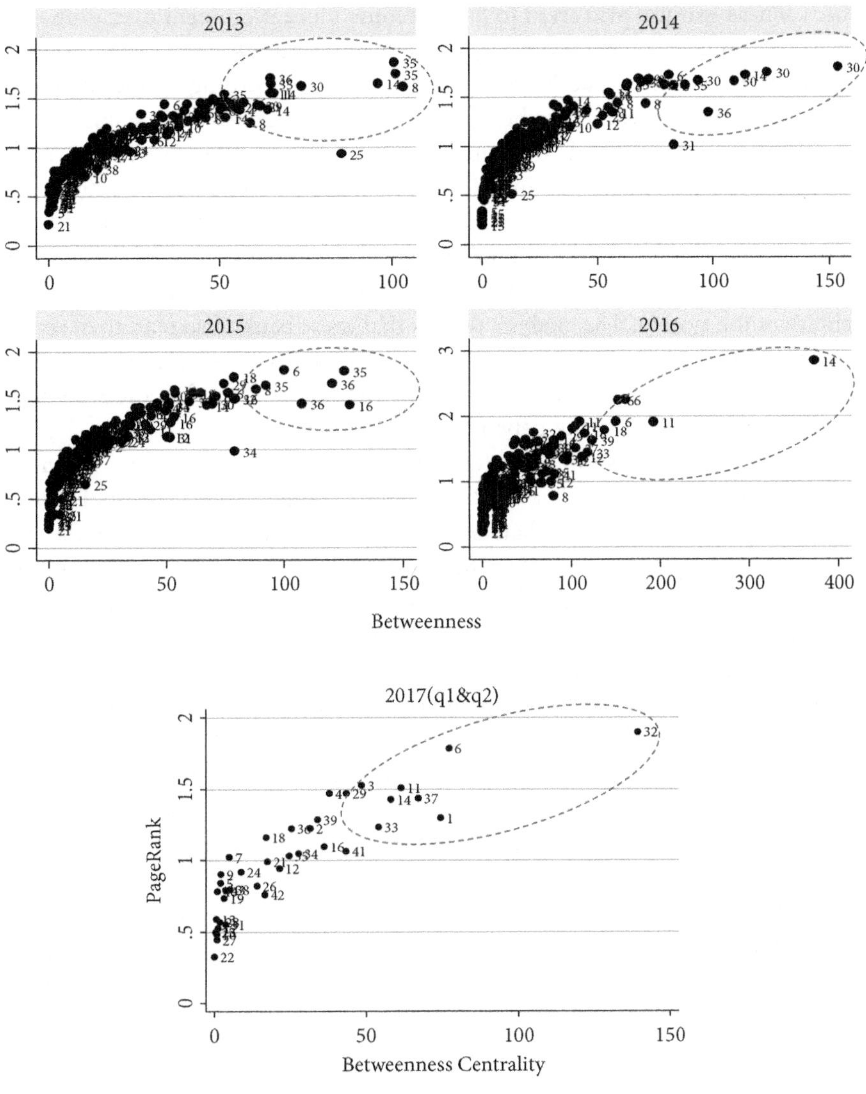

Figure 18.20 PageRank and betweenness centrality

interbank network suggest that interconnectedness among the banks generally fell from about 2012. This is demonstrated by the lower levels of the network density, clustering, closeness, and higher concentration of contracts and transacted volumes. The evidence points to an increase in importance of some banks in the network overtime, as shown by an increase in some centrality measures.

Overall, the interbank market's network is incomplete and has a decentralized structure with some banks having a relatively higher degree of connectivity than others. These features also seem to have become more prominent over time. The concentration of links in a few nodes leads to an overall topology that consists of local clusters with hub-like banks in the network. According to the literature, networks exhibiting core-periphery features are associated with stability with respect to the random breakdown of nodes, but are vulnerable to removal of the very few well connected nodes. In the context on the interbank market, this would mean that the banking system is relatively robust with respect to domino effects caused by the random breakdown of individual banks. However, the existence of the hub-like banks means their removal would have a dramatic impact on the stability of the system. The analysis reveals that these banks also tend to have low clustering coefficient, which implies that their counterparties have few substitute trading partners. The use of the network metrics allows identification of some of the most central banks in the network in each period.

Although the results show the interbank structure is largely incomplete, with a density of about 0.25, each bank can be linked to all other banks in the network in no more than three steps (two banks in between). While this may imply that the core potentially provides an efficient shortcut for most peripheral banks for accessing and/or providing liquidity in the network; the short-path length suggests that contagion can also spread with ease. An average maximum distance of three steps means that exposure is about two banks away.

From the foregoing, the Kenyan interbank market has not developed deep enough to allow a reliable price information. The level of segmentation, and increase in interest rate spreads and volatility, limits the extent to which the central bank can rely on price-based instruments as intermediate targets for monetary policy. Part of this can be attributed to developments in the fiscal space. Variations in the net position of the government increased substantially from 2013. Such rise in volatility of liquidity supply limits the ability of the Central Bank to make effective decisions on timing and size of its liquidity providing and absorbing operations; and hence the development of conditions for smooth functioning of the interbank market.

Appendix

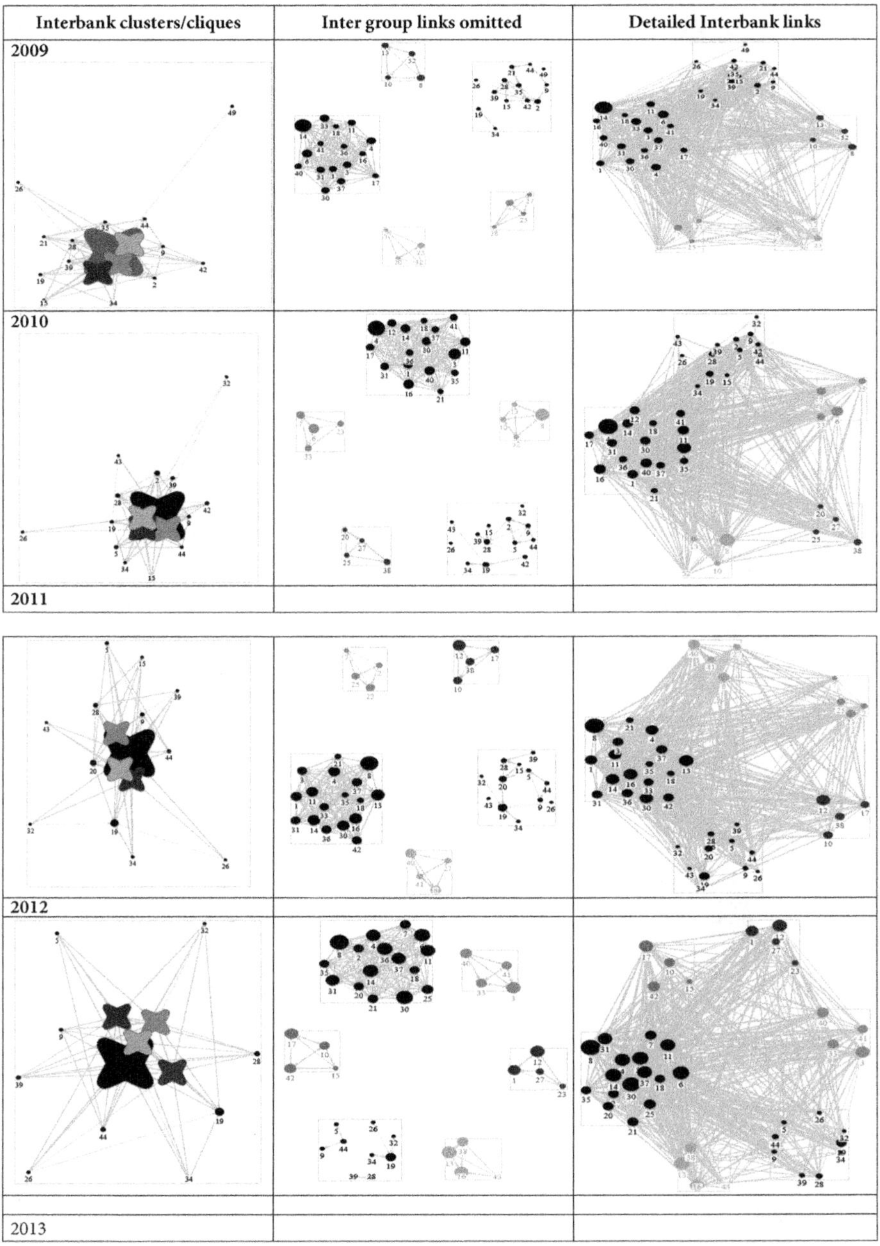

Figure A18.1 The interbank exposure for 2013–16

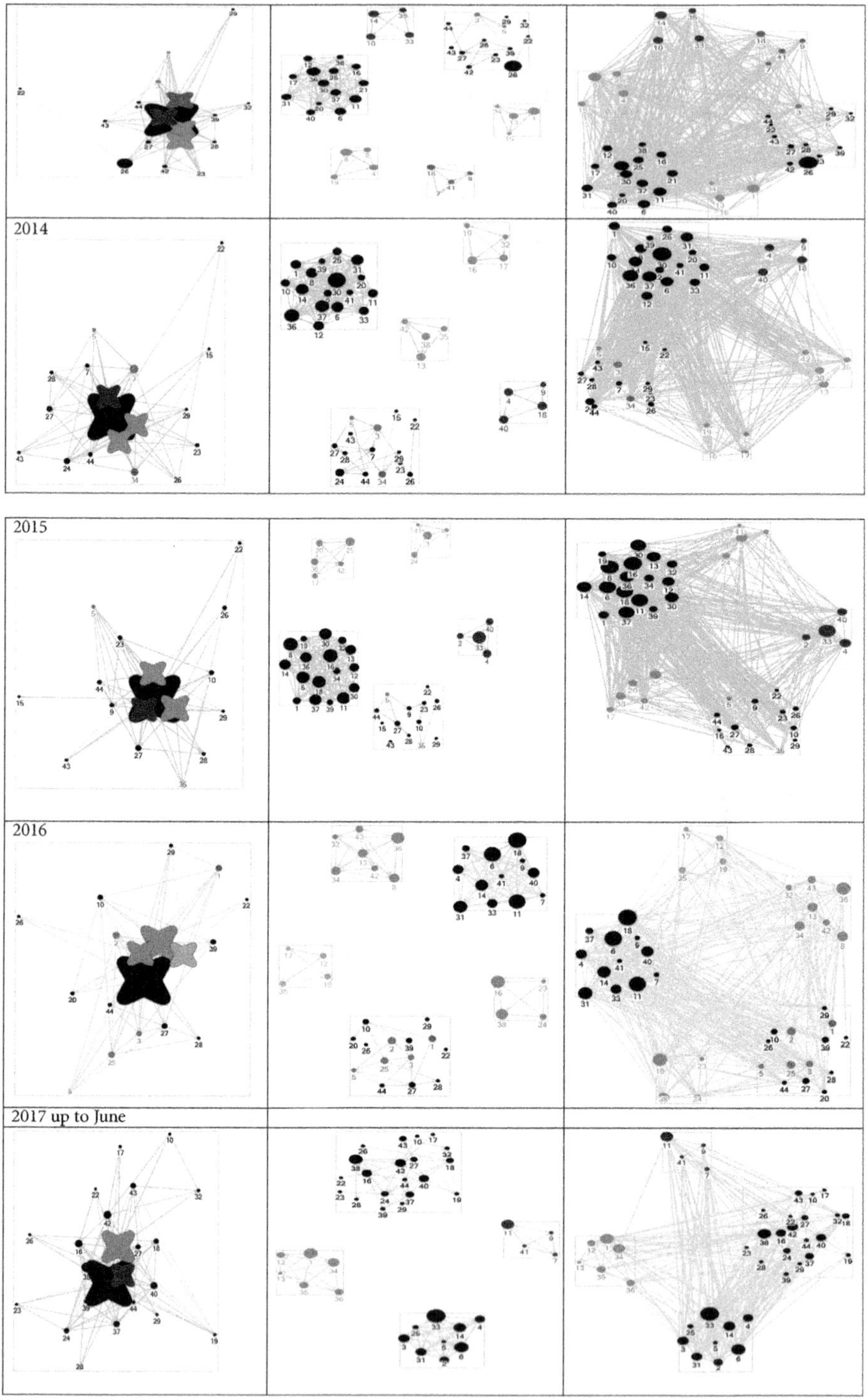
2014
2015
2016
2017 up to June

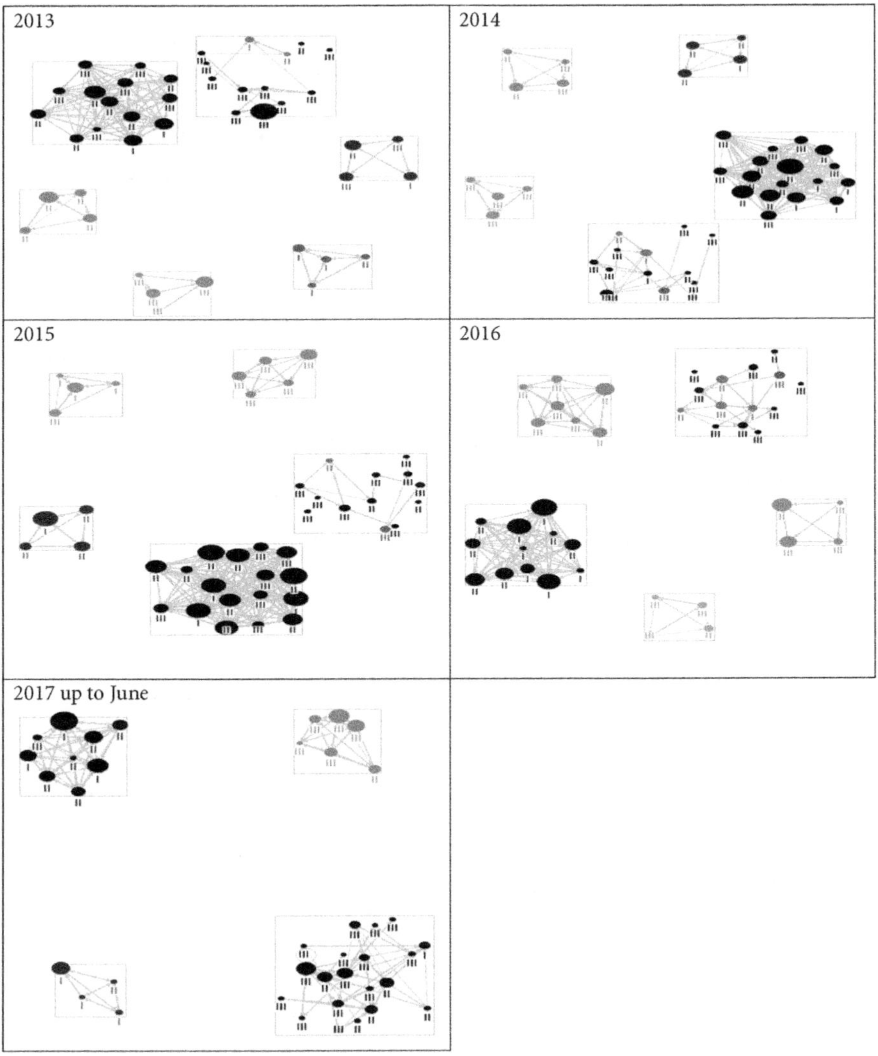

Figure A18.2 The interbank exposure for 2013–16

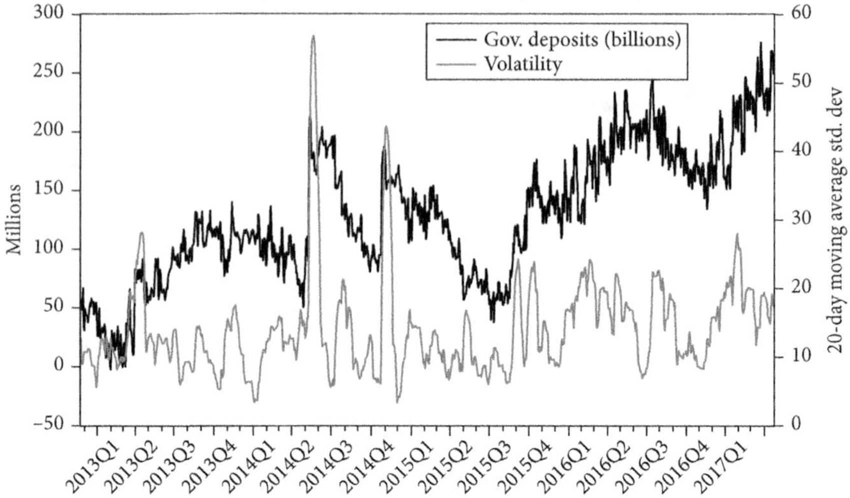

Figure A18.3 Trends in level and volatility of government deposits, 2013–2017q1

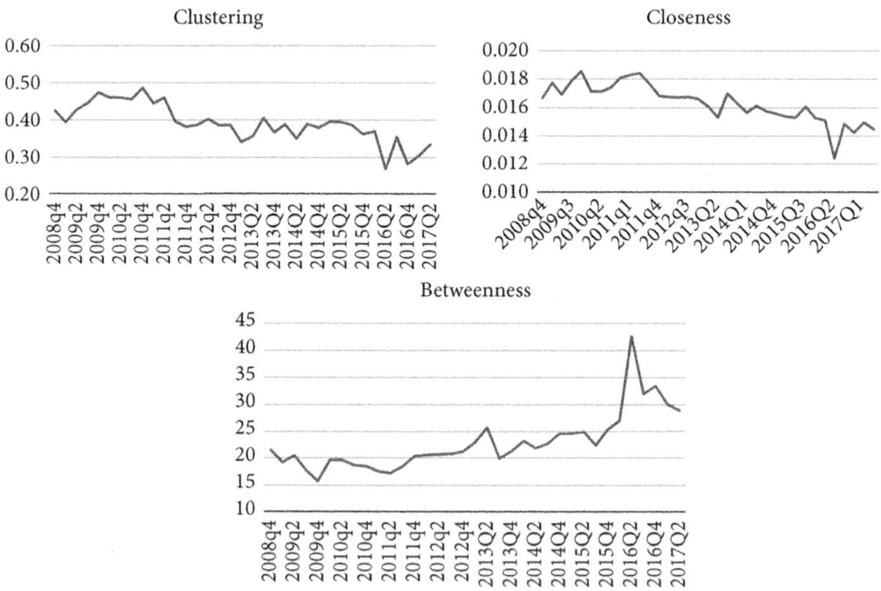

Figure A18.4 Trend of clustering coefficient, closeness and betweenness centrality

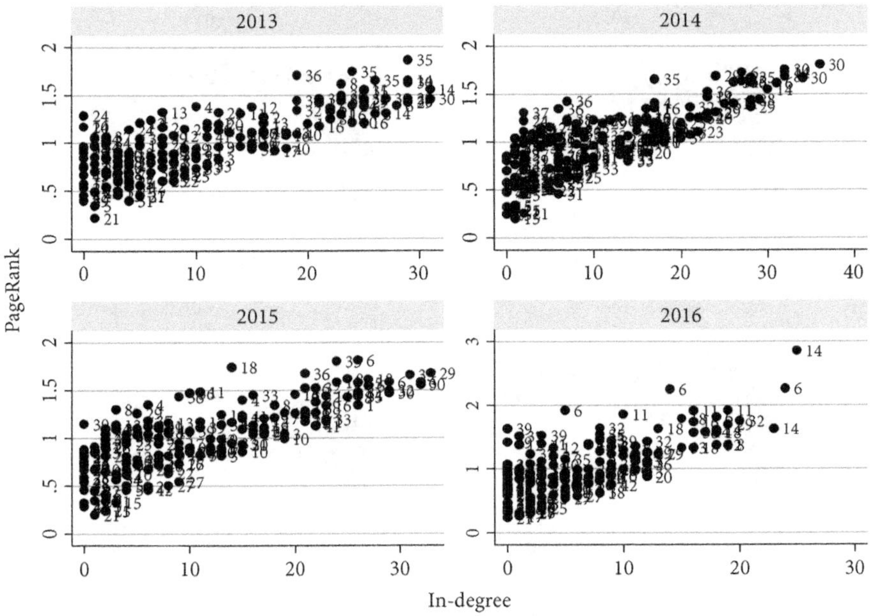

Figure A18.5 PageRank and in-degree centrality

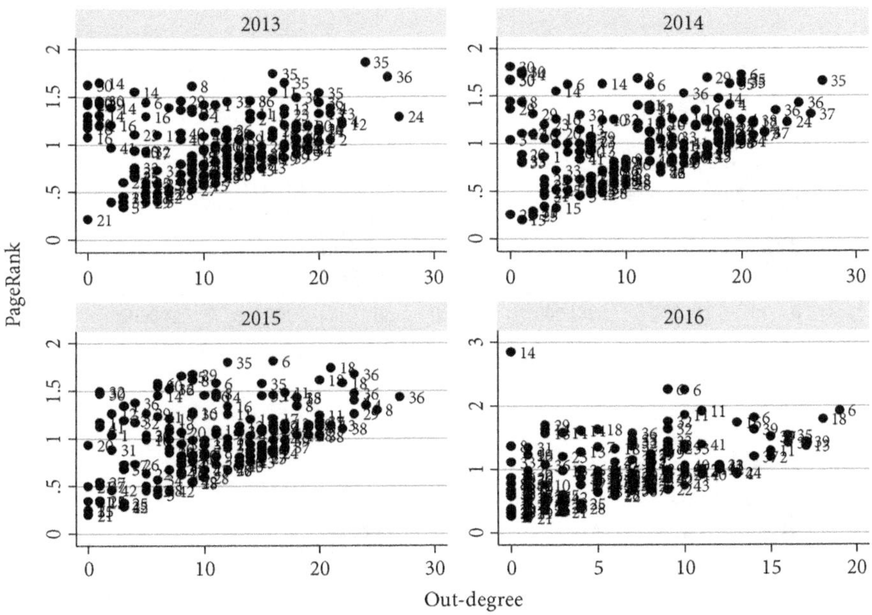

Figure A18.6 PageRank and out-degree centrality

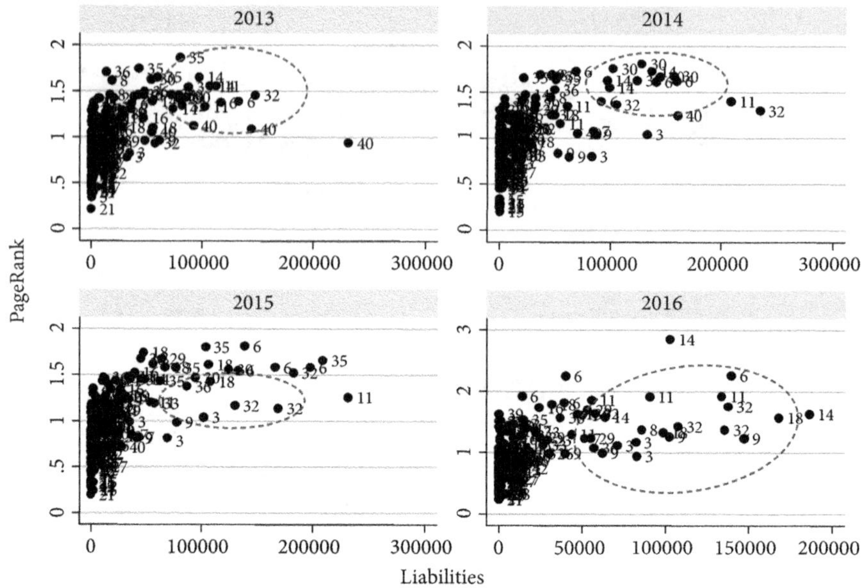

Figure A18.7 PageRank and liabilities

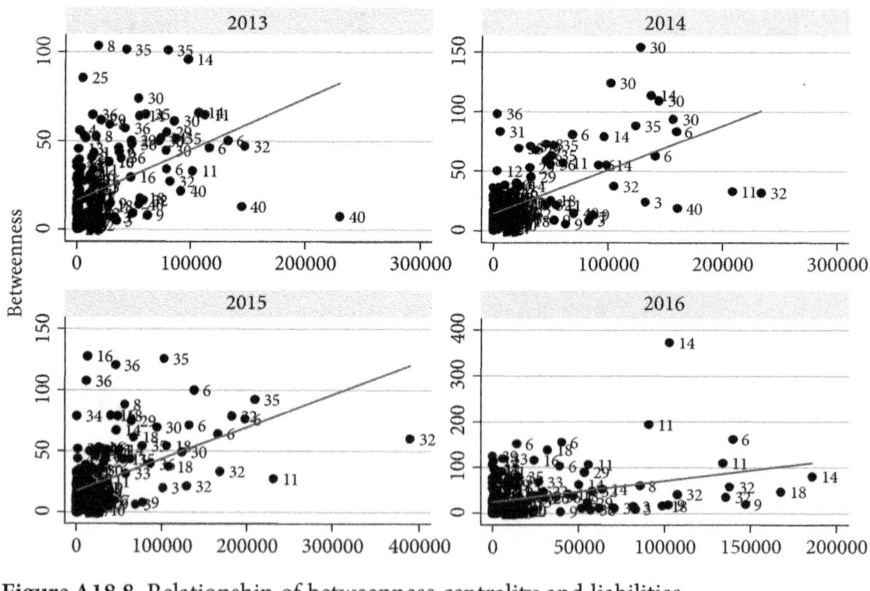

Figure A18.8 Relationship of betweenness centrality and liabilities

Table A18.1 Policy actions to reform the open market operations, 2006–15

Date	Policy action	Objective
June 06	The facility was extended to reverse the repos. The trading time was modified to run from 10.00 am–11.30 am insteads of 9.30 am–10.45 am. CBK entered into master repurchase agreement (MRA) with commercial banks.	Support the vital repo programme for monetary system liquidity management and intra-day liquidity facility transactions.
August 06	The Trading was changed to 10.00 am to 11.00 am and repo period modified to between 7 to 40 days. The tenor of the securities was previously between 5 and 21 days.	To stop the commercial banks from using repo as an overnight facility. Signal that when the CBK is in the market to inject liquidity, it would only accept bids subject to CBR being the maximum applicable rate.
October 06	The trading time was modified between 10.00 am and 1.00 pm	
June 07	The tenor was again modified to between 3 and 90 days.	Lengthening maximum maturity to signal to banks repos could be considered as an alternative investment as it made it possible to get a bill virtually equivalent to the 91 day Treasury bill. Shortening the minimum maturity reduced the period during which banks could hold excess balances to meet clearing obligations.
Aug 07	The threshold bid was reduced from Ksh. 50 million to Ksh 20 million.	Increase flexibility in liquidity management
Sept 07	A late day trading facility introduced to the repo window to run from 2.00 pm to 2.30 pm. It was allowed to trade repo bills overnight at 150 basis points below the day`s weighted average repo rate derived from the competitive morning auction.	Capture excess cash reserves received by banks late in the day not drained in the early repo window to help CBK meet its reserve money targets.
Dec 07	Tenor for late repo was changed from overnight to a minimum of 3 days The threshold amount was lowered to Ksh.10 Million Margin on the late repo yield narrowed to 100 basis points.	Increase participation in late repo window
May 08	Term Auction Deposit Facility (TAD) was introduced with a maturity from 3 to 90 days Minimum threshold of Ksh 20 million for the morning auction and Ksh 10 million for the late auction. Late deposit bid prices at 100 basis points below the weighted average TAD rate.	Increase the scope of liquidity management after the stock of existing repo securities were exhausted.

Continued

Table A18.1 *Continued*

Date	Policy action	Objective
Sept 08	Introduction of the Horizontal Repurchase Agreements between commercial banks	To help banks overcome the problem of limits to lines of credit, thus promoting more efficient distribution of liquidity in the interbank market.
Dec 08	Cash ratio requirement reviewed from 6 per cent to 5 per cent	To encourage expansion in net domestic assets
May 09	Review of the tenors for repos, reverse repos, the late repo and the TAD to a single tenor of 5 days.	Improve liquidity management
July 09	Tenor of the repo transactions lengthened to a single 7 days period. CRR reviewed downwards to 4.5 per cent	CRR reviewed to promote credit expansion.
August 09	The time of repo trading starts was shifted to 10.00–11.30 am	
Sept 08	Introduction of the horizontal repurchase agreements between commercial banks	Deepen money markets and enhance distribution of liquidity in the interbank market
May 09	Repo and TAD tenure fixed to 5 days	Improve liquidity management
July 09	Repo and TAD tenure fixed to 7 days. Recourse by banks to reverse repo only after interbank and horizontal repo opportunities exhausted	Improve liquidity management
Mar 11	Modification of the monetary programme from using reserve money as the operating target to use of the net domestic assets (NDA) and net international reserves (NIR). As part of daily liquidity management, NDA was to be supported by monitoring of reserve money, interbank rates, liquidity distribution in the banking sector and deviations of broad money from target.	Consistent with the Extended Credit Facility, NDA ceiling was set as the operating target in place of the reserve money to address the weaknesses of unstable velocity and money multiplier.
May 11	Late repo tenure fixed at 4 days and CRR raised to 4.75 per cent.	Improve liquidity management CRR raised to contain domestic credit expansion
July 11	Introduction of weekly averaging on cash reserves instead of the daily. Banks were also allowed to deviate from the 4.75 per cent provided the five-day average of 4.75 per cent was met.	To facilitate banks liquidity management

Aug 11	Expanded averaging of cash reserves from weekly to monthly, from 15th of the previous month to 14th of the current month, subject to a CRR daily floor of 3 per cent. Banks utilizing the CBK Overnight Window were charged the CBR plus a penalty of six percentage points from 3 percentage points.	To facilitate banks' flexibility in liquidity management
	Review of the monetary policy operations framework the CBR the reference rate for pricing monetary policy operations.	To align the interbank rate more closely with the CBR
	Banks maintain their CRR based on a 30-day average with a floor of 3 per cent	To facilitate commercial banks' liquidity management
Oct 11	CRR raised to 5.25 per cent, effective from 15 December 2011	Tighten liquidity conditions
November 2011	Introduction of new monetary operations framework-All Central Bank market operations were based on the CBR as the reference rate	To enhance clarity and certainty in the market.
April 12	Introduction of an interest rate band for the interbank rate around the CBR (±2).	Move towards using market-based instruments for monetary policy. Aim was to use the CBR to guide the interbank market rates to achieve the NDA operational target.
June 12	Introduced longer tenor TADs (14-day, 21-day and 28-day)	Tighten liquidity conditions
October 2015	The interest rate band for the interbank rate around the CBR (±2), temporarily discontinued.	High volatility in the interbank market made it difficult to follow the corridor.

Source: CBK (adopted from Murinde et al., 2012).

References

Albert, R. and Barabási, A. L. (2002), 'Statistical mechanics of complex networks'. *Reviews Modern Physics*, Vol. 74, No. 2, pp. 47–97.

Albert R., Jeong, H., and Barabási, A.L (2000), 'Error and attack tolerance of complex networks'. *Nature*, Vol. 406, pp. 378–82.

Barabási, A. L. (2009), 'Scale-free networks: A decade and beyond'. *Science*, Vol. 325, No. 5939, pp. 412–13.

Bech, M. and Atalay, E. (2010), 'The topology of the federal funds market', *Physica A; Statistical Mechanics and its Application*, Vol. 389, No. 22, pp. 5223–46.

Bech, M. L. and Atalay, E. (2008), 'The topology of the federal funds market'. ECB Working Paper No 986.

Becher C., Millard, S. and Soramäli, K. (2008), "The network topology of CHAPS Sterling", Bank of England Working Paper, no. 355.

Boss M., Elsinger, H., Summers, M. and Thurner, S. (2004), 'The network topology of the interbank market'. *Quantitative Finance*, Vol. 4, No. 6, pp. 677–84.

Bräuning, F. and Fecht, F. (2017), 'Relationship lending in the interbank market and the price of liquidity'. *Review of Finance*, Vol. 21, No. 1, pp. 33–75.

Brink, N. and Georg, C. P. (2011), 'Systemic risk in the South African Interbank system'. South African Reserve Bank Discussion Paper 11/01.

Cajueiro, D. O. and Tabak, B. M. (2008). "The role of banks in the Brazilian interbank market: Does bank type matter?" *Physica A: Statistical Mechanics and its Applications*, 387(27):6825–6836.

Clauset, A., Shalizi, C. R., and Newman, M. E. J. (2009), 'Power-law distributions in empirical data'. *SIAM Review*, Vol. 51, No. 4, pp. 661–703.

Craig, B. and Peter, G. von (2014), 'Interbank tiering and money center banks'. *Journal of Financial Intermediation*, Vol. 23, No. 3, pp. 322–47.

Fricke, D. and Lux, T., (2015), 'Core–periphery structure in the overnight money market: Evidence from the e-MID trading platform'. *Computational Economics*, Vol. 45, pp. 359–95.

Green, C., Bai, Y., Murinde, V., Ngoka, K., Maana, I., and Tiriongo, S. (2016), 'Overnight interbank markets and the determination of the interbank rate: A selective survey'. *International Review of Financial Analysis*, Vol. 44, pp. 149–61.

Haldane A. (2009), Rethinking the financial network. Speech delivered at the financial student association in Amsterdam.

Hale, G. (2012). 'Bank relationships, business cycles, and financial crises'. *Journal of International Economics*, Vol. 88, No. 2, pp. 312–25.

Henggeler-Muller, J. (2006), 'The potential for contagion in the Swiss interbank market'. PhD thesis, Universitat, Basel, May 2006.

Iazzetta, M. and C. Manna, C. (2009), 'The topology of the interbank market: Developments in Italy since 1990'. *Temi di Discussione* (Working Paper) 711, Bank of Italy, 2009. Available at: https://www.bancaditalia.it/pubblicazioni/temi-discussione/2009/2009-0711/en_tema_711.pdf?language_id=1

Imakubo, K. and Soejima, Y. (2006), 'The transaction network in Japan's interbank money market', Financial System Report Bank of Japan.

Martinez-Jaramillo, S., Alexandrova-Kabadjova, B., Bravo-Benítez, B., and Solórzano-Margain, J. (2012), 'An empirical study of the Mexican banking system's network and its implications for systemic risk'. Working Papers series of Banco de Mexico 2012–07.

Murinde, V., Bai, Y., Green, C. J., and Mwega, F. (2012), Consultancy Report on Interbank Market Operations in Kenya. Central Bank of Kenya.

Mwega, F., Murinde, V., and Green, C. (2012), 'Interbank market operations in Kenya'. Paper 1 of a Consultancy Report on Interbank Market Operations in Kenya. Central Bank of Kenya.

Newman, M. E. (2003), 'Mixing patterns in networks'. *Physical Review* E, Vol. 67, No. 2, pp. 1–14.

Newman, M. E. (2010), *Networks: An Introduction*. New York: Oxford University Press.

Newman, M. E. and Girvan, M. (2004), 'Finding and evaluating community structure in networks', *Physical Review Letters,* Vol. 69, No. 2, pp. 02611.

Noldus, R. and Mieghem, P. V. (2015), 'Assortativity in complex networks', *Journal of Complex Networks,* Vol. 3, No. 4, pp. 507–42.

Oduor, J., Sichei, M. M., Tiriongo, S. K., and Shimba, C. (2014), 'Segmentation and efficiency of the interbank market and their implication for the conduct of monetary policy'. African Development Bank Working Paper 202.

Peltonen, Ta., Scheicher, M., and Vuillemey, G. (2013), 'The network structure of the CDS market and its determinants'. ECB Working Paper Series 1583.

Puhr, C., Seliger, R., and Sigmund, M. (2012), 'Contagiousness and vulnerability in the Austrian interbank market'. OeNB Financial Stability Report 24.

Silva, T. C., Stancato de Souza, S. R., and Tabak, B. M. (2015), 'Network structure analysis of the Brazilian interbank market'. Banco Central Do Brasil Working Paper Series 391.

Soramäki K., Arnold J., M.L. Bech, W.E. Beyeler and R.J. Glass (2006), 'The Topology of Interbank Payment Flows', Federal Reserve Bank of New York Staff Reports, no. 243.

Soramäki, K., Bech, M. L., Arnold, J., Glass, R. J., and Beyeler, W. (2007), 'The topology of interbank payment flows'. *Physica A: Statistical Mechanics and its Applications,* Vol. 379, No. 1, pp. 317–33.

Watts D.J. and Strogatz, S.H. (1998), 'Collective dynamics of small world networks'. *Nature,* Vol. 393, pp. 440–42.

Index of Names

Note: Tables are indicated by an italic '*t*' following the page number; 'n.' after a page number indicates the footnote number.

General Index

Note: Tables, figures, and boxes are indicated by an italic '*t*', '*f*', and '*b*' following the page number; 'n.' after a page number indicates the footnote number.